Interpretations of Erasmus c 1750–1920
Man on His Own

During his lifetime Erasmus was one of the most controversial figures of Renaissance and Reformation Europe. In the 450 years since his death his reputation has undergone a series of fluctuations that reflect the attitudes of successive periods in European, and eventually North American, theological, historical, and social thought.

In his earlier work, *Phoenix of His Age*, Bruce Mansfield followed the fate of Erasmus' reputation broadly from his death to the middle of the eighteenth century when the first full biographies of the humanist were published, biographies already reflecting the outlook of the Enlightenment. Now, in *Interpretations of Erasmus c 1750–1920: Man on His Own*, he carries the story to the 1920s when other famous biographies appeared, such as those by Preserved Smith and Johan Huizinga.

Mansfield aims to relate changing interpretations of Erasmus to the historical contexts and experiences of those who wrote about him. He explores the influences in turn of the Enlightment, romanticism, religious revival, and the emergence of liberalism.

However, despite the preoccupations of specific eras, certain issues of continuing interest to students of Erasmus transcend the shifts in contemporary view. Mansfield also examines the treatment of these issues, revealing how, through the centuries, Protestant writers, for example, continue to focus on Erasmus' relationship to the Reformation.

In the twentieth century, Mansfield concludes, more modern ways of studying Erasmus have emerged, notably through seeing him more precisely in his own historical context. He argues, nevertheless, that the Enlightment liberal interpretation of Erasmus remained the dominant one through the whole period and that, despite its weaknesses, it did succeed in revealing essential aspects of Erasmus as a historical personality.

BRUCE MANSFIELD is Visiting Professor, Department of History, University of Sydney.

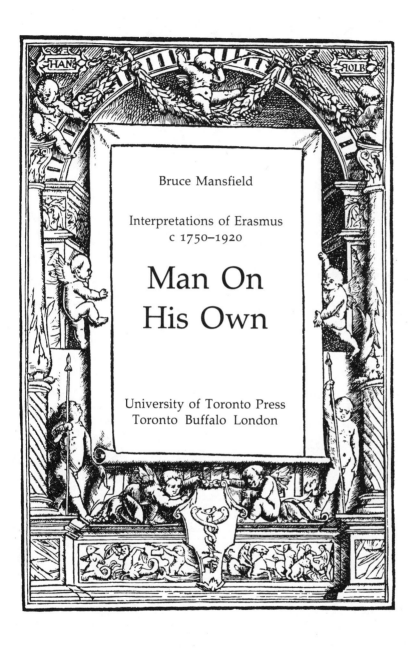

Bruce Mansfield

Interpretations of Erasmus
c 1750–1920

Man On
His Own

University of Toronto Press
Toronto Buffalo London

© University of Toronto Press 1992
Toronto Buffalo London
Printed in Canada

ISBN 0-8020-5950-3

Erasmus Studies 11

Printed on acid-free paper

Canadian Cataloguing in Publication Data

Mansfield, Bruce, 1926–
The reputation of Erasmus c1750–1920

(Erasmus studies ; 11)
Sequel to: Mansfield, Bruce, 1926–   . Phoenix
of his age.
Includes bibliographical references and index.
ISBN 0-8020-5950-3

1. Erasmus, Desiderius, d. 1536 – Criticism and
interpretation – History.   I. Title. II. Series.

PA8518.M35 1992   199'.492   C92-093218-5

This book has been published with the help of a grant
from the Canadian Federation for the Humanities,
using funds provided by the Social Sciences and Humanities
Research Council of Canada.

TO MACQUARIE UNIVERSITY 1965–1985
and three of its graduates

Contents

Acknowledgments / ix

Illustrations / xi

1
Introduction / 3

PART ONE
ENLIGHTENMENT, ROMANTICISM, AND
REVOLUTION

2
Introduction to Part One / 11

3
Erasmus and Enlightenment / 14

4
Romanticism and Revolution / 69

PART TWO
THE NINETEENTH CENTURY AND AFTER

5
Introduction to Part Two / 121

6
From Restoration to the Revolutions of 1848:
Erasmus as Critic, Publicist, and Rebel / 123

7
Nineteenth-Century France:
Erasmus as Writer and Moralist / 134

8
Liberalism:
Erasmus as Sceptic, Rationalist, and
Modern Man / 152

9
Nineteenth-Century Catholicism:
Erasmus' Relation to Catholic Orthodoxy,
the Catholic Tradition, and Scholasticism / 186

10
Nineteenth-Century Protestantism:
Erasmus and the Reformation in Modern History / 238

11
Into the Twentieth Century / 297

12
Conclusion / 373

List of Abbreviations / 377

Notes / 379

Bibliography / 455

Index / 485

Acknowledgments

This work is a sequel to my *Phoenix of His Age: Interpretations of Erasmus c 1550–1750*. I have had the encouragement of Ron Schoeffel and James McConica throughout the preparation of both volumes. I hope that I have benefited from both the encouragement and the criticism of reviewers of the first.

As before I acknowledge the interest and support of many friends and colleagues. I must mention Brian Fletcher and Deryck Schreuder, who eased my return to writing, and Geoffrey Dickens and John Tonkin because of our happy exchanges on Reformation historiography. Roslyn Pesman, Robert Scribner, and Leighton Frappell, who were once my students, have more than returned any benefit through their writings and conversation. Len McGlashan helped with some difficult German.

Both Macquarie University and the University of Sydney have provided research grants, especially for the acquisition of microfilm and photocopies. Colleagues in Europe and North America can hardly appreciate our dependence at this distance on microfilmed materials. I must pay tribute to the inter-library loans section of the libraries of both universities and especially to Reingard Porges who (her change of institution coinciding with mine) has been a guardian angel to the project in the two places. Other collections used included the British Library, the Gemeentebibliotheek, Rotterdam, and earlier the Yale University Library, and I express appreciation for courtesies in each case.

I am grateful to the Renaissance Society of America and the editors of the *Australian Journal of Politics and History* and the *Journal of Religious History* for permission to reproduce passages from articles published in their respective publications, as detailed in the notes.

Joyce Acheson typed the bulk of the text. She began when working as my secretary at Macquarie University, but continued well beyond the line of duty after my retirement – out of friendship to the work and its author.

The typing was completed by my wife Joan who has also read the text and commented fruitfully. She did much of the detailed work on the final version. The first volume was dedicated to her and the completion of the second also has depended on her constant support.

This volume is dedicated to the institution to whose progress in its first twenty years I had a strong commitment, and to my sons Martin, Paul, and Nicholas.

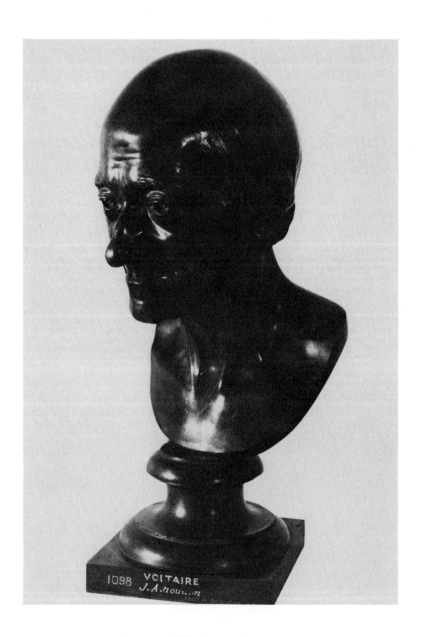

Voltaire, 1778.
Bronze bust by Jean-Antoine Houdon (1741–1828).
Reproduced by permission of the
National Gallery of Victoria, Melbourne, Australia

Mark Pattison (1813–84), Rector of Lincoln College Oxford.
Drawing by C.W. Cope, 1865.
Reproduced by permission of Lincoln College Oxford

James Anthony Froude (1818–94).
Photograph taken in 1880

Charles Beard (1827–88).
Reproduced by permission of Liverpool University Press

Johannes Janssen (1829–91).
Frontispiece to *Johannes Janssens Briefe*, Volume I (1920)

ERASMUS REDIVIVUS

SIVE

DE CURIA ROMANA HUCUSQUE INSANABILI.

SCRIPSIT

CONSTANTINUS SCHLOTTMANN.

Non enim possumus aliquid adversus
veritatem sed pro veritate.
Ep. II. ad Cor. 13, 8.

HALIS
SUMPTIBUS ORPHANOTROPHEI
MDCCCLXXXIII.

Title-page of Constantinus Schlottmann's
Erasmus redivivus, 1883.
Reproduced by permission of the
Gemeentebibliotheek Rotterdam

ERASMI ROTERODAMI

SILVA CARMINUM

ANTEHAC NUNQUAM IMPRESSORUM.

GOUDA, 1513.

REPRODUCTION PHOTO-LITHOGRAPHIQUE.
AVEC NOTICE SUR LA JEUNESSE ET LES PREMIERS TRAVAUX D'ÉRASME.

PAR

M. CH. RUELENS,

CONSERVATEUR-ADJ.-HON. A LA BIBLIOTHÈQUE ROYALE DE BRUXELLES.

BRUXELLES,
T.-J. I. ARNOLD, LIBRAIRE-ANTIQUAIRE,
12, RUE DE L'HÔPITAL.
—
1864

Ch. Ruelens, title-page of
Erasmi Roterodami, *Silva Carminum*, Brussels 1864.
Reproduced by permission of the
Gemeentebibliotheek Rotterdam

Basel University in the 1870s.

Left bank with (left to right) 'The Blue House' (Rheinsprung 16), the Old University, and St Martin's Church. Photo by A. Varady. Reproduced by permission of the Staatsarchiv Basel

Döllinger and Acton (far right) with Gladstone and his family at Tegernsee, 1879. Photograph by Herbert Paul

Robert Fruin (1823–99),
photographed in 1878 by J. Goedeljee.
Reproduced by permission of the
Rijksuniversiteit te Leiden

Johan Huizinga (1872–1945).
Drawing of Huizinga as Erasmus by J.A.J. Barge
on a copy of the menu of an anniversary dinner
at Leiden University, 8 February 1933.
Reproduced by permission of the
Rijksuniversiteit te Leiden

Friedrich Paulsen (1846–1908)

INTERPRETATIONS OF ERASMUS

Introduction

Erasmus had in his own time a great reputation as scholar, church reformer, and social critic. He was a vigorous polemicist. He attracted the loyalty of colleagues and disciples but he also made enemies. He had an ironic temperament which could not always forgo a witticism at the expense of an acquaintance, there was in his personality a mixture of warmth and reserve, and he could be needlessly defensive or touchy. The controversies about him that had begun in his lifetime continued after his death but they were also quickly reshaped or distorted by changing historical circumstances.

Above all, the divisions in Christianity – showing few signs of healing before the twentieth century – fixed attitudes about Erasmus as about much else. He had been caught in the beginnings of that controversy but in his darkest hours could not have foreseen the finality of the division or the wreck it would make of his own reputation. The division and the wreck went together because Erasmus' scholarly enterprises, the reforms he urged on church and society assumed the continuing unity of Christian Europe and an unhampered flow of news and exchange of opinions among its intellectual leaders.

What needs explanation is the interest of succeeding generations in this solitary figure. In the two centuries after his death a vast literature gathered about him and by the middle of the eighteenth century three substantial biographies had appeared.[1] For one thing, his writings had retained currency; naturally some did so more than others, depending on the differing interests of various times and various places. The *Praise of Folly (Moriae encomium)* remained a cause of scandal – thrilling to some, disgusting to others – over the two centuries. Its finer points, especially its religious passion, were invariably missed.[2] Nevertheless, as the bitterness passed from the confessional struggles, his works of piety, with their understanding of faith as an inward and personal possession (rather than a credal statement or a ritual act) and their sturdy moralism, came to be appreciated again in some quarters. Even in the bitter moments kindred spirits appealed to his irenic and pacifist writings, though generally Erasmus' political works were little quoted before the eighteenth century with its intimations of revolution or at least liberal change.

In every development of literary and biblical criticism, however, he was recognized as a predecessor. The fact is that the academic tradition to which he belonged – the classical humanist – kept its vitality until well into the nineteenth century. At the lowest level some of his writings were constantly reprinted, if in bowdlerized form, as schoolbooks. More generally, he could only continue in honour among the heirs of the classical revival of which he was a luminary.

Above all, Erasmus remained a talking-point because of a continuing fascination with the age in which he lived. For six generations Europe was coming to terms with the consequences of the Reformation. Here was an inspiration for some and a cautionary tale for others. Besides, the historiographical thesis that modernity begins with the sixteenth century was not an invention of nineteenth-century historians; there are senses in which it was a creation of the sixteenth century itself.[3] Erasmus – if talk about him could do him any good – was a beneficiary of these preoccupations.

They were limiting preoccupations. As well, the nature of the writings in which Erasmus was portrayed helped determine judgments about him. A high proportion of the works treating Erasmus up to 1700 were theological and in some way related to confessional controversy. The histories were mostly ecclesiastical and the biographies of his contemporaries were, if not of ecclesiastical personages, at least of those – like Thomas More – who had a definite ecclesiastical significance. Biographical studies of Erasmus himself appeared in the constricted setting of biographical dictionaries and gazetteers.

It is not surprising, therefore, that questions like the following dominated the literature. What were Erasmus' relations with the theological authorities of the past – the church Fathers and scholastics – and the ecclesiastical authorities of his own time? Was he a good Catholic? What were his views on the test doctrines of Christianity: the Trinity, the authority of scripture, the atonement? How did he stand to Luther? Did his devotion to the classics represent a revival of paganism? Or was it a foretaste of intellectual and religious enlightenment?

The Erasmus emerging from the writings of two centuries was then essentially ideological. Naturally, there was discussion of his personality and a recurring fascination with certain biographical details: his illegitimate birth and especially the status of his parents at his conception; the circumstances of his entering and leaving a monastery in his youth and young manhood; his relations with the great of his time, with kings like Henry VIII of England or Francis I of France, and popes like Julius II or Leo X; his friendships especially with those who, like John Colet or Thomas More, themselves posed delicate problems of confessional definition; his travels and attachments to places; and finally his death in one problematic place, the Protestant city of Basel. But the structure into which all these fitted was plainly doctrinal or ideological.

Those choosing to write about Erasmus after the middle of the eighteenth century had ready to hand a number of standard interpretations. At the risk of grossly oversimplifying, I might characterize these briefly. There was Erasmus the true pioneer of Catholic reformation, the friend of Thomas More, teaching a purified, but essentially orthodox, form of faith and practice. There was Erasmus the corrosive agent, the enemy of scholasticism and so of the indispensable structure of Catholic theology, the mocker (especially at those whose status, whatever their personal faults, deserved reverence, like monks and bishops) and the doubter (especially of the Trinity, which made him a late Arian or an early Socinian). The first of these interpretations was standard among the friends and associates who survived him; it persisted in places where, as in the southern Netherlands, life remained in the Christian humanist tradition, or some kind of ecumenical contact was possible. The second had great vogue in the Society of Jesus and was indeed dominant in the Catholic church after the Council of Trent. It began to pale before its rival only at the beginning of the eighteenth century when confessional bitterness started to ebb away and a change in religious sentiment might be observed – towards more intimate forms of devotion with an emphasis on purity of life.

On the other side, there was Erasmus the reformer, the predecessor of Luther and scourge of ecclesiastical abuses, laying the foundations of the new (Reformation) doctrinal structures. This interpretation came in two versions, one at least discernible in Protestant Basel, where there was an enduring attachment to Erasmus' memory, and also strong among the Arminians of Holland, and the other entrenched in the main Protestant churches, the Lutheran (though the heirs of Philipp Melanchthon cast a lingering look on the alternative) and the Calvinist or Reformed. The first saw Erasmus as the real reformer and the Reformation as deformed by the intolerance and dogmatic obsessions of Luther and the rigidities of Calvin and his heirs. In the second, Erasmus was touched by the light but – from vacillation, or cowardice, or attachment to his friends, or conservatism – he turned his back on it. In this view, he both promoted the Reformation and betrayed it.

Finally, there was an inverted form of the Jesuit and post-Tridentine denunciation. Erasmus did abandon the more unbelievable elements in traditional Christian doctrine, like the Trinity; he sought a more rational religion and directly challenged ecclesiastical authority of all kinds. He was the father of enlightenment. This interpretation had its beginnings in the anti-Trinitarian writers of the sixteenth century and an observer in the eighteenth might easily guess that it had a great future.

There were, of course, writers about Erasmus who stood to an extent outside these stereotypes. Pierre Bayle and John Jortin among the Protestants, for example, accepted the Reformation as a liberation and Erasmus' relation to it as generally positive, while treating his separation from it in an understanding way and without serious blame. This amelioration arose from their particular historical settings and experiences.[4] Bayle in the remarkable essay on Erasmus in volume VI of his *Dictionnaire historique et critique* settled a number of biographical questions although, until problems in the dating of correspondence were resolved, much would remain confused, as the contemporary 'Life' by Jean Le Clerc recognized.[5]

Above all, the big two-volume biography of Jean Lévesque de Burigny (1757), *Vie d'Erasme*, a major work in all the Erasmus literature, went beyond the stereotyping of the previous two centuries and set a standard for the writers who were to follow. Burigny knew his predecessors and tested for himself their results.

His picture was closest to that of the pre-Tridentine Erasmians –
Erasmus was a true Catholic but a critical and at times indiscreet
one. But Burigny's sense of living in an enlightened age enabled
him to treat all the warring parties of Erasmus' time with a certain
detachment and even-handedness and to consider Erasmus, within
limits, in his own terms. The limits were, of course, set by 'enlightenment' itself.

Those who followed would depend on Burigny and the others.
They, like all their predecessors, would also be writing about
Erasmus and the controversies surrounding him in awareness of
the controversies, the religious changes, and cultural shifts of their
own times. Earlier I have said that Erasmus remained 'someone
to be reckoned with in the great debates of European history' and
that this kind of study is given its liveliest form when the subject
is 'drawn into the encounters of the generations and the parties
and the traditions with one another.'[6] The approach – setting
Erasmus in contemporary controversy – is valid at least to the
late nineteenth century when professionalism began in Erasmus
studies. It would be foolish to imagine that even after that the
impulse to use Erasmus for present purposes, constructive or controversial, was quite dead.

This is not the place for a systematic summary. Here are some
unsystematic indicators. Erasmus is mentioned in some of the
great documents of the Enlightenment, the *Encyclopédie* and Voltaire's *Essai sur les moeurs*, for example. He is used as a symbol
in the conflict between classical restraint and romantic fervour in
late eighteenth-century Germany. Correspondingly, those who
wrote about Erasmus and his age amid the turmoils of revolution
and the uneasy peace of the Restoration were easily tempted in
various ways to draw parallels and historical analogies: French
Revolution and German Reformation, Erasmus and Voltaire, religious wars and Napoleonic conquests. Movements of national
liberation or national self-assertion were the staple of nineteenth-
century politics. How might the pacifist and cosmopolitan Erasmus fare in the age of nationalism? Might its excesses provoke
an interest in distant apostles of internationalism? Similarly, might
writers in touch with liberal and constitutional movements in the
nineteenth century have their interest stirred in the political writings of one who could say: 'If no more than an ordinary man is
presented (things being what they are nowadays), then monarchy
should preferably be checked and diluted with a mixture of ar-

istocracy and democracy ...'7 Through the whole period runs a sequence of theological changes not unconnected with the broad development of intellectual life – the theology of the Enlightenment, romantic theology, the theology of the evangelical revival and 'Awakening,' Hegelian theology, neo-scholasticism, and theological liberalism. Representatives of all of them had their encounters with Erasmus.

Nineteenth-century historiography of Erasmus had two marked, if contradictory, features. On the one hand, liberalism was a strong, often dominant, voice. Erasmus was made an initiator of liberalizing tendencies, especially in religion, which were thought still to be working themselves out. On the other hand, religious revivals of various kinds reopened the Reformation debates; denominational loyalties were reinforced. Erasmus found himself again the victim of confessional conflict. In retrospect it can be seen that twentieth-century scholarship (with notable forerunners) had the task of escaping liberal simplicities on the one hand and confessional narrowness on the other. Ecumenism assisted, perhaps also the massive secularization characteristic of the century, but the latter carried the threat of leaving stranded Erasmus and his predominantly religious concerns. Growing professionalism brought to writing on Erasmus scholarly substance which no previous age could rival. Above all, the vast correspondence of Erasmus and his contemporaries was at last reordered and presented in an exemplary and monumental work of editing. The most promising way forward in the early years of the century was, through study of that correspondence, to trace Erasmus' associations throughout Europe, his influence on his contemporaries, not least on those in power. Both greater precision and a clearer sense of Erasmus' world became possible. Larger questions could not, of course, be evaded. How might the interpretation of Erasmus be affected by the twentieth-century crises of that Western civilization of which he was for many a leader, a model figure, or symbol? In this volume that question may just be broached.

PART ONE

ENLIGHTENMENT, ROMANTICISM, AND
REVOLUTION

TWO

Introduction to Part One

There is a pattern to the history of Erasmus interpretations over the two to three generations 1750–1820.[1] Advances in the scholarship of the subject were rare;[2] there were few subtle or discriminating analyses. One could hardly claim that understanding was significantly deeper at the end of the period than at the beginning, if the measure were (as it should be) a greater awareness of complexity (in the man and his thought), a recognition, through a tracing out, of the innumerable links between the man and his time and place, or an appreciation of the distinctive character of his society and mental world. The interest lies rather in the effects on Erasmus interpretation of the substantial cultural shifts of the period. Once again, Erasmus was used – as example or as warning – in other people's controversies.

In the second half of the eighteenth century he was taken as a model, or at least a forerunner, of the enlightenment that educated men were then claiming for themselves. His exact role was determined by the attitude one took to the Protestant Reformation. On one view, he worked along with the Reformation, itself seen as the first stage of the Enlightenment, for the liberation of the human mind. On another, he was the herald of a distinct, more radical religious revolution than the Protestant Reformers envisaged or, at any rate, achieved. In this case the Reformation was seen as a continuation of medieval civilization, with its authoritarianism and dogmatism, or even its reinforcement. But on either view, Erasmus was associated with moral virtues or social values held to be admirable; they were tolerance, restraint, moderation, a certain reticence or even scepticism, sincerity, openness, reasonableness.

Well before the end of the eighteenth century there was a moral and cultural shift and what had been virtues became vices. At least different names could be given to the Enlightenment values: tolerance and restraint became fearfulness, scepticism lack of faith, and openness frivolity or emptiness. Now the stress was on commitment and sacrifice and authenticity. Erasmus was held to lack these virtues. In romanticism, especially when in harness with nationalism, the search was for heroic qualities and the sixteenth century offered heroes enough to outshine the timid Erasmus; in Germany there were, above all, Hutten and Luther. Indeed, character, the force and vitality of a personality, replaced the virtues as the main preoccupation of biographers. Romanticism bequeathed this preoccupation to the nineteenth-century writers on Erasmus.

The upheavals of the revolutionary era in their turn rearranged the pattern. For some the parallel between the Reformation and the French Revolution reinforced the condemnation of Erasmus as too fearful and indecisive; in both cases, the times required upset and cleansing and that meant forceful leadership. Others, even some who had earlier exalted the heroic and authentic, were shocked by revolutionary violence and appealed for moderation. For them, again, Erasmus became a model of toleration and civility. Under the Restoration, in particular, there were writers (especially among Catholics) who saw him as a survivor in times of violence and calamity; that is how they also saw themselves. In this phase the tendency was to separate Erasmus from the Reformers, whereas most writers of the Protestant Enlightenment had had the two working together, as we have seen. Of those who wrote about Erasmus in reaction against the Enlightenment and the Revolution, only S.T. Coleridge – in the most important contribution of the period – avoided sectarian division and wrote about Luther and Erasmus with equal sympathy.

The religious revivals of the revolutionary and post-revolutionary eras were neither clear loss nor clear gain for Erasmus' reputation. Where, under the influence of romanticism, the emphasis was on feeling and sentiment, Erasmus, with his call for a piety inward and sincere, could seem a pioneer. However, the intensity of feeling and the insistence on doctrinal correctness in both the evangelical and Catholic revivals worked against him. While liberals and liberal Protestants persisted with the heritage of the Enlightenment, those of stronger denominational loyalty were to revive the harsh judgments of the confessional age.

THREE

Erasmus and Enlightenment

🐦

'Within limits, the Enlightenment was what one thinks it was.'[1] The writers of the Enlightenment, whom for the sake of simplifying we may call the *philosophes*, were not of one mind and 'carried on an unending debate with one another' on matters both fundamental and ephemeral.[2] But they did have common preoccupations and these had consequences for their judgments on past ages and individual figures of the past. They were sceptical about the supernatural and concentrated on the subcelestial world; they rejected present dogmatisms and exercised their critical faculties on the authoritative institutions and the authoritative books of the past; within the somewhat severe limits set by contemporary theories of the mind and personality, they were interested at one and the same time in the workings of individual psychologies (as they were also in the multifarious operations of the natural world) and in the character and destiny of 'humanity' beyond the compartments – ecclesiastical and political – in which it had hitherto been confined; they were political in that they sought to change existing institutions, to check arbitrariness in government, extend and safeguard toleration, put down superstition, open opportunities (again within limits that varied from *philosophe* to *philosophe* and from situation to situation); in observing human affairs and human history they could vacillate between pessimism and optimism but over all they believed in a progress – at least in recent times – from 'barbarism' to civilization.

One would expect writers with such preoccupations to take an interest in Erasmus and view him sympathetically. To identify his 'philosophy of Christ' with the outlook of eighteenth-century *philosophes* would be a great distortion, but he did attack a religion that relied excessively on rituals and condoned superstitious practices; he did criticize dogmatic theologians and prefer humane action to doctrinal exactitude; he was ecumenical and cosmopolitan and satirized the boorish values of many of the princes and aristocrats of his time; he advanced critical studies and contributed to a mood of 'renaissance.' In fact, the references to Erasmus in some of the classic works of the Enlightenment are disappointing. They are neither subtle nor substantial. Much about him that had been recovered by earlier writers was again lost or overlooked. Compared with the writers of the late seventeenth and early eighteenth centuries who genuinely honoured him, says Werner Kaegi, those of the encyclopedists' generation 'cited Erasmus, but scarcely read him.'[3] It is, sadly, not by the brilliant writers of the Enlightenment but by the more plodding church historians that the proper study of Erasmus is advanced in this period. We begin with the chief literary monument (the *Encyclopédie*) and the dominant voice (Voltaire) of the Enlightenment in France.

I

The *Encyclopédie, ou Dictionnaire raisonnée des sciences, des arts et des métiers* (1751–72) gave a name and a character to a generation. It was 'a repository of technological information, which could thus be preserved and disseminated' and 'an anthology of "enlightened" opinions on politics, philosophy and religion, whatever disguises contributors had to adopt in order to hoodwink their somewhat somnolent censors.'[4] To it the many-sided Diderot gave much of his working life. Unfortunately its main contribution on Erasmus – in the article on Rotterdam in volume XIV – is mostly a plagiarism. Otherwise he appears only in the very first volume (1751) in an article by Mallet on Arianism. This heresy, Mallet says, had been extinguished throughout the Middle Ages, 'when at the beginning of the sixteenth century Erasmus, in his commentary on the New Testament, seemed to wish to revive it.' To enemies who accused him of sowing Arian glosses and interpretations in this work he replied simply that there was no more defunct heresy than the Arian, an assertion belied by developments after the appearance of Servetus. This is but an echo of previous controversies about the purported Arianism of Erasmus.[5]

The article on Rotterdam is the work of Louis, Chevalier de Jaucourt (1704–80).[6] Jaucourt belonged to an old aristocratic family of Burgundy converted to Protestantism in the sixteenth century.[7] He studied at Geneva and Cambridge and took a medical degree at Leiden (1730). Though he joined Diderot's team only after the publication of the first volume, he finished by writing over a quarter of the total number of articles in the *Encyclopédie*. He earned nothing for his efforts – the publishers treated him shabbily – and he did not particularly have the respect of his collaborators though they had to recognize his devotion. 'This man,' Diderot wrote in 1760, 'has been for six or seven years at the centre of four or five secretaries, reading, dictating, working thirteen to fourteen hours a day, and this situation has not yet wearied him.'[8] Unhappily the conditions under which he worked made him a 'ruthless compiler.'[9] 'In general,' said Naigeon, 'this compiler knew the good sources well enough and most of his articles in the *Encyclopédie* are copied word for word from our most celebrated authors.'[10]

The article on Rotterdam conforms to that picture. Almost everything of substance in it is borrowed from the *Dictionnaire* of Pierre Bayle. There is some summary of Bayle but much is also quoted verbatim. The article on Erasmus in Bayle's dictionary, supplemented by references in his own article on Rotterdam, had been a milestone in the study of Erasmus.[11] Its erudite notes settled a number of questions in Erasmus' biography. Despite some studied ambiguities reminiscent of Erasmus himself, the picture comes through clearly: Erasmus shared Bayle's own hatred of party spirit and intolerance in religion; he feared the appearance of these in the Reformation and, after an early welcome to Luther, underestimated the good the Reformation would do. The *philosophes* generally did not understand the combination of the Protestant and the sceptic in Bayle, born as it was from the controversies in and around late seventeenth-century French Calvinism. In a sense they captured him for their own more direct assault on superstition and even on religious belief itself. 'They pillaged no book more freely, more often' than Bayle's *Dictionnaire*.[12] Even Jaucourt's Protestant associations failed – at least in the piece on Erasmus – to take him beyond his colleagues' half-understanding of Bayle. And the work of pillaging itself was done indifferently. The selection is arbitrary and the intellectual energy which gives a sense of direction to the apparent chaos of Bayle's notes is lacking.

The omissions are as interesting as the inclusions. Bayle's extended treatment of Erasmus' literary controversies, those with J.C. Scaliger, for example, is not included and this diminishes Bayle's depiction of Erasmus' place in the republic of letters. The circumstances of his conception – an appealing subject to an Enlightenment relatively liberated in sexual matters – are not discussed. But Jaucourt repeats Bayle's rather ponderous reflections on Erasmus' chastity.[13]

The article begins – appropriately, given its titular subject – with matter on the town of Rotterdam, but its core is the two columns on Erasmus. Rotterdam was the country of Erasmus and has erected a statue to his memory – that is the town's glory. What follows about Rotterdam's claim to be the birthplace of Erasmus and its affirmation of that claim is taken virtually word for word from Bayle's article on Rotterdam.[14] Erasmus' life – his monastic experience, his visits to England and Italy, his attachment to Emperor Charles V and later to the city of Basel – is summarized from Bayle on Erasmus. The notes plagiarized are those on Erasmus' praise of the English nobility and its learning (praise confirmed by Bayle for his time and reiterated here) – fifteen lines are also quoted from Erasmus' famous letter about the ready kissing of English noblewomen, naturally without the censoriousness of earlier (clerical) writers; on Rome's offer of a cardinalate which he had within his grasp if he had but chosen; on his dissertation on the proverb *Dulce bellum inexpertis*; on Holbein's portrait and Beza's epigram about it.[15] The borrowing from Bayle's crucial note T on Erasmus and the Reformation[16] shifts the emphasis from the Reformation itself to the attacks on Erasmus by both sides and indeed by 'all the sects.' To that marginal extent Bayle is revised in an Enlightenment sense. The main judgment is an elaboration of Bayle's:

It would be superfluous to say here that Erasmus was one of the greatest men of the republic of letters. We owe principally to him the rebirth of the sciences, criticism and the taste for antiquity in our country. He was one of the first to treat religious matters with the nobility and dignity befitting the Christian mysteries ('nos mysteres'). He was tolerant, loved peace and knew all its value.[17]

The words added to Bayle – the two middle sentences of this passage – smack of Burigny, whose biography was published eight years before the appearance of this volume of the *Encyclopédie*, and, more generally, of writers sympathetic to Erasmus in both the Catholic and Protestant traditions. But in this setting and in association with a Bayle plagiarized for purposes not quite his own, Erasmus, too, emerges – however sketchily – as an Enlightenment man.

The comparison between Erasmus and Voltaire has been a historical commonplace since the nineteenth century. 'It is impossible in reading Erasmus not to be reminded of the rationalist of the 18th century,' wrote Mark Pattison in 1878.[18] Sixty years later a professor at the University of Amsterdam took the comparison as the subject of his inaugural lecture.[19] Peter Gay has taken up an idea of Edward Gibbon's[20] and actually brought the two together in a somewhat implausible dialogue in defence of the Enlightenment.[21] Voltaire himself made the comparison. In a letter praising Burigny's lives of Erasmus and Grotius, he wrote: 'The two men [Erasmus and Grotius] were fortunate to have come before the present age. Something a little stronger is necessary for us today. They came at the beginning of the meal. We now are intoxicated, we ask for wine from the Cape and water from Barbados.'[22] At other times he was to see the age of Erasmus in a more sombre light.

In an entry in his notebooks belonging probably to the first half of the 1750s Voltaire put Erasmus in a characteristic setting:

> Ridicule succeeded in discrediting what the morals of the ecclesiastical courts had already made odious. Reuchlin, Hutten, Erasmus contributed to that. Rabelais came afterwards. The French arrive last in everything. The Italians treated the Germans as barbarians; the latter took their revenge and wished to prove that in religion, in morals, in government it was the Italians who were the barbarians.[23]

Erasmus belonged to the effective scoffers.

Correspondingly, Erasmus appears in Voltaire's great history

of medieval civilization, the *Essai sur les moeurs et l'esprit des
nations*, in connection with the crisis at the end of the Middle
Ages over the state of the church.[24] Throughout the Middle Ages,
says Voltaire, the papacy had aggravated the confusions of Christian civilization. Pope Leo X (1513–21), on the contrary, believed
that he had restored the order of Roman days. He combined 'the
most refined taste with the most finished magnificence.' Voltaire's
tone is half-approving, half-ironical. 'We should recognize that
this [papal] court civilized [poliçait] Europe and made men more
sociable.' Troubles over religion were being calmed and 'the majority of Christians lived in a happy ignorance.'[25]

   The real contradictions remained, however, unresolved. The
luxury of the papal court and the abuses in the church generally
were an offence to ordinary people: 'Most fathers of families who
worked unceasingly to provide a modest living for their wives
and children ... saw with pain monks surrounded by the pomp
and luxury of princes.'[26]

   A deeper irony attached to the pope's achievement: 'in encouraging studies he gave arms against himself.' The rebirth of
letters which he favoured began the ruin of the spiritual monarchy. Men in northern Germany, whom the Italians treated as
barbarians, first accustomed minds to condemn what they had
revered. 'Erasmus, though long a monk himself – or rather because he had been a monk – cast on the monks a ridicule from
which they never recovered.' Such ridicule prepared the way for
a more serious revolution which Leo X did not anticipate. It began
actually in a quarrel among German monks over the profits from
the sale of indulgences and was soon out of control: 'this little
monkish interest in a corner of Saxony produced more than a
hundred years of discord, frenzy and misfortune for thirty nations.'[27]

   In the chapter on the German Reformation which follows there
are two further references to Erasmus. Voltaire touches on the
controversy between Erasmus and Luther. In the midst of the
maelstrom of theological controversy the issue of freewill – that
trap for the human reason – 'mixed its inexhaustible spring of
absurd quarrels with a torrent of theological hatreds.' Further, he
compares the historical influence of the two men. If it were only
a matter of injuries done the church Luther would have achieved
less than Erasmus. But Luther, unlike Erasmus, created a party

which challenged not only the scholastic dogmas but all the claims of the papacy and took a large part of Europe out of its obedience.[28]

In this treatment Erasmus is associated with the revival of learning but much more with a severe assault – by ridicule – on ecclesiastical abuses. He was an essentially negative if cleansing force. He is given no particular historical dignity; indeed, he arouses less interest as a human being than the nameless 'fathers of families' who engage Voltaire's sympathy and ours.

In fact, in this and other respects the treatment of Erasmus is characteristic of Voltaire's historical writing in general and the *Essai* in particular. He was interested relatively little in the psychology of individual figures of the past; but in a kind of social history which turned attention to the affairs of ordinary people he was a pioneer. He was vividly aware of the endless suffering that makes up human history and attributed men's misfortunes, above all, to intransigence, dogmatism, and intellectual self-assertion: 'it is the power of opinion, true or false, sacred or profane, which has filled the earth with bloodshed during so many centuries.'[29] Important, too, were the evidences of progress, of a dawning enlightenment, no matter how wan and grey: 'amid a background of horrors and follies of every kind, mankind gradually makes progress.'[30] There Erasmus has his modest place.

The bitter reference to the free-will controversy has its irony. While writing the *Essai* Voltaire was preoccupied with the problem of determinism – indeed it tormented him – and examples of the various answers he attempted may be found in the *Essai*.[31] That the tumults of the Reformation and the sufferings of peoples and nations could arise from a money-changers' dispute among monks was a disturbing instance of the problem of small causes and great effects.

In his historical works Voltaire shows little sympathy for the Reformers, essentially because the theological quarrels they aroused ended in religious war. The doctrines of the Reformers are ignored or treated with irony or contempt.[32] Yet, Voltaire saw in the Reformation a model – no matter how distorted – of the renovation he wished to bring about in Western civilization. The little Reformation of the sixteenth century must be followed by a great one, in the name of a tolerant theism.[33] 'I have done more in my time than Luther and Calvin. We see them, by a fatal error, oppose abuse to abuse, scandal to scandal. Among the factions hot to throw themselves on one another, they condemned the pope and wished to imitate him. By them all, Europe was desolated for a long time. They troubled the earth, and I have consoled it.'[34] Unlike Gibbon and a number of nineteenth-century writers, he did not in so many words associate Erasmus with the larger reformation.

By the time of the second edition of the *Essai* in 1761 Voltaire was in full cry against '*l'Infâme*' by which he meant fanaticism and more generally 'the intolerance practised by organized churches and inspired by Christian dogmas.'[35] His 'Conversation de Lucien, Erasme, et Rabelais dans les champs élysées' (1765) belongs to the most militant phase of his writing.[36] In the world of the dead Lucian falls into conversation with Erasmus, despite his feeling of repugnance for the barbarous race to which the latter belonged. He found that Erasmus' vocation was identical with his own, turning a salutary ridicule against the whole human condition ('vous vous êtes moqué de tout'). But Erasmus, calling himself a 'poor theologian,' explains dejectedly how circumspect he had to be in his time and place: Lucian had to deal with a religion of play-acting ('des dieux qu'on jouait sur le théâtre') and with philosophers as light-weight as their gods; he had to deal with real fanatics and 'I needed great care not to be burned by the one or assassinated by the other.' Vain notions – there is a passing reference to the sacramental controversy – turned men into sombre fanatics. A man of his profession was thought unnatural if he did not take sides between the two factions.[37] Here Voltaire is in the line of Bayle: the enemy for both is party spirit.

What was Erasmus' profession? He was a 'Dutch monk.' What did that mean? The language turns savage: it meant having no real profession, 'being bound by an unbreakable oath to be useless to the human race, to be absurd and enslaved, and to live at the expense of others.' How could Erasmus enter a condition so dishonouring to human nature? In reply he offers a brief autobiography: 'Being very young and having neither relations nor friends, I let myself be seduced by beggars who wanted to increase the number of those like themselves.' 'What consoles me,' he adds, 'is that everybody in the age when I lived had reached the last stage of madness; they can only return from it and some among them finally rediscover a little reason.'[38] So much for the Renaissance and the age of reason! To this gloomy Erasmus, speaking for one side of Voltaire, progress was relative and limited.

Lucian's laughter at Erasmus' long list of his contemporaries' follies draws a new character on to the stage: 'Where there is laughter, I am welcome.' It is Rabelais whom Voltaire had rejected in the past as too gross and unrestrained but whose comic style he now in his militant phase found useful for polemic against *l'Infâme*.[39] Voltaire's Rabelais in fact expresses the double nature of the *philosophe*: he plays the fool and to a besotted people, as the French were in his time, he seems a mere clown but underneath the frivolity is a hard ridicule which men of discernment understand. By this double play Rabelais escaped the persecution which even Erasmus suffered. Erasmus' comment is: 'He was bolder than me and more humorous; but he was a priest and could take more liberties than me, a monk.'[40]

There follows a three-way conversation on the ecclesiastical tyranny of popes and cardinals who, says Erasmus, studiously put down reason, which was beginning to raise its head. Lucian concludes that it was better to live in his time than in theirs; the fables of Jupiter, Neptune, and Pluto which he mocked were respectable when compared with the lunacies of arrogant cardinals, infallible popes, and fawning monks. The conversation finishes in a dialogue between Erasmus and Rabelais. Rabelais considers that, despite differences between them in their lifetimes – the one being too reserved and the other too bold – he and Erasmus now think alike; yet a difference of mood persists. When they see arriving in the Elysian Fields a teacher who has exhausted himself in vain studies all his life, Rabelais laughs but Erasmus remains melancholy. The man is undeceived too late. 'The great pleasure is to show the way to friends who are going astray; the dead ask their way of no one.' Here Erasmus speaks for Voltaire, urgent publicist for the Enlightenment.[41] The three figures are joined by Jonathan Swift, much loved by Voltaire for his combination of sharp polemic and classical restraint,[42] and the four go off to dine together. Looking back over the whole conversation, one feels that this disenchanted Erasmus, sketchily presented as a historical figure, speaks for the side of Voltaire weighed down by the seemingly ineradicable follies of mankind. Only in the expressed hope of recalling friends who are losing their way, does vivacity flicker up in this Erasmus.

Erasmus who, against the odds in the fanatic world of his time, turned folly and tyranny to ridicule: that is the Erasmus to emerge from the pages of Voltaire. In late writings other sides are briefly suggested. In 1767 when he was seventy-two Voltaire added a fresh controversy to those in which he was already engaged. Early in the year Jean François Marmontel published a didactic novel *Bélisaire*, its hero being Belisarius, general of the Byzantine emperor Justinian. The fifteenth chapter of the book dealt first with a classic problem in theology, the destiny of virtuous pagans: Belisarius, Marmontel's mouthpiece, says that he expects to find the good Roman emperors in heaven. In the second half of the chapter, Marmontel takes the more daring path of defending civil toleration. Why, he asks, do rulers take it upon themselves to persecute people over speculative teachings unconnected with essential morality? Undistinguished as a literary performance, the work nevertheless expressed its author's strong personal feeling on these matters and immediately attracted the hostile attention of defenders of the traditional position that the state was obliged to uphold revealed truth. The 1760s were a time in France when public opinion and opinion in government were turning away from that position.[43] The Sorbonne, still a bastion of orthodoxy, saw an opportunity for a test of strength with its enemies. It represented the work as camouflaged propaganda for deism, which was to make Marmontel more extreme than he was. In time Voltaire and the *philosophes* also accepted the trial of strength and the *Bélisaire* affair became 'the pretext for a renewed dispute of imposing and perhaps unparalleled proportions between the *philosophes* and the church.'[44] But even in the early stages (April 1767) Voltaire came to Marmontel's support with his *Anecdote sur Bélisaire*. Preoccupied with recent cases of savage persecution of Protestants, he saw in any suppression of Marmontel or recantation by him the danger of overweening arrogance in the Sorbonne and an entrenchment of intolerance. The *Anecdote* was prepared easily and rapidly – composed, printed, and despatched within six days.[45]

The scene is an after-dinner conversation at the house of a learned magistrate and the protagonist a recently licensed monk called Triboulet, who had dined too well with the servants and now chose to attack one of the magistrate's guests, a member of the Academy. The attack opens on the theme of the virtuous pagan. Marmontel – for he is the academician – had villainously presented God as the 'father of all men.' Finally, through Belisarius he had pronounced the impious words: 'What attaches me most to my religion is that it makes me better and more human.'

Such words appeal (in Voltaire's summary of the philosophic movement) to good women, educated soldiers, just judges, and 'men of letters unhappily more filled with taste and sentiment than theology.' Triboulet blusters and threatens: 'Know that we damn everybody when we are on the bench; that is our pleasure.' He rejoices that among millions on millions who are damned only two or three thousand are saved. To all this Marmontel replies with ironic disdain. Triboulet returns to the charge: the *philosophes* preach benevolence and go so far as to say that God is good. In the Renaissance this fallacy was taught by Erasmus: 'We well know that in the century when reason, which we had everywhere proscribed, began to be reborn in our northern lands, it was Erasmus who renewed this dangerous error, Erasmus who was tempted to say: Holy Socrates, pray for us; Erasmus to whom they raised a statue.'[46] In the seventeenth century the sceptic La Mothe Le Vayer took it up.[47] There should be no leniency to preachers of this error. Here the dialogue touches the deeper issue of toleration but then finishes in the magistrate's admonition to the monk ('do not insult an excellent writer; go on making bad books and leave us to read good ones'), the latter's retreat, and Marmontel's conclusion that everybody is really of his opinion but most hide it out of envy or interest.[48]

Erasmus, as he appears in this context, has become more than a master of ridicule; he taught a generous idea of God and the possibility of salvation for all mankind. Voltaire had come to the verge of associating him with his desired reformation.

Also in 1767 Voltaire returned – in his letter 'Sur les Allemands' – to the subject of the other Reformation. This short piece – one of a number on literary figures of the past and the present – contains pleasantly detached and ironic portraits of figures in German intellectual history during and since the sixteenth century, especially those accused of irreligion, including Erasmus. 'The famous Erasmus was suspected equally of irreligion by the catholics and by the protestants because he ridiculed the excesses into which the one and the other had fallen. When two sides are wrong, he who remains neutral and who consequently is right is harassed by both. The statue which has been erected to him in the square at Rotterdam, his birthplace, is his revenge on Luther and the Inquisition.'[49] Melanchthon was in the same case as Erasmus; he was 'moderate and tolerant' but accused of indifference. Voltaire goes on to Leibniz and to Wolff the contemporary rationalist theologian. This is a return to the Erasmus of Bayle, enemy of the warring parties, sceptical holder of the middle ground, victim of fanatical excess. There is a touch of warmth missing in the earlier picture of Erasmus, scoffer at superstition: the way of the reasonable man, the neutral, was hard. But a later generation – as the repeated reference to Erasmus' statue suggests – recalls his memory with pleasure.

Voltaire left, as we have seen, only fragments on Erasmus. The evidence is then too brief and too diverse to create a finished portrait; interest lies in establishing the nature of Erasmus' appeal to Voltaire. In fact the Erasmus that emerges expresses aspects of the many-sided personality of Voltaire himself. Dominant is scorn and ridicule for the superstitious, the charlatan, the dogmatist, the persecutor. More appealing is the sense of a man battling against odds, almost defeated by the murderous passions of the religious parties. Voltaire may have seen Erasmus as a forerunner but in circumstances far less favourable than his own. He saw Swift as 'le Rabelais de la bonne compagnie.'[50] His Erasmus might be considered the Voltaire of hard times.

II

The Enlightenment gave a high place to history.[51] Works of history are among its masterpieces. Much of its polemic was historical. It did not resolve satisfactorily the contradiction between scholarship and the restraint necessary for historical judgment on the one hand and polemic against the Christian or feudal past on the other. The case of Voltaire makes that clear. There were differences, however, and in some works and writers we are brought close to that sense of the past and the methods and approaches necessary for understanding it which are usually and rightly attributed to the great historians of the nineteenth century like Leopold von Ranke. This is true of the Scottish cleric and historian William Robertson.[52] His vocation and outlook as well as the subjects he chose for historical enquiry made the history of the sixteenth century important to Robertson and so he came to deal with Erasmus.

His vocation was that of a minister of the Church of Scotland, and he did not treat lightly the doctrines of the Presbyterian church.[53] He was chief of a party, the so-called Moderates, who led but by no means dominated the Church of Scotland in the second half of the eighteenth century, and in that way represented the Enlightenment in its peculiarly Scottish form.

The Moderates had a comprehensive view of the church; their ideal was 'a Church occupying a central place in the national life, Established yet politically independent, disciplined yet comprehensive and tolerant, committed to "progress" yet conforming to the existing structure of Scottish life.'[54] A cultural openness went along with this way of seeing the church. The Moderates detached themselves from the stricter Calvinist tradition, from theocratic notions and puritan restraints; as to the last, some of the younger Moderates made 'an express design' – of which attendance at the theatre was a demonstration – 'to throw contempt on that vile species of hypocrisy which magnified an indecorum into a crime, and gave an air of false sanctimony and Jesuitism to the greatest part of the clergy, and was thereby pernicious to rational religion.'[55]

The Moderates stood for good order, cultural progress, and a reasoned faith. Tensions, even contradictions, between these values were possible. In Robertson they were kept in balance. As Moderator from 1763 to 1780 he combined respect for authority with independence of the political powers. His election as principal of the University of Edinburgh in 1762 had demonstrated the sympathy of those same political powers – in the country and the city – for his Moderate principles and indeed for the Scottish Enlightenment.[56] Of 'mild conciliatory temper,' he was long 'honourably employed in healing the divisions of a church torn with faction, and in smoothing the transition from the severity of puritanical manners, to habits less at variance with the genius of the times.'[57]

Robertson was a perfect representative of the distinctive character of the Scottish Enlightenment. It was not anticlerical; it associated the national church with cultural progress and did not reject the Christian past.[58] His attitude to the Reformers will, therefore, be very different from Voltaire's.

The sobriety, judgment, good order, and independence of mind that Robertson admired in church and society, he aimed for also in written history. He shared with the *philosophes* the assumption that history tended towards a more refined society and the rule of reason.[59] The assumption underlies his famous introduction to his *History of the Reign of the Emperor Charles V* (1769), 'The Progress of Society in Europe.' But, unlike most of his *confrères*, he could refer to providence without a smirk or equivocation. Above all, Robertson saw no contradiction between his preconceptions about progress or the divine purpose and scholarly historical enquiry. Not only in his perception of a European political system where the great powers were held together by a balance of power did Robertson anticipate Ranke. He made strides towards the critical historiography of the nineteenth century. He was, within limits, an archival researcher; he made 'accuracy' a watchword. He eschewed conjecture and speculation and scorned literary flourishes. He was aware of the dangers of anachronism and of the complexity of historical causation.[60] His gravity and insistence on the 'dignity' of history have raised smiles.[61] But precisely that seriousness of mind helped distinguish history from journalism and *belles lettres*. Hume saw that in Robertson gravity of style and soundness of judgment went together.[62] By the standards of the age he was non-partisan. Of his *History of Scotland* (1759) he wrote to a friend: 'I have not spared to speak truth of all factions and parties.'[63]

Robertson's treatment of the Reformation – an extended interlude in his *Reign of Charles V* – may be taken as a measure of his approach and achievement. Much of what has been said above is reflected there. It demonstrates that gravity of manner and concern for authenticity are not the same as dryness or emotional shallowness. Dugald Stewart's perceptive remark applies to the Reformation section: 'His own imagination was warm and vigorous; and, although in the conduct of life it gave no tincture of enthusiasm to his temper, yet, in the solitude of the closet, it attached him peculiarly to those passages of history which approach to the romantic.'[64]

A charge of thinness or superficiality has been laid frequently against Robertson's treatment of the Reformation. These have been said to arise either from a lack of appreciation of spiritual forces or from a wish to separate clearly civil and ecclesiastical history and to concentrate attention on the former, on political history.[65] The charge cannot be sustained.

Robertson recognized the Reformation as a spiritual upheaval, 'a revolution in the sentiments of mankind, the greatest as well as the most beneficial that has happened since the publication of Christianity.'

To overturn a system of religious belief founded on ancient

and deep-rooted prejudices, supported by power, and defended with no less art than industry; to establish in its room doctrines of the most contrary genius and tendency; and to accomplish all this not by external violence or the force of arms, are operations which historians the least prone to credulity and superstition ascribe to that Divine Providence which, with infinite ease, can bring about events which to human sagacity appear impossible.[66]

He recognized the personal force of Luther: he was serious and learned, his 'naturally sound' understanding was soon disgusted with the frivolities and subtleties of scholasticism, he had a 'warm and impetuous temper.' Even those traits thought 'in ages of greater moderation and refinement' to be defects – his fierceness of spirit, arrogance, scurrility, and buffoonery – counted in his favour with a people bearing the burden of papal tyranny. Nor did Robertson overlook the theological foundations of the Reformation. Luther's theological progress was gradual; in confuting indulgences he was 'obliged to inquire into the true cause of our justification and acceptance with God' and was led on to question the position of the clergy and the papacy.[67]

Certainly Robertson attended to the surrounding circumstances, including the political circumstances. Others had propagated opinions like Luther's before but had failed; 'at that critical and mature juncture when he appeared, circumstances of every kind concurred in rendering each step that he took successful.'[68] In fact, Robertson's presentation of the Reformation is a dialectic of doctrine and circumstance, Luther's progress a dialectic of conscience and politics.

Robertson spoke with the voice of the Scottish Enlightenment, as some of his expressions make clear: the Roman authority stood 'in direct opposition to the dictates of reason and the determinations of the divine law'; Luther 'had ventured to assert the liberty of mankind'; men 'listened with joy to the first offer of procuring them deliverance!' The work of the Reformation was intellectual emancipation, the liberation of the human mind. 'The charm which had bound mankind for so many ages was broken at once.'[69]

It is not surprising, therefore, that Robertson saw the revival of learning as 'a circumstance extremely friendly to the Reformation.'[70] Already in the *History of Scotland* he had said dra-

matically: 'The human mind felt its own strength, broke the fetters
of authority by which it had been so long constrained.'[71] But
science and philosophy, for all their progress, worked slowly;
generally, they are better fitted to undermine an established false
religion than to replace it. Something more precipitate was required and that Luther provided.[72]

As an Enlightenment historian Robertson took a positive view
of the Reformation. Certainly it brought on the 'fatal calamities'
which preoccupied the mind of Voltaire but it also served 'to
increase purity of manners, to diffuse science, and to inspire humanity.'[73] He saw as mutually reinforcing the Renaissance, or
revival of leaning, and the Reformation. This is one of the standard Protestant interpretations but now heavily overlaid with 'enlightenment.' The same may be said of Robertson's account of
Erasmus.

Erasmus' influence – the combination of his high reputation
and the character of his writings – was 'one of the circumstances
which contributed considerably towards Luther's success.' Like
other controversialists of the time – Reuchlin and Hutten – he
had turned with bitterness against the corruptions of the church.
His particular sphere was theological controversy. 'Erasmus having been destined for the church, and trained up in the knowledge
of ecclesiastical literature, applied himself more to theological
inquiries than any of the revivers of learning in that age. His
acute judgment and extensive erudition enabled him to discover
many errors both in the doctrine and worship of the Romish
church. Some of these he confuted with great solidity of reasoning
and force of eloquence.' The opening words of this passage give
more value to Erasmus' monastic and scholastic training than was
customary. His use of ridicule – an 'irresistible torrent of popular
and satirical wit' – was a more familiar theme. There then follows
a sentence which takes the Protestant Enlightenment's identification of Renaissance and Reformation as far as it could go. 'There
was hardly any opinion or practice of the Romish church which
Luther endeavoured to reform, but what had been previously
animadverted upon by Erasmus, and had afforded him subject
either of censure or of raillery.' Consequently Erasmus appeared
to be on Luther's side in his earliest controversies; 'he courted
the friendship of several of his disciples and patrons, and condemned the spirit of his adversaries.' Indeed he openly agreed
with Luther in his attack on the scholastics 'as the teachers of a

system equally unedifying and obscure.' 'He joined him in endeavouring to turn the attention of men to the study of the Holy Scriptures, as the only standard of religious truth.'[74]

For this line of argument Robertson acknowledged his dependence on Hermann von der Hardt's *Historia literaria reformationis* which had been prepared for the Reformation anniversary of 1717 and presented the revival of learning and the Reformation as two stages of but one advance towards enlightenment, with the dethronement of scholasticism as an indispensable first step; both the dethronement and the revival were Erasmus' work.[75]

What follows demonstrates Robertson's debt to authors of a somewhat different stamp, Veit Ludwig von Seckendorf, the orthodox Lutheran, who was sympathetic to Erasmus and recognized his part in the great renovation but condemned his failure to stand by Luther unreservedly, and John Jortin, the English latitudinarian, who was more sympathetic still and defended Erasmus warmly against his detractors but yet regretted the final separation between him and Luther.[76] Erasmus, says Robertson, held back for various reasons. Some of them are more brutally stated than either Seckendorf or Jortin would have allowed.

> The natural timidity of his temper; his want of that strength of mind which alone can prompt a man to assume the character of a reformer; his excessive deference for persons in high station; his dread of losing the pensions and emoluments which their liberality had conferred upon him; his extreme love of peace, and hopes of reforming abuses gradually and by gentle methods, all concurred in determining him not only to repress and to moderate the zeal with which he had once been animated against the errors of the church, but to assume the character of a mediator between Luther and his opponents.

The moralizing tone anticipates Protestant writers of the nineteenth century. But Robertson does not linger over these judgments. He returns to his main line of argument. Erasmus was Luther's 'forerunner and auxiliary.' 'He first scattered the seeds which Luther cherished and brought to maturity.' So he was seen by the defenders of the old church in his time; so he must be seen by every informed observer.[77] The zigzag progress of Robertson's treatment is characteristic of enlightened Protestant discussion: Erasmus prepared and promoted the Reformation; yet he failed to stand by it; yet again without him it might have failed. Robertson, says the *Dictionary of National Biography*, lacked the 'suggestive cynicism' of Edward Gibbon.[78] There is, not cynicism necessarily, but a many-sided suggestiveness to Gibbon's references to Erasmus in the *Decline and Fall of the Roman Empire*. In subject they range from Erasmus' comments on the ecclesiastical controversies of antiquity to his relation to the revolutionary ferments of Gibbon's own time.

Gibbon's most extended comment on Erasmus is to be found in his journal for September 1762 and arose from his reading of Burigny.[79] It deals mostly with Erasmus' contribution to learning. This is natural because – ahead of all his contemporaries, of the other philosophical historians – Gibbon gave a high value to erudition; he defended the antiquarians and *érudits* of previous generations against their airy dismissal by the *philosophes*.[80] Erasmus' reputation for learning in his own time, says Gibbon, was enormous. 'All the scholars, and all the princes of Europe, looked upon him as an oracle.' The character of the age encouraged such adulation; it was a time of first awakening after a long sleep, when 'all orders of men applied themselves to letters with an enthusiasm which produced in them the highest esteem and veneration for one of their principal restorers.'[81]

Erasmus' achievement was real but limited. Despite a wandering life, ill health, and a vast correspondence, he produced numerous editions which evince his mastery of the ancient authors.

> And besides, those convenient compilations of all sorts, where a modern author can learn to be a profound scholar at a small expense, did not then exist; every thing was to be sought for in the originals themselves. But besides this learning, which was common to many, Erasmus possessed a genius without which no writer will ever descend to posterity; a genius which could see through the vain subtleties of the schools, revive the laws of criticism, treat every subject with eloquence and delicacy, sometimes emulate the ancients, often imitate them, and never copy them.[82]

The limits – again partly set by the age – were suggested to Gibbon by his reading of Erasmus' *Ciceronianus*, the work satirizing those intellectuals who made a fetish of Cicero's language and style.

Despite his justified scorn for the Ciceronians, Erasmus himself remained a prisoner of the ancients. He did not break through to a coherent modern idiom. 'Perhaps the natural conclusion from these various difficulties, where either freedom or correctness must be sacrificed, was, that instead of that ungrateful labour upon a dead language, it would be better to improve and cultivate the living ones. But this conclusion was too much for the age of Erasmus.'[83] In asides in the *Decline and Fall*, Gibbon speaks of Erasmus' 'admirable sense and freedom,' 'vivacity and good sense,' and 'taste.'[84] Yet his good sense was 'sometimes vitiated by an excessive love of antiquity.'[85] Gibbon is sharper with Erasmus' 'prudence' in admitting the Trinitarian interpolation at 1 John 5:7. The word suggests that Erasmus should have known better and indeed did know better; that separated him from the 'honest bigotry' of other editors. They yielded to their own prejudices, he to those of the times.[86]

On Erasmus' character Gibbon's judgment was unusually harsh. 'As to his morals, they had the poor merit of being regular. In the nobler part of his character I find him very deficient. Delicacy of sentiment he had none. A parasite of all the great men of his time, he was neither ashamed to magnify their characters by the lowest adulation, nor to debase his own by the most impudent solicitation to obtain presents which very often he did not want.'[87] This judgment had not come from Burigny. It derived from an uncharitable, indeed unjust, reading of Erasmus' (admittedly sedulous) letters to his patrons on whom in his early days at least he was completely dependent, not only for the means of life but also for making a career. Protestant observers like Jean Le Clerc had said that Erasmus abandoned Luther for fear of losing his pensions but Gibbon's condemnation is more sweeping and, coming from a gentleman of independent means, unfeeling.

Gibbon returns to a predictable warmth when he treats Erasmus' role in the Reformation. He was a conspicuous divine and all parties wanted to attract him. To which did he belong?

The Catholics claim him, though they acknowledge that he was often indiscreet. Le Clerc challenges him for the Protestants, though he blames him for not professing what he knew to be the truth; and attributes his reserve solely to timidity and self-interest. Erasmus has certainly exposed all the grosser superstitions of the Romish worship to the ridicule of the public: and had his free opinion been taken, I believe that he was a Protestant upon most of the contested points.[88]

But for Erasmus uncertainty was a tactic necessary, not for saving his own skin, but for defining, no matter how indirectly, his own cause. He believed that 'any speculative truths were dearly purchased at the expense of practical virtue and public peace.' That is close to Bayle's: 'he loved peace and knew its importance.'[89] A Catholic upbringing, the authority of the Fathers, 'a natural inclination to scepticism' might restrain him from joining the Lutherans. 'Add to all this, that really disapproving many things in the Protestant communion, though more in the Romish, by remaining in the loose situation of a man who was unwilling to quit the religion of his ancestors, he could blame many things in it with freedom; whereas had he deserted it, he must either have set up a standard himself, or else have enlisted blindly under that of Luther or Oecolampadius.'[90]

The reference to Erasmus in chapter LIV of the *Decline and Fall* makes this equivocation the starting-point of a religious tradition. This curious chapter follows the history of the so-called Paulician heresy from its beginnings in Asia Minor in the seventh century. The Paulicians sought a drastic simplification in rite, sacrament, and creed; they also shared the Gnostic or Manichaean belief in two rival principles, two gods, one of goodness and the spirit, the other of evil and matter; their growth was an 'obstinate vegetation of fanaticism and reason.' In the eighth century the heresy entered Europe; by the twelfth it had penetrated the West and become an expression of resistance to the papacy, eventually under the name 'Albigensian.' The bitterest persecution left nevertheless a 'latent succession' of those 'who protested against the tyranny of Rome, embraced the Bible as the rule of faith, and purified their creed from all the visions of the Gnostic theology. The struggles of Wickliff in England, of Huss in Bohemia, were premature and ineffectual; but the names of Zvinglius, Luther, and Calvin are pronounced with gratitude as the deliverers of nations.'[91] Thus Gibbon introduces the Reformation as the successor of the Paulicians in their various manifestations. The Reformation appears out of sequence, as a kind of digression, and that necessarily limits the scope of Gibbon's discussion.[92] He is concerned with a philosopher's, not a historian's, question: from what articles of faith *'above* or *against* our reason' have the Reformers enfranchised Christians?[93] The conclusion is: 'After a fair discussion we shall rather be surprised by the timidity, than scandalized by the freedom, of our first reformers.' They clung to the Hebrew scriptures with all their prodigies; on the Trinity they were 'severely orthodox'; only slowly have the reformed churches abandoned a corporeal or real presence in the sacrament. Yet, unsympathetic though he may be, the philosopher must admit an obligation to these 'fearless enthusiasts.' They levelled 'the lofty fabric of superstition'; they broke 'the chain of authority.' Each Christian henceforth acknowledged 'no law but the scriptures, no interpreter but his own conscience.' But freedom was the consequence, not the design, of the Reformation. The Reformers were as authoritarian as their predecessors. They could not, however, sustain the part. 'The nature of the tiger was the same, but he was gradually deprived of his teeth and fangs.' Popular discussion and the appeal to private judgment made the restoration of ecclesiastical authority impossible.

Erasmus appears at this point. 'Since the days of Luther and Calvin, a secret reformation has been silently working in the bosom of the reformed churches; many weeds of prejudice were eradicated; and the disciples of Erasmus diffused a spirit of freedom and moderation.' In a note to this passage, Gibbon defines an apostolic succession of rational theology. Erasmus may be considered its father; after 'a slumber of a hundred years' it was revived by the Arminians of Holland from Grotius to Le Clerc, by Chillingworth and the English latitudinarians. Gibbon in effect proposes the idea of two Reformations, the limited but well understood Reformation of Luther and Calvin and the more profound and far-reaching Reformation begun by Erasmus.[94] The outcome of the latter has been liberty of conscience and religious toleration, at least in Holland and England where the protection of the law has been 'enlarged by the prudence and humanity of the times.' Presumptuous questions that preoccupied a more childish or less civilized age have been set aside. 'In the exercise, the mind has understood the limits of its powers, and the words and shadows that might amuse the child can no longer satisfy his manly reason.' If Enlightenment scepticism dominates this sentence, there is, too, a haunting echo of Erasmus' rejection of the insensitive boldness of scholastic disputations on ultimate questions: 'the mind has understood the limit of its powers.'

Here the discussion takes a new direction. There is another, more menacing succession. With the progress of rational theology, orthodoxy is overthrown. 'Yet the friends of Christianity are alarmed at the boundless impulse of inquiry and scepticism.' Gibbon is not completely divorced from these 'friends of Christianity.' 'The predictions of the Catholics are accomplished, the web of mystery is unravelled by the Arminians, Arians, and Socinians, whose numbers must not be computed from their separate congregations; and the pillars of revelation are shaken by those men who preserve the name without the substance of religion, who indulge the licence without the temper of philosophy.' To shake the pillars of revelation in the cause of rational theology is one thing; to indulge the licence without the temper of philosopher, to cry freedom without moderation, is, especially in a time of instability, quite another. A note refers the reader to two passages which, according to Gibbon, 'betray the ultimate tendency' of Joseph Priestley's *History of the Corruptions of Christianity*. One will make the priest, the other the magistrate tremble![95]

The questions raised by this remarkable passage are not easily answered. They are in the last resort questions about Gibbon and his world, about his relation to the religious traditions, to the Enlightenment and revolution. Is there a straight line from Erasmus to Priestley or is there a turn which might have been avoided? Does Gibbon see a dark side to the Enlightenment or is his fear of revolution a failure of nerve?

On one side, Gibbon seems to stand above or beyond any religious persuasion or conviction. After his adolescent conversion to Rome – bewildered as he put it by Bossuet's controversial skill, especially in exposing 'the faults and follies, the changes and contradictions of our first reformers' – and reconversion to some kind of residual faith ('acquiescing with implicit belief in the tenets and mysteries which are adopted by the general consent of Catholics and Protestants'), he found a model in Pierre Bayle as understood by the Enlightenment: 'he balances the *false* religions in his skeptical scales till the opposite quantities (if I may use the language of algebra) annihilate each other.' Gibbon from this side was a follower of the 'universal Pyrrhonism' of Bayle.[96]

On the other side, Gibbon remained obsessed with the religious questions that had attracted him in his youth.[97] He was 'so deeply interested in religion that he could neither leave it alone nor rest satisfied with its conventional expressions as provided by the Churches.' His railing against Christianity arose in part from disappointed hopes. His rejection of intolerance and bigotry was complete. But he had not broken with all the Christian traditions. In much that he said he remained in the line of liberal Protestants like Jean Le Clerc.[98] The phrase 'only supposed infidelity,' used of him by his friend William Hayley, may have been his own.[99] So one must understand his appreciation of Erasmus. He has not secularized Erasmus. He genuinely admires Erasmus' religious sincerity, openness, and universalism.

Similarly, it was not by chance that Erasmus came to mind when Gibbon confronted the upheavals in France.

> I beg leave to subscribe my assent to Mr. Burke's creed on the revolution of France. I admire his eloquence; I approve his politics; I adore his chivalry; and I can almost excuse his reverence for church establishments. I have sometimes thought of writing a dialogue of the dead in which Lucian, Erasmus, and Voltaire should mutually acknowledge the danger of exposing an old superstition to the contempt of the blind and fanatic multitude.[100]

Gibbon disliked Priestley, apparently because he insisted on indulging in religious polemics on the one hand and seditious trumpetings on the other.[101] He admired Erasmus because Erasmus saw the dangers in both stunted orthodoxy and revolutionary enthusiasm. Erasmus helped define a moderate conservative response to the French Revolution.[102] All this may represent the love of an eighteenth-century English gentleman for a quiet life.[103] It also expresses a deep conviction about the true sources of human happiness and unhappiness.

It has proved impossible to discuss either Robertson's or Gibbon's interpretations of Erasmus without fairly extensive reference to their views on the Reformation. His significance can be established only through that reference. This they have in common but otherwise, on the points at issue, Robertson and Gibbon represent alternative versions of the Protestant Enlightenment. For the former Erasmus anticipated and furthered the Protestant Reformation; for the latter he represented, in a sense began, a second, more complete reformation whose outcome has been the intellectual emancipation of the eighteenth century. The limits of reformation and emancipation, recognized by Robertson's Moderate churchmanship and Gibbon's Burkean response to the Revolution, can also be determined by reference to Erasmus. The interest in these writings is less in the person of Erasmus than in the larger historical movements (of his own time and later) with which he can be associated. The same can be said of the Protestant Enlightenment historians in Germany.

III

Compared with Gibbon, if not with Robertson, there is an air of the pulpit and the lectern about the German historians of the Enlightenment. Each held a place, as professor of church history, history, or theology, in one of the many universities maintained by the rival German states. These universities generally were small and conservative institutions which limited rather than expanded the horizons of German intellectual life.[104] Nevertheless, changes came with the new foundations – Halle in Prussia and above all Göttingen in Hanover (founded in 1737): the interest of the bureaucracy which promoted more up-to-date studies and made appointments on merit; the revival of university attendance among young noblemen; a reform of legal studies and a moderating of confessional intransigence in the theological schools, which had a liberating effect on biblical and historical studies.[105] History itself was emerging only gradually as an independent scholarly discipline. To the middle of the eighteenth century church history, taught in a rhetorical and confessional way, remained preparatory to theological or other studies. Around 1750 it was incorporated into theological instruction itself.[106] Similarly, the jurists were accepting history as a necessary adjunct in their studies. At Göttingen, history was said to be essential to a sound political formation. The ground was being unobtrusively prepared for the historical revolution of the nineteenth century.[107]

In Germany the Enlightenment seems a mutation on the Christian tradition. The slower pace of intellectual change and the less dramatic conflicts and contrasts than in France were related in part to the cultural dominance of France itself, at least until late in the century, in part to the provincial character of German political society, divided into states of differing weights and sizes, with the towns static and quiescent and the courts and the bureaucracies in the ascendant.[108] In theology there was a slow march from orthodox dogmatics or the inner certainties of pietism towards rationalism. A first stage was represented by Christian Wolff at Halle who allowed rights to reason but assumed an easy partnership between reason and revelation. In the next stage, the so-called neologians, whose literary vehicle was Nicolai's *Allgemeine deutsche Bibliothek*, subjected revelation to reason. At the end rationalism abandoned the very idea of revelation.[109]

A representative figure of the mid-century was the minister and schoolmaster Johann Jakob Brucker (1696–1770) and a representative book his *Historia critica philosophiae*, the first German attempt at a history of philosophy. Brucker's secure relation to the Protestant tradition – informed by the common sense of the early Enlightenment and a pietist concern for personal religion – is demonstrated by the argument made many times in his book that the revival of philosophy, for all the efforts of the Italians of the Renaissance, ultimately depended on the renovation of religion by the Protestant Reformers.[110] The enemy was scholasticism which darkened minds with ill-founded speculations but its overthrow was beyond those preoccupied with philosophical questions alone; it had to be cut at its theological roots. The Reuchlin affair 'showed how deeply German minds were immersed in the mire and that they would never awake from their torpor unless movements for the reformation of the church began to overturn all things.'[111]

Erasmus, Brucker says, belonged to those who feared a general upset and sought a lighter medicine than was strictly necessary. Nevertheless, he saw clearly that the scholastic theology and philosophy were the root of the evil and put every effort into turning them out. Divine providence was in the efforts of Erasmus and his fellows to heal the long-running sores of Christianity. Some worked by denunciation, Erasmus more by laughter and satire. Altogether he was no philosopher and devoted himself wholly to sacred and profane philology and to interpreting the scriptures; he 'strove nevertheless to bring his readers, at various places in his writings, an understanding of the better philosophy.' Thus in his incomparable *Moriae encomium* (*Praise of Folly*) he depicted scholastic 'pseudophilosophy' in lively colours and displayed its deformities to the readers' scorn; so it merited the distaste even of inattentive readers. Erasmus had great authority among the Germans since none surpassed him in abundance of reading, refinement of mind, and excellence of learning. Still a youth, he challenged the scholastics when no one else was moving a finger to reform religion or correct sacred learning. They responded with enmity but others took Erasmus' example and, 'while he was occupied with other things, advanced further than he and worked not only to cure these sores but also with all their strength to restore fallen philosophy.'[112]

Such a location of Erasmus in the history of thought was to be expected from an enlightened Lutheran teacher who believed in the progress – under providence – of the human mind and the scrutiny of intellectual and ecclesiastical authorities by the kindly light of reason.[113] Brucker drew on earlier writers who had made mild and appreciative judgments of Erasmus and – allowance made for changing circumstances – who shared his view of the world: Melanchthon, Melchior Adam, Fabricius, Le Clerc, and von der Hardt.[114]

In Johann Lorenz von Mosheim (1693–1755) – long a theological professor at Helmstedt in Braunschweig, church and school administrator in that principality, and adviser and mentor to the new foundation at Göttingen to which he came at last in 1747 as chancellor and professor of theology – there was a combination of Enlightenment faith in moral and intellectual progress (again under providence) and an anticipation of the nineteenth-century quest for objectivity in historical study, with an accompanying recognition of how elusive the goal of objectivity could be.[115] Mosheim abandoned the idea, dear to anticlericals and pietists, of the decline and fall of the church through its history. He was attracted by the alternative idea of progress but, as well, he recognized the distinctive form of church and society in each age and – unusually for a Protestant theologian – saw the Middle Ages as having their own validity and as more than a lost era in the history of civilization, though he readily made a butt of scholasticism.[116] His supreme aim was impartiality. Historical writing was saturated in party spirit. 'Each loves the faith which he himself confesses and hates opinions contrary to it. Part of this love and hate is transplanted on the people who share the doctrine with us or teach otherwise.'[117] Not even the pietist Gottfried Arnold, who exalted the persecuted, the heretic, the outsider (and consequently praised Erasmus), had the purest of motives; he sought less to bring truth to light than to blacken the reputation of the persecutors of heretics.[118] In his awareness of a relativity which affects all observers including himself, Mosheim draws near to his historicist successors of the nineteenth century.

His histories retain the annalistic character of earlier forms of historical writing; he holds to the humanist view that history must be a useful, salutary, and sociable study; his interest lies in individuals and particulars rather than in larger interpretative ideas – he does not organize his material around concepts like 'Renaissance' or 'Reformation,' for example. All this represents but a small advance on the past. But in his deft, searching, sceptical handling of the critical method, in his preoccupation with causes and effects, in his recognition of the church as a historical phenomenon affected by its social and cultural setting in every age, Mosheim is very much the modern historian.[119]

The combination of Protestant Enlightenment sensibility and critical historical methods is apparent in Mosheim's treatment of Erasmus and his world. Towards the end of the third book of his *Institutionum*, Mosheim deals with the revival of learning in fifteenth-century Italy, the degenerate condition of the church at the time, and the first modest attempts at reform.[120] Of the religious fraternities of the age none was more worthy of commemoration or more useful to Christianity than the Brethren and Clerks of the Common Life. On this subject Mosheim made an original contribution by reference to unpublished records.[121] The community was in two sections held together by strong bonds – the studious clerks and the unlearned engaged in manual labour. 'The schools, that were erected by the *Clerks* of this fraternity, acquired a great and illustrious reputation in this century. From them issued forth those immortal restorers of learning and taste that gave a new face to the republic of letters in *Germany* and *Holland*, such as Erasmus of Rotterdam, Alexander Hegius ...'[122] The Brethren attracted the hatred of monks and priests, who disliked studies. The revival of learning and the criticism of its condition at the beginning of the sixteenth century left the church largely unscathed because the critics accepted papal authority.

The revival of learning dispersed the shades of ignorance and kindled the love of truth and freedom in many minds; many, as the example of Erasmus and others shows, smoothly and cleverly scorned and reproved the perversity of priests, the superstitions of the age, the vices of the Roman court, the rude manners and barbarity of the monks. But none dared courageously attack the root of every misery and public calamity, the canon law of the popes and that ancient opinion about the settling of Christ's vicar at Rome.[123]

Mosheim, like Brucker, believed that change depended on a correction in religion, the Reformation which, for good and ill, has been behind every transformation in religious and civil affairs in recent times. Luther could have debated fundamental articles of the faith provided that he did not challenge the pope and the hierarchy; the first was allowed to doctors of the church but certainly not the second. Meanwhile Erasmus had earned his own opprobrium by exposing the aversion of the mendicant orders to learning.[124]

Mosheim says that the sixteenth century generally brought significant progress in theological, and especially biblical, studies; it began 'what was afterwards more happily finished' and laid the foundations of the 'striking superiority' of modern divines over the ancient. In the Roman church the situation was mixed; the Jesuits, for example, continued the revival of learning on the one hand but confirmed the baleful dominance of Aristotle on the other, while the popes and the Council of Trent restored the authority of the Vulgate despite its errors. But there was another, if weaker, tradition. 'One may name some who were strong in wisdom, who rejected empty mysteries and who strove to follow the literal sense of scripture alone. The first place among these was held by Erasmus of Rotterdam who, as is well known, translated the books of the New Testament into Latin clearly and elegantly and explained them with discernment.'[125] These references to Erasmus betray Mosheim's preoccupations – the emergence of critical methods in scholarship and theology, liberation from ecclesiastical authority and hierarchy, the assertion of the reasonable and ethical over the ritual and mysterious in religion. Much here belongs to the Protestant tradition but the Enlightenment is anticipated also. Mosheim went to school in Lübeck, he was a student at the University of Kiel, he was a friend of J.A. Fabricius in Hamburg. In these circles the humanist tradition remained strong, there was a bias against fanaticism and the *odium theologicum* (which confirmed a temperamental aversion of Mosheim's) and in favour of mediating theologies and irenic endeavours.[126] A factor was the connection of the north German centres with the liberal societies of Holland and England. Mosheim himself was interested in the Arminians of Holland and wrote a work challenging the synod of Dordrecht which had condemned them; he was praised by Jean Le Clerc, Erasmus' Arminian editor and defender.[127] He was the one Lutheran theologian of the time well-known in English-speaking lands, he translated Ralph Cudworth's work against atheism (1678) and felt an affinity with the English latitudinarians, while denouncing the deists. His associations, in short, were all in places where Erasmus' memory was cherished. His independence of the assertive parties of his time – the orthodox, the pietists, the deists – was Erasmian in its way.[128]

Mosheim had as followers two figures – long-lived, well-known in their time as teachers and writers, prolific, and, for that time, authoritative: Gottlieb Jakob Planck (1751–1833) and Johann Matthias Schröckh (1733–1808).[129] In them the historiography of the Protestant Enlightenment was rounded off. Those who followed were to break more radically from the Protestant tradition and from the compromises of the moderate Enlightenment. Schröckh studied with Mosheim at Göttingen. Like his master, indeed like all historians since the Renaissance, he believed that history had a practical and pedagogical purpose – to guide contemporary institutions, to shape the minds of a new generation of leaders. He taught at Wittenberg (professor of poetry 1767, of history 1775), Luther's university, now – but for Schröckh's own reputation – in decline. He shared the Enlightenment faith in progress but curiously returned to the idea, beloved of pietists like Gottfried Arnold but rejected by Mosheim, of the fall of the church. On both counts the Reformation was critical to his historiography; with it came the first light after a long age of darkness; from it spread modern progress.[130] The corruption of the church after its pure beginnings came from the institution of authorities to interpret its sacred texts, from the appeal to emotion through cult and ceremonies, from the spiritual monarchy.[131] The Reformation brought its own danger in the renewed concentration on the sacred text. In all this, in his view of religion as essentially personal piety, Schröckh was a disciple of the pietists. Indeed, his historical method was predominantly biographical; he organized the periods of church history about great personalities, so foreshadowing the historiography of romanticism. Schröckh had a wide appeal in his time. He was read even in the Catholic seminaries and copied by the Catholic writers.[132] His moderation, best exemplified for our purposes by his praise of Burigny, Erasmus' Catholic biographer, counted there.[133] His death – from a fall in his library while working on his history of the Reformation – struck contemporaries as a martyrdom to scholarship.[134]

Planck came to Göttingen as an established scholar (professor of church history 1784). The association between the man and the university was a congenial one. The value Göttingen gave to historical studies ensured for Planck a place of honour in the institution over his long tenure, to which was added from 1791 high office in the Hanoverian church.[135] In theological matters he shared the Göttingen preference for middle ground. He remained true to the Wolffian confidence in the harmony of reason and revelation, learnt in his student days at the University of Tübingen.[136] He believed that historical studies would not invalidate the Christian revelation. He warned his own students, one of them later reported, against 'shallow, heartless rationalism, obstinate orthodoxy, mystical sentimentalism and speculative corruptions.' His natural bent was towards the Kantian emphasis on the practical and the ethical. Even amid the political excitements of the German war of liberation against Napoleon, he gave 'the impression of a sympathetic but serene and circumspect observer,' a stance which did not always please his students.[137] He was physically impressive, a sense of humour sweetening his irregular features and naturally severe expression.[138]

Planck was an innovator in historical studies. He was the founder of the comparative history of the different Christian confessions, indeed of the serious study of Protestant theology itself. His characteristic restraint and avoidance of polemics was essential to his success.[139] The obligation of the historian, he said, was 'moderation, human feeling and cool assessment.' He would not conceal the fact that he was a Lutheran but he strove to be fair to the other parties and acknowledged weaknesses on his own side. It is an exacting task to discern God's hand amid the complexities of human affairs, in the record of man's intolerance and inhumanity. 'No wonder,' he exclaimed, 'that such studies produce [Gottfried] Arnolds!'[140]

Planck, like Schröckh, gave the Reformation pride of place in his understanding of church history. Indeed, the discipline of church history was in his view a creation of the Reformation, since the first Reformers wished to recover the true visage of the ancient church.[141] Controversy stimulated free enquiry on both sides. Among the Lutherans especially, the historical–critical method developed; with the coming of a new age in the history of Christianity in the middle of the eighteenth century and a general moral and spiritual progress, there would, he believed, be another rapid advance in critical enquiry.[142] It is not surprising that Planck's temperament and scholarly interests should excite a sympathy for Erasmus.[143]

Planck's study of Erasmus is to be found in his history of Protestant thought in the sixteenth century, Schröckh's in part 30 of his church history and in the first part of the sequel, his church history since the Reformation.[144] The common ground between these two last representatives of the Protestant Enlightenment is substantial. For both, the Reformation was a more predictable event, a more natural outcome of what had gone before than Protestant historians commonly supposed. An observer of the start of the sixteenth century, says Schröckh, could not doubt that religion, theology, and the church would be reformed.[145] For Planck, the extent of the change had been exaggerated, and preparatory and accompanying circumstances had been overlooked, by pious authors who wished to attribute the success of the Reformation to God's direct intervention. The changes in ideas had, in fact, been long and variously prepared. Planck actually calls them 'enlightenment' [Aufklärung]. With the Reformation came a 'confluence of favourable circumstances,' by which 'the enlightenment which had begun among the wise' spread through all peoples; 'as soon as the general enlightenment had reached a certain point, it was impossible that [the system of belief on which the papacy rested] could endure any longer.' Learning and the arts were alive and in ferment in the fifteenth century. Before Luther appeared thousands believed what he came to believe only later.[146]

Erasmus, says Planck, was among those who thus anticipated the Reformation though, like others in the religious orders who recognized the errors of the existing system, he preferred to work indirectly and quietly since, in his view, direct attacks on the papacy would achieve nothing and even damage the truth. 'It is certain that Erasmus had no less insight into the failings of the Roman system, no less knowledge of its disordered places, no less desire to expose these or zeal to reform them than the most fiery of our Reformers.' In the circle of his trusted friends he spoke frankly but he was a shrewd and diplomatic man who measured each step carefully. Planck's Erasmus is an apostle of gradualism, advocating a 'step by step preparation for the general enlightenment.' He acted on his own conviction and should not be condemned because that was different from Luther's. The circumstances which came together at the beginning of the sixteenth century were effectively exploited by Luther. Yet Luther, for all his courage and zeal, would in other circumstances and among other men not have achieved what he did in so short a time. Erasmus and his party were essential to Luther's success, preparing the way and creating the immediate circumstances. Thus, out of Reuchlin's personal controversy over the Hebrew books which Erasmus supported there developed a declared war between the forces of light and the forces of darkness in the German nation.[147]

Schröckh uses much the same language. Erasmus' understanding of Roman corruptions developed so rapidly that already at the beginning of the sixteenth century he was seen as taking the lead in proclaiming the necessity for a thoroughgoing reformation of the church. His works were such a proclamation. The *Enchiridion* challenged those who reduced religion to ceremonies.[148] The *Ratio* criticized the scholastics and recommended a theological method which, while not perfect, far excelled all that had gone before. Erasmus recognized that biblical studies were the foundation of all religious knowledge. Here he marked out a road which every religious reformer must tread. Again, the purpose of his *Paraphrases* was to ease the way for theological reform.[149] He was attacked from various quarters. 'But at bottom all men of spirit, learning and candour who longed for a better order of things were on his side.' Posterity honours him as the greatest of those who used the revived learning of antiquity to the advantage of theology and religion itself. He deserves the name of reformer of the church, if not in the fullest sense, since he lacked the unconquerable courage to face all the dangers of the great undertaking and the clear-sightedness to see that, not mere corrections, but a complete reconstruction of the building was necessary.[150]

An important difference remained between Schröckh and Planck, a difference which had run through all Protestant writing on Erasmus from Melanchthon to their time. Both recognized the support Erasmus gave to Luther in his early controversies and appreciated his pleas for moderation. He had defended Luther when all the obscurantists of Europe were after his own blood and when Luther's friends were trying tendentiously to identify him with their cause. At the same time, he expressed candidly his mistrust of Luther's violent zeal. Nor did he hide his views from the Roman authorities.[151] Further, both Planck and Schröckh sympathized with Erasmus' stand in the free-will controversy against Luther's extreme determinism which, says Schröckh, the modern Protestant church does not feel committed to defend. His choice of theme showed Erasmus to be both honourable and sharp-sighted. If his own position was not defined with complete clarity because of an excessive anxiety to safeguard himself on all sides, he could still show strikingly a weakness in Luther's position.[152] Planck goes further; he is outraged by Luther's handling of Erasmus in this controversy. Luther's hard, confident tone, so different from the modest, uncertain speech of his opponent, won the support of all those consumed by party spirit and incapable of seeing or testing both sides of a question.[153] This remark illustrates the difference between the two historians. Schröckh stands by the narrower Lutheran definition of the Reformation. In the last resort Erasmus, who avoided decisive or final commitments, lay outside the Reformation. He did not wish to rebuild the church from the foundations up but, 'while continuing to dwell in it, sought to secure it against collapse, to cleanse it of abuses and, where possible, to beautify it.'[154] By contrast, Planck brought the Reformers and their forerunners together in the one enlightenment. He would have preferred a Reformation which embraced Erasmus and his associates.[155]

I V

In Planck and Schröckh, despite their differences, Protestantism and the Enlightenment remained in easy association. In two of their contemporaries, Heinrich Philipp Konrad Henke (1752–1809) and Johann Salomo Semler (1725–91), disassociation began; the bond was breaking. Neither Henke nor Semler was wholly with the rationalists; each remained attached to the Protestant tradition but the attachment was looser. They were more independent, more critical. As a consequence, the balance in their appreciation of the Reformation on the one hand and the Renaissance and humanism on the other changed. Planck, like Robertson, wished to bring the Reformers and their forerunners together. For Henke and Semler the forerunners had their own historical importance; indeed, in them – and in Erasmus above all – rather than in the Protestant Reformers may be found the beginnings of modern enlightenment. In this Henke and Semler were close to Gibbon; they were also moving towards the liberal historiography of the nineteenth century.[156]

Henke published the German edition of Burigny's life of Erasmus.[157] His notes and addenda to the great work make a study in cultural contrasts and associations. Burigny commended Erasmus to Catholic readers deeply affected but not carried away by the Enlightenment. By the time he wrote his life of Erasmus he had returned from a rationalizing youth to the Catholic fold though he kept his commitment to tolerance and moderation. He had, says Henke, imbibed something of the Erasmian spirit; yet, for all his frankness, he made Erasmus as orthodox as possible and, when it came to the condition of the church, he dwelt on outward abuses and failed to see that they were but expressions of false teachings, superstitions, and clerical pride and tyranny.[158] Henke himself was concerned to drive a wedge between the religion of the New Testament and all later orthodoxies and to separate the person of Jesus from all his interpreters as one to whom men might respond as moral and reasonable beings. For him, too, Christian teachings were self-evident but by orthodox standards he drastically reduced the scope of those teachings.[159] His notes and commentaries would represent a radicalizing of Burigny and of Erasmus.

Henke goes beyond writers of the Protestant Enlightenment like Planck and Schröckh in three respects. First, he offers a straight defence of Erasmus against his Lutheran critics without shuffling or reserve. The latter charged him, for example, with theological imprecision. On the contrary, says Henke, it was a fundamental position for him that one should avoid too fine distinctions in Christian theology. If Erasmus had been left to establish religion in any community, he would have prescribed few articles and stated them with simplicity: 'his followers would have been latitudinarians.' He may have held to the old church but let us remember that 'the main source of his way of thinking as of his whole conduct in the turmoil of that time in the church was a quality deserving of the highest praise, his love of peace.' We excuse the Reformers much, says Henke. Why then should the harshest judgments be reserved for Erasmus? He, too, believed that he was advancing God's cause by working in quietness and

hoping for better times. One can be courageous without swim-
ming against the stream or throwing oneself into the fire. Erasmus
knew that he would have to suffer much in his struggle against
abuses in the church without casting his lot with Luther. He saw
that one could correct only gradually abuses – like the honouring
of saints – that were general and popular. Interest – his English
pensions, for example – did not determine him to write against
Luther. He had commitments to friends and patrons, certainly,
but he was also alarmed by the Protestant promotion of unrest
and violence. He may have expected too much in looking for
peaceable dispositions in the professors of the new gospel but to
ask for a correspondence between faith and life did credit to his
character. All this excuses his writing against Luther which he
did with discretion and deliberation. Besides, he did not attack a
central feature of the Lutheran Reformation – Henke's remark
shows how distant the eighteenth century was from the Reformer
– but rather an idiosyncrasy and philosophical error of
Luther's.[160]

Secondly, Henke, more emphatically than Planck and Schrockh,
proclaims Erasmus a genuine reformer of the church. He was one
of those men destined by providence to work a great transformation in the human mind. His struggles 'are to be seen as a war
of light and darkness in which ignorance, superstition and monk-
ery exert all their powers to disperse the beautiful light of morning
shedding itself over the human spirit.' He came at a time 'of
restoration in learning, of purification in taste and of the glorious
beginnings of the reformation in the Christian church which continues still.' On fundamental matters like confession, the basis of
priestly power, he spoke as freely as the Reformers. He held his
position consistently to the end – reform must be gradual but
thorough. He did not become a Protestant before his death in
Basel – to do so would have done him no honour. But he gave
no comfort to the Romanists since he died, as the monks said,
'sine crux, sine lux, sine Deus.'[161]

Henke develops Erasmus' character as reformer especially in
a long appendix on his biblical work. On this subject, he says,
Burigny needs to be expanded and corrected. Later critics like
Richard Simon should have remembered that Erasmus worked
virtually without predecessors and that they in their turn could
outstrip him only by treading for a start in his steps.[162] Lorenzo
Valla had opened the way to enlightened biblical criticism in his

Annotationes but Erasmus' work was far more comprehensive and therefore, in the theological atmosphere of the time, more risky. He did not rush unprepared at the task but was not a slow-moving pedant either, since he recognized that the world could not afford a long wait for this book. His translation, despite unavoidable errors and some unnecessary corrections of the Vulgate, was a masterpiece, his notes revealing 'the sound, pertinent and candid student of the Bible, the exact and learned linguist.' He was not overawed by authorities and past reputations. How much slower the reformation of faith and piety would have been without his work![163]

Thirdly, Henke brought a new and striking relativism to his judgments on the Reformation controversies. That Luther went beyond Erasmus in his attacks on Rome was due to a different temperament but also to different experiences. Erasmus, treated with respect in Rome, was sensible to hold the middle ground and hope for a response to his appeals for reform. 'Luther could not with a good conscience behave like Erasmus, nor Erasmus like Luther.' Inevitably they drew apart; they were not running on parallel lines. Unjust accusations of one against the other marked a failure in mutual understanding, in appreciation of how each could hardly do other than he did. Erasmus had his own cause, deriving from his own experience and commitments, and he remained faithful to it. 'Why should he be a martyr for Luther's teaching?' Providentially he remained an eloquent witness in the old church to the need for church reform. Henke occasionally swings away towards the more traditional Protestant positions: moderate counsels, as the example of Erasmus himself showed, earned only hatred and persecution for their authors.[164] But his frank statement of the relativist position made the rejection, or even criticism, of Erasmus from the old Protestant standpoint impossible. More drastically than previous writers like Johannes Klefeker he established the independent validity of Erasmus' conscience: he could do no other than he did. Thus finally the modern historical outlook brings Erasmus deliverance from the rigid categories of the confessional age.

J.S. Semler was the most considerable figure among the German intellectuals treated here. His works were a watershed in the history of German Protestant thought.[165] He had Mosheim's appreciation of historical development, the distinctiveness of past epochs, and the inescapable relativity of all historical judgments.[166] Every community, every text bore the mark of its time; none were immune from historical change; all deserved the scrutiny of the historian. The primitive church, the sacred text were no exception – to assert this was to go beyond his predecessors and to make Semler the true founder of the historical-critical method in the study of the Bible. In such studies and in the history of mind generally there was advancing enlightenment; Christianity was itself open to historical progress.[167] There could be no body of doctrine given once for all.[168] Semler's youthful studies had liberated him from the intellectual and emotional constraints of both orthodoxy and pietism. Like Mosheim he knew the English thinkers. Student and teacher at Halle, he secured that university's leadership in critical scholarship. It has been said that he took the neological tradition to its limits, to a crossroads where rationalists and supernaturalists must part company. For himself he resisted the rationalist challenge to the apostolic witness to the death and resurrection of Jesus, which he saw as the secure foundation of faith. In his sense for historical development, Semler anticipated the historical philosophers of the next generation, the Fichtes and Hegels. Friedrich Schleiermacher, we might also observe, was a student at Halle. There were elements of Semler in Schleiermacher: the sense (once again) of the historical, the freedom from dogmatisms of all kinds, and (to be noted in what follows) the high value given to individual religious experience.[169]

For Semler Erasmus was more than a figure in history or even an intellectual influence. His debt was established early and was personal and intimate. In the second part of his autobiography, Semler recounts how he came to work in the then largely unoccupied field of historical theology and in particular the history of biblical interpretation. He began, he recalls, in a Protestant Germany where – against the teachings of the Reformers themselves – the inerrancy of the scriptural text was taken for granted and critical methods were largely unknown. While still a student he owned and read industriously Erasmus' 1519 edition of the New Testament and its annotations. His own liberation in fact began there. 'Scarcely anyone since had taken the right path in research with so little party spirit and with so purely an historical approach as Erasmus.' Semler went on to study Erasmus' *Ratio verae theologiae* which had begun as a foreword to the first version of his New Testament edition but which Erasmus later turned into a manifesto for the reform of theology in the spirit, says Semler, of the best in late-medieval mysticism, especially the writings of Johann Tauler and Meister Eckhart.[170] These early encounters helped fix the two distinct aims of Semler's scholarly activity – a critical, historical appreciation of the Christian texts, where change and variety were recognized, and an understanding of Christian faith defined not by authoritative voices from the past or even by the enquiries of theologians, themselves subject to contention and variation, but by personal experience and inward conviction in response to revelation.[171]

The best part of a lifetime later – in 1782 – Semler issued a new edition of the *Ratio*. In preparing his autobiography he had come across his youthful notes from the work. 'I felt myself affected,' he says in a preface, 'by a great and almost holy desire – the wonder I am used to feeling at Erasmus' name – so that I at once determined to spare no effort to bring out this work deserving of canonical recognition.'[172] These were in fact testing and emotional days for Semler. In controversy with more radical neologians, he provoked the anger of a Prussian minister, who supported them, and was deposed as director of the theological seminary at Halle.[173] His aim, Semler said, was to maintain the established practice of the Christian religion, while also encouraging in professional theology the critical methods appropriate to an enlightened age. Like Erasmus who in his time feared that wilder spirits would ultimately set Christianity aside, Semler opposed those seeking radical departures.[174] Like so many embattled figures before him – moderates, Arminians, Jansenists, pietists – Semler compared himself with Erasmus, hard pressed on every side over the last fifteen years of his life and belaboured by both revolutionaries and reactionaries.

In his *Ratio*, says Semler, Erasmus defined the true character of the Christian religion. His call to theologians, 'Let this be your sole aim ... that you be changed, that you be carried away ... that you be transformed into what you are studying,' breathes a Christian spirit and expresses God's word.[175] This was no wild religious enthusiasm. Luther and Melanchthon nowhere wrote better. The book was a beautiful *summa*, making men inwardly Christian. The sign of true piety was to recognize one's own lack of piety – this teaching of Erasmus, which Semler often repeated, should represent the experience of all Christians. Luther had taken it up; indeed, much in the Augsburg Confession was drawn from this writing of Erasmus. Erasmus taught that the whole New Testament was faith and love, not ceremonies. Semler does not doubt that Luther and more especially Melanchthon built on these masterly contentions in putting Christ's teaching to the people. It is then all the more remarkable that after them a new scholasticism, with all the faults of the old, should emerge among the Protestants. Thus Semler identified Erasmus as the true source of the Reformation which Luther and others completed and distinguished Erasmus, the Reformers, and himself from the orthodoxy which followed.[176]

Erasmus, says Semler, urged a free exercise of the critical intelligence and a thorough reformation of the church; he rejected the whole of monasticism, indulgences, prayers to saints, relics, pilgrimages, and so forth long before Luther and Zwingli appeared. 'With a giant's power Erasmus, almost alone, pulled the old papacy from its place by means of a quite different understanding of church affairs.'[177] Without him the achievements of Luther and Zwingli would be scarcely thinkable. That he did not abandon the Roman church is no justification for suppressing the recognition he deserves. The same may be said of Luther's argumentativeness in his work against Erasmus' book on free will; of the two works Semler prefers the latter. Luther was too much influenced by Augustine and too severe in his handling of those who took a different view.[178] When the intransigence of the parties threatened breakdown and bloodshed, Erasmus wrote a book on mending the peace of the church.[179] He sought a reconciliation, says Semler, but he wished also to preserve the essence of the great reform which he had initiated and which a new dogmatism was threatening to distort. Thus, on the main point of contention, he said that grace was primary but true faith also bore fruit in good works.[180]

These judgments on Erasmus as a historical figure belong to an interpretation of the Reformation distinct from the standard Protestant interpretation and consistent with Semler's commitment to the critical historical method. Luther did not have a unique authority, the Reformation was not uniquely a work of God or a miraculous recovery of primitive Christianity. It emerged from the reform movements of the fifteenth century and was very much of its own time.[181] Indeed, the innovating power of various fifteenth-century groups and individuals was a major theme in Semler's historiography.[182] Among the Reformers – Semler here reiterates an Enlightenment preference – Melanchthon best sustained the original impulses.[183] Those who made authoritative every word of Luther's did not understand that the Protestant Reformation was but a beginning.[184] What mattered, despite setbacks like the revival of dogmatism in Protestantism itself, was the progress in enlightenment since the Reformation and especially in recent times.

Semler makes a distinction, crucial to his thought, between inner religion and various external forms. Inner religion is free and common to Christians in all times and places. It is untrammelled by needs of public order. It consists in motions of the spirit and requires no outward expression. By contrast, religious observances and organizations established by external authority for the public convenience have their character determined by time and place ('characterem publicum, historicum, localem'). Similarly, the work of theologians is critical and intellectual; it leaves the inner core untouched. Theologians should not impose on all the standards appropriate to their professional studies; nor – even worse – should they embroil other Christians in their vehement scholarly disputes. True religion does not reside in the books of controversial theology. In such matters, says Semler, the eighteenth century enjoys an advantage over its predecessors. Theological uniformity is no longer the ground of civil unity.[185] One recognizes the distinction between erudition, which is freer than ever before, and religion; the former belongs to the few, the latter to all.[186]

It is not an accident that these expressions appear in Semler's introduction to his edition of Erasmus' *Ratio*. Erasmus' writings were, he says, not only 'limpid sources of theological learning'; they nurtured a personal religious growth which was quite independent of the ecclesiastical order under which Christians lived. Erasmus was a herald of that inner Christianity which was, for Semler, at the heart of human destiny. In associating Erasmus so fully and explicitly with this utterly free form of Christianity, Semler took the Protestant Enlightenment interpretation of him (which is to be found also in Gibbon, as we have seen) to its very limits.[187]

V

Semler had dedicated his edition of Erasmus' *Ratio* to the emperor Joseph II, 'best father of the fatherland, protector of the public

religion and teacher of the private.' This apostrophe to the doc-
trinaire reformer of the Habsburg lands in the later eighteenth
century calls to mind a curious element in the history of Erasmus'
reputation, the association of his name with the Habsburg dynasty. Beatus Rhenanus had dedicated the first biography of Erasmus to the emperor Charles V and depicted Erasmus paying
honour 'to the most noble House of Austria, cradle of so many
Caesars.' Hermann von der Hardt at the beginning of the eighteenth century made the great dynasty the midwife of the renewal
of letters of which Erasmus was the glory.[188]

Joseph II was not without personal religion but he was hardly
a teacher of faith.[189] His interests lay elsewhere, in the rational
use of the state's resources to benefit its subjects and enhance its
power. This pragmatic absolutism certainly had consequences for
the Catholic religion. The emperor's personal commitment to religious toleration seems of the pure essence of eighteenth-century
philosophy: 'Fanaticism shall in future be known in my states
only by the contempt I have for it ... Tolerance is an effect of that
beneficent increase of knowledge which now enlightens Europe.'[190] But the famous Edict of Toleration (1781) bestowed upon
the religious minorities – by favour of the state – 'equal and
equally limited rights.'[191] In speaking of the monks, the chancellor Kaunitz, one on the architects of the Josephine reforms,
could use Erasmian expressions: 'It is universally known that the
Church existed for more than three centuries before anyone knew
anything about monks. Consequently their introduction was quite
arbitrary and had nothing to do with the essence of Christianity.'[192] But the suppression of the contemplative orders in Josephine Austria was more a condemnation of a way of life deemed
useless by the absolute state.[193] The intellectual background to
these efforts was mixed and included the optimistic rationalism
of a Protestant theologian like Wolff.[194] One expression of the
Josephine spirit – as found in the writings of Justinius Febronius
(Johann Nicolaus von Hontheim) – was a kind of gallicanism, a
call for the restriction of papal authority to spiritual matters alone,
for a national church and the prerogatives of the episcopate.

The historian Michael Ignaz Schmidt (1736–94) belonged to
this atmosphere. Schmidt was the first to attempt a general history
of the German people, its cultural and moral progress, somewhat
on the lines of Voltaire's *Essai sur les moeurs*.[195] At the beginning
of the first volume of this *Geschichte der Deutschen* Schmidt states

his purpose: 'to show how Germany has received its present moral condition, enlightenment, arts and sciences and above all its excellent constitution in church and state, in short how it has become what it really is.' His idealizing of German conditions in his time sprang from his idealizing of the Habsburg house. A nation's good fortune, he said, depended on the soundness of its laws and religion which in turn exposed the capacity of its rulers.[196] Even before his own translation to Vienna he had found a hero in the Habsburg emperor from the time of Erasmus' youth, Maximilian I, and had identified himself with Austrian ambitions. He came to the Austrian capital in 1780 from Würzburg, where he had been schooled in gallicanism and had reformed the education system, to become director of the Habsburg archives and a member of the censorship commission.

Schmidt was a publicist for Josephine ideas and on church–state relations a Febronian. His rejection of the larger claims of the papacy affected his historical judgments. He sided with the medieval emperors; he was suspicious of the religious orders (he was himself a secular priest); he was sympathetic to the conciliarists of the fifteenth century; he opposed the Jesuits (though educated by them). Of course only in a limited sense was Schmidt an Enlightenment historian. He held to the idea of Christendom, of a Catholic church embracing all nations and cultures, and, in anticipation of one aspect of romanticism, he admired much in the medieval world. He expressed a warm, if tolerant, piety.

With values like these Schmidt was bound to have a complex view of the Reformation.[197] Erasmus is an important witness for Schmidt. In volume 5, which deals with the first part of the reign of Charles V and the Reformation, he presents Erasmus as a reformer who expressed his views freely, who criticized the false security induced among the people by church practices like indulgences, though he was to be overtaken by another who was more earnest and violent.[198] In volume 6 Schmidt attempts a retrospect and summary judgment of the Reformation.[199] He begins chapter 22 with the question: did the advantages brought by the Reformation (he will later speak of these) make up for the outpouring of rivers of blood? Soon after Luther began, says Schmidt, Erasmus, 'one man who deserved to be heard,' wrote a letter to his friend and patron Mountjoy declaring that he would prefer to be in error on some points than to fight for truth at the cost of a world upheaval. 'Erasmus,' Schmidt goes on, 'had not seen the hundredth part of all that would follow from Luther's innovations.' What if in spirit he had seen the Thirty Years' War?[200]

Schmidt then turns to the eighteenth-century Protestant view of the Reformation. He seems to accept the idea of two Reformations; the one – led by Luther – was more limited, the other – associated with Erasmus (though how far he held the radical views attributed to him, for example on the Trinity and original sin, remained uncertain) – more expansive. Luther, having taken innovation so far, wanted to shut the door behind him. It is strange, says Schmidt, that modern Protestants should claim Luther as forerunner. In fact they are closer to Erasmus, whose 'party' was equally distant from the fanaticism of the Reformers and the monachism and spiritual tyranny of the Catholics and, correspondingly, was suppressed by both sides. Now in the eighteenth century it has reappeared on both sides but under the name of Enlightenment. Luther would indeed be surprised by what is taught among his followers. Here Schmidt is both puncturing Protestant pride in Luther as the bringer of enlightenment and needling the Protestants about how far contemporary 'Enlightenment' had taken them away from their beginnings.[201]

Logically, the next question is: if Erasmus and his friends were more radical than Luther, would not they have produced even more dire effects (more rivers of blood, etc.)? Not necessarily, replies Schmidt, and that partly because Erasmus and more recent reformers did not bring in the mob ('Pöbel'), for whom Schmidt like other spokesmen for enlightened despotism had both fear and disdain, and partly because violence was not inherent in the situation but had to be aroused by Luther. Certainly the Protestants freed themselves from pope and infallible church and from a hierarchy stifling to the spirit. But how real is this freedom? The Protestant authorities and the mob have been more intimidating than any pope. Erasmus – under the pope and surrounded by the enmity of the monks – proceeded cautiously. Schmidt accepts and justifies that caution. When the Protestants – in the face of political authority or the mob – fall silent or behave prudently, they demonstrate, says Schmidt, how little their freedom, bought at so high a price, amounts to. Schmidt is here the victim of a double standard. From this point on he follows a zigzag course: Protestantism is heading towards deism and naturalism; however, the Reformation created, not freedom of thought, but a new scholasticism and intolerance. Practical religion gained when the Reformation replaced outward ceremonies by inner faith; however, there was much superficial faith and relaxed morality, a predictable outcome of so-called Christian freedom. Erasmus had seen the danger and of these things he was a reliable witness.[202]

Finally, in chapter 23 Schmidt asks again about the relation between Reformation and Enlightenment, the issue that preoccupied his Protestant colleagues. The Reformers did well, he says, to make languages the foundation of their study of the Bible. But the revival of letters had not begun with them. Their violence and the violence they aroused damaged the cause. Schmidt ends disenchanted with both parties. Luther's exaggerations led to exaggerations on the other side. Each sought, not to find the truth, but to defend a system. With the triumph of the Jesuits, the 'Mönchs-System' emerged stronger than ever. Studies became suspect. 'Erasmus himself, to whom popes, cardinals and bishops paid compliments in his life-time, had his writings branded after his death.'[203]

For Schmidt, Erasmus was a genuine reformer of the church. He preferred to work by persuasion since he saw the dangers in tumult and violence. In this sense he was less revolutionary than Luther. However, he aimed at a larger intellectual freedom, anticipating the freedoms enjoyed in the eighteenth century itself. Erasmus would not have cut progress off by a new scholasticism, as the Lutherans had done. In that sense he was more revolutionary than Luther. There are unresolved ambiguities here. Was Erasmus the forerunner of the benign Enlightenment only or of the destructive one also? Schmidt has no clear answer because – like many of his Catholic predecessors – he is less interested in Erasmus for his own sake than in using him as a witness against the Reformers.

What is distinctive in the Josephine historian's case against the Reformers is the claim that they were wanting in enlightenment. His critics attacked him at exactly that point. Schröckh in a review in *Allgemeine deutsche Bibliothek* suggested this reply to Schmidt's question: what if Erasmus had foreseen the Thirty Years War? 'Without doubt he would as a wise man have said that the persecuting spirit of his own church, not the Reformation, had produced this and a thousand other sad consequences.' As for the charge of neo-scholasticism, the spirit of critical enquiry was, according to Schröckh, the outcome of the Reformation. What, after all, had been the fate of free spirits like Valla, Savonarola, Reuchlin, and Erasmus in the old church?[204]

A Protestant, J.F. Gaum, republished the relevant section of *Geschichte der Deutschen* under the title 'Luther und die Reformation' and added his own correcting notes. To Schmidt's use of Erasmus as a witness to the undisciplined violence of the Reformers, Gaum retorts that Erasmus was as much for Luther as against him; the humanist attack on scholasticism and on Rome itself was indispensable to the success of the Reformation.[205] Between Gaum and Schmidt is the difference between the Protestant Enlightenment's identification of Erasmus with the Reformation and itself, and a Josephine or gallican claim to Erasmus as forerunner of a distinctive, eighteenth-century form of Catholicism and of an intellectual freedom which was more secure in the old church than among the Protestants.

V I

Johann Gottfried Herder's fierce attack on Erasmus in defence of his militant critic Ulrich von Hutten takes us beyond eighteenth-century academic controversies and already announces the revolutionary age that is to come. Hutten and Erasmus had been comrades in the literary warfare against scholastic learning. This was a friendship between an older man with an established scholarly reputation and a young firebrand. Hutten was a gifted propagandist, especially for German patriotism and against Roman abuses. In Luther he came to see a hope of realizing his and Erasmus' program for the reform of the church and the restoration of Christian piety. But he sought also the vindication of his own troubled class (the imperial knights) and the establishment of a strong political authority in Germany through the emperor, especially as a counterweight to Rome. After Luther's condemnation at the Diet of Worms he promoted a civil war against the Romanists in the Rhineland. The attempt was a fiasco. Ailing and defeated, Hutten came to Basel where Erasmus showed an understandable, if distressing, reluctance to see him. This and Erasmus' refusal to side with Luther provoked bitter recriminations from Hutten on his deathbed, his friends, and his apologists through the generations.[206]

Hutten was a natural hero for the young Herder of the *Sturm und Drang*. When Herder (1744–1803) wrote his panegyric of Hut-

ten and resumed his hero's complaint against Erasmus (1776), he
was in his early thirties and about to begin his service with Karl
August, duke of Weimar (1775–1828), as superintendent of
schools, chief pastor, and court preacher. Behind him lay a pietist
upbringing, study at Königsberg, where he was taught by both
Kant and Hamann – the latter reinforcing his preference for the
subjective and intuitive over the formal and rationalistic – ordination, teaching and preaching at Riga, a journey to France where
he moved among the *philosophes* (1769), the beginnings of his
friendship with Goethe, marriage, and a variety of writings in
literature and philosophy. On one side he was possessed of 'inexhaustible energy ... a tremendous sensitivity and a pedagogical
èlan'; on the other he could lapse into 'gloom and despondency'
and express a 'sardonic bitterness.'[207] The *Sturm und Drang* was
much more than a matter of temperament but the strains in Herder's personality were not uncharacteristic. Its search was for
spontaneity and authenticity in personal and social life, for a
genuine cultural growth in native soil; its target was the artificial
and conventional in literature and life and especially obsequious-
ness towards a dominant French culture. There were bound to
be contradictions.[208]

In his essay in the *Teutsche Merkur* of July 1776 Herder presented Hutten as a heroic figure who had sacrificed everything
in the struggle for the good.[209] This is the portrait of an authentic
personality, true and guileless. In contrast were the double-
dealers ('Falschen') who became his relentless enemies and ridiculed and defamed him. Hutten, Herder says, died 'with love
for the fatherland and with lion-like courage against the liars and
smotherers ['Verkleisterer'] of the truth.' Hutten was no author
of a pedantic kind; all was alive in his writings.[210] Hence the
contrast with Erasmus. The full-blooded satire on scholastic obscurantism, the famous *Epistolae obscurorum virorum (Letters of
Obscure Men*, 1515), could, Herder adds, come only from his pen,
never from that of Erasmus. The fearful, two-faced Erasmus might
laugh over the letters but he hoped to cover his tracks as well.
'To laugh over them, to enjoy them for himself, in laughing to
break a deadly abscess, to learn by heart some of the more striking
letters – all this the faint-hearted Erasmus, who always lived
simultaneously on land and water, could well do. But when once
he thought more carefully, he discovered so many risks and fearful "buts" that – out of sheer pitiful fear – he ... praised to the

heights Ortwinus Gratius [a butt of the letters].' To ascribe the letters to Erasmus would be like making him a martyr or a fisheater and he had a wish to be neither.[211]

Hutten, Herder goes on, dared all in his challenge to the papacy. He prepared the way for Luther. 'Here is Germany's Demosthenes in all his greatness.' His appeal to the German princes was abortive but he stood by Franz von Sickingen, a leader of the imperial knights who fell in the Rhineland war, not for some phantom of political freedom, but for 'truth, light, justice, religion, Christ.'[212] After the defeat Hutten came to Basel seeking deliverance, not least from Erasmus who earlier, at the height of his fame, had cultivated him.

But on the road to calamity he found a man of refinement ['einen schönen Geist'] and so-called friend, who completely broke his heart. Erasmus was also at Basel and not only shunned and denied the poor, hunted or, as he put it, shabby nobleman, whom previously he had exalted to the heavens, but he wished on the other side to Hutten's friends to be considered a friend of Hutten's, lied, put the blame on Hutten's sickness [syphilis – innocently acquired, said Herder] that he did not speak to him, etc.

Erasmus tried – by threat or flattery – to silence Hutten's final expostulation against him, but in vain. His reply, the *Spongia adversus aspergines Hutteni*, offered a wretched bolt-hole ('Schlupfwinkel') for a mere critic and classical wit.[213]

The contrast between these two portraits is bald. The psychology and morality is of an elementary kind. Erasmus, according to Herder, was fearful, devious, self-regarding, a bloodless intellectual; Hutten was a hero, clear as light, straightforward, a fighter in the world's arena. Ten years before at Riga, in his earliest writings on language and literature (*Ueber die neuere deutsche Litteratur: Fragmente*), Herder had made an analogous contrast between Erasmus and Luther; it went along with a rejection of Renaissance humanism and an assertion of the national principle in language. The domination of Latin weakened the vernaculars. Would that the revival of the ancients had led, not to a recovery of their thought and language, but to a stimulation of ours! Luther, he goes on in a famous and arresting phrase, awakened the German language, 'a sleeping giant.' It was no discredit to Luther that Erasmus, 'the nicest pedant' the world had seen, accused him of doing violence to Latin literature; he had broken the unwholesome connection between Latin religion, scholastic learning, and Roman speech.[214] In this contrast of hero and pedant *Sturm und Drang* (and even romanticism) is already announced.[215]

At another point in the *Sturm und Drang* Herder made the contrast between depth and surface. He was discussing determinism. The deeper man's awareness of the possibilities of freedom, the more he recognizes his bondage. Nevertheless, some more superficial minds feel as free as gods. 'Luther with his "bondage of the will" declared the half-wise an offence and the half-virtuous a folly; this teaching proved Luther's deep feeling for mankind's bonds. Even the fine Erasmus did not understand him ...' Herder's understanding of mankind's bonds was very different from Luther's but he was affirming his preference for a high doctrine of determinism (Luther) over mere refinement and rationality (Erasmus).[216]

Herder's view of Erasmus was challenged precisely by a voice which represented the most refined form of the German Enlightenment, that of Christoph Martin Wieland (1733–1813). Wieland had in fact given Herder the opportunity for his outburst. In 1773 he founded a literary journal, the *Teutsche Merkur*, to serve the middlebrow reading public of the German-speaking lands. The *Teutsche Merkur* was not devoted to an interest, a program, or a speciality. It was the successor to the eclectic journals of the early eighteenth century rather than a forerunner of the professional publications of the nineteenth century. Its role in the mind of its founder was educative and popularizing. Contributors came from many sides and spoke in their own voices, without editorial constraint. The tone was tolerant and undogmatic.[217]

In 1776 at a time when his relations with the young men of the *Sturm und Drang* were at best uneasy, Wieland began publishing in each number a pen-portrait of a German hero of the sixteenth century. His own piece on Hutten in February was largely derivative and without fire. Herder's lightning-strike followed in July. Wieland was shocked into an immediate reply; he did not edit Herder but added a note. In reviving memories of Hutten, Wieland said, he did not want to disturb the peace in Germany; on the contrary, he wanted Catholic readers, too, to admire 'the man of true German blood and heroic heart.' No German author was better fitted than Herder to recall Hutten and his essay made a worthy memorial. But the Catholic half of the German population would be more than human if they did not find him partisan. He was right to do justice to Hutten but not, three centuries after his death, to revive his bitter tones. 'From zeal for Hutten to blacken the memōry of the milder, weaker but, truly, in his way and in his own circle of influence, no less good and noble and deserving Erasmus, who was loved by the best men of his time – those who think this right may do it; I can neither do it nor approve it.' That men deal unjustly with one another in times of disturbance and agitation is natural; there is no reason why we, says Wieland, living in times of peace and of balance guaranteed by the fundamental laws, should not do justly by all.[218]

Here Wieland in face of the stormy proceedings of his younger colleagues (he and Herder were together in Weimar in 1776) – speaks for an Enlightenment that has become established, a cultural status quo. His note shows the strain between two men, two temperaments, and two outlooks. 'The man is like an electric cloud,' he said of Herder. 'The meteor may make a very imposing effect at a distance, but Devil take such a neighbour close up.'[219] Wieland's relations with the *Sturm und Drang* had not been good for some years. To them he belonged to an effete tradition and was too dominated by French culture. He did indeed distance himself from, say, Voltaire and paid homage to national distinctiveness in literature; the pen-portraits in the *Teutsche Merkur* of 1776 were part of that homage. But he rejected attempts at a complete break from tradition, at complete spontaneity, at a purely German literature or scholarship; he adhered to the humanist, more universalist tradition and appealed to the wider educated public in its support.[220]

Wieland determined to reiterate his point by including an essay on Erasmus himself in the *Teutsche Merkur* series.[221] Besides reproducing the Holbein portrait which gave an accurate impression of both sides of Erasmus' character – his intellectual acuteness and his sensitive feeling – Wieland wanted that character to be seen more justly than was possible under the unforgiving light of religious partisanship. Half the essay is given over to Erasmus' place in the Reformation controversies. Each side believed itself disadvantaged by his stand, despite his own wish to do right by both. Catholics blamed those youthful achievements which actually give him an honoured place among the noblest and best: his frankness in unmasking abuses, his attack on intellectual barbarism, his merry but effective satire. Protestants, too, overlooked these achievements in regretting that he did less than they had hoped for their cause. Together they conspired to deny his virtues: disinterestedness, discretion, love of peace, sense of fairness, and moderation.[222]

Wieland advocates a moral discrimination which recognizes that all characters are not strictly comparable: 'spirits of such different kinds should not be put against one another.' It is not just to allow one whose traits and achievements were so different form theirs to be overshadowed by larger-than-life figures like Luther and Hutten. He had his own warmth and light to shed. Wieland in short defends a kind of relativism. There is some justice in Luther's reproaches: Erasmus temporized for the sake of his reputation, security, and rest. But conviction and heroism are not always in a man's power to command. Erasmus was not suited by birth or training to play the hero's role in fierce conflicts; unlike Hutten he was not led by a hard destiny to the gambler's throw of pitting all against all.

Erasmus favoured and furthered the good cause, so far as his conviction took him, so long as he saw it as pure, as the cause of humanity and the grace of God; and drew his hand back only when he saw or believed he saw that the human was too much winning the upper hand over the godly; when he saw that personal passions, politics, bureaucratic purposes of the powerful, etc. were mixed in too strongly, and that the fierce heat with which it was carried through and which was quite contrary to his naturally mild nature, would lead to a schism – something he always wished greatly to avoid.

Must everyone, Wieland asks, take sides? Is it not wise for some to hold themselves in reserve, hoping to preserve peace and check civil war? What appears great in Hutten is not all virtue. What appears small in Erasmus is not all dishonourable or mean. The observer – in a phrase that would appeal to the historians of the next generation – must think his way into the circumstances of the person he would judge.[223]

So Wieland goes into Erasmus' circumstances, his birth, upbringing, and education, following the earliest biography by Beatus Rhenanus. His bodily constitution was weak, which in part explains his temperamental preference for the golden mean (the *aurea mediocritas* of Horace) and for all that is measured and restful in nature and life and his distaste for everything pretentious and extravagant, Platonist illusion and Stoic arrogance. Wieland's sympathy for this temperament is unmistakable; he is stating here both a humanist and an Enlightenment ideal. Through an account of the monastic years, his travels and writings and rising reputation, Wieland traces Erasmus' other commitment, to his spiritual freedom.

All this, says Wieland, explains why, in the Reformation controversy, Erasmus had to be himself. Wieland is close to the Protestant Enlightenment historians in saying that Erasmus and Luther each had his own role to play. Erasmus was justified, but 'where would we be if Luther had thought like him?' Erasmus showed courage in attacking the monks, the scholastics, and church abuses. His satires did more to overthrow superstition than many a solemn, long-winded disquisition. He could not reasonably be asked – an aged and ailing man – to throw himself into the Reformation maelstrom. If he had been born twenty years later – Wieland repeats an old Protestant belief – he would have been as warm for Luther as his friend Melanchthon.[224]

Erasmus was not a casual interest for Wieland. In his essay, for all its smoothness and lightness of tone, there was a warm feeling for its subject. Wieland had been wounded by Herder's outrages against Erasmus. The natural affinity between the two men has often been remarked. Wieland found in Erasmus, says Friedrich Sengle, 'a perfect symbol of his own spiritual being.' For Wieland (as for Erasmus) tolerance and moderation did not arise from indifference but from a serious and often energetic ethic.[225] In the history of Erasmus interpretations the significance of Wieland's 'Fragment' lay in its concentration on questions of 'character'; for the nineteenth-century writers these were to become an obsession.

Wieland's defence of Erasmus was not the last word between Wieland and Herder. In time relations between them improved. More important for us is the amelioration in Herder's attitude towards Erasmus which began almost immediately.[226] In an essay of 1779, which a biographer calls 'a masterpiece of essayistic style,'[227] on the relation between the humanities and specialized studies, Herder abandoned the suspicions of the *Fragmente* and gave Latin back its priority. Erasmus was included among those who had appreciated the mutual dependence between the two kinds of study and had treated the higher studies in the true spirit of humanity. A teacher of the humanities in that tradition refines his students' taste and imagination but above all guides them to love mankind and seek its true good – 'the best influence in the higher studies and the great art of living.'[228]

Herder also came to value Erasmus' biblical work. In a handbook prepared for their use around 1780 he warned the theological students of his diocese against turning to biblical paraphrases rather than the text. But he made an exception of Erasmus who had worked in different circumstances and had to rescue both the ancient languages from barbarism. By his easy paraphrases he led scholars form scholasticism to the Bible. 'He aimed at this and performed it in an ongoing reformation through his writings bright as sliver: his paraphrases remain therefore by their clear thinking and beautiful expression worth their weight in gold.'[229] Herder was more and more identifying religion with the poetic and claiming the Bible as poetry's highest expression. In a letter to a young Swiss student, Georg Müller, who was passing through a crisis of faith, he developed this idea and pointed to Erasmus who, like Jerome, had a fine sense for the poetic in the Bible, those places 'where mingle image and deed, history and poetry.'[230]

By the last decade of the century Herder's mind had moved away from assertions of individuality and distinctiveness and towards a universalism to which both the pietists and the Enlightenment contributed. The fundamental concepts of book 15 of his *Ideen zur Philosophie der Geschichte der Menschheit* (1784–91) have been defined as 'law ..., fine cohesion, balance, order, harmony.'[231] The dominant idea was that of *Humanität*. It was associated with ideas of continuity and unity. Both individuals and communities are formed organically over time; individual and community depend on one another and indeed participate in the process of human development generally. Harmony between nations – still seen, of course, as indestructible human units – was an essential part of the progress of mankind.[232]

The revolution in France cut deeply into Herder's reflections on these matters. Twenty years before he had abandoned enlightened despotism for a more popular understanding of the state.[233] At first he welcomed the revolution but by the time he published his *Briefe zur Beförderung der Humanität* (*Letters for the*

Advancement of Humanity) in April 1793 his view had changed
and the sympathetic expressions included in earlier unpublished
versions of these letters had been excised.[234] It is no surprise that
Erasmus, lover of peace and concord and critic of the revolutionaries of his own time, should be mentioned. A poet, says Herder
in one letter, should not be too deeply involved in politics. Thus
the poet takes sides, circumstances change and he is swept aside
– much better to remain in a higher realm, the sphere of humanity
where all political ideas are reconciled. 'We, my friends, would
build the garden of the graces and muses in tranquillity. Wise
Homer, noble Pindar and the men of gentleness and wisdom –
Pythagoras, Socrates, Plato, Aristotle, Epicurus, Zeno, Marcus
Antoninus, Erasmus, Sarpi, Grotius, Fénelon, St Pierre, Penn and
Franklin – shall be the godly inhabitants of our peaceful garden.'
For Herder as for Erasmus peace was a positive human value.
Humanitarian reform was endangered by turbulence, promoted
by calm reflection: 'the seed in the earth needs rest and mild,
refreshing rain.'[235]

Herder has arrived at a kind of quietism but a quietism qualified
by passionate commitments. In particular he was an unyielding
opponent of dogmatic, authoritarian religion. He argued for an
open, tolerant, universal form of Christianity. The last words of
his *Christliche Schriften* (1794–8) capture his intention: 'What name
did Christ give himself? The Son of Man, that is, the name of a
simple, pure human being. Purified of dross, his religion cannot
be called otherwise than the religion of pure human kindness,
human religion.'[236] Little wonder there was a change in his attitude to the Reformation from the time of his 'Hutten.' Now he
states a preference for moderate spirits and for the 'progressive,
natural, reasonable evolution of things,' rather than revolution.[237]
In the fourth volume of the *Christliche Schriften* (1798), he returned to the free-will controversy and spoke against exaggerations of the contradiction between nature and grace, for which
he blamed Augustine and the Augustinians. 'Augustinianism came
needlessly into Lutheranism; certainly the struggle which broke
out between Luther and Erasmus over human free-will brought
nothing to Christianity.' After Luther's death his best helpers
(presumably Melanchthon, the friend of Erasmus) were reviled
and persecuted as synergists, while the extreme determinists reduced man to a block.[238] A new dogmatism and scholasticism

were born from which escape came only in the eighteenth century.

In this last phase Herder revised the piece on Hutten and the changes he made are startling.[239] He now described the original version as a 'wild growth' ('diesem etwas wilden Gewächse') whose purpose was to present Hutten not as others – in his own time or in the present – saw him but on his own terms. The picture is still clear, since Hutten did not hide his aims or his faults, and Herder believed that he acted 'for the good cause of the fatherland, for religion and truth.' But others worked for the same ends in their fashion: 'I am so far from denying the merits of the great and widely honoured Erasmus because of Hutten's personal enmity that in other regards he and Grotius have been my idols for many years.'[240] Critical passages about Erasmus disappear in the new version – the fearful Erasmus who lived on both land and water, his incapacity for writing anything so vigorous as the *Letters of Obscure Men*, the 'wretched bolt-hole' of his *Spongia*. Many expressions are moderated: the sarcastic 'man of refinement and so-called friend' applied to Erasmus' final refusal to see Hutten is replaced by the mild 'former friend.'[241] Notes which make the treatment more even-handed are added. Thus Herder would not wish to deny that wild fire as well as noble flame burned in Hutten – the spirit of his turbulent class.[242] In a revolutionary age when for Herder tolerance, moderation, humanity, even civilization itself were at risk, he rejected heroics and turned to the man he saw as undogmatic, civil, reforming, the man of the harassed middle way.

In that company Herder rejoined Wieland. Wieland was at heart republican but after 1789 he warned against attempts to realize political ideals absolutely.[243] He was the enemy of 'fanatics, ideologues and prophets.'[244] Through a fictitious correspondent Wieland questioned himself in the *Teutsche Merkur* in 1793 about his attitude to the revolution. Would Wieland, his ostensibly radical interrogator asked, have been on the side of the Tarquins, the Austrians, the pope, or Alva if he had lived respectively in the times of Brutus, William Tell, Luther, or Egmont? Wieland replied: 'If I had, for example, been Luther's contemporary (as I have many times frankly said), I would have taken the party of Erasmus; and I confess this, though I know that I have a large majority against me.'[245]

The revolution forced a reappraisal of Erasmus by Herder, as by Gibbon. That Herder in effect adopted Wieland's view of Erasmus showed how substantial the reappraisal was. Erasmus retained for Wieland and Herder the qualities admired in the Enlightenment, above all critical penetration in studies, openness in religion, spiritual freedom. Now was added a pragmatic conservatism for facing a time of turbulence and change. The experience of revolution gave a new force and dignity to Erasmus' mediating position in the Reformation, which the controversialists of the past had mostly seen as a sign of defeat.[246]

At the beginning of the eighteenth century Erasmus seemed – after two centuries of confessional strife in which his reputation suffered badly – to be rejoining the cultural majority, going with the prevailing trends.[247] That was due above all to changes in religious thought and sensibility. Through the century diverse writers found in him congenial themes: a critique of Catholicism and of authoritarianism in religion generally (for the present purpose one may overlook sharp differences about his role in the Reformation), a religion of individual inner experience, a historical/critical approach to the biblical texts, a liberation from the scholastic strait-jacket in philosophy and theology, a sense of enlightenment and progress, a commitment to social and cultural reform but a rejection of violence and revolution, a faith in mutual toleration. Erasmus may not have been seen true; he was certainly not seen whole. But there were genuine points of contact between Enlightenment preoccupations and the historical figure and his thought. By the end of the century, as a new social order struggled into being and the old Europe of monarchies and aristocracies began its long decline, new cries and slogans were heard: social equality, political rights, national liberation. Words of Erasmus could be turned to some of these causes. But the surrounding turbulence of war and revolution would not favour his reputation. Erasmus could appear as the hero of a passing generation. The old Herder and the old Wieland were possibly making true criticisms of revolutionary pretensions but they could also be seen as spokesmen for a cultural order that was fading away. The young Herder had prefigured the passions of the nineteenth century in his essay on Hutten. The history of Erasmus' reputation was entering a new and problematical stage.[248]

FOUR

Romanticism and Revolution

I

At the beginning of the last decade of the eighteenth century with
revolution already begun in France, two biographies – the first
since Burigny's in the middle decade of the century – summed
up the Protestant Enlightenment's judgment of Erasmus. In that
judgment Erasmus was presented as a liberator – sometimes the
chief liberator – of both the intellect and Christian piety from
medieval bondage. The Middle Ages appeared uniformly dark
and scholasticism was everywhere the enemy. Erasmus, it was
said, freed the intellect by his daring satire on clerical pretensions
and the abuse of ecclesiastical power and by his critical work on
the biblical texts. He taught a Christian piety more personal, more
sensitive, more expansive and tolerant. That was seen as a liberation of the spirit. Between Erasmus and the Protestant Reformers was an essential solidarity. The issues that mattered in
the Reformation were issues for him, too – indeed he first stated
many of them. They are the womb of the modern world. Erasmus
and the Reformers drew apart – not on any matter that the Protestant Enlightenment could consider fundamental – but on the
pragmatic question: how could reformation best be carried forward? Here, say the eighteenth-century Protestant writers, the
Reformers were right – more was needed than the power of words.
There was a misjudgment (more or less serious) on Erasmus' part,
a misjudgment sometimes related to weaknesses of character but
more generally seen as an honest mistake. Only with Herder and
Wieland did the question of character take the central ground it
was to occupy through the nineteenth century.

Both biographies were published in Zürich where the German Enlightenment theologians had long had a profound influence. Historical interests – in part for patriotic reasons – had also developed in eighteenth-century Zürich, and an interest not least in the Zürich Reformation. One writer, Hans Rudolf Maurer (1752–1805), presented Zwingli as the forerunner of the Enlightenment, sent to break the yoke of superstition.[1] It is not surprising that in these circumstances and under these influences the minds of Zürich theologians should turn to Erasmus. Among the biblical interpreters recommended to the Zürich pastorate Erasmus and Grotius had pride of place.[2] Attachment to Erasmus was to be found widely among educated Swiss. Peter Ochs, who played a controversial role in the French invasion of Switzerland and the destruction of the old Swiss confederation in the later 1790s, had in 1782 composed a dialogue wherein Erasmus appealed to natural simplicity against the faded sophistication of the age.[3] Twenty years earlier the Platonist philosopher from St Gallen Jakob Wegelin (1721–91) had included in his dialogues of the dead (*Religiöse Gespräche der Toten*) a dialogue between Erasmus and Luther on the true form of reformation, Erasmus arguing for reformation by persuasion after careful preparation of minds and hearts; otherwise, he says, there comes schism and anarchy followed by a new authoritarianism and scholasticism. The dialogue ends unpolemically with a prayer for the renewed purification of the church.[4] Meanwhile, Basel with its classical educated businessmen reminded the English traveller William Coxe of the 'noble Erasmus.'[5] A German teacher took satisfaction from translating the *Moriae encomium* of 'our Erasmus' while staying in Basel.[6]

Johannes Gaudin's life of Erasmus was dedicated to a society of learned friends in Zürich, although Gaudin himself (1766–1833) was a Vaudois, pastor at Nyon and professor of botany at Lausanne Academy.[7] From the standard sources and works of the preceding century from Bayle to Wieland, it recounts Erasmus' biography in annalistic form. It is instructive that Gaudin singles out Planck for special praise.[8] His views of both history and Erasmus are expressed in the language of the Enlightenment. Everywhere in Europe in Erasmus' time darkness and enlightenment, ignorance and knowledge were in conflict. Erasmus' book in praise of marriage, *Encomium matrimonii*, did honour to his enlightenment. More generally, 'his writings and the partial enlightenment [die halbe Aufklärung] they produced, at least among a certain class of readers, without doubt facilitated the work of church reform [Kirchenverbesserung].' Zwingli himself attested that Erasmus was one of the first to promote a purer religious knowledge because he restored the authority of the scriptures.[9]

The Protestant Reformation dominates this biography of Erasmus. Gaudin confesses his sympathy for the moderate reformation espoused by Erasmus by taking as his book's motto Erasmus' remark: 'I know that it is sometimes pious to conceal truth or not to proclaim it in all circumstances and at all times before all and sundry and without qualification.'[10] On the one hand, Erasmus blamed the arbitrary proceedings of the Lutherans who disturbed the public peace for a reformation which might have been achieved without disturbance, if more gradually. On the other, he frankly called on the pope to reform the church and resisted subservience to the Roman system, while warning Rome that it would do itself no service by lumping him in with the Lutherans. But through the 1520s his middle ground came more and more under attack from both the parties and his beautiful appeal for Christian unity, *Liber de sarcienda ecclesiae concordia* (1533), found favour with neither. Gaudin's appreciation of Erasmus' stand is real and avowed but in the end he reverts to the standard Protestant position: Luther's stubbornness was indispensable for the recovery of Christian freedom from Roman tyranny – to treat with Rome then (as now) jeopardized that freedom.[11]

Of Erasmus' many controversies, Gaudin says perceptively enough that he would have saved his own reputation and left his opponents' in deserved obscurity if he had resisted the temptation always to respond.[12] Conflict with Hutten was unavoidable, the one man being restless and violent, the other mild and peace-loving. In his controversy with Luther, Erasmus had to choose his ground with care. He could not attack the Reformation which he had himself prepared or defend church abuses of which he had been the chief critic. Correspondingly, Luther's bitter tone towards one who had prepared his own way and long carried the burden of the struggle against the monks was inexcusable. Erasmus to his great honour chose to vindicate the rights of humanity against Luther's harsh and offensive teaching on the human will. Erasmus tried but could not maintain a spirit of moderation in his dealings with Luther. Their mutual recriminations were 'highly prejudicial to the good cause' and left Erasmus suspect to Protestants down to the present time.[13]

Events in Basel also contributed to that outcome. In the mid-1520s Erasmus saw with alarm the religious innovations in the city and knew that his Catholic enemies would turn his residence there against him. To stay, he said to Oecolampadius, would be to give the religious revolution his blessing. Gaudin wants, despite these difficulties, to show a mutual respect between Erasmus and Basel. The circumstances of Erasmus' death in Basel fit his purpose admirably: Erasmus wished no priest, confession, or sacrament – fortunate was he then to be dying in a Protestant town. The city has continued to honour his name.[14]

For Gaudin Erasmus was first among the pre-Reformers. He anticipated the Reformation, indeed advanced most of its causes and lacked only the single-mindedness, obstinacy, or belligerency of Luther. He was in important ways alienated from the old church – he wanted to replace ceremonies by 'evangelical piety,' he made scripture the source of faith, he rejected Catholic 'superstitions' and even on the eucharist, while adhering most of his life to established doctrine, he was shaken by the arguments of Oecolampadius.[15] But this reformation was identified by the passwords of the Enlightenment: enlightenment itself, tolerance, freedom, and humanity.

On Erasmus' character Gaudin echoes 'the great Wieland.'[16] He was naturally anxious and fearful but never so much that he would deny his own opinion. He was modest and restrained and, despite the princes' attraction to his wit and urbanity, his preference was always for the middle-class ('dem glücklichen Mittelstand'). His life expressed a certain wholesome simplicity, the tone of his writings was unforced and natural and both life and writings were free of affectation. He loved peace and concord – indeed too much – and was never an aggressor.[17]

The two-volume biography of Salomon Hess is a more substantial and scholarly work than Gaudin's. It was the first extended biography in the German language and, with Jortin and Burigny, a standard work for nineteenth-century writers.[18] Hess (1763–1837) came from a patrician family of Zürich, whose fortunes had been founded on the trade in wool and silk and which provided the city with a succession of pastors and theologians, including Salomon's uncle Johann Jakob Hess (1741–1828), a pioneer in the quest of the historical Jesus.[19] In 1801 he became pastor in the ancient parish church of St Peter where he had as predecessor the attractive and controversial Johann Caspar Lavater, another participant in the Erasmus story.

Hess's biography is, like Burigny's, rather formless. It has marginal headings but no chapters. The treatment is chronological. Like Jean Le Clerc, Erasmus' editor whose 'Life' of 1705 followed the ebb and flow of his friendships and associations through the correspondence Le Clerc was then editing, Hess devotes most space to Erasmus' personal relations – with friends, patrons, rivals, and enemies. Thus, explains Hess in his first volume, a study of his work on the New Testament shows how many patrons and friends but also how many enemies it acquired for Erasmus. Similarly, Hess says that he has recounted Erasmus' various controversies at greater length than earlier biographers. These struggles – those within his own 'party' in the first volume, those with the other (Protestant) party in the second – throw light on his character but they also (here Hess in his turn adopts the language of the Enlightenment and sums up the view of Erasmus which has occupied us so far in this volume) reveal the gradual awakening of learned criticism in his time and the larger conflict between darkness and the light of truth.[20]

Erasmus' early life is recounted from accepted sources in simple biographical form without much attention to the historical background. Knowing Knight's account of Erasmus' English friends, Hess makes more than his immediate predecessors had done of the relationship with John Colet, who is presented as Erasmus' tutor in biblical and theological studies and an enemy of scholasticism.[21] Shortly after his encounter with Colet Erasmus wrote his *Enchiridion*, a warm commendation of Christian virtues and condemnation of false religion. It was welcomed by 'rational Christians' ('vernünftige Christen'), though the enthusiasts thought it too cold and the orthodox found heresies. Another early influence was that of the Italian critic Lorenzo Valla and indeed Erasmus – despite his disingenuous disclaimers – owed much in general to Italy.[22]

Through his first volume Hess presents Erasmus as the enlightened critic. His *Moriae encomium* (*Praise of Folly*) brought light to darkened minds and prepared the way for the religious reformation. Sadly he so took to heart the reproaches of his enemies that he later wished that he had never written the work. His edition of the New Testament spread a purer religious knowledge and helped uproot superstition and prejudice.[23] For many of his patrons he was too candid and so, as Le Clerc said, 'more agreeable in his writings than in his person.'[24] But his sharpness of wit came out in his writings, too, as in his annotations to the New Testament. In his controversies he was often too sensitive and too ready to justify himself. The controversies over the New Testament with those considered his scholarly equals were an example. Still, he could hold his ground under pressure – he explained himself in controversy over the authority of the pope 'with a dignity and good nature which do honour to his character.' The preface to his edition of Hilary (1523), where he touched on the Trinitarian question, aroused hostility not only for its free expressions about dogma but also for its boldness in treating one of the church Fathers critically like any other author. An impartial observer, Hess says, finds laughable the anxiety of Erasmus' Catholic defenders to establish his orthodoxy. They rely too much on his apologetic writings where he is rarely natural. Were then his enemies right to call him Lutheran, Arian, or Pelagian? Hess replies 'no'; Erasmus may have points in common with various parties but he is bound to none. 'His faith is not subject to testing by systems'; rather he relies on a reasonable interpretation of scripture.[25]

For all his inordinate prudence and sensitivity, Erasmus never denied his better understanding and in the Luther controversy remained true to his principle of tolerance.[26] Hess writes thus at the end of his first volume and this spirit – close to Gaudin's – informs his discussion of Erasmus' relations with Luther in the second volume, 'the most interesting part of his life,' Hess adds, in a characteristically Protestant presumption.[27] Burigny, his Catholic predecessor, recognized, Hess says, that in recounting such controversies a balance must be struck between Erasmus' strengths and weaknesses.[28]

In fact – and here Hess builds on the more advanced Enlightenment positions and anticipates, if mildly and fleetingly, a case that nineteenth-century liberal writers would develop – Erasmus saw more deeply than Luther into the needs of the church and the truths of scripture; he saw more clearly the distinction between the papacy and 'Christus-religion.' He was 'a declared proponent of sound philosophy.' If he had but had Luther's force and courage, the Protestant church would have freed itself earlier than it did of the vestiges of popery which still cling to it. But in that sphere Erasmus remained temperamentally behind Luther. He had a different idea of the vocation of religious reformer; he stood by a 'Christian prudence' and did not believe that truth should be proclaimed in all circumstances. He was also careful of his reputation, tranquillity, and security. He believed his methods would be effective for reform; he had, for example, faith in the reforming intentions of the rulers of the age. He adjusted to Roman beliefs of which he was doubtful because he feared for the public peace and hoped for a gradual reformation of ideas.[29] On this point, the Reformers were right: Erasmus' way would have avoided great tribulations but, as Le Clerc had seen, the world would have remained in darkness. He had both personal and doctrinal grounds for opposing Luther and his choice of the matter for debate – free will – was an honourable one. Unhappily, controversy unhinged him and he covered the Reformers and their friends with unjustified calumnies.[30]

Erasmus, Salomon Hess concludes, was 'the restorer of literature.' Further, he never lost sight of the chief end of his studies – to make the scriptures available to the people and restore practical Christianity. His call was for a briefly stated, simple and unforced faith. This practical theology cannot be linked with either or any party. His party could only be one of his own creation but that was far from his thoughts. He did not aspire to spiritual dictatorship. He had many enemies – those who defended barbarism and superstition, those who wanted to break the yoke immediately, whatever the cost to the peace of the church. His defensiveness towards these enemies might be criticized but, as Wieland saw, character traits are not always at a man's command.[31] This final reference to Wieland makes it possible to locate Hess's biography with fair precision – incoherent though its argument sometimes is – within the ambit of the late Enlightenment.

If Wieland's mild and appreciative judgments were taken up by Gaudin and Hess, the heroics of Herder's early essay on Hutten were emulated in a life of Erasmus published at Leipzig in 1802 and written by Gottlob Heinrich Adolf Wagner (1774–1835).[32] Not surprisingly Wagner followed this work with a life of Hutten (1803).[33] Here already romanticism (of a certain kind) is in full flood. Only blindness or prejudice, says Wagner, could explain the height at which Wieland placed Erasmus. One does not need

to make allowances – from circumstances or contemporary standards – for really great men. 'Every great man puts his stamp on
the age. Men on whom the age, to the contrary, puts its stamp
are surely small and insignificant.' Erasmus cannot be compared
to Hutten and Luther who did conform to the heroic pattern.
Besides, his weaknesses were condemned out of his own mouth.
Luther's own judgment of Erasmus 'seemed hard and unfriendly
to the weakling, but was so just and true and great that the small
anxiety that party spirit might have entered into it was quite vain
and mischievous.'[34]

Wagner, who is dependent on Gaudin, Burigny-Henke, and
more particularly Hess, does not attempt a chronological narra-
tion. Indeed, his loose presentation – so he says – corresponds
to the character of his subject! His primary interest is in Erasmus'
relation to the Reformation, one of those great events which, he
says, shape human destiny and in which religious men will see
divine direction. Erasmus went along at first but fell back the
more the undertaking was advanced by men of spirit and courage.
He made a contribution in studies but could not go further. He
was admittedly many-sided but Wagner makes a main theme of
his work the contrast between weak many-sidedness (Erasmus)
and strong simplicity (Luther).[35]

Wagner chafes to give a romantic colour even to the unsympathetic Erasmus. He calls the love of his parents, about which
in fact little can be known, 'rare true love,' 'passionate impetu-
osity.' Like other children born out of wedlock Erasmus was a
pupil of destiny, 'that dear, strict but sure teacher.' In part his
destiny led him into bad ways. Against the unwelcome pressure
of his guardians he learned the art of dissimulation. His studies
taught him to value a fine and polished style but he was more
interested in form than in substance and was thus lukewarm to
the things that matter.[36] Yet fortune also smiled. Friendships –
as in England – prepared his way.[37] Erasmus made friends easily,
accommodating himself to each. By temperament, as well as from
his circumstances, he needed the support of friends and patrons.
Indeed, the praises of his patrons gave him a higher opinion of
himself than he deserved. He was in return sometimes impatient
and unthankful. His friendships were 'more for reputation and
possible advantage than a selfless friendly devotion.'[38] The picture is of a shallow, self-centred, talented but directionless man.

Erasmus' works fit into this picture. The *Enchiridion*, which

Hess thought a warm commendation of piety, offered an insipid comparison of the soldier and the Christian – the human spirit cannot be touched by rhetorical exercises of this kind. His work on Greek texts was commendable in the difficult circumstances of the time but his judgments were often misguided and empty. In the affair over Reuchlin, when the boldness of a Hutten was needed to defend Reuchlin against his enemies, Erasmus was again lukewarm. Religious learning for him was an exercise-ground where questions were debated from various sides but without one's ever penetrating to the heart of the matter. His mockery revealed more the rashness of his nature than a genuine freedom of spirit.[39]

At the height of his fame, Erasmus was overtaken by the Reformation. He could not plunge into the stream, he could only disport himself on the bank. There was common ground between Luther and Erasmus – a rejection of scholasticism and clerical abuse, a search for true piety, scriptural standards. 'But Erasmus loved a rhetorical expansiveness, Luther a solid brevity and simplicity.' He could not, like Luther, powerfully and from a full heart speak out for 'the cause of humanity or the nation.' This striking conjuncture – humanity and nation – makes clear that we stand at the beginning of the nineteenth century. Erasmus' responses in the Reformation crisis, Wagner goes on, betray the lightness and fearfulness of his character. His literary achievements – his defence of good letters and his classical and biblical editions – were recognized by contemporaries and by Luther. But Luther also saw how incomplete his theological work was and how damaging to the godly cause his equivocations, which Erasmus called 'prudence, moderation and gentleness.' Here Hess and Wagner run together along the German Protestant main line. If Luther had followed Erasmus' advice, 'then there would not have been such great conflict but the nation would never joyously have been freed from the heavy yoke.' Hutten – 'true German' – saw through Erasmus and in his writing drew him to the life.[40]

In the Reformation controversies Erasmus was characteristically evasive. Over free will he sought a middle way. Luther by contrast exalted faith and spirit and what God achieves in those who have faith and spirit – a curious romantic inversion of Luther's 'by grace alone'! On the sacrament, Erasmus was indecisive and 'slippery,' denying the spiritual understanding he had previously taught.[41]

In sum, Wagner's Erasmus lacked the capacity to define himself personally and historically. He was all flexibility. He had thrown himself into the newer studies and so was caught up in the tempestuous life of his time. 'But his powers were too weak for him to remain dominant in that sphere. This and circumstances meant that he came to grief.'[42]

These three biographies – Gaudin and Hess on one side, Wagner on the other – define the rival views the nineteenth century was to inherit from the latter part of the eighteenth, at least within Protestant historiography. The conflict in values is clear, a preference on one side for moderation, restraint, and tolerance, on the other for commitment, devotion, and single-mindedness. Much in the history of the nineteenth century could be written around this conflict. It is central to the nineteenth-century debates about Erasmus. It identifies one tradition or cluster of values which, all allowances made, may be called 'liberal' and another which may be called 'romantic.'

II

One would not expect the name of Erasmus to be much used by apologists for the French Revolution, although the relation – comparison or contrast? – between the Reformation and the revolution was frequently discussed from the time of the revolution itself and became a favourite theme for nineteenth-century writers, as we shall see.

An early example was the eminent Scottish philosopher Dugald Stewart (1753–1828), who gave Erasmus a modest place. It has been said that in Stewart 'the Scottish philosophy of common sense acquired the dignity of an institution.'[43] His interest was above all in human mind, empirically studied, and the expansion of its powers. His influence was 'less purely speculative than moral and practical' and exercised above all through his teaching.[44] In religion he continued the tradition of natural theology begun with Locke, rejecting both those who associated political liberties with atheism and those who exalted revelation at the expense of reason, and in politics he derived liberalism 'from his general doctrine of the propriety of fully recognizing individual instincts and tendencies as normal social forces.'[45] Robert Burns, who was a friend, said: 'I think his character, divided into ten parts, stands thus: – four parts Socrates, four parts Nathanael, and two parts Shakespeare's Brutus.'[46]

In the post-revolutionary era Stewart combined an unabated faith in progress, and especially intellectual emancipation, with a distrust of the revolution. 'From the Revival of Letters to the present times,' he said in his historical dissertation intended to accompany an edition of the *Encyclopedia Britannica*, 'the progress of mankind in knowledge, in mental illumination, and in enlarged sentiments of humanity towards each other, has proceeded not only with a steady course, but at a rate continually accelerating.' Though a Whig and an early sympathizer, he did not on reflection include the revolution – as it actually happened – in this acceleration. It showed the 'extreme danger' of exhibiting Utopian ideas to the passions of the multitude.[47]

Stewart showed no sign of the amelioration in attitudes towards the Middle Ages going on among his contemporaries. They were in his view 'the most melancholy blank ... in the intellectual and moral history of the human race.' At the revival of letters the 'progress of useful knowledge was extremely slow' for one pedantry (the scholastic) was but replaced by another (the antique). Still, the classical materials, if often gathered in an unprofitable or undiscriminating way, were 'much more favourable to the development of taste and of genius than the unsubstantial subtleties of ontology or of dialectics.'[48] The new studies formed men like Erasmus, Vives, and More 'who, if they do not rank in the same line with the daring reformers by whom the errors of the Catholic Church were openly assailed, certainly exhibit a very striking contrast to the barbarous and unenlightened writers of the preceding age.'[49]

The Reformation for Stewart was one among a number of contemporaneous changes preparing the way for modern liberalism and it ranked equally with them. The renunciation of theological opinions long reverenced 'could not fail to encourage, on all other subjects, a congenial freedom of inquiry.' Important above all was the undermining of Aristotle's authority about which Luther spoke 'with most unbecoming asperity and contempt.' The Reformers' use of printing and the vernacular removed the unique authority of oral teaching, which was always more constricting, and destroyed the hoary prejudice which had 'long confounded knowledge with erudition.' These changes opened knowledge to the 'lower orders' as economic progress opened wealth. At the same time the Reformers revived a practical and common-sense morality. 'The Genius of the human race seems, all at once, to have awakened with renovated and giant strength from his long sleep.'[50]

How did Erasmus and his fellows fit into this awakening? In a long note Stewart combines a standard view of the Protestant Enlightenment (Erasmus had intellectual priority among the reformers of his time, but tougher spirits were needed to carry reformation through) with his distinctive libertarian interests. 'The writings of Erasmus probably contributed still more than those of Luther himself to the progress of the Reformation among men of education and taste; but, without the co-operation of bolder and more decided characters than his, little would to this day have been effected in Europe among the lower orders.' Erasmus' hope of gradual improvement could be realized only in a 'perfect freedom of literary discussion' and after an educational reform which 'would give complete scope to the energies of the human mind,' but these could not be expected. On the contrary, 'where books and teachers are subjected to the censorship of those who are hostile to the dissemination of truth, they become the most powerful of all auxiliaries to the authority of established errors.'[51] Erasmus' friend Thomas More was 'unhinged' by the Reformers' attack on existing establishments and Erasmus, too, became a persecutor and began in his old days, as Jortin says, 'to act the zealot,' affected perhaps by a desire to keep the favour of persecuting kings and princes.[52] Stewart concludes:

> Something, it must at the same time be observed, may be alleged in behalf of these two illustrious persons; *not*, indeed, in extenuation of their unpardonable defection from the cause of religious liberty, but of their estrangement from some of their old friends, who scrupled not to consider as apostates and traitors all those who, while they acknowledged the expediency of ecclesiastical reform, did not approve of the violent measures employed for the accomplishment of that object.[53]

Erasmus could have been the liberator of the human mind, but entrenched prejudice and his own timidity or preference for the gradual hindered him. Yet, against the more determined characters who made the Reformation, he had a point: with violence comes danger to the cause of Enlightenment. Behind this remark are no doubt troubling recollections of the revolutionary violence of 1793–4. Over all, Stewart's pattern of analogy between the Reformation and the French Revolution is: intellectual preparation (Erasmus/the *philosophes*); revolutionary thrust (Luther/ 1789); reaction against violence (Erasmus/1794).

Stewart's Erasmus is essentially that of the Protestant Enlightenment.[54] Novelty lies only in the setting – a thoroughgoing statement of the idea of progress. Despite his political interests, Stewart had nothing to say about Erasmus' political writings. By contrast the English essayist Vicesimus Knox (1752–1821) brought him into the political arena. He used him not so much to defend the Revolution as to restrain counter-revolution. In 1794, with England at war with regicide France, he published a translation of Erasmus' essay on the adage *Dulce bellum inexpertis* under the title *Antipolemus; Or, the Plea of Reason, Religion, and Humanity, against War. A Fragment. Translated from Erasmus; and addressed to aggressors*. On 18 August 1793 Knox – staunchly Whig throughout his life – had preached at Brighton a sermon against offensive war.[55] A few days later he and his family were hounded out of the Brighton Theatre by a party of indignant militia officers. He took the precaution of publishing at Philadelphia his book against the *Spirit of Despotism* (1795).[56]

Knox was introduced early to Erasmus for as a boy he often spent his holidays in the vicarage of Dr John Jortin, Erasmus' genial biographer.[57] The humanist attracted Knox on two counts. The first was his championing of classical culture – headmaster of Tunbridge School (1778–1812), Knox was a 'zealous advocate for classical education,' and his *Essays Moral and Literary* were recommended by Samuel Johnson and generally esteemed, not only for their sound morality, but also for their 'correct critical taste and scholarship.'[58] The second was his advocacy of peace. Knox was not alone in feeling this attraction. His adoption and publication of Erasmus belonged to a broad anti-war movement situated at the liberal end of politics and, on the religious side, including both rationalist and evangelical Christians.[59]

In his long and highly declamatory preface, Knox describes Erasmus as an instrument of providence for his own and later times. It pleases God to raise up men extraordinary in both ability and virtue to shine, 'like the nocturnal lamp of Heaven,' in the 'dark night of ignorance and prejudice.' Obscured for a time by the clouds of envy, self-interest, and bigotry, they at last come shining through. Erasmus had God-given abilities which he industriously trained to gather a store of knowledge which, by uncommon eloquence, he disseminated over the darkened world. But God also gave him 'a GOOD and FEELING HEART,' a 'warm philanthropy' which prompted him to write for an age 'when man, free-born but degraded man, was bound down in darkness, with double shackles, in the chains of a twofold despotism, usurping an absolute dominion, both in church and in state, over the body and the soul.'[60]

Knox made a clear continuity between the striving of Erasmus' time and the revolution. 'Liberty acknowledges him as one of her noblest assertors.' Had he not appeared, Europe, 'instead of enjoying or contending for freedom at this hour,' might still have been sunk in servitude. He exposed the despots 'to the derision of the deluded and oppressed multitude.' He took the side of human nature and promoted 'the GREAT SOCIETY of all human beings united under ONE KING, their common Creator and Preserver.' So he was against war. 'On the rock of Religion,' says Knox in a curiously ill-advised metaphor, 'he planted the artillery of solid arguments against it.'[61]

We owe the religious Reformation to Erasmus: that, says Knox, is the view of all the Protestant *literati*. But his struggle against war is not yet complete. In his own time he was opposed by 'sordid worldlings' and 'opulent dunces;' war-making kings would like to have domesticated him but he preferred his freedom. In our time, Knox goes on bitterly, there will never be lacking 'in countries where prime ministers possess unlimited patronage' pamphleteers and journalists to defend war.[62] Despite modern Enlightenment, refinement in manners, arts, and letters and 'a most liberal philosophy,' war rages with unabated ferocity as is shown by the duke of Brunswick's bloodthirsty manifesto against the revolution (August 1792). 'What signifies,' Knox asks his fellow-clerics, 'a zealous vigilance over *thirty-nine articles*, if we neglect ONE ARTICLE, the law of charity and love ...?' The French, 'as it is usual to bend a crooked stick in the contrary direction in order to make it straight,' have gone too far – further than they intended – in correcting the errors of bigotry and superstition. But such excess should be rectified by persuasion. The real revolution, concludes Knox in an affirmation wholly of the Enlightenment, is going on in the mind of man, who is emerging from the degenerate state in which 'base policy and tyranny' have put him and reassuming his natural character and 'original excellence as a rational being.'[63]

Knox makes Erasmus the progenitor of modern pacifism and of progressive politics generally. He uses him in support of political reform.[64] The political use of Erasmus had been rare in previous centuries: from time to time he had been made a propagandist for Habsburg dynasticism but only by Claude Joly in the aftermath of the Fronde a political reformer.[65] Knox's essentially rhetorical performance made an innovation in the history of Erasmus interpretations. He bequeathed a political Erasmus to the nineteenth century. Generally, as we shall see, the bequest was neglected.[66]

The argument for a positive analogy between the French Revolution and the Reformation is to be found in the work by Charles Villers (1765–1815) which won the prize offered by the Institut de France in 1802 for an essay on the following question: 'What has been the influence of the Reformation of Luther on the political situation of the different states of Europe, and on the progress of knowledge?' Like Dugald Stewart, Villers held a progressive view of history but he envisaged, not linear progress or ever accelerating advance, but rather a process of birth and rebirth, of maturation in the womb of time, of spirit realizing itself, thrusting upward through the apparent catastrophes of history. He looked, amid the diversity of human interests and passions, for 'a single force, which is that of the human race, that of an universal spirit, which concealed in the lapse of ages, governs and directs them.' Any revolution in human affairs is but a manifestation of it.[67]

While an émigré from the revolution Villers had been attracted by German idealism.[68] At Göttingen (where he was later a professor) and at Lübeck in the 1790s he deepened his knowledge of German literature and philosophy, through reading and the acquaintance of representative figures. He came to see as his life's work an intellectual and spiritual mediation between the French and German cultures and peoples, above all through the introduction to France of German spiritual and idealist philosophy. His first book (1801) was on Kant and included an attack on materialist philosophies. German romanticism also provided him with a better sense of the distinctive development of different historical communities than the French Enlightenment could offer.

Villers' primary judgment of Erasmus relates to his view of history as tumultuous and catastrophic but progressive and pregnant with spirit. Even in apparently catastrophic events like Luther's Reformation providence, he says, is opening a way forward: 'After those deplorable commotions, in which so many individuals are sacrificed, it is not uncommon to see a better order of things arise, to behold the race itself advance more freely toward the great end which is pointed out to it by its intellectual nature, and obtain a new expansion of its improvement by every new explosion of its powers.' In every such revolution there are those who cannot trust providence or discern the shape of a new and better order amid the turbulence. These are 'men of temperate natures' who wish amelioration without commotion and, where there is conflict, blame both parties, often deciding against him who gave the first blow to peace, though he was the victim of oppression. That is true of some opponents of the French Revolution, 'a set of virtuous and upright men who shuddered at the shock of parties.' It was true of Erasmus who called the Reformation the 'Lutheran tragedy': 'It was because the piece announced itself as a tragical one, that this discerning and cautious man, whose favourite motto was, *otium cum dignitate*, refused to become an actor in it. But to expect that good should be wrought out of good only, is to make of human nature a romance, to turn history into a pastoral, and the universe into an Arcadia.'[69]

Despite his failure in the crisis, Erasmus had, according to Villers, a notable part in preparing it. Reformation comes, he says, when external structure and inner spirit are too discordant, as had become the case with medieval Christendom.[70] Part of the preparation for the Reformation of the sixteenth century was a renewal of literature, and to the forefront in that 'the public voice had placed the modest and ingenious Erasmus of Rotterdam.' Villers follows Enlightenment historians in having Luther hail, and associate himself with, the revival of literature and, in dealing with the last part of the Institute's question, takes a very positive view of the Reformation's influence on 'the progress of knowledge'; by its own direct action, as well as by the debates it aroused, Luther's Reformation accelerated intellectual improvement. Here Erasmus, he says, failed to follow through. He and his associates condemned scholasticism. 'But how, remaining as they did in the bosom of a church to which the scholastic philosophy had become an indispensable auxiliary, could they labour successfully in demolishing that supporter?' Success was possible only to Reformers who courageously broke with the old church and established a new one based 'on the pure principles of the Gospel and of reason.'[71]

Here Villers, despite his idealist and catastrophic view of history, begins to sound like the Protestant historians and his tone is, in English terms, decidedly Whiggish.[72] His London editor James Mill (1773–1836) welcomed that element in Villers but was cold to his more metaphysical side. The translation and editing of Villers' work came at the beginning of Mill's literary career. Of humble origins Mill had, with the help of patrons, studied for the Scottish ministry at the University of Edinburgh. There he was introduced to the Scottish philosophers, including Dugald Stewart whose eloquence he admired.[73] Their influence is apparent in his preface and notes to Villers' book.[74] He welcomed as a 'memorable proof of the extraordinary progress of reason and liberty' that a learned institute in a Catholic country should propose for assessment the beneficent effects of the Reformation. The work itself, he said, demonstrated the vices of the papal system and impartially represented 'the happy tendency and effects of the Reformation.' Villers' views of human rights and improvement were, in Mill's judgment, 'liberal and just' and at neither the revolutionary nor the conservative extreme.[75] This language reflects the moderate Whiggism of Mill's Scottish mentors and their tempered optimism about the revolution.

Mill expresses surprise that Villers is silent on the comparison frequently made in England between the influence of the *philosophes* in the eighteenth century and that of Erasmus in the sixteenth. 'The analogy is strong between the complaints against these authors, and those of the partisans of the church of Rome in the sixteenth century, against Erasmus, who, they said, laid the egg which Luther only hatched. The question has been asked, with great propriety, what were the circumstances by which Erasmus and others were prepared and formed to write as they did; and the people to listen to them?'[76] The answer would no doubt include the illiberalism of the Roman church. Mill accepts Villers' distinction between the two kinds of reformers and his association of Erasmus with those too much inclined to timidity. Indeed, in his view both parties (the timid and the rash) in following their natural bents produce ill consequences. 'Reason,' he concludes in the tones of the Scottish Enlightenment, 'not natural temper, on either side, is the proper guide in this momentous concern.'[77] Mill accepts Villers' case for progress in history but not its metaphysical underpinnings.[78] On the case for acclaiming the revolution's benefits, as those of the Reformation could be acclaimed, he considers the evidence not yet all in. 'Hereafter it will form an important object to the philosophical historian to compare both the good and bad effects of those two events, the greatest in themselves, and the most pregnant with consequences in the history of modern Europe.'[79]

A more considerable figure than any so far considered, Samuel Taylor Coleridge (1772–1834), also made a conscious contrast between Erasmus' time and the revolutionary era. In the first number of his short-lived periodical, *The Watchman* (1 March 1796), Coleridge expounded a progressive philosophy of history. With the revival of letters in Europe came 'the first scanty twilight of knowledge,' sufficient to expose the horrors arising from ignorance. 'This incipient diffusion of truth was aided by the Lutheran schism, which roused the Clergy of Europe from their long doze of sensuality, and by the keen goading of religious controversy forced each party into literary exertion.' The enemies of popular enlightenment – despotism, aristocracy, and priesthood – saw their danger and entered a vigorous struggle against it.[80] Coleridge, at the age of twenty-three, was writing still under the influence of the unitarianism and political radicalism (associated with the name of William Godwin) he had embraced as an undergraduate. He still hailed the revolution as he had done in his youthful poem on the fall of the Bastille:

> When slum'bring FREEDOM raised by high DISDAIN
> With giant fury burst his triple chain![81]

But by the time he had finished with the *Watchman* a change had occurred; he was doubtful about the revolution and rejected Godwin.[82]

When Coleridge launched another periodical, *The Friend*, in 1809, he was still interested in the connection between the sixteenth-century Reformers of the church and the revolutionary spirits of his own or the immediately preceding time. The relation was now one of surface similarities and fundamental contrasts. In general, the *Friend* was intended to penetrate more deeply than the *Watchman*, be more philosophical and avoid ephemeral politics.[83] Its theme was 'the illumination of principles in all fields of life; from this light the reader could "kindle his own Torch" [as Coleridge himself put it] and with it examine whatever objects he chose.' It was an experiment 'in testing wisdom by experience, the Platonic tempered by and reconciled with the Baconian discipline.'[84] It thus represented a stage in the emergence of Coleridge's mature thought. He himself recognized its importance and in 1818, with the outlines of that thought settled, reissued it in three volumes, after significantly rearranging the material. The essay on the Reformers which had first appeared in number 8 of 5 October 1809 was now included in what Coleridge called the first 'Landing-Place,' a small miscellany of essays for the reader's amusement and retrospect after an arduous first section of sixteen essays ('an initiation into general principles') and his preparation for the next advance.[85]

The pleasure of studying history, says Coleridge heading into the comparisons he intends to make, is like that of listening to a skilled musical composition.

The events and characters of one age, like the strains of music, recal [sic] those of another, and the variety by which each is individualized, not only gives a charm and poignancy to the resemblance, but likewise renders the whole more intelligible. Meantime ample room is afforded for the exercise both of the judgment and the fancy, in distinguishing cases of real resemblance from those of intentional imitation, the analogies of nature, revolving upon herself, from the masquerade figures of cunning and vanity.

Coleridge's interest is in the comparison between those whose characters at first view seem very dissimilar but who have in their different times produced similar effects 'and this by the exertion of powers which on examination will be found far more alike, than the altered drapery and costume would have led us to suspect.' Coleridge goes on: 'Of the heirs of fame few are more respected by me, though for very different qualities, than Erasmus and Luther: scarcely anyone has a larger share of my aversion than Voltaire; and even of the better-hearted Rousseau I was never more than a very lukewarm admirer.'[86] Coleridge leaves no doubt – in appreciation of their respective talents – of his substantial preference for 'the two purifiers of revealed Religion, now neglected as obsolete, over 'the two modern conspirators against its authority, who are still the Alpha and Omega of Continental Genius.' Yet, leaving aside the issue of good and evil and taking into account only the effects and the means of producing them, Coleridge is struck by the comparison of the two 'clusters,' Erasmus/Luther/Munster (probably Thomas Müntzer, the radical religious leader of Luther's time) and Voltaire/Rousseau/Robespierre.

Those who are familiar with the works of Erasmus, and who know the influence of his wit, as the pioneer of the reformation; and who likewise know, that by his wit, added to the vast variety of knowledge communicated in his works, he had won over by anticipation so large a part of the polite and lettered world to the Protestant party; will be at no loss in discovering the intended counterpart in the life and writings of the veteran Frenchman. They will see, indeed, that the knowledge of the one was solid through its whole extent, and that of the other extensive at a cheap rate, by its superficiality; that the wit of the one is always bottomed on sound sense, peoples and enriches the mind of the reader with an endless variety of distinct images and living interests; and that his broadest laughter is every where translatable into grave and weighty truth: while the wit of the Frenchman, without imagery, without character, and without that pathos which gives the magic charm to genuine humour, consists, when it is most perfect, in happy turns of phrase, but far too often in fantastic incidents, outrages of the pure imagination, and the poor low trick of combining the ridiculous with the venerable, where he, who does not laugh, abhors. Neither will they have forgotten, that the object of the one was to drive the thieves and mummers out of the temple, while the other was propelling a worse banditti, first to profane and pillage, and ultimately to raze it. Yet not the less will they perceive, that the *effects* remain parallel, the *circumstances* analogous, and the *instruments* the same. In each case the *effects* extended over Europe, were attested and augmented by the praise and patronage of thrones and dignities, and are not to be explained but by extraordinary industry and a life of literature; in both instances the *circumstances* were supplied by an age of hopes and promises – the age of Erasmus restless from the first vernal influences of real knowledge, that of Voltaire from the hectic of imagined superiority. In the voluminous works of both, the *instruments* employed are chiefly those of wit and amusive erudition, and alike in both the errors and evils (real or imputed) in Religion and Politics are the objects of the battery. And here we must stop. The two *Men* were *essentially* different. Exchange mutually their dates and spheres of action, yet Voltaire, had he been ten-fold a Voltaire, could not have made up an Erasmus; and Erasmus must have emptied himself of half his greatness and all his goodness, to have become a Voltaire.[87]

This is an Erasmus of good sense and depth of feeling, in touch with the real life of his time. His work had character; he expressed himself authentically and addressed the people on matters of substance. He was genuinely a reformer of the church, a pioneer of the Reformation. Here the Renaissance and the Reformation are connected and continuous. The comparison with Voltaire is decisive: he was, by contrast with Erasmus, superficial, contrived, destructive, trashy.

The second comparison – between 'the heroic LUTHER, a Giant awaking in his strength! and the crazy ROUSSEAU, the Dreamer of lovesick Tales and the Spinner of speculative Cobwebs' – is both more complete and less decisive. In this case there is more similarity of character: 'Each referred all things to his own ideal'; they produced similar effects by the same 'serious and vehement eloquence, and an elevated tone of moral feeling.' But they served very different causes and here Rousseau can be linked to Voltaire, as Luther to Erasmus. Happily for Luther 'he had derived his standard from a common measure already received by the good and wise: I mean the inspired writings, the study of which Erasmus had previously restored among the learned.' Rousseau, by contrast, 'steered by the compass of unaided reason.' Thus Coleridge declares his solidarity with the Reformation against the 'age of reason,' asserts the scriptural principle and associates with it both Luther and Erasmus.[88]

Both men, says Coleridge in passing, deserved more serious and critical historical enquiry. A life of Luther to the measure of the subject, of Luther the man as well as of Luther the theologian, was a *desideratum* of English literature, 'though perhaps there is no subject for which so many unused materials are extant, both printed and in manuscript.' Similarly, 'the affectionate respect' in which Coleridge held John Jortin – a 'Nursling' like Coleridge himself of Jesus College, Cambridge – could not stand in the way of his declaring that such a life of Erasmus was also a *desideratum*: 'every Scholar well read in the writings of Erasmus and his illustrious Contemporaries, must have discovered, that Jortin had neither collected sufficient, nor the best, materials for his work: and (perhaps from that very cause) he grew weary of his task, before he had made a full use of the scanty materials which he had collected.'[89]

Erasmus and Luther – this is the point of importance – were not a casual or merely historical interest for Coleridge. It is not by chance that they appear in the first 'Landing-Place' which in the structure of Coleridge's work fulfils the function of a landing-place in a great staircase. The last two essays in this miscellany (IV and V) introduce, in the direct wake of his discussion of Erasmus and Luther, his fundamental concerns – the condemnation of mere expediency, the necessity in the actual business of life of principles 'grounded in reason,' properly understood, the distinction between 'Understanding' and 'Reason.'[90]

A brief (and inadequate) explanation is necessary. 'Understanding' for Coleridge is that 'faculty by which we generalize and arrange the phaenomena of perception: that faculty, the functions of which contain the rules and constitute the possibility of outward Experience.'[91] It masters both scientific knowledge and practical living and its triumphs in the modern world evoke wonder and admiration.[92] But the tragedy of modern civilization has been the annexation by the Understanding of spheres beyond its limit or capacity, religion and morality. These belong rather to the Reason or 'higher reason,' 'the organ of the Super-sensuous,' 'an organ of inward sense' by which man has the power of acquainting himself with 'invisible realities or spiritual objects.'[93] Here the whole being – understanding, feeling, will – confronts reality in all its dimensions; the only possible response – again of the whole being – is faith which confirms its ground in the existence of God, the conscience, immortality. Coleridge had taken elements in the Platonist tradition and the language of Kant and married them with Christian orthodoxy, associating the whole with St Paul and the Reformers, especially Luther. Thereby he challenged the religion illegitimately spawned by the Understanding – natural theology, so-called rational religion, the theology of evidences, unitarianism.[94] Erasmus as presented in the *Friend* is well on the right side of this great divide while Voltaire is at the worst extremity.

In the winter of 1818–19 Coleridge delivered at the Crown and Anchor Tavern in the Strand a series of public lectures in the history of philosophy. In the lecture on the Reformation period (Lecture X) he repeated in quotation-marks the passage on Erasmus from the *Friend*.[95] The explanation for this self-plagiarism was the difficulties under which he laboured in offering these lectures. Among other things, books for the tenth lecture, which Coleridge thought his worst, did not arrive or arrived too late to be useful.[96] In general, the lectures fell awkwardly between an effort at popularization and reflections for the better informed.[97] But one is inclined to accept also that the repetition demonstrated Coleridge's satisfaction with his portrait of Erasmus in the *Friend*.

The interest of the philosophical lectures for us lies in their location of the Reformation material and personages in a historical sequence. Coleridge's view of history is developmental and providential: each stage has its significance.[98] 'It is a great error,' he said of the past, 'to idolize it, but a still greater to hold it in contempt.'[99] Thus scholasticism – condemned by all other Protestant writers – is given serious attention. It served two great purposes: it introduced to the Gothic nations the interconnectedness of Graeco-Roman thought and language; it addressed problems in the philosophy of mind. Coleridge was persuaded that 'to the scholastic philosophy the Reformation is attributable, far more than to the revival of classical literature.' Nevertheless, scholasticism lost its utility as it concentrated on mere forms and the classical revival gave 'a general impulse and awakening over society.' In fifteenth-century Italy there was an enthusiasm for eloquence and a philosophy appropriate to the time – Neoplatonism.[100] 'You must,' says Coleridge, coming to the Reformation, 'draw a picture full of incongruities to represent fairly the state of things in Europe,' on one side 'genius in all its splendor,' on the other 'barbarism in all the details of social life,' including a susceptibility to delusions and superstitions of every kind. 'But a glorious period, which has left seeds that cannot perish, took place under the first operation of these chaotic causes. The trumpet in the revolution was blown and prepared by whatever was great and excellent; and with it no doubt, even the vices and the follies of mankind were forced into the same services.' Luther was the 'immediate agent,' Erasmus the 'pioneer.'[101]

Thus Coleridge, who now repeats the *Friend* material, again makes Erasmus integral to the wholesome, purifying, invigorating transformation of his time. The point is not removed by his reiteration of the standard Protestant view, heightened no doubt by a romantic colouring, that something more than Erasmus' wit and 'gentle raillery' was needed, viz Luther's earnestness (just as, for the work of destruction, Rousseau's earnestness must supplement the frivolity of Voltaire).[102] Already Coleridge had summed up: 'the Erasmuses, the Luthers – the men who have made us all we are, and whose works if well studied would make us a great deal better.'[103]

Other aphorisms of Coleridge on Erasmus have been reported. His *Moriae encomium* was his 'most pleasant Book.'[104] His paraphrase of the New Testament is 'clear and explanatory; but you cannot expect anything very deep from Erasmus. The only fit commentator on Paul was Luther – not by any means such a gentleman as the Apostle, but almost as great a genius.'[105] Here is a combination   Coleridge's personal preference for Luther and a long-established Protestant judgment, which must be read against Coleridge's more considered opinions. Finally, there is the well known and sad: 'Such utter unlikes cannot but end in dislikes, and so it proved between Erasmus and Luther.'[106]

Coleridge's essay on Erasmus and Luther was the most interesting piece in the history of Erasmus interpretations since Bayle's article over a century before. The biographies, even the greatest, though much more extended, seem repetitive and unimaginative by comparison. As Bayle (however unwittingly) prepared an Erasmus for the Enlightenment – the hater of intolerance and partisanship – Coleridge, though his lead was hardly followed, composed an Erasmus for the post-revolutionary and post-romantic age. It was indeed part and parcel of his reaction against the Enlightenment and the revolution. In the longer history of Erasmus interpretations it has lasting significance. The mind of this Erasmus has both a sense of reality and depth, true perceptions of the social life of his time and a grasp on (essentially biblical) truth, and the capacity to express these in language alive with images. He belonged to, indeed he pioneered, a rejuvenation of the human spirit and thus helped make an epoch in the history of mankind. He and Luther were together in this cause. Coleridge transcended the confessional inheritance in two ways – by setting aside the tired re-examinations of how far Erasmus was 'Protestant' and how far 'Catholic,' and by recognizing that the renaissance to which Erasmus and Luther belonged drew on resources from both the medieval and classical pasts. These were insights of which the nineteenth century was to make but patchy use.

III

We have seen that a Christian presence remained in the historical literature of the 'age of reason' and consequently in the writings on Erasmus. If to many writers of the Enlightenment Christianity was at best a matter of indifference or contempt or at worst an enemy, there were others for whom theology and piety were chief concerns, no matter how – in the view of their romantic, evangelical, or neo-scholastic successors – they might have attenuated the substance of Christianity. Robertson, who saw Erasmus as a link between Renaissance and Reformation, was leader of a party in the Church of Scotland. The German writers who made Erasmus the pioneer of Luther's Reformation or, more radically, of a larger, still continuing, religious revolution, were almost all professors of theology and church history. Erasmus' first English biographers were faithful pastors of the established church. At the same time – the middle of the eighteenth century – expressions about Erasmus could be found in varieties of English religion other than the Whiggery of Samuel Knight and the latitudinarianism of John Jortin. On the one hand was the sombre Anglicanism of Samuel Johnson, on the other the evangelical revival in its first formative years.

Samuel Johnson's acquaintance with Erasmus began early. From the age of seven at the Lichfield Grammar School he learned Latin from the *Familiaria Colloquia* of Christopher Helwig or Helvicus (1581–1617), of whose fifty dialogues, thirty-three were taken from Erasmus' *Colloquia*. He 'observed that we learned Helvicus a long time with very little progress' and, indeed, in face of the difficulties, he 'got an English Erasmus.'[107] The influence survived. Soon after his marriage in 1736, Johnson himself set up an academy at Lichfield and proved, to Boswell's satisfaction, 'that he was not so well qualified for being a teacher of elements, and a conductor in learning by regular gradations, as men of inferiour powers of mind.' But, Boswell goes on, that he knew the 'proper course' was clear from his scheme for the classes of a grammar school where, after their mastery of the formation of nouns and verbs, the pupils were directed to 'Corderius by Mr Clarke' and 'Erasmus with an English translation by the same authour.'[108]

Erasmus' name occurs a number of times in the diaries of the mature Johnson. The entries mostly exhibit his preoccupation with Christian orthodoxy in its Protestant form. In a note from 7 August 1774 during his journey to North Wales, he praised Erasmus' distinction − in interpreting the injunction: 'But when ye pray, use not vain repetitions ...' (Matthew 6:7) − between vain repetitions and those caused by 'ardent and vehement passion' in prayer. On the same day he read the letter (1607) of Dominic Baudius, the Leiden professor, on Erasmus for he noted Baudius' remark that posterity was infinitely indebted to him.[109] A week later he was finding the *Epistola consolatoria in adversis* to the nuns of a Franciscan house near Cambridge too 'full of mystick notions, and allegories.'[110]

Erasmus accompanied Johnson into old age. On 5 October 1777 he sat by a waterfall at Ashbourne reading the *Enchiridion* and asked his correspondent: 'Have you got that book?'[111] Seven years later he wrote of a coach journey to Lichfield: 'in the coach I read Ciceronianus, which I concluded as I entred Lichfield. My affection and understanding went along with Erasmus, except that once or twice he somewhat unskilfully entangles Cicero's civil or moral, with his rhetorical character.'[112]

Why did Johnson have a 'great regard for Erasmus'?[113] He was devoted to the classical tradition and the Latin tongue and literature with which, among the moderns, Erasmus was supremely associated. 'Consider, sir'; he cried at the suggestion that Goldsmith's epitaph at Westminster should be in English, 'how you should feel were you to find at Rotterdam an epitaph upon Erasmus *in Dutch!*'[114] He had projected a history of the revival of learning 'containing an account of whatever contributed to the restoration of literature ... with the lives of the most eminent patrons and most eminent early professors of all kinds of learning in different countries.'[115]

We may assume, too, a common commitment to a practical piety and morality. Johnson belonged to the line which joined the classical moralists, the wisdom literature of the Bible, the Renaissance humanists and seventeenth-century divines, and the modern essayists from Montaigne to Addison. He drew also on 'a large internal fund of accumulated experience and reflection' to assist his readers – especially of essays like those in the *Rambler* (1750–2) – to face the disappointments, avoid the snares, and eschew the vanities of life.[116] In this connection he made his longest comment on Erasmus. The *Rambler* essay for Saturday 30 March 1751 dealt characteristically with our use and misuse of time and the invalidity of the excuses we make for frittering it away. Great works may depend only on an accumulation of small parcels of time, even amid much distraction, and on diligence.

> A great part of the life of Erasmus was one continual pere-grination; ill supplied with the gifts of fortune, and led from city to city, and from kingdom to kingdom, by the hopes of patrons and preferment, hopes which always flattered and always deceived him; he yet found means by unshaken con-stancy, and a vigilant improvement of those hours, which, in the midst of the most restless activity, will remain unen-gaged, to write more than another in the same condition would have hoped to read. Compelled by want to attend-ance and solicitation, and so much versed in common life, that he has transmitted to us the most perfect delineation of the manners of his age, he joined to his knowledge of the world, such application to books, that he will stand for ever in the first rank of literary heroes. How this proficiency was obtained he sufficiently discovers, by informing us, that the *Praise of Folly*, one of his most celebrated performances, was composed by him on the road to Italy; *ne totum illud tempus quo equo fuit insidendum, illiteratis fabulis terreretur*, lest the hours which he was obliged to spend on horseback, should be tattled away without regard to literature.[117]

Here Erasmus is presented not only as a hero of literature but as an epitome of the self-control essential to moral progress and Christian character.

It would be speculation to go further and find in Johnson sym-pathy for Erasmus as a kindred tormented spirit (for that is how he is himself now seen).[118] The evidence is lacking. But the idea remains attractive that the profoundly pessimistic streak in John-son responded to the disappointments and broken hopes of Er-asmus' life.

Johnson's relation to Erasmus was then, like all his literary relations, personal and passionately felt though his expressions can also be attached to a long-standing and sympathetic tradition in Anglicanism which was to continue – again in an individual manner – in Coleridge. The evangelicals, by contrast, belonged to a large public movement which changed the character of English religion and to an extent its historiography. The role and character of a historical figure like Erasmus had to be described in language appropriate to the new way of seeing the church and the world.

Judgments in the Wesleyan phase were mild. In the minutes of the first annual conference of the Methodist connection (29 June 1744), John Wesley listed books for reading by lay assistants: the classical authors, some church fathers, and moderns like Pascal and the pietist Francke were joined by Erasmus and another sixteenth-century figure, Castellio, the publicist for toleration.[119] The list demonstrates the intellectual openness of early Methodism. Wesley rejected the high Calvinist doctrine of predestination and sided with the Dutch Arminians who had, as we know, Erasmian associations and loyalties.[120] There were in the 1770s heated theological controversies about this issue among those broadly to be called evangelicals.[121] Wesley's colleague John Fletcher (born Jean Guillaume de la Flechere in Nyon in Switzerland in 1729 and converted by Methodist preaching while on a visit to England in 1752, becoming the devoted and much loved vicar of Madeley in Shropshire in 1760[122]) sought common ground between at least the moderate Calvinists and the Wesleyans. When the Reformers, he said, threw off the papal yoke, they did not restore the balance between grace and justice, faith and works. Luther denied free will and thus struck a blow against justice, 'a rash deed, for which Erasmus, the Dutch reformer, openly reproved him, but with too much of the Pelagian spirit.' Cranmer restored the balance in England, Arminius on the continent went some way and English divines followed, but ultimately success belonged to Wesley who reconciled free grace and human responsibility.[123] For Fletcher Erasmus, who could rightly claim the title of reformer of the church, was a useful corrector of Lutheran exaggerations, if not an honoured name; he served in the struggle for theological balance.

By the end of the eighteenth century when the evangelicals had become a powerful party in the Church of England itself judgments, not least of Erasmus, had become more categorical.

Representative of, indeed largely responsible for, the evangelical understanding of the Christian past is *The History of the Church of Christ* by the brothers Joseph and Isaac Milner.[124] The book had a vogue in the early nineteenth century commensurate with the prominence of the brothers in evangelical Anglicanism. After a sharp attack on its methodology, especially in the treatment of medieval heresy, by S.R. Maitland (1832), it was again briefly conspicuous and reissued in a single volume (1847), but was outclassed by the more critical historical writing of the second half of the century.[125]

Joseph Milner's plan for the whole work makes its standpoint clear. His interest is in the evangelical succession; he will write a history of those 'whose dispositions and lives have been formed by the rules of the New Testament,' no matter what their ecclesiastical allegiance. In every age there has been a remnant of real followers of Christ. In identifying them the author would 'have frequent occasion to state what the gospel is, and what it is not' and to show God's providential care for his people.[126] This is the characteristic language of the evangelical party which was – it has been said – largely fashioned by Joseph Milner.[127] Existing church histories like Mosheim's were, says Milner, more civil than religious in character and silent on the history of godliness. The Protestant martyrology of John Foxe and the fiercely polemical Magdeburg *Centuries* were exceptions to the general run of church histories, which seemed more interested in wickedness than in piety.[128]

Joseph Milner (1744–97) was converted to an austere Calvinist faith after his appointment as master of the town grammar school at Hull. This conversion strained the loyalty of his erstwhile supporters in the corporation and he was accused of methodism and dissent. 'Few persons who wore a tolerably good coat,' he said, 'would take notice of him when they met him in the street.'[129] Physically delicate, gentle by nature, sober in temperament, intellectually precocious, he had risen by his own talents and the help of friends and patrons from impoverished beginnings and now by the exercise of those virtues gradually turned hostility aside. He made his school a home of evangelical piety; from it, said his brother, went out a 'succession of truly worthy and evangelical preachers.'[130] Milner was distantly related to Wilberforce who attended the school as a small child. Years later (1797), he was – by Wilberforce's influence – preferred to Holy Trinity Church in Hull where he had long been an afternoon lecturer (from 1768).[131]

Isaac Milner (1750–1820) said of his brother that he had 'never met with any person who resembled him in ... an extreme ignorance of the ways and manners of mankind in their ordinary intercourse with each other, – and an utter and absolute rejection of disguise in all its shapes.'[132] Isaac's was a different personality; he represented another, more worldly, stage in the history of the evangelical party. His rise was quick and spectacular: usher in his brother's school, 1768; sizar at Queen's College, Cambridge, 1770; first place in the mathematical tripos with the accolade *incomparabilis*, 1774; FRS, 1776; college tutor and priest, 1777; the first professor of natural philosophy at Cambridge, 1783. Later, he was to become president of Queen's. (1788), a largely absentee dean of Carlisle (1791) and vice-chancellor of Cambridge (1792) and to occupy Newton's chair of mathematics (1798).[133] One observer indeed thought his success too complete. Fortune, said James Stephen, 'bestowed on him the rewards of eminence, such as wealth, leisure, reputation, and authority, without exacting the appointed price of toil and self-denial.'[134]

Isaac Milner was convinced of evangelical religion as a young man. 'Though full of levity on all other subjects,' he was, Wilberforce recalls, 'never backward in avowing his opinions, or entering into religious conversation,' which he did with 'the utmost seriousness.' 'By degrees,' Wilberforce concludes, 'I imbibed his sentiments.'[135] As president Milner was determined to make Queen's – Erasmus' Cambridge college – a reservoir of zeal and talent for the evangelical party. 'Evangelical parents sent their sons, young Evangelicals seeking ordination came from all parts of the country.'[136] He himself became the intellectual chief of the party: 'the members of it resorted to him at Cambridge, there to dispel doubts, and thence to bring back responses, oracular, authoritative, and profound.'[137]

There was a dark side to Milner's character. He was a hypochondriac, 'haunted by imaginary maladies and ideal dangers.' His customary manner, however, was ebullient. He was tall and corpulent, awkward and indolent but made alive by company. 'He had,' says James Stephen, 'looked into innumerable books, had dipped into most subjects, whether of vulgar or of learned inquiry, and talked with shrewdness, animation, and intrepidity, on them all. Whatever the company and whatever the theme, his sonorous voice predominated over all other voices, even as his lofty stature, vast girth, and superincumbent wig, defied all competition.'[138]

If there are occasional glimpses of the different personalities of its two authors, the *History* is distinctive for a common evangelical piety. Europe at the beginning of the sixteenth century, it says, 'presented nothing that was properly evangelical.' There was 'the grossest ignorance of the nature of gospel-grace.' The doctrine of justification had been lost for many ages. Nevertheless, there remained a bewildered remnant: 'Persons truly serious, – and such there ever were and will be, because there ever was and will be a true church on earth, – were so clouded in their understandings by the prevailing corruptions of the hierarchy, that they could find no access to God by Jesus Christ.' Luther's attempt to restore the gospel was 'more evangelically judicious, more simply founded on the word of God' than any since St Augustine. He was led on by circumstances far beyond his intention – in short, he was an instrument of providence. He was concerned not with abuses, like his ineffective predecessors, but with doctrines. He had self-knowledge, an understanding of scriptural truth, disinterested zeal, undaunted courage. The sober Joseph added: he had two characteristic faults – anger and facetiousness.[139]

Naturally, the Milners have a particular interest in Luther's conversion. The account follows the evangelical sequence: 'a deep and solid conviction of sin, leading the mind to the search of scripture-truth, and the investigation of the way of peace, was the main-spring of Luther's whole after-conduct.' He accidentally found – the Protestant legend is repeated – a Latin Bible in the monastery library. 'In reading the word of God with prayer, his understanding was gradually enlightened, and he found some beams of evangelical comfort to dart into his soul.'[140]

Where does Erasmus stand to the faithful remnant and the rediscovered gospel? Joseph Milner is reluctant to include him among those 'who have shewn no particular predeliction for the pure gospel of Jesus Christ.' 'His great learning, his elegant taste, and his acute understanding; are all unquestionable; neither is there any doubt how very serviceable his writings proved in preparing men's minds to approve the bolder and more decisive measures of Luther.' Such expressions remind us that Joseph Milner, for all his simplicity of spirit, was no rustic; he was himself a learned man, a classicist, who admired the great pioneer of humane studies and shared his scholarly tastes and discriminations. Yet evangelical austerity and the absolute claims of the gospel break in. 'But still, in my judgment, the proofs of his love of ease, of fame, and of the esteem of persons of rank and consequence, are far more numerous, than any example which can be produced of his sincere regard for the essential doctrines of christianity, or of the evangelical humility of his own mind.' Joseph Milner is suspicious of accommodating spirits: Erasmus was of help to Luther but let us remember 'that timid and artful politicians were never employed, to any good purpose, in the service of Jesus Christ.'[141] The judgment that Erasmus, for all his services to literature and religion, was too prudent, calculating, and even time-serving was not new; it had been heard from Protestant critics since the sixteenth century. However, the standard of 'evangelical humility' and gospel simplicity was distinctive of the unworldly, plain-hearted evangelicals of Joseph Milner's generation.

The section written predominantly by Isaac Milner gives more than thirty pages to the controversy between Erasmus and Luther over the freedom of the will. It begins by repeating – in a somewhat more light-hearted way – Joseph Milner's judgments. Erasmus' conduct offers both instruction and amusement to the student of the Reformation. Of his services as a restorer of learning one cannot speak too highly. 'It is the purity of his Christian principles, and the integrity and conscientiousness of his motives, which are called in question.' Seckendorf thought that no one did more injury to Luther's cause. The Catholic magnates played on his pride and ambition and 'natural timidity.' They saw his value to the church in its perilous position.[142] They persuaded him reluctantly to write against Luther.

Erasmus' diatribe on free will is, Milner says, 'the production of a man who has scoured the surface of his question, but by no means penetrated into its substance.' An experienced (one should add evangelical) observer notes 'a firm attachment to some degree at least of the Pelagian tenets.' For his part, Luther recognized Erasmus' services to church reform. He saw his weakness – 'he had repeatedly declared that the church wanted reformation, but would never run any risk to further the good cause' – but feared the weight of his reputation on the other side. Reluctantly he, too, came into the controversy to counter that authority. Luther demonstrated his superiority in both matter and style; his treatise was 'abundantly more orderly, perspicuous and nervous.' Above all, his evangelical statement of human incapacity was 'peculiarly offensive to Erasmus; and so it must ever prove to the pride of every human heart, which is not yet brought, through a sense of its unworthiness, to deep contrition and penitence at the cross of the Saviour.' In summary, Erasmus was 'a very superficial theologian, doubtful in his sentiments, and indeterminate in his expressions.' By contrast, Luther's religion was 'vital, practical, and experimental in the highest degree.'[143]

Not without an unconscious irony, for he had been accused of levity himself, Isaac Milner finishes with a section on 'The Inconsistency and Levity of Erasmus.' He showed – in his reply to the Sorbonne, for example – 'an artful mixture of submission, sarcasm, and menace.' There was no end to his contradictory declarations. The key to his character was timidity and irresolution. Despite this, Milner adds, his Pelagian or half-Pelagian views 'secure him but too favourable a reception with many modern divines.'[144]

The contrast between Luther and Erasmus suited the Milners' purpose admirably for, among other things, it was made to parallel the contrast between the latitudinarians and the evangelicals in their own time. The language is telling. On one side, all is artful, evasive, accommodating, and in theological matters superficial; on the other side all is undaunted, decisive, and experimental, ie based on genuine evangelical experience.

The *History* was not a work of great scholarship. James Stephen's judgment was dampening: the Reformation sections

> have been extolled as containing the most comprehensive and authentic account of the Reformation in Germany, and of the character of the great German Reformer; a praise to which it is impossible to subscribe, for this, if for no other reason; that neither the Author [Joseph] nor the Editor [Isaac] had ever seen, or would have been able to read, one line of the many volumes written by Luther in his mother tongue, and even yet untranslated into any other.[145]

The Milners relied on Seckendorf, Sarpi – the historian of the Council of Trent – Sleidan, de Thou, Melchior Adam, the Reformation history by the Huguenot exile Isaac de Beausobre (1659–1738) and Jortin, all works of long standing by the last decade of the eighteenth century.[146] Isaac quoted extensively from the two treatises on free will and Erasmus' letters in the Le Clerc edition. Yet, despite its limited scholarship, the work is of considerable interest. Its significance in Reformation historiography lies in its restoring attention to the doctrinal issues.[147] For us it presents a familiar figure – the Protestant judgment on Erasmus – in new clothing, the language of the evangelical revival. Its opinions on Erasmus and Luther are thus not new but they are rephrased.[148]

Both evangelicalism and the rationalism it opposed assumed truths which could be objectively established and defended. Running parallel to, though sometimes intersecting, these tendencies was another tendency – towards a religion grounded in inner awareness and experience, suffused in subjectivity.[149] One can trace the emergence of this religious sensibility from the beginning of the eighteenth century. It had its source – or one source – in pietism but it was refined, associated on occasion with the aesthetic sense and generally given an individualistic character in the Enlightenment. The divine drama was played out in the individual human heart, human feeling was the conduit of the divine spirit. The physiognomy of Johann Caspar Lavater belongs to this religious stream.[150]

Lavater's physiognomic studies attempted to trace the characters of historic personages from their features through the scrutiny of portraits.[151] There was a deeper purpose: to find in the character the image in some sense of God, a microcosm of the divine, one expression of the manifold nature of divinity. The work was 'a hymn to the grandeur and divine worth of humanity.'[152] *Physiognomik,* said Lavater himself, is a 'godly alphabet.' Between temperament and expression, mind and body, the inner and the outer is an intimate bond, a harmony and analogy.[153] Physiognomy was to be both a science and an inspiration. The purpose, said Lavater, is not merely to amuse the reader but to ennoble him, to do honour to humanity and to the divine wisdom and goodness which reveals itself in the least of human beings.[154] Lavater would draw on a common fund of human feeling.

How had he arrived at this apparently humanist, optimistic religiosity, this religion of feeling? It is a complex and distinctive

story. Johann Caspar Lavater (1741–1801) was born of a patrician
family in Zürich and grew up in a strongly biblical faith. Trav-
elling in Germany as a young man, he was influenced by the
Enlightenment theologians. The influence from them which lasted
was a belief in divine immanence in the human spirit, for Lavater
soon threw off the secularizing, rationalistic shell of Enlightenment theology. He broke with rationalist colleagues in Zürich,
where he was preaching from 1769, denounced deism, and said
that, if Semler were right, Christ was unseated from his throne.[155]
He began drawing together the two main strands in his development – the biblical and pietist faith of his youth and the optimistic humanity of the Enlightenment.

The writers of the *Sturm und Drang* responded to Lavater: for
Herder his religion had 'an inner apostolic character,' he spoke
the 'truth of the heart.' In turn he took up, notably in the *Physiognomische Fragmente*, their idea of genius, but genius for him
grasps not only poetic, social, and human truths but also the
divine truth. He came to preach a religion of immediate encounter
between Christ and man or, to repeat his own expression, a direct
'community' of God with men through Christ.[156] The seat of this
community was the human heart. For Lavater feeling was the
criterion of truth. 'Where feeling is, there is strength; so much
feeling, so much strength.'[157] The ambiguity of the divine and
the human in this theology was repeated in Lavater's influence
on his own and the next generation; he was the apostle both of
a new humanism and of evangelical enthusiasm.[158]

Of interest to us is the influence of his *Physiognomik* on nineteenth-century ideas of character and personality. It is ironical
that Lavater, for whom the human spirit was unconfined and had
limitless possibilities, should bequeath a particularly static stereotyping to nineteenth-century writers on Erasmus.

In a fragment on scholars and thinkers in book II Lavater takes
five heads of Erasmus, four of them versions of Holbein's late
portrait at Basel. Erasmus' face is, he says, one of the most ex-
pressive he knows. In all five portraits he finds three traits: '(a)
the fearful, cautious, timorous disposition; (b) the drollness in the
expression of the mouth; (c) the subtlety in the look.' The finest
of the five are the two closest to the Holbein portrait. In both
Lavater finds 'the same expression of intellectual versatility, fearfulness, naivety, wit.'

No impulse of an onrushing, destructive audacity.
In his eye the serenity of the subtle, eagerly attentive ob-
server.
This half-closed eye ... the eye of a subtle and clever schemer.
The nose ... is ... of one sharp in thinking but soft in feeling.

'The delicately closed mouth, the broad but not flat or fleshy
chin' express 'pensiveness and placid activity.' The creasing of
the brow is not usually a good sign, being a mark of weakness,
negligence, lightness, and indolence. Of a final vignette based on
a Holbein woodcut (Erasmus half-length with his hand on the
head of the god Terminus), Lavater says: 'how evident the expression of calculating reflection! Who does not see in the posture –
and hand – the subtle, the prudent, the shrewd and the faint-
hearted!'[159]

Lavater's observations are, one suspects, less independent discoveries in the portraits than a continuation of a literary tradition,
the hostile Protestant tradition which explained Erasmus' refusal
to join the Reformers by weaknesses of character – timidity,
overrefinement, softness. At that point he touched hands with
the Milners in their very different world. The pseudo-scientific
claims of physiognomy, its physico-psychological determinism,
were powerfully to reinforce the moralizing prejudices of nineteenth-century biographers.[160] Sadly Lavater missed the opportunity of finding in Erasmus, as he might have done, a forerunner
in teaching inner, experienced religion.

At the beginning of the nineteenth century the religion of feeling found a more powerful exponent. For Friedrich Schleiermacher (1768–1834) the feeling of utter dependence was the core
of the religious experience and the subject-matter of theology.
This perception had great authority in the nineteenth century.[161]
Schleiermacher referred to Erasmus not in this connection directly
– though a connection can be made – but in his lectures on church
history.

When Schleiermacher took up that discipine – at Halle in 1806,
the year Prussia was crushed by Napoleon – he had already made
a full, if by no means definitive, statement of his distinctive view
of religion, his *On Religion: Speeches to Its Cultured Despisers* (1799),
whose second edition was to appear in 1806 itself.[162] He returned
to church history in a series of lectures at Berlin, to whose new
university he had gone as professor of theology in 1810, when

the political future of Prussia and Germany hung in the balance. The lectures were delivered in the academic years 1821–2 and 1825–6 under a political restoration for which he had little sympathy. Schleiermacher had been thinking of the church as a historical formation for several years; he had supported the union of the Reformed and Lutheran churches in Prussia promoted by King Friedrich Wilhelm III (1817) but later became disillusioned with the domineering attitude of the Prussian state towards the church and with the reactionary confessionalism of the Lutherans.[163]

The lecture on the Reformation, where the reference to Erasmus occurs, belongs to the series of 1821–2. The lectures were published six years after Schleiermacher's death by a former student from his own and others' notes and the papers of Schleiermacher himself.[164] Schleiermacher valued history as a discipline: if he were ten years younger, he said at the time of the first Berlin series, 'I would throw myself exclusively into this discipline for several years.' But he never became a specialist and the value of his lectures is in the insights they afford into his understanding of Christianity as a historical phenomenon.[165]

In the introduction to the lectures as published, amid a variety of reflections on the practice and methodology of church history, Schleiermacher introduces a double dialectic whose interest for us will become clear when we consider the role he attributes to Erasmus. One is the dialectic of inner and outer. The history of the church is essentially the working out of the new beginnings in Christ, of the inner spiritual power he brought. The historians' question is: 'How has this – from inside out – found historical expression.' With outward expansion, with the mass conversions necessary for the church's survival, came corruptions. These could be checked only by a return to origins.[166] The second dialectic is that of unity and diversity. There is in Christianity a drive towards unity, indeed towards ever larger unity – Schleiermacher shares the romantics' view of all historical communities, including the church, as growing and developing organisms.[167] But the divisions between languages and peoples are natural and unavoidable and distinctions within Christianity may also be wholesome; there are honest and salutary differences of opinion.[168] Of such, the Reformation is the great example in the history of the western church. The old unity rested on the dominance of Latin speech and a Latin hierarchy. The scholastic theology secured the domination of the clergy in general. Medieval unity was inimical to national consciousness and vernacular piety, ie to the forces promoting healthy diversity. The Reformation was prepared in the contradiction 'between the unity of the church and the struggle – through the division of the church in the form of a free community – to bring about a greater inward sincerity in Christianity.'[169]

For Schleiermacher there is always a tension in the church between the drive to adhere to or realize the original, unifying, spiritual principle and a natural liveliness which is itself a manifestation of the spirit. The leadership of the church should restrain sterile controversy while encouraging healthy differences and individual self-expression, though – unhappily – the actual churches are almost invariably confessional and sectarian, a tendency reinforced in Germany by the intervention of the state, to which a freer, more spiritual, more individual religion is suspect.[170] At the last, all differences will be taken up in a higher unity; Schleiermacher's earliest experience was among the Moravians, in a religion which was 'in principle synthetic, with a Christianity beyond the historical differentiations of Christianity, with the bold idea of a union before union comprising the various confessions merely as various choirs or divisions of the one Church of Christ.'[171] But ultimate unity is grounded in the absolute and unrealizable in history. There can be no definitive statement of the Christian faith; there will always be possibilities for growth and development. Speaking with one voice cannot be forced.[172] Least of all should the Reformation be seen as closing off Christian history. 'The Protestant view of the Christian church,' Schleiermacher said, 'includes this essential characteristic: that we think of it as a totality in movement, as something capable of progress and development.'[173]

All this shows that Schleiermacher's reference to Erasmus – despite its brevity – is significant and makes him a major religious figure, a Christian hero. Schleiermacher begins his lecture on the Reformation with the circumstances favouring reformation. They included the creation of new universities as rivals to the monastic foundations and the philological study of the Bible, which undermined the scholastic theology. The Reuchlin affair in particular showed how weak the credit of traditional theology and church authority had become. The support of Hutten and Erasmus for Reuchlin turned a small controversy into a major affair and printing spread the critical ideas far and wide, as with Erasmus' edition of the New Testament.[174]

These references to Erasmus are unremarkable for their time. Different are those which follow Schleiermacher's next questions – not only, what favoured these reforming movements? but also, why were they shortly checked, so that there was no reform of the whole church? Critical was the failure to hold in balance or in tension the principle of unity on the one hand, that of diversity on the other. In various ways, this theme occupies Schleiermacher through most of the lecture. Luther and Emperor Charles V, in one sense great rivals, agreed that there must be uniformity of teaching, a *corpus integrum doctrinae*.

> On the other hand, I cannot but say that Erasmus, though much is to be said against him, had very free views on this point and also expressed them; in his work, *De amabili ecclesiae concordia*, he seeks to show how diversity in teaching could well persist so long as generally a barrier was set against practical abuses, until better instruction gradually extending makes the necessity of such impure teaching disappear of its own accord. That is the idea of a purer reformation. If one imagines this possibility and a way of securing it, one cannot indeed deny that Erasmus had the purest view of a reformation. This is really the pure evangelical spirit.

Erasmus was wrong in not taking part in the actual, rather aggressive Reformation since, as long as awe of the papacy continued inviolate, his own idea could not succeed.[175]

The failing was nevertheless a minor one. Otherwise, Erasmus had the heart of the matter. He would hold unity by not pressing too hard on doctrinal differences, allowing diversity, emphasizing inwardness, and checking outward abuses, letting time and the spirit do the sifting and the healing. Unity and diversity were not in contradiction. Properly understood, held in balance, each was dependent on the other; otherwise unity would degenerate into oppressive uniformity, diversity into destructive divisions. That is how, in fact, it turned out. In Luther's Saxony the state asserted its authority over the church; confessions set limits to belief and checked further development; in the controversies over the sacrament unity, even among Protestants, was irretrievably broken. Attempts at reunion failed. Schleiermacher finishes the lecture by praising the smaller, freer, more spiritual religious communities.[176]

Schleiermacher's Erasmus owes something to pietism and something to the Enlightenment. He wanted both more inwardness in religion and more open competition in ideas. But there was a newer element also: Schleiermacher associated Erasmus with the idea – partly of romantic origin – that history (including the history of the Christian church) was a process of growth where errors were discarded and strengths added without a break in continuity.

IV

We have seen how Herder's essay on Hutten and Erasmus signalled a change in the moral climate. Toleration, mildness, rationality were the values of the Protestant Enlightenment. The essay of 1776 – though not, as we have also seen, the older Herder – by contrast asserted daring, heroism, and self-sacrifice. The moral confrontation of Hutten and Erasmus became a commonplace of the literature about them in the next two generations.

An essay on the two men in the periodical *Patriotisches Archiv für Deutschland* in 1787 was less extreme than the young Herder's outburst but the two writings had a historical judgment and, to some extent, a moral tone in common. Through this periodical the retired Hessian minister Friedrich Karl von Moser (1723–98) offered contemporaries instruction of a patriotic kind in political morality and history. Moser was a man of strong feelings and opinions who had belonged to pietist circles as a young man and in maturity had written more than one book on how an administrator could keep a clear conscience in his work. He believed in improvement through administration and was an admirer of Emperor Joseph II but not of Frederick the Great's more militarist version of enlightened despotism.[177]

The essay was a twenty-page introduction to the letter of appeal Hutten wrote to Erasmus from the Ebernburg castle on 13 November 1520, which had not previously been published.[178] The frontispiece, in which a large figure in armour overshadows a smaller clerk with the caption 'The greater the man, the greater his shadow,' and the opening sentence, 'Letter, one will say, of the lion to a hare,' pose the Herder-like contrast. 'How far does one deserve his praise and the other his blame?' Moser asks.[179]

Moser disclaims judgment (God alone can judge); he will but share his own thoughts and feelings about the two men. Enough touched by the Enlightenment to say, 'Doubt is not error, often rather the search for truth,' Moser yet condemns Erasmus for adding so many 'buts' to truth that something quite different from truth emerged. Hutten's claim to glory rested less on his character – Erasmus was easily able to point to his sins (sins which Erasmus himself, 'dry, weak and fearful,' was not capable of committing) – than on his cause. Erasmus had in his own way served the good cause through the revival of learning and the call for church reform. But he lacked the single-mindedness of the high-spirited Hutten who thought one only had to speak the truth for others to believe it. Erasmus was 'too conscientious to blaspheme and go backwards and loved honours and the favour of men too much to go forward, he always wavered – under fear and hope, profession and dissembling – up to the grave.' Erasmus was a bookworm, Hutten full of living emotion; Erasmus struggled for intellectual freedom, Hutten for freedom of conscience and political freedom; Hutten lost all, Erasmus kept his riches and reputation.[180] Despite these summary judgments, the influence of Wieland checks that of Herder: one must take account of Erasmus' temperament and his circumstances. He was fearful but not a Judas as Luther said. His letter to Luther of May 1524[181] was that of 'an unsure, prudent but honourable man, no scoundrel or traitor.' So Mosheim might have written to Luther. Herder's piece was less a reasoned statement than a 'sentimentale Declamation.'[182]

At base Moser accepts Herder's contrast but is more restrained. He shared the taste for high spirits and devotion to causes but had a commitment to reason and conscience which made Erasmus appealing to him. He balanced Enlightenment discrimination and romantic feeling.

With the emergence, during the revolutionary and Napoleonic wars, of nationality as an issue and for many a dominant value, the German past required re-evaluation. The year 1817, the three-hundredth anniversary of Luther's posting of the ninety-five theses, provided an occasion for a re-evaluation of one episode in German history. A study of the most famous commemoration, the festival of the German student organizations at Luther's retreat of the Wartburg in October 1817, demonstrates a variety of interpretations of the German Reformation.[183]

The values of the preceding epoch had not been generally abandoned: the Enlightenment understanding of the Reformation was still influential in 1817 – the Reformation was an intellectual liberation, a work essentially of enlightenment and moral purification. Those who saw the Reformation in this way – even when they associated it also with national liberation – kept the Protestant Enlightenment's favourable judgment of Erasmus.

Thus, Heinrich Wilhelm Rotermund (1761–1848), pastor at Bremen cathedral, commemorated the Reformation as a delivery of the gospel from papal tyranny but also wrote sympathetically of the men who stood apart from Luther or even opposed him, including Erasmus.[184] For Rotermund Erasmus was a model of the autonomous individual. If from his earliest years he cultivated the rich and powerful, his aim was personal and financial independence. Indeed, for long he remained poor and relied only on his own talents and industry. In later life he did not accept the professorships and bishoprics pressed upon him because his great literary undertakings could be carried through only in leisure and freedom.

To this free way of life corresponded the independent part he played in the affairs of his time.

> Through the new way he took in theology, through the bold truths which he declared to the teachers of his church, through the mockeries which could touch them more than the truths themselves and through the great support he manifestly gave the reformation then breaking out in Germany and Switzerland – even if it were one not fully after his own intention – he was much hated by the zealots of his church; it required all the respect which he enjoyed among the leading princes and the popes themselves, but also all the grandeur of the new light then streaming over many European lands to prevent his being suppressed by his opponents.

Independence of mind won him no favour: supporters of the old church accused him of betrayal, friends of the Reformers of hypocrisy. He had nevertheless the support of men of spirit, candour, or learning and posterity has within limits justified him.[185]

The limits are, of course, Protestant: that must be expected even of a liberal-minded Protestant in 1817. Posterity, says Rotermund, honours Erasmus as the most renowned of those who used the revival of learning in the service of theology; it accords him the honoured name of reformer of the church but not in the fullest sense since he lacked courage to face all dangers and did not clearly see that the ruined building could not be restored or propped up but must be completely demolished and a better one built. The age, with its great reforming movements, gave him prominence – or, to put this romantic notion in Christian terms, providence singled him out as an instrument of the good cause.[186]

Also in the line of the Protestant Enlightenment, Gottfried Wilhelm Becker in his *Luther und seine Zeitgenossen* of 1817 saw the Reformation as the fulfilment of Renaissance humanism.[187] Erasmus, Reuchlin, and Hutten worked in the one cause and Luther benefited from, if he did not belong to, their association. Becker introduces national liberation as the natural companion and not the rival of the renewal of letters. The union of enlightened and learned friends who supported Reuchlin against clerical despotism was like the union of Germans against Napoleon.[188]

Erasmus and Reuchlin, says Becker, brought an enlightenment which Hutten spread into the homes of the people. Wyclif and Hus a century before could not shake church authority but their successors had the double advantage of printing, through which one might say 'the word will conquer the world,' and the classical revival. Erasmus and Reuchlin already made a reformation in restoring the biblical languages, opening the best sources, not only to the learned, but also to simple laymen who more and more shook themselves free of clerical domination. The attempt by ignorant monks to suppress Reuchlin divided Germany and Europe into two parties, the friends of light and slaves of darkness. Hutten, 'liberator of his fatherland, defender of German freedom,' finished the work.[189] This was one of the interpretations, Becker's was one of the voices of 1817: Renaissance, Reformation, and Enlightenment made a sequence; the religious, intellectual, and national liberations were in harmony with one another.

There were other voices of 1817. One was that of revived orthodoxy, which rejected secular idealism and presented Luther as a man of God and the Reformation not as liberation, but as spiritual regeneration. Another tendency made a religion out of nationality and exalted German ways and ostensibly German values – honour, courage, fidelity – revealed in both the Reformation and the war of liberation.[190] This turned Luther into a national hero and found a perfect expression in Hutten. It is instructive that Wagner, whom we have met as a particularly unsympathetic biographer of Erasmus, also wrote – soon after the turn of the century – an enthusiastic biography of Hutten.[191] There came, during and after the wars of liberation, a small spate of Hutten biographies, carrying forward the themes of Herder and Wagner: moral grandeur and the liberating word belonged, not to Erasmus, but to Hutten. C.J. Wagenseil's biography of 1823 presented Hutten as 'martyr for the truth, freedom's noble, strong defender, powerful poet and orator, ardent friend of the fatherland.' By contrast, Erasmus was two-faced, hypocritical.[192]

Appeals to fairness were made even at the height of the patriotic fever. In 1813 Johann Jakob Stolz – admittedly a Swiss – published translations of Hutten's and Erasmus' broadsides against each other and called for a better balanced, less partisan judgment of the two men than had been common in the past. It should be possible to do justice after three centuries. Reconciliation would have been a possibility but for the meddling of third parties. It was unreasonable of Hutten to ask Erasmus to side with Luther: why not let Erasmus be himself? His neutrality would, says Stolz, have served the cause better than a forced adherence. And the violence of Hutten's attack was beyond reason: 'In several places he treated Erasmus only as one treats a man one wants, morally speaking, to slay.' Erasmus did himself credit by making a measured, not a heated, reply. His *Spongia* is a work of great skill, if not without sophistry. Stolz regrets that Erasmus still pursued Hutten after his death and acknowledges some weaknesses of character, but in the main accepts Erasmus' justification and his individuality.[193]

Defences of Erasmus became more common under the Restoration after 1815, especially among Catholic writers. He was a sympathetic subject for those who had endured and survived the revolutionary era, who still felt threatened and who clung to the precarious balance of the Restoration settlement. Such people were sceptical of the heroic ardour which the previous generation had found attractive in Hutten. Thus, Carl Kieser, priest in Heckfeld, decided on his study of Erasmus and Hutten when the latter – as he thought a traitor to his civil and ecclesiastical rulers and to himself – was offered anew to German youth and manhood as a model. He had no respect for elders, rulers, teachers, or friends, called the people to rebellion, and threatened his fatherland with rapine. 'Truly,' concludes Kieser, who saw the Reformers as forerunners of contemporary revolutionaries, 'it reveals the deep degradation of our age that one dares to depict such a character as an example for young people.'[194] Erasmus, by contrast, showed true greatness in the troubles which descended on him and of which he was the innocent occasion. With all right-thinking people of that time, he approved Luther's first writings against the monks but he stood by the Catholic church and abhorred separation from it as the greatest evil. Admittedly his satirical writings were misconceived: satire embitters, rather than cures, the afflicted heart and undermines the respect subjects owe their superiors. But he did not make personal attacks on the leaders of the church and worked for its betterment, not its overthrow. He was no flatterer but 'a moderate and candid friend of the truth.'[195]

Another writer entered a defence of Erasmus against the charges commonly made by Hutten's admirers, drawing on readily accessible works like Hess's biography and Schröck's history and arguing that Erasmus' faults had been greatly exaggerated in recent literature in order to place him in the most odious light, while Hutten had been praised beyond his deserts and the faults of the other Reformers overlooked.[196] Thus his table of contents includes: Erasmus loved the truth and was not fearful; he abhorred flattery; he was steadfast in character and sought only to assist good letters; he did not wish to be involved in the Lutheran struggle and was not persuaded into it by promises and gifts; in that struggle he remained true to his convictions and counselled only moderation; he was not inordinately ambitious; he did not live a life of luxury. The picture is of a reformer who worked by wit and sobriety rather than grossness and extravagance, who persisted courageously in his criticisms, even of the great, who supported every effort at reform until he observed too large an infusion of passion and private interest. His struggle was to introduce a truer appreciation of the classical writings, to give theology a new foundation and open the Bible to all Christians, and he won a response.[197]

The relationship between Hutten and Erasmus, the work concludes, had been much misunderstood. Hutten early won the friendship of Erasmus who admired his great qualities. They gave one another mutual support against enemies and critics. Unfortunately, Hutten's restless way of life denied him the calm necessary for developing his gifts and Erasmus' refusal to side with Luther alienated him. Of the débâcle in Basel in 1522 it is asked: how could the peace-loving Erasmus – counsellor of the empire – be expected to receive the lawless, turbulent fugitive?[198]

Hutten and Erasmus were useful symbols in the era of revolution and restoration. Hutten had conducted a pamphlet war – for which he had the flair of genius – against foreign intervention in German affairs; he had also run the risks of taking up arms against the enemy. Germans rallying against Napoleon or resentful of the post-Napoleonic settlements, which left national hopes unrealized, recognized in him a forerunner and a hero. Those who supported the settlement and feared rather a continuing disorder and instability, when they turned to the equally disturbed era of the Reformation, found a predecessor in Erasmus, a reformer by persuasion, an advocate of restraint and moderation, a lover of concord who preferred imperfect order to the hazards of war and rebellion.

V

The first substantial biography of Erasmus in the nineteenth century – by Adolf Müller (Berlin 1828) – registered the changes in the intellectual climate since Gaudin and Hess published their biographies in Zürich around 1790.[199] They wrote still under the influence of the Protestant Enlightenment and before the revolutionary upheavals and saw Erasmus as the apostle of tolerance and rationality and enlightenment. Müller, by contrast, not only lived through the great upheavals but also came under intellectual influences which led him to value not tolerance but a sense of commitment, not rationality but intensity of feeling, and to understand enlightenment in a markedly different sense from his eighteenth-century predecessors. He thought not of a dawn gradual and benign but of the spirit brooding over the earth and of dramatic historical confrontations.

There was much in Müller typical of the time; he also expressed – indeed partly determined – the tone of much nineteenth-century Protestant writing about Erasmus. But however typical, his book was also a very personal document, a kind of testimony to a highly individual faith. Müller had experiences in childhood and youth which taught him the value of personal stability and strength; they also lifted his eyes to wide historical horizons and taught him to speak of mission and destiny.[200] About the former his own father was a warning, an unsteady man who could not properly care for his family; about the latter he was instructed by the fate of Germany in the Napoleonic wars – the French entry into Berlin in 1806 made a deep impression on the child of eight, while the boy of fifteen had a fast faith in Prussia's victory in the wars of liberation. His patriotism was enriched when, after mastering his craft of instrument maker, he entered on his 'Wanderjahre' and learnt, as he put it, wisdom in the company of the common folk. Then in January 1819 he suddenly lost his sight. He was said later to have rejoiced in this searing experience because it taught him to be content with his lot – a remarkable example of self-mastery.

After a naïve but successful appeal for financial support from the king of Prussia, he began studies at the University of Berlin in 1823. It was the time of Schleiermacher and Hegel and the influence of both may be found in Müller's work on Erasmus. On one occasion he made a parallel between the progression from scholasticism through humanism to the Reformation and that from Protestant orthodoxy through the Enlightenment to the recovery of living, experienced faith – presumably as in Schleiermacher.[201] The biographer, he said on another occasion, has the Hegelian mission of describing the relation of his subject to the Idea and their interaction.[202] After two years of Hegel's lectures, he was drawn to submit an essay on the question set by the philosophical faculty – 'Ut vita Erasmi Roterodamensis atque quid ille litteris praestiterit exponatur' – not by any attraction to Erasmus' personality initially but in the belief that Erasmus in his life exemplified an Hegelian parallel between the destiny of the individual human being and the history of mankind.[203]

Twenty years later, a seventeen-year-old pupil of Müller's, Helene von Hülsen, heard from him *dicta* which help to explain his judgments of Erasmus. 'We have objective truth; see that for you it becomes experienced truth'; his relation to God alone determines a man's worth – only from love for God and the truth comes strength of character; the ideal is eternal, the real mortal; the Greeks sought divine oracles but those Christians who bear God in their hearts do not need an outward oracle: they must follow blindly the inner command; the struggle against sterile orthodoxy turns on the issue: 'absolute submission to human authority, or subjective development of the individual'; the intellect, however brilliant, is mortal and preoccupied with the transient, spirit alone grasps the essentials.[204]

The Renaissance was the intellect, the Reformation the spirit of mankind's history – thus in a detached but related essay Müller begins his life of Erasmus. He makes a still more intricate analogy between the individual and mankind. The earliest peoples and civilizations, like the child, lived in an innocent simplicity but gradually the rebellious intellect ('Verstand') set adolescent mankind on a restless search. In Christianity, the manhood of humanity, the mature conscience, true reason ('Vernunft'), an unforced adherence to the right, asserted itself. But mankind did not wish to rest in conscience; 'Verstand' continued its agitated, unsatisfying search, doing all in its power to solve mankind's problems and so remain its master. It failed; indeed proud intellect called up its contrary, superstition. From their conflict arose a third, purifying, restorative power. The late Middle Ages were mankind's experience of anxiety, guilt, self-disgust, the Reformation its second birth, the restoration of conscience.[205]

While Luther was – in the hand of God and in the fullness of time – the instrument of this restoration, Erasmus, Müller says, stood for 'Verstand.' 'He really sought the best both for himself and for his fellow men; only he could never find it, since he sought it with his understanding alone (eben nur mit dem Verstande) and did not grant a higher power any direct influence on his life.' Anxious to instruct his contemporaries in the rediscovered classical learning, he spread himself rapidly over many works and failed – as in a narrower, more penetrating attack – to reach down to firm unshakeable truths.[206] In his writing on ethics, the same superficiality. There is much good advice but no deep inner principle which would make good advice unnecessary. Erasmus and John Colet – his chief mentor after Lorenzo Valla – were as one in having true and pious things to say but also in their prudence in saying them. The *Enchiridion* could not be a handbook for the true Christian striving for perfection but only for one who has a natural morality and an education in Christian language. Erasmus' moral ideal is one of outward respectability and a blameless reputation before the world.[207]

The same domination by 'Verstand' explains Erasmus' role in the Reformation. He could not be Luther's John Baptist[208] because he lived too much for himself and lacked the submission to God's will necessary in a prophet and reformer. He judged Luther's case superficially, seeing on the one side established authority in its brilliance and power and on the other a mere monk, 'ein Sandkorn am Meeresgestade.' The intellectual man did not discern the spirit of God, the genius of humanity which brooded in this monk's affairs. The realm of the free spirit was closed to Erasmus; for him there was only the visible world, the world of intellect. On another side, his dry intellectualism closed to him the life of the common people and the beauties of the physical world and of art. His rationalism misunderstood the passion and commitment behind Luther's teaching on the will which Erasmus treated like any pagan philosophy. Müller concludes with an unabashed statement of his historicist theme: as unhoped-for light can break from outside into the deepest being of a man struggling to ennoble his life, so mankind in the sixteenth century was failed by those who promised it salvation from its own intellectual resources, only to have an unquenchable light break within it in Luther's Reformation.[209]

Throughout the book runs the subsidiary but reinforcing theme of Erasmus' character. Failings of character are held to explain his role in history. The sensitive, fastidious Erasmus, says Müller, lacked precisely those qualities which make man and not woman the master of the world: courage, self-confidence, and, characteristically, 'Vaterlandsliebe.' His bodily did not keep up with his intellectual training and a weak body cannot stand manfully in a great crisis. He was the product of the over-tender care of an anxious mother. This was not Müller's only attempt to provide Erasmus with a psychological history: the violence and deception of his guardians in inveigling him into a monastery made him chronically mistrustful.[210] Generally Müller goes for big effects: Erasmus could have turned even the monastic life to advantage if he had had more trust in God – Luther and Thomas à Kempis drew strength even from the sluggish spirituality of the time; he was incapable of true friendship because his own inner being was unsteady, he lived on the surface and took the colour of his surroundings. 'He had a great deal, but he was very little.' This unflattering portrait is largely confirmed by the circular procedures of Lavater's *Physiognomy*; one read into Holbein's portraits the expressions one had come already to expect – 'no impulse of an onrushing, destructive audacity.'[211] Lavater and Adolf Müller together were to be a quarry of abusive expressions for hostile Protestant writers throughout the nineteenth century.

The theme of this chapter has been the effect of new values and new sensibilities in the late eighteenth and early nineteenth centuries on the reputation of Erasmus. Of course, he continued to be defended by the heirs of the Protestant Enlightenment; he also had, especially under the Restoration, orthodox Catholic apologists, on the rebound from the perils of revolution. The newer kind of thinking valued commitment and liveliness and feeling, though forms of expression differed greatly – from the evangelicals' response to grace to the aggressive patriotism of Hutten's defenders.

The new style could work either way for Erasmus. Coleridge praised his sense for the vivid social life of his time and his commitment to the highest principles, so making a distinctive contribution to the story of Erasmus interpretations to which today one may profitably return. Mostly, however, the new sensibility found Erasmus uncongenial and his popularity in the Enlightenment counted against him: he was said to be too sceptical, too cool, moderate and tolerant to a fault.

The fact is that the Enlightenment writers and the new writers basically saw Erasmus in the same way, the former with favour, the latter with distaste. He was the man of rationality and open-mindedness. Save for Coleridge, all underestimated his depth of feeling (feelings about church abuses apart). Exaggerated ideas about his weakness of character confirmed the portrait of the calculating, superficial, unfeeling man. Nineteenth-century writers inherited, indeed carried the burden, of this picture.

PART TWO

THE NINETEENTH CENTURY AND AFTER

FIVE

Introduction to Part Two

Writings about Erasmus since his death had produced by the beginning of the nineteenth century four stereotypes. Two had come down virtually unchanged from the confessional age. These were the hostile and rejecting judgments of Protestant and Catholic orthodoxy. Critics from the two camps shared a suspicion of his reputed scepticism with its corrosive working on dogmatic and ecclesiastical structures, but the Protestants condemned his refusal to join the religious revolution (despite, as they claimed, his actual sympathy for it) and the Catholics his betrayal of the old religious authorities. Such judgments were ready to hand for the representatives of orthodoxy in each generation.

The third stereotype had its origins in the Reformation era – actually in Christian humanist circles both around the Reformers and in the old church (especially the former). Erasmus was seen as one of the sources, indeed for many the primary source, of a growing enlightenment dispersing the darkness of superstition and intolerance. This picture was given sharper outlines and altogether enlarged during the Enlightenment. Those still within the Christian tradition made him a beginning – or the beginning – of its wholesome purification and renovation. The others saw him as early – or first – into the breach against *l'Infâme*: consciously or half-consciously he began the dismantling of the old dogmatic order.

The beginnings of the fourth stereotype might be traced in the first two but mostly it was a creation of romanticism. The preoccupation was with alleged weaknesses in Erasmus' character; he was represented as a pale shadow of a man compared with the heroes of his age. Hence came his refusal to take sides finally in the Reformation controversies.

Plainly much writing about Erasmus since the late seventeenth century cannot be reduced to these stereotypes. Scale alone guaranteed escape in some cases. A biography like Burigny's or Hess's breaks out of the strait-jacket through the variety of its subject-matter and the diverse standpoints its author must assume in presentation. Some authors – several at the beginning of the eighteenth century and Coleridge at the beginning of the nineteenth – had the subtlety and sensitivity to produce a living if incomplete portrait. And one must always recognize the effects of cultural change; Enlightenment was able to recover features buried beneath the ice in the confessional age and so – from the standpoint of modern scholarship – make genuine advances.

Nevertheless, the attraction of the stereotype was enormous. It drew on the dependence of authors on one another, on the relatively limited range of sources brought seriously into the account, on the persistence of cultural patterns, especially in the religious or ecclesiastical sphere, despite changes elsewhere; to all this one should add the effects of an understandable intellectual laziness and the power of smart or telling formulations from the past, no matter how inaccurate or unjust they might be.

A cynic might say that what we have in the nineteenth-century literature is but a refinement or a reshuffling of the four stereotypes. Certainly there is much evidence of their continuing power but that power was not absolute. Nineteenth-century movements had their own preoccupations and the portrait of Erasmus was adjusted to these as earlier it had been adjusted to Enlightenment and romanticism. Above all, the canons of critical historical scholarship were being more securely established. Better-founded treatments of Erasmus appear though, naturally, preconceptions and prejudices abound. Work done in the second half of the century prepared the way for P.S. Allen's fundamental reworking of Erasmus' correspondence and scholars began recasting Erasmus' portrait. It is possible to recognize in the literature not only the tendencies in nineteenth-century life and thought to which that portrait was being adjusted but also some present, recognizably modern problems in Erasmus scholarship. The terms and structure of our discussion can be set by both.

SIX

From Restoration to the Revolutions of 1848: Erasmus as Critic, Publicist, and Rebel

Modern scholarship has recognized that Erasmus, far from being a withdrawn scholar, was one of the great shapers of public opinion in his time. Naturally one thinks first of educated opinion. Erasmus' works are found in large numbers in the libraries of thinking clergy and literate laymen.[1] But in the great propaganda battles of the sixteenth century his words and his person were also used in appeals to the 'common man.' One woodcut, 'The Divine Mill,' which turned a familiar image of the doctrine of transubstantiation into Protestant propaganda, depicts Erasmus supervising the processing of biblical truth for the people. Luther and a believing peasant stand beside him and together they confront a resistant pope, cardinal, and monk.[2] Erasmus' writings were translated into the vernaculars and, above all, into German; that his was the name to be conjured with is indicated by its prominence on title-pages even when vernacular works had an intermixture of others' labours. As a German author Erasmus was second only to Luther and their popularity followed a remarkably similar course reaching its peak in the heady years 1521–2. In the period between 1519 and 1525 there was, on the one hand, a broad reforming movement, variegated in character but not yet divided into mutually exclusive camps, within which Erasmus was a leader and, on the other, an agitated public – literate and semi-literate – devouring the productions of authors, translators, and publishers as they appeared.[3]

It is not surprising that this Erasmus – the journalist, commentator, publicist – should be clearly identified in the first half of the nineteenth century, in the period between the Restoration and the European revolutions of 1848. The Restoration was an attempt to establish equilibrium by judicious compromises and to defuse the revolutionary dynamism of the last generation. It was unsettled not least by the extension and increasing activity of the political press, the wider discussion of unresolved political issues among a larger reading public. The revolution of 1830 in Paris was begun by a protest of journalists and its high moments were battles between police and printers' workmen around the presses.[4] Political censorship and the freedom of the press was a primary issue through the whole period 1815–48.[5] The 1840s saw the gradual commercializing and popularizing of the press in France, and in Germany – politically more fragmented and retarded – its association with a more active, indeed at times effervescent, public life.[6] The revolutionary summer of 1848 itself produced a new press – 'full of polemics and fiery speech, crude and witty popular sheets, others more crude than witty, satire, broad folk-humour, constructive and destructive, libellous or seriously political.'[7] It was at a distance reminiscent of the *Flugschriften* of the Reformation time.

This importance of public opinion and the printed word in the revolutionary events both of his own time and of the less literate age of the Reformation was appreciated by the main creator of modern critical history, Leopold von Ranke. This is apparent in his portrait of Erasmus in the *History of the Reformation in Germany*, one of two great works of the 1830s demonstrating Ranke's maturity as a historian (the other was the *History of the Popes*). For the first time in this book Ranke used the *Flugschriften* and popular songs as sources.[8] His position in the 1830s helps explain the peculiar stamp Ranke put on the Erasmus portrait and in particular the recognition he gave to the role of public opinion in the Reformation drama, Erasmus appearing in the prologue.

From early in life Ranke had had a strong attraction to the academic calling.[9] He began – characteristically for the time – with philological studies which laid the foundation for his enthusiasm for the classical world.[10] Only gradually did modern history emerge as his chosen sphere but, when it did, it was accompanied by an intense sense of vocation expressing a distinctive, if not wholly orthodox, piety: he could not, he said, when his first historical work appeared, abandon his historical studies 'without killing myself'; years later, when he was beginning the German *History*, he wrote that he thanked God daily for his vocation but recognized that he could never rightly fulfil it.[11] Not unexpectedly his famous characterizations of historical figures often include an awareness of or sense for their subjects' historic vocations. This is true, as we shall see, of the Erasmus portrait, though Ranke's view of Erasmus' vocation mingled attraction and distaste. Naturally, Erasmus' skill in language, his dedication to the classics and the ancient world, were part of his attraction to Ranke.

Central to Ranke's development both personal and professional was his search for a resolution of the apparent contradiction between his two commitments: one was to historical enquiry – scrupulous, impartial, well documented – into particular events and developments in all their manifold variety, to which he was devoted and for which he is famous; the other was to larger, even universal patterns in human affairs. By the time of his writing his *History of the Popes* in the 1830s he had arrived at an optimistic position about holding in focus general themes and particular facts.[12] The opening section of the *History of the Reformation in Germany*, within which his Erasmus portrait appears, is a case of such holding in focus.

Ranke resisted illegitimate generalizing which for him meant the application of general theories from above without research into particulars. There was an analogy in his approach to politics. He saw much liberal and revolutionary politics as an attempt to make society over by general principles without regard to the peculiar histories and characters of the different peoples. Revolutionary politics and especially the stirring of public opinion were revived with the fall of the monarchy in France and its European reverberations in 1830, which broke the Restoration equilibrium. The negative traits in his Erasmus portrait are related to these events and Ranke's reaction to them.

Erasmus appears in a chapter on the origin of the religious opposition; it begins with the state of religion in the fifteenth century and ends with the appearance of Luther. The vitality of Latin Christendom, says Ranke, was unimpaired at the end of the fifteenth century but faced one major threat. The unusual energies of western civilization arose from the unceasing rivalry and balancing of religion, with its universal claims, on the one hand and the European states, as particular political formations, on the other. But in the later Middle Ages the balance became seriously disturbed; one side in the rivalry made a claim for – and indeed went far towards realizing – an exclusive domination.

By the thirteenth century limitless authority was being ascribed to the papacy, by the fifteenth – most clearly in Germany – all intellectual life was moving in courses determined by ecclesiastical authority.[13] 'For it was all a single structure, grown from the shoots planted in earlier centuries, in which spiritual and temporal power, fantasy and arid scholasticism, tender devotion and brute force, religion and superstition met and mingled, held together by a secret quality common to them all.'[14]

The deepest need – ultimately to be met in Germany – was to bring the heart of the Christian religion again to light from beneath the many accidental forms which hid it. Other reforms were pressed. The attempt around the beginning of the sixteenth century to reform the constitution of the German empire failed through political weakness but the opposition to Rome, with which it was associated, was more and more alive in the popular mind. There was public revulsion at the condition of the clergy. In its first beginnings, German popular literature expressed this revulsion but went further. It brought all aspects of social life before the judgment of sober good sense, expressing a simple, honest bourgeois morality and a grasp on social realities. Learned literature, Ranke goes on, took a similar direction. Admiration for antiquity – fired by the revival of classical studies in Italy – was expressed, above all, in the founding of schools. These were not so much seats of higher learning as creators of public opinion; a literate, critical public appeared to which, as scholasticism stood its ground and there began the clash between the old learning and the new, Erasmus made his appeal.[15]

An agitated public opinion, the pressing of reform demands, a spate of books popular and learned, above all the clash of educational ideologies – this is the historical moment that met Erasmus. He was 'the first great writer of the opposition in the modern sense.'[16] Writers of the opposition were familiar and not particularly congenial figures to Ranke in the 1830s. In the revolutionary age they had set the historical agenda. Ranke's Erasmus is a journalist, a critic, a shrewd judge and skilful master of public opinion.

Erasmus' early life was in 'ceaseless inner contradiction' with established views and interests: his parents' inability to marry, his own imperfect schooling, the pressure to enter a monastery, the encounter with scholastic learning at Paris. These contradictions made him what he was. But in their very midst he was already conscious of his personal powers. While still a boy, he followed the first traces he received of a new and better method of study 'with the sure instinct of true talent.' He commanded a light, fluent style, not by imitation of the ancients, but by an inner disposition to correctness and elegance.[17]

He cut himself off from the world of cloister and university and began to live the life of the free writer. He was dependent at first on patrons but more and more he developed a sense for what the public liked and wanted. In all his writings he showed himself master of the fine observation which at once both instructs and delights. But his real attraction for the public was the tendency of opposition running through the work. He poured out his bitterness – acquired by experience and become habitual – against the forms of piety and theology in his time, not usually in direct attacks but, rather, obliquely in bursts of satire and humour.

The centre-piece of Ranke's presentation of Erasmus is a treatment of the Folly (Moriae encomium). He reads it essentially as a satire on all social classes but, above all, on the clergy, as connected therefore with the popular literature then burgeoning in Germany. It presented, though with unusual wit and terseness and in a literary form, matter already in wide circulation. It had an indescribable effect, confirming the mind of the age in its anticlerical tendency.[18]

To popular criticism Erasmus added the more scholarly. He agreed with the Italians that Greek studies opened prospects beyond the narrow confines of western ecclesiastical learning and that sciences were to be learned from the ancients but he took the further step of demanding that theology be learned, not from the scholastics, but from the Greek Fathers and, above all, the New Testament. He pointed, Ranke concludes, to the simple origins of the complicated and towering structure of contemporary theology. The expressions are reminiscent of Schleiermacher with whom Ranke was associated at the University of Berlin.[19] Erasmus cultivated his public like a liberal, not a revolutionary, publicist. He claimed to be working only for reforms and improvements, which he represented as easy, and took care to conceal the abyss yawning beyond. It is not clear how Ranke sees this abyss – was it revolution? a division in the church? a breakdown in faith? – or what foresight he attributed to Erasmus. At any rate Erasmus avoided challenging articles of belief to which the convictions of the faithful were attached.

As a writer he had the skills of the journalist, capable of winning quick command over the public mind. He worked rapidly
and published immediately what came from his pen, since he
lacked the patience to revise, but this added to the charm for
contemporary readers who felt directly in touch with Erasmus'
mind – 'a mind rich, fine, witty, bold and cultivated.' Public opinion, for which he was a pathfinder, crowned him with laurels.[20]

Ranke finishes suddenly with a brief pen-portrait whose sources
may be traced without difficulty. 'His person was small, with light
hair, blue, half-closed eyes, full of acute observation, and humour
playing about the delicate mouth; his air was so timorous that
he looked as if a breath would overthrow him, and he trembled
at the very name of death.'[21] There are elements here from Beatus
Rhenanus but the tone comes mostly from Lavater and Adolf
Müller.[22]

Ranke's Erasmus is a telling depiction of a liberal publicist, one
who led public opinion but also attuned himself to it. In that the
critic and satirist are highlighted and the *Folly* given a special
place, there is much in common with the Erasmus of the Enlightenment. Its recognition of the effectiveness of his attack on clerical
abuses and its somewhat unfriendly handling of his style and
person link this portrait to a longer Protestant tradition about
Erasmus. What is missing, and might have been expected from
one of Ranke's interests and sensitivities, is any study of Erasmus'
piety.[23] The outlines of the portrait have been determined by the
role Ranke has given Erasmus to play.

What follows reinforces this conclusion. Ranke moves to the
universities where battle between the old learning and the new
was joined in an unexpected quarter, over the Hebrew studies of
Johann Reuchlin, of whose person and thought Ranke gives a
much warmer picture. Reuchlin's philological work had ultimately a religious purpose; for this Ranke had, unfairly, found
no counterpart in Erasmus. Still, the public opinion which Erasmus had created to support the new learning protected Reuchlin
against his scholastic attackers. The literary opposition sensed
victory. History, however, took another course, though the literary revival, especially as it affected the study of scripture, was
not made superfluous. The great historical renovation arose, not
from outside, but from within the theological tradition itself – in
the person of Luther.[24]

The contrast between the essentially literary Erasmus and the theological Luther was long familiar, especially among Protestant writers. Ranke's contribution was not there but in his presentation of Erasmus as a public figure, as a maker, not just of books, but of public opinion.

A book of the 1840s by Karl Hagen (1810–68) called *Deutschlands literarische und religiöse Verhältnisse im Reformationszeitalter* was seen by contemporaries as a counterpart, from the democratic side of politics, to Ranke's *History*.[25] Noteworthy for our purposes is the common interest in public opinion which, says Hagen, was the real subject of his study of the Reformation: public opinion created and carried Luther.[26] Hagen also used the *Flugschriften* of which he found a rich collection in the town library of Windsheim. The three-volume work began as a study of Willibald Pirckheimer, the Nuremberg patrician and humanist, but it was never really a biography and, by the second volume, Pirckheimer's name had disappeared from the title.[27] Nor was it a general history of Germany during the Reformation or a formal kind of literary history. Hagen's interest was in reforming ideas or 'tendencies' which, emerging in Germany in the fifteenth century, made their greatest impact around 1520. Of these ideas Hagen had a very distinctive appreciation, as we shall see.

Hagen and his book belong to the pre-revolutionary ferment in the Germany of the 1840s. He had been influenced by his father, a free-thinking pastor, and educated at Erlangen and Jena, where he was taught by Heinrich Luden, historian of medieval Germany, enemy of the conservative post-1815 settlement, and 'ardent patriot of the era of Liberation.'[28] When his book appeared, he was a popular teacher at Heidelberg. He was to be active in the events of 1848, to go to the Frankfurt Assembly as Heidelberg's representative, and to sit with the extreme left. The failure of the revolution destroyed his career at Heidelberg but in 1855 he was appointed to Bern, where he again became a much-loved teacher.

According to Hagen, the reforming movement began in Germany around the middle of the fifteenth century.[29] It was a movement towards a freer, more expansive, more spontaneous religious and social life. In its learned or humanist form, it sought freedom from the old, scholastic authorities and a genuine cultivation of heart and mind, instead of a repetition of scholastic formulas. It wanted to relate school learning to social life and the needs of the nation. This linked the learned to the popular form of the movement, for the latter sought to judge every form of pride and conceit by natural good sense and a simple human understanding.[30] The expression reminds one of the 'sober good sense' Ranke attributed to the German popular writers.

The movement also took a theological form. Indeed, it mastered the theological field and transformed it. Just as the renewed study of the classics provided literary forms for expressing the learned movement's aspirations, so the classics had a refreshing influence on theology, since the critical study of the scriptures, the foundation of all theological endeavour, depended on the knowledge of languages. In theological speculation and biblical criticism, reason became the standard; Hagen could find in the reforming movement anticipations of Strauss and Feuerbach – these anachronisms are the measure of his radical understanding of the Reformation controversies.[31]

Erasmus' historical achievement was to be the unifier of the movement in its three forms – popular, humanist, and theological. He became the focus ('Brennpunkt') for all three and had the talents for attracting a broad public to the new ideas. Like Ranke, Hagen found the source of Erasmus' opposition to established interests in his early experiences: from childhood he suffered frustration and restriction and, through irony and satire if not by direct assault, expressed his hatred for the institutions that hemmed him in.[32] For Hagen, however, Erasmus is more than an opposition figure; he also embodied the hopes and aspirations of the reforming movement.

Above all, he expressed its religious ideas clearly and comprehensively. Hagen sets out to establish this by an analysis of the *Enchiridion*. Here Erasmus went beyond any predecessor in applying the new learning to theology. He allegorized scripture not like the mystics and scholastics but like the present-day rationalists, seeing a truth, an idea behind the biblical picture. He brought a social sense to religion, finding the Christian life not in ceremonies but in a pious loving spirit. He broke the dividing wall between priests and laity, since Christ was the same for all. He may have had the prudence to disseminate radical views without appearing to break with the church but he must fundamentally have been a sceptic about church traditions.[33]

If the *Enchiridion* combined the humanist and theological forms of the movement, the *Folly* drew together the popular and the scholarly tendencies. It was the best example of the use the humanist opposition could make of the popular tone. In it, as in the popular *Flugschriften* of the time, the ostensible wisdom of the scholastics was confronted by nature and reason – so the apparently wise appeared the greatest fools.[34]

The reforming movement reached its high-point in these works. Luther's appearance brought not, as for Ranke, a new, creative, and decisive phase in the renovation of western Christendom but a rapid decline and disintegration. In the 1520s, Hagen says in his third volume, the three streams which had run powerfully together in the first years of the century drew apart again. The popular movement rejected learning as vanity, and so alienated the humanist scholarly movement. More important, a deep division appeared between the scholarly and theological movements, indeed within the theological movement itself. A harsher, more dogmatic strain, increasingly indifferent to the classics and rigidly biblicist, drew apart from the freer, more mystical, or more rationalist strain, which sought an inner Word in human reason and retained some of the freshness of the early popular and humanist movements. Luther was an ever more stubborn spokesman for the dogmatic, biblical view.[35]

In fact, Hagen took to its limits the Enlightenment distinction between the original impulse for reform and the Protestant churches that emerged from the Reformation: 'Protestantism, as it found expression in the new churches with their new dogmas, seems to me more or less a back-sliding from the original free reforming movement.' He had no wish to preserve the Protestant church but rather hoped that the original idea would again sweep the nation. Not Luther but the sects maintained that idea and they had their counterparts in the freer religious movements opposing a dominant orthodoxy and pietism in Hagen's own time.[36]

Apart from the sects, Erasmus, more than any other leader, continued the original movement. He saw the dangers in the new orthodoxy. What help was it to put new dogmas in the place of the old? Outwardly, he adhered to the old church, but to the end he thought and wrote on religious things more freely than any theologian in the new churches: he questioned the Trinity and the sacraments and declared that there was much not authentic in the scriptural books. He even shared certain views of the popular movement, against Christians' taking oaths, for example.[37]

Hagen stated a paradox which many liberal writers were to

adopt in the nineteenth century. He enlarged the Enlightenment understanding of Erasmus as a freethinker; at the same time he repeated the old Protestant judgment on Erasmus' character: he was fearful, vacillating, cowardly. Erasmus was a bold thinker, but a weak man, his weakness arising from childhood experiences which broke a naturally lively spirit. The two sides are exposed in Hagen's treatment of the controversies with Hutten and Luther. In the first, Erasmus appears as weak and devious, Hutten as a straightforward soldier, avenging a betrayal and entering a preventive war against an ally threatening to go over to the other side. In the second, ie in the controversy over free will, Erasmus broke with the dogmatism and biblicism of Luther's party and confirmed his role as spokesman for the true reforming tendency.[38]

Erasmus was for Hagen the most forward-looking man of his age, the pioneer of modern thought. He was best able to lead and unify the various expressions of the reform movement because he understood and appreciated their variety and the mutual forbearance that variety required: 'he grasped the spirit of the time in its depth and very essence, and was thereby more tolerant towards differing views.' This is like Schleiermacher's interpretation of Erasmus' significance. Even though his motives were mixed in the 1520s – fear of disorder, envy of Luther as a more prominent leader – and outwardly he could do no better than a swinging neutrality, inwardly he remained true to his convictions: his critical, rationalist, radical convictions.[39]

There is, after all allowance has been made for Ranke's great superiority as writer and historian, one similarity and one dissimilarity between his and Hagen's views of Erasmus' historic role. Both saw him as an opposition figure, driven by various psychological needs, and constrained by the historical situation, to attack the literary, educational, theological, and ecclesiastical establishments. Ranke, however, saw his as a preliminary campaign, destroying outworks but no more. The real battle had to be fought on another field and the renovation of Christendom secured on other foundations, Luther's theological discoveries and spiritual vitality. For Hagen, the real reformation was the one led by and embodied in Erasmus: it pointed forward to the free society. Luther's 'reformation,' by contrast, was a retreat into dogmatism and authoritarianism.

None of these views was in essence new. Both Protestantism

and the Enlightenment had appreciated Erasmus' achievements as a critic of the old order. Ranke's view of his relation to Luther was a thoughtful restatement of the Protestant tradition and Hagen's a radical extension of a line taken in the Enlightenment and picked up by many liberal writers in the nineteenth century, as we shall see.

What is new and a significant contribution to Erasmus studies was their interest in his appeal to and relationship with different sections of opinion in contemporary Germany and public opinion generally. This gave a dynamic character to their appreciation of his historic role which goes well beyond the static categorizations – Protestant? Catholic? literary? theological? – which dominated writing about Erasmus before the historical revolution of the nineteenth century.

SEVEN

Nineteenth-Century France: Erasmus as Writer and Moralist

❧

We scarcely need reminding that the relation of form and substance, words and things, was a preoccupation of the sixteenth-century humanists. There was, they believed, no casual connection between what was said and how it was said; noble thought demanded noble expression; pure words exhibited a pure mind. Even in spheres hitherto seen as essentially technical and professional – theological controversy, for example – form and substance were held to be inseparable: how theological issues were presented was critical to the validity of their treatment; form and expression always carried religious and ethical overtones.[1] Recent studies have demonstrated that the thought of Erasmus himself may easily be misunderstood if studied apart from the literary or rhetorical forms chosen for its expression.[2]

Nineteenth-century observers, preoccupied with the Reformation controversies and the popular, especially the patriotic, movements associated with them, were interested mostly in what Erasmus had to say, in content or substance. Nevertheless, an awareness can be found of the relation between form and content, or at least a double interest in the ethical and the literary. This is especially so among French writers of the period. We are dealing with a kind of essayistic tradition which combines moral reflection with a sense of style and genre. J.M.N.D. (Désiré) Nisard (1806–88), for example, in a flamboyant essay whose well-turned phrases held a dangerous fascination for later authors, assessed Erasmus' character and influence but also used him in a controversy with the romantics.

The revolution of 1830 was a watershed for Nisard.[3] He inherited from a Bonapartist father hatred of the Bourbon restoration, he wrote for the opposition newspaper, the *Journal des Débats*, and fought at the barricades in July 1830. His political and literary commitments reinforced one another. He shared in 1828–9 the alienation of the younger romantic writers from the régime. He began as a supporter of the new Orleanist monarchy and a king (Louis Philippe) who, in his own words, 'worked instead of hunting and who had neither confessor nor mistress.'[4] But within two years his ardour had cooled; the new régime was not aggressive enough in supporting French interests abroad.

A literary change accompanied the political. Indeed, the ardour previously put into politics he now turned to literature. He rejected the romantics and especially their taste for the exotic and, as Saint-Beuve put it, deliberately set himself to defend French against foreign literature, established ages, reputations, and glories against the moderns – in short, the classical tradition against its recent challengers – and prose against poetic forms. He wrote literary historical works which were – again in Sainte-Beuve's words – erudite manifestos against modern poetry.[5] Nisard himself described the return to classical French language and literature (the literature of the seventeenth century and the language of Bossuet) as a corollary to pursuing a national policy abroad. All men of natural good sense, he declared, however led astray by contemporary literary caprice, would return eventually to the classical values. His own admiration for the classics, which would in a less combative age have remained in obscurity because without contradiction, must now become a lively, restless, aggressive faith, like all contested faiths.[6]

Erasmus does not make a neat fit with these preoccupations. Indeed, Nisard's different preoccupations – admiration for the Roman classics and sixteenth-century humanism, devotion to French seventeenth-century literature, and an aggressive patriotism – relate to one another somewhat uneasily. Nor had Nisard – in form or substance – abandoned romanticism as fully as he intended or imagined: patriotic fervours and the anecdotal, speculative, literary style of his essay on Erasmus demonstrate that. His heightened tones betray a self-consciousness essentially romantic.

Nevertheless, the essay on Erasmus, which first appeared in the *Revue des deux mondes* in 1835, gives evidence of the transition he had set for himself. Its primary purpose was to associate Erasmus with a tradition – in literature but also in behaviour – which had begun in the classical age, had been in Nisard's view the source of every subsequent renewal of civilization and was now the guarantee of its future. This Erasmus has much in common with the Erasmus of the Enlightenment. There are frequent comparisons with Voltaire and in an approving, not Coleridge's disapproving, sense. Nisard belongs to the 'liberal tradition' of nineteenth-century writing about Erasmus, whom he sees as anticipating a more open, rational, and tolerant religion and society. Behind the Enlightenment and liberal civilization for Nisard was the classical order of which Erasmus was a model and defender.[7]

Nisard intended his essay, not as biography, a genre of which he had a poor opinion, but as history, which would do justice to the complexity of the person, the restless activity of his life and its connections with the larger movements of humanity.[8] Nevertheless, he uses two episodes in Erasmus' life to build up the picture of the man of classical civility: his encounter, first, with the monks and, secondly, with Luther. Through all runs the contrast of the man and the age, the one, though under pressure, moderate, calm, and controlled, the other turbulent and tumultuous.

Nisard's depiction of Erasmus' association with the monastery follows the latter's own blackest account of it: he was introduced there by violence and deceit. His brother, who was physically strong but dim-witted and cunning and, therefore, well suited to be a monk, even before becoming a novice, had a hand in this misfortune. His early experiences determined Erasmus' attitude to the monks, which was one of implacable enmity, though prudently expressed. He constantly contrasted their drunkenness, ignorance, and hypocrisy with the ideals of the founders of their communities, which he admired. His colloquies against the monastic vows, at once prudent and daring, recall certain dialogues of Voltaire.[9]

Erasmus' relations with his age, on which the monks had still a dominant influence, were, Nisard says, ambiguous. He was so fearful of public opinion, of which in time he was to become a leader, indeed the master, that when he left the monastery he continued to wear the habit. He could both flatter and make fun of his patrons: 'sad contradictions of poverty, which posterity ought not to judge after dinner.' He was a 'timid and anxious' man; he longed for rest but was constantly forced into action; mild and benevolent, hating quarrels, he had constantly to take them up; he was physically small and weak with a constitution as brittle as glass. He was not naturally at home in his robust, embattled, and contradictory age.[10]

Of that age two classes of men were the type, 'the one representing material disorder, the other ignorance': the soldier and the monk. On the latter subject, Nisard used colourings drawn from his romantic inheritance. His monk is a Gothic monster:

> The monk, a person without parent or child, without past or future, wholly given to the present and its material pleasures, a kind of pilgrim camped as master in a foreign land; ... mixture of intolerant ignorance, of cunning, of cruelty, of debauchery, of superstition, of gross indolence, of stupid piety; ... restless, wild, in the midst of the general revival of literature and the arts, lowering his heavy eyelids before the light like a bird of the night before the day.

Erasmus could not help being the enemy of the monks; he had towards them, says Nisard, the rancour of one whom they had deprived of his natural disposition and his self-possession. They in return hated him more for his labours in recalling antiquity than for his insinuations of doubt in established dogmas. They feared religious controversy less than intellectual enlightenment. The man of letters was hated more than the church reformer.[11]

In such a world Erasmus could not enjoy the 'peaceable universality' of a Voltaire, rich, independent, not under pressure but with much leisure 'and no serious enemy.' Yet, paradoxically, in contradiction though he often was to his age, Erasmus may also be seen as the man for the time, a moment from which there was to flow a long succession of nobler times, and his significance lay there rather than in any personal or literary genius.[12] The reference to better times reveals Nisard's acceptance of the liberal idea of linear progress in history. Elsewhere, in assessing Erasmus' significance, he presents a more subtle view of how historical periods relate to one another.

Erasmus did not willingly sacrifice the present for the future: that is one key to Nisard's understanding of his conflict with Luther, to which all of the second part of Nisard's essay is devoted. The other key is the depiction of him as the man of classical restraint and moderation. The presentation here is not theologically sophisticated: while Luther was still a zealous Catholic, says

Nisard, Erasmus had already treated all the points of belief over which the Protestants would separate from the church. When Luther first spoke out, Erasmus had already won all enlightened people to the reform ideas. Despite these convergences, there was a stark contrast between the two men: Luther was an ardent reformer, appealing to the passions, Erasmus above all a philologist and incidentally a moderate reformer addressing the intelligence. Like all moderates, Erasmus wanted to give both sides their due; the complete victory of either party would be evil. He wanted to check the ambition of the one by giving due praise to the other. In this he was 'a model of that *civility* which he wanted so much to see in the Germans,' but this approach earned him the displeasure of both sides.[13]

Besides, Nisard adds, the moderate man often intervenes to bad effect in violent controversies; he hesitates too long and finally comes on 'rather as an actor, arrived after the raising of the curtain, throws over his shoulders the first costume that comes to hand, in order not to keep the audience waiting.' So Erasmus did not tackle Luther's new scholasticism head on but took up what, for a nineteenth-century liberal, was an incidental question, free will. Nisard praises Erasmus' eloquence 'nourished and seasoned with a certain, natural atticism,' the instrument of Demosthenes and Cicero; but the issue was a dead one.[14] What mattered, Nisard concludes in expressions reminiscent of Pierre Bayle, was his distinctiveness; he was neither Protestant nor Catholic, though sentiment and custom inclined him towards Catholicism. 'He remained the man of everything durable which human passions had hidden under formulae become battle-cries.'[15]

Erasmus was not one of those who does evil today for the sake of a good delayed for two centuries; he did not have the 'baneful foresight of our assassins of 1793, who dedicated themselves to being execrated for ten centuries in order to be rehabilitated and deified in the eleventh.' Nisard tilts at metaphysical history which blandly discerns good arising from evil and which asserts that, since Protestantism, despite its violence and passion, engendered the Enlightenment and the triumphs of 1789 and 1830, it should be embraced by all men of superior mind. In fact, the promise of the future rested with Erasmus (the man of sense and toleration) rather than with Luther (the man of force and passion): 'Which has the more life to-day, the philosophy of Christ or Lutheranism, dogma – either Protestant or Catholic – or the Christian ethic, the sects or liberty of conscience?'[16] Nisard is asserting, on the one hand, an unchanging morality by which historical characters in their own time should be judged and, on the other, the possibility of progress towards a more civilized and moral society.

There was a kind of heroism about Erasmus' last years in Basel. He was a martyr to his work. As the head of the moderate party, which by its very nature required of its adherents unceasing reflection and discussion, he remained at his task to the end without drawing breath, oblivious of time and season. His importance, like Voltaire's, lay in his drawing together and expressing the nobler aspirations of his time.[17]

Erasmus was not in Nisard's view a man of one idea; his mind was fluid, responsive, complex. His writings show imagination, intelligence, and a lively spirit. Though they fell short of classic art, which requires the expression of essential human truths in the matured forms of a native language, born of the nation and the soil, Erasmus had the best of the argument with the Ciceronians, because for him Latin was a living, personal language needing continual adjustment to new truths and new realities. He condemned servile imitation and spoke up for freedom and originality in using even the best of models.[18]

Erasmus knew how to address the public; he had the secret of making ideas at once agreeable and useful. 'He had ... the instinct of a thing for which Voltaire had the genius.' Nisard is close here to Ranke. The *Adagia*, in its recovery of classical wisdom, was a decisive book for the future of the European literatures. It was the first revelation of the double truth that modern humanity was heir to the ancients and that literature is essentially a deposit of the practical wisdom of mankind.[19]

It is hard to overlook the rhetorical exaggerations of Nisard's essay. This is not a work of scholarship and, in providing colourful phrases to later writers, it perhaps impeded fresh thought about Erasmus. Ideologically it added to Enlightenment views only its polemic against the metaphysical historians (like Villers). For all that, there is an appreciation of the true nature of Erasmus' social and cultural influence – pragmatic, sceptical, concrete – which is reminiscent, momentarily, of Coleridge. For Nisard himself, the association of this influence with the classical literary and cultural heritage was the point of importance.

True to his principles, Nisard criticized the lack of order and method, and blamed the 'lyrical exaltation' of Jules Michelet's

Histoire de France.[20] The romantic colouring he condemned in Michelet was not, as we have seen, altogether absent in his own writing and the two men shared a view of the Renaissance as a liberation of humanity. The first six volumes of the history of France covering the medieval period – in Gooch's view 'his most perfect and enduring work'[21] – appeared in the 1830s and early 1840s when Michelet (1798–1874) retained his early sympathy for medieval Catholicism. He returned to the volumes on the Renaissance and Reformation only after an interruption for the writing of his famous history of the French Revolution. During this interruption Michelet changed considerably. He broke with Catholicism and indeed Christianity. He came to believe that human spontaneity and solidarity, as expressed for example in the family, are endangered by religious institutions and dogmas. Christianity, a religion of grace rather than justice, nurtures an arbitrary and inequitable society. The work on the French Revolution expressed Michelet's new commitments. Henceforth, he was to recognize but one great actor in the historical drama – the people – and history itself became a progress (with detours and set-backs) towards humanity's full control over its own destiny.[22]

In the Renaissance, Michelet says in the seventh volume of his *Histoire de France* (1855), two Romes confronted one another, the false Rome erected on the fraudulent decretals of the canon law, and the eternal, civilizing Rome of antiquity. He sees the recovery of antiquity as a challenge to the false Rome: thus, the first printings of Virgil, Homer, Aristotle, and Plato were a 'holy work.' The new spirit undermined Christianity, although that was not a deliberate intention. Europe ran innocently, like a child, into the arms of its mother, antiquity. Michelet himself – he makes a characteristic personal aside – had prayed to 'Saint Virgil' before he was aware that one had done so already in the sixteenth century.[23]

The Renaissance was an immense act of the will, a creation out of nothing, because the civilization of the Middle Ages, lovingly re-created in Michelet's earlier volumes, was now moribund or dead. There was no prelude to the Renaissance as the Enlightenment was prelude to the French Revolution. The darkness deepened before dawn. The great effort of will was directed – the phrase was to become famous – towards the discovery of the world and of man.[24] Curiously, Michelet, historian of the people, attributes the effort and the achievement to heroic individuals –

Columbus, Luther, Copernicus; the surrounding society and civilization were too degenerate to restore themselves, and the people were held in the shrouds of ignorance and superstition, capable
of only sluggish movements towards renewal.[25]

Michelet includes Luther among the heroic individuals who
pioneered the restoration of humanity. He takes (in volume VIII
of the history) a positive view of the Reformation. In the Renaissance humanity, through its lively contact with antiquity and
the drive of its intellectual leaders towards discovery, was renewing itself. But it faltered, hesitated like a traveller on the edge
of the primeval American forest. The Reformation had to concentrate its forces and assert its principles, if the whole enterprise
were not to be aborted. 'The conscience of the time was in Germany.' When Rome was itself taking possession of the Renaissance, Pope Leo X was offering friendship to Erasmus, and
Germany was being bought and sold by politicians and indul-
gence-sellers, Luther gave powerful voice to the spiritual longings
of his people. Amid dark and threatening skies was a point of
piercing, steely blue. Here was the true renaissance, 'the renaissance of the heart.'[26]

Years before, Michelet had edited a book of materials on Luther.[27] He there admired Luther's frankness and personal force,
though he rejected his doctrine of grace as (like all forms of determinism) inimical to human freedom, and kept his sympathy
for the old church in its comprehensiveness.[28] Michelet did not
in fact arrive at an integrated portrait of the Reformer, at once
the liberator of consciences and the sworn enemy of the freedom
of the will. There were unresolved issues here for Michelet himself
in 1835. By 1855 there had been a resolution. Michelet's own
commitments had changed and the portrait of Luther was correspondingly simplified.[29] Now he is seen to have brought 'heroic
joy.' The Christianity of the Middle Ages and of antiquity lacked
joy. Luther's assurance of pardon released humanity for action
and freed it from vain terrors. Besides, his whole manner – whatever his teaching – suggested light and freedom. He was the
herald of broad daylight: 'this is an awakening in May at four
o'clock in the morning.' He was the father of modern man.[30]
Luther has become a hero in two senses: he represents the en-
lightening, progressive thrust of the Renaissance; he is close to
the people, an expression of the popular will.[31]

The presentation of Erasmus makes a great contrast to this. He

was not one of the heroes whose acts of will made the Renaissance, and yet he was critical to the story. When flood-waters
have gathered, one drop more is enough to break the dykes. The
publication of Erasmus' *Adagia* in Paris in 1500 was the final drop.
No masterpiece was ever received with greater enthusiasm. It
offered antiquity between the covers of a single book.[32]

Returning from Italy in 1838 Michelet had visited Basel. He
called it 'the Geneva of Erasmus,' city of Protestantism and rationalism, and there felt himself remote from the Italy he had just
left. Basel, he noted on a later visit, was a base for the modern
tradition which he defended: Erasmus, Luther, Shakespeare,
Montaigne, Rousseau, Voltaire. 'They have established freedom
of enquiry and prepared the guarantees of all kinds which make
for our security and dignity.' Erasmus stood at the beginning of
this tradition. At Basel the moral balance was struck between the
'philosophe' Erasmus, who taught the freedom of the human will
and its power to act, and the Protestant theologians who said
'faith alone.' Erasmus was really the *genius loci*; his bust stood
alone in the room where the Council of Basel had met and in the
cathedral his monument overlooked the communion table.[33]

All this presents a favourable picture of Erasmus, but the limits
to Michelet's admiration are severe. In the Luther *Mémoires* and
in the *Histoire de France* twenty years later the characterization
is the same. 'A critical and negative spirit,' he received Luther's
approaches coldly, with timid precaution (1519); in the debate
on free will (1524), 'cold and clever,' he struck some shrewd blows
against Luther. Intellectually Michelet inclined to the partisan of
free will but he responded unsympathetically to Erasmus' personality. He associated Erasmus with the Swiss and Rhineland
Protestants, the Zwinglis and the Bucers, in his view 'hard and
cold logicians,' who would destroy what Luther was struggling
to protect, 'the old Christian poetry.'[34]

Even in his own most characteristic works Erasmus was cold
and with little verve. His paradoxes often left good sense behind.
The *Praise of Folly*, says Michelet indignantly, if obtusely, even
includes the child among the fools and 'sees in love, in the sacred
mystery of generation, a ridiculous folly!' This is sacrilege.[35] The
revival of antiquity itself, where the less vigorous ancient works
(like Cicero's *De Officiis*) were chosen, could issue in a feeble
educational and cultural ideal, that of the 'honnête homme,' much

loved by French middlebrows but of little use for the education of the people.[36]

Michelet's Erasmus belongs to the Enlightenment; this is apparent from his association with the so-called 'modern tradition' and his link across the centuries with Voltaire. The liberal and anticlerical Michelet approved his restoration of antiquity as a standard by which his own degenerate age could be judged. The romantic and populist Michelet, however, found Erasmus unheroic and out of touch with the vital energies released by Luther. Michelet, in other words, shared the prejudice of religious, even clerical, writers among his contemporaries against the element of reserve, of scepticism – so-called coldness – in Erasmus' character. In separating him so completely from the popular life of his time, he missed points taken by Coleridge and even by Nisard.

Gaston Feugère (1836–90) wrote one of the two full-length studies of Erasmus to appear in French in the 1870s. Both were Catholic works but Feugère, who later taught the first class at the lycée Saint-Louis and whose book was crowned by the Academy, was especially interested in Erasmus as a writer. He was drawn to the sixteenth-century writers by his father, Léon-Jacques Feugère (1810–58), whose *Caractères et portraits du XVIᵉ siècle* was published posthumously. Nisard's liveliness and sympathy for his subject also attracted him.[37]

Feugère would like to have arranged Erasmus' writings according to the contemporary academic division into genres but concluded that this was impossible because a mixing of genres was characteristic of the Renaissance writers. Only one of Erasmus' works, the *Moriae encomium*, belonged exclusively to one genre, the satiric. The *Adagia* were typical of the rest, mixing theology, ethics, pedagogy, satire, erudition, even personal reminiscence.[38]

In seeing the *Folly*, for all its lightness and elegance, as a destructive and pagan work, Feugère followed a pattern set by Erasmus' critics in his lifetime and by the Enlightenment. He was aware of Folly's rapid transformations but did not fathom the work's different levels; for him, its last word was the pagan counsel to avoid seeming wiser than other men and disturbing one's rest with the futile hope of trying to reform them. The satire of the Renaissance moved away from the warm-hearted raillery and childish angers of the Middle Ages and approached the sectarian bitterness of the Reformation pamphlets. Thus, Erasmus may not have attacked the monastic principle, but his satire on the monks' lives was so mordant as to threaten monasticism as such.[39]

Erasmus' theological writings are, for Feugère, essentially of historical interest – for their criticism of scholasticism on the one side and of the Protestant Reformation on the other. His book on preaching (*Ecclesiastes*), despite its lack of organization, did have fine moral and psychological observations. The *Methodus* was not in fact a work of systematic theology; Erasmus' appeal for the direct study of scripture opened the way to individual interpretation. Erasmus' New Testament anticipated Bayle and Lessing by disguising audacious criticism in the modest forms of erudition, the indiscreet question and daring argument covered in qualifications.[40]

Feugère did not embrace the neo-scholasticism of some other Catholic writers in the second half of the nineteen century. Indeed, as we shall see, he shared to some extent the humanists' rejection of scholasticism. But he agreed with the neo-scholastic criticism of Erasmus for undermining the piety and Christian civilization of the Middle Ages. *Folly* weakened monasticism; the *Colloquia* were familiar, easy, delicate, mocking, 'à la Lucien'; the *Enchiridion* as a work of piety was cold (a reminiscence of Loyola's judgment).[41] Ceremonies and pious practices, which Erasmus condemned, are an effective forward defence for religion and to scorn them is to disturb the faith of the people. Once again, Feugère says, Erasmus was like Bayle who did not penetrate the sanctuary but came right up to the wall, measured its height, and placed ladders for rationalism to scale. As a kind of 'Montaigne théologien,' he insinuated doubts about the teaching of the Fathers. He assisted the Reformation but may also be linked across two centuries with Voltaire. As Bellarmine and Possevino had shown, he had an affinity with the Arians. Feugère associates him above all with the deists.[42]

In his political writings, on the education of princes or on war, Erasmus drew on classical commonplaces. They were none the less praiseworthy in sixteenth-century circumstances, and those against war achieved real eloquence because of the deep indignation infusing them. Erasmus, discontented rather than revolutionary, satirized abuses in government but had no program for removing them. In his writings political satire was still at an early stage. They were, like classical declamations, too vague and prolix. To be effective, political satire needs more practical application to affairs of state, and that in turn requires a more open political society.[43]

Erasmus stood, according to Feugère, at the beginning of the secularization of morality. Deductive ethics drawn from dogma were giving way to an ethics of conscience where faith, as Pascal said, was the point of arrival rather than of departure. The revival of antiquity brought forth a human and universal morality to challenge the exclusive claim of the Christian and theological. In Erasmus, the two streams, the pagan and the Christian, ran together; he did not want to uproot the theological tradition but rather to graft the green bough of antiquity on the dry, scholastic wood. Is there, Feugère asks, a tendency in Erasmus to confine the supernatural and turn religion into 'un spiritualisme conciliant'? He accepted dogma with resignation rather than confident faith, relegating it to an inaccessible height and surrounding it with respectful silence. Where Erasmus scored, Feugère recognizes, was in practical ethics. Like other empirical moralists, he found in marriage and the family the most favourable environment for the development of practical virtues. He had a sensitive appreciation of the needs of women and children. In his analysis of Erasmus' book on Christian marriage, Feugère is at his most responsive, making an interesting contrast with Michelet. The pedagogical writings evoke a similar sympathy, though the *Ciceronianus* is seen as missing the point that Latin could not survive as an everyday language and the hour of the vernaculars had come.[44]

In fact, Feugère is not, over all, unsympathetic to Erasmus and shows himself attentive to some of his subject's finer moral and psychological observations. Thus, he says, in perusing the 'calm and sensitive pages' of the work on Christian marriage, one can only regret that Erasmus did not live in more peaceful times which would have 'allowed his happy talent as a lively and penetrating moralist to be truly displayed.' Yet Feugère's whole presentation is shaped by a theological judgment, as the preceding paragraphs make clear. Though always prudent, Erasmus took a very free attitude towards the church: 'like the dove, he will fly away from the Ark but will leave a window open for his return.' Erasmus resisted the constraints imposed by both the doctrines and the institutions of the church. To that extent he prepared the way for rationalism and secularization.[45]

Historically, Feugère says in linking his life and his writings, Erasmus needs to be related to the two great controversies of his time, that of the Renaissance against scholasticism and that of the Reformation against the old church.[46] On the first, Feugère uses the language of the liberals, the language of darkness and enlightenment: thus, at the time of Erasmus' birth, the darkness was lifted only in Italy, though in northern Europe there were glimmers.[47] Feugère accepts the war against scholasticism – by the fifteenth century sterile and oversubtle – as a war of liberation. The question was: would this be a liberation into paganism, as for many in Italy? Or would a new Christian balance be struck, scholasticism adapting itself to the renewal of antiquity, the men of the Renaissance moderating their demands upon it? Erasmus did not come up to the measure of this opportunity. His criticism was too free and too equivocal to be a sure support for Christianity in the new age.[48]

The second controversy swallowed up the first. Just as the critics of French society in the eighteenth century did not foresee the revolution of which they were eventually to be the victims, Erasmus and his associates did not expect anything like Luther's appearance. In Germany at least, the Renaissance was the victim of the Reformation. Feugère recognizes that Erasmus' position was not a simple one: the historian must go beyond culling texts, which might prove him completely orthodox or a Lutheran before Luther, and try to arrive at a whole impression.[49] His dispositions were mobile, fluid, contradictory. Feugère is saddened by Erasmus' evasiveness in the early years of the Luther affair; he shares the post-romantic preference for those who enter boldly into the action, at the cost even of failures and mistakes. He adds that Erasmus' love of peace was deep and genuine.[50]

The contrast between Luther, passionate, dominating, appealing to the masses, and Erasmus, prudent, timid, appealing to an élite, is predictable. Less so is the argument that, since some of its causes – the general restlessness of the human spirit, the guelf-ghibbeline rivalry between Germans and Italians – were unrelated to Erasmus, his role in the Reformation must be seen as limited. In the free-will controversy (as his account proceeds, Feugère becomes more sympathetic), Erasmus represented good sense and, indeed, the human conscience. In attacking Luther on this question, he showed real courage. He was the ancestor of the Catholic minority who stood for toleration and – to an extent – freedom of thought during the wars of religion later in the century.[51] In the controversies of his last years he was moderate and resigned. He cared for the victory or defeat of neither party. Enough strong and lively writing came still from his pen for one to associate him with Cato who refused to allow bodily weakness to curb his spirit.[52]

Feugère takes care over his sketches of Erasmus' personality, his 'moral portrait.' There are some familiar traits. Thus he quotes (from Adolf Müller) Lavater's physiognomic study. Surprisingly (since it was a great favourite with nineteenth-century biographers), he calls it little-known. At the same time he shows some subtlety and understanding. One cannot impose unity on Erasmus' mind and personality. He had a 'supple vivacity.' He was full of contradictions, at once bold and timid, loving peace but making sharp sallies against his opponents. Despite his attacks on superstition, he prayed to St Genevieve against the plague, like a man who, when evening comes, slips into church to light a candle before the image of a saint he has ridiculed at midday. The contradictions arose from his environment and his experience; the hard circumstances of his early life made him both dependent on his society and resentful of it. Feugère accepts Erasmus' own suggestion that the pressures imposed on him as a boy justified his rancours against the monks, but he rightly rejects Müller's association of his nervous irritability with an essentially feminine upbringing. He loved friendship and has been unfairly charged with flattering the great – he was less obsequious than Voltaire.[53]

Erasmus cannot, Feugère concludes, be categorized, nationally or confessionally. He is best described as a citizen of the republic of letters. He was like the Renaissance itself – 'a confused and powerful activity, spreading, extending and dispersing itself on every side.'[54] Rigorous critical method must be abandoned if one is to judge aright this abounding life. Erasmus' intellectual work was the inquiring, impatient activity of a man of letters rather than the profound searching of a thinker. In the end his passion for letters gave unity to his life. He may be compared with Michelangelo throwing himself with fury on the marble.[55]

Feugère has touched something important here and has, of course, escaped the stereotyped contrast between the cold and rational Erasmus and the passionate Luther. The German critic Ludwig Geiger considered the book a collection of more or less good essays rather than a truly scholarly work.[56] Like the other writers considered in this chapter, even Michelet,[57] Feugère belonged in the tradition of literary and ethical reflection. Though his theological judgments are, when summarily defined, as severe as those of other Catholic critics, a certain benevolence is cast over the whole portrait by Feugère's personal response to Erasmus' own moral perceptions and his sympathy for the psychological strains imposed by his life and circumstances.[58]

This chapter, which began with Désiré Nisard, will end appropriately with Emile Amiel whose *Erasme: Un libre-penseur du XVIe siècle* combines, as Nisard's essay had done, a liberal, progressive view of history and a commitment to classicism. Amiel's book was the last to sustain that particular combination.

Amiel (1824–97) was a councillor in the Côte d'Or with a special interest in educational questions.[59] He argued for the streaming of pupils, the gifted into classical schools, those with more utilitarian interests into professional schools. Erasmus was relevant to this controversy because, said Amiel, to him the West owed its classical system of secondary schooling. France in particular was the heir to Latin culture and her mind would be impoverished and she would be deprived of her élite if the classical tradition, already threatened, were weakened further. The classics were best fitted to inculcate in youth 'the general and primordial sentiments of humanity, virtually the same in all ages.'[60]

The other line of thought in the book makes Erasmus the pioneer of modern religion and, to an extent, of the liberal political system. He 'secularized the mind; he created free research in religious and social science.' Before Descartes he applied 'the modern method which allows only demonstrable truths.' Sceptical and freethinking, he began the work which Voltaire crowned.[61] The strictures of Luther and Aleander, papal legate in Germany at the height of the Luther affair, are to be read as praises by the modern mind: Erasmus had freed himself from the confines of orthodox Christianity. But he was not an atheist or materialist. His aim was to 'generalize' the Christian faith, to restore antiquity certainly but also to preserve the purity and clarity of the Sermon on the Mount, 'ce résumé sublime d'une morale exquise.' His Christian philosophy was a composite of metaphysics and morality comparable to philosophic deism. He was the ancestor of Renan. He also foreshadowed the anticlerical ideology of the Third Republic.[62]

Amiel's presentation of Erasmus' various writings is consistent with this view of him. He gives, as did Michelet, an exaggerated importance to the first edition of the *Adagia*. It was, according to Amiel, composed when Erasmus was already committed to church reform and joined with John Colet in an attack on scholasticism, which had become useless verbiage, 'a complete nothing.' It revealed a critical, sceptical, and 'frondeur' tendency of mind. Amiel interprets *Moriae encomium (Praise of Folly)* as a reform manifesto and a call to battle. Michelet lacked his usual sagacity when he condemned it as cold. Erasmus' light-hearted treatment of sex was but a lead-in to his real objective, an attack on the abuses of the church. His *Colloquia* express a modern naturalism – one can imagine oneself listening to a contemporary of Condillac and Helvétius.[63]

In the last report Erasmus rejected both sides in the Reformation struggle. He was alienated from the old church. 'Despite some light retractions to which he descended in order not to give himself away completely, he was not and did not wish to be within the Catholic tradition.' Nor did he side with the Reformers. 'Convinced by neither side, at bottom sceptical on many points, was it a crime for him to refuse to sacrifice the repose of his old age to quarrels that left him indifferent?'[64]

This conclusion determines the relative places Amiel would give Erasmus and Luther in the progress of the human mind. Erasmus was far ahead of Luther in that freer spirit which (like Abelard's) accepted Socrates among the saints. 'Abelard and Erasmus were the men of the future; Luther, for all his glory, was only the apostle of the past, Christian and even Hebrew.' Appearances here easily deceive. Luther was revolutionary by temperament; he moved the masses by means not at the command of the more prudent and tractable Erasmus. Yet in the long run Luther's 'Jéhovisme' obstructed progress. Erasmus, less revolutionary in avowal and by temperament, was more so in fact.[65]

Amiel showed an unusual interest in Erasmus' political writings. Erasmus' political expressions were, he says, democratic, a foretaste of reforms long demanded in vain, 'comme un programme anticipé de notre 1789.' Erasmus was a liberal; his preferred constitution was a model of the Charters of 1815 and 1830. With that analogy there could be no inconsistency in calling him a 'conservateur' in the best sense. He did not encourage social disorder. If he openly declared his convictions, he also aimed, in his moral teaching, at keeping the people – for its own sake – within the bounds of custom and obedience. In antiquity he saw the source not of unrest but of 'practical reason and good sense.' He was not in sixteenth-century circumstances a supporter of unbridled freedom of the press whose inconveniences, Amiel adds, we experience today. He was prudent and one of the sources of the *politique* party which sought later to moderate the confessional struggles.[66]

Unlike most nineteenth-century writers, Amiel was not preoccupied with Erasmus' character and its alleged weaknesses. He was sceptical about Lavater's physiognomy. He rejected Müller's charge that Erasmus learned dissimulation from his pre-monastic and monastic experiences. In friendship – again contrary to Müller – he was not cold and self-seeking. The German biographer's judgment was, says Amiel, distorted by Erasmus' refusal to join Luther. In controversy, he could sometimes lack sang-froid but elsewhere he shows 'the suppleness and the freedom of a man who will neither break nor yield.' He would have made a superb diplomat.[67]

Compared with much nineteenth-century writing, these are subtle judgments. That is, of course, 'relatively speaking.' They are a large part of Amiel's modest contribution to the history of Erasmus interpretation. His use of Erasmus in defence of the humanist tradition in education links him to Nisard and other writers with predominantly literary or rhetorical interests. Otherwise, anachronisms abound: Erasmus and Renan, Erasmus and the Charters of 1815 and 1830. His religion is, so to speak, vaporized and his politics are given a precise constitutional form appropriate to the nineteenth but not to the sixteenth century. The mix suits well a conservative republican and anticlerical of the second decade of the Third Republic. This Erasmus was 'well devised for advancing the struggle against clericalism on the one hand and for restraining social disorder on the other.'[68]

•

The writers considered in this chapter present a consistent picture of Erasmus and his historical significance: he attacked scholasticism, broke with authoritarian religion, prepared the way for modern toleration, even for rationalism and deism. For Nisard and Amiel this was a matter for praise, for Feugère of complaint, while Michelet hailed the achievement but was left cold by the personality. The picture derived from the Enlightenment and was, by the nineteenth century, an orthodoxy.

These writers – Michelet apart – judged Erasmus' character less severely than German writers obsessed by the antithesis: the weak Erasmus, the heroic Luther or Hutten. The difference was not, however, due to nationality or confession; it related rather to the whole approach of the French writers. Excessively rhetorical, often superficial, discursive rather than rigorous, they nevertheless had the great virtue of seeking moral guidance and illumination from their study of Erasmus and so touched the core of his being. They also recognized that there was a connection between the wholesome things he taught and his sincerity and integrity as a writer. This led them to a more thorough appreciation, in the literary sense, of his writings. The combination of moral and literary reflections did some justice to Erasmus and anticipated the more subtle discussions in this century of the relation in his work between substance and form.

EIGHT

Liberalism: Erasmus as Sceptic, Rationalist, and Modern Man

꿌

During the confessional age nothing in Erasmus' writings was used against him more often than his association of himself with ancient scepticism: 'So far am I from delighting in "assertions" that I would readily take refuge in the opinion of the Skeptics ...' Luther's retort, 'The Holy Spirit is no Skeptic ...,' has been repeated by Protestant controversialists to the present day.[1] Catholic observers have accused Erasmus of corroding – through doubt and uncertainty – the dogmatic substance of the faith. It has recently been argued that to take the sceptical position was not to state a preference for doubt but rather to follow a method in matters of controversy, the method of comparing opinions, testing them in moderate and courteous discussion, and deciding for the more probable.[2]

Heirs of the Enlightenment, in seeking to claim Erasmus for themselves, took scepticism in their sense and attributed to him their doubts about all forms of dogmatic religion. This was the reverse of the confessional coin: they praised what the dogmatists (Catholic and Protestant) had blamed. Erasmus so seen was a congenial figure to nineteenth-century liberals.

Over the last three centuries, said Lecky, 'a certain cast of thought or bias of reasoning' had gained a marked ascendancy in Europe: 'it leads men on all occasions to subordinate dogmatic theology to the dictates of reason and of conscience, and, as a necessary consequence, greatly to restrict its influence upon life.' He called this tendency the 'spirit of Rationalism.'[3] The subordination, even rejection, of dogmatic, authoritarian religion is one ingredient of the liberalism to which, in different ways, the authors to be treated in this chapter subscribed. A second is a progressive view of history. Modernity became a value and standard by which past episodes and individuals might be judged. In the mainstream of Whig historiography, the Tudor and Stuart despotisms, the events of the 1640s and 1650s and the Glorious Revolution of 1688 had to be related to both the medieval and the modern constitutions. There was a consensus in favour of a substantial continuity in constitutional development from the thirteenth to the nineteenth century, though significant differences in philosophy and in the interpretation of individual events could remain.[4]

In the works that interest us, the Reformation was the problematic event. Where did it stand on the scale of modernity, in relation to the 'cast of thought or bias of reasoning' which subordinated dogmatic theology to 'the dictates of reason and of conscience'? The writers of the Protestant Enlightenment had already shown that, within a broad consensus that counted the Reformation as progress over the Middle Ages, very different answers could be given to this question. Among nineteenth-century liberals the harsher judgment of the Reformation prevailed. At best it was a 'negative revolution,' necessary, that is, 'to the destruction of discredited ideas and institutions in order that a new and higher order might succeed'; at worst it was 'obscurantist reaction,' destroying, by its revival of religious enthusiasm, the seeds of progress and enlightenment produced by the humanism of the Renaissance.[5]

Erasmus was a key piece in the assembling of these interpretations. Above all, he could be presented as the preferred option: he was said to have cut loose from the authoritarian and dogmatic religion which still, to a degree, held fast the Reformers. Gibbon and Semler had seen him so already in the eighteenth century. His name could be associated with other nineteenth-century developments which liberal writers counted as evidence of progress and of the triumph of reason and conscience over dogma and superstition: the advances in the critical and historical study of the scriptures, the widening of religious toleration and, generally, the opening up of religious questions to free enquiry and discussion. For all this were antecedents, at least from the time of Bayle and Le Clerc. Erasmus' relation to political liberalism – an extension of political rights without threatening the constitutional order – remained to be explored; up to the nineteenth century his 'political' writings had attracted little notice. It was unlikely that much connection would be made between him and the most revolutionary of all changes in nineteenth-century thought, those in natural science.

Certain liberal presuppositions were widely diffused in the nineteenth century, above all the idea of progress towards a larger toleration and a freer society. One can speak of liberal Anglicans and liberal Protestants. Writers in these categories – seeking accommodation between liberal and Christian presuppositions – will appear in a later chapter. Those considered here are substantially free either of the main Christian tradition altogether or of the Trinitarian formulation of it.

Henry Hallam (1777–1859) was the most self-effacing of the Whig historians, separated from the public (unlike Macaulay) by a 'dignified reticence and absorption in severe studies.'[6] Private fortune, inherited from his father who had been a canon of Windsor and dean of Bristol, and undemanding public employment enabled him to withdraw from legal practice and pursue studies which issued in his *View of the State of Europe during the Middle Ages* (1818) and *Constitutional History of England from the Accession of Henry VII to the Death of George II* (1827). Personally reserved, Hallam shared the confident vision of the Whig historians, generally and of the Whig society in which he moved: despite the darkness of past epochs – Middle Ages, Reformation, Tudor and Stuart despotism – an ordered liberty had emerged early in England and, through all vicissitudes, had been providentially preserved and refined.[7] Hallam's confidence in the future of the constitution was not heedless, however; he recoiled from the French Revolution, 'had little confidence in the instinctive wisdom of the people,' and opposed the Reform Bill of 1832.[8]

Hallam's Erasmus appears in a work very different in character from his *Constitutional History*: the *Introduction to the Literature of Europe in the Fifteenth, Sixteenth, and Seventeenth Centuries*. Yet, the constitutional struggles and the revolution are by no means absent. With the previous generation – the Gibbons, Herders, Wielands, and a host of lesser fry – he saw the Reformation across the revolution. Strains of scepticism and pessimism about aspirations for change appear in his attitude to both.[9] A figure whose relations with the Reformation were at best ambiguous was bound to arouse his interest and sympathy.

The *Introduction to the Literature of Europe* is a work of remarkable range. On reaching the period 1520–50, Hallam broke his material into separate chapters by genre, the chapter titles covering 'ancient literature,' 'theological literature,' 'speculative, moral, and political philosophy' (and jurisprudence), 'the literature of taste,' and 'scientific and miscellaneous literature.' Though he saw himself in the succession of the encyclopaedic writers, like Possevino, Morhof, Bayle, Brucker, and Eichhorn, he insisted that the work be not used 'as a book of reference on particular topics' but read rather 'as an entire and synoptical work,' a daunting thought, given its scale and form, even for readers of his own time.[10]

Hallam claimed – justly, by all accounts – to have quoted 'no passage which I have not seen in its own place.'[11] For Erasmus, he used the letters and works in the Leiden edition; he knew the essays by Bayle and Le Clerc and the biographies of Jortin and Burigny; he knew at least some of the literature on the Hutten controversy. On the Reformation, he referred to the established histories by Sleidan, Seckendorf, Gerdes, Sarpi, von der Hardt, Schmidt, and Mosheim. He considered the evangelical Milner 'highly prejudiced.' A note in a late edition (1847) paid tribute to Ranke, 'as impartial as he is learned and penetrating.' He quoted Luther's *Table Talk* in the English translation.[12]

Erasmus first appears, with Guillaume Budé, as the pioneer – at the cost of 'incessant labour' and much privation – of Greek studies in northern Europe and as the author of the *Adagia*, 'doubtless the chief prose work of this century beyond the limits of Italy.' Hallam's opinion of the state of learning in the last part of the fifteenth century was cast in the language of the philosophical historians, though typically judicious: there was in the north an active and progressive spirit, and classical learning and the invention of printing promised a future harvest, but the progress of the human mind in the fifteenth century was limited.[13] In the new century, Erasmus – again with Budé – was the leader. In the quarrel between the two men, Erasmus was the aggressor, having the 'unlucky inability to restrain his pen from sly sarcasm,' so multiplying the enemies that another trait in his character, 'its spirit of temporising and timidity,' was always raising up.[14]

Despite these and other failings, it was Erasmus who gave lustre to that age. His superiority rested on 'his quickness of apprehension, united with much industry, his liveliness of fancy, his wit and good sense. He is not a very profound thinker, but an acute observer; and the age for original thinking was hardly come.' There seems here an echo of Coleridge. Erasmus' Latin, if short of classical elegance, was suited to his qualities – 'fluent, spirited, and never at a loss to express his meaning.'[15]

Of all Erasmus' works, Hallam deals most fully with the 'political' essays in the 1515 edition of the *Adagia*. These touch closely Hallam the political historian and conservative Whig. He saw justice in Erasmus' invective – he, like More, had 'a just sense of the oppression of Europe in that age by ambitious and selfish rulers.' However, his bitterness and freedom of language were excessive: he hates kings and priests 'with the fury of a philosopher of the last century' (this is in reference to the 'Sileni Alcibiadis'); nothing 'in the most seditious libel of our own time' was more cutting against regal government than the picture of the eagle in 'Scarabeus aquilam quaerit.' At the end of that essay he represents the monks as beetles 'with equal bitterness and more contempt,' though Hallam adds the justification that 'Erasmus knew that the regular clergy were not to be conciliated, and resolved to throw away the scabbard.'[16] The judicious Hallam saw an irony in these declamations. The fact that their author was tolerated, indeed honoured, by the 'tyrants' suggests a more favourable view of them than his; with princes and nobles, he was throughout his life a privileged person.[17]

Hallam's commentary on these essays was not particularly penetrating. He was too quick to judge them from his standpoint. But he did a service in drawing attention to them – they were, he believed 'very little known.'[18] It will be important to ask how far his nineteenth-century successors followed his lead.

That he saw in the controversies between the old and the new learning a war between darkness and light links Hallam to the historiography of the Enlightenment. 'Through all the palaces of Ignorance went forth a cry of terror at the coming light – "A voice of weeping heard and loud lament." The aged giant was roused from sleep, and sent his dark hosts of owls and bats to the war. One man above all the rest, Erasmus, cut them to pieces with irony or invective. They stood in the way of his noble zeal for the restoration of letters.' His *Folly* was directed above all at the mendicant monks and was welcomed by all who hated them and loved merriment, although 'grave men, as usual' (like Dorpius) were uneasy at the use of ridicule.[19]

The Reformation bulks large in Hallam's book, though he came to it unwillingly and had little sympathy for it. He makes an explicit analogy between the Reformation and the French Revolution and its aftermath which reveals his conservative Whiggish preference for controlled change. Both were against the ordinary course of human history, where traditional notions and sentiments dominate.

> In each, the characteristic features are a contempt for antiquity, a shifting of prejudices, an inward sense of self-esteem leading to an assertion of private judgment in the most uninformed, a sanguine confidence in the amelioration of human affairs, a fixing of the heart on great ends, with a comparative disregard of all things intermediate. In each there has been so much of alloy in the motives, and, still more, so much of danger and suffering in the means, that the cautious and moderate have shrunk back, and sometimes retraced their own steps rather than encounter evils which at a distance they had not seen in their full magnitude.[20]

A movement so described could not be attractive to Hallam, though the depiction had the merit of recognizing that the Reformation, as a 'great working in the public mind' and a 'revolution in religious sentiment,' could not be reduced to particular theological controversies.[21] Luther had behind him the 'prodigious force of popular opinion'; no great revolution can be carried forward without popular passion and, Hallam adds, folly.[22]

Hallam expected what he called 'unreasonable cavilling' at his views on Luther and the Reformation. In a long note in the 1847 edition of his book he defended them against Luther's English apologists, especially Julius Hare. Luther was, he agreed, 'an instrument of Providence for a signal good,' but his teachings were paradoxical, antinomian, 'preposterously contradictory to natural morality and religion,' and had the Anabaptist fanatics as 'their legitimate brood.' Luther was no liberal.[23] Hallam had not any real sense for the dynamics of Luther's thought; he judged it from the standpoint of a broad natural theology.

A religious revolution of a popular and violent kind under a leader passionate, dogmatic, and contradictory: this is the background to Hallam's last references to Erasmus. His summary is: 'He was the first conspicuous enemy of ignorance and superstition, the first restorer of Christian morality on a Scriptural foundation, and, notwithstanding the ridiculous assertions of some moderns that he wanted theological learning, the first who possessed it in its proper sense, and applied it to its proper end.'[24]

Erasmus did not, like Thomas More, go 'violently back to the extreme of maintaining the whole fabric of superstition.' He could fairly claim to have prepared the way for the Reformers and shared some tenets and certainly some enemies with them. His *Colloquia* of 1522, for example, spared neither the clergy nor the practices of the church: 'No one who desired to render established institutions odious could set about it in a shorter or surer way.' There were opinions of the Reformers he did not share and he condemned their violent language; he feared the evils arising from 'the presumptuousness of ignorant men in judging for themselves in religion' and sincerely wished to preserve the unity of the church, 'which he thought consistent with much latitude of private faith.' The Reformation, he concluded, promoted neither virtue nor learning.[25]

This mixed response to the Reformation expressed both character traits and a cast of mind. Erasmus' letters, admits Hallam, reveal his failings. 'An extreme sensibility to blame in his own person, with little regard to that of others; a genuine warmth of friendship towards some, but an artificial pretence of it too frequently assumed; an inconsistency of profession both as to persons and opinions, partly arising from the different character of his correspondents, but in a great degree from the varying impulses of his ardent mind.' That mind could easily see different points of view on any subject. His learning as well as his disposition kept him indecisive.[26]

Hallam's location on the range of Erasmus interpretations can best be determined by recognizing that he shared the Enlightenment prejudice against medieval religion and at the same time rejected the attachment of contemporary evangelicals to the Reformers.[27] He recognized the magnitude of the Reformation as a historical movement but did not approve it. It is reasonable to infer that, like Gibbon, he would have preferred an alternative reformation under the sign of Erasmus. Change in both church and government should arise from debate within the educated élite and occur by persuasion. He admired the sceptical temper, especially when applied to disputes over dogma, party strife, and popular agitation.

Hallam's comments on individual works confirm his portrayal of Erasmus as a lively mind, a sensitive observer, and a prudent reformer. The *Ciceronianus* distinguished, 'in a spirit of sound taste,' between just imitation and servility. 'The object of the Italian scholars was to write pure Latin, to glean little morsels of Roman literature, to talk a heathenish philosophy in private, and leave the world to its own abuses. That of Erasmus was to make men wiser and better by wit, sense, and learning.' In the *Colloquia* one finds a morality without austerity and a piety without superstition. 'The dialogue is short and pointed, the characters display themselves naturally, the ridicule falls in general with skill and delicacy; the moral is not forced, yet always in view.'[28]

In Mark Pattison (1813–84) there is a more thorough scepticism than in Hallam. The latter had, certainly, the Enlightenment's contempt for both superstition and enthusiasm. He was always ready to judge and few escaped his censure.[29] Yet, despite the failings of individuals, events took mostly a good turn; beneath the troubled, murky surface wholesome currents flowed. One can speak of a general progress of the human mind. For Pattison every victory was hard-won and might be short-lived. Bitter experiences of life, both public and private, and an insecure personality produced a liberalism more precarious than the grave Whiggery of Hallam. Affirmation was snatched from doubt and despair.[30] The view of history was more catastrophic.

His experience of Tractarianism in the 1830s and 1840s was decisive for Pattison's attitudes. He saw clear correspondences between the destinies of Erasmus' generation and his own. He entered Oriel College, Oxford, as an unseasoned undergraduate from a north-of-England evangelical home at a moment comparable – so he later thought – with the third decennium of the sixteenth century. Then reaction and obscurantism and sterile theological controversy had submerged nascent humanism. 'The *"sacrificio d'intelletto"* of Loyola took the place of the free and rationalising spirit with which Erasmus had looked out upon the world of men.' So in the years after 1830 liberals gave way to Tractarians at Oriel, 'the "Tracts" desolated Oxford life, and suspended, for an indefinite period, all science, humane letters, and the first strivings of intellectual freedom ...' That is how he saw Tractarianism in the last year of his life; but at the time he was its devotee and Newman's disciple and associate. He was, he said, less convinced by argument than compelled by 'the inner force of an inherited pietism of an evangelical type.'[31] When the crash came with Newman's conversion in 1845, that impulse had spent itself; he was ready, as he saw it, to come out from under the shadow of fanaticism. Another principle had been taking root in Pattison, faith in the rational faculties and in the sole efficacy of the life of the mind. From the fiasco of his association with Tractarianism, he emerged believing 'in the power of the intellect as the sovereign expression of an almighty hand.'[32]

Thus he treated his own experience and Oxford's as a type for the history of the European mind from the fifteenth to the nineteenth centuries. In each case, the beginnings of enlightenment were put out by revived dogmatism and fanaticism. The outcome for both Erasmus and Pattison was the same: they were left isolated and defensive. It is tempting to find in Pattison a more personal bond with Erasmus, a sense of shared misfortunes (though of very different kinds) and an envy of certain characteristics of the great humanist, his sociability and openness to the world. Pattison suffered much: his father, a Yorkshire rector, became mentally unstable and violent in 1851; he (himself) failed, through intrigue among the electors, to become, as he and the College expected, rector of Lincoln College, to which he had devoted his energies; ten years later, he made an unhappy marriage. He was alienated from his family, in a sense from Oxford (though finally elected rector in 1861) and, at a deep level, from the church, though he continued to officiate. The picture was not wholly black: he had success as a teacher and in university reform; he deliberately chose the life of study.[33] But contemporaries found certain character traits dominant: he was bitter, sardonic, unable to give or receive affection, restless, morbidly introspective.[34] The bitterness cannot be understood without reference back to the Tractarian experience. 'It made him hate what he had left, and all that was like it, with the bitterness of one who had been imposed upon, and has been led to commit himself to what he now feels to be absurd and contemptible, and the bitterness of this disappointment gave an edge to all his work.'[35]

Pattison's Erasmus is then a determined anticlerical. 'As he

loathed fish so he loathed clerical fanaticism.' Like all the learned
of his age, he wanted to see the power of the clergy broken, 'as
that of an obscurantist army arrayed against light.' He also recoiled from the 'new fanaticism' of the Reformers. 'Theological
historians' have condemned him as a trimmer or as one who,
though Protestant at heart, declined to avow this for fear of losing
his worldly advantages. In fact, he was 'one of those natures to
which partisanship is an impossibility.' Theological questions did
not attract him and became odious when infused with party passion. Not timidity, but reasonableness kept him neutral. 'His mind
had no metaphysical inclination; he was a man of letters, with a
general tendency to rational views on every subject which came
under his pen.'[36]

Pattison's view of Erasmus' larger historic role appears in the
familiar comparison with Voltaire. The two stood in very different
relations to the church and Christianity. It was not possible for
Erasmus in his age like Voltaire in his to create a substitute for
Christianity. But he achieved unintentionally what he could not
deliberately envisage: he shook the structure of the church in all
its parts. Erasmus was a Voltaire in spite of himself. If he 'was
unlike the 18th century rationalist in that he did not declare war
against the church, but remained a Catholic and mourned the
disruption, he was yet a true rationalist in principle. The principle
that reason is the one only guide of life, the supreme arbiter of
all questions, politics and religion included, has its earliest and
most complete exemplar in Erasmus.' He does not announce the
rights of reason dogmatically so much as exercise them practically.
His writings are pervaded by an 'unconscious freedom' and this
is their great attraction. Erasmus represents for Pattison an un-
selfconscious stage of the Enlightenment.

It is not surprising that he made a somewhat severe judgment
on Erasmus' learning but qualified it immediately by referring to
his connections with the real life of his time. His Latin was 'far
removed from any classical model' but had qualities well above
purity. Latin was for him a spoken, not a dead language. His page
had the 'flavour of life and not of books.' He 'was not a "learned"
man in the special sense of the word' but far more, the 'man of
letters,' 'the first who had appeared in Europe since the fall of
the Roman empire.' His acquirements in learning 'were all brought
to bear upon the life of his day.' 'In editing a father, or a classic,
he had in view the practical utility of the general reader, not the

accuracy required by the guild of scholars.' In fact, his editions are full of blunders. He had, in Pattison's strait-laced opinion, the misfortune of being best known by his slightest works, the *Colloquia* and *Moriae encomium*. The *Adagia* demonstrates perfectly the balance sought by Pattison, man of learning divorced from, but envious of those in touch with, the real world. This was 'a mere commonplace book' but just what the public wanted, 'a manual of the wit and wisdom of the ancient world for the use of the modern.'

Similarly, Erasmus' edition of the New Testament has no value as critical scholarship though, if he did nothing to solve the critical problem, he at least had the honour of first propounding it. Its significance lay in its influence on opinion. 'It contributed more to the liberation of the human mind from the thraldom of the clergy than all the uproar and rage of Luther's many pamphlets.' The exposure of errors in the Vulgate gave a shock to the credit of the clergy comparable to that given by the astronomical discoveries of the seventeenth century.[37]

For Pattison, then, it was Erasmus' usefulness to the social life of his time that made him interesting and important. He was useful in two ways: he transmitted the wisdom of the ancient world, he challenged what was oppressive and stultifying in his society and especially in the church. That Erasmus, for all his vast reading, was no bookworm and had a living connection with contemporary society had been seen by Coleridge; Ranke and Hagen had recognized his appeal to public opinion. It is a tribute to Pattison's sensitivity that he, as one for whom, in the judgment of contemporaries, study was its own object and turning it to practical use was to corrupt it,[38] should emphasize the practical side of Erasmus' genius. There was here some attraction of opposites.

Pattison could, by contrast, find a personal likeness in his portrait of Erasmus as a free man, ie the detached Erasmus. The latter kept his cherished independence by a life of constant movement, never settling and becoming dependent, and also by the careful management of his finances, above all by attracting and not putting at risk the presents and pensions that in middle life were showered upon him. In the opening columns of his essay, Pattison is preoccupied with these two topics. The life of movement met a psychological need in Erasmus. Until he was fifty, 'the agitation of locomotion, new places, and fresh faces were a necessity to him. An over-excited nervous sensibility was at the bottom of this feverish restlessness.' If he was cautious not to give offence to the powerful in church and state, he was also 'most anxious to avoid dependence on any individual. It suited him to be always competed for, and never to sell himself.'[39] That Erasmus valued his independence and in that sense lived for himself had been observed in his lifetime and often reiterated. The image of the free man appealed to writers affected by romanticism. No one before Pattison had sought a consistent psychological explanation.[40] Pattison's introspection, his own restlessness, expressed not in constant movement but in ceaseless mental activity, predisposed him, one must conclude, to giving this account of Erasmus' personality.[41]

What is impressive is the link Pattison makes between the psychological traits of Erasmus, as he describes them, and the openness to the world that gave him his historical importance.

His highly nervous organization made his feelings acute, and his brain incessantly active. Through his ready sympathy with all forms of life and character, his attention was always alive. The active movement of his spirit spent itself, not in following out its own trains of thought, but in outward observation. No man was ever less introspective, and though he talks much of himself, his egotism is the genial egotism which takes the world into its confidence, not the selfish egotism which feels no interest but in its own woes.

In this remarkable portrait the neurotic, self-pitying elements are washed away and all that is positive and life-affirming drawn out. Erasmus, Pattison concludes, was a man of many moods but not inconsistent. Underneath is unity of character. 'His seeming inconsistencies are reconciled to apprehension, not by a formula of the intellect, but by the many-sidedness of a highly impressible nature.'[42]

Erasmus not only enjoyed but used his freedom. He directed his satiric raillery, not only against priests and monks, but also against nobles, princes, and kings. 'No 18th century republican has used stronger language than has this pensioner of Charles v.' How, Pattison asks, did he not suffer for such outspokenness? He died while the Catholic revival 'with its full antipathy to art and letters' was still in its infancy; he carefully remained in the empire where (compared with the more violent Reformers and revolutionaries) he 'passed for a moderate man.'[43]

This essay was one of the seven Pattison contributed to the ninth edition of the *Encyclopaedia Britannica*.[44] John Morley considered them 'all terse, luminous and finished' and took the piece on Erasmus in particular as demonstrating the highest type of criticism which recognized the duty of going beyond 'texts or abstract ideas or general movements or literary effects' and of conveying the 'moral and intellectual configuration' of its subject. Pattison's own debts are indicated in his bibliography: he recognized Le Clerc's 'Life' as the common foundation of the long list of modern biographies, which have all told essentially the same story.[45] Thus his own intention, as Morley rightly saw, was less to recount the biographical details than to sum up a personality and a historical presence and influence.

What most attracts the modern reader and may be counted as Pattison's distinctive contribution is his depiction of Erasmus' personal style, his literary personality, which was different in important ways from Pattison's own. He was lively, practical, sociable, and outgoing. Otherwise, Pattison's interpretation is tied firmly to liberal presuppositions: the Reformation was a clash of dogmatisms; Erasmus could not be indifferent to the religious issues or cut loose from the church – Pattison recognizes the danger of anachronism – but he was temperamentally averse to dogma and metaphysics; he was 'in principle' a rationalist, a practical rationalist who made reason 'the one only guide of life.' This linked him to the Enlightenment and nineteenth-century liberalism.

The most complete statement in the nineteenth century of this view of Erasmus is to be found in its most important biography, the two-volume work by the Scottish Unitarian R.B. Drummond (1833–1920), which Pattison quoted with approval. One significant difference subsist between Pattison and Drummond: the latter is closer to the main Protestant position on Erasmus' relation to the Reformation, which was, for Drummond, more than a rival dogmatism – Erasmus, he says, failed to see its liberating force. The tone of this book, which is a relatively youthful work,[46] is cool, somewhat olympian and detached, with an irony less pessimistic than Hallam's or Pattison's but with an equal disdain for religious fervours – in the sixteenth or the nineteenth century.

Drummond is in fact too detached to capture the intensities of Erasmus' life – Pattison could better understand his vulnerability and admire, without being able to emulate, his openness to the world. Yet his interest in the episodes of Erasmus' life, even in minor anecdotes, conveys an impression of the swift, crowded flow of that life. Drummond attempts two characterizations, one of the younger man towards the beginning of his first volume and the other of the fully mature one at the end of the work. For the former he relies mostly on the familiar portrait of Beatus Rhenanus: 'of small but well-built and elegant person, with a pleasant expression of countenance, and of grave deportment, as became his profession ... His voice was thin and weak, but his pronunciation was beautifully accurate ... and all through life he was subject to and easily affected by slight external changes, as of food or climate.' But Lavater, too, seems to have had an influence, if unrecorded: 'The expression of his face might indicate something of natural timidity, while the pointed nose and large flexible mouth, which must have been much the same then as they were afterwards when Holbein drew them, marked the shrewd observer and the keen humorist.'[47] Behind the Erasmus, so depicted as he entered the household of the bishop of Cambrai, lay a childhood not altogether unhappy, since he left the school at Deventer, despite its still barbarous instruction, well equipped in Latin literature and having a gravity of demeanour later reflected in the colloquy 'Youthful Piety'; there were also his monastic years – again, despite Erasmus' own grim account of them, spent not without profit and 'some degree of inward satisfaction.'[48] Drummond is thus prepared to correct Erasmus' own very unfavourable account of these experiences (in the *Compendium vitae* and the letter to Grunnius).

The larger portrait at the end of the work must be related to the role Drummond gave Erasmus to play, that of liberal reformer. He was open, flexible, generous, 'keenly observant and unceasingly active.' He was not 'great-souled' or cast in a heroic mould. He could not have defied the world like Luther. He was 'too broad, too liberal, he saw too much good in things the most evil, too much evil in the best things, to be sternly consistent or absolutely unyielding' or to commit himself single-mindedly to a cause. He could be mean, as in the mendicancy learned in his early years, he was over-sensitive to criticism but not sycophantic, as some have said, or in any way jealous, though sometimes too bitter in controversy, as with Hutten. He was not an original genius; rather he had the range of learning, the industry, the command of languages, the taste – 'classical but without pedantry' – which those times required. His most distinctive faculty was his humour. He understood the true function of satire – to expose men to themselves as they were and to provoke them to correction and reform. He did not have Swift's disgust at all things human. From this he was saved 'by his faith in humanity and his sincere and heart-felt piety.' He did not confuse superstition and true religion.[49] There are debts to Hallam and anticipation of Pattison in this depiction, but Drummond's tone is throughout more optimistic, without any trace of gloominess or bitterness. In Erasmus he is characterizing a liberal mind as understood at the height of the Victorian age.

The anachronism is real, indeed avowed. This is the great weakness of Drummond's work, as contemporary critics recognized.[50] Its purpose, Drummond says, is to show Erasmus' part in the great conflict, 'the issues of which, for his own age, were the triumph of letters and the Protestant Reformation, and of which the ultimate issue – still in the future – is the entire emancipation of the human mind from every form of intellectual and spiritual bondage.' Erasmus belonged in many respects rather to the nineteenth than to the sixteenth century. His struggles were not essentially different from those of liberal churchmen in England against evangelical orthodoxy with its inerrant Bible and infallible interpreters. His position was that of a Broad Churchman of the nineteenth century who had outgrown the church into which he had been born without abandoning it. He embodied in himself the 'modern spirit,' the spirit of doubt, enquiry and investigation.[51]

Drummond's account of Erasmus' religion is affected by this anachronistic judgment. There is in Drummond a mixture of an almost ahistorical disdain for the dangers of anachronism, which is associated – somewhat inappropriately – with a liberal, progressive view of history, and a shrewdness and good sense in the judgment of people and writings which give the book standing even in modern scholarly company. The first is apparent in the association already noted of Erasmus with the modern Broad Church. Erasmus' hopes of preferment were comparable with those of modern dissenters within the church; such people are 'not the stuff of which bishops or even deans are made.' It is apparent also in a comparison between Erasmus and Jerome, which prefaces an appreciative review of his great edition of 1516. There were, Drummond admits, many differences between the 'grim old Father,' withdrawn to the desert, and 'the self-satisfied and by no means ascetic German man of letters'; for example, Jerome believed in the monastic life and virginity and Erasmus denied both. When, however, allowance has been made for the difference between an age of deepening darkness and one of increasing light, enough can be found in common to justify the conclusion 'that Erasmus would have been a Jerome had he lived in the fourth century, and Jerome an Erasmus had he lived in the sixteenth.' Above all, both held 'moderate and common-sense views of religion.'[52]

Despite a readiness to relocate his subjects in time, Drummond held the standard liberal, progressive view of history. His book opens with a depiction of mid-fifteenth-century Europe plunged in darkness. The subsequent history is of broadening enlightenment, to which Erasmus, of course, contributed. 'The life, the movement of the new age was, as it were, impersonated in Erasmus.'[53] Personal vocation and the destiny of an age were associated.

The movement was, above all, towards more rational religion and there Erasmus made his greatest contribution. Naturally, he had first to find his own way out of the shadows. His vow to St Genevieve while stricken with a fever in Paris and his cure are, Drummond says, recounted in a style half-serious and half-humorous, 'probably not inconsistent with some degree of faith, or half-faith, in the power of the saint.' Similarly, a later vow to St Paul offered 'another curious illustration' of the difficulty even the most rational minds find in escaping the influence of a superstitious age, especially in sickness.[54] In time Erasmus escaped from even the traces of such superstition. The monks were guided by 'a perfectly true instinct' in condemning him, for he was in spirit wholly separated from Rome, even if his heresies were 'of that intangible kind which it is always extremely difficult to bring within the letter of a written law.' Catholic ceremony was rightly absent from Erasmus' deathbed; 'priestly mummeries' would have been strangely incongruous there. Throughout he had remained true to himself and his own objects and was not thrown off balance – hurrying into excess and then suffering reaction – by the convulsions around him. He was in his time 'the great apostle of common sense and of rational religion,' whose care was for 'practical Christianity.' The key to Erasmus' position, Drummond concludes, is in the character of his mind – a sceptical rather than an asserting mind. He held to the church as an external standard because he sensed how far, without that, his inquiring mind would take him.[55] He doubted the doctrine of the Trinity and inclined towards Arianism. He may have been sceptical of the biblical miracles; he was far from literalism, 'the common evangelical view of Scripture.'[56] Drummond's Erasmus would like to have slipped his moorings in dogmatic Christianity (and, for that matter, in his own age) but prudence forbade it.

Drummond's comments on Erasmus' works are consistent with his picture of the man but he is saved from too simplistic judgments by common sense and a sound scholarly instinct. In any case, he stays close to the texts which he quotes at length. The *Enchiridion* demonstrates how freely Erasmus handled dogma from the beginning and teaches an essentially practical religion. Its view of man is Platonic; salvation comes from virtue which is in man's power. The *Moriae encomium* is reminiscent of Lucian in its contempt – 'mirthful rather than fierce or indignant' – poured on all human activities. Folly's part is well sustained, except when she becomes too earnest in denunciation of the follies of the world. For Drummond, lightness of touch is the key to the satire's success; like most of his contemporaries, he failed to understand the final, ecstatic section of the work. Indeed, he sympathizes with those offended by it: 'the free way in which Scripture is handled, and even the most sacred names introduced, while it shows certainly great want of taste, if not even want of reverence, might reasonably have given offence to persons who were neither very superstitious nor very bigoted.' Drummond gives little credence to the political writings of Erasmus– they add nothing to the wisdom of a nineteenth-century liberal beneficiary of the constitutional revolutions since his time. The precepts of the *Institutio principis christiani* are admirable but 'tolerably obvious.' It offers no guarantees against tyranny. The *Querela pacis* argues for peace at any price, 'on the plain mercantile principle that to purchase peace will always cost less than to carry on war.' Drummond decently adds that 'he urges also the higher motive that it is more Christian to forgive than to take vengeance,' but the whole treatment understates Erasmus' anger.[57]

The Reformation, as we have seen, posed a dilemma for nineteenth-century liberals: was it part of the progress of the human mind, did it advance enlightenment? or was it a reversion to dogmatism and intolerance? How one saw the relation between the revival of learning and the Reformation, between Erasmus and Luther, was critical to answering these questions. The central Protestant position was that only the apparent extremism of Luther and his associates could break the medieval mould. Drummond, who devotes his second volume to Erasmus and the Reformation, accepts that position. This seems at first sight surprising, since much in Luther's religion was distasteful to him and Erasmus was for him the true ancestor of modern rational religion. He has accepted two arguments popular – as we shall see – among nineteenth-century Protestant writers. One had a romantic, the other a democratic colouring. First, men 'of more heroic mould' than Erasmus were necessary to carry out the church reform. Secondly, 'it is not from the learned and the wise, as was said in the beginning, and as many an example since compels us to confess, that the help of humanity comes ... Out of the heart of the people the great movements of humanity come.' This is a change of tone and standpoint as if a constitutional liberal had thrown in his lot with revolution. Erasmus' hope of reformation by learning and persuasion and without dividing the church or overthrowing authority was vain. Drummond's liberalism is on this point pragmatic, even ruthless. He is sympathetic to Erasmus' rejection of Luther's doctrine of justification, but this had the great merit of crushing 'the pretensions of the priests.' Erasmus' role was honourable and consistent; he did not hold to Rome for worldly reasons. His ready mind and quick sympathy responded to Luther's case. In recoiling from the evils the Reformation produced, he failed, however, to see that, by mild measures and a spirit of conciliation, the ultimate gains – liberty of conscience, freedom of the press – would be lost.[58]

It is not possible to do justice to Drummond's book by tracing only its dominant themes. Its ironic asides, even – perhaps especially – the anachronistic ones, its unpretentious comments on other authors and scholarly difficulties, its extensive quotation of Erasmus' letters and writings on the model of the great Victorian biographies, made it attractive to a contemporary readership used to summary judgments about Erasmus and without a full biography in English since Jortin's imperfect performance of one hundred years before. It remains attractive, not least for the often

perceptive accounts of Erasmus' relations with patrons, colleagues, and friends.[59]

Drummond's views on Erasmus' relation to the Reformation
or, more generally, on the relation of the Reformation itself to
modern thought were challenged by a reviewer in the Unitarian
journal where his work had first appeared. This was Charles
Kegan Paul. Drummond and Kegan Paul represented rival liberal
views of the Reformation. The matter can, the latter said, be put
in a nutshell: 'Erasmus was always and remained a Catholic,'
though of a liberal kind, say in the manner of Döllinger. He broke
with Luther when the latter became as dogmatic as the old church.
Erasmus anticipated freer thought and a new kind of church.
Luther 'perpetuated while he changed dogma; but Erasmus, imposing of himself nothing new, laughed away what should be
demolished, and prepared the way for greater changes still.' The
question in the Reformation was: this dogma or that? The modern
question is: dogma or none? Erasmus began to pose that question.[60] This is the most extreme version of the liberal view (first
expressed by Gibbon and Semler) that the Reformation was but
an episode in the history of Christian thought and that intellectual
liberation had other sources. For Drummond, both Erasmus and
Luther were liberators, for different purposes and in different
ways. For Kegan Paul, Erasmus, not Luther, was the pioneer of
modern freedoms. It is possible to relate these views to the point
Kegan Paul had reached in his own strange career. Educated at
Eton and Exeter College, Oxford, ordained in 1852, he became,
under the influence of Kingsley, Maurice, and the Christian So-
cialists, 'broadly high church in doctrine, given to ritualism, and
a radical in politics.' Interested successively in mesmerism, veg-
etarianism, and Positivism, he became associated, while vicar of
Sturminster Marshall in Dorset, with a body of broadly unitarian
views, the Free Christian Union: 'an Unitarian theology,' he recalled, 'had long been unconsciously mine.' At that stage he wrote
his comment on Drummond; a year later he threw up his living
in the Church of England and moved to London, becoming a
distinguished publisher and eventually a Catholic convert.[61]

The Theological Review, where Drummond and Kegan Paul published, was edited between 1864 and 1879 by a Unitarian preacher
and writer more famous than either at that time, Charles Beard
(1827–88). He, too, wrote on the history of the Reformation and

on the relation of Erasmus, Luther, and others 'to modern thought and knowledge.'[62] In the liberal debate Beard stands somewhere between Drummond and Kegan Paul. The key to the ambiguity, if it may be so described, is in Luther's inner conflicts, as we shall see. The account of Erasmus' place in the pattern is comparatively straightforward.

Beard's career coincided with the high Victorian age and he shared its openness and optimism.[63] He associated its most important and characteristic intellectual achievement, the theory of evolution, with the more familiar idea of progress. Beard had from his father, John Relly Beard,[64] both his classical education and his liberal Unitarian faith. Knowledge of the ancient world was for him 'part of the intellectual air we breathe.'[65] Faith should, he believed (without underestimating the difficulties), accommodate both the higher literary criticism and the idea of evolution. He urged comprehensiveness and resisted sectarianism, to the extent of preferring not to use the term 'Unitarian,' though it accurately expressed his own commitments.[66] In broad terms, he postulated the progress of the human race from barbarism to civilization and a continuing, if not unchecked, refinement of the latter. Beard can sound like Dugald Stewart.[67] He accepted the evidences of progress in his own times. Though he knew political turbulence – at Manchester in the years of the Chartist movement and at the University of Berlin during the revolutions of 1848–9 – he enjoyed a long and productive ministry in a relatively settled and prosperous era. He was pastor at Renshaw Street chapel in Liverpool from 1867 to his death in 1888. He believed in the great city as a civilizer. He was not, however, complacent: he was active against social evils and, notably as a leader-writer on the *Liverpool Daily Post*, supported political reforms.

Beard associated the Reformation with the social and scientific movements of his own time or, rather, related both to a larger secular development of human powers. 'The Reformation was part of a mightier movement than itself – the manifestation upon religious ground of the intellectual forces which inspire the speculation and have given us the science of to-day.' What has been the nature of this movement which 'has gone on with accelerating rapidity to the present moment'?

It has been, in the first place, an effort to bring both traditional and new knowledge to the test of reason, rejecting as untrue whatever will not stand it, and building up all that it approves into a compact system of fact and inference; in the second, a slow struggle towards a state of society in which every man is permitted to think and speak as he will, without incurring legal penalty or social disability. ... Every science in turn has abandoned the principle of authority, and now expects belief only for what it can prove. And liberty of thought, speech and life is the practical corollary of the scientific method ... First, toleration – next, equality before the law – last of all, social equality – are stages of progress in the art of life necessarily involved in the development of the scientific spirit. The final consummation will be reached when all belief rests upon adequate evidence, and none affects a man's relations to his neighbours.[68]

The movement began as a reaction against the ecclesiastical domination and the monolithic culture of the Middle Ages. Its first expressions – tentative, out of season, certainly abortive – were the various late-medieval reform movements, but its true beginnings were in the revival of letters in Italy and Germany. The Renaissance – Beard considers the word appropriate – was a rebellion against medieval culture, against scholastic philosophy and ascetic theories of morals. He uses the familiar images of light and darkness and indeed more specific images that had become current in the liberal literature: 'the schoolmen blinked, like owls in sunshine, in the light of the new learning.'[69] The Renaissance made the Reformation possible – indeed, for Beard the latter is the religious expression of the former. The two were, however, distinguishable; the Reformation was the more short-lived, and petered out, while the Renaissance tide continued still to flow in the nineteenth century. While theology was trapped in a new scholasticism, philosophy, science, and history made triumphant progress.[70] That way of seeing modern history determines for Beard the historic relationship between Luther and Erasmus.

Erasmus was, says Beard, the summation of the classical revival in northern Europe. His service to 'scientific theology' cannot be overestimated. His Christian belief was sincere and his biblical and patristic work intended to place 'before men's eyes, in as unadulterated form as possible, the records of Christian antiquity.' The Reformers Luther and Tyndale depended on this work. Erasmus, too, wanted the literary revival to end in the reformation of the church – he especially hated the monastic system which 'had robbed him of both his patrimony and his personal liberty' – but he did not acknowledge any necessary connection between these and Luther's specific teachings. Justification by faith was abhorrent to him. His own theology, to be found in the *Enchiridion*, was strongly ethical and for Luther without substance. Yet, historically the two were allies: Erasmus himself recognized this, while explaining it variously.

To put the emphasis on Erasmus' 'personal and intellectual timidity,' his wish to stand well with all the world, especially his high patrons, and his reluctance to imperil his intellectual supremacy would be to take a superficial view of his character and action. Beard's key to both is in the sentence: 'He believed in the dissolvent power upon old abuse of intellectual culture.' Its workings would be gradual and without uproar or violent breaks with the past. Luther swept this dream aside. That was the immediate need, but the last three centuries have also vindicated Erasmus. Without Luther's vigour and the simplifying impact of a doctrine like justification by faith, reform would have faltered at the start. But Erasmus cannot be blamed for not acknowledging this or 'for not being Luther.' Events have justified both. 'The Reformation that has been, is Luther's monument: perhaps the Reformation that is to be, will trace itself back to Erasmus.' This is probably the most famous formulation of the doctrine of the two Reformations, first stated by Gibbon and generally accepted by nineteenth-century liberals, if with variations. Erasmus stands for the modern, scientific spirit, risen to supremacy already in the nineteenth century. Luther may convey personal inspiration; 'the spirit of Erasmus is the life of scientific criticism, the breath of modern scholarship.'[71]

Beard associates the Renaissance with a straightforward rationalism, the Reformation with something more clouded and ambiguous. Of the first, Erasmus was representative. Thus, on biblical matters, his annotations 'often anticipate the results of modern criticism'; he doubted the texts used to establish the Trinity or refute the Arians; he admitted errors by the apostles and questioned received authorships.[72] On doctrinal matters like the Trinity or the sacraments, he was hardy or even unorthodox. 'Upon Eternal Punishment he was still more hopelessly rationalistic.' So, Beard concludes, one may show that 'the Renaissance, in the hands of serious men, was prepared to bring Scripture and the Creeds to the test of sound reason, and that, but for the action of other and opposing forces, many of the questions which we are apt to think exclusively characteristic of our own age, might have taken shape and received at least a tentative answer three centuries ago.' As for the Reformers, Beard takes a more positive view than Gibbon of their 'relation to reason and liberty.' They were, 'in a very true sense, rationalists without knowing it'; they had audaciously taken their religious fate into their own hands; to have broken the religious monopoly of the old church was in itself a liberation. At Worms in 1521 Luther had made an independent appeal to reason.[73] But reaction soon set in, towards biblical literalism, a traditional view of the sacraments, the restriction of reason to the things of this world. Among Beard's most telling passages is his long account of the struggle of faith and reason in Luther. The very violence of Luther's language demonstrates for Beard that he was pulled both ways; here was 'a rigorous process of self-suppression,' 'struggles in which the whole peace of his life was at stake.' Faith won the battle in Luther and the Reformation. 'But who can tell what might have been the effect upon the Reformation, and the subsequent development of the intellectual life of Europe, had Luther put himself boldly at the head of the larger and freer thought of his time, instead of using all the force of his genius, all the weight of his authority, to crush it?'[74]

As it was, Erasmus, not Luther, anticipated modern intellectual life. This is characterized by free enquiry and the application of the critical intelligence to every sphere. Philosophical speculation, scientific discovery, and historical criticism have mental processes and intellectual assumptions in common. That is why Erasmus can be confidently linked with modern studies remote from his own interests and attitudes: his work, too, was 'scientific.' Erasmus believed that the Reformation's retreat from the more open and critical way was indicated by the renewed dominance of polemical theology and the relative neglect of humanist studies among the Protestants.[75] Religion stood apart from modern progress and the present need, according to Beard, is for another Reformation with the mission of testing religious attitudes 'by the surest knowledge of our own day.'[76] It would be, as we have seen, under the sign of Erasmus.

This is an Erasmus wholly devoted to the life of the mind. An irony of Beard's work is that the charm of Erasmus' personality, the liveliness of his commentary on the social world – noticed by Coleridge and others – is barely suggested. The Reformation in his name, for all his acuteness, would be a dull affair. The appealing personality in Beard's book is Luther's – he had a naïve satisfaction in domestic life and his very contradictions and inner conflicts betrayed a rich humanity.[77] Beard was not unusual among nineteenth-century liberals in responding to Luther, hero and house father, while linking with the long curve of progress, not his name, but Erasmus'. Otherwise, Beard's work is without ironies or paradoxes or contradictions. His mind is inclusive:[78] there is one modern, scientific movement; one sap runs in all the branches of knowledge. Growth is sturdy, continuous and continuing. With Beard, Erasmus belongs to the side promised a total victory.

As with Mark Pattison, both the mind and career of James Anthony Froude (1818–94) were much influenced by his reaction against the Tractarian movement. Indeed, Pattison thought that Froude had an easier passage to scepticism: 'J.A. Froude had made much shorter work with it than I could possibly do, not having had in youth that profound pietistic impression which lay like lead upon my understanding for so many years of my life.'[79] That was to underestimate Froude's anguish. Besides, his early life had been exceptionally hard: his mother dead during his childhood, his father remote and austere, an older brother (Hurrell) brilliant but cruel. There followed an oppressive schooling and undergraduate years of self-doubt and self-recrimination.[80] Controversy almost always surrounded his accomplishments in later life, from his autobiographical novel exorcising his youthful religious allegiances (*Nemesis of Faith*, 1849) to the successive volumes of his great *History of England* and his life of Carlyle.[81]

Froude was drawn to Newman in the 1840s, without being personally close to him. He felt the power of the straight choice: Catholic faith or infidelity, there being no middle ground.[82] Yet, he held back from a full commitment and in the end broke away. He arrived at a position well short of Pattison's scepticism; he retained 'a deep and abiding faith in God' and always considered himself a member of the Church of England.[83] What he condemned henceforth was dogmatism or rather a preoccupation with doctrine or theology. Religion as he accepted it was summed up in the idealized picture he gave of the church in England during his youth, before the Reform Act and the disastrous conflict of liberals and Tractarians: 'It was orthodox without being theological ... The institution had drifted into the condition of what I should call moral health. It did not instruct us in mysteries, it did not teach us to make religion a special object of our thoughts; it taught us to use religion as a light by which to see our way along the road of duty.'[84] Froude is attracted by the morally robust, repelled by the theologically fastidious. Carlyle, with his preferred test 'is it alive?' rather than 'is it true?' was already an influence upon him in the 1840s.[85]

His theological reductionism, his emphasis on the ethical, his resistance to speculative assertions in religion gave Froude common ground with the liberals. These views also, as we shall see, pointed him to Erasmus and, in part, determined the kind of Erasmus he found. Thus his *Life and Letters of Erasmus*, first presented as lectures at Oxford in 1893–4, may appropriately conclude this chapter. In much else, Froude was unsympathetic to liberal values and preconceptions. He did not share the Whig 'prejudice in favour of constitutionalism.' He accepted the Tudor despotism and admired Henry VIII. He rejected liberal optimism and laissez-faire individualism in the manner of the Tory radicals.[86] Yet, the hero of the English story for him was Protestantism. To accept that, even when linked with a residual theology like his own, was to give religion an un-Whiggish importance. Nevertheless, the Reformation, for all its ambiguities, retained a place in most liberal accounts of human progress. Froude was at once free from and bound to the liberal tradition.[87]

Correspondences could be found between his experiences and personal traits and those of Erasmus. The hatred of theological speculation instilled by Tractarianism could be readily turned against the scholastics, the fear of legalism and authoritarianism in religion turned against the monks whom Erasmus satirized. Erasmus' rejection of the extremes, his search for middle ground, was more problematical for Froude. On the one hand, there was a side of Froude that admired a staunch, uncomplicated adherence to principle and – on one view of him – Luther, rather than Erasmus, fitted that ideal. On the other hand, he was distrustful of zealots, men of an idea, and recognized the ambiguities in the best of causes. Erasmian irony was no stranger to him. Years after his death, Mary Kingsley wrote of him to his daughter Margaret:

'Ironic toward opinion and toward the *appearance* of human actions, because he realized the immense variety of possibilities surrounding everything we say and think, or *think* we think, and everything we do.'[88] Unhappy childhoods incline their victims to pessimism and over-sensitiveness, for which irony is a controlled release: Froude and Erasmus had that in common.

Froude's publications on Erasmus both derived from series of lectures, one of three to the Literary and Philosophic Society at Newcastle in January 1867 – 'Times of Erasmus and Luther' – and one of twenty at Oxford in the academic year 1893–4, when he was Regius Professor at the very end of his life. The brush-strokes in the former are cruder. Erasmus is seen from the standpoint of the Reformation. The Reformation was misunderstood by two kinds of contemporaries – the Tractarians and the secularizing 'liberal philosophers.' By the beginning of the sixteenth century the once beautiful Catholic ideal was corrupt; ritual and speculative theology had replaced practical religion. There were but two practicable policies of reform: to create a new tone through education and literary culture; to bring in the people.[89]

Erasmus was associated with the first: 'the breadth of his culture, his clear understanding, and the worldly moderation of his temper, seemed to qualify him above living men to conduct a temperate reform.' The portrait is shallow. Froude, like Drummond and others, seemed to be listening, as he put it, 'to the wisest of modern broad Churchmen.' But, he argues, 'this latitudinarian philosophising, this cultivated epicurean gracefulness' would have had, for the times, too devastating an effect. It would have made the educated into infidels and left the multitude to 'a convenient but debasing superstition.' 'The sceptical philosophy is the most powerful of solvents, but it has no principle of organic life in it; and what of truth there was in Erasmus' teaching had to assume a far other form before it was available for the reinvigoration of religion.'[90]

The reinvigoration came from the passionate convictions of Luther. The course of history, says Froude – somewhat naïvely for one who understood well enough the circumstantial constraints on individual action – would have been better if Erasmus had sided with Luther. He would have led the educated to support the Reformers, who had already won the multitude. Erasmus had brilliant gifts and tireless industry; he remained true to himself; he was 'even far braver than he professed to be.' 'And yet, in his special scheme for remodelling the mind of Europe, he failed hopelessly – almost absurdly ... Literature and cultivation will feed life when life exists already ... When there is no spiritual life at all ... then, for the restoration of the higher nature in man, qualities are needed different in kind from any which Erasmus possessed.'[91]

In reading this version of the encounter between Erasmus and Luther, it is important to recall that Froude was the disciple, friend, and biographer of Carlyle and that Carlyle had included Luther in his *On Heroes, Hero-Worship and the Heroic in History* under the title 'The Hero as Priest.' Protestant writers had long contrasted Luther and Erasmus to the latter's disadvantage, essentially because he had not accepted the truths Luther taught. For Froude, Luther's superiority lay not in the doctrines he taught but in the fact itself of his being a man of faith, by which he meant not belief in dogmas, but 'belief in goodness, belief in justice, in righteousness, above all, belief in truth.' Such men stake all, and ask others to stake all, by being 'true to the common light which God has given to all his children.'[92] So also Carlyle had called all the true men who had ever lived 'soldiers of the same army, enlisted, under Heaven's captaincy, to do battle against the same enemy, the Empire of Darkness and Wrong.'[93] They were distinguished by a passionate awareness of the difference between sham and reality; beyond that, their authenticity derived less from specific teachings than from their sense of conviction and their steadfastness. By contrast, Erasmus – for Froude in 1867 – was a shallow intellectual who misjudged the needs of his time, overestimating the influence of literary culture and the prospects for temperate solutions. This was a return to the Enlightenment view of Erasmus, as unfavourably interpreted by the romantics.

The twenty lectures which Froude delivered to students reading history at Oxford in the academic year 1893–4, and then revised for publication, offered a more favourable view of Erasmus. They would, he said in the last sentence of this, his last published work, best understand the Reformation era 'if you will look at it through the eyes of Erasmus.'[94] The relation with Luther is again a major theme, as we shall see. But much of the book is devoted to presenting Erasmus himself through translations, often in paraphrase, of his letters. The object of his work, he says, is 'rather to lead historical readers to a study of Erasmus' own writings than to provide an abbreviated substitute for them.'[95] Even

so, he is less interested in the works than in the life. After quoting
Erasmus' lively account of a journey from Basel to Louvain, Froude
remarks that those who believe that history consists of actions
'attributed to wooden figures called men and women, interpreted
successively by philosophic writers according to their own notions
of probability, and arranged to teach constitutional lessons' would
not consider such an account history; but it is very historical to
those who seek 'as much as we can learn of the character and
doings of past generations of real human creatures who would
bleed if we pricked them.'[96] This was the familiar distinction, as
he saw it, between the Whig and the Carlylean approaches to
history. Constitutional lessons for the present are not the best
reason for studying history. 'To understand the past we must look
at it always, when we can, through the eyes of contemporaries.'[97]
Yet, Froude would not deny – it will become plain – that history
had lessons, especially moral lessons, to teach the present; he
shared that presupposition with the Whigs and most other nineteenth-century historians.

The letters rather than the works bulk large in Froude's lectures. One lecture was devoted to the *Moria* and the *Julius Exclusus*, which Froude attributed to Erasmus and of which he gave
a translation.[98] He confused the chronology of the *Moria* and
associated it both in time and purpose with the edition of the
New Testament: they 'were the voice and protest of the Christian
laity against the parody of a Church which pretended to be their
spiritual master.'[99] *Moria's* satirical character is established, its
final mystical section overlooked. The *Enchiridion* is said to be
'the finest of Erasmus's minor compositions' but not analysed.[100]
Only the earliest edition of the *Adagia*, with its 'light good hu-
moured wit,' is mentioned: already 'the clergy felt the presence
of their natural enemy.'[101] The *Colloquia* attracted Froude most;
they expressed the spirit of the more interesting letters and offered
'pictures of his own mind, pictures of men and things which show
the hand of an artist in the highest sense, never spiteful, never
malicious, always delightful and amusing, and finished photo-
graphs of the world in which he lived and moved.'[102]

For Froude, who had, as he saw it, himself come out from
under the shadow of clericalism, Erasmus' biography to middle
life is a story of freedom and integrity secured. There was 'no
likelier spot in Europe' than among the free Netherlands towns
'to be the birthplace of a vigorous independent thinker.' At school,

he was quick and conscious of superior abilities, perhaps insubordinate. There was a counterpoint between such a spirit and his guardians' efforts to place him in a monastery. After finally submitting (as the letter to Grunnius recounts), he 'was like a handcuffed prisoner in the clutches of the police.' Escape was a necessity. He found it in study at Paris under the patronage of the bishop of Cambrai. His life there was free and companionable, the atmosphere essentially secular: 'he wished to see what the world was which religious men denounced as something so terrible, and of which he was as yet only on the confines.'[103]

He showed the same sociability on his first visit to England (put at 1497–8). He was studying in libraries intensely, and his talk, eg his famous improvisation about Cain at an Oxford dinner-table,[104] exposed a brilliant intellect; yet, he was observing the real world as much as he was pursuing book-learning. He did not like his reputation of 'brilliant adventurer,' but freedom was his 'breath of life': 'He was a wild bird, and would not sing in a cage.'[105]

Part of his struggle was for financial independence and Froude shows throughout an interest in his material fortunes. His early condition was miserable; of all the virtues, economy was the least possible to him. Pedants might criticize his shifts for obtaining support but he had no choice: 'Erasmus starving in a garret might have been as dull ... as they.' He was tempted by the offers made him in Italy. 'Yet, strong as the inclination might be to yield, his love of freedom was stronger – freedom and the high purpose of his life, which must be abandoned for ever if he once consented to put on the golden chain.' His English patrons (Warham and Mountjoy) finally gave him security, though at his return to England in 1509 he was disappointed in his hopes of Henry VIII. He could now defeat efforts to bring him back to the monastery. He had a universal reputation. His squalid and struggling years came to an end triumphantly with his edition of the New Testament; he blazed before Europe as a new star.[106]

The appearance of Erasmus, Froude declares, was associated with a vast secular change in human history. The old ecclesiastical order was played out. He explained this commonplace of Protestant historiography in two ways: first, like Carlyle, he said that the life once present in medieval civilization had, by the beginning of the sixteenth century, gone out of it, reality had become sham and only a façade was left; secondly, like the liberals, he could say that the whole had rested on false foundations, had been a complete distortion of the original impulse of Christianity – so, rituals and ceremonies had replaced moral duty and the service of God. The second argument called up for Froude reminiscences of Tractarianism: 'This extraordinary system rested on the belief in the supernatural powers which they pretended to have received in the laying on of hands'; the teaching was of 'some preposterous legend or childish superstition, varied with the unintelligible speculations of scholastic theology.'[107] Froude uses the language of the Enlightenment, though again not without an ironic reference to Newman: 'the long night of narrow ecclesiasticism was drawing to an end; ... the shell was bursting; the dawn was drawing on of a new age, when, as Newman said of our own time, the minds of men were demanding something deeper and truer than had satisfied preceding centuries.' Nevertheless, he does not hold the liberal idea of progress. Historical development is for him less sure and predictable, it is more of a lottery. Most new ideas, he says in an aside, are nonsense but 'the odd one will be the egg which contains the whole future in it.'[108]

For all his sympathy for him, Froude did not see Erasmus' reform program as so seminal. He did not adopt the two Reformations doctrine of Gibbon and many liberals. The true Reformation remained Luther's. Even so, the power and attraction of Erasmus' program comes out more clearly in 1893–4 than in the earlier lectures of 1867. Its heart was the editing of the New Testament and the Fathers. Erasmus' purpose was to point up the difference between past and present. Ordinary Christians could for the first time compare early Christianity with 'the Christianity of the Church with a Borgia pope, cardinal princes, ecclesiastical courts, and a mythology of lies.' It was, in a sense, a literary program and the controversies arising from the New Testament edition were often over issues of language and interpretation. But its effect ought not to be underestimated; the New Testament caused a 'spiritual earthquake.'[109] Erasmus was not planning a catastrophe; he had the favour of the pope and could reasonably expect a peaceful reformation. Reform could come, he thought, without diminishing the church which 'was, or might be, a magnificent instrument of human cultivation, and might grow with the expansion of knowledge.' On that Froude says, exposing the blunt, tough side of his historiography: 'the devil is nòt expelled by rose-water.'[110]

Force must be met by force, at least emotional force: this is the lesson Froude draws from his extended discussion of Erasmus' response to Luther. It links him with the romantics. He here mixes sympathy for Erasmus' moral and theological positions with scepticism about his effectiveness.

> He had no passionate emotions of any kind, and rather dreaded than welcomed the effervescence of religious enthusiasm. The faults of the Church, as he saw them, were oblivion and absolute neglect of ordinary morality, the tendency to substitute for obedience to the Ten Commandments an extravagant superstition chiefly built upon fiction, and a doctrinal system, hardening and stiffening with each generation, which was made the essence of religion, defined by ecclesiastical law, guarded by ecclesiastical courts, and enforced by steel and fire. His dream was a return to early Christianity as it was before councils had laid the minds of men in chains; a Christianity of practice, not of opinion, where the Church itself might consent to leave the intellect free to think as it pleased on the inscrutable mysteries; and where, as the Church would no longer insist on particular forms of belief, mankind would cease to hate and slaughter each other because they differed on points of metaphysics.

He saw in Luther the same disposition to dogmatic assertion as in the old church. Dogma confronted dogma and the end was religious war. By the nineteenth century, after the exhaustion of the struggle, the world had come round to Erasmus' view, and one asked 'why all that misery was necessary before the voice of moderation could be heard.' Froude answers: 'I suppose because reason has so little to do with the direction of human conduct. I called Erasmus's views of reform a dream ... Reason is no match for superstition. One passion can only be encountered by another passion, and bigotry by the enthusiasm of faith.'[111]

Erasmus, says Froude, could not side with Luther but did not wish to denounce him either. He had the moderate's natural resentment at the intrusion of the radical but still spoke to the authorities in Luther's defence. That was creditable, since he was risking the loss of protection and support 'in a cause with which he had imperfect sympathy, and for a man whom he thought headstrong and unwise.' He feared anarchy and thought the outcome of revolution unpredictable. He looked for a lead from above; his hopes were to prove vain in the end but he had, Froude judges, a case so long as there seemed a possibility that pope or council would bring in reform and greater intellectual freedom.[112]

Even when, in the free-will controversy, Erasmus broke with Luther, he did not condemn him utterly; according to Froude, he never disputed the correctness of Luther's criticisms of the old church. Froude rejects the common view that in free will he found an abstruse theological issue away from the main scene of conflict; what he most disliked and feared was the construction of a new dogmatic theology and he saw that, for Luther, denial of the freedom of the will was the cornerstone of such a theology. Other moderates, including the emperor Charles V himself, were equally dismayed by the emergence of a rival dogmatic system.[113]

Froude's picture of Erasmus' last years is, naturally enough, sombre. He had the continuing hatred of the monks; only at the very end, under Paul III, did he again find sympathy in Rome.[114] He was burdened by age, by illness, by the pressures of work. Froude, who himself had suffered much and whose own life was drawing to a close, speaks of him to his students as of a friend: 'He might complain, and complain he did loudly enough, but he had a tough elastic spirit underneath it all, and complaint did not mean weakness. It is well to mention these things if I am to make you respect him, as I hope you will.'[115]

To repeat: Froude's treatment of Erasmus' relation with the Reformation is contradictory. On the one hand, he is wholly sympathetic to Erasmus' religious views as he understood them, to his theological reductionism, his emphasis on practical religion and morality, his moderation, his plea for mutual tolerance. On the other hand, Luther, not Erasmus, created Protestantism which, for Froude, was the liberating and constructive force of modern history. He saw Protestantism, less as the fierce dogmatism which Erasmus resisted, than as the easy and natural, but serious and dignified, form of practical Christianity he had found among Irish Protestant friends in the 1840s.[116] He still felt that, to produce that outcome, Luther's passion and intensity, indeed his dogmatism, were necessary. He excused in him what he could never excuse in Catholics or Tractarians.

His understanding of Erasmus' religious views, one must also say, was limited. He attributes to Erasmus, if not the muscular Christianity, at least the call to duty and the strenuous morality characteristic of the Victorian age: 'To Erasmus religion was a rule of life, a perpetual reminder to mankind of their responsibility to their Maker, a spiritual authority under which individuals could learn their duties to God and to their neighbour.' He missed the elements of religious passion, even of effervescence, in Erasmus himself.[117]

If, then, there is a certain thinness in Froude's presentation of Erasmus' religion, the same cannot be said of his depiction of the personality and the immediate social setting. Partly because of his extensive quotation from Erasmus' correspondence, Froude succeeds in conveying the appeal Erasmus' personality had for him. One recognizes and responds to his liveliness of mind, his good humour, his sociability, his ironic detachment from the human community which never negates his strong commitment to its reform and betterment. You could not do better, said P.S. Allen, than turn to Froude's pages 'for a vivid and penetrating sketch of Erasmus' attractive personality.' 'There was much in common between the biographer and his subject; in charm of character, in variety of experience, in brilliance of gifts ... the outlines are boldly and truly drawn, as so remarkable a figure merits; and the reader feels throughout that he is reading of a real man.'[118]

It is strange, perhaps even perverse, to complete a chapter on nineteenth-century liberal interpretations of Erasmus with an extended discussion of James Anthony Froude. Froude was hostile to important elements in liberalism: its linear idea of progress, its faith in constitutional government and the free market, its broadly optimistic view of human nature and the human condition. In one respect, but that of the greatest importance, he aligned himself with the liberals: he opposed dogmatism and authoritarianism in religion; he saw the decay and division of medieval Christendom as a liberation of humanity; he gave religious freedom a very high place among social and political values. Even here, he was distinctive. He was not a secularist, he remained a 'devout theist'[119] and, despite his agonies of the 1840s, a Church of England man. This meant that he saw the Reformation differently from most liberals.

The difference was over such questions as these. Did the Reformation produce a dogmatism not much better than the one it replaced? Did it consequently become sterile? How quickly did this reversion take place? There was a further question: how necessary to modern religious freedom and intellectual progress was an alternative line beginning with Erasmus, a second reformation?

Actually, the various writers considered in this chapter gave different answers to these questions. Hallam condemned what he saw as the violent populism of the Reformers: Erasmus, in his view, rightly opposed them and represented a saner approach to reform. Pattison, too, saw Erasmus as standing apart from the clashing dogmatisms of the sixteenth century and anticipating the Enlightenment and modern religious liberalism, indeed scepticism, not so much by producing a complete program as by applying his natural critical intelligence to the social and ecclesiastical life of the time. For Drummond, however, Erasmus, while certainly anticipating a later, more placid era, could not have carried the work of liberation through in the perilous conditions of the sixteenth century; a more determined, extreme, and popular figure was necessary. Kegan Paul challenged Drummond at that point: there could be no advantage to the liberal cause in moving from one dogmatism to another. Of these writers, Beard made the most complete statement of the two Reformations doctrine: for reform in the sixteenth century, Luther's passion was indispensable; but of the larger, liberating movement, in which the Reformation was but an episode, and which was still gathering force, the true pioneer was Erasmus. Froude was closer to Drummond: he shared the outlook of Erasmus, but the historical movement which made the great change began rather with Luther.

All recognized Luther's vigour; they differed over how far its effects were beneficent or malign. They differed, too, in their responses to Erasmus' personality but, generally, admired the quickness and openness of his mind and spirit. All were agreed that he stood for values essential to liberalism: toleration, restraint, a sceptical temper, resistance to the unthinking dogmatist on one side and the unthinking enthusiast on the other. They saw only part of Erasmus, of course, but within limits they saw true.

NINE

Nineteenth-Century Catholicism: Erasmus' Relation to Catholic Orthodoxy, the Catholic Tradition, and Scholasticism

🕉

Erasmus' attitude to the church and the relation of his writings and ideas to Catholic orthodoxy were a matter of controversy in his lifetime. Critics of his edition of the New Testament and the writings associated with it, for example, took up textual and philological issues, but they also questioned his soundness on doctrines central to the Catholic faith.[1] These bitter and ominous controversies dogged the last twenty years of his life. Of course, they continued after his death and clouded his reputation for many Catholics throughout the sixteenth and seventeenth centuries.

The debate is not dead in our own time, in a sense cannot be dead, although participants might be well advised to recognize the intrinsic difficulties of such a debate. Joseph Lortz, the famous and, as is generally believed, irenic church historian, made a sharp attack on Erasmus as a Catholic and defended the severity of his judgment: asking about the 'Christian' element in any historical agent means assessing his attitude to an absolute and binding demand. Erasmus had, Lortz claims, an imperfect awareness of the teaching church, was indecisive and relativist.[2] The rival view of 'a profoundly Christian Erasmus fully orthodox and Catholic' has been frequently and reasonably argued.[3] The argument has, of course, been easier to make since Vatican II.[4]

The question 'was Erasmus Catholic?' is not, historically speaking, a simple one. It can be broken down into various questions of different kinds. There are his actual, personal relations with the hierarchy of the church and ecclesiastical authority. There is his attitude to scholasticism, however its relationship with Catholic doctrine is defined. If Erasmus is seen as a leader or representative or even symbol of northern humanism, its character is drawn into the argument, its dependence on or alienation from scholasticism, for example, or, for that matter, its relation to medieval culture generally. When this last topic is considered, very broad historical questions arise, indeed have arisen in the literature: is modern culture a degeneration from the Catholic Christian civilization of the Middle Ages? Is modern history a decline or in some sense a progress and liberation? An alternative to the liberal idea of progress, equally one-sided and simple-minded, can be and has been put. Erasmus and humanism have been seen as heralds of decline.

There have in theological terms been more sophisticated questions. A defence of Erasmus against the charge of heterodoxy has been entered in these terms: before the Council of Trent many issues remained unsettled and Erasmus ought not to be accused of indecisiveness on matters that were still undecided. What then was Catholic orthodoxy in Erasmus' time and what degree of freedom did the believer have? The critics return with questions of a looser kind, questions about Erasmus' intentions and dispositions. Did he think as a Catholic? Before long the ground along this way becomes very treacherous.[5] A related question arises from Erasmus' and others' criticism of abuses. Where is the line to be drawn between exposing abuse and damaging the institution itself? How far could Erasmus attack the failings of the monks without calling monasticism into question?

The nineteenth century was bound to be an important and distinctive stage in the history of Catholic interpretations of Erasmus. In the aftermath of the revolution and the attacks, during its course, on the church and Catholicism, with the successes of liberalism and the appearance of an aggressive secularism, the church and the faith could seem in peril.[6] Historical times of peril and critical voices from the past attracted attention. On the other side, the church responded with its own aggressions: the Catholic sense of mission revived, new orders were established, education became a battleground between the church and its enemies, while in ultramontanism, with its call for enhanced papal authority, embattled Catholics found a principle of organization and an object of devotion appropriate to their circumstances. There was a revival of interest in scholasticism. Again, a figure like Erasmus who had no taste for clerical aggression, who had been a severe critic of scholasticism and who yet had remained faithful to the imperilled church would, among those interested in the era of humanism and especially in the comparison between the revolution and the Reformation, attract both critics and defenders. He had always done so among Catholics, of course, but the nineteenth century brought new urgency and important nuances.

It is possible to speak of two traditions of Erasmus interpretation among Catholics, the moderate and favourable and the intransigent and unfavourable, but to group our authors under two heads in that way would not do justice to the range and complexity of views. So, in this chapter writers are grouped more loosely and, indeed, a certain counterpoint is set up between the more severe and the milder critics of Erasmus, between his friends and enemies.

I

Charles Butler (1750–1832) came from an old English Catholic family.[7] He was educated in Catholic schools in England and at the English college in Douai, where the instruction was devout and classical. Education abroad enhanced Butler's patriotism, a consideration not irrelevant to his part in the controversies thrown up by the campaign for Catholic emancipation in England.[8] Even his Catholic enemies accepted that he was personally devout, even ascetic.[9] He became interested in Erasmus (and Grotius, with whom he associated him) early in life but included a *Life of Erasmus* among his other voluminous publications only in 1825, when he had long been a prominent and, to some, controversial figure in the English Catholic community.[10]

Butler experienced in himself both Catholic disability and Catholic emancipation. Accomplished in the law, he could work only as a conveyancer until the relief act of 1791, when he became the first Catholic barrister in England since 1688. He was secretary of the Catholic Committee of 1782 formed to press the cause of emancipation.[11] Butler's movement was lay in character and Gallican in sentiment; the object was to integrate Catholics with the English political community whose values, understood in a Whiggish way, Butler shared. Without qualifying the tenets of the faith, he wished to convince his compatriots of Catholic harmlessness on points that still troubled Protestant spirits – adherence to a foreign power, papal interference in English affairs, and so on. He was, therefore, willing to make compromises on matters like the oath of allegiance and a governmental veto on episcopal appointments, where other Catholics demanded intransigence. His chief opponent was John Milner, vicar apostolic in the Midlands, who treated Butler with extreme bitterness: Butler was one of the 'false brethren,' who aimed at subjecting the priesthood 'to unrestricted lay and even heterodox control.'[12] At issue then were the respective roles of lay and clerical leaders in the church; one might, on the face of it, expect these debates to find some expression in a biography of Erasmus.[13]

Despite a busy, and at times wearing, public and professional life, Butler persisted with his scholarly and literary labours throughout his life. There is the attractive picture of him stealing 'from his home, even in mid-winter, at four in the morning, taking his lantern, lighting the fire in his chamber, and setting doggedly to work till breakfast-time.'[14] In these circumstances, the finished products could show a certain thinness, and this is true of the *Life of Erasmus*. It is a little chronicle based on a reading of earlier biographies (Beatus Rhenanus, Le Clerc, Bayle, Knight, Jortin, and Burigny) and of familiar epistles, including the *Compendium vitae*, and adorned with a sober commentary and, at times, homely asides. Thus, Butler repeats the apocryphal story of Erasmus' stealing pears from a tree in the monastery garden and putting the blame on another monk, adding the remark: 'How greatly are we interested in the actions of illustrious men, even this trifling story!'[15] Butler is interested in Erasmus' literary achievements, his friendships, and, generally, his relations with places and people, those in England occupying, as in Knight and Jortin, a disproportionate space. (Erasmus' English friends were, says Butler at one point, his best supporters.)[16] In this work Erasmus is set, above all, in the context of the literary revival, as the opening sentence reveals: 'In considering the character of Erasmus, we shall find that nothing reflects so much honour upon his memory, as the services which he rendered, by his example and labours, to sacred and profane learning.' The first chapter offers 'Historical Remarks on the State of Literature during the Middle Ages' which, while praising the high scholastics and arguing for a beginning to the literary revival earlier than is commonly supposed, generally put a progressive view, the 'spirit of free inquiry' arising in the fourteenth century and being ever thereafter 'on the increase.'[17]

Though this work's centre of interest is the literary revival, it can still be read as a Catholic interpretation of Erasmus, Catholic in line with Butler's outlook and experience. The former pupil of Douai comments on the holy atmosphere among the Brethren at Deventer. He deals at a little length with Erasmus' experience of conventual life but not with his attitude to the monastic institution. Scholasticism, as taught at Paris when he was a student there, had little attraction for him; but later Colet 'and probably his own inclination' directed him to theology, not of the scholastic kind, but 'on a large and liberal plan which, excluding the subtleties of the schools, comprised all that could serve to explain or illustrate the doctrines or the history of Christianity.'[18] Butler mildly challenges Erasmus' sarcasm at the expense of pilgrims to Becket's tomb at Canterbury:[19] 'But was it not much better, both for the poor and for society, that the artisan should have been employed in the workmanship of them? Were not both art and science served by it?' Like others, Butler found in love of freedom a clue to Erasmus' life; even England, to which he was attached, could not hold him.[20]

In his treatment of Erasmus' works, Butler makes a salute to orthodoxy but holds to a liberal, generous judgment wherever he can. Thus he says of the works connected with the New Testament edition: 'It may be said of them, as of his other writings, those even which are most valuable, that they contain some doubtful and some reprehensible positions; but that the general fund is excellent.'[21] He praises the *Colloquia* for their depictions of life and manners, of characters whom the reader seems to see and know. At the same time, he goes on, a Roman Catholic finds the teaching and practice of his church often misrepresented there, and that at a dangerous time for the church. Erasmus' worst fault was that he made abuses universal, which they were not. His defenders argue that, writing before the Council of Trent, he should not be bound by later orthodoxy; Butler declares himself willing to give Erasmus every advantage of that defence. 'All lovers of learning must ever wish to find Erasmus in the right; and, when he is not quite in the right, to find him very excusable.'[22] Butler does not share Erasmus' preference for Jerome over Augustine. The latter's speculations were more sublime and his piety of a more amiable nature. The language of this old English Catholic is – in such a comment – touched by romanticism and the religion of feeling. Similarly, the *Enchiridion*, which aimed at identifying religion, not with ceremony, but with 'true piety and the practice of Christian duty,' contained some expressions failing in theological accuracy and, further, 'considering it as a work of devotion, it does not speak sufficiently to the hearts.' On that point, Butler agrees with Loyola. *Moriae encomium*, an 'almost unrivalled effusion of wit' and not actually condemned by the popes of Erasmus' time, still included indefensible propositions.[23]

Butler has less to say on the Reformation than the nineteenth-century Protestant writers. Erasmus, he writes, at first saw in Luther only 'an indiscreet and too ardent a Catholic' but later believed he was driving everything to extremities; his later moderation earned the displeasure of both sides. To both contributions to the free-will debate he applies Milton's line; they 'found no end in wandering mazes lost.' 'In fact the subject is above human reason.'[24] It is an appeal to common sense congenial to Butler's countrymen. As for Erasmus' Catholicity, he 'repeatedly and explicitly' disclaimed every opinion contrary to the church's faith; his death in a Protestant town was by chance, for he intended to settle in a Catholic country. In short, his will was Catholic; he was, in the last resort, a reformer in the Catholic mould.[25]

Butler represented a long-established tradition of Catholic dissent in England. It was faithful in its own way, sharing with the surrounding society its dominant values, including tolerance and reasonableness in religion, not strongly Roman, or even particularly obedient to the hierarchy. Butler liked Erasmus because of his services to learning and because, despite his theological inaccuracies and inadequacies, he stood for moderation amid clashing enthusiasms and dogmatisms. Those Catholics who grew up in a time of fierce reaction against the French Revolution and of romantic intensity in religion, often associated with enthusiasm for the Middle Ages, saw the church and the world differently. For them Erasmus' virtues (as interpreted by Gallicans and liberals) became vices: openness to pagan culture, tolerance of religious differences, reserve towards institutional authority.

In his first book, *Les pèlerinages de Suisse*, Louis Veuillot (1813–83), the gifted, abrasive, uncompromising Catholic polemicist and journalist, blamed Erasmus (among others) for the loss of Basel to Catholicism.[26] He gives a picture of a Catholic city, indeed of medieval civilization, subverted by intellectual pride. On one side lies a world of trusting faith and social unity, on the other side a fractured community, spiritual restlessness, and a cold individualism. Erasmus and his associates, examples of the 'vanity of knowledge and reason' when unattached to faith, were the bridge between. The picture has its origins partly in romanticism, in a longing for the imagined wholeness of medieval society, of which both the Renaissance and Protestantism are seen as enemies.

The same picture is to be found in the first volume of Ignaz von Döllinger's history of the Reformation. In this there is a great irony. At the first Vatican Council in 1870, Veuillot was to be the mouthpiece of the party pressing for the decree of papal infallibility, while Döllinger saw the decree as a break with primitive Catholicity, a new dogma not supported by either scripture or tradition. He was among the more prominent of its opponents. A comparison has been made between Döllinger and Erasmus, moderate men in an age of extremes.[27] Döllinger himself wrote to Acton that, among the historical characters of the sixteenth century, he would rather be an Erasmus or a Michel de l'Hôpital (the mediating French chancellor) than a great Counter-Reformation pope like Pius V.[28]

That was in 1881 when Döllinger (1799–1890) was cut off from the Roman church. In the 1840s he appeared differently: a professor at Munich University, where a strongly Catholic spirit prevailed, a member of the Görres circle, which combined an intense spirituality with a sense of the church as a historical formation. 'The central theme was the renewal of life through the power of faith, as understood by the Catholic church, after the catastrophes of unbelief, in revolutions, wars and breakdowns of every kind.'[29] Of Döllinger himself, Acton said: 'The cause he pleaded was the divine government of the Church, the fulfilment of the promise that it would be preserved from error, though not from sin, the uninterrupted employment of the powers committed by Christ for the salvation of man.'[30] During the revolution of 1848, soon after completing his work on the Reformation, he spoke out for the rights of the church, especially for its independence from the state, and was active in Catholic political organization.[31]

If, as has been suggested, Döllinger intended his book on the Reformation to be a reply to Ranke's history,[32] the outcome was very different from what might have been expected. This is no narrative or analytical history of the Reformation but, as Döllinger himself said in the foreword, an assessment of its inner meaning, an investigation of its inner springs. The third volume is a confrontation with Luther's doctrine on justification.[33] The first is essentially the testimony of witnesses who had at the beginning had sympathy for the movement and then turned against it. At the head stands Erasmus.

Much of this opening essay of the work carries a judgment on Erasmus himself. In the early years of the sixteenth century, Döllinger begins, he had an unexampled place among the learned of Europe. Like other humanists, he believed that the intellectual hegemony in Germany and the education of the rising generations belonged to them rather than to the theologians and religious. He ridiculed superstitions and abuses, but not without striking at the institution itself. So, 'without this exactly being his intention, he prepared the way for the Reformation by the tone and content of his writing.' His way of handling theological and church questions was superficial and scattered doubts and suspicions far and wide. It was well fitted 'to prepare souls for a great disruption of the church and to make them receptive to a new teaching.'

Erasmus was, Döllinger believes, deceived by the apparently secure position of the church; he was as far from desiring a violent upset as a man who has seen only smooth seas can anticipate a storm. Later, when the seed he had sown had brought forth its fruit a hundredfold, he withdrew, directly or indirectly, much of what he had said. One acquainted with Erasmus and his writings would explain his early utterances by the fact that he was not a man of firm convictions and his distaste for scholastic theology had left him weak in systematic thought.[34]

The role which Erasmus played in the years 1518–23, years critical for the church, could only confirm the belief of his contemporary critics, like Aleander, Alberto Pio, and Sepulveda, that he had prepared the way for Luther. Döllinger quotes the famous letter of May 1519 to Wolsey[35] and goes on: Luther himself knew how many of Erasmus' views he had taken over and how large a part of his success he owed to him. He spoke favourably of Luther's commentary on the psalms, which contained much of his heretical teaching. He praised Luther even to those whose reaction he would have occasion to fear if they took it badly, like the archbishop of Mainz.[36]

A change came only in 1523–4, Döllinger says, quoting Duke George of Saxony's remark about Erasmus' diatribe on free will that the church would not be in such a plight if Erasmus had spoken up earlier. He was convinced by what he observed as moral decline among the adherents of the new teaching. He used ever stronger expressions, notably in letters to Melanchthon: 'I see new hypocrites, new tyrants and not a grain of the gospel spirit.' Moral decline and divisions among the Protestants led him to expect the movement's speedy disappearance. A long quotation from Erasmus' *Epistola contra quosdam qui se falso iactant evangelicos* is the point to which Döllinger's discussion has been leading: Erasmus is a witness against the Protestant Reformation.[37]

Without carrying Veuillot's suggestions of the corruption of a whole civilization, Döllinger's interpretation of Erasmus points in the same direction as that of the ultramontane journalist: misled by vanity and a mistaken optimism, unprotected by strong character, firm conviction, or sound theological preparation, he opened the way to a disruption of the church and a break in the Catholic tradition, which he himself came in time to deplore. While this picture naturally had much in common with earlier unfriendly Catholic interpretations, it also had, in its criticism of Erasmus' carelessness or indifference toward the hitherto unbroken, as it were organic, continuity of Catholic tradition, the particular colouring of the Catholicism of the romantic era.

The attitudes of mid-century Catholicism, which are to be found in Döllinger's work on the Reformation, are also expressed in one of the most important and influential articles on Erasmus published in the nineteenth century. That this was so is in itself remarkable since the author, Moritz Kerker, was otherwise not widely known.[38] The attitudes mentioned were a strong sense of the continuity of Catholic history and of the life of the church as an organic unity and a revived enthusiasm for the Middle Ages. Kerker's article can be seen as a product of the Catholic theological faculty set up in the Protestant University of Tübingen in 1817 by the government of Württemberg in order to promote cooperation between the confessions. It was published in the journal *Theologische Quartalschrift*, founded in 1819 to represent that faculty's academic interests.

Moritz Kerker (1825–1900) studied at Tübingen, 1843–7, was ordained in the fateful year 1848, and himself taught at Tübingen in the early 1850s. He spent his later career as an educational administrator in Swabia. When he published his article on Erasmus in 1859, he was pastor at Kleinsüssen and inspector of schools.[39]

An interest in church history was characteristic of the Tübingen school, an interest going beyond the history of the ecclesiastical institution, its hierarchy and bureaucracy. For J.A. Möhler, one of the leaders of the school, the church was a community created by the Spirit, capable of development, embracing a variety of gifts. His idea of synthesis owed something to Hegel. Also, Tübingen rediscovered scholasticism after its neglect in the eighteenth century, even before a strong wave of neo-Thomism came in from Italy.[40]

The two ideas – the synthesis, or at least the reconciliation, of different movements of thought and the recovery of scholasticism – are put plainly at the beginning of Kerker's article, 'Erasmus und sein theologischer Standpunkt.' The humanists, Kerker begins, condemned the scholastics as barbarians and, even before Luther, the modern stereotype of the Middle Ages as a time of darkness and servitude had been set up. For their part, the scholastics rejected the humanists as pagans and their studies as worldly and unchristian. For the church, it was a misfortune that matters went to such extremes and two exclusive worlds faced each other in mutual incomprehension. Certainly, the force of scholasticism had been weakened in the later Middle Ages with the nominalist school, whose language hardly made theological study attractive to gifted minds. The refreshment of theology by the study of languages, the classics, and the Fathers was desirable. On the other side, how greatly humanism needed correcting and completing by Christian theology! Pico della Mirandola, who warned against rejecting all scholasticism because of the later, more corrupt forms, was ignored. Most humanists turned away from theology and Christianity itself.[41]

The need, then, was for mediation between humanism and theology. Erasmus, Kerker concludes, seemed called to this task; he himself, according to his lights, saw it as his mission. His writings and editions demonstrate the point.[42] In his *Ciceronianus*, he attacked the paganizing humanists and, to his great honour, defended the Christian uses of Latin. Kerker asks: may we not, therefore, expect from Erasmus a reconciling stance towards scholasticism? The need was exactly for an explanation of the scholastic use of language, since that most repelled the humanists. The *Ciceronianus* had prepared that explanation: it is more Ciceronian to adjust one's speech to one's Christian themes than to distort them in the language of pagan antiquity.[43]

Yet Erasmus was, says Kerker, the most unrelenting enemy of scholasticism. This was not, in fact, a matter of language. Erasmus would not have found Scotus, Durandus, or Ockham attractive if they had come clothed in the language of Cicero, Varro, or Quintilian. His objection was to the substance, 'the philosophical [speculativ] treatment of theological teachings, their sharp and distinct definition and development, the explicating of dogmatic content, the systematic and deductive method in dogmatics and ethics,' to which he was completely hostile. By this line of attack, he struck the spirit of the Middle Ages, which was a philosophical, speculative one, to its heart. In comparing (as he saw them) the noble, living speech and the ethical interests of the Fathers with the speculative concerns of the scholastics, he represented scholasticism and all medieval dogmatics as a degeneration from, and not an unfolding of, Christian teaching. 'The common suspicion, which suspected the Middle Ages of falsifying the simple Christian faith, first gained currency through him.' Luther took it over from him. His theological work tuned in with the age's preference for the tangible, the easily understandable, and the popular.44

Erasmus' attack on scholasticism meant a missed opportunity for reconciling two intellectual traditions, the humanist and the scholastic. It went further. Döllinger, says Kerker, rightly concluded that Erasmus so ridiculed abuses as to strike at the institution itself. The attack was thorough; Erasmus denied the whole scholastic achievement, the great names and periods as well as the lesser or corrupt, and blamed scholasticism for the decline of the church. The question arises for Kerker: if theology was as degenerate as Erasmus said, must not the whole dogmatic system of the church have been contaminated, for in the Middle Ages the two could hardly be separated? In other words, must not Erasmus' attack move from one to the other? Kerker replies: 'In all seriousness, he proposes to revise dogmatic teachings which are already established in the church.' He raises questions about marriage as a sacrament, oral confession, and the papal primacy, not merely for debate, but as an expression of doubt over the substance of the received doctrine.45

The sharp tooth of the 'sceptical humanist' (Kerker uses a favourite image of Catholic critics of Erasmus since the sixteenth century) began gnawing at the dogmatic web woven in the christological controversies of the first centuries. These were, for Erasmus, needless controversies over words. But his attack was not limited to language. The very idea of dogmatic definition was unwelcome to Erasmus. He hoped that the fall of scholasticism would take with it the more elaborate dogmatic structures.[46] He wanted a greater intellectual freedom.[47] The limits set by scholasticism had to be broken. Often he spoke of scripture as the one source of faith, beside which tradition was human and imperfect, but scripture itself had to be freed of human additions.[48]

Kerker is prudent and distinguishes between Erasmus' conscious belief and the principle of doubt at work in his writings, which broke through from time to time, to his own surprise. His enemies, Catholic and Protestant, were wrong to call him an Arian. Rather, he sought a simpler, more rationalistic faith and drew back, frightened, when he saw the consequences. Like other sceptics, he then called on the authority of the church or asked for certain questions to be left to the last judgment. Such appeals, says Kerker, betray a lack of firm faith and clear thought.

Similarly, his call for theology to have a purer, practical piety as outcome was praiseworthy in its way. But piety and theology should not be confused. Kerker found distasteful the scorn of Erasmus, a man of study with (as Kerker believed) no feeling for popular needs, for the piety of the people. His attacks on monastic disciplines and on so-called works righteousness anticipated Luther, indeed the Lutheran fideism, from which the rationalistic tendency in him otherwise recoiled.[49]

At the end of his article, Kerker returns to the relationship between humanism and the church generally and puts an apparent paradox. The revival of classical pagan forms was not in itself a danger to the church. Certainly, the frivolity and indifference of the Italian humanists had baleful effects, but humanism in Italy saw itself as a worldly, literary movement and stood apart from theology; it would be too much to fear a revival of paganism from that quarter. Many manifestations of the antique were childish rather than dangerous and, in any case, some Italian humanists became orthodox reformers. The danger arose where humanism 'wants to be Christian, where it undertakes the reform of theology.' It arose because there humanism stood in contradiction to the Middle Ages and, in condemning the theology of that time, called into question the continuity of dogmatic development. It arose, in short, with Erasmus. His humanism rejected, not only medieval language and form, but the very substance of the medieval achievement.[50]

There is fair intellectual power in Kerker's article. It has a sustained argument: Erasmus' resistance to dogmatic definition, to the association of philosophy and theology, his preference for piety over dogma, represented an attack on the fund of theological and dogmatic resources the church had inherited from the Middle Ages. In the sixteenth century – and in the nineteenth – it still needed to draw on that fund. The threatened break in continuity put the church in danger as never before. Kerker raised an important question: Erasmus' relation to scholasticism. His answer was determined by certain assumptions; that scholastic theology and the doctrinal system of the church were inextricably associated and, therefore, in a sense scholasticism was indispensable to the church; that scholasticism was in decline in the later Middle Ages but that this, in itself, did not excuse its critics; that an association between humanism and scholasticism was possible or, more exactly, humanism could claim to be Christian only where, theologically speaking, the priority of scholasticism was accepted. To summarize Kerker's judgment on Erasmus: he failed to take the opportunity offered him by his situation because of a deeply implanted suspicion, indeed hostility, towards the definition and elaboration of doctrine in the church. There is another assumption present here: that a man's conscious intentions are less important for his historical significance than the tendency or principle at work in his thought and writings, even beyond his intentions. In Erasmus' case, the tendency, in Kerker's view, was toward rationalism. But to accept this assumption is to cut historical enquiry short. Kerker did not ask what, in his experience and background, led Erasmus to his views on scholasticism and church dogma or how real an alternative the cooperation of humanists and scholastics would be for him.[51]

II

As Döllinger's changed attitude demonstrates, the tendencies represented by Kerker's article – rediscovery of scholasticism, enhanced insistence on the teaching authority of the church – were not the only elements in the Roman church's situation as its nineteenth-century crisis approached in 1870. There were contrary voices. Some spoke against exclusiveness and sought to widen, rather than reduce, contact with the non-Roman churches. Others wanted at least to keep to moderate tones. Erasmus and others of a tolerant, irenic disposition in the sixteenth century were attractive subjects to Catholic scholars of the 1860s and 1870s who had this outlook.[52]

Friedrich Wilhelm Kampschulte (1831–72) may be taken as representative, not least in the personal tragedy the events of 1870 brought him.[53] He believed that the Vatican decrees falsified the faith in which he had been brought up in Westphalia, resisted them publicly, and subsequently adhered to the old Catholic church, the body of those who could not accept the decrees. He was denied the last sacrament. Earlier he had turned from training for the priesthood to history and had studied with Ranke at Berlin and Cornelius, a friend of Döllinger's, at Bonn. His studies of sixteenth-century history served his Catholic convictions but also showed his bias towards the irenic. His Bonn dissertation was on Witzel, the irenic thinker, one of the authors of the moderate church ordinances in the Duchy of Cleves and Erasmus' friend.[54] He was later to write on Calvin, but his first substantial work was a history of Erfurt University in the age of humanism and the Reformation.

The subject was an appropriate one for Kampschulte because the lines between scholasticism, humanism, and the Reformation were more fluid there than elsewhere in Germany.[55] In its beginnings, humanism in Erfurt had, according to Kampschulte, a mild temper. But the fierce controversy over Reuchlin and the Jewish books, in which Erfurt was caught up, suggested that the humanists would be satisfied with nothing less than the complete destruction of the old learning. The chief exponent of this feeling was Mutian. More moderate natures in fact recoiled from his extremism and looked to Erasmus. Admittedly in *Moriae encomium* he had done more to damage the reputation of scholasticism than any other writer but by nature he preferred to avoid extremes: the new learning should be introduced gradually, not suddenly and violently, with the aim of purifying, not destroying, the old learning. The Reuchlin affair confirmed Erasmus in these feelings which he expressed thereafter publicly and clearly.[56] He began to exercise a direct influence on Erfurt after his return to the Netherlands in 1516, at a time when the leadership of the humanist circle there passed from Mutian to the moderate Eobanus Hessus who revered Erasmus and made a pilgrimage to him in late 1518. Kampschulte pictures an idyllic brotherhood of scholars in Erfurt around 1520 under the name and sign of Erasmus; Hutten lost all influence there and Mutian himself was

reconciled. The humanist circle took the lead in a peaceful transformation of the university in the Erasmian spirit.[57]

The interest of Kampschulte's study is in its portrayal of Erasmus' irenicism and moderation, even towards the scholastics about
whom he had spoken earlier with great bitterness. The most complete statement in the nineteenth century of the irenic side of
Erasmus was made by a student of Kampschulte's, Philipp Woker,
who was born in 1848, also in Westphalia, and studied with
Kampschulte at Bonn in the later 1860s. His dissertation was
entitled *De Erasmi Roterodami studiis irenicis.* Woker's *prooemium*
deals with two points: first, the inevitability of conflict between
scholastics and humanists, since the former defended their corrupt doctrines 'with blind tenacity' and the latter were on the
attack, even to the point of endangering the authority of the
church; secondly, the early experiences of Erasmus, including his
forced entry to the monastery and his encounter with the scholastics at Paris, which filled him with bitterness against the state
of the monasteries and of studies and the condition of the church
generally. The *Moriae encomium* expressed this mood. Having by
diligence and natural gifts risen above the handicaps of his early
life and become a public figure, he threatened to confront the
church in a completely negative spirit.[58]

There came, according to Woker, a change of direction in Erasmus' life after the *Moriae*; it was the last of his essentially negative
and censorious works. The cause was his association with English
friends, especially John Colet and Thomas More, who not only
despised the condition of the church but believed that it could
be corrected and purified.[59] Erasmus was led into their 'studiis
pacificis' the more easily because he was 'by nature mild and
peaceful, cautious, nay timid, in spirit, not one who undertook
perilous struggles with ardour and tenacity.' There were two sides
to this change in Erasmus, as Woker describes it: he had moved
from attacking the church to correcting it; he believed that this
must be done, not by vituperation and threats of violence, but
gradually, by peaceful persuasion. Correction must be in studies
and in ways of life. The change did not lead to neglect of his
humanist studies; rather they were now directed towards the benefit of religion and theology. It bore fruit in his edition of the
New Testament.[60]

How had the degeneration occurred from the pristine state of
the Christian church to its present deformed appearance? Woker

follows Erasmus' argument in his anti-war tract, *Dulce bellum inexpertis*: in their controversies with the heretics, Christians drew on the worldly wisdom of the ancients; Aristotle and even Roman law became mixed in with the Christian philosophy. As faith and true piety wavered, dogmas and ceremonies multiplied. Thus, Erasmus returns to his starting-point, his attack on scholasticism, though now for the sake of pure religion rather than secular learning.

He made this attack, Woker adds, without impugning church authority. Woker wishes to safeguard that authority at least in its pre-1870 form: Erasmus did not question the power of councils, he did not deny that the pope was the vicar of Christ, but he did resist scholastic exaggerations like papal inerrancy in matters of faith and morals. Since the mark of the church was unanimity and concord, reform should begin with the rulers and proceed with the consent of the church. Woker through Erasmus expresses old Catholic preferences – for an earlier consensus about papal authority without the 'exaggerations' of 1870 and for the avoidance of controversy between extremes.[61]

In the Reuchlin affair Erasmus counselled both sides to moderation. He adhered to Reuchlin and his supporters and saw the source of the conflict in the scholastics' hatred of good letters but he approached even the Cologne scholastics with mild words. He disapproved of the calumnies of the *Letters of Obscure Men*. No doubt he had personal reasons for wanting conflicts assuaged – the tranquillity of his studies and the amenity of life generally. But above all he saw the conflicts as an impediment to the kind of church reform he wanted, a change of heart and correction of life requiring a time of peace.[62]

Of course, he faced an even greater controversy, and more than half Woker's study is given to the period after Luther's appearance in 1517. He held apart from the Lutheran party and hated Luther's 'seditiosa studia' but he did not want peace restored by the forcible suppression of the Lutherans. His own studies and reform would be in danger if Luther's were suppressed. Though his natural timidity kept him away from the diets (Worms in 1521, Augsburg in 1530), he gave advice, in writing or through intermediaries, always along the same lines, to Emperor Charles v and to the popes: the conservative theologians should be restrained and the affair treated with clemency, not severity; certainly, the authorities should suppress seditious and libellous writings; otherwise, consciences should be allowed liberty in matters not affecting piety or the dignity of rulers. His advice was in vain and on the other side, says Woker following Döllinger, Luther was producing the turbulence and dissension Erasmus most wished to avoid. The free-will controversy was for him less a matter of dogma than of piety.[63]

In the mid-1520s Erasmus, under attack from both sides, felt his isolation. Later he resumed his search for peace, hoping that God would calm passions, though his swings of mood continued to the end. He was encouraged by younger irenicists, with whom he was associated in preparing the Cleves ordinances and who urged him to be active publicly for reconciliation, especially Julius Pflug and Georg Witzel. His response was the *De sarcienda ecclesiae concordia* of 1533 which summed up his mediating position and expressed principles long held: piety is to be preferred to dogma, reform is, above all, for the correction of ways of life and should be led from above.[64] He no longer hoped for a return to a golden age but for the restoration of at least a tolerable condition; yet he spoke of peace and concord with the same emotion as in the *Complaint of Peace* of twenty years before.[65]

Woker was well read in Erasmus' writings and in previous commentators.[66] His position among Catholic writers of the nineteenth century is distinctive but not, of course, unique. He is anti-scholastic and out of sympathy with those who made essentially defensive responses to the reform demands of the early sixteenth century. He makes no criticism of the Erasmian shift from dogma to piety. He shares Erasmus' love of concord. He makes barely a reference to the events of his own time, but the tone of his work and his association with Kampschulte, to whom the dissertation is dedicated, indicate where he stands; he is irenic, not exclusive, moderate, not intransigent.

Moderate judgments of Erasmus and appreciations of *his* moderation are to be found also in France.[67] They are voluminously expressed in the longest work (so far as I know) written on Erasmus in the nineteenth century, the immense *Erasme: Précurseur et initiateur de l'esprit moderne* by H. Durand de Laur. One may delay for a moment over its dimensions. The first volume, on Erasmus' life, has 689 pages and thirty-five chapters; the second, on his work and writings, is somewhat shorter. The division between life and work makes for repetition, as nineteenth-century critics observed.[68] More seriously, the critics said, Durand de Laur's methods failed to bring Erasmus adequately into encounter with his times. He made little use of other writers on Erasmus or the sixteenth century and showed no familiarity with sources other than Erasmus' letters and writings.[69] The work can be seen as a vast paraphrase of Erasmus with accompanying reflections. The biographical volume in particular lacks shape; there is a kind of undifferentiated narrative following the ebb and flow of Erasmus' correspondence, though occasionally a link between events is made by a glance back or forward. It is essentially a work of cumulation. Yet these remarks may give a misleading impression. There is also evidence of care and acumen. A note on the chronology of Erasmus' correspondence carries conviction: only by patient investigation, claims Durand de Laur, has he been able to order Erasmus' letters sufficiently to throw adequate light on the earlier parts of his life; he had some success.[70]

Durand de Laur's book is contemporary with Gaston Feugère's, which has been treated here in another chapter. The separation is perhaps artificial. The works are not markedly different in tone. Both writers were Catholics and had, presumably, similar vocations, since they both taught in distinguished *lycées*.[71] Nevertheless, Feugère made a more extended and explicit assessment of Erasmus' literary performance, and so it seemed reasonable to consider him within that peculiarly French tradition of interpretation which combined moral reflection with a sense of style and genre.[72] The point of greatest interest, for a history of Erasmus interpretations, in the vast mass of Durand de Laur's work is its handling of the religious question, its definition of Erasmus' religious standpoint and, to a degree, its own standpoint. Both Erasmus, as described by Durand de Laur, and Durand de Laur himself, at least on the evidence of this book, could be called 'moderate Catholics.' The expression has many difficulties but serves to define those who accepted the teaching authority of the church and the substance of Catholic dogma, while arguing for comprehensiveness, for a shift in emphasis from the dogmatic and institutional to the practical and ethical, and for toleration of other Christians.

It is not easy to give an account of the biographical volume because of its form. The author's conclusions are submerged in the mass of paraphrase and quotation from Erasmus' correspondence. Analysis is rare and interpretations have to be wrested from the narrative. In some cases the sources quoted point to different conclusions: Erasmus' school at Deventer was still barbarous but also the fruitful nursery of literature and the learned languages; Erasmus left his monastery with general approval but Willem Hermans wrote that, had he known about his departure, he would have hindered it.[73] When the terrain is described evenly and comprehensively, high points and landmarks are hard to identify.

Nevertheless, Durand de Laur describes Erasmus' entry to the monastery as the 'decisive moment' of his life. To ask why he sees it so will help in establishing the main themes of his work. Erasmus' entry to the monastery is recounted as in the famous letter to Grunnius: the unscrupulous pressure of guardians, the treachery of his brother, the self-interested persuasion of a friend.[74] Life in the monastery was an irritation to one of Erasmus' temperament. There could be no easy resolution between his sceptical spirit and the monastic discipline. The strains were heightened by his nervous sensibility and natural irritability. The case, says Durand de Laur, demonstrates the folly of imposing a vocation against nature. Erasmus developed an implacable hatred for the monastic life which he later ridiculed. His own vocation was for studies and for literature; to enter on it and fulfil it required freedom and especially freedom from the monastery.[75]

From the beginning, adds Durand de Laur, Erasmus was a bold thinker and attracted to predecessors like himself. Already in the monastery, he defended Lorenzo Valla against the criticisms of his friend Cornelis Gerard. This was Erasmus' intellectual point of departure. His boldness remained – Durand de Laur frequently uses the expression 'hardi' – but around 1500 he turned towards theology and the sacred literature. That was under the influence of his English friends and especially of John Colet, whom Durand de Laur depicts as a radical: 'a theologian of great capacity and pure morals, but independent and daring in his opinions,' a forerunner of the Reformation.[76]

The outlines of Durand de Laur's Erasmus portrait are apparent here: a highly strung, even irritable temperament, a passionate devotion to studies, a longing for personal freedom, and a bent towards daring and independent thought.

The boldness of his thinking and his over-sensitivity became apparent as soon as he was embroiled in controversies, initially on literary themes. Too prone to explain and defend himself, he got drawn into interminable debates where, certainly, 'he displayed a remarkable suppleness of mind but which soon absorbed precious time and ended by overwhelming him.' This combativeness – in part unnecessary – was qualified by his moderation and love of peace. The paradox of the peace-lover who found himself in constant conflict may (glimpsed through the fog of words) be counted a main theme of Durand de Laur's work. Erasmus had a flair for friendship but could not help playing on differences in character and style between himself and fellow scholars like Budé.[77] While supporting Reuchlin, he encouraged the Reuchlinists to moderation; he overlooked such advice, however, when attacked himself.[78]

These contradictions threatened from the beginning the balance he wanted to keep in the Luther affair, a balance between his boldness and his moderation. He wanted reform and was a genuine innovator; yet, he abhorred violence and turbulence. Reform must come, therefore, through legitimate authority. Thus he could not in the end make common cause with Luther but, at the same time, he feared the intransigence of Luther's opponents and wanted the popes to institute reforms.[79] The balance, says Durand de Laur, was upset partly by Erasmus' instability of temperament and weakness of character.[80] But the moderate Catholic position was inherently difficult to maintain – not only in turbulent times like the early sixteenth century but at any time. One may draw that conclusion from Durand de Laur's depiction of Erasmus' plight. His relations with the popes were ambiguous.[81] On some subjects, the thrust of his own thinking threatened to carry him beyond the bounds of Catholic doctrine, in particular, on the eucharist, though mostly he held the line. He died in Basel, a Protestant town which had helped secure his independence, but he died with pious, possibly specifically Catholic, expressions on his lips.[82]

The bearing of Erasmus' religious thought is the main subject of volume II. The crux is once again the difficulty of maintaining a moderate Catholic position. The reader cannot tell whether that was a personal difficulty for Durand de Laur in the time of ultramontanism and the Vatican Council. Contemporary references are rare in this work.[83] The dilemmas of Erasmus, however, are made plain. Before returning to that theme, we should notice other features of this volume when contrasted with its predecessor.

The discussion generally is more analytical. Thus, in the second and longest chapter in the volume, Durand de Laur asks what characteristics of Erasmus made him uniquely the propagator of the Renaissance in Europe. He answers: first, Erasmus was without a family, in a sense without a homeland – hence his 'humeur voyageuse,' fitting him for a cosmopolitan role; secondly, he was a monk and priest, allowed liberties not accorded the layman (the remark is strange, since the contrary would seem equally plausible); thirdly, he enchanted the lay world itself with 'his profane ways, his light and mocking spirit, his free manner, his language without prudery, his surface clarity, his easy fluency'; finally, he had the printing-press at his disposal.[84] There follows an account of the works through which Erasmus popularized the Renaissance, the *Adagia* and the *Colloquia* in particular. His translations served the same purpose; he opened up Greek literature like a 'new world.' Durand de Laur turns to the polemical works, notably the *Antibarbari*, Erasmus' most bitter and aggressive composition 'against the ignorance, hypocrisy, and corruption of the monks and priests of his time,' a work of youth, fierce and immoderate.[85]

He asks further: why had Erasmus so commanding an influence, so that 'all, friends and enemies, applied themselves to speaking his language and imitating his way of thinking and writing'? More than any other biographer before the twentieth century, Durand de Laur was interested in the spread of 'Erasmianism' – in England, Germany, and France but also in Spain, where Erasmus was read avidly and the Erasmians translated his works for the people, and in eastern Europe. Budé, he remarks, had more substantial scholarship but lacked his rival's powers of communication. His name recalls only 'an admirable scholar,' Erasmus' name 'a solemn moment in the march of the human spirit' (the comment is reminiscent of Hallam's).[86]

In a somewhat overdrawn picture, Durand de Laur represents Erasmus as the 'president' of the republic of letters, uniting the learned of Europe through correspondence and mutual criticism and support. He returns to the heart of his Erasmus portrait when he asks about the handicaps on Erasmus' leadership of the humanist movement and identifies certain faults of character (irritability, levity, lack of discretion) and a failure in the moderation he commended in his writings.[87] His censures of institutions and doctrines were excessive. Thus in his *Ratio verae theologiae* he rightly sought to bring theology back to its true sources in the scriptures and the Fathers. But he was too fearful of metaphysical questions and too harsh on scholasticism, whose vigour he underestimated (it had a sturdy frame, says Durand de Laur, but lacked flesh and blood).[88] So we are brought back to the problem of Erasmus' Catholicism and to the strains on one of whom Durand de Laur says at one point: his moderation is one of his finest claims to glory.[89]

In fact, Erasmus – in this author's view – contributed to the frustration of the reform in religion and theology to which he himself was devoted. He was carried, by his nature and the thrust of his ideas, beyond the moderate ways he recommended to others. He let sarcasm have its head. He provoked a reaction among monks and theologians who, failing to see that the movement needed responsible leadership and mixing tares and wheat, condemned Erasmus entirely. They thus delivered the field to the Protestant Reformers. A similar pattern appears in Erasmus' biblical work. He was sincere in saying that his work was not destructive of the faith or the authority of the sacred books. Nevertheless, he raised questions 'heavy with storms.' The seeds of modern criticism, Durand de Laur goes on, are in his writings on the New Testament. 'While claiming to remain in the bosom of Christianity and the church, was Erasmus not in a certain measure the precursor and the father of modern scepticism?'[90] The question is prudently worded but Durand de Laur himself has difficulty in keeping the balance he wants in his judgment of Erasmus. Here he veers towards the Enlightenment view of Erasmus as 'father of modern scepticism.'

In explaining Erasmus' relation to the Reformation, he repeats the metaphor of Erasmus the sower of seeds; the growth was Luther's. Thus the *Enchiridion*'s teaching of the inwardness of scriptural teaching was not inconsistent with Catholic doctrine but in the Reformation it was taken to excess and Erasmus himself had written there with insufficient restraint. Similarly, Folly's actual criticisms were justified but the spirit of irreverence with which she expressed them prepared the way for Luther.[91] Erasmus' intention was a Catholic reformation which maintained the unity of the church and respected its hierarchy but his lack of judgment gave their opportunity to those who wanted something more drastic. 'In him there were two men, one clear-sighted, moderate, conciliating, the other passionate, personal, satiric.'[92]

Durand de Laur is making two criticisms of Erasmus: a temperament which often took him beyond his own intention; a failure to recognize the consequences of his ideas.

Durand de Laur is able to keep his balance to the end of his long work. For him, in the last resort Erasmus was not made for theology. He lacked the necessary rigour and precision and even dryness, all predicated on the teaching authority of the church.[93] The simplification of doctrine for which he called threatened a crippling relaxation. He tended to inconsistency on fundamental questions though his intentions were Catholic and his good faith shone through.[94]

Nevertheless, there were issues and situations where his gifts were appropriate, indeed – for the church in that age – providential. Of the requisite qualities for debating free will with Martin Luther, Erasmus had only one, but it was all-important: 'good sense and feeling for reality.' His diatribe was more than a book, it was a deed, the protest of good sense and human conscience against determinism. Erasmus modestly promised a discussion of the issue, not the demonstration of a dogma.[95] Unlike Luther, he understood that liberty of conscience and toleration could be grounded only on a sense of moral responsibility predicated on free will.[96] In his writings on government and war, like his friend Thomas More, he set a Christian ethical standard, even if their amalgam of Platonism and the gospel teaching went beyond the bounds of possibility in that age of perfidious princes.[97]

For Durand de Laur Erasmus' intention ultimately was to open Catholicism and the modern world to one another. Hence the subtitle of his book: 'précurseur et initiateur de l'esprit moderne.' The phrase seems to belong to the liberals whom we have discussed elsewhere. The intended marriage between modern mind and Catholic tradition distinguishes this vision from theirs. Erasmus 'wished to remain Christian, which distinguishes him essentially from Voltaire. He wished further to remain Catholic, which separates him profoundly from Luther ... On the threshold of the modern world, Erasmus, with penetrating gaze, saw the vast transformation which was in preparation and at the same time the great problem which was presenting itself: how to reconcile the life of the Church to the new spirit, to knowledge and liberty?' Unlike Luther and Voltaire, he wished to maintain the whole chain of tradition, to associate pagan wisdom with Christian truth, 'et, de cette union conclue sous les auspices des *Muses*, faire sortir l'esprit moderne.'[98]

III

Those who, in the second half of the twentieth century, wish to present Erasmus as fully Catholic and orthodox might well consider Durand de Laur's judgment of him essentially unsympathetic and the characterization of this writer as 'moderate Catholic' seriously misleading. Yet, it is a defensible description of one holding the views he did in a time of aggressive ultramontanism, when the strictures of the young Döllinger and Moritz Kerker were well known to informed readers. Much the same can be said of a group of Belgian Catholic writers who wrote about Erasmus in terms like Durand de Laur's: although Erasmus made mistakes in theology and inadvertently prepared the way for more revolutionary and destructive thinkers, his intentions were wholly Catholic and he served notably, indeed uniquely, the revival of letters and, within limits, the reform of the church and of Christian society.

In the Belgium which freed itself from Dutch administration in the revolutions of 1830 one finds debates, characteristic of the century everywhere in western Europe, over the place of the church in the polity and movements – secularism and anticlericalism – aimed at diminishing that place.[99] At the same time, one is not surprised that Catholics associated Belgian nationality with Catholic sentiments or that Catholic writers on Erasmus should interest themselves in his sojourns in and relations with their homeland. They had an interest in demonstrating a continuous national identity from the Middle Ages, through the times of humanism, Catholic reformation, and Habsburg government, to the reconstitution of the nineteenth century.

Thus, Pierre F.-X. de Ram (1804–65), who was to become first rector of the reconstituted University of Louvain (1834)[100] and, later, president of the Académie Royale des Sciences, des Lettres et des Beaux-Arts (1857), had under the Dutch administration promoted efforts to compete with Protestant proselytizing literature in the Flemish language and himself published four volumes of lives of the Netherlands saints. He also took up a project of publishing acts of the provincial and diocesan synods in Belgium since the Council of Trent. He sought, during the revolution, to secure the independence of the church and was principal author of a petition from the primate to the constituent assembly renouncing the ecclesiastical privileges of the past and seeking guarantees of the church's freedom under the new constitution.[101]

De Ram was interested in Erasmus. He published a number of short papers on him in the *Bulletin* of the Academy. The longest concerned Erasmus' relations with Basel, and its standpoint is unmistakable from the first page. The Reformation of Luther and Zwingli brought discord and violence to Switzerland, and Basel shared this unhappy fate. Between Erasmus and the city there had been a mutual attraction and love. Even when the Reformation had driven him to Freiburg, he kept his connection with Basel and especially with Froben's printery. In de Ram's view, Erasmus was not wholly sound as a Catholic; he trusted too much in his own inspirations in theology. But he was prepared to sacrifice his residence in Basel rather than accept the religious revolution. Above all, he died Catholic. Erasmus did not choose to die in a Protestant town. After returning to Basel in 1535, he was confident of going on to Brabant but was taken unawares by his last illness.[102]

De Ram's article includes three hitherto unpublished letters touching on Erasmus' death.[103] He dealt with that subject in a separate brief article 'Note sur Lambert Coomans, secrétaire d'Erasme.' He wanted to challenge Adolf Müller's depiction of Erasmus dying in 'cold indifference for the succour and consolations of religion'; some, he says, had anachronistically turned him into a *philosophe* of the eighteenth century. Doubts about his fidelity to the church, de Ram goes on, should disappear when one observes that he had, as personal secretary in his last years, a Catholic priest, Lambert Coomans, who acted as a kind of chaplain.[104] According to an eighteenth-century book on Turnhout, Coomans' birthplace, Erasmus had died in the latter's arms saying: 'O mater dei, memento mei.' The story was said to be confirmed by two old (unspecified) manuscripts in Turnhout. It was, we can now see, not well founded.[105] Its importance for de Ram was its witness to the essentially Catholic character of Erasmus. The spirit of de Ram's writings on the great humanist is admirably expressed by the comment of a friend: 'Everything which serves to establish the religious sentiments and the orthodoxy of intention of this celebrated man should be received with alacrity.'[106]

Later writers for the Académie Royale concentrated on Erasmus' relations with Belgium but they maintained de Ram's spirit. Like him, they noted theological weaknesses but accepted, indeed emphasized, his 'orthodoxy of intention.' In 1854 the Academy crowned a memoir on the life and works of Erasmus, considered in their relations with Belgium, by Eugène Rottier. The author (born 1829) was an advocate from Ghent for whom Erasmus was an amateur enthusiasm.[107] His work betrays its amateur character: it is written in a strong, precipitate style but is badly arranged, with serious displacements in chronology, errors of fact, and even contradictory judgments.[108]

Rottier's study has two main themes: its association of Erasmus with Belgium, its moderate judgment of him as a Catholic. Erasmus' attachments in the Netherlands, Rottier says, were not narrow. He accepted the political and cultural unity of the Netherlands later to be divided in two; as the passions roused by the Restoration and the revolution of 1830 recede, Rottier believes, the historic unity will be valued once again. Erasmus was the 'faithful servant' of the house of Austria; he did not share the resentment, admittedly often justified, of his compatriots in Holland against the Burgundian inheritance. At the end of his life, he looked to Brabant, 'his dear country.'[109] The gravity and sobriety of tone which marked his early works came from the Netherlands ('la pieuse Belgique'); he lost these in Italy, which intoxicated him with its 'voluptuous breath'; gravity gave way to verve, elegance, finesse, and 'a dangerous spirit of raillery came to dominate him.' This highly coloured account, which would seem, even to contemporaries, to reverse the accepted pattern of Erasmus' development (ie from the more frivolous toward the more serious), is presumably intended to explain the fissures in his work between the Christian and the pagan, the constructive and the destructive. The new spirit brought benefits to literature in Belgium itself. In a work like the *Praise of Folly*, Erasmus introduced lightness and elegance and restored to the imagination its rights.[110]

In religion Erasmus was, on Rottier's account, a divided man. In the *Enchiridion*, for example, there were some rays of pure light but otherwise a dark disorder, where Christian faith and philosophical boldness met and clashed. One can even find the idea of the equality of religions, 'an audacity bordering on impiety,' worthy of a free thinker. The *Praise of Folly* offended both morals and taste by introducing sacred subjects into a satire and was also

disfigured by its violence against the monks. Yet these weaknesses should not obscure its elegant satire on our vanities and
ambitions, its generous indignation against injustice and oppression. Certainly, says Rottier, Erasmus was too single-minded in
asserting primitive against modern Christianity, apostolic poverty, for example, against papal wealth. This is Rottier's main
point: by giving way to his flair for ridicule and by his extreme
judgments, Erasmus called into question the very things he wished
to defend.[111]

Rottier was unaffected by the revival of scholasticism in his
time. For him, it was 'false science.' In Erasmus' days, even at
Louvain, it was approaching its end, and Erasmus' biblical work
indicated how it was to be replaced. Perhaps Erasmus opened
the way to individual interpretation of the Bible but to rank him
among the heretics on that score would, Rottier says, be like
accusing of a crime the artisan who forged the weapon with which
it was committed. In fact, Erasmus, Reuchlin, and others were
bringing in a gradual reformation which obstinacy on one side
and rebelliousness on the other destroyed. For Rottier, a moderate
reform by men who were and remained Catholic, whatever their
weaknesses or the unintended consequences of those weaknesses,
had been a possibility.[112]

Drawing together his two themes, Rottier says at the end: Erasmus prepared the way for reformation, if not for heresy; this was
a 'perilous glory' which more enlightened Catholics have not
dared to condemn, since they recognized his pure intention. But
the theologians of Louvain saw the danger and helped defend
the country against it. 'One did justice to the beauty of style, to
the nobility of thought, but one feared the temerity, the restlessness, the need to innovate, and to all that anguish of spirit which
hesitates and doubts one preferred the naive and superstitious
faith of the past.'[113]

It is not easy to bring Rottier's various comments and judgments into a consistent focus. Erasmus appears as the pioneer, at
one point, of true Catholic reform, at another almost of godless
scepticism. What associates Rottier with the moderate Catholic
group in my view is the distinction he makes between intention
and effect. It is, of course, not original with him; it is a useful
distinction for writers wanting to maintain a claim to Erasmus,
while accepting many of the criticisms made of him by Catholics.
His intentions were orthodox and Catholic, but circumstances,

misjudgment, personal weakness, or self-indulgence led him beyond the bounds. The other point of interest in Rottier's work is,
of course, Belgium itself; Erasmus had many associations there;
he is also judged by its standards, the standards of 'la pieuse
Belgique.'

The most important of the Belgian Catholic commentators on
Erasmus was Félix Nève (1816–93). Like de Ram he was a man
of Louvain, indeed one of the first students of the reconstituted
university. He was a polymath, a productive scholar in a number
of fields, some exotic: Indian, Armenian, and Christian oriental
studies and the history of scholarship in Belgium (in this last he
was influenced especially by de Ram). There were, it has been
said, both patriotic and Catholic motives behind his work: his
more popular writings were directed at the education of his countrymen and all his scholarship had a Christian apologetic purpose.
His praise of another scholar could be applied to himself: 'he
intended to serve scholarship without prejudice to the faith.'[114]

Nève's commitments are apparent in the introductory essay
on the Renaissance he wrote for a volume reproducing, with minor amendments, two essays originally published in the *Revue
Catholique*, essays on Erasmus' sojourn and studies in Brabant
and on his modern historians. A Catholic writer can, he concludes,
treat the Renaissance with restrained sympathy and without sac-
rificing his Christian judgment.[115] Rome's interest in the classical
revival was not contrived, as Michelet claimed. It had its origins
in the Christian Middle Ages whose reputation, says Nève, contemporary scholarship is rehabilitating. Michelet's mistake was
precisely that of confining the Renaissance to the sixteenth century.[116] Nève also criticizes historians who judge a break from
scholasticism to have been unnecessary or misguided (one notes
how this comment distinguishes his views from those of, say,
Moritz Kerker). A new order was coming into being – national,
vernacular – and the refinement of the ancient languages, which
in due course promoted the vernaculars, served its purpose.[117]
Above all, Nève distinguishes Renaissance and Reformation, the
renovation of literature and the revolution in religion. Catholicism, not Protestantism, was the companion of the literary revival.
It has been shown, Nève reports, that already, in the Catholic
Germany of the fifteen century, schools of pure Latinity were
appearing.[118] By contrast, studies declined in the Protestant lands
(as Döllinger demonstrated).[119]

To a Catholic observer in the nineteenth century, Nève remarks, the sixteenth century seems much like his own. It was an
age of inquietude, attractive, compelling in its agitations and contradictions but dangerous. These observations help define the role
of the Catholic scholar: 'His first duty is to bring to the study of
such an age rectitude, firmness and the strength of a truly Christian conscience.'[120]

These views of the Renaissance and its relation to the Reformation must make Erasmus a central and problematic figure for
Nève. In any case, he recognizes him as the leader of the classical
revival in Belgium who, he says, gave Latin 'un accent moderne'
and exercised an immense ascendancy.[121] Naturally, Nève has a
special interest in Erasmus' relations with his *alma mater*. His
standpoint is, in fact, that of Erasmus' more courteous critics at
Louvain, respecting his qualities and achievements but critical of
his character and ideas.

The unhappy course of Erasmus' relations with Louvain (despite his friendships there) is, according to Nève, explained primarily by his own character and disposition. He had worked
untiringly for the Trilingual College and had supported and encouraged the younger humanists, of many of whom (together
with his other friends) Nève gives pen-portraits.[122] He had the
favour of Jean Sauvage, chancellor of Burgundy. Yet his attachments were loose; he was jealous of his freedom, seeking a location where he could work on opinion without constraints and
according to circumstances.[123] Underneath was what Nève calls
his 'esprit frondeur,' against which there was resentment at Louvain; there was also unwillingness to forgive his satire against
the theologians. He attacked the scholastics, Nève judges, without
understanding them and did not distinguish between the great
doctors and mere dialecticians.[124] Much of the early controversy
between Erasmus and the Louvain teachers was courteous and
turned on an issue of importance, the place of the scriptural text
in theology. But after Luther's appearance, there was less willingness at Louvain to overlook 'la liberté de badinage' which
Erasmus invoked in his defence.[125] Besides, less congenial figures,
like Edward Lee and Egmond (Nicolaas Baechem), came to the
fore. Erasmus' alienation from Luther, Nève says, is apparent by
1519. But, duped by personal vanity, he did not side with the
theologians of Louvain when they condemned Luther; he wanted
to separate himself from Luther in his own way and at his own

time. Indeed, concludes Nève, he indulged himself with 'the presumptuous hope that he would some day be the supreme arbitrator.'[126] Instead of defending the church as requested by Adrian VI, he proposed reforms contrary to the traditions of the church. At the end, he regretted having left Brabant but, to justify himself, he exaggerated the enmity he would meet there. As always, he wanted to preserve his freedom of action.[127]

Nève's article on the recent historians of Erasmus, after commenting on such as Drummond, the Protestant writer Stichart, Nisard, Durand de Laur, and Feugère,[128] reiterates the claim of Belgium or at least the historic Netherlands (Burgundy) to Erasmus. Ambiguities about Erasmus' nationality are not justified, Nève says: all his life, Erasmus remained the loyal subject of one state, Burgundy.[129] Nineteenth-century painters, Nève adds, have recognized this association better than Erasmus' biographers and historians.[130]

In the remainder of his article, Nève treated three issues: the nature of Erasmus' Christianity, his criticisms of the social order, and his literary talents and achievements. Nève's summary on the first point reads: 'If he was bold in his attacks and inconsistent in his conduct, he more than once protested against excesses; he never openly separated from the Catholic church, against which he had long seemed to struggle; he even became its defender, but he never turned to it with a filial confidence and submission.' He approached theology, especially scholastic theology, in a highly critical spirit but stopped short of complete negation. He was a natural polemicist but, despite his severity on incumbents, did not deny the institution of the papacy or the hierarchy. Unlike the old Catholics of the nineteenth century, he was not a schismatic and kept the idea of the one true church. He opposed Luther on free will but was generally indecisive on dogma. His was a case of ambiguity, not of apostasy. The tolerance shown his ambiguities was due partly to the religious situation of his time – the pre-Tridentine situation – with the better part of the clergy wanting reform and many points of doctrine still to be defined. Ambiguity was also part of his character. By and large, he had Catholic convictions, but feebleness of character made for equivocation. Nève's treatment of these questions is a balancing act with statements and qualifications on them carrying virtually equal weight.[131]

Nève's appreciation of Erasmus' social criticism is more positive. He sees it as an expression of Christian ethics, a form of moral philosophy drawing on practical experience and the wisdom of the ancient world, not inconsistent with theology but naturally closer to real life, of which Erasmus was a shrewd observer. He was one of the first to speak out for the lay mind ('l'esprit laïque'). He rightly denounced injustice; if sometimes carried away by the force of his own criticism, he did not play the demagogue; he was no utopian.[132]

Nève's judgments on individual works of Erasmus are reasonably typical of Catholic opinion in the nineteenth century. He emphasizes the critical, satiric traits of the *Adagia*, *Colloquia*, and *Moriae encomium* and praises the 'sure taste' of the *Ciceronianus*, a Christian witness against paganism. He admires the natural tone of his writing, its liveliness and penetration; his letters in their improvisatory character correspond admirably to the febrile agitation of Erasmus' life. He showed how a language no longer that of the people could be turned to contemporary use. Nève finishes with a classical qualification: his work would have achieved the level of art, if it had been more controlled.[133]

These Belgian writers occupy a stage in the history of Erasmus scholarship. De Ram and Nève worked with original materials; they were part of a movement towards more exact scholarship, which was to culminate in P.S. Allen's magisterial edition of Erasmus' letters. Their own achievement was mixed; they not surprisingly lacked the thoroughness of modern scholarship. Of most interest to us are their commitments. A mixture of patriotism and religious loyalty led them to study the leading role of Erasmus in the revival of letters in Belgium and his part in the controversies which, as they saw it, helped set the character of modern Belgium. From the debates in and around Louvain, from the Reformation struggles and the civil wars that followed, Belgium emerged a Catholic country. In their view this was a Catholicism different, because of the literary revival itself, from the clerical and scholastic culture of the Middle Ages, a tempered Catholicism, to whose modern character Erasmus – for all his theological errors and inadequacies – had made a contribution.

IV

On 28 April 1875 the young Ludwig von Pastor, later historian of the papacy, reported to his teacher, the Frankfurt historian

Johannes Janssen (1829–91), a conversation with Alberdingk Thijm, professor of the history of Netherlands literature at Louvain. Thijm had defended Erasmus. 'He was,' recalls Pastor, 'somewhat taken aback when I quoted your opinion that Erasmus was the Döllinger of the sixteenth century.'[134] In the following year (1876) there appeared the first volume of Janssen's history of the German people at the close of the Middle Ages (fifteenth to seventeenth centuries). That work expressed a view of Erasmus and a general outlook different from those of the Belgian Catholics we have just been considering, whose opinions Thijm no doubt represented. Janssen was writing amid the repercussions of the Vatican Council in Germany. His own commitments were strongly Roman, if not ultramontane.[135] His acceptance of the universal claims of the church is reflected in Pastor's report that he avoided using the term 'Catholicism' because every '-ism' became a particularism.[136] Product of a pious home in the Rhineland, he was influenced by the romantic poets as much as by his academic teachers at Münster, Bonn, and Louvain.[137] He became a much loved, if exacting, teacher at the Frankfurt gymnasium but, following an ambition from childhood, he was also ordained priest (1860). Despite his commitment to historical scholarship, which imposed strains on a delicate health, he thought of spending his last years as a simple pastor of souls.[138]

Janssen's patriotism was expressed initially in a devotion to the old empire but, unlike many other Catholics, he supported Prussia in the 1860s. A reversal came when the new Bismarckian empire, in the aftermath of the 1870 decree, declared war on the Roman church (the so-called *Kulturkampf*). Janssen was elected to the Prussian diet as a defender of the interests of the church in 1875, when he was preparing the first volume of his history for publication. The intensity of the controversy surrounding especially its later volumes, where Janssen deals with the Reformation, and its publishing success can be explained only by the passions aroused by the *Kulturkampf*. Janssen himself saw his book as meeting the need for a Catholic history of his country (he was at the same time always insistent on his objectivity). Its place in modern historiography rests on other grounds, its primary interest in social and cultural history, marking a break from the predominantly political historiography of the age.

Janssen forced a reassessment of the fifteenth century in Germany. Liberal and Protestant writers had mostly seen it as a dark

age. For Janssen, by contrast, social life was still healthy and
Catholic piety still vibrant. Corruption had already begun – the
expansion of the money economy and the love of money, the
ambitions of the secular princes, sharpened by the jurists' rediscovery of Roman law and its notions of sovereignty – but the
heart was still sound. Breakdown was hastened (the Fall is Janssen's model for the destiny of the German people in the sixteenth
century) by an intellectual revolution. The first generation of humanists gave way to a new breed of whom Erasmus was the
leader and type, constructive gave way to destructive studies.

In the older humanists we find a sober enthusiasm for the
classics; yet they still 'contemplated classical antiquity from the
point of view of absolute faith in Christianity, and ... pressed the
classics into the service of their creed.' Certainly they condemned
the barbarous Latin and theological hair-splitting of the late scholastic theologians, but they did not, for this reason, throw over
the whole medieval tradition. Thomas Aquinas was for them 'a
beacon light.' They were also patriots and encouraged the vernacular literature. All their labours were coloured by a strong
national as well as religious spirit. They wanted reform of the
notorious abuses in the church but without abandoning the ground
of the Middle Ages or qualifying their devotion to pope and Christian emperor.[139]

The new generation of humanists, by contrast, was not devout
but irreverent, devoted not to both the classical and the Christian
past but to the classical past alone (according to whose lights they
condemned the living past of the Christian Middle Ages), not
sober but rebellious, too lawless and too egotistical to be either
good Christians or good patriots. For Janssen, Erasmus is the
model of the restless, alienated intellectual. He travelled Europe
'in the spirit of a mere book-student, never as an observer of
national life.'[140] Despite his obligations as monk and priest, his
religious observance was lax. Janssen reports in a decidedly unfriendly spirit the letter to Servatius Rogerus, in which Erasmus
excuses himself from returning to the monastery. He was avaricious and stooped to the grossest 'literary toadying'; affluence
was his reward. Vain, he had the highest regard for his own
opinions and became irritable if they were in any way challenged.
'He met all attacks on himself not only by completely ignoring,
but with intentional disregard for, the truth; and used any weapon
that came handy to annihilate his opponents both as men and

writers.' Worse in this respect than the Italian humanists, he covered his malice with the cloak of sanctity.[141]

His influence on his times was considerable but malign. He had great knowledge and skills, 'swift and universal perception,' and remarkable intellectual versatility; but he lacked depth and his influence arose above all from the cultivation and projection of his self-image. 'Manly dignity, warmth of feeling, self-sacrifice, love of his country and his Church appear as little in his writings as in his life.' He came to the abuses in the church in a spirit, not of sober or even anguished regret, but of 'scorn and derision.' He thus prepared the way for the ruin of the church. 'The "Praise of Folly" may almost be called a prologue to the great theological tragedies of the sixteenth century.'[142] His religion was at once too intellectual and too vague. To 'the hard and fast limits of dogmatic teaching' he preferred 'elastic and liberal methods.' 'His want of firm, unalterable convictions,' says Janssen, 'was on a par with his want of courage.' At the same time, he ridiculed the piety of the common people which Janssen finds earnest and deep. His vaunted respect for scripture had no depth; he allegorized the text as he would the ancient myths and sagas. He confounded pagan and Christian teachings, eg on death. 'The moral of it all is that human cleverness rules life, and views death, because it cannot escape from it, with philosophic resignation.'[143] In sum, Erasmus led the new generation of humanists towards the destruction of the Christian tradition. Even a comparison with Voltaire is not lacking, although Janssen adds amiably that the 'dark side of his counterpart was undoubtedly of a blacker shade.'[144]

Janssen's use of the Erasmus sources is predictable: the *Enchiridion* for his rationalistic allegorizing, the *Colloquia* for the revival of paganism. Among secondary writers, he does not rely only on his Catholic predecessors. He uses for his purpose liberal and Protestant writers: Müller, Stichart, and Drummond on Erasmus' irreverent handling, and Hagen on his rationalistic interpretations, of scripture, for example. There are references to Nève, Feugère, and Durand de Laur, but it is Kerker who is said to go to the heart of the matter.[145]

Janssen's judgment on Erasmus' personality is the harshest in the modern literature. His account of his influence belongs to the long, unfriendly Catholic tradition going back to Erasmus' lifetime and reinforced by an inversion of Enlightenment interpretations:

the rationality it praised, he condemned. Historically, this account rests on two assumptions, one broad, the other more specific: that the early modern period was a time of cultural, as well as religious and ecclesiastical, catastrophe, and that the appearance of a new generation of humanists was a large part of the explanation for this. Janssen's debt to romanticism's love of the medieval is apparent. His distinction between the two generations of humanists is indefensible.[146] He contributed little of substance to Erasmus interpretations but had a great influence.

Pastor's authoritative voice conveyed Janssen's judgment to a new generation. He accepted the distinction between older and younger humanists and, speaking of Erasmus' role in the Luther affair (1520), condemned the 'temporizing disposition and vague theology of the highly gifted scholar.'[147] H.J. Allard began a long and unfriendly word-portrait for Dutch readers with praise for Janssen's 'calm objectivity.' He aimed to follow Janssen and emphasize what would especially interest the Dutch, since Erasmus was a Netherlander, though 'no great patriot.'[148] Many expressions in Allard's essay recall Janssen directly: Erasmus' failure to speak regretfully of the circumstances of his birth was characteristic of the second-generation humanists, who spoke lightly of such matters and had pagan inclinations; he seldom participated in the services of the church and showed a lack of good faith in his response to his superior Servatius Rogerus; he had great talents and a profound influence on his age, concentrating many of its scholarly achievements in himself, but his writings were full of ambiguities and he was 'a veritable chameleon'; his *Folly* was a prologue to the theological tragedy of the sixteenth century.[149] Allard gave a Netherlands application to Janssen's judgments. As a man of the study Erasmus had not the least knowledge of the common folk, showed no interest in popular life and only contempt for the vernaculars. 'We Dutch,' commented Allard sententiously, 'who cherish our beautiful mother tongue, must and can never forgive that in our Rotterdam compatriot.' In seeking to have humanist rhetoric replace the firm structures created by scholasticism, Erasmus was 'a type for our modern Protestant divines, who consider themselves bound to no formulas or dogmatic canons.'[150]

Allard is relentless against Erasmus' character. Despite his so-called humour and love of mockery, he was oppressed by a dreary scepticism and a sad lack of resolution. He showed throughout

his life a 'boundless vanity and repulsive overvaluing of himself.'
Especially in his last years, this was paired with maliciousness
towards his opponents. For him as for Voltaire, ridicule was a
favourite weapon. The two had character traits in common: both
were 'ice-cold egoists.'[151]

Despite his avowals, Erasmus was for Allard no Catholic at
heart. He 'understood the church as a human institution, which
could prescribe or abolish dogmas according to the changing needs
and opinions of the times.' He prepared the way for the Protestant
attack and his criticism of the Reformers was a case of the beam
and the mote in the eye. Under Christian-sounding expressions,
the *Enchiridion* offered nothing but a naturalistic morality 'without real Christian foundations.' His change to a better direction
late in life (in itself still indecisive) came too late. 'The tares he
had sown with full hands had thrown roots too deep in the hearts
of many for them not to spring up luxuriantly.'[152]

The virulence of Allard's attack on his famous countryman
(following Janssen's) shows how far the bitterness of the later
nineteenth-century controversies over the church's place in modern society could carry some Catholic observers in their handling
of those who, in past conflicts, had taken a critical, moderate, or
irenic stand. This is not the portrait of a living man; it is, as Allard's
own expression (already noted) indicates, the depiction of a type,
the image of the mocking, empty, corrosive anticlerical who
everywhere in western Europe (as Janssen and Allard would see
it) threatened the church and Christian civilization. Underneath
is an idealization of the Middle Ages which is assumed in Allard,
though, naturally, explicit in Janssen. It derived from romanticism
and the Catholic revival and, in the Netherlands as elsewhere,
continued to the end of the century, indeed in a book like Remy
de Gourmont's *Le Latin mystique* (1892), with its catholicizing
preface by J.-K. Huysmans, took on a *fin de siècle* colouring. One
influential reader of that work rejoiced in the triumph in the
Netherlands of medievalism over the 'spirit of Erasmus,' who was
seen as rhetorical, arid, and pedantic.[153]

As we have often seen, the hostile image – Erasmus as sub-
verter and even destroyer of Catholicism – never had a monopoly
of Catholic opinion and Janssen's attack provoked disagreement
as well as support. The most notable critique was by Frank Xavier
Funk. Having painted the fifteenth century in too light colours,
says Funk (who does not undervalue Janssen's broader achieve-

ment), Janssen makes the early sixteenth century too dark. The younger humanists cannot be given the fateful role he attributes to them. An unprejudiced reading leads to different conclusions about the *Moriae encomium*, for example. Erasmus was not attacking the faith and order of the church in themselves, or even the religious orders, but abuses and superstitious outgrowth. As for the papacy, his criticism was of persons, not of the institution, and was deserved. There is no mockery of the Bible in the last part of the work as Janssen claimed. Funk found the *Enchiridion* so Christian that he could, he says, have ascribed it to one of the church Fathers. On the central doctrines of the faith Erasmus was sound: he related the call to a virtuous life to the baptismal vow and Christ's death for us; he presented the Crucified as our wisdom and our light. Funk rejects charges of unsoundness on the authority of the church, the Trinity, the deity of Christ, and original sin.[154] He makes the telling observation that much of Janssen's case against Erasmus is assembled from nineteenth-century Protestant writers beginning with Adolf Müller.[155] A well-rounded biography of Erasmus from the Catholic side is, Funk concludes, still lacking. Janssen was wrong in making him a forerunner of the Reformers; Catholics should claim him for their own.[156] Funk's is a restatement of the old moderate Catholic tradition about Erasmus and a wholehearted defence. He does not exhaust the issues on the main problem: how to distinguish an attack on abuses from attack on the institution itself. He reiterates an argument that goes back at least to Jacques Marsollier's *Apologie, ou justification d'Erasme* at the beginning of the eighteenth century: how could one who had the friendliest relations with the noblest figures and the religious leaders of his time be accused of speaking frivolously of sacred subjects?[157]

Janssen did not respond to Funk in either of his substantial replies to his critics.[158] He concentrated on his Protestant opponents, of whom there were many. He defended his objectivity and reiterated in the strongest terms his assertions about the younger humanists.[159] He was especially bitter against the Reformed theologian August Ebrard (1818–88).[160] In defence, Ebrard returned sarcastic questions and propositions about Janssen's boasted objectivity and took Erasmus as the test case. Far from promoting paganism, Ebrard says, Erasmus defined his life's work as penetrating with the Christian spirit a humanist culture that in Italy was all but pagan. Is it then 'objective' of Janssen to speak of a younger school of humanists who turned their backs on Christianity? Is it 'objective' to stay silent over pagan Italian humanists and their protector Pope Leo X and to attribute revolutionary designs to those like Erasmus who were affronted by this degeneracy of the Christian religion and fought pagan tendencies with all their strength?[161]

Ebrard cited the most elaborate defence of Erasmus against the kind of attack mounted by Janssen and his followers. This was Constantin Schlottmann's *Erasmus redivivus sive de Curia Romana hucusque insanabili* and came from the Protestant side; its essential context was the *Kulturkampf*. The Vatican Council, says Schlottmann, worked a revolution in the Catholic church, the relationship between the papacy and the bishops was changed profoundly and a servile spirit was brought in everywhere. The civil power, he adds, was right to protect its independence, especially in the new German empire, towards which Rome was hostile. Among the causes of conflict was the refusal of German authorities to act against Döllinger and other old Catholics who had resisted the Vatican decrees.[162] This mixture of religious liberalism and German patriotism was characteristic of Schlottmann (1819–87). At Berlin he had been taught by August Neander, the student of Schleiermacher and progenitor of the 'mediating school' of theology, which sought a middle path between biblical literalism and strict confessionalism on the one hand and rationalism or philosophical idealism on the other. His professional field was Old Testament (he was a lively teacher at Halle from 1866 to his death). His scholarly position was conservative but, as a participant in the revision of the German (Luther) Bible, he resisted paternalistic attitudes in the church authorities. Meanwhile he had greeted 1848 with patriotic verse, served the German Protestant community in Constantinople as embassy chaplain (in the 1850s), and welcomed the founding of the Second Empire in 1870.[163] When sections of *Erasmus redivivus* dealing with the *Kulturkampf* were published separately in advance, he was heavily attacked by members of the Centre (Catholic) party in the Prussian parliament.[164]

Schlottmann had long been interested in the humanists; at Bonn in 1860–1, he had published monographs on Melanchthon and the origins of the republic of letters. While Erasmus was then no stranger to him, an explanation is needed for his use of Erasmus in a polemic – at once religious and patriotic – against the

Centre party and the Vatican decrees. It derives from his interpretation of modern European history. After the Reformation, he
argues in his introduction (his second volume is also largely given
to this theme), the conservative, monastic, Jesuitical forces triumphed in the Catholic church. The vestiges of the Erasmian
spirit were suppressed and Erasmus himself given a bad name.
In the nineteenth century after the French Revolution, and not
without the sympathy of the European powers, there were freer
stirrings among Catholics. Some German Catholics, of whom Döllinger was chief, while accepting the hierarchy, wanted reform,
a freer outlook, and more openness to the Protestants. The ecumenical hopes of the early eighteenth century (as furthered, eg,
by Leibniz) were revived. In response, the Jesuitical party re-
gathered its strength and, in the Vatican Council, again triumphed.
The worst fears of the would-be reformers, says Schlottmann,
have been realized: clericalism, on the one hand, and neo-
paganism, as a reaction among the disillusioned on the other, are
in confrontation.[165] In these circumstances, he has thought to
bring forward Erasmus, who wished to associate unity with liberty, religious faith with cultivation of liberal studies, old traditions with new values. There are lessons here also, Schlottmann
adds, for Protestants. Among them, Luther's unfair judgments of
Erasmus have prevailed, though not to the point of monopoly.
Now in the nineteenth century Erasmus' fame is being restored
by writers in England, France, and Germany.[166] Schlottmann sees
himself in fact as promoting a revival that is already under way
in both confessions.

Even in Italian humanism, Schlottmann says, as he sets the
background to Erasmus' appearance, there was some preparation
for the reform movement. In contradiction to the mixture of reaction and neo-paganism at the court of Leo x, which not even
Janssen could deny, stood those, with Erasmus at their head, who
looked for renewal through a combination of humane literature
and genuine piety. Schlottmann sets out to prove Erasmus' essential consistency and his great influence over his contemporaries. He used his standing, earned by his unrivalled mastery of
the ancient literatures, to further the cause of piety. Scarcely anyone, says Schlottmann, since the Greek Fathers of Alexandria and
Antioch had defended with such freedom of spirit and such erudition the double truth: the church cannot do without learning,
learning cannot do without religion. Drawing widely on Erasmus'

writings, he identifies his main concerns: to open the scriptures to everybody; to make this effective by improving education; to have the gospel rightly preached, without legalism and scholastic subtleties.[167]

On Erasmus' influence, Schlottmann takes up the familiar comparison with Voltaire. He combined the brilliance of Voltaire with the seriousness of Leibniz; his was a nobler nature, more anxious about building up than pulling down.[168] Schlottmann wants to convey the warmth of relationships in Erasmus' circle. He rarely failed in friendship, he drew his contemporaries like pilgrims, he saw a Christian brotherhood among men of learning. In dealing with his enemies he showed a variable temper but public, not private, concerns (above all, his care for the revival of spiritual religion) moved him most deeply.[169]

Naturally, Schlottmann deals at length with Erasmus' relations with Luther. Partly he reiterates the old Protestant position: reform does not come by the peaceable pursuit of learning alone but by the fire of God's spirit at work among the people, expressed in this case in Luther. But he also has more independent and interesting things to say. He emphasizes the continuity between Erasmus and Luther; right-minded contemporaries were correct to hail them as fellow-workers. It is mistaken to say that Wittenberg owed nothing of substance, but only a method, to Erasmus. 'Both sought to extend the powers of the human mind as much as possible, but in such a way that they all serve the kingdom of Christ.' Erasmus, Schlottmann says, in writing freely and candidly to Pope Leo X, put the blame for the church crisis largely on Luther's adversaries. After Worms in 1521 Erasmus' doubts about Luther grew, although he did not altogether overlook what his heroic spirit could do for the reform of the church. In the end, Rome succeeded in dividing both the learned community and Christians in Germany.[170]

Schlottmann blames both Luther and Erasmus for the breakdown between them. More and more they looked to what divided, rather than to what united them. Before Luther, says Schlottmann, Erasmus had taught that Christ was the centre and end of Christianity; he had rejected Pelagianism and anticipated the teaching of justification by faith. Luther, he thought, in making the latter the heart of Christian doctrine, had added hard doctrines, eg about the human will. Erasmus saw his own teaching on the will as close to that of the Greek Fathers. In Schlottmann's view, he bound the transformation of human nature more closely than they had done to redemption through Christ crucified. The 'philosophy of Christ,' he adds, was not a new kind of religion but the faith of the early church. Luther, while making fair criticisms, did not see all that was sound in Erasmus or even recognize his own blindness on the subject. In the controversy on free will, both used biblical texts in a way uncongenial to modern minds. Luther was particularly unjust in charging Erasmus with scepticism towards the gospel itself.[171]

Schlottmann's huge book, for all its polemical origin and purpose, was a work of learning, as is demonstrated by his references to Erasmus' letters and writings and to a range of works about him. He makes Erasmus a defender of the essential Christian gospel, of a Christocentric religion where, as has been seen, human renewal depends, not on moralizing, but on the divine action in Christ. In this, the work anticipates modern writing on Erasmus' theology.[172] There is here a rejection of the judgment on Erasmus offered by Janssen and his followers: Erasmus the archsceptic, inwardly alienated from the Christian faith, lax in its observances, doubting its central doctrines. But, it is important to note, certain Protestant views of Erasmus are also rejected: again, Erasmus the sceptic, who wanted to replace the gospel by a mere moralism, or (alternatively) Erasmus the crypto-Protestant, who broke with Luther only out of fear. While admitting that he was excessively cautious, Schlottmann challenges most nineteenth-century Protestant writing on Erasmus' character; even Ranke exaggerated unjustly his timidity.[173] Schlottmann's book belongs with the Catholic controversies about Erasmus in the nineteenth century, because it challenges the long hostile tradition restated – in the atmosphere surrounding the Vatican Council and in an especially virulent form – by Janssen and his followers. It also belongs to the *Kulturkampf* and sides with the Bismarckian empire in its struggle with the German church and with Rome.[174] Erasmus seems to us quite remote from that world. Yet Schlottmann used the occasion to produce an account of Erasmus more positive and generous than can otherwise be found in either the Protestant or the Catholic literature in the nineteenth century.

V

By the beginning of the twentieth century, rival and contradictory Catholic interpretations of Erasmus stood side by side in the literature. In one, Erasmus was the underminer, or even the destroyer, of the Catholic faith. He replaced faith by, at best, a shallow moralism, at worst, a cold egoism. He was hostile to structures, dogmatic and ecclesiastical. He prepared the way for the catastrophes of the sixteenth century and, indeed, for the worse catastrophes of the revolutionary and secularist age that began in the late eighteenth century. In the other, Erasmus, though constrained by hesitations and uncertainties and even drawn to doubt on some teachings, was a Christian reformer in the main tradition. He wanted the church to be purified by a return to its origins and its sources. He had the essence of the gospel and was an enemy only of corrupt or overelaborate structures.

In the Erasmus article in the *Dictionnaire de théologie catholique* (1911), P. Godet offered a restrained version of the critical interpretation. His account of Erasmus' life is sympathetic (the first two volumes of Allen's edition of the letters were available to him), but his portrait of the man is in the end unattractive. Like many before him, he found in the Holbein portrait at Basel a version – in his case a Catholic version – of what Lavater had found: 'the unconquerable application of the humanist to study, his talent and flair for criticism, his taste for mockery, his shrewd prudence deriving no doubt from timidity but not excluding, when necessary, pride and courage; yet,' he goes on, 'there is not reflected there any largeness of soul, any religious enthusiasm, any mystical yearnings.'[175] Erasmus was a great and powerful mind; he had not much of a heart.

Godet knows to avoid the cruder forms of anachronistic judgment. Erasmus was not a sceptic or a freethinker in the modern sense of the word. Such scepticism was out of the question in the early sixteenth century. Godet approves Janssen's description of the *Praise of Folly* as the prologue to the sixteenth-century tragedy; he finds in the book an 'unheard-of boldness.'[176] Yet within the church Erasmus was not a rebel but a malcontent. Ideas and interest kept him a Catholic. He was not without faith, but as a priest he was without vocation and without piety.

Godet's judgment of Erasmus is rigorously theological. Erasmus had an imperfect understanding of tradition. The centre and pivot of his theology was his phrase *simplicitas doctrinae*. He was frightened by dogmatism; he treated metaphysics as an enemy and hated medieval scholasticism with 'an implacable hatred.' 'To seek for dogmatic precision was for him,' says Godet, 'not to progress but to decline.' 'In his hands,' Godet concludes in a phrase which would do as motto for the whole anti-Erasmus school, 'Catholic dogma volatilizes itself.'[177]

The second interpretation had representatives not least in England.[178] The most enthusiastic defence of Erasmus as a Catholic was made by a Benedictine monk, Francis Neil (Dom Aidan) Gasquet (1846–1929), who began his ecclesiastical career as a vigorous and reforming prior of the Benedictine school and community at Downside and finished as cardinal with high responsibilities in Rome.[179] Gasquet's historical writings, beginning with *Henry VIII and the English Monasteries*, were acclaimed at their appearance and did indeed offer both new facts and fresh insights; but they were also disfigured by many inaccuracies and misjudgments, in which Gasquet persisted and which became the subject of bitter controversy.[180] The portrait of Erasmus in *Eve of the Reformation* is, of course, not central to these controversies. It epitomizes the favourable Catholic tradition and also gives expression to a combination of the Catholic and the liberal that was especially English. When allowance has been made for the great and obvious differences, there remains some affinity between Gasquet and Froude, to whom he was in any case indebted.

> Such men [as Erasmus] held that the best service a true son of the Church could give to religion was the service of a trained mind, ready to face facts as they were, convinced that the Christian faith had nothing to lose by the fullest light and the freest investigation, but at the same time protesting that they would suffer no suspicion to rest on their entire loyalty of heart to the authority of the teaching Church.[181]

Outspoken, sometimes injudicious, Erasmus was consistently loyal to the pope and ecclesiastical authority. He was 'a reformer in the best sense,' wishing to improve the present system, courageous in pointing out faults, but no iconoclast. The popes and other Catholic contemporaries did not misunderstand his intentions but looked upon him as a faithful, 'if perhaps a somewhat eccentric and caustic son of Holy Church.' His enmity to the religious orders – a point of difficulty, one might think, for an English Benedictine – arose from abuses and was not a 'wholesale sweeping condemnation of the system of regular life.' Gasquet had read Janssen and, in a minor way, *Eve of the Reformation* was doing for England what Janssen's history did for Germany, depicting a Catholic community where faith was still alive and productive, though corruption and breakdown were imminent. Unlike Janssen, Gasquet did not see Erasmus as furthering that corruption. *Folly* was not for him the prologue to the tragedies of the sixteenth century; blessed by Thomas More, it was but 'a playful, if somewhat ill-judged and severe lampoon, on some patent abuses.'[182] Gasquet has a straightforward solution to the problem Catholics might have with Erasmus: he attacked the real but fortuitous abuses in the church; the essentials he left inviolate.

It is regrettable that another, and even more controversial Catholic figure, Lord Acton, has left only a few paragraphs on Erasmus. The humanist, with his critical and independent mind, might have attracted a treatment that was fresh and distinctive from one who, while never breaking with the faith he inherited, had strained or stormy relations with ecclesiastical authority for much of his life, who followed the passage of his friend and mentor Ignaz von Döllinger from ultramontanism to liberalism and eventual exile, who against the evidence of his own time accepted the compatibility of Catholicism and liberty, and for whom religious toleration was the touchstone of a civilized society. One might have looked for a fuller portrait of Erasmus in Acton's projected history of liberty but, as is well known, he never fulfilled his plans for that work, crippled – observers have thought – by contradictions in his own outlook (between, for example, his hopes for freedom and his deep pessimism about the human condition) and his commitment to the severest judgment on moral failure and the crimes of history, his intransigence producing in the end a break with Döllinger and a terrible sense of isolation.[183]

Erasmus is mentioned in Acton's essay of 1863 on 'Ultramontanism.'[184] The rise of the ultramontane school, Acton says, with its ignorant and sometimes dishonest opposition to modern knowledge, depended on the separation of Catholic from Protestant and scientific thought at the beginning of the nineteenth century. The intellectual revival of that time was distinct from religion and was thus reminiscent of the classical revival at the Renaissance: 'the mental exertion of the period of Goethe, like that of Erasmus, had no definite practical end to attain, no reward to earn but that of literary enjoyment, no mission to fulfil but that of satisfying the thirst for knowledge.'[185] Acton's appeal was for a Catholicism which, without diminishing the core of faith, was yet ready to adjust the outer rings – philosophical, scientific, political – to accommodate change and progress in the world beyond the church. He had already argued for this mutual exchange between church and world, religion and science, in an essay on the Catholic academy which Cardinal Wiseman was establishing in England in 1861. Learning, he says there, 'is an ally to the Church that would be more powerful if it was more trusted.'[186] The fifteenth-century revival of ancient learning, he goes on, evoked three different responses at the time: there were those, including the most illustrious prelates, 'who knew that all the resources of criticism and learning belong to the armoury of the Church'; there was a party which chose paganism instead of Christianity; there were, finally, 'those whose conduct justified the attacks it drew down on them, who feared and deprecated the introduction of the new studies.' It would, he adds, be unjust to place Erasmus in the second party, 'because his satire of the clergy that so readily accepted the doctrines and precepts of the Reformation was at least redeemed by his dogmatical opposition to Luther.' Acton's attitude to the Renaissance is approving but reserved.[187] His compliment to Erasmus is backhanded: despite appearances, he did not join the paganizers or the Protestants; by inference, he belonged to the first, wholesome party, advocating critical enquiry and the advancement of learning, not against the church but for its sake. In an essay on Sarpi, also written (1867) before the testing events of the Vatican Council, Acton associates Erasmus' reforming zeal with that of Dante and Giberti, the reformer of Verona.[188]

Of the history of liberty, to which Acton turned after the trauma of the Vatican Council, where he had worked passionately for the defeated side, only two fragments – both given as lectures in 1877 – have survived, 'The History of Freedom in Antiquity' and 'The History of Freedom in Christianity.' In the latter, Erasmus is associated, first, with those who in antiquity and the Middle Ages had asserted liberty of conscience and, secondly, with those who raised the cry of social equality, which Acton still saw as a threat to liberty. He is described as 'the most celebrated precursor of the Reformation.'[189] In that connection, he is mentioned in an exchange ten years later between Acton and Mandell Creighton over Acton's proposed review of volumes 3 and 4 of Creighton's *History of the Papacy during the Reformation*. Acton was anxious to demonstrate Rome's responsibility for the Reformation. The disruption was ultimately due to the papal absolutism developed (though unexplained by Creighton) 'between the days of Kempis and of Erasmus.'[190] Rome – in defence of these inordinate claims – resisted Luther on a point (indulgences) whose theological validity was widely doubted among Catholic divines themselves:

> Supposing, therefore, there had been men of influence at Rome such as certain fathers of Constance formerly, or such as Erasmus or Gropper, it might well have been that they would have preferred the opinion of Luther to the opinion of Tetzel, and would have effected straightway the desired reform of the indulgences for the Dead ... I must, therefore, cast the responsibility on those who refused to say, in 1517, what everybody had said two centuries before, and many said a century later. And the motive of these people was not a religious idea, one system of salvation set up against another; but an ecclesiastical one.[191]

Here Erasmus appears as the Catholic reformer, to Acton a figure of sympathy. In the famous Inaugural Lecture on his appointment as Regius Professor of Modern History at Cambridge (1895), Erasmus appears, along with Columbus, Machiavelli, Luther, and Copernicus, as one who helped bring in the new order of modern history. But, curiously, while the others represented the rupture or innovation, which Acton considered characteristic of the time, the very language used of Erasmus suggests continuity: he 'diverted the current of ancient learning from profane into Christian channels.'[192]

Erasmus comes as the climax of the lecture on the Renaissance in the series on modern history which Acton delivered to his students in 1899–1900. He was, says Acton, 'eminently an international character.' More than any other, he could appreciate 'the gradual ripening and enlargement of ideas' which the classical, and especially the Hellenic, revival brought. He lived in an easy intimacy with previous ages which others had struggled to bring to light. Yet, with parts of the Renaissance achievement he had no sympathy, being 'indifferent to art, to metaphysics, to antiquarian pedantry.' His interests were practical and spiritual; from classical and Christian antiquity, he drew equally 'the same lessons of morality and wisdom; for he valued doctrine chiefly

for the sake of a good life and a happy death, and was impatient
of subtle dialectics and speculative disputations.' He was, though
using irony and abstaining 'from the high horse and the big word,'
an earnest reformer; he believed that 'reform of the Church depended on a better knowledge of early Christianity, in other words,
on better self-knowledge, which could only result from a slow
and prolonged literary process,' involving the replacement of the
scholastics by the Fathers and systematic theology by spiritual
religion. Despite his mildness, he aroused many enemies. Intellectually, he belonged 'to a later and more scientific or rational
age,' not the Enlightenment but the scholarly generations of the
seventeenth century, which resumed his work after interruption
by the Reformation tumults. In those troubles, Erasmus – for a
time – saw Luther as continuing his work, but for Luther himself
Erasmus and the Renaissance (in his view, rationalizing and
Pelagian) were the enemy.[193]

The purity of moral standards which Acton asked students of
history to apply may be associated with the nineteenth-century
preoccupation with character (or the Victorian preoccupation with
rectitude) which, as we have seen, affected writing on Erasmus
in that period, not always for the better. Counteracting that tendency was the sense of history or of historical circumstances which
could mitigate severity of judgment. Failings and weaknesses,
Wieland had said in his controversy with Herder, must be related
to the difficult circumstances of Erasmus' life. On the development of the sense of history in the nineteenth century Acton was
an informed, if critical, commentator.[194] Unfortunately, he left
nothing on these dilemmas in the interpretation of Erasmus. As
we have them, his snatches of writing on Erasmus offer us the
picture of a moderate Catholic reformer, one who, against the
tide of rising absolutism in church and state, gave promise of a
reconciliation between Catholic tradition and liberty of conscience, Acton's two great goods.

The most moving account of that interpretation of Erasmus
was by a French Catholic scholar, Pierre Imbart de la Tour
(1860–1925). It appears in his magisterial four-volume work on
Les Origines de la Réforme (left incomplete at his premature death),
whose most original and significant part was the third volume
subtitled L'Evangélisme (1521–1538) and published in 1914. His
contribution – not fully appreciated in the later literature[195] – was
to identify the diverse spiritual and intellectual movements at

work in Catholic Europe, and especially in France, in the uncertain, fluid period (1520s and 1530s) before Reformation and Counter-Reformation secured dominance in their respective territories. The subject of 'Evangelism' (in the special sixteenth-century sense of a search for the renewal of religion through direct contact with the scriptures, while, on the one hand, retaining a sense of Catholicity and, on the other, being sensitive to the issues of sin and grace and justification) has been of great interest to historians in the last generation.[196] Erasmus' role has been assessed variously. For Imbart de la Tour it was central.

Sharing with nineteenth-century historians a strong patriotic feeling, Imbart de la Tour found the open, mediating character of 'évangélisme' especially congenial to the French character and genius. His sense for the life of the people had something in common with Janssen's. Also, like Janssen, he distinguished two sides to the humanist movement, the one paganizing and the other essentially and devotedly Christian, but he reversed the movement described by Janssen; the generation of Erasmus was sound. While Janssen's was a Catholicism coloured by ultramontanism, the decrees of 1870, and the *Kulturkampf*, Imbart de la Tour was free of clericalism and, in a France which had survived the controversies over the church around 1900, no longer defensive about the faith.[197] He also confronted the dilemma of Catholicism and freedom over which Acton had agonized. That was one of the issues posed in the encounter between different solutions to the problems of the church at the beginning of the sixteenth century. In its depiction of historical movements and figures in confrontation with one another, in its use of climaxes, turning-points, and critical moments, Imbart de la Tour's historical style is essentially dramatic.

Just before 1520 on every side in Christendom, he says, except among the conservatives of the theological schools, people were longing for the recovery of the pure and pristine gospel. All the forward-looking movements of the time ran together to make the single powerful current with Imbart de la Tour calls *Evangélisme*. But the brutal irruption of Luther split the stream again. It posed before the men of the time a fateful choice; they might join either those who with Luther rebelled against the church or those 'who hoped to regenerate without destroying, to restore the Christian society, not to break the structure of its laws and government.'[198] Soon, for those who remained Catholic a second fateful choice presented itself; for the crisis divided Catholics themselves – and, says Imbart de la Tour, the division has lasted to our own day; on the one hand were the intransigents and, on the other, those who, as he puts it, looked for conciliation and progress. In this dramatic encounter there were, in short, not two parties but three, the conservative, the reformist, the revolutionary.

Now, Imbart de la Tour seems to say, historians – and even Catholic historians – have applied a two-party model prematurely. There were Catholics and there were Protestants. But this was to overlook the 'reformist' group, to see in it only a weak, inconsequential, and cowardly precursor of Protestantism. In fact, this group was the true reformation in the French church – and we become aware again of the patriotic dimension – uniting in itself the élite of the land. 'We can say that the soul of our race breathes in this great party which, between 1530 and 1538, saves intellectual liberty, takes up the Renaissance into the old faith, sketches out a national policy within, of tolerance, without, of balance of power, and restores Catholicism itself in helping to raise to the head of the church, the greatest of the sixteenth-century popes, Paul III.'[199] In the very existence of this party, for which Imbart de la Tour thus makes the largest claims, is to be found the reason why France remained Catholic.

Erasmus – together with Lefèvre d'Etaples – was the inspiration and the leader of this party. His was the dream of a renewal of Catholicism without destroying its historic structure and government. Imbart de la Tour evokes that dream and the sense of a rising dawn which the New Testament of 1516 inspired in the Erasmians. Sadly and retrospectively he shares that dream. How different then his picture of Erasmus must be from that of Janssen! The church criticisms of Erasmus were those of a scoffer and sceptic set on ruining the church? No; Erasmus 'desired reform only by and along with the hierarchy.' Erasmus would adore the classical writers and by them throw off the yoke of Christianity? No; he would purify religion in his studies by bringing it into contact with the scriptures and the Fathers; he would rejuvenate the church by reconciling faith and culture, the idea of tradition and the idea of progress. Erasmus had no firm convictions? No; in breaking with Luther he followed out the deepest tendencies in himself. 'In taking his stand, the great scholar had but to be true to himself.'[200] To be true to himself was to desire to be, and in fact to be, orthodox.

At this point Imbart de la Tour's argument becomes more elaborate. More than once he has said that Erasmus and his party would restore intellectual liberty to Catholicism. What is meant? How is the delicate balance between orthodoxy and freedom achieved? What it demanded was that a clearer distinction be made between dogma (which is divine and inviolable) and mere opinions, the opinions of the schools (which are human and changeable). Only by making this distinction, by letting the criticism of the all too human opinions of the schools run free, could change take place without revolution. Erasmus in fact thought of three stages, that of dogmatic truth (which was beyond discussion), that of theological truth (where the church alone may decree and to its decree all must submit), and that of opinion (where liberty must prevail). Standing on the third stage, Erasmus fought the old-style theologians for intellectual liberty. Standing on the first two, he fought Luther for the old church. He defended the essential principles of that church, its universality and its unity. To him in fact Imbart de la Tour attributes his own lyrical conception of the church:

Truly universal society, whose large and flexible frontiers enclose lives, doctrines, traditions, individuals or peoples, at the same time one and many, permanent and in movement, in the inexhaustible richness of its great men, of its saints, a living body plunging back into the past without becoming imprisoned there, adapting itself to the future, without becoming deformed, like an embryo which is born, grows, evolves in retaining the identity of its nature and its form.[201]

According to Imbart de la Tour Erasmus was Catholic. He certainly lacked the dogmatic assurance to become the decisive force in the great crisis of Christianity but his influence was lasting and profound, in the papacy, at the Council of Trent, and above all, of course, in Catholic France. In the end, Imbart de la Tour's portrait is without shades. The drama proceeds like a vast but simple morality play. To Erasmus is given a noble and moving part. For once, in the history of its influence on interpretations of Erasmus through the nineteenth century, romanticism has found a voice favourable to Erasmus.

The twentieth century inherited the two Catholic interpretations of Erasmus that have occupied us in this chapter and they have remained – at least until recent times – alive and vigorous. Reduced to their basic parts they are, first, that Erasmus, through his careless or malicious criticisms and his theological looseness, undermined Catholic institutions and threatened the continuity of the dogmatic tradition and, secondly, that, without necessarily being sound on every point of doctrine, he sought the renewal of the church and of religious life in a thoroughly Catholic spirit. Each interpretation requires a view of the religious character of northern humanism and its relation (including Erasmus' relation) to the Protestant Reformers. There are difficulties about both interpretations, but the first is especially unsatisfactory. It identifies Catholicism with structures, dogmatic and ecclesiastical, and – to put it mildly – cannot easily accommodate one who, while not in the last resort denying them, had a bias of mind against them. On the whole, writers on this side deal too lightly with the evidence for Erasmus' adherence to the church, acquaintance with the theological traditions, including scholasticism, and religious seriousness and evangelical purpose. They have too narrow a vision of Catholic faith and are not sufficiently alive to the dangers of anachronism mentioned in the opening remarks of this chapter and always present in discussions of this kind. It is, of course, understandable that the intense controversies within and around the church in the nineteenth century concentrated the vision of many Catholics and tempted them to apply the expectations of nineteenth-century ultramontanism to a sixteenth-century intellectual.

The second interpretation has the great virtue of recognizing Erasmus' claims as a religious thinker and, often because of the commitments of its adherents, escapes the trap of anachronism, at least on the side of clerical and ultramontane severity (liberalism, even Catholic liberalism, has, as we know, its own dangers, especially the temptation to sentimentalize and to find forerunners of the modern). Most rightly recognize a problematical element in Erasmus' attitude to authority but they underplay his astringency and abrasiveness and make him too much of a pietist. As a result, they miss something of his liveliness and vigour. Part of the explanation is that nineteenth-century writers generally do not think outside the categories of Reformation and Counter-Reformation as they actually occurred: these are for them the real and, in the last resort, the only options in the sixteenth century. When another possibility is allowed for, a Catholic but open and thorough reform and renewal of the church (as, briefly, in Acton and in Imbart de la Tour), Erasmus can come into his own.

Nineteenth-Century Protestantism: Erasmus and the Reformation in Modern History

'The sad business of Luther had brought him a burden of intolerable ill will; he was torn in pieces by both sides, while aiming zealously at what was best for both.'[1] So wrote Erasmus of the effects of Luther's Reformation on his life in his abbreviated autobiography of 1524. All biographers of Erasmus down to our own time have divided his life at Luther's appearance. Protestants, especially, have made his attitude to the Reformation a test of his integrity. Did Erasmus change position after 1517 or 1520? Did he moderate his criticisms of the existing order and embrace what he had previously condemned? Or is there an essential consistency in his ideas despite the attacks of both sides? Was his break with Luther inevitable or fortuitous, on an essential or a peripheral issue? Did he deal fairly with the Swiss and south German Reformers? Is it significant that he died in a Protestant town?

Modern scholars find such questions less straightforward than their predecessors, because they are aware, first, of the difficulties of interpreting past polemics, of which the conventions and expectations need to be understood, and, secondly, of the dangers of anachronism, in particular of giving a premature solidity to words like 'Reformation' and 'Protestant.'[2] Even when the questions were more simply stated and understood, however, answers were various. The so-called Reformation took many different forms and each pattern of Reformation in the sixteenth century had its own historiography and its own interpretation of Erasmus.[3] Enlightenment writers held a common historical model: light broke in on darkness at the Renaissance and broadened as the years passed; but there were differences among them over how the

Reformation is to be related to this growing enlightenment and how Erasmus is to be related to both. He could be seen as the true herald of enlightenment and the Protestant Reformers as authors of a stultified, if not aborted, reform; or, their Reformation could be interpreted as a pre-Enlightenment and Erasmus as its pioneer and supporter, more or less willing.[4]

The nineteenth-century Protestant writers inherited the Enlightenment model; almost without reflection, they used the image of light breaking on darkness. They added what they owed to romanticism and a deepening sense of history – a belief in historical necessity, often expressed in providential form. Luther's Reformation was the need of the hour, partly because of the conjuncture of historical forces, partly because the divine will was propelling humanity forward. Erasmus was to be judged by his responsiveness to this historic moment. Thus, there was also among the nineteenth-century writers a strong interest in the individual and his life's decisions, consequently in character, its strengths and weaknesses. The polemics around 1800 over Erasmus and Hutten set a pattern. What kind of character should a nineteenth-century Protestant Christian admire most?

None of this should suggest that a single view of Erasmus had emerged among the heirs of the Reformers in the nineteenth century. The old variety remained, a continuation of the original patterns of Reformation reinforced, sometimes changed, by contemporary movements of thought. Many Protestant writers on Erasmus were heavily influenced by a dominant liberalism. Others belonged to the evangelical revival, at work throughout western Europe in the first half of the nineteenth century. By the end of the century, writing on Erasmus was being affected by another expression of the century's interest in history, the attempt to recover the pristine religious of Jesus or essence of the Christian religion, freed of later dogmatic accretions.

I

We might begin in Geneva, Calvin's town, where, after the Napoleonic wars, an evangelical movement developed in reaction against the state church, whose pastors had been trained in an essentially rationalistic theology. It formed an evangelical organization within the state church ('Société évangelique de Genève' 1831) and its own theological school (1832), and established independent congregations and eventually a free denomination (1849).[5] The leading theologian was Jean Henri Merle d'Aubigné (1794–1872) whose *History of the Reformation in the Sixteenth Century* was a nineteenth-century best-seller, not least in English-speaking lands. He was born near Geneva of a French merchant family, Huguenot refugees. In 1817 he was ordained pastor, converted to the evangelical awakening ('Réveil') with its strong sense of personal redemption, and, while visiting the Wartburg during the Luther anniversary celebrations, whose importance for the revival of enthusiasm for the Reformation we have already noticed, decided to write a history of the Reformation. It was to be scholarly but aimed also at arousing a devout spirit. Merle d'Aubigné's was not a narrow outlook; he studied at Berlin under August Neander, the student of Schleiermacher, who was, as we will see, to have a great influence on the mediating theologians of mid-century. He absorbed something of his irenic spirit and shared his distaste for dry orthodoxy. He served as pastor of the French congregation in Hamburg and at Brussels, returning to Geneva after the 1830 revolutions. He became a leader among the evangelicals and separated from the state church in the year the first volume of his *History* appeared, 1835.[6]

Merle d'Aubigné wishes to present the Reformation as a creative event in the history of Christianity, while avoiding needless polemic against the Catholics. Like other French-speaking Protestant writers on the Reformation in the nineteenth century, he takes a providential view of the event.[7] Historians, he says, are no longer satisfied with enumerating a 'lifeless series of events'; some adorn history with the liveliness of art, others with philosophical reflections, but his purpose is to declare the power of God. The Reformation as a 'great revolution,' an emanation of God's power and the offspring of faith, must be distinguished from negative protest and from modern Protestantism which is vague, lukewarm, and rationalistic.[8]

Such views determined and diminished the role of one whose relations with the Reformation were reserved and problematical. To Merle d'Aubigné, Erasmus has been 'overrated by some and underrated by others'; he was not and never could have been a reformer, but he 'paved the way for others' by fostering 'a spirit of research' and by satire. He took a giant step beyond the Italians by returning theology to its sources, a step, this nineteenth-century pietist says characteristically, 'of more importance to humanity' than that lately taken by Columbus. By his New Testament, theologians were able to recognize the purity of the Reformation doctrine.[9] In later editions Merle d'Aubigné drew for his Erasmus study on Ranke, whose first volume had appeared in 1834. Thus, Erasmus was 'the great writer of the opposition' at the beginning of the sixteenth century; his *Folly* served more than any other work 'to confirm the age in its antisacerdotal tendency'; his lively, bold, intelligent writings poured in flowing streams upon contemporaries. The pen-portrait of the man is wholly Ranke's: 'That little fair-haired man, whose peering blue eyes keenly observed whatever came before him, and on whose lips a somewhat sarcastic smile was always playing, though timid and embarrassed in his step.'[10]

Erasmus and Luther represent, says Merle d'Aubigné, the two parties apparent at every moment of decision, the prudent and the courageous. Erasmus failed to see that the Spirit of God could not restore Christendom without great commotion. He lost courage, forsook the gospel, and, consequently, forfeited the esteem of the noblest men of his age and deprived himself (this kind of writing is not backward in judging) of 'those heavenly consolations which God sheds in the hearts of those who conduct themselves as good soldiers of Jesus Christ.' 'Erasmus was powerful as an instrument of God, but when he ceased to be so, he was nothing.' This style might best be described as evangelical–romantic. Merle d'Aubigné's interpretation of Erasmus' relation to the Reformation combines the romantic condemnation of his lack of heroism and failure to discern the march of history with the Protestant tradition that he had really accepted the Reformation gospel and then forsook it. To this mix has been added a pietistic and moralizing flavour: 'He was, first of all, a learned, and in the second place only, a Christian man.'[11] Merle d'Aubigné had fixed this appreciation of Erasmus in countless Protestant minds in Britain, Europe, and North America by the 1850s.

Theses by students in training for the ministry at the Protestant Faculty of Theology at Montauban demonstrate how well entrenched Merle d'Aubigné's views were in evangelical and Calvinist circles throughout the nineteenth century. Theses for the baccalaureate in theology are likely to express received doctrine and, more important, represent the views of at least two generations, that of the teachers and that of the young men whose careers as pastors were just beginning. Interpretations they offer are likely to be acceptable over a great span of time. Montauban's Faculty of Theology, destroyed under Louis XIV and restored under Napoleon (1808), was the centre of orthodox Calvinist studies in France in the nineteenth century. There was bad blood between that faculty and the Genevan authorities who, with their rationalizing (one would say later 'liberal') theology, had denied Genevan pulpits to Merle d'Aubigné; the rupture was complete between 1828 and 1870, Montauban finding its Genevan connection in the evangelical school of theology founded in 1832.[12]

Three theses on Erasmus' relations with the Reformation were defended at Montauban, by Marius Addi, W. Bauer, and Paul Boyer respectively in the years 1869, 1878, and 1886.[13] No significant change occurs in the interpretation of Erasmus over the seventeen years. Although, without adopting his views, these candidates love and repeat the colourful language of Désiré Nisard, their interpretation is substantially Merle d'Aubigné's. Erasmus, they say, prepared the Reformation and, if he had had more courage and theological rigour, he would have adhered to it; but, from timidity, conservatism, theological confusion, he denied it. He prepared the Reformation by denouncing Roman and monastic abuses: in scourging the papacy, he sounded like a Huguenot; his holy·anger anticipated Luther's and even Pascal's. In the *Adagia* he spared neither priest nor prince. He also prepared essential Protestant positions by asserting the rights of conscience and claiming the open Bible for all. His devoted work on the biblical texts supported these claims. But the appearance of Luther exposed his weaknesses of character and conviction. In his criticisms of the church, offence to good taste counted for more than affront to faith.[14] His thought lacked sure foundation and firm structure: it was 'un syllogisme perpétuel sans conclusion.' In confronting Luther, he was indecisive and cowardly; his sympathy was with the Reformation but he would not avow this openly. If the free-will controversy exposed a weak side of Luther (he carried his awareness of human frailty and divine grace through to an inexorable determinism), Erasmus' views lacked conviction and were semi-Pelagian.[15] In the words, virtually, of Merle d'Aubigné, Erasmus is said to have been primarily a humanist and only secondarily a Christian: 'In his heart, the gospel has a place, but not the central place.'[16]

The intention of these thesis-writers is clear: to affirm the Reformation as a recovery of the essentials of the Christian faith. Erasmus, they say, concurred in this affirmation but he retreated from it, much as modern, sceptical, rationalizing theologians have done. In the way they make their points, there is, however, an incoherence: they want to make Erasmus a precursor and supporter of the Reformation, a prophet of some of Protestantism's dearest convictions, and, at the same time, to write him down as sceptic, aesthete, *philosophe* before his time.

The three-part pattern is characteristic of evangelical and orthodox Protestant writers on Erasmus in the nineteenth century: he prepared the Reformation; he betrayed it; that was because he was weak in character and superficial or indeterminate in theology. How far there are incoherences in the pattern depends on where the emphasis is put among its different components. The Milners at the beginning of the century had emphasized, in contrasting it with Luther's rediscovery of the gospel, the latitudinarian character of Erasmus' theology.[17] Arthur Robert Pennington (1814–99) was a Cambridge graduate in the evangelical line of the Milners and rector of Utterby in Lincolnshire for forty-five years (1854–99).[18] His *Life and Character of Erasmus* makes the predictable division in Erasmus' life at Luther's appearance. Had Erasmus but died in 1517, his reputation would have stood higher![19] Before that, says Pennington, he had done much for reform, more, one might add, than the Milners had recognized: his New Testament had opened the scriptures to his generation; it was 'the instrument in God's hand' for disseminating truth and overthrowing spiritual bondage. He held before his contemporaries the ideal of conformity to Christ. In the *Enchiridion*, he taught a genuine practical piety. He saw many teachings of the church as 'condemned alike by reason and by revelation.'[20] Yet, even at his best, he was deficient as a reformer. His hopes for a peaceful reformation were 'a mere chimera.' Even an evangelical can sound like Charles Villers or the Hegelians in accepting catastrophe as both inevitable and salutary. 'A change so great as the one now before us,' says Pennington of the Reformation, 'could not be accomplished without terrible commotions. If we wait till we can prevent evil from mingling with the good, we shall have to abandon many of those high and holy enterprises which have for their object the amelioration of human society.' Erasmus failed to see that stifling the outburst would produce a greater explosion. The teachings of the *Enchiridion* itself fell far short of evangelical truth. 'He does, indeed, allude to Adam's transgression, and to our redemption by Christ Jesus; but he does not make these truths the foundation of his system ... We learn also from this treatise that he held the meritoriousness of good works; ... and that he could not accept that doctrine of justification by faith in Christ's righteousness, which Luther calls the article of a standing or falling church.' He was then divided from Luther over doctrines like original sin, the role of law, the atonement; he also lacked Luther's moral courage. Anxious, especially over his standing with the powerful people of the day, holding 'very confused notions' on church authority, he took a neutral position which, Pennington concludes with Victorian solemnity, brought him only suffering: 'He now went heavily all the day in the bitterness of his soul.'[21] More than his personal qualities was at stake. His mind was 'essentially sceptical'; regrettably, 'a rationalistic spirit constantly appears in his writings.'[22] We notice again: the evangelicals condemned what the liberals praised, Erasmus' reputed rationalism. Pennington's biography was contemporary with Drummond's; indeed, it was nearly completed when Drummond's work appeared.[23] The difference in outlook is marked, and also in tone: Drummond's irony, which makes his book readable still, is missing.

In Germany, Lutheran orthodoxy had long condemned Erasmus for not siding with Luther. A variety of explanations for this defection were offered – from doctrinal differences to the hold of patrons upon Erasmus. For nineteenth-century writers, as we have already seen, weakness of character was an appealing explanation. In the nineteenth century also, historicism, the sense of the historical necessities of a given time (usually related to the forward movement of history), accompanied, even overshadowed, theological judgments of Erasmus. Hegelian language abounded. The leading Hegelian historian at the University of Berlin in the 1820s and 1830s, Philipp Conrad Marheineke (1780–1846), caught (to some extent set) the tone of partisan Protestant judgments of Erasmus, in the history he wrote for the Luther anniversary of 1817: Erasmus 'had more fear of men than of God'; only momentarily did truth shine in him; he could not understand Luther's heroic soul.[24] We find a full statement of the historicist theme in an influential article of 1866 by G.L. Plitt (1836–80), who was a student at Erlangen and Berlin, and teacher at the former from 1862. He was devoted to the Lutheran church; it was characteristic that his main scholarly work was a study of the Confession of Augsburg. He did not, however, see the confessions he studied or the Reformers' teachings as final and inerrant. Much less was he bound by the existing condition of the Lutheran churches, especially their dependence on the state; like his teacher at Erlangen, J.K. von Hofmann, he wished to see that bond loosened (both Plitt and Hofmann were attached to the liberal side of politics). His commitment was to the church as historical reality, whose confessions would, in fact, become more significant for its life and unity as dependence on the state lessened, and whose vitality must continually be renewed in experiences like, if not on the scale of, the Reformation.[25]

The progress of humanity in the sixteenth century, Plitt says, depended on the Reformation. In this it was representative, for all human progress begins with the Christian church, which is to history as the soul to the body. In the sixteenth century, Luther spoke the refreshing word, for he 'felt in his heart the renewing creative power of God.' With him historical progress could begin again. Other figures and movements must be judged by how they responded to that lead. 'Whoever wished really to take part in the progress of mankind must attach himself to the Reformation movement; only in so far as he did, could he have a lasting influence.' The demand was posed by the time itself. To refuse was to cut oneself off from history's forward march. For those already active in, say, church reform, the choice was a difficult one; they had to renounce their own claims to leadership and allow their activity to be transformed by a new spirit. The humanists especially had to submit to this experience, for already it was plain that the longed-for reform could not come from humanism.[26]

Erasmus is then, in Plitt's article, being judged by a dynamic measure, by how he related to a historical movement of unique significance. His case, says Plitt, is instructive for the fate of the tendencies he typified, for he may be taken as a type for the aims and the failures of humanism. Fifty years old, confirmed in his weaknesses, he was unable to respond to Luther as did the younger Melanchthon, otherwise much like Erasmus. But a static measure is also applied: 'The true essence of Christianity remained foreign to him.' He may have used evangelical expressions and sounded like the Protestant Reformers but he stopped, really, at admiration for the fruits of Christianity (the moral life), without tapping its roots. He spoke of faith, but his was not the faith by which the Reformers overturned the world. (The argument is, of course, satisfyingly circular: Erasmus, whatever he says, cannot mean his avowals of faith because he has not been like the Reformers or done what they did.) He spoke of devotion to scripture but was not in an 'inner living relation' to it.[27]

The terms of Plitt's interpretation of Erasmus' relation with the Reformation are set by his view of the Reformation itself, as both a leap forward in human progress and a recovery of the essence of biblical Christianity. Standard Protestant judgments on his religion and his character are fitted into this scheme without difficulty: Erasmus lacked conviction and, needing support somewhere, he clung to the Roman church; his fearfulness was excessive, as was his love of peace at any price. Plitt does not deny that Erasmus prepared the way for Luther's Reformation: on the negative side, his satires were justified and effective, if lacking in 'deep earnestness and wounded moral feeling'; on the positive side, his work on the New Testament delivered powerful weapons into the hands of the Reformers. Yet, his wish to remain outside the struggle was 'historically unrealizable and morally unjustified'; the situation required a decisive 'Either–or.' Among the humanists, only an ageing minority remained true to Erasmus; to his sorrow, the younger, more lively spirits left him for Luther. He was a living example of Luther's assertion that Christian wisdom does not come from a knowledge of Latin and Greek.[28]

Plitt's article was an epitome of evangelical, orthodox Protestant views on Erasmus in the nineteenth century. It took an old, simple Protestant idea – Erasmus turned his back on the light of the gospel – and reinforced it with nineteenth-century dynamism, a belief in progress and in moments of inescapable historical decision (the decisive 'Either–or'). Erasmus resisted the current or, better, was content to linger in shallows by the shore. Franz Otto Stichart's *Erasmus von Rotterdam: Seine Stellung zu der Kirche und zu den kirchlichen Bewegungen seiner Zeit* is a more static treatment than Plitt's, composed of long quotations from Erasmus' writings, usually presented without reference to biographical or historical context, and interspersed with short bursts of interpretation, mostly hostile to Erasmus. Stichart (1810–83) was a Saxon pastor (at Reinhardsgrimma near Dresden), who wrote, as well as local histories and school books, works in defence of Luther and the Protestant church.[29] The time of his book's

publication (1870, the year of the Vatican Council) is revealing:
the present era of confessional conflicts is appropriate, Stichart
says, for presenting a specific study – hitherto lacking – of
Erasmus' relation to the church. His purpose, he adds, is to test
his oft-repeated assertion of his loyalty to the old church.[30] Stichart, as his book itself reveals, has a second aim – to use Erasmus
as a witness against that church. Thus, towards the end he blesses
providence that, whatever Erasmus' personal loyalty, he demonstrated in his writings the necessity of and the justification for
the Reformation.[31] The two aims are not completely compatible;
to emphasize constantly, from every stage of Erasmus' life, his
unfavourable judgments on the church, its cult and practices,
seems to exclude the possibility of arguing (as many Protestants
had done) that he changed his mind or that he was drawn in two
directions, having a kind of love-hate relationship with the church.

In fact, in pursuing his first aim, Stichart depicts Erasmus as
wavering and indecisive. Thus he could (as in the essays of social
criticism in the *Adagia*) represent the church as the Christian people, that is in a reasonably democratic way. Yet, he insisted that
the church should be reformed from above, with and through the
papacy. There was the same uncertainty, says Stichart, in his
judgments of individual popes and on matters like devotions paid
to the saints, celibacy, purgatory, and even the sacraments.[32] Yet
the weight of quotation Stichart draws from Erasmus' writings,
on the matters mentioned and on the priests, monks, and theologians generally, indicates not indecisiveness but a fixed hostility
towards the old church and its ways; that suits Stichart's second
purpose – to vindicate the Reformation by demonstrating the
entrenched evils of the old church. Those evils could not, as
Erasmus vainly hoped, be cured by intellectual enlightenment:
'If all his contemporaries had thought like that, the state of the
church would perhaps be no brighter or more Christian now than
it was then.' In so far as Stichart recognizes a contradiction, he
explains it, as we might expect, by Erasmus' character, his excessive love of peace and his timidity about disturbances to the
status quo.[33]

The contradiction between the presentations of Erasmus as, on
the one hand, a committed witness against the old church and,
on the other, a man caught in uncertainties and ambiguities remains in Stichart's treatment of his relation to Luther's Reformation. It is said at one point that he played the part of Nicodemus,

the implication being that he accepted the (Protestant) gospel but chose not to follow it.[34] Earlier, Stichart had attributed to him the Protestant principle of asserting nothing not clearly expressed in scripture. Stichart's qualifications on this claim move Erasmus towards liberalism and rationalism. Thus, as an interpreter of scripture, Erasmus was very free; at the end of *Praise of Folly*, he went so far as to ridicule Bible passages. Similarly, he was untrustworthy on the great doctrines of Christianity like the Trinity; his consolations in death were mostly pagan; his views on the salvation of pious pagans were 'Liberalismus.' Overall, he was more concerned with ethics than with doctrine; his was neither a dogmatic, nor a deeply religious nature.[35] On all these points, Stichart sounds, across the confessional division, much like Janssen and Allard.

The true reformer, Stichart concludes (as we would expect), must have a firm grounding in the truth and courage to make it prevail. Erasmus had neither. On one point Stichart makes an original (if contestable) claim: the idea of the invisible church was foreign to Erasmus; so he clung to existing authority. Stichart picks up the language of Adolf Müller: 'One sees that Erasmus had absolutely no appreciation of Luther and his great work; this world of the free spirit was closed to him; for him, there was only a visible world, a world of the rational understanding.'[36]

II

Protestant opinion on Erasmus in the nineteenth century swung between two poles. One was the orthodox and evangelical judgment expressed – in a more or less consistent fashion – by the authors we have just been considering: Erasmus may have helped prepare the Reformation but at decisive moments he failed the good cause because he lacked firmness in both character and theological direction.[37] The other pole was the liberal interpretation which either liberalized the Reformation and turned it into a pre-Enlightenment or removed it from its privileged position and made a freer form of religion the true bearer of human progress. In either case, Erasmus became a central, not a marginal, figure, either by representing the bond between Renaissance enlightenment and the Reformation or by being a progenitor of the freer form of Christianity. On this interpretation the hypothesis of a change of direction at Luther's appearance was not necessary;

thus Erasmus appeared more consistent as a Christian reformer. Not many nineteenth-century Protestants approached the full liberal position. But some at least swung towards that pole.[38]

The acceptance of Erasmus' essential consistency saved the more liberal writers from a logical difficulty in which the orthodox and evangelical writers were caught. For the latter, too, Erasmus prepared the way for the Reformation and anticipated it; in a sense, he was a Protestant before the time. In that case much in his thought must have been sound. How then could he be condemned, as they wished to condemn him, for theological inadequacies of a very serious kind, for superficiality and frivolity, for unsoundness on central tenets of the faith? Heinrich August Erhard (1793–1852) escaped the difficulty in his article – one of the most solid pieces on Erasmus in the nineteenth century – in the general encyclopaedia edited by J.S. Ersch and J.G. Gruber (1842). He did so by separating Erasmus from the Reformation, by seeing him as distinctive and independent, though, in comparison with Luther, inadequate (no nineteenth-century Protestant writer could say less than that). He abandoned the pattern by which Erasmus anticipated the Reformation and then betrayed it. In giving him more historical independence and, one might say, dignity, Erhard approaches to a degree the liberal interpretation of Erasmus.

Erhard was archivist at Münster and made his reputation with a three-volume work on the revival of scholarship, especially in Germany, up to the beginnings of the Reformation (1827–32).[39] The traces of the earlier work are to be found in the article on Erasmus. Thus, Erhard says, Erasmus' edition of Valla's notes on the New Testament (1505) was an event of the greatest importance in modern letters because, with it and Reuchlin's work on Hebrew, the revival of the scholarly study of the Bible began. Unlike other humanists, Erasmus did not, in reaction against scholasticism, renounce theological work permanently but turned his skills to the study of the Bible. That was due, above all, to the influence of John Colet. Erhard, who has a nineteenth-century bureaucrat's interest in place, rank, and position, recognizes a certain restlessness and a love of personal freedom in Erasmus. He considers his appointment as councillor to Charles V very advantageous to his scholarly work, for it gave him pay and honours sufficient for his dealings with other highly placed scholars but left him free and undisturbed. Erasmus was, Erhard says, the one scholar of the age whose life was given wholly to scholarly activity. It served as a lesson in the independence of the life of learning.[40]

The Reuchlin controversy offers Erhard a first opportunity for assessing Erasmus as a historic figure. In his reserve, he was, Erhard says, acting true to his character. As leader of the German learned world, he held it beneath his dignity to fight 'under another's flag.' He could claim with justice to have done more for learning than some who threw themselves into the struggle and, in any case, the weapons used (ridicule without finesse) were not to his taste.

In Erhard's assessment of Erasmus' distinctiveness, sensible expressions are mixed with psychological colourings from Müller and Lavater. As a figure in European intellectual history, Erasmus has, for him, a real but limited significance. To an unusual richness of knowledge and great gifts for imparting it, Erasmus joined, he says, a tireless industry, an insight into the needs of learning in his time, and the will to meet those needs. All had, however, to be without risk to his personal serenity. He lacked the willingness to give up everything for the truth, the one quality capable of 'making him really what in many respects he flattered himself to be, the first man of his age.' His thought was essentially practical; he had distaste for speculation not directed at the improvement of life. He was prudent, somewhat cold, not aiming beyond his capacity; 'it was not his nature to ascend in courageous flight to unknown regions.' In the higher qualities he was – the comparisons are predictable – behind Reuchlin and Luther.[41]

In his primary sphere, philology, he was not an innovator. Yet, he was a landmark; no one knew the ancient writings better or could better convey their contents to his contemporaries. Erhard, like other nineteenth-century commentators, is uneasy with Erasmus' attitude to the vernaculars. He makes a wider criticism of humanist education for its emphasis on formal qualities and for its authoritarianism; taste and values were set by the teacher for the pupils. These are debatable readings of Erasmus' *De ratione studii* and *De pueris instituendis*.[42] They also seem to contradict Erhard's presentation of Erasmus as a philosopher-theologian who avowed an essentially practical wisdom and resisted a morality of abstract, impersonal rules. As a critic of church and theology, he deserved the highest praise. In speaking of the *Enchiridion*, Erhard goes further and makes Erasmus a powerful, beneficent force in the religious life of his time. The book, he says, had a

very wide circulation, which was to be attributed to the fine writing but also to its dominant spirit of 'serious gentleness and noble
liberality of mind.' It was 'one of the happiest harbingers of the
reform of the church.'[43]

Erhard does not accuse Erasmus of making a reversal with the
coming of the Reformation or, for that matter, notably harden his
own judgment. This, as we have seen, separates him from the
evangelical and orthodox writers. So long as Erasmus stood alone,
he says, it was clear that he had a more worthwhile message than
all his contemporaries; at Luther's appearance, the true character
of his theology was revealed. The contrast exposed its limitations.
Modern observers, Erhard goes on, can understand the mutual
alienation of Luther and Erasmus better than contemporaries and
do not need to attribute purely self-regarding and worldly motives
to Erasmus. For Erasmus Christianity was fundamentally a moral
system. He expressed his views, according to circumstances, in
different ways. Anxious to keep his independence from both sides
in the Reformation crisis, he lost firm footing, fell into contradictions, and sacrificed both inner and outer peace.[44]

When he comes to particularities, Erhard veers towards the
standard Protestant judgments, indeed creates a tension between
his conscientious exposition of the contents of Erasmus' works
and his own accompanying commentary.[45] Thus, Erasmus' treatment of Hutten was 'dishonourable.' Luther's reproaches after
1524 may have been excessive but Erasmus deserved many of
them, 'through his lack of decisiveness and of depth and earnestness in his treatment of faith.' On the sacramental teaching,
he hid his true opinions, which were close to those of the Swiss
Reformers. His complaints about the Protestants and their unruly
way of life were 'partly gross exaggerations, partly manifest calumnies.' In his controversy with the ministers of Strasbourg, he
proved unwilling to endure even the most restrained and justified
contradiction.[46]

In the last resort, therefore, Erhard, who was both well read
and well intentioned, was a case of reversion to type. He finishes
by defending the old Protestant positions and treating Erasmus
as a rather malicious enemy, though remarks earlier in his essay
showed more independence and more understanding. We might
expect such independence and understanding from the theologians of the so-called mediating school of the mid-nineteenth
century, a number of whom wrote about Erasmus. How far did

they escape reversion to type? On the face of it, Erasmus would be a sympathetic study for these theologians. He had sought the middle ground and at the end, very much against the odds, sought reconciliation between the parties (what Erhard called 'well-meaning pious hopes,' which rightly failed to win the Protestants from their allegiance to scripture).[47]

The theologians of the mediating school rejected exclusive or extreme positions, on the one side biblical literalism or strict confessionalism, on the other rationalism or philosophic idealism.[48] They tried to embrace all the positive, fruitful tendencies of their time: they believed in the value of historical enquiry for theological studies; they wanted a less dogmatic, more personal, ethical, and practical theology. They rejected rationalism but valued and defended free, scholarly enquiry; they resisted confessionalism but sought for what was still living and relevant in the church tradition. Schleiermacher was the teacher directly or indirectly of the mediating theologians, though generally they were less critical and more churchly than he. They owed to him their concern for the cultural relevance of Christianity and their theological order of priorities: religion was not primarily systematic theology but something inward and experienced. In church history the chief influence was August Neander, who had been a pupil of Schleiermacher. Neander has been praised for his responsiveness to the historical subject, his wide sympathy, though said to be lacking a sense for the dramatic and demonic.[49] All the mediating theologians had to bear the reproach of showing more goodwill than intellectual rigour. They shared the reproach with Erasmus himself. In their age and his, attempts at comprehension were readily associated with lack of conviction. This could make for sympathy with him as a historical subject, as could these theologians' emphasis on a biblically based and personally experienced religion.

Adolf Müller's biography was the occasion of the first pronouncement on Erasmus by one of the mediating theologians, Carl Ullmann (1796–1865). That book, it will be recalled, fitted Erasmus into a large historical scheme whereby, in an intricate analogy between individual biography and the history of the race, the Renaissance (and Erasmus) represented the intellect, the Reformation (and Luther) the spirit of humanity. The intellect, though restless and searching, was unable to resolve mankind's problems or meet its needs. Thus Erasmus, who did not understand the forces at work, responded ineffectively to Luther's Reformation, a response in line with his weak, over-sensitive character.[50]

Ullmann and Müller were much of an age; they had had teachers in common but their paths in scholarship were quite different. Unlike Müller, Ullmann was not captivated by Hegel. 'My path in scholarship,' he himself said, 'is that of historical research; it moves, not from the general to the particular, but from the particular to the general.'[51] Naturally he was cool to Müller's organic analogy between the growth of the individual and the destiny of the race. History was the realm of freedom, not of natural necessity. It was better, Ullmann said, to do without these uncertain speculations and remain in the domain of demonstrable facts, where admittedly the freedom of the observer was decisive but where there was a greater likelihood of certainty and unanimity. Ullmann applied this better sense of historical possibilities to Erasmus, insisting that false demands should not be made of him; he was essentially a scholar with a clear and sharp vision of the real world. He was neither a philosopher nor a prophet and could not be expected to set a new course for humanity.[52]

Ullmann met the theology of Schleiermacher and the history of Neander at Berlin in 1819. From these and his earlier teachers – the Christian humanist Creuzer at Heidelberg, for example – he learned, like Müller, that faith was a personal response, and not primarily exact theology, but did not succumb to the pietistic and romantic enthusiasm which we find in Müller. Against rationalism on the one side and the old supernaturalism on the other, he came, like Schleiermacher, to believe that a reconciliation between faith and culture was possible. In his inaugural lecture delivered at Halle in the same year as his review of Müller appeared, Ullmann declared that revelation and reason were not themselves in contradiction, provided that revelation was understood in its purity and right reason, not one-sided intellectualism, was applied to it.[53] Optimistic, expecting a renewal of the church from the new theology and teaching a Christianity open to culture, Ullmann as church historian was drawn to the more practical and less assertive pre-reformers of the fifteenth century and to Erasmus.[54] Müller was, he said, mistaken to see Erasmus as a rationalist, a mere theologian of the intellect. Erasmus lacked Luther's depth but he shared the standpoint of the Reformers – Christianity consists of living faith in Christ, not of human works and merits – and spoke out with warmth and feeling, not only against errors and superstitions, but also for true Christianity.[55]

The mediating theology gave Ullmann an insight into the positive traits in Erasmus's thought. It also made possible a more sympathetic judgment than Müller's of his character and his role in the Reformation. Erasmus, Ullmann said, did not stand off from the church struggle out of mere prudence or self-regard. To have thrown himself into it would have been an 'affectation.' His independent stand demanded a strength of character not within the capacity of the effeminate disposition which Müller attributed to him. A weak man would have run to join one or other of the parties.[56] Ullmann knew in his own experience the perils of Erasmus' situation. Heidelberg, when he returned to it in 1819, was not a happy place for a teacher of his views. Those who wished (in his own words) 'to hold to the simple gospel without addition or taking away and to treat theology in an historical scholarly way' were caught between the rationalists on the one side and the philosophical idealists on the other.[57]

By his theology and by his temperament and situation, Ullmann was sympathetic to Erasmus. Yet the pull of the mediating theology was not strong enough to counteract that of the traditional Protestant judgments, of which Müller's book had been a naïve reformulation. For all his sympathy Ullmann could not appreciate Erasmus for his own sake. The positive traits he found in him were anticipations of the Reformation and in the last resort Ullmann lacked neither Protestant historicism nor character-judgment. Erasmus, a scholar and philologist, had no sense for the deep religious currents of his time. He was in conflict 'with the nobler spirit of the age.' If one cannot ask a man to step forth as a hero one can at least ask him to join the better side. Unlike Melanchthon, Ullmann said, Erasmus failed because he was without a feeling for firm, absolute truth.[58]

Ullmann's review, which set the pattern of interpretation for the mediating school, was published in the second volume of *Theologische Studien und Kritiken*, the organ of the school which Ullmann himself founded and edited. Another theological journal offered a congenial environment for a sympathetic treatment of Erasmus, the *Zeitschrift für die historische Theologie*, which was founded by C.F. Illgen (1786–1844) in Leipzig in 1832. Illgen preferred moderate and comprehensive positions; historical scholarship, he believed, was the way to advance them.[59]

The article on Erasmus by W.E. Eberhardi, pastor in Weimar, which appeared in *Zeitschrift für die historische Theologie* in 1839, was very much in Illgen's spirit. It posed the typically Protestant question (or 'riddle' as Eberhardi put it): why did Erasmus, who not only castigated abuses and superstitions but also broke in a number of ways from Catholic doctrine and, by his work on the Bible and his writings on theological studies, sent light streaming in darkness, not adhere to the Reformation whose cause he had served? But untypically it left open the further question: whose conduct was the better guide in the disturbed religious and political conditions of the present day, for example in the conflict between rationalism and supernaturalism – the courageous Luther or the gentle Erasmus? At least the mediating position of Erasmus deserved closer study. Protestant judgment, Eberhardi said, would be milder than was customary if the surrounding circumstances and the whole course of Erasmus' life were taken into account.[60]

Weakness of character was not the sole explanation of Erasmus' refusal to join Luther. Eberhardi broke from Müller and the main Protestant tradition at this point. Erasmus was held to the old church by many bonds of respect and gratitude, not as Protestants liked to say by avarice and ambition. To break them would have required an uncommon heroism. Erasmus' receptive temperament and his physical weakness did not allow a rude breaking of bonds, especially in his old age. Besides, between him and Luther there were genuine doctrinal differences. Eberhardi believed that in their controversy over the freedom of the will Erasmus made the better case and regretted that even down to the present day the Lutheran faith was loaded with Luther's more extreme assertions.[61] Like all Protestant writers, Eberhardi condemned Erasmus for being too anxious and fearful and contrasted him in the customary way with Luther, representative of all that was best in the German character – 'integrity, fidelity and sincerity.' Thus Eberhardi came back to character but found not only weakness to explain Erasmus' role in the Reformation but also one estimable trait, his love of peace, which was both genuine and strong.[62] Within the limits set by the question he asked (not 'What did Erasmus stand for?' but 'Why did he not join Luther's Reformation?'), Eberhardi was led by a sense of history and the preference for moderate, middling positions characteristic of the mediating school to a judgment of Erasmus as sympathetic as was possible for any German Protestant in the time between the wars of liberation and the revolutions of 1848 when Erasmus' rivals, Luther and Hutten, appeared as national heroes.[63]

III

In view of the prominence, from Hallam to Froude, of liberal interpretations of Erasmus in nineteenth-century Britain and of the tone of its public and religious life generally, it is not surprising that much Protestant writing on Erasmus there swung towards the liberal pole. Henry Hart Milman (1791–1868) represents the liberal Anglican position.[64] In 1859 he published an essay on Erasmus in the *Quarterly Review*, a journal to which he had contributed for nearly forty years. After starting as a poet and dramatist, Milman turned to biblical history with a *History of the Jews* (1829), which aroused antagonism because it applied the usual canons of historical criticism to Old Testament accounts and attempted, as Lecky said, 'to separate in the sacred writings the parts which were essential and revealed from those which were merely human and fallible.'[65] The controversy put his career under a cloud but in 1849 he was advanced by a Liberal government to the deanship of St Paul's, where he officiated with distinction.

The essay on Erasmus was a work of Milman's old age. It may have been a fragment of the history of Teutonic Christianity which would have concluded his series of many volumes on the history of religion in the West but which he did not live to write.[66] Milman took as his subject not the history of the church as institution and certainly not the history of dogma but rather the interplay in history between religion and civilization. The object of his *History of Christianity* was 'to portray the genius of Christianity of each successive age in connection with that of the age itself; ... to mark ... [the] progress [of different beliefs] from their adaptation to the prevailing state of opinion or sentiment; ... in short, to exhibit the reciprocal influence of civilization on Christianity, of Christianity on civilization.'[67] In every age Christianity must under providence accommodate itself to the development of human institutions and the progress of the human mind. It had adapted itself with 'wonderful versatility in the past, but with a faithful conservation of its inner vital spirit, to all vicissitudes and phases of man's social, moral, intellectual being.'[68] The age of the Reformation and his own age both demanded, in Milman's view, a radical adjustment of Christianity. In the nineteenth century it must recognize the discoveries of science and of literary and historical criticism and embrace them without any fear of their damaging its essential truth. The Reformation had been Christianity's accommodation to the mind's liberation from the tutelage of the medieval church.[69] Milman's Erasmus is a stage in that great accommodation.

It was then not enough for Milman to present Erasmus in himself, to explore the affinity which existed (so Lecky suggested) between Erasmus' mind and his own.[70] The question to be put was: what did he contribute and how did he stand to the Reformation? Milman answered: he was, like Savonarola, its herald. In at least one respect he went far beyond Savonarola, who was a monk and wished to reform the world by turning it into one vast cloister. If Erasmus fell short of reinstating, like Luther and the English Reformers, 'the primitive Christian family as the pure type, the unapproachable model of Christianity,' he yet hated and rejected monkhood, a system 'of which he was never the votary, and refused to be the slave, though in a certain sense the victim.'[71] He was the enemy equally of scholasticism and superstition; his biblical work challenged the uncritical veneration of the Vulgate, which took 'no common courage or honesty.' Had he departed the scene in 1520, he would, says Milman, have been honoured as the most illustrious of the precursors and prophets of the Reformation. As it was, his last years dimmed his reputation. One may not judge severely an ageing man's hesitation and weakness, but Erasmus failed to see that Christian liberty, on which 'the civilization of mankind' depended, was at issue; an impenitent Latin, he failed, too, to recognize a Teutonic and vernacular reformation.[72]

Milman has to this point repeated a familiar Protestant interpretation: Erasmus prepared the Reformation but at its full appearance – for one reason or another – drew back. It flowed on and beyond him, leaving him stranded and powerless. But for a liberal Anglican problems remained. Had not Erasmus anticipated the modern critical study of the scriptures, of which Milman himself was an embattled champion – less in response (so he said) to German influences than out of faithfulness to a sound Anglican tradition? Had not Erasmus prefigured his own attempt to distinguish the essential from the extraneous in religion and to arrive at 'a comprehensive, all-embracing, truly Catholic Christianity?'[73]

Would he not have sided with Erasmus in the debate with Luther over the freedom of the will? In surmounting these problems Milman does not arrive at the ultimate liberal position, that Erasmus, not Luther, was the pioneer of modern religious ideas. Rather he makes new use of the principle of accommodation. Luther's doctrine of predestination was appropriate to a revolutionary moment. Nothing less than total concentration on Christ could arouse mankind from its torpor, break the servitude of centuries, and 'inaugurate the manhood of the mind.' But in more serene times and places Erasmus resumes his influence. 'Erasmianism, as soon as the religious world calmed down, and so long as it is not in a state of paroxysmal struggle, usually renews its sway.' On the issue in dispute with Luther, 'almost all the most learned, very many of the most pious of our Church, including John Wesley and his disciples,' have in England sided with Erasmus.[74]

An Oxford price essay of 1874 (winner of the Lothian Prize) also identifies later Christian thought more with Erasmus than with Luther. Milman was among the writers acknowledged by its author, Arthur Lionel Smith (1850–1924), an exhibitioner at Balliol College, who had taken firsts in classical moderations (1871) and *literae humaniores* (1873) and who was – in 1874 – reading modern history.[75] Other debts were to Jortin, Gibbon, Coleridge, and Hallam but Drummond's was the strongest influence on this fluent, readable, and opinionated piece. A friend and contemporary, R.H. Roe, commented on Smith's natural skill, when writing undergraduate essays, at weaving together thoughts collected in a miscellaneous and voluminous reading. Smith's wife and biographer described the essay as 'a rugged piece of work [which] shows traces of the writer's keen study of Carlyle.'[76] To a modern reader there is less angularity, less sense of the precipitate and catastrophic course of history than that comment might warrant; there is more of the liberal, progressive Protestantism suggested by the names mentioned above. Smith's wife refers to the free thought influential in Balliol in his undergraduate days; it influenced him, she says, without making him a 'scoffer'.[77] In fact, the essay on Erasmus, in its depiction of the latter's calm spirituality and social idealism, suggests Smith's adherence to a comprehensive and ethical, but still recognizably Christian, liberal Protestant religion.

Like the liberals, Smith sees the Renaissance 'as an anti-ecclesiastical, anti-scholastic revolution' and Erasmus as its most representative figure. At least from his own days in the monastery, his kind of religion was in contradiction to that of the monks and the scholastics: 'His sensible and spiritual view of religion would offend them no less than his satirical temper and devotion to learning.' Later studies and associations, including the friendship with Colet, strengthened his predispositions against them.[78] In passing, one might notice a certain poignancy in Smith's account of Erasmus' childhood, which is drawn from the standard sources: he, too, had a childhood without parents, his father dead, his mother living abroad.[79]

What he says about Luther and Erasmus best characterizes Smith's position. Erasmus, he says, wanted 'gradual reform by education and diffusion of the Gospel.' Now, in the nineteenth century, it is possible to see the dangers of Luther's more violent way, while Erasmus appears as 'the prophetic representative of the moderation, reticence, and luminous sense of the best modern teaching.' This is the reticence of those who do not wish to claim certainties where certainty cannot be had. Erasmus, Smith adds, was indifferent to dogma but respectful of tradition and authority. The diatribe on free will was 'the expression of a man of moderation and sound sense, not denying the doctrine of grace, but pointing out the difficulties of denying free-will in the face of the Scripture exhortations and its teaching of a God of justice and love.'[80] Thus in his dealings and controversy with Luther he tried to avoid extremes, and moderns (modern Protestants presumably are meant) must also avoid extreme judgments and recognize their debts to both men.[81] The appeal is in a sense routine; through the essay, it is Erasmus who – in the liberal manner – is associated with the best in modern thought.

Marcus Dods, the liberal-minded professor of New Testament criticism and exegesis at New College, Edinburgh, thought the nineteenth century robbed of its best hope of a satisfying Erasmus biography by the untimely death of its prospective author, James Hamilton (1814–67). The latter had, Dods said, the 'needed culture, diligence, humour, sympathy with the subject.'[82] Hamilton came in 1841, still a young man (he had graduated at Glasgow in 1835), to be minister of the National Scotch Church at Regent Square, London. He spent his life, often overtaxing his strength, as preacher, editor, writer, committeeman, and the much-loved pastor of a congregation divided and depleted by the charismatic proceedings of his brilliant but stormy predecessor, Edward Irving.[83] In an interlude from his editorial work in 1860, he bought for £7 the Leiden edition of Erasmus and began to read him through; it was, he told a correspondent, 'capital reading.' He planned a 'Life and Times' but work and controversy drained his energies and the project had reluctantly to be abandoned.[84] He left only a general lecture and two essays on Erasmus' early life.[85] They are not without attractions or clear perceptions but, in their essentially literary presentation (ranging from the finely tuned to the overblown) and their broad – sometimes superficial – judgments, they are closer in style and spirit to an occasional piece like A.L. Smith's prize essay than to the complete biography anticipated by Dods.

Distinctive in Hamilton is the attempt to provide Erasmus with a psychological history. The tone and pathos are Victorian: his infancy was 'hapless,' his entry into the world 'forlorn and unwelcome.'[86] 'Like other hunted creatures, he grew keen-scented, sharp of sight and hearing, very timid, somewhat coy and secretive, affecting neutral tints and twilight hours.' The outcome was a great versatility of mind and temperament but also a way of going about reform: it needed no Darwin, Hamilton tells his audience of earnest young men, to show 'that this mild little rodent will never develop into a leonine Luther, or rhinocerostic Hutten.'[87]

Erasmus' character as a reformer was, according to Hamilton, determined, first, by his studies and his experience of the monastery. Without elaborating, he anticipates those twentieth-century students of Erasmus who have made the piety of the Brethren of the Common Life (or the *devotio moderna*) a seminal influence on his mind. His teachers in the school at Deventer, says Hamilton, were disciples of Thomas à Kempis, who was 'a reviver of devotion rather than a restorer of learning' but contributed much to the cause of letters, 'for the worst foes of knowledge are grossness and apathy.' When he entered the monastery (an event recounted as in the letters to Grunnius and Servatius Rogerus), his piety was already formed. He sought to serve the living God; the monastic devotions seemed 'an idle mummery.' Generally, 'the love of letters, the love of reality, and the love of liberty' made the monastic life 'irksome captivity.' The experience made Erasmus a fixed enemy of the monks: 'In its treatment of Erasmus, monasticism prepared its own Nemesis.'[88]

Secondly, Erasmus was greatly influenced by his English friends and especially by John Colet.[89] Again, Hamilton touches a question of interest to later scholarship – Erasmus' intellectual or spiritual debt to Colet; a contemporary, Frederic Seebohm, was already preparing his book on the *Oxford Reformers* which would profoundly influence the next generation of biographers. Colet, for Hamilton, was a characteristic figure of that Tudor England which he saw, in the Froudean way, as springing into 'sturdy manhood.' 'Encumbered by no sentiment, and capable of no great subtlety, all matters submitted to his judgment he looked fully in the face, and, making up his mind on their own intrinsic merits, he was little influenced by the voice of antiquity on the one hand, or the allegations of casuists on the other.'[90] He turned Erasmus, hitherto merely a man of letters, to serious study of the Bible. Samuel Knight in his biographies of the two men had underestimated Erasmus' debt to Colet; without him, 'we should probably have lost altogether the Biblical critic.'[91] The biblical work defined the reform that Erasmus wanted, indeed to a degree the Reformation that actually occurred in England. In Hamilton's view, Colet was a proto-Protestant; had he lived beyond 1519, he might have carried Erasmus into the English Reformation. In any case, Hamilton associates Erasmus with that event much as Edward Stillingfleet, the Anglican divine and apologist, had done 150 years before. 'It was not Luther who started the Reformation in England, nor Zwingle, but the Greek New Testament published by Erasmus; and during the remainder of that century no single mind had such influence on the theology of the pulpit and the people as the author of the "Paraphrase." '[92] Erasmus stood for 'a religion at once rational and spiritual,' where intelligence and piety supported one another; his *Enchiridion*, for example, revealed a mind 'sagacious and sensible rather than glowing or imaginative,' but not lacking in evangelical spirit.[93]

Hamilton might be described as a liberal evangelical. He felt a bond with the Puritans of the seventeenth century and the evangelicals of the eighteenth; he sympathized with the disruption of 1843 in the Church of Scotland over patronage and state interference in church affairs. As one would expect from these associations, he was strongly biblicist in outlook; he was a literalist, though he opposed the culling of texts practised by some evangelicals, because it fragmented the scriptures and obscured their overriding themes.[94] All this gave him an appreciation of Erasmus' biblical scholarship; no doubt he was reluctant to follow the critical impulse too far. Marcus Dods (1834–1909), Hamilton's admirer, was much more at ease with the critical revolution of the nineteenth century. Indeed, he used his expository gifts to popularize modern critical views about the Bible. More than once his views on verbal inspiration were scrutinized by his presbytery or by the general assembly of the Free Church to which he belonged. His appointment to the chair of New Testament criticism at New College was taken to indicate an acceptance of critical studies by that church.[95] He was 'one of the most outspoken representatives of critical liberalism who had frankly disavowed the idea of the inerrancy of Scripture and advocated the broader view of inspiration.'[96] In dealing with his opponents he was candid but restrained.

One can discern a natural sympathy in Dods for Erasmus. The latter's mind, he says, tended away from abstractions and dogmatic theology. But to reject dogmatism was not to lack faith. Drummond was wrong to call him an Arian. 'Erasmus knew his own mind; he had not attained to that sentimental laudation of the spirit of doubt which characterizes our own day, nor had he learned to prize investigation more highly than the truth it discovers.'[97] His object was to restore Christianity in Europe. The edition of the New Testament, his main instrument for that purpose, was long in preparation and not as rushed as some have suggested, though hurriedly put through the press; as a critical enterprise, it had serious imperfections, but it began to elucidate and make available the true text. He had as a result great visibility as a reformer; few authors have found so wide an audience in their lifetimes. Naturally, he was alienated by the dogmatism of the Protestant Reformers but, in looking for a gradual reform, he put too much faith in Rome. It was, Dods adds, a mistake for Erasmus to debate with Luther one of the most abstruse philosophical and theological questions – better to have simply asserted his right 'to know nothing but the historical data of Christianity, and the simple lines of truth delivered in the Apostles' Creed.'[98]

Dods' essay was ostensibly a review of Seebohm's book and Drummond's and first appeared in the British and Foreign Evangelical Review. He found Drummond 'a modest, unostentatious, painstaking, competent writer,' the best in English, but he regretted the lack of restraint in his contemporary references and especially in his handling of the evangelicals, with whom he was unhealthily obsessed.[99] The tone of Dods' own treatment of Eras-

mus is set by his comment on Erasmus' portrait (among nineteenth-century writers such a comment seemed obligatory): 'one
of the great faces of the world, to be ranked with that of Dante,
or of Newman.'[100] There is a welcome dignity about this description after the cranial mysticism of Lavater and Hamilton's
extravagant psychologizing, and the comparisons are fresh and
interesting. Dods rejected many of the conventional Protestant
views of Erasmus. His 'diligence in his proper vocation as a literary man' has never been surpassed. He stood between the ancient and modern worlds 'as a kind of gentleman-usher,' bringing
forward the best or most-needed authors.[101] In assessing his character, one should remember his nervous temperament. A reader
of the *Adagia* or the *Julius exclusus* is struck by his boldness, not
by the timidity of which so much has been made. He did not
sacrifice robustness for refinement; he was no mere bookworm.
'Each of his writings has its motive in the real world around him,
and all of them are alive with the characters he was daily seeing.'
His *Ciceronianus* made a vigorous defence of Christianity. For him
culture was the way to faith.[102] In emphasizing positive traits,
Dods appears as a liberal evangelical version of Coleridge.

Common to the British Protestant writers of liberal outlook we
have been considering here have been (apart from the familiar
Protestant association of Erasmus with the repudiation of medievalism and especially monasticism) an inclination to support
Erasmus in his debate with Luther and, above all, praise for his
critical work on the text of the scriptures. In both respects he was
seen as a precursor of modern attitudes. He was, in other words,
fitted into a generally progressive view of modern religious history.[103]

'A characteristic specimen of the vocation of the scholar and
the man of letters': that was how principal John Caird (1820–98)
presented Erasmus to students of Glasgow University in an opening lecture to the session of 1877.[104] Erasmus, if a mind not of
the very highest order, demonstrated how far intellectual liveliness and diligence could go. Of equal interest to Caird, who 'taught
a reasoned and explicit idealism' in the Hegelian mould, was
Erasmus' 'devotion to the cause of letters and liberal thought in
an age of religious conflict.'[105] His interest in the relationship of
religion and secular culture removed Caird somewhat from the
liberal evangelical circle which enclosed Hamilton and Dods.
Erasmus' very nature, lacking in fervour and enthusiasm though

religious in a sober way, and the sphere of his achievement, literature with some applicability to ecclesiastical ideas and institutions, make him 'a sort of living test of the measure in which the Church and its traditions and institutions are in harmony with the spirit of culture.' This is, for Caird, a question about the church's capacity to accommodate modernity. Erasmus' response was a model: to support critical investigation and reasoned discussion of the religious books and ideas, but to stand clear of the clashing dogmatisms and irrationalities. He recognized the place of both change and continuity in cultural and spiritual life.[106] He exemplified the cultivated mind, the 'spirit of culture.' 'It is at once progressive and conservative; it has in it elements both of hardihood and timidity – a critical audacity which seems to rank its possessor on the side of revolution, and yet a fastidious moderation, a recoil from violence and vulgar iconoclastic zeal, which to a superficial observer gives him the air of the reactionary and the obstructive.'[107]

Caird's is a more secularized picture of Erasmus than that of the liberal evangelicals previously considered. His discussion of culture and religion is reminiscent of Milman's appeal to the principle of accommodation. In him the demands of modernity, of modern, liberal, scientific culture, seem more urgent. Yet the relation of Erasmus to modernity in some form, at least that of the critical historical study of the scriptures, concerns all these writers. By most of them he is expected also to be a guide though the dilemmas of Christianity and civilization in the nineteenth century.

IV

The liberal strain in Erasmus interpretation was strong among Swiss Protestants in the nineteenth century.[108] In Zürich liberal reforms in state and education in the 1830s and their aftermath find an echo in an essay on Erasmus published in Friedrich von Raumer's *Historisches Taschenbuch* in 1843. Indeed, this piece reflects the tense time before the outbreak in 1847 of the civil war between the liberal and conservative cantons of Switzerland. Apart from the historical justification for studying Erasmus (his part in preparing the Reformation), says its author Heinrich Escher, there were contemporary reasons for considering one of his outlook, one who taught an essentially practical religion and resisted oppressive dogmatism. Ultramontanism was seeking to re-establish Roman domination and threatened the liberty of both the state and scholarship. On the Protestant side, too, a dogmatic party was seeking to impose its own views and rejecting those who – even though meritorious – did not 'carry its colours and swear to all its articles of belief.' Materialism posed a third threat.[109]

Escher (1781–1860) had long been an influential figure in the Zürich educational system when, in 1839, conservative and pietist forces barred David Friedrich Strauss, author of the controversial *Life of Jesus*, from taking up the chair of dogmatics in the newly created university. His view of these people is plain from his essay on Erasmus. Escher was a figure of the establishment, coming from an old Zürich family and entering the ministry of the church there at the age of nineteen, but he was also active in the educational reforms of the 1830s, subsequently teaching in both the gymnasium and the university. His background in critical scholarship included study with the great classicist F.A. Wolf at Halle (1802).[110]

Much in Escher's essay may be seen as a rejection of Adolf Müller's pietist strictures on Erasmus. Thus, the *Enchiridion* which, in a frank and unprovocative spirit, expressed the practical character of Erasmus' religion (learned in part from his study of classical thought) has not been well received by all. In his time and ours, Escher remarks, there have been well-meaning souls 'for whom the content of the work – clear, directed above all at moral and religious practice, at an active Christianity – appeared as no more than instruction in an outwardly respectable life, since it offered no support for their disposition to a pious enthusiasm.' He explicitly rejects Müller's criticism of Erasmus' neglect of the vernaculars. For Erasmus, he says, Latin was virtually a mother-tongue and, besides, concentration on it was necessary if he was to fulfil his vocation of advancing the classical revival. He was not at all ignorant of the common life of his time – his writings report his keen observations.[111]

Erasmus saw his classical, especially his philological, studies as a way to the restoration of theology; but all, Escher repeats, was a means to the end of reviving practical Christianity among the people. He did not misuse scripture, as some later Protestants have done, by picking texts to back up preconceived dogmas.[112] Escher puts Erasmus in opposition to the dogmatists among both Catholics and Protestants.[113] He is one of those liberal Protestants who sees the New Testament edition as 'decisive preparation, or rather as the beginning of the Reformation itself.' Escher is not uncritical of Erasmus' response to Luther's Reformation: his search, through learning, for a reasonable, undogmatic, practical religion could overlook the deeper springs of religious feeling. But the warring parties were unjust in trying to force him into their mould. He rightly saw that Luther's dogmatism was destructive of practical Christianity and was but scholastic complexity in another form. His refusal to join Luther did not arise only from lack of courage; he differed from the Roman church on important doctrines but – his concern being practical religion – he saw no reason on that ground for making a break.[114]

Similarly, Escher recognizes Erasmus' weaknesses of character (he, too, quotes Lavater), arising from his early experiences and his unenviable position between two warring parties: mistrust, slyness, fearfulness. But there is, he says, another side. One who showed the enthusiasm Erasmus did for virtue and learning cannot be called a cold egoist. Like Wieland, Escher says that Erasmus must be taken as he is and not asked to exhibit Luther's qualities. His great work in learning and religion depended on the qualities he actually possessed and would have been crippled by the qualities others have sought to impose upon him.[115]

Escher's essay is, for its time, a notable defence of Erasmus as the apostle of practical religion and interesting because of its setting, the struggle between liberals and conservatives in Zürich and Switzerland.[116] At the theological faculty of Basel in the same period, there was a mixture of traditions and influences, as is demonstrated by differences over the call of the critical scholar W.M.L. De Wette, the colleague of Schleiermacher and Neander at Berlin, to a chair there in 1822. De Wette in time reshaped the faculty. Under his aegis a young Basel scholar, Karl Rudolf Hagenbach (1801–74), was appointed to teach church history in 1822 (he took the chair from 1829). Hagenbach epitomized the spiritual mixture in Basel: his father, a member of the medical faculty, was attached to the ideals of the Enlightenment; he received strong pietist influences from the Basel church; he was drawn to German idealism, as a student taking from Herder the notion of Christ, not as transcendent being, a metaphysical riddle, but as a realization of what all men could be – sons of God – and, later, visiting Goethe at Weimar. He studied in Germany, at Bonn, and then at Berlin with Schleiermacher and Neander; Bonn confirmed the biblical, orthodox element in his thought, Berlin the place of the subjective, of cultivation of the spirit and its expression in ethics and life.[117] From the beginning Hagenbach saw his vocation as reconciling Christianity and the idea of humanity. One would expect his attitude to Erasmus to be revealing of this balance in his thought.

Hagenbach was the first, but not the only Basel scholar in the nineteenth century to write about the great humanist's relation with the city where he had felt most at home and where his reputation was long treasured. His essay was part of a projected series on figures connected with the history of Basel University. Erasmus had not been a member of the university, but his presence in the city added to its renown. He came to Basel, Hagenbach says, seeking the best printer possible for his New Testament edition. Finding him in Froben, he stayed there for most of the last twenty years of his life. Basel was able to do what the papal and royal courts could not do, 'to tie down this wandering star.' However, the Reformation there unsettled the calm life of scholarship he had planned. A familiar romantic colouring infuses Hagenbach's account of Erasmus' response to the Reformation: 'he was a spoilt child of the muses, while Luther and Zwingli were sturdy sons of mother nature and men of the people.' He gave wavering advice to the Basel council in 1525, forgetting that the stream of history cannot be controlled like the canals of his homeland. Yet in his last illness he showed the patience of a sage and a Christian.[118]

The rather cloying tone of this small piece was no doubt set by its homiletic aim of inspiring the middle-class youth of Basel: they should follow his good example in studies, while recognizing his lack of the more forceful and heroic qualities. Hagenbach was to write more substantial passages on Erasmus, while other writers were pursuing in a more scholarly way the theme of his relations with the city. Immanuel Stockmeyer (1814–94), who became *Antistes* in the Basel church from 1871 and professor of theology at the university from 1876, had as a young man published an essay on Erasmus' friendship with Bonifacius Amerbach (1495–1562), who had himself been professor (of law) in the university and five times rector.[119] It was based on a fund of more than ninety letters, only two of which had appeared in Le Clerc's edition of Erasmus' *Opera omnia* at the beginning of the eighteenth century. They had been discovered in the 1770s and published in 1779 by another Basel professor, Johann Wernhard Herzog, under the title *Epistolae familiares Des. Erasmi Roterodami ad Bonif. Amerbachium,* but neither Hess nor Müller – the most influential biographers of the first half of the nineteenth century – had noticed them. Now they had been passed from the church to the university library by the *Antistes* Emanuel Merian, the orthodox professor of New Testament and sometime professor of mathematics.[120] This story of archival recovery is worth telling because it records the interest of the Basel élite of all persuasions in Erasmus and the city of his time.   ·

Stockmeyer's own interest is in the personality of Erasmus in his last years (almost all the letters were written from Freiburg), but the relationship with Amerbach and Basel naturally bulks large. Despite incidents (recounted in the letters) which aggravated the differences between Erasmus and the Protestant Reformers (whose cause Basel had joined in 1529), and played on Erasmus' suspiciousness, Erasmus' friendships in Basel were not significantly disturbed. Among them, that with Amerbach was the closest and the most untroubled. Erasmus assumed an identity in religious outlook between himself and Amerbach who, in fact, long delayed his adherence to the Reformation.[121] As for Erasmus' personality (his stated interest), Stockmeyer asserts the correctness of Müller's judgments but his actual conclusions are closer to the moderate Basel tradition than to Müller's high censoriousness. Admittedly Erasmus' over-sensitivity increased in his last years and it is, says Stockmeyer, sad to see an old, sick man needing repose but caught up in struggle on every side and indeed attracting more enmity to himself. Stockmeyer does not doubt the sincerity of Erasmus' religious position. He told Amerbach that only the fall of the old faith could bring him to leave Basel, but that was enough; he gladly abandoned a town that had changed its faith. This for Stockmeyer was proof of how unjustly those had condemned Erasmus who considered him a convinced Protestant holding back from a public avowal of his inner convictions out of fear. Erasmus never shared Luther's conclusion that the Roman church was not the church of grace. Only on secondary issues did he hold views in common with the Reformers. He wanted to be, and to be seen to be, a good Catholic. He may have been over-anxious and have equivocated but ultimately his stand corresponded to his convictions. As a form of Protestant judgment this is milder than that which assumes Erasmus' support and then betrayal of the Protestant cause. His fault, says Stockmeyer in a final section of his essay, lay in seeing only a pestilence, not the birth-pangs of a better age, in the troubles of his time; he failed to make God's cause his own.[122] Thus Stockmeyer adheres in the end to the Protestant historicism of writers like Merle d'Aubigné and, later, G.L. Plitt.

In 1850 the first number of the *Basler Taschenbuch*, a new periodical, carried a further essay on Erasmus' residence in the city. The author was its editor Wilhelm Theodor Streuber (1816–57), who cut a different figure in Basel from Hagenbach and Stockmeyer.[123] He was a layman, who did not have so secure an academic career and supplemented his income by journalistic work, editing the *Basler Zeitung* from 1847 to 1856. His scholarly sphere was classical philosophy, in which he taught and wrote over a wide range; but he was active also in the history of Basel, and the *Basler Taschenbuch* (1850–7) was intended to cultivate that field. Basel's history, says Streuber in the first number, was distinctive and instructive but must be seen in connection with the wider history of the times (a prescription to which his own essay on Erasmus in the same number conformed).[124] He was of delicate constitution, if of hardy spirit, resented the materialism of the age, and died young. This life of some frustration and difficulty provided perhaps a better setting for assessing Erasmus' Basel years than the more magisterial experiences of Hagenbach and Stockmeyer.

The standpoint of Streuber's essay is made clear at once by his remark that Erasmus' relation to the scholarship of his time has been more accurately judged (notably by Ranke) than his relation to the church, and by his praise for Escher and his condemnation of Müller. Basel, says Streuber, attracted Erasmus through the scholarly spirit dominant there and the character of its inhabitants and he, in turn, drew other scholars to the city. The Basel Reformation had both religious and political elements and was in fact a revolution. Erasmus could, Streuber adds, have precipitated events by siding with revolution but he stood by a program of reform; his principle was that no church should act unilaterally within the body of Christendom. Even so, he used – in advising the setting aside of various 'human ordinances' – expressions that were 'decidedly liberal.' The advice he gave the Basel Council as the crisis was developing in 1525 was not unfavourable to the Reformation: book censorship but only for seditious and libellous writings, not for Lutheran books; maintenance of church practices but removal of accompanying superstitions; allowance of clerical marriage; and leaving the decision on fasting to the individual conscience. This advice, with its accompanying call to avoid tumults, was, in Streuber's view, a 'masterpiece of moderation and intelligence,' justifying the faith the Basel government put in the man of learning.[125] Even after the revolution of 1529, Streuber adds, Erasmus avoided enmity with the leaders of the Reformation in Basel and the city retained its respect for him. About his departure he was regretful but firm. His return six years later was a step towards returning to his homeland, but he bore the intervening (and fatal) illness 'with Christian patience and resignation.'[126]

This somewhat detailed account has been necessary in order to convey, first, the solidity of Streuber's treatment of Erasmus' encounter with the Basel Reformation and, second, the humanity of his depiction of Erasmus himself, which is not seriously qualified by the borrowing of some expressions from Lavater.[127] To return to Hagenbach is to revert to the theologically oriented Protestant interpretation. There is in fact a mystery about Hagenbach's attitude to Erasmus. His own thought was open and irenic. It was Schleiermacher's thought, said his pupil and successor Rudolf Stähelin, modified in an orthodox direction to distinguish between the object of belief and the subjective working of belief. He emphasized what modern Catholics and Protestants, especially in German-speaking countries, had in common. More broadly, as we have seen, he sought to harmonize the eternal truths given in Christianity with a broad cultivation of the human spirit freed, as far as possible, from prejudices and preconceptions. He was seen as the leader of the mediating theology in Switzerland. His historical work, which he saw as closely bound to his theological, expressed the same spirit, as is revealed in the notes of his most famous student, Jacob Burckhardt, who retained great affection for his first teacher. 'Humanism and Christianity,' Burckhardt could conclude from his lectures on recent church history, 'if not always identified with one another, still stood – especially after the reawakening of an Erasmian theology in the eighteenth century – in close agreement.'[128] It is then surprising that Hagenbach's picture of Erasmus himself is initially quite unsympathetic.

One explanation is that, when he prepared his lectures on the

Reformation (first published in 1833), he was much under the influence of Müller. So Erasmus' character bulks large in his seven-page treatment and there is many a familiar expression. The combination of spoiling (by his mother) and toughness in his childhood and youth gave him a weak and devious character. His experiences, which brought him no joy but in his books, made him a bookworm, the client of the great, rather than a free man. He himself admitted that as a young man he shuddered at the name of death.[129] Despite a reference to the attractiveness of his clear and cultivated mind and his sensitive spirit, unappealing traits predominate in Hagenbach's portrait. His religion stayed on the surface. It consisted in a respect for the good rather than an inner, living connection with Christ. As in Müller, Schleiermacher's religion of inner feeling and personal dependence is used here to make a judgment on Erasmus: neither his study of antiquity nor his philosophical religion had prepared him for finding himself only in connection with the whole, God's kingdom, or for surrendering himself to that kingdom. To preparing the Reformation he brought intellectual enlightenment and satire, mostly cold stuff. Hagenbach in these lectures uses an array of metaphors to depict this inadequacy: the scholarly revival was more like the light of the moon than warming, enriching sunlight; Erasmus' wit was more like summer sheet lightning than a purifying storm; his criticism of the church reached only the outworks, not the citadel, the extremities, not the heart.[130]

A later essay – in the *Realencyclopädie für protestantische Theologie und Kirche* (1855) – in part escaped the Müller influence and drew closer to liberal Protestant interpretations of Erasmus. It is said, for example, that in the *Enchiridion* Erasmus opposed a sound Christian piety to the superstition of his time. Hagenbach, like other liberal and mediating writers, also recognizes the connection between Erasmus' work on the New Testament and modern textual criticism; he followed a fine critical instinct rather than fully worked out principles. His positive role in preparing the Reformation is now brought out (in the lectures, too, it had been said that the scholarly revival had created a freer intellectual atmosphere in which Luther's Reformation could take wing, whereas Hus' a century before had gone to ground). Hagenbach now uses expressions like Ullmann's: 'he presented scripture as the pure source of Christian faith which must be offered to all and pointed to Christ as the ground of salvation.' Here Erasmus shows a feeling for the people and their religious needs. That he looked more to the wisdom which Christianity shared with antiquity than to the working of the Word in the depths of the soul does not justify denying him an earnest Christian disposition or calling him the Voltaire of his time.[131] Hagenbach sets out the familiar contrast between Luther the man of conscience and the people and Erasmus the man of enlightenment and the intellectual élite, but in this essay the tone has lightened appreciably and we have an Erasmus interpretation more or less in line with liberal Protestant preconceptions and the depictions by other writers of the mediating school.

Rudolf Stähelin (1841–1900) takes the same standpoint as Hagenbach (to whose chair he succeeded in 1875) but has a more positive feeling for Erasmus. He was scion of a Basel merchant family belonging to the Moravian brethren, whose active piety made a lasting impression upon him. A second influence came from the Basel gymnasium – the classical humanist educational ideal. The combination of scholarship and piety was characteristic of the man; it was reinforced by theological studies in Germany where the influence of Schleiermacher ('a guide to the sanctuary,' said Stähelin) was primary. Stähelin was the student of Hagenbach and the son-in-law of Stockmeyer, devoted like his elders to university, church, and community in Basel (he once declined a call to Marburg). His open and tolerant disposition, it was said, represented the best traditions of old Basel. Theologically he adhered explicitly to the *via media* and was associated with the mediating school.[132] In interpreting Erasmus (in his probationary lecture of 1873 and the article 'Erasmus' in the second edition of the *Realencyklopädie*), he expressed this, not so much by exalting the middle position in itself, as by balancing alternative opinions, the old Protestant view (Erasmus was the precursor and then the opponent of the Protestant Reformation) and the humanist Enlightenment view (Erasmus was a progressive force in his own right).

What is new, reflecting an important change in the Erasmus literature in the last third of the nineteenth century (to this we will return in the next chapter), is an awareness of the power Erasmus exercised over contemporaries, of the existence in other words of an Erasmian party. We are no longer dealing with a solitary scholar. Stähelin knew Frederic Seebohm's *Oxford Reformers* on the so-called fellow-work of Erasmus, Colet, and More;

Erasmus learned, he says, much from Colet: how humanist study can be put to the service of theology and the renewal of religious life; how the Bible should stand at the centre of theology; how (this was much less palatable to a Protestant writer) reform could be pursued within the existing church order.[133] At Basel, Stähelin continues, taking further the theme which had already occupied so many Basel historians, Erasmus gathered about him an eager, youthful circle, giving its members new views and aims and uniting them in common work and achievement. In Germany between 1509 and 1519 a defined party of Erasmians appeared which saw in Erasmus the leader not merely of a scholarly but also of a religious renewal; excepting Luther himself, almost all significant leaders of the later Reformation were of this party.[134]

Recognizing Erasmus as a positive force but continuing to judge him from the standpoint of the Reformation forced on Stähelin a clearly defined pattern of interpretation. Erasmus is a case of approach and backsliding. His early career was a power for light and liberation. Indeed his life to 1509 was a model of that emancipation and rejuvenation which he anticipated for humanity. He fought his way out of the double darkness of his own miserable circumstances and the old religion.[135] In the years that followed he unfolded, especially at Basel, a powerful and fruitful reforming activity, whose climax was the great edition of the New Testament in 1516 – less a work of scholarship than of practical reform. He prepared the Reformation in quite specific ways, moving scripture into the central position and using christocentric expressions very reminiscent of Luther's. 'In his work,' Stähelin concludes, 'Reformation faith and evangelical freedom have become conscious of their divine right.'[136]

Yet Erasmus turned away from the light which he himself had produced. The evangelical principle once released, the alternatives were to follow it to the end or to backslide. How is Erasmus' backsliding to be explained? Stähelin is free of the intense, romantic language of Müller and Hagenbach, who claimed to peer into the void of Erasmus' inner being, but still attributes his historic failure in part to his character. He was fearful and preferred peace and personal well-being to the truth. But Stähelin recognizes deeper grounds of difference. Luther's Reformation was Augustinian, Erasmus was Pelagian; for the one, Christ was redeemer, for the other, example. At this point Erasmus' affinities are less with the Reformation than with the Enlightenment.[137]

Stähelin's Erasmus is a marriage between the typical Protestant preoccupation with Erasmus' failure to recognize the historical necessity of the Reformation and an admiration, characteristic of the mediating school, for the defenders of intellectual freedom, however they might be judged theologically. Stähelin regrets Erasmus' alienation from the Reformation: his freer spirit might have saved Protestantism from its own scholasticism.[138]

The church historians of the mediating school – in Switzerland as in Germany – are, as commentators on Erasmus, disappointing, in that they failed to break free of the traditional Protestant framework of interpretation. For them, as for other Protestant writers, the Reformation was a great and necessary work in the history of the church and of civilization. Erasmus must be judged from its standpoint. Nevertheless, their theological commitments and personal dispositions to reconciliation and the middle way made Erasmus attractive to them. Among the Basel church historians we have just been considering, the consequent amelioration in judgment of Erasmus was furthered by the attention given to the circumstances in Basel itself. This is to be explained by the character of the Basel Reformation. After the initial shock of revolution, there was, in the 1530s and 1540s, a gradual return – under the leadership of men like Bonifacius Amerbach – to a moderate and, in many respects, 'Erasmian' position. By sixteenth-century standards reformed Basel was unusually tolerant and latitudinarian.[139] There was no need then for the Basel historians – unlike their German Lutheran colleagues – to defend the hatred and irascibility of Luther towards the Dutch humanist.

V

There were sharp differences of opinion over Erasmus in the Netherlands in the first half of the nineteenth century. Indeed this had been so since the time of the Revolt and the seventeenth-century controversies over Calvinist doctrine and the relations of church and state. On the one hand, Erasmus was a suspect figure to many Calvinists of a rigidly dogmatic or intensely pietistic type. Writers like Adolf Müller and Merle d'Aubigné were congenial to them. On the other hand, there was a sturdy tradition running through some of the leaders of the Revolt (including, probably, William of Orange himself), the Remonstrants and writers of the Enlightenment which associated the practical piety, irenicism, and religious toleration those people favoured with the name of Erasmus.[140] Between this tradition and nineteenth-century liberal Protestantism a link could easily be made.

Early in the century, a standard work of church history (by Ypeij and Dermout) claimed Erasmus as 'the first, the greatest reformer of the church': 'He it was whom we ... cannot thank enough for the light which he enkindled for the reform of the church and with which he led the way for the rest of the reformers, giving precedence to none.'[141] An essay of about the same time in a literary magazine had the primary purpose of presenting Erasmus as an example of those who had surmounted difficulties to achieve eminence in life, but it also saw him as an admirable exponent of the Christian faith: his way of thinking was wise and moderate, filled with faith in the divine word, indifferent to dry speculation, ardent and vigorous in praising goodness and peace. Admittedly, this author adds, he was condemned by both sides in the Reformation struggle, but he had the honest conviction that the church should be reformed from within, which pleased neither the defenders of the old ways nor those seeking larger convulsions. Basel was right to give him – in life and death – an honoured place.[142] Another essay in the same magazine took the contrary view, directly challenging Ypeij's large claim for Erasmus, by assembling the evidence for denying him the title of reformer of the church, let alone that of first and greatest reformer. The author quotes Luther's remark to Oecolampadius that Erasmus would, like Moses, die in Moab and not enter the promised land. He has, in other words, his own achievements and his own renown (especially in letters and studies); he ought not to deprive Luther of the title of church reformer, which belongs properly to him. Erasmus did all he could (his expressions against schism make this clear) to prevent the setting up of the reformed church. How then can he be its founder?[143]

Those who accepted, indeed advanced, Erasmus' claim to the title 'church reformer' raised another question which struck a chord of Dutch nationalism but also echoed contemporary scholarly interest in the 'forerunners of the Reformation' (as demonstrated by the popularity of Ullmann's book on that subject): how far did Erasmus' program – in style and substance – continue or belong to a Netherlands reforming tradition? How far was it distinctively Dutch? The voice of humanity against superstition was first raised in the Netherlands, said J.J.F. Noordziek (1811–86), deputy librarian in the royal library, in a lecture of 1841, adding expansively: 'what the other Christian peoples have seen and done, they have seen and done on the lead of the Netherlands.' All Europe admired Erasmus' achievements. The main subject of this lecture is Erasmus' humour, his distinguishing characteristic (as Lavater had already shown). Noordziek gathers a number of anecdotes – most, unhappily, apocryphal – to demonstrate Erasmus' humorous disposition. More seriously, he relates his wit to his understanding of the waywardness of the human heart and also suggests that, in the struggles for reform, his amiability did not flee away: his aim was to better, not embitter.[144] This lightweight piece at least has the virtue of indicating the sunnier side of Erasmus' personality, a relief from the preoccupation, apparent especially among those who rejected his claim to be a reformer, with his weaknesses of character.

That there was such a debate in the Netherlands in the nineteenth century was due not only to the persistence of traditions in Erasmus interpretation going back to the Arminian controversy and beyond but also to the contemporary cultural and religious situation. A revival of Calvinist orthodoxy was reinforced by romanticism and anti-revolutionary politics. Thus the distinguished historian Groen van Prinsterer (1801–76), a leading figure on this side of Dutch cultural and political life for half a century, became convinced under the Restoration that 'the Protestant faith as professed by the orthodox in the Republic since the 16th century ought to be the starting-point and permanent standard in estimating all matters both spiritual and material.' At work here was less the attraction of dogmatic strictness in itself than an intense reaction against the optimism and rationalism of the Enlightenment, including enlightened liberal Protestantism. Groen, for example, was a reader of the conservative political theorists beginning with Burke.[145] It is possible to describe the Dutch version of the Protestant 'awakening' (Réveil), whose Genevan expression we earlier encountered in Merle D'Aubigné, as 'in fact theologically vague, full of tears and fervent sentimentalism.'[146] Writers affected by this mood were unlikely to find Erasmus – seen as cool, rationalistic, and latitudinarian – a congenial figure. In its historical thinking, the romantic and orthodox school was hostile to the regent class of Holland which ruled the country after the Revolt (if not without challenge) and which had sympathy for the Remonstrants and appealed to a tradition of reli-

gious tolerance and conciliation thought of as 'Erasmian.'
On the other side in the nineteenth century were the heirs of
that tradition and, to a degree, of the Enlightenment, the so-called
Groningen movement, gathered about a group of theology professors at the University of Groningen. Their outlook can be described as a different kind of romanticism from the dark, intense
emotionalism of the orthodox party; it was optimistic, lyrical,
conciliatory. They held also to a different version of Dutch history:
'They discovered a truly national Dutch Reformation, that of the
Brethren of the Common Life and of Erasmus whose example
they sought to follow, as opposed to that of foreigners like Luther
and Calvin.'[147]
By mid-century, therefore, it was a lively issue in Dutch intellectual life how far the Netherlands Reformation had an Erasmian origin and how the balance in Dutch civilization was to be
struck between the orthodox Calvinist tradition and the alternative, variously associated with the pre-reformers, Erasmus, the
Remonstrants, Grotius, and the regent class of Holland. In 1843
the Haagsch Genootschap tot verdediging van de Christelijke
Godsdienst (the Society for the Defence of the Christian Religion
at The Hague) offered a prize question on Erasmus as Netherlands
church reformer. The author of the successful submission was
Barend Glasius (1805–86), minister at Geertruidenberg, the historic fortress town on the Maas; it was published in 1850. He had
thought for a long time before responding to the society – there
could be more qualified participants, the issue was controverted
but the form of the question seemed to suggest that the answer
was assumed. He was, however, reassured by the closer definition
of the question: it required study of what Erasmus had in common
with other pre-reformers in the Netherlands and of his continuing
influence on the Netherlands church, including that part which
remained Catholic.[148]
Glasius' work falls then into three parts: first, to establish what
was distinctive in Erasmus' approach to church reform; secondly,
to relate this to his character and formation as a Netherlander;
thirdly, to trace how far his continuing influence on the Netherlands churches flowed from a natural affinity between the reformer and his countrymen.[149] On the first, he emphasizes above
all the biblical character of Erasmus' program. His way to reform
'is the biblical, better said that of the New Testament, wed to the
scholarly and bearing fruit in the ethical and religious.' From the

Bible he could derive not mere correction for this abuse or that within the church but a reform program over the whole field. For this purpose, 'none before him had thrown so rich, so pure and so broad a light on the holy scriptures, nor promoted their study so powerfully.' His whole intellectual development, beginning in Hegius' school, was towards a deeper and more understanding study of the Bible. Always the gospel became clearer to him; there he was 'as at home.' And what the Bible was for him it should and could become for all people.[150]

A reform flowing from the Bible, Glasius continues, would in Erasmus' view be a gradual, long-term process. It would reshape the church and Christendom without breaking or dividing them; the light would spread and the seed would grow without violent disturbance. There was, in Glasius' estimation, a paradox: none before Erasmus had spoken as freely as he about reform but he remained attached to the old church order. Those who, after Luther's appearance, looked to him to take an unambiguous stand for or against the Reformation misunderstood this combination.[151]

In what sense then was Erasmus a church reformer? He had, Glasius concludes, the key to reform; he accepted the fundamental principle, viz the renewal of the church according to the Bible. The present church must be judged by the New Testament church, by the standard of the gospel. That was the source of moral reform. If one might hesitate to call Erasmus a mystic as Hofstede de Groot of the Groningen school had done, he cannot be dubbed a rationalist or humanist reformer either; the biblical principle was too strong in him for that. He began at the right place but failed to achieve his end, a thoroughgoing reform in church and Christendom, because he did not challenge the hierarchy. For this reason he cannot be called a church reformer in the fullest sense but otherwise – as one who recognized the fundamental principle, as a reformer of morals and teaching – he deserved the title. In practical terms he was indispensable to reform. Even as things stood – after his break from the Reformers – he influenced many to look critically at the state of the church and promoted Catholic reform; within the old he advised tolerance and moderation.[152]

How then did Glasius decide between the rival views of Erasmus' relation to their Reformation among Dutch Protestants? (He is also aware of the conflict among Catholic writers between those who saw him as an essentially Catholic reformer and those who treated him as an enemy. In Glasius' view he was in many ways alienated from church teachings, but his attachment to the hierarchy makes it unjust to brand him a heretic.) He can join neither those who consider Erasmus the greatest of the reformers, so exalting him too far, nor those who treat him as of no importance to the Reformation, so abasing him. He is with those who honour him as serving reform in indispensable ways, but without taking the necessary step of breaking with the hierarchy. It is indicative that Glasius considers Ullmann and Eberhardi more just than Hagenbach and Merle d'Aubigné and is severe on Müller.[153]

His second question – the relation of Erasmus' role as reformer to his formation as a Netherlander – Glasius treats historically. There had been in the Netherlands a long reforming tradition – among clergy, ruler, and people. His question is: can Erasmus be seen 'as the last and most vigorous interpreter of that struggle'? The movement had a distinct historical character. From the beginning it was ethical and biblical. In time it added on the one hand strongly practical and on the other scholarly interests. To all this Erasmus was heir; he can indeed be seen as the climax of the movement. His initial connection with it came through Hegius at Deventer and behind him Rudolf Agricola.[154] In all he built on the work of his predecessors and went beyond them: in scholarship, biblical understanding, moral reform, and the correction of abuses. He shared with them, too, his wish for peaceful reform without being disloyal to the hierarchy. Glasius uses a nineteenth-century political analogy: 'they ranged themselves under the banner of the liberal-minded but still conservative party; they did not belong to the thoroughgoing radicals.' Erasmus was by nineteenth-century standards a liberal conservative. It is not surprising that Glasius, writing in the 1840s, should introduce the idea of national character; the piety, prudence, and practicality of the early reformers and, supremely, of Erasmus himself were part of the Dutch character. Love of peace was another characteristic quality but Glasius adds, in a tribute to Erasmus' strength of character unusual at the time, his enemies discovered that he 'belonged to a nation that did not let a muzzle be put on its convictions.'[155]

Glasius' third section deals with the influence of Erasmus on the subsequent religious history of that nation. It is apparent in the mutual toleration among the different kinds of Protestants in the early stages of the Netherlands Reformation. This tolerant disposition – so close to Erasmus – cannot be explained by circumstances, say the intensity of Catholic persecution; Erasmus was a direct and positive influence. The confession adopted as late as the Antwerp synod of 1566 was seen as a basis of union, not a prescriptive rule of belief. Later, of course, the movement was to split into liberal and Calvinist wings; the Remonstrants, who were close to Erasmus and honoured him, were heirs to the former. But even in the Calvinist Reformed Church itself there have been, Glasius concludes, traces of the great compatriot's influence. It appears in the attention given to practical religion but, above all, in biblical studies which have gradually become freer and more vigorous and, by the nineteenth century, a dominant force in Reformed religion.[156] Correspondingly, in the continuing Catholic community in the Netherlands signs remained of the tolerance Erasmus taught and, again, of his concentration on the scriptures.[157]

The controversies in his homeland over Erasmus' role as Netherlands reformer produced, in Glasius' book, a work of real worth, substance, and character. It is highly structured (as perhaps befits a prize essay), possibly too repetitive but always analytical. Unlike the more discursive, essayistic writings on Erasmus, this book puts and pursues its questions in a clear and determined way. If to some in the twentieth century Glasius' interest in the national origins and character of the various reformations would seem a false trail,[158] he anticipated the better work of the later nineteenth century and much writing in the twentieth century by associating Erasmus with a broad, constructive reforming movement of a distinctive kind and by effectually setting aside the image of the solitary scholar, introverted and self-regarding. In Reformation historiography the two-party model was still dominant; he – as early as 1850 – escaped it and, in that, anticipated the historians of évangélisme and Imbart de la Tour. The national approach, for all its difficulties, thus justified itself.[159]

V I

The differences among Protestant writers which Barend Glasius recorded and to a degree moderated at mid-century subsisted throughout the nineteenth century. Variations were considerable

but, with some violence to the finer points, two alternative interpretations can be put as follows. On one side – in a line going
back at least to Gibbon – were those who saw Erasmus as the
progenitor of the Reformation as it actually occurred or, more
probably, of an alternative reformation which was in the long
run to prove more liberalizing and more drastic for established
institutions and beliefs. On the other side, he was seen as at best
preparing the Reformation; history in fact passed by the man and
what he stood for, a moralizing, theologically shallow reform.
The controversy was not easily resolved because differences over
very large historical constructions (medieval Catholicism, humanism, Reformation) were entangled in it. At one level progress
would be possible when scholars obtained a command of Erasmus' correspondence sufficient for tracing securely his connections and associations in the different parts of Europe. He would
cease to be an isolated scholar. Up to a point Glasius had freed
him from his isolation, as we have seen. Other writers had done
the same through studies of his relations with, for example, Belgium and Basel. The next chapter will indicate other advances
along this line before the end of the century, notably through the
work of Wilhelm Maurenbrecher on the Catholic reformation
(1880); but it is with the first fruits of P.S. Allen's work on the
correspondence early in the new century that the command mentioned began to be possible. On the eve of that development,
there was a new burst of controversy, the old alternatives being
stated in their most sophisticated form so far.

   Before coming to that controversy, we should turn to the last
full-length biography of the nineteenth century, Ephraim Emerton's *Desiderius Erasmus of Rotterdam* (1899) in Putnam's series
'Heroes of the Reformation.'[160] It was the first substantial American work on Erasmus; only at one point, however, does Emerton
refer to his own nationality, in a defence of Luther's revolutionary
proceedings. 'Let us, citizens of a nation to which revolution has
meant only the entrance into a larger and a better-ordered public
life, admit frankly that the action of North Germany in the years
following 1520 was, so far as church matters were concerned,
revolutionary, and that only as such can it be justified or understood.'[161] After studies at Leipzig and Berlin, Emerton (1851–1935)
had returned to the faculty of Harvard University in the time of
President Eliot, becoming the first Winn Professor of Ecclesiastical History in 1882 and teaching (by the seminar method)

primarily the history of the Middle Ages, Renaissance, and Reformation.[162] As the series required, he intended to relate Erasmus primarily to the Reformation. He would concern himself with Erasmus' 'very peculiar and often elusive personality' only to the extent of explaining 'his attitude towards the world-movement of his time.'[163] These expressions indicate the standpoint of the work: with many nineteenth-century writers Emerton takes a low view of Erasmus' personality; the Reformation he sees, in a way reminiscent of Charles Beard, the English unitarian, as a 'world-movement,' part of a great readjustment with which Erasmus was intellectually in sympathy.

Emerton's Erasmus is an unattractive figure – querulous, hypochondriac, and self-absorbed. His personal sensitiveness was acute; he had 'joy in the idea of being persecuted'; his disease (the stone) brought him 'great bodily distress' but also 'great moral comfort.' He cherished his individuality; in this at least he was representative – his exaggerated sense of personal importance was 'the especial mark of the Renaissance scholar.' He had no loyalties to country or locality and had a dread of anybody or anything that might make lasting claims upon him.[164] At a time then when other scholars are emphasizing Erasmus' connections and associations, tracing the networks to which he belonged and even speaking of an Erasmian movement, Emerton reproduces the picture of the isolated scholar in an exaggerated form. Erasmus, he concludes, 'never aimed to form a "school" and he left no followers behind him.'[165]

At the same time he did not lack serious purpose. By nature, Emerton says, he was drawn to the 'brilliant shallowness' of the Italian humanists; but partly under Colet's influence he devoted himself to scholarship, not exclusively for its own sake but for the purification of religion.[166] This intention made the link between Erasmus and the Reformation or the larger, more shadowy change of which it was part. 'The special function of Erasmus in the Great Readjustment was, as he conceived it, to bring men back to the standards of a true Christianity by constant reference to the principles of ancient learning, and by an appeal to the tribunal of common sense.'[167] The argument of common sense Emerton, like other theological liberals in his time, associates, perhaps equates, with 'the plain teaching of Jesus.' The *Enchiridion*, he says, opposed it to the formal righteousness of the time. If Erasmus' first appeal, according to Emerton, was to common

sense, his second was to nature. In various works he asserted 'the
essential rightness of what is natural.' Folly represented an un-
calculating and beneficent nature. The work on Christian marriage asserted 'the higher value of the life of nature as compared
with any life of mere formalism.' The writings addressed to Christian ruler took society to be part of a divinely established order,
a moral organism.[168]

Emerton does not explore the relation between this teaching
about nature and the Christian tradition. At one point he argues
that Erasmus did not wish to attack forms and institutions in
themselves but only their misuse; yet, he adds, his treatment
made them dispensable. Ultimately it remains uncertain how revolutionary this Erasmus is. A bigger contradiction runs through
Emerton's whole work, as he himself recognizes in his conclusion.

> Now one may well ask: How is all this nobility and elevation
> of purpose to be reconciled with the obvious personal lim-
> itations of Erasmus' character? How does this profound in-
> terest in the welfare of human society go with a self-centred,
> nervous dread of criticism which rises at times to the hys-
> terical point? How account for the fear that the very ideas
> he seems most to cherish might be spread abroad among
> the very people for whom they seem especially intended?
> ... Such a personality, we are tempted to say, is beneath our
> honest contempt. It is the very negation of all the ideals of
> which the man tried to pose as the champion.[169]

Emerton relies in part on the traditional, indeed rather tired, Protestant distinctions between Erasmus and Luther as personalities.
Hence the paradox of the free-will debate: Erasmus, the man of
the Renaissance, the 'apostle of light,' approached the subject
with the timidity of a scholastic, referring it finally to the judgment
of the church authorities, whereas Luther, the man of feeling,
'who gloried in being the slave of a higher will, comes out here
in reality as a champion of the boldest liberty of human judgment.'[170] Erasmus was not merely timid, for he felt himself 'the
spokesman of a cause greater than himself – the cause of free
and sane scholarship'; but he did not wish to break with the
established order. All he could offer Luther were 'commonplaces
about moderation and gentleness.' So he finished in the total

isolation congenial to his personality. 'The time for his "ifs" and "buts" was past.'[171]

In themselves these familiar expressions are not satisfying or convincing. Emerton's final paragraph adds a new element – 'the perpetual mystery of genius.' 'Erasmus partially solved the problem for us when he declared that while he was at work a certain demon seemed to take possession of him and to carry him on without his will ... Just as his powerful will compelled his frail and suffering body to do the bidding of his unconquerable spirit, so the literary impulse carried him on to utterances far beyond the capacity of his personality to realize in action.'[172] In fact Emerton's problem is insoluble. There is no way a personality so self-absorbed could stand for the things or play the historic role he attributes to Erasmus. The oddity is that he wrote at a time when scholars – some known to Emerton, others apparently not[173] – were drawing Erasmus from his isolation and integrating him and his values with the whole life of his time. Emerton's case reminds us that not only traditional Protestants and the austerely orthodox condemned Erasmus as a personality. It was possible for liberal Protestants to do so, though they had then to face Emerton's dilemma – unattractive man, attractive values and influences.[174]

This dialectic of character and ideas or achievements – 'a great scholar but a petty-minded man'[175] – appears time and again in the Protestant literature of the nineteenth century. In an article in the *Hibbert Journal* in 1905, 'The Triumph of Erasmus in Modern Protestantism,' it is used to expose the dilemmas of many, especially younger, liberal Protestants at that time. The author, Henry Goodwin Smith (Cincinatti, Ohio), contends that, after years of condemnation of both his ideas and his character, modern Protestantism has at last done justice to Erasmus. On the points of difference between him and Luther, Protestants would now side with Erasmus: they take his kinder rather than Luther's harsher view of the papacy; they regret that Luther did not heed his advice about the methods of reform; they share his convictions about religious toleration, which he defended with courage and on which he took the 'essentially modern' view (Luther meanwhile clinging to principles no different from the pope's). The same may be said of the free-will controversy, to which Smith, in any case, gives little importance.[176] Above all, they take Erasmus' attitude to dogma. 'The modern tendency in Protestantism

toward a "short creed," or simple statement of fundamental beliefs, is quite in the Erasmian way ... Although Luther was the
champion of Protestantism, Erasmus was really maintaining the
more logically Protestant position of freedom from the authority
of all dogma.'[177] However, Smith continues, the rehabilitation of
Erasmus has extended to his darker side, his lack of conviction,
his shiftiness, his call for conformity to the church. Here Luther
'towered above him as the rugged champion of honesty and personal liberty.' In Smith's judgment, many liberal teachers and
preachers of his time were covering their difficulties with Erasmian morality. They believed things inconsistent with the doctrinal standards they had undertaken to maintain; so they spoke
indirectly, even evasively. This crypto-liberalism (as Smith calls
it) was neither honest nor Protestant. It would be better to attack
the dilemma in Luther's spirit, if not with his ideas. Biblical criticism, the influence of non-Christian religions, and scientific ideas
had made obsolete the old Protestant doctrinal systems, whose
authority was still asserted in ordination vows. These old systems
should be completely recast. 'If it is true to itself, Protestantism
will tear away the tissues and glosses with which the Erasmian
morals have entangled it. Progressive Protestantism will come
forth courageously from its bondage to the old Protestant letter.
It will defend the noble ideas of Erasmus in the spirit of Luther.
It will never speak with power and persuasion until it does.'[178]
Smith has accepted the dialectic of ideas and character (morality)
and used it in an argument about liberal strategy in the Protestant
churches of his day.

The idea that Erasmus was the precursor of a modern, freer
form of religion was given classic reformulation by Wilhelm Dilthey (1833–1911) in a famous essay of 1891–2 which had considerable influence among liberal Protestants. For Dilthey,
establishing a morality independent of religious dogma was the
primary work of the age of Renaissance and Reformation.[179] In
this development Erasmus represented an important stage. Dilthey's Erasmus is a reiteration in sophisticated form of much that
was commonplace in the nineteenth century, but the colouring
over all is liberal and progressive. He was 'the Voltaire of the
sixteenth century' and, having been oppressed by the monks from
the beginning, led the anticlerical movement for a generation. As
a writer he was an improviser, but every work of his is filled with
a sense of what the time needed. Its multifarious tendencies found

expression in his writing, which drew all eyes upon him. He defended tolerance; to believe that the word was the one legitimate weapon in religious strife was natural to this mild, physically weak man 'with the half-closed blue observant eyes.' He subjected everything to critical thought. 'The joy of the self-conscious intellect in its sovereign power' lit up his whole person (as the *Moriae encomium* above all indicates). He placed the problem of true Christianity at the centre of his critical activity; by study of the text, he wished to separate the simple, essential teaching of Christ from dogmatic accretions.[180]

The Reformation, too, was a stage in the development from the dominant, theistic metaphysics of the Middle Ages to the moral autonomy of the seventeenth century and the Enlightenment; but, as with the liberal writers, Dilthey must determine the respective contributions of Erasmian humanism and the Reformation to the new morality. In Luther and Zwingli, he says, there was a mixing of old and new. They spoke of inner, personal faith in the unseen God which expresses itself, not in outward rituals or institutional practices, but in an active life in the world, through the natural relations of human society. Yet at the same time they remained bound to dogma; indeed, they saw dogma as the necessary precondition of the Christian life as they described it. Further, the Reformation, as it developed, became more, not less, dogmatic and authoritarian. The outcome was Lutheran orthodoxy.[181]

Erasmus for Dilthey – as for Gibbon, Hagen, and Pattison – was at the start of an alternative tradition; he was 'the founder of theological rationalism,' by which Dilthey means an insistence on rational enquiry into the substance of faith, combined with a sceptical awareness of the limitations of reason. *De libero arbitrio* was the first classic work of theological rationalism. If he hedged somewhat ('an accommodation of the first rationalist'), in the end he showed his good sense in all its strength by requiring reliance on the facts of inner experience alone and by his scepticism about every plunge into metaphysics. Prudently but with quiet determination he undermined dogmatic structures, including Trinitarianism and sacramentalism, in the interest of a universalist theism. 'From Erasmus goes a straight line to Coornhert, to the Socinians and Arminians, and thence to the Deists.'[182]

Dilthey's essay offers a refinement of the tradition in liberal Protestantism that Erasmus stood to the left of the Reformers and anticipated modern attitudes in ethics and religion. The view that he stood to their right, fell short of them, remained essentially Catholic and medieval, or offered at best superficial solutions to prevailing problems was also restated in the 1890s. Friedrich Lezius' inaugural lecture at Greifswald in July 1894 – later published as *Zur Charakteristik des religiösen Standpunktes des Erasmus* – argued that moralism and biblicism were the two distinctive features of Erasmus' religious outlook.[183] Both, as Erasmus presented them, belonged essentially to the Middle Ages or were at least 'unprotestantisch.' Actually Lezius' evidence (drawn from writings like the *Enchiridion* or the materials gathered in Stichart's book) does not always confirm such categorical judgments or at least the conclusions seem sharper than the preceding discussion warrants.

Thus Lezius considers the term 'moralism' appropriate because Erasmus – notably in the *Enchiridion* – presents Christ above all as teacher and example (this was, he adds, a way of thinking Erasmus shared with many serious-minded contemporaries). But, Lezius admits, Erasmus can also use the language of the mystics and Augustine, he speaks of the hope of heaven and fear of hell and makes Christ a help as well as an example: 'What there is of virtue in us we should ascribe to grace.'[184]

Nevertheless, for Lezius this moralism defines Erasmus as a reformer and a historic personality. It determined his relations with the order and teaching of the church. Once again, Lezius' conclusions seem at a tangent to his discussion; his Erasmus can sound like Dilthey's but is then pulled back into the Middle Ages. Erasmus was, he says, indifferent to dogmas of every kind, the definitions of the early church as well as scholasticism. Doctrinal controversy was not worth the sacrifice of public peace. On the matters in dispute – like justification – his views were, however, Catholic. Like Valla he challenged the monk's claim to religious superiority; in all callings one may strive for perfection. Thus he taught a lay piety, rejecting celibacy and defending marriage; but it fell short of the Protestant doctrine of vocation (true 'good works' are in fulfilling a worldly vocation); he retained a 'monkish-medieval' outlook.[185]

Erasmus' biblicism also, according to Lezius, contributed to his alienation from the religious practices of his time. Scripture was normative; it should be made accessible to all. He could even say: faith comes from hearing.[186] This scriptural and christocentric teaching affects Erasmus' understanding of the church (it is for him not a hierarchy but the whole Christian people) and, above all, of the sacraments. His moralism is also relevant to his sacramental teaching; the efficacy of the sacrament is dependent on the disposition of the recipient. Yet, for all the incipient radicalism of this doctrine, he did not openly reject the Catholic sacraments or break from the medieval order. Speaking of penance, he said that Christ alone absolves, but he did not deny the priestly power of absolution; scripture, he said, did not support the idea of an indelible character conferred in ordination, but he did not think of setting aside the hierarchy; he was indifferent to transubstantiation but expressed his true opinion of the eucharist (close to Zwingli's) only in private and otherwise used symbolic language familiar to medieval theologians.[187]

This Erasmus seems to point in different directions. Lezius' intention is to locate him firmly in the late Middle Ages; he was a humanistically inclined reforming Catholic of the fifteenth century. Here is the point of greatest interest and originality in his study; it makes a sharp alternative to Dilthey's case for seeing Erasmus as the pioneer of modern attitudes. When Lezius moves on to consider his relation to the Reformation, the characterization is painfully familiar: he lacked the higher seriousness of the Protestants, their strength of will and courage of conviction; he had a 'fanatical love of peace,' and so forth.[188]

Erasmus, precursor of the modern religious outlook defined as lay, independent, rationalistic, or Erasmus, representative of a late medieval piety whose time had passed by the end of the fifteenth century: these were the rival views among Protestant writers at the beginning of the twentieth century. For a time the former had the upper hand. Erasmus was treated as a major figure in the history of the West; at least in retrospect one could speak of an 'Erasmus renaissance.'[189] The church historian of Giessen, Breslau, and Tübingen Karl Müller (1852–1940) in his *Kirchengeschichte*, the great philosopher of history and religion Ernst Troeltsch (1865–1923), who was then (1894–1915) professor of systematic theology at Heidelberg, and Troeltsch's associate in their first days of university teaching at Göttingen Paul Wernle (1872–1939), who was appointed to the chair of church history at Basel in 1905 after publishing in the previous year a short work on Erasmus and the Christian renaissance, all present Erasmus as an independent and distinctive force for the reform of church and culture.

Of the three, Müller is closest to the traditional Protestant positions on Erasmus; nevertheless he sees him, at least for the period before his break from Luther, as 'a spiritual world power' through the influence he exercised on contemporaries.[190] His devotion to the classics, Müller says, was not one-sided or pedantic; 'he lived not in the fancifully revived forms of the ancient world but in the present.' His studies were intended to make primitive Christianity accessible to his contemporaries; they were a means to but, of course, not the substance of the reform he sought. Müller like Janssen distinguishes Erasmus from the older humanists but he finds the difference in Erasmus' refusal to identify the Christian religion with the apparatus of the church. For him (as for Colet) Christ was central, 'the middle-point and the one theme of scripture.' Certainly he saw Christ primarily as teacher and example but, adds Müller, there are in his writings impressive places where human works are denied any value and faith in Christ is presented as the one and only way of pleasing God. His christocentrism radicalized his understanding of the church. Laymen had been offered a richer devotional life in the fifteenth century but the dominant tone still was monastic. Erasmus in effect erased the distinction between lay and clerical by concentrating wholly on Christ and the plain teachings of the gospel. He did not wish to overthrow the existing structures, but ultimately everything could disappear beyond the direct working of Christ on the human spirit.[191] Such expressions draw Müller towards Dilthey but his remarks on Erasmus' relation to the Reformation are more traditional: in the crisis of German humanism brought on by Luther's emergence, Erasmus was left a lonely figure, drawing within the structure of the old church while holding, as far as he could, to his earlier religious positions.[192]

Troeltsch's views on Erasmus, expressed in a section ('The Humanist Theology') of an extended essay on 'Protestant Christianity and Church in Modern Times,' were much closer to Dilthey's, though they were arrived at independently. From his first scholarly work in 1891 (on reason and revelation in Gerhard and Melanchthon), Troeltsch had argued that the outlook of the Protestant Reformers was essentially medieval; the corollary was that the breakthrough to the modern world came not with the Reformation but with the Enlightenment; of the latter Troeltsch found anticipations in 'the humanist theology.'[193] For him, as for Dilthey, that theology represented an original idea in the history of Christianity, though its working was delayed a century and a half by Luther's domination over the immediately following generations. In his *Enchiridion* Erasmus passed from the misconceived Paulinism of the Florentine Neoplatonic circle to the religion of the Sermon on the Mount, a change made instinctively and without awareness of contradicting Paulinism, but 'the historic root of later rationalist theology with its "pure teaching of Jesus" and its "Christianity of Christ" none the less. Erasmus was the teacher of a theistic universalism which, interpreting the gospel as 'only the divinely revealed high-point of universal religion,' made by one concession to medieval supernaturalism, that the universal religion of humanity needed such an ultimate authorization. Rejecting the Augustinian dualism of elect and ungodly, Erasmus was bound to oppose Luther's *servum arbitrium*. Their conflict was not one between religious depth and moralistic superficiality; rather it was the first challenge of modern religious thought, universal and antisupernatural, to the resurgent dualism and supernaturalism of the Middle Ages.[194]

Paul Wernle began in New Testament studies. First attracted to history by Treitschke at Berlin, he – like Dilthey and Troeltsch – accepted it as in some sense 'the teacher of the present.'[195] Both elements in his background are expressed in his assertion that the heart of the 'Christian renaissance' as Erasmus conceived it was the recovery of the Sermon on the Mount and that this has an abiding significance. 'As long as the Sermon on the Mount has a place in the New Testament,' he says at one point, 'a simple ethical lay theology, as Erasmus represented it, has a right to be heard among Christians.' The question could be asked of the present as of Erasmus' time: is there a way back to the pure teaching of Jesus beyond the interpretations and elaborations of the Reformers, the scholastics, the Fathers, Paul? (Lutheran readers too easily forget, Wernle remarks, how the New Testament can be read in other ways than Luther's.)[196] 'Erasmus issued the call: back to Jesus, and made the gospels, the Sermon on the Mount the measure of Christian faith and life.' This is said of the New Testament edition which is for Wernle the high point of the Christian renaissance; it was, he says, no mere humanist edition but rather a reforming act; it was meant not only for scholars and theologians but for the whole Christian people.[197]

Three main themes emerge in Wernle's study: the reform program of Erasmus was positive, liberating, life-enhancing; it was a genuine rival to Luther's, which must then be seen as only one of the options for reform in the sixteenth century; it exercised a creative influence on the minds of many contemporaries. Since Christianity must always be expressed in theological forms and since such forms often become rigid and outdated, any Christian renaissance requires a reform in theology. In this case, for Wernle as for Troeltsch, it begins with fifteenth-century Neoplatonism or, more precisely, with the double interest in Plato and Paul. This revival, for all its internal contradictions, took on a robust, deeply devout character in England in the thought and person of John Colet (the influence of Seebohm is apparent in all this early twentieth-century literature). Erasmus quickly appreciated that Colet's lectures on Paul's letters promised the restoration of primitive Christian thought and a revolution in contemporary theology. One cannot, however, expect to find Luther's single-minded commitment to theological reform in Erasmus; he worked, says Wernle, on a broader front. His call was for a simple, practical lay piety, whose setting was a Christian community bound together by mutual love. This is the theme of the *Enchiridion*, 'the first fruit of the Christian renaissance, whose beauty and power – surprising for its time – we still feel today.' The Sermon on the Mount imposed the demand of perfection on all, not only on monks.[198]

These ideas had a great influence, Wernle says, in Switzerland and southern Germany. The Christian renaissance so defined had, he adds, internal contradictions: the Roman church did not respond as Erasmus hoped; a program founded on scripture was bound to be beset with conflicting interpretations: 'From the one liberating expression "Bible Christianity," "Christianity of the New Testament," sprang forth a whole bunch of interpretations of Christianity.'[199] That is, however, not to deny its historical importance and its continuing interest and influence.

This way of seeing Erasmus gives his thought a life-affirming character. It makes easy the link with modern culture seen also as world-affirming rather than world-denying. Obviously it identifies a break from medieval culture, which – it was said – diminished this world and the present life, and from Luther with his concentration on sin and judgment, on the transcendent and eschatological. The alternative view of Erasmus – that his outlook was essentially medieval – was also firmly put in the first decade of the twentieth century, most notably by Martin Schulze (like Karl Müller, a teacher at Breslau) in a study of Erasmus' influence on Calvin's thought about eschatology and the next world. Schulze could not stand at a greater distance from Dilthey, Wernle, and Troeltsch. Yet he agreed with them in one thing, that Erasmus' religious thought was to be taken seriously, in itself and for its influence on contemporaries and on posterity. Theologically he cuts deeper than they. At one point he remarks that his appreciation of the seriousness of Calvin's thought has not been diminished by recognizing the influence of Erasmus upon it.[200]

Schulze's study is based on Erasmus' writings on death and the afterlife[201] and, of course, on Calvin's *Institutio*. He appreciates the influence of Plato on Calvin (the subject of a previous study of his); he also understands that much in Calvin's thought might be traditional, but even that could pass to him through Erasmus.[202] Schulze finds in Erasmus as in Calvin a deep pessimism about the present life, deriving not so much from its sufferings as from its transitoriness. Both see this life as a preparation for the next; indeed, only by holding this life in low esteem can love of the next world (and Christian faith itself) grow. 'In a word this concerns – in Erasmus as in Calvin – a monasticism of the disposition.' The morality is negative; no particular value or dignity attaches to the possessions or affairs of this world; they are to be used in passing, so to speak, and as though they were not being used. There is an emphasis on the inner life but also a mystical and eschatological element: the spirit strains towards the next world. Calvin and Erasmus differ from Plato in their psychology and anthropology – the corruption of sin and the need for rebirth in the Christian sense – but they share with him a commitment to the spiritual and the transcendental.[203]

Schulze breaks from the whole Protestant way of seeing Erasmus, liberal as well as orthodox. He had been accepted as close to the Protestant Reformers on church issues (monasticism, ceremonies, even the papacy and the hierarchy). But both orthodox and liberals had seen him at a great distance from the Reformers in theology. Schulze brings Erasmus and Calvin close theologically. This, he says ingenuously, puts the humanist in an unusual light. In his religious writings, Erasmus' overwhelming interest is in grace, not in human powers; our struggle and victory is Christ's struggle and victory in us. Christ is no mere teacher and example; he brings us a new status – children of God – and immortality. One cannot, of course, speak of identity but on numerous issues the parallels, Schulze says, are close, to the point sometimes of suggesting that Calvin had Erasmus' words in front of him while he wrote.[204]

Erasmus, concentrating on the supernatural and the transcendental, despising the things of this world, linked therefore to the medieval ascetic, world-denying ethic: that is in broad terms Schulze's picture. It marks a break from many nineteenth-century assumptions and preoccupations and a sharp confrontation with the views of Dilthey, Troeltsch, and Wernle (as many contemporary observers noted). A broader argument for locating Erasmus in the medieval world was made by Heinrich Hermelink (then, after studies at Tübingen, *Privatdozent* at Leipzig) in his *Die religiösen Reformbestrebungen des deutschen Humanismus* of 1907. The problem of Erasmus (which remains unresolved despite the attention he is now attracting) can be overcome, says Hermelink, only by relating him to the movement of which he is part, German humanism, and this, in turn, can be understood only in relation to the late medieval movements for church reform. Its aim was a simpler and more personal religion; in that it expressed the aspirations of an increasingly self-conscious laity.[205] The argument so far is unexceptionable; indeed it opened a line of enquiry rewarding for twentieth-century scholarship.[206] Hermelink then makes a less secure move: he links both humanism's aim of simplification through return to the sources and the lay drive for more direct participation in the church's life to one strand in scholasticism, the so-called *via antiqua*.[207] He mistakenly makes Erasmus a student of the *via antiqua* in Cologne.[208] Hermelink's substantial argument is for seeing Erasmus as an end rather than a beginning. He was deeply committed to the reformed piety – he propagated it with both learning and journalistic flair. But he had not created anything new; he deepened the stream and made it flow faster, but it continued to flow in the same direction. Contrary to Troeltsch's view, he was not the father of a distinctively modern spirituality; nowhere, for example, does he distinguish sharply between the religion of Jesus and the religion of Paul. His 'Christ-piety' was in fact in line with the ethical ideal of medieval Catholicism. He accepts its dualism; life is an earthly striving for a heavenly reward, if a reward bestowed ultimately by grace. Hermelink then retreats to familiar ground by making Luther once again the standard by which Erasmus is to be judged: Luther saw that a dualism of doing good works and hoping on grace was thoroughly Catholic, assumed the authority of the church, and brought no religious liberation. Erasmus died – more or less as usual for Protestant writers – in the land of Moab.[209]

Nevertheless, he became the subject of genuine historical debate in these years. This is apparent from the critical reception the books just surveyed received. Thus Troeltsch, in a review in *Göttingische gelehrte Anzeigen* in 1909, praised Hermelink's attempt to provide German humanism with a historical context, but he rejected the thesis that its seed-bed was the *via antiqua*; that was to underestimate the influence of Italy and the originality of at least Erasmus. This thesis, Troeltsch says, serves the needs of Lutheran confessional apologetics: only Luther could be the creator of the new age, humanism remaining stuck in medieval moralism. Troeltsch reiterates (from Dilthey) the essential modernity of Erasmus' critical work and the view of him he shares with Wernle: 'Erasmus is an independent type of the reform, whom one can and should evaluate quite impartially as such.' It adds little, Troeltsch says, to say that Erasmus stands still on medieval ground; various ways led from the Middle Ages to the Enlightenment and modern culture (including the religious individualism of the Reformers); Erasmus' way was the rediscovery (through a critical use of the sources) of the simplicity of primitive Christianity and its similarity with the best in ancient thought.[210]

Meantime Walter Köhler, a student of Troeltsch's, had published a long review of Schulze's monograph in the *Theologische Literaturzeitung* (1903). He accepted the case for Erasmus' influence on Calvin, asking only whether it was as exclusive as Schulze suggests or perhaps indirect (through Martin Bucer, for example). As for Erasmus, Köhler welcomes the lighting up of a side of him hitherto neglected. But, he goes on, for all the points of contact between Erasmus' *philosophia christi* and the Reformers' religion of Christ, the differences should not be neglected. For them, all is darkness outside Christ; for Erasmus, as Dilthey saw, enlightenment spread far. He concludes: rationalism (if not of the purest kind) and supernaturalism here confronted one another.[211]

On the other side, Johannes von Walter (1876–1940), in a review essay of 1911, criticized the tendency represented variously by Maurenbrecher,[212] Karl Müller, Wernle, and Troeltsch.[213] Walter sides rather with Lezius and Hermelink: Erasmus was essentially a late medieval figure. Much in the Middle Ages, he says, anticipated Erasmus' criticism of the religious practice of his day and his turning to the writers of ancient times and, for that matter, to Jesus himself. Erasmus only said more clearly and elegantly, and with greater effect, what had been said already. His acceptance of the papacy and the authority of the church was wholly medieval. Walter sees Erasmus' 'lay religion' (as described by Wernle and Troeltsch) discounted by his aristocratic prejudices and his distaste for popular intervention in religious debate. Finally, he accepts the arguments of Schulze's book; Erasmus' teaching on grace and the Pauline and even Thomist elements in his thought were far from rationalistic and this-worldly.[214]

This debate was inconclusive as one would expect. The explanatory instruments – 'late Middle Ages,' 'Enlightenment,' 'modern culture' – were too large, awkward, and undiscriminating for elucidating the delicate balances of Erasmus' mind. Progress in understanding Erasmus, his thought, and historical role depended on placing him more precisely in his time, establishing his many associations and connections, and tracing the pattern of influences on and from him.[215] The image of the isolated, ineffective scholar, the pathos of which appealed to nineteenth-century tastes (as Emerton's biography again demonstrates),[216] had to be discarded. At the same time, his proper independence must be safeguarded. In Protestant circles he must be freed from the double prejudice, that Luther was right and his contemporaries must be judged by his standard and that the Reformation was an act of providence or a historical event of a special kind.

Here the succession of Dilthey, Wernle, and Troeltsch made its contribution. Erasmus was seen as a historical force in his own right or as part of a movement which worked large changes in culture and society, even though these were later overlaid by the Reformation and Counter-Reformation. The weakness lay in tying Erasmus too much to the future, to the religion and morality of the Enlightenment, even to modern secularism. That, too, pulled him out of his own time, made an abstraction of him. Enlightenment and liberal writing on Erasmus had had this tendency since the time of Gibbon.[217]

The strength of the other side, as represented especially by Schulze, lay in its close attention to the Erasmus texts. What it demonstrated unquestionably was the depth and seriousness of his religious thought. Wernle's representation seems shallow, even vapid, by contrast. It was, however, an error to make that thought wholly or mostly traditional. The incoherence of Lezius' account betrays in fact the inner tensions of Erasmus' thought; to these none of the participants in this debate could do full justice. Using their categories, one may say: there are intimations of modernity in what Erasmus had to say about the Bible and the lay vocation as well as a profound traditionalism in his personal piety.

The debate brought more gain than loss. That was because it lifted minds above the nineteenth century's preoccupations with Erasmus' character and his relation to the Protestant confessions. It also suggested conditions for an advance in understanding; apart from the necessary scholarly labours on his writings and correspondence, there needed to be studies of Erasmus' associations with contemporaries, of contemporary situations and settings where his influence was felt, of the effects of his activity and ideas. Reviewing the developments we have just been considering and those to which we now come, Gustav Wolf remarked in 1915 that progress in interpretation of Erasmus occurred when interest in his doctrines receded and gave way to interest in his practical influence. To categorize or schematize his thought was to distort his intentions; his aim was practical and pedagogical rather than dogmatic.[218] The perception was to be a fruitful one.

ELEVEN

Into the Twentieth Century

In his review of the literature in 1915 Gustav Wolf identified features of the transition from nineteenth- to twentieth-century scholarship on Erasmus. There was liberation from confessional concerns and from the related preoccupation with alleged weaknesses of Erasmus' character. The argument may be extended thus. If the later seventeenth and the eighteenth centuries had replaced the confessional depictions of Erasmus with a picture more human and realistic but still (in its enlightened and progressive traits) somewhat superficial, the religious and theological revivals of the first half of the nineteenth century refastened the grip of confessionalism. Erasmus' relation to the Reformation again became the dominant issue. Judgment of his purported equivocations came easily to those whose own allegiances were clear. The preoccupation with character owed something also to romanticism's search for heroes, and for many, at least on the Protestant side, images of Luther and Hutten lay ready to hand.

For Wolf the important shift was from dealing with Erasmus under broad headings of doctrine or theology (often in terms set by his adversaries) to estimating his influence on circles of contemporaries. Therefore, Kampschulte's study of the Erfurt circle was, he believed, an innovation, although Ranke, for whom Erasmus was not unfortunately of primary interest, had already (because of his greater interest in actions than in doctrines) noticed his public influence. Even Janssen, says Wolf, approached Erasmus in this way but in a negative spirit. Wilhelm Maurenbrecher was the first to concentrate on Erasmus' constructive influence.[1]

We will follow Wolf and begin here with Maurenbrecher's history of the Catholic Reformation. Between 1880 and 1910 activity then developed on three fronts: first, there were studies of Erasmus' influence on contemporaries and his connections with friends and colleagues in many locations and settings; secondly, his significance for education and pedagogy became a favourite theme; thirdly, already well before the end of the nineteenth century had begun the scholarly labours on Erasmus' correspondence whose culmination and crowning was to be the magisterial edition of P.S. Allen. Errors passed from biography to biography were to be corrected.[2] There was (as in Luther's case) a special interest in the young Erasmus and the spiritual and intellectual influences upon him.

These developments (which determine the sections of this chapter) may be counted as progress in Erasmus studies, not only because of the greater scholarly sophistication just mentioned, but because they marked a break from the simple constructions of the past, doctrinal and biographical. To make the picture more complex was to give it more credibility and authenticity. Complexity came from peopling the picture with Erasmus' friends and associates, from placing his thought in its contemporary setting, from recovering the real world (domestic, social, and political) he inhabited. This is not to say that stereotypes from the past did not have a continuing life in this century or that the twentieth century would not produce orthodoxies and even illusions of its own.

I

Wilhelm Maurenbrecher (1838–92) was directed to work on sixteenth-century Catholicism by his teacher Heinrich von Sybel but he approached the subject in a different spirit from his master's. Sybel was devoted to the Prussian monarchy, saw Catholicism as an enemy of German nationality and liberal principles in scholarship, and supported Bismarck in the *Kulturkampf*.[3] Maurenbrecher by contrast stressed the obligation on a Protestant historian to deal objectively with Catholic history, shared Ranke's view of the common origins of the Protestant and Catholic Reformations, and, indeed, chose the term 'Catholic Reformation' as indicating a positive reforming tendency rather than a merely defensive response to the Reformation. His original plan was for a history of Spain's role in the Counter-Reformation and he spent a year (1862) in the Spanish archives at Simancas but he came to recognize that the roots of that history went back to the reforming attempts (in Spain and western Europe generally) at the beginning of the sixteenth century. The first (and only completed) volume of his work dealt with those attempts. More than most Protestant writers of the nineteenth century, Maurenbrecher devised a scheme which made possible an appreciation of Erasmus' influence as a constructive reformer.[4]

Maurenbrecher's Erasmus is the pioneer and proponent of a Catholic reformation. Before 1517 he took impulses for reform already present in humanism and the 'Oxford reformers' (as de- picted by Seebohm) and made them a force in European affairs. This is a different Erasmus from the delicate, satiric, evasive spirit behind half-closed lids evoked by other Protestant writers. At the time of *Folly* he stood 'in full command of his intellectual powers, in the strong, unhindered exercise of his fully matured talents, an incomparable writer.' Maurenbrecher insists that, along with his negations, Erasmus offered a very positive teaching, in fact Christian preaching and teaching in its primitive form. He sought influence over the whole cultural world and he succeeded. He became 'a European power.'[5]

Maurenbrecher recognizes that there were setbacks, some se- vere. Younger humanists (the grouping is different from Jans- sen's), for whom Hutten was spokesman, exaggerated the critical, negative components of Erasmus' reform program and divested it of serious religious purpose. His hopes of 1516 for peace among the European states were blasted and Luther, urging a more dras- tic, more penetrating reform, outstripped Erasmus in appeal. What, however, distinguishes Maurenbrecher's from almost all other nineteenth-century interpretations in his insistence on Erasmus' continuing influence. The time after 1520 was not one simply of defeat and withdrawal. His appreciation of the different strands within the Catholic reform movement saves Maurenbrecher from that distortion. Alongside the demand for a renewal of the me- dieval Catholic spirit went the Erasmian call for reform through learning. Winning ground for the latter required from Erasmus a clear break with Luther since it was already handicapped by the fear that it threatened church authority. That is why the clash between Erasmus and Luther made a deep impression on con- temporaries. Erasmus rallied a following especially in Germany among the bishops, though for a time the Erasmians were influ- ential also in Spain. Far from withering, therefore, Erasmus' influence was growing around 1530, in the councils of Charles v, in the episcopacy, in a number of German states. The heart of the reform program had always been the restoration of Christian piety and practical morality; in the later 1520s the need was for a council to recover Christian unity and press reforms; meanwhile, moderation and tolerance should be shown the dissidents. Maurenbrecher's summing-up of Erasmus' position around 1530 is thus: he shared with Protestants awareness of the necessity of reform; he held to Catholic principles about the church. He worked tirelessly for mediation between the parties. This, Maurenbrecher adds, is not work for a coward and weakling. Here he breaks from dominant Protestant views of Erasmus' character: 'His firm and principled assertion of the middle way amid the frenzied struggle ... revealed, as is often the case, an unusual energy of will and character.'[6]

The Erasmian party had in the long run limited success, in the empire and in German states like the Duchy of Cleves where Erasmus' principles were written directly into the church ordinances. To recognize the limitations is not, however, to deny the reality or the persistence of Erasmus' influence in the German lands.[7]

In two respects Maurenbrecher rejected the image of Erasmus as a lonely neurotic scholar (as presented by Ephraim Emerton, for example): he showed the power over contemporaries of his ideas and personality; he identified places where his influence worked distinctive changes; thus Maurenbrecher anticipated major works of the twentieth century. While in some quarters the old Protestant judgments were reiterated in response to Maurenbrecher (Erasmus' reform plans lacked substance, they melted away like mist, history itself passing judgment on them, as Luther meanwhile broke the domination of the church and opened a new epoch of human history),[8] the influence of his work can be widely observed. Traces can be found in two essays published in the journal which Maurenbrecher edited from 1882, *Historisches Taschenbuch*, one on the colloquies of Erasmus, the other on his relations with the popes of his time. They were written, respectively, by Adalbert Horawitz (1840–88) and Karl Hartfelder (1848–93), friends and colleagues who cooperated on ventures in the history of humanism, including the publication of the letters of Beatus Rhenanus.

Horawitz belonged to a brilliant circle of students at the Uni-

versity of Vienna, though he failed (to his bitter disappointment)
to win a chair there. He was intellectually lively and active in
teaching, journalism, contemporary letters, and, later, historical
scholarship, including the editing of Erasmus' letters. Spread thin,
his work was criticized for errors in detail, though it (with Hartfelder's) earned the praise of P.S. Allen.[9] His last great project
was a life of Erasmus to which he devoted many years. He did
not live to complete it. Hartfelder assumed the task but also died
before its completion. He, too, was a teacher (professor in the
Heidelberg gymnasium from 1882) and indeed had a primary
interest in educational history, his most substantial work being
Philipp Melanchthon als Praeceptor Germaniae (Berlin 1889).[10] He
had, said one observer, a better grasp than Horawitz of the pedagogical side of humanism. He was passionately committed to
the proposed Erasmus biography, but in vain.[11]

The two essays were a mixture of conventional judgments and
the fresh understandings of Maurenbrecher. The colloquies, Horawitz argues, were distinctive to Erasmus and had no obvious
antecedents; yet they also give an insight into 'the intellectual
movements of that time.' Erasmus was both reacting against existing conditions and seeking renewal in a purer form of Christianity. The colloquy 'Convivium religiosum,' Horawitz adds, with
its searching discussion among devout friends, refutes the contention that Erasmus lacked feeling. His condemnation of forced
entries to monasteries was 'a great moral act' with incalculable
consequences for the age.[12] How, Horawitz concludes, is the paradox to be explained, that Erasmus saw the work as advancing
religion and morality, yet many contemporaries saw it as an offence to both? Despite some of his expressions, he has been unjustly linked with the encyclopaedists. As Maurenbrecher saw,
he deserved a place among the Catholic reformers; at the same
time he must be accepted as a pioneer of the Reformation.[13]

This conclusion, which has Erasmus pointing in various directions at once, is consistent with Horawitz's judgment of ten
years before which accompanied his first collection of Erasmus'
letters. Erasmus, he says there, was not a party man. Hence among
contemporaries and in posterity different parties viewed him differently: 'Here one seeks out the latent "Lutheran" in him; there
one defends the reputation of the misunderstood "Catholic." ' In
fact, in sixteenth-century terms he was neither Catholic nor Protestant; to side with Luther would be to surrender his individuality;

to side with the conservatives would be to commit a kind of intellectual suicide. Maintaining his critical independence was not easy; he was forced into various equivocations and contradictions, but these were due, not to weakness of character, but to circumstances.[14]

Horawitz's emphasis on Erasmus' intellectual independence recalls Ranke's picture of the free-ranging critic and oppositionist. He at least safeguards his distinctiveness and avoids dubbing him either a Protestant or a Catholic who denied his cause. In contrast to Maurenbrecher, however, he returns him to isolation. Hartfelder was interested in Erasmus' associations and explored some of them but without escaping Protestant presuppositions. His exploration of his relations with the popes is reduced to the question: why did Erasmus remain Catholic? From the beginning, Hartfelder answers, even in the way he freed himself from the monastic burden, he showed a preference for legitimacy. He wanted reform but without challenging the structure of the church. He was (unlike Aleander) not wholehearted in the Roman cause; he had doubts, indeed raised doubt 'to a literary power.' Yet his personal bonds to the popes held him. Even with Aleander his enemy he made no final break, as a stronger man would have done.[15]

A warmer picture emerges from a second essay of Hartfelder's, on Erasmus' relations with the humanist circle at Constance. It is a set of portraits of the members of that circle – men like Johann von Botzheim, Michael Hummelberg, Johann Menlishofer, and Johannes Fabri.[16] Hartfelder suggests the attractiveness of this circle, the intellectual excitement within it, the delicacy, even tenderness, of the relations among its members. He makes apparent their respect, even love, for Erasmus who, said Hummelberg, was their sun in whose light every question was decided. This, says Hartfelder, was an 'Erasmuskultus.'[17] The high-point in the circle's life was Erasmus' own visit to Constance in September 1522, which he described in a famous letter.[18] But, Hartfelder concludes, those meetings were lit by afternoon light. The Constance circle was broken by the Reformation.[19]

Though disappointing in some ways, these small-scale pieces by Horawitz and Hartfelder at least reinforced the impression Maurenbrecher gave of Erasmus as a power and influence among contemporaries. One could envisage a shift of interest from Erasmus to Erasmianism. Erasmus' influence on education, says Hartfelder in his contribution – on humanist pedagogy – to K.A. Schmid's history of education, was universal. It was not a matter merely of book-learning, since his educational writings revealed his keen eye for the common life. Nor was his influence destroyed by the break with Luther; it continued even in the Protestant lands.[20] These declarations of Erasmus' influence on his times and on posterity provided one of the threads later continued in the Erasmus interpretations of Karl Müller, Wernle, and Troeltsch; another came from theological liberalism, as we have seen. It was possible to speak of a third force, a Christian humanist reform competing with the Protestant and Catholic Reformations, only if there were evidence forthcoming of Erasmus' hold on the minds of contemporaries. Maurenbrecher and his successors were believed to have provided this.[21]

Even where views (traditional among Protestant writers) hostile to Erasmus and dismissive of his character still prevailed, there was talk of a 'Christian renaissance' under his auspices. Friedrich von Bezold (1848–1928) cannot simply be associated with traditional Lutheran positions. He was not at ease in the atmosphere of Erlangen, the citadel of Lutheran orthodoxy, where he was teaching when his *Geschichte der deutschen Reformation* was published in 1890. The work was commonly compared with Ranke's; it was less theological, social and economic history bulked larger, and less attention was given to European, more to German national themes. Bezold grew up in the relatively liberal atmosphere of Munich in the third quarter of the century; he was a friend of Döllinger and critic of Janssen, an opponent of the Wilhelmine Reich.[22] He saw a liberating force in Erasmian humanism. Erasmus' achievement was to turn the work of his humanist predecessors towards practical religious reform. He was, Bezold says, dedicated less to the revival of antiquity than to the renaissance of Christianity. The critical spirit of Lorenzo Valla, the religious feeling of the Florentine Platonists, the burgeoning studies of the scriptures and the Fathers met in him. On the other side, his scorn for the existing society, his unflattering comparison of monarchy with the civic spirit and love of peace of the town democracies promoted revolutionary feeling.[23]

Yet what Bezold gives with one hand, he takes away with the other. The religious renaissance, for all its sense of a rising dawn, did not produce real reformation. Erasmus had no feeling for the sufferings and the needs of the people. Bezold approves a remark of Drummond's that Erasmus clung to the authority of the church, for he did not know otherwise where his scepticism would lead him.[24] He returns, almost word for word, to Lavater's, Adolf Müller's, and Janssen's disparagements of Erasmus' character and turns the by now familiar comparison with Voltaire to his disadvantage: 'There is in Erasmus not the slightest trace of the fine human traits of Voltaire, of his capacity to love and fight for others.' Bezold sees the Reformation as a revolutionary event, Luther – at least in the early days of the movement – as a revolutionary figure.[25] He recognizes Erasmus as having influence in his time but not, through intellectual and personal limitations, on its crucial religious and social revolution.

There is a narrow common ground between Bezold and Maurenbrecher. The sphere of Erasmus' influence is for the former much confined. On the great humanist's limitations, especially on his weaknesses of character, he is one with orthodox or pietistic Protestant writers whose attitudes to the study of the Reformation he did not share. The true heirs of Maurenbrecher were those who studied Erasmus' relations with and influence on contemporaries in specific historical settings. To a selection of such writers we now come.

The subject of Erasmus' association with his homeland and his countrymen has naturally attracted Netherlands writers up to the present day. There has especially been, from Glasius' work on, a search for affinities between Erasmus' views and Netherlands religious traditions. In general, characterizing him as a Netherlander has counteracted tendencies to attribute to him a colourless cosmopolitanism. Conrad Busken Huet (1826–86) awards Erasmus a chapter in the preliminary volume of his great book on Netherlands culture in the seventeenth century *Het Land van Rembrand* and makes his Dutch origins one of its themes. Though from his mid-twenties he was a resident more of Europe than of the Netherlands, he never lost the traces of that origin: 'The Netherlands revealed him to himself, and such impressions are indelible.' To have produced so talented a child was an honour to the lower clergy and the servant class of the fifteenth-century Netherlands. With the painters of the seventeenth century he represented, in contrast to the well-known warriors of the republican period, the arts of peace of his countrymen.[26]

Huet takes, in this work, a broad conception of the task of cultural history.[27] He asks what circumstances stood in the way of the emergence of higher education in the northern Netherlands and finds in its late medieval piety an ascetic, anti-intellectual strain. Erasmus, he concludes, represented the overcoming of the negative elements in that tradition. His writings formed the first 'invisible academy' in his homeland, even if the times were not yet ripe for a visible institution.[28]

Erasmus was not divorced from the religious leanings of his countrymen. On the contrary, his turning the stream of the Renaissance into religious channels explains the influence he had over contemporaries, especially in the Netherlands. This influence, Huet says, was to persist. If as Napoleon said 'France is of the religion of Voltaire,' one could also say 'Holland is of the religion of Erasmus.' Once the revolutionary movement of the sixteenth century had worked itself out, much Dutch opinion, as is evident from the religious moderation of regents and intellectuals, ranged itself on the side of the Rotterdamer. For more than three hundred years the religion of Erasmus, despite the Reformed state church, has been 'the quiet common way of thinking of the Netherlanders.'[29]

Huet linked Erasmus' religion to modernity. In this as in much else he was at one with the liberals. He himself had abandoned his clerical career and left the church, tending in the end to agnosticism.[30] He found in Erasmus the openness of mind and spirit he sought for himself. In his opinion dogmatic Protestantism was dead, while liveliness emanated still from Erasmus' religious thought. Luther's denomination, he says, is but one among a number; it has 'nothing by which it lives on as a distinct flower of European civilization on its own stem.' Luther's writings were but a branch of the Christian devotional literature of the ancient and medieval worlds. Here Huet anticipates Ernst Troeltsch but not, of course, the Luther revival of the twentieth century. By contrast, he adds that something in Erasmus' mind was attuned to the present time. If alive he would be a friend of the modernists, of those of an ethical-irenic tendency, of the biblical critics and men of science of his homeland.[31] To Huet he was, in short, forward-looking. Hence he emphasizes the gulf between Erasmus and the more ascetic, penitential, and world-denying writers who preceded him, men like Thomas à Kempis and Sebastian Brant, even if he also sees his work as rooted 'in the mysticism of the time and of the land.'[32]

Huet depicts Erasmus as positive and life-affirming. This man, he says, turned to advantage even the difficulties of his early life. Experiences that would have made others misanthropic – poverty, begging for favours, the cloister itself – were transmuted into art in some of his letters and in works like the *Colloquia* and *Moriae encomium*. Disadvantage and disappointment nurtured rather than weakened his sense of humour. Confident in his talents, he sought through all his early struggles the liberty to exercise them.[33]

Huet offers a consistent and suggestive psychological portrait of Erasmus. He rejects the common criticism of Erasmus' character, that he was weak and cowardly, for example. 'We do not take it amiss that Luther and Calvin died in their beds, though they both had innocent blood on their consciences. But Erasmus, who never hurt a fly or asked for another sword than his pen, we call cowardly because he shrank from the stake.' Erasmus, Huet concludes, was not a universal genius; his genius lay rather in literature. He was not notable as philosopher, jurist, or historian; he was something of a dilettante in dogmatic theology and biblical interpretation and, in politics, he was a dreamer. He nevertheless embodied 'the healthy, sound understanding' of the age. Huet concludes (in a way, he says, flattering to the Dutch patriot) that only three times did a single name so dominate European intellectual life: the times of Petrarch, Erasmus, and Voltaire.[34]

Leiden church historians of the earlier twentieth century, notably Fredrik Pijper (1859–1926) and Johannes Lindeboom (1882–1958), put afresh the argument for Erasmus' association with a religious reform movement distinctive to the Netherlands. Pijper's work as editor (with S. Cramer) of reform writings in the Netherlands for the series *Bibliotheca Reformatoria Neerlandica* (1903–14) equipped him to argue points that had been put forward by earlier writers but without the scholarly support he could bring.[35] Those points were that there was a distinctive reforming movement in the Netherlands, especially in the early years of the sixteenth century, and that Erasmus had a large hand in determining its character. The first had been obscured by the inclination of scholars to seek influences from outside, from Saxony, Zürich, or Geneva. Of tracts and pamphlets published in his *Bibliotheca* Pijper says: they are not Lutheran, Zwinglian, or Calvinist; they are 'Netherlandish.' There were various contributors to this Netherlandish stream – the schools of the Brethren, the writings of the mystics, and, of course, the activities of the Protestant

Reformers. The movement itself was diverse; the early reformers in the Netherlands, Pijper says, did not all teach the same things but they shared the same spirit.[36] On that spirit Erasmus had an unmistakable influence.

The nature of that influence is revealed, not so much in the familiar works of Erasmus like the *Folly* or the *Colloquia*, as in his theological handbook, the *Ratio verae theologiae*. That work, says Pijper, is biblicist, it gives theology the task, above all, of preparing preachers, it presents Jesus more as prophet and pioneer of a new order than as the world's redeemer from its sins. The emphasis is on the Sermon on the Mount.[37] The reference suggests common ground (in appreciation of Erasmus' theology) between Pijper and the liberal theologians of Germany and Switzerland. But Pijper's interest is primarily in the connection between Erasmus' theology and the reforming interest in the Netherlands.

Three groups were subject to his influence: rectors of the Latin schools who began reading his literary and pedagogical works but were led on to his theological ones; those who occupied middle ground in the controversies of the age – the mediating theologians but also statesmen like (later) William of Orange; above all, the first Netherlands reformers who shared much of Erasmus' outlook, who were biblicist, inclined to a symbolic view of the sacraments, sceptical of ceremony, teaching a form of justification by faith, but not faith without love.[38] In the last part of his essay (which had begun as a lecture and retained some of the rhetorical flavour of that form), Pijper traces parallels between the writings of Erasmus and those of the early Netherlands reformers. The heirs of these men, he concludes, finished as a minority in the independent Netherlands (where Calvinism became dominant). That is a subject for neither grieving nor rejoicing; but there is satisfaction in giving recognition to the influence of Erasmus so long overlooked.[39]

Johannes Lindeboom read theology at Leiden 1902–8 and was a student of Pijper's.[40] His doctoral dissertation of 1909 was a full-length study of Erasmus' theology but it also accepted his place in a Netherlands tradition of religious reform. His writings, Lindeboom says early in his dissertation, were a major source of the mediating tendency in sixteenth-century thought which was especially strong in the Netherlands.[41] This way of seeing Erasmus presupposes his distinctiveness as a religious thinker and Lindeboom's purpose – baldly stated – is to define that distinctiveness.

He also argues for a substantial consistency in his thought, while not denying the impact of circumstances and gradual change. At many points he wishes to qualify the one-sided judgments of his predecessors. As a result his work may seem a series of 'buts': Erasmus was anti-dogmatist but he was not a freethinker;[42] he was a critic of church abuses but he was never alienated from the Roman church; he had some points in common with Luther and for a time defended him but on his own terms.

Lindeboom draws three main conclusions from his study of Erasmus' theology. First, Erasmus was a biblicist. For him 'the Bible is the starting-point and guideline for all true theology,' it is the foundation and norm for the Christian life. Even in translation it should be in the hands of all Christians. Lindeboom says, in criticizing those who associated him too much with the Enlightenment, that Erasmus believed unreservedly in the direct inspiration of the Bible, though he was also engaged in critical work on the text.[43] Secondly, he was devoted to the church not only as the community of believers but in its visible Roman form. That had always been so, but the commitment deepened in the Reformation years. Certainly he was a strong, at times it would seem a root-and-branch, critic of church abuses but he usually avoided confusing the abuse and the institution. There were in Erasmus, Lindeboom sums up, two ideas of the church, as community of believers and as Roman hierarchy; he held to both.[44] Thirdly, his piety was moralistic and centred on the faith that works by love. Faith for him (as against Luther's wholly passive and receptive trust) was both intellectual conviction and practical application. His Christ was (for Lindeboom as for Pijper) above all a teacher and leader in the good way. Erasmus may not, Lindeboom concludes, be fairly called a Pelagian; theologically he gave grace the primary place. But his attention was concentrated on the moral strife.[45]

From this set of complex theological judgments Lindeboom turns, in a final section, to Erasmus' 'religious personality.' This summation makes it easier to see where he locates him in the history of religious thought. In Erasmus, he says, the Renaissance takes on a distinctive biblical and religious colouring. It is mistaken to see him (in expressions like 'Saint Socrates, pray for us') adhering to the universalist theism of some Italian thinkers; he was 'too much the biblical Christian' for that. His piety may have been one-sided in its moralism but it was nevertheless personal, conscious, and distinctive. Lindeboom asks how far that piety had an autonomous, self-directing character. Erasmus' indifference to dogma, his refusal to use the weapons of traditional dogmatics, suggested such a character. That is qualified (one is struck by the arbitrariness of these judgments) by the lack of any sense of inner struggle in Erasmus' piety; his writings 'breathe an irenic calm.' 'It is noteworthy how little the ideas of conscience and struggle of conscience are expressed in his work, how comparatively little even the word "conscience" appears there.' A moralist piety, according to Lindeboom, needs the backing of church authority. In the Luther affair, Lindeboom says, Erasmus was consistent. He welcomed Luther only as a reformer along his own lines; he maintained his loyalty to the church; he sought mediation and peace but more and more feared uproar and anarchy, for which he blamed the Lutherans. There was a mystical side to Erasmus' piety, a 'Christ-mysticism,' an inner imitation of Christ, seeking rest and security in Christ. Lindeboom concludes: Erasmus was the father of those attitudes of a 'peaceable, mediating and latitudinarian piety' which played a great role in Netherlands religion in the sixteenth century.[46]

That is the point in Lindeboom's work (following Pijper's) which interests us at this stage of our discussion. Generally it was the most thorough investigation of Erasmus' theology to that time. As we have seen, Lindeboom sought very deliberately to give a balanced account and pressed qualifications on every generalization. But the overriding notion – in so far as there is an overriding notion – of Erasmus' moralism links his account, perhaps against his intention, most to that of the liberals.[47]

If we can trace Erasmus' spiritual bonds with the land of his birth, we also know that for northern intellectuals of his time and type the Italy of humanists and printers was a homeland of the mind. The desire to go there dominated his early adulthood. His eventual visit, his Italian associations, the mutual influences which ensued deserved closer attention and received it before the end of the nineteenth century in a small work that may be counted a minor masterpiece of Erasmus scholarship, the *Erasme en Italie: Etude sur un épisode de la Renaissance* of Pierre de Nolhac (1859–1936). It contributed to Erasmus biography; it also notably advanced the study of his friendships and associations. A half-century later Augustin Renaudet found that it needed little supplementing or correcting despite the intervening advances in scholarship; it was 'un guide sage.'[48]

In Italy, as Nolhac's narrative brings out, Erasmus had dangerous and disheartening experiences, including the (for him) monstrous sight of a pope (Julius II) entering a city as conqueror, a threatening encounter in the streets of the same city (Bologna), and fear of starvation from the frugality of his Venetian host, Andrea Torresani of Asola.[49] But above all the book conveys an impression of the pleasures of the Italian journey. The pervading atmosphere is of calm afternoons devoted to learning or learned dialogue. The climax of the journey and of the book is the visit at Rome to Cardinal Domenico Grimani which Erasmus recounted twenty years later in a famous passage.

> There was no creature to be seen either in the court or in the vestibule. It was afternoon. I gave my horse to my servant, and mounting the stairs by myself, went into the first reception-room. I saw no one. I went on to the second and third. Just the same. I found no door closed and marvelled at the solitude around me. Coming to the last room, I found one person, keeping watch at an open door ... At last he asked my name, which I gave him. As soon as he heard it, he went hastily in without my noticing it, and coming out directly bade me not to go. Without further delay I was fetched in, and the cardinal received me not as a cardinal, and such a cardinal, might receive a person of humble rank, but as he might a colleague. A chair being placed for me, we talked together for more than two hours.[50]

The Italian journey, says Nolhac (this is a theme of his work), left on Erasmus' mind 'ineffaceable memories and endless regret.' He notes how the biography by Beatus Rhenanus confirms the place it had in Erasmus' memory. Already before his departure his friends knew the power Italy would have over him and feared he would not return. In fact he was left with a strong nostalgia which Nolhac conveys and, so to speak, shares.[51]

Our primary interest now is in Nolhac's account of Erasmus' connections with humanist circles in Italy. He met the Bologna humanists and began with Paolo Bombasius, who helped him with Greek, one of the closest friendships of his life.[52] At Venice he was intimate with the circle of Aldus Manutius whose printing-house, says Nolhac somewhat extravagantly, was at times 'truly the intellectual centre of Europe.' The 1508 edition of the *Adagia* owed much to that circle. He represented transalpine scholarship in the so-called Aldine academy. In Rome he lived in the world of the Roman curia, then 'so hospitable to scholars and artists.'[53]

For Nolhac Italy completed Erasmus' intellectual formation, ripening his talents as writer and completing his grasp of the new ideas which he, more than any other, would propagate in the north. Sharp observations on Italian life are scattered throughout his later works.[54] Of the physical remains of antiquity he, like other savants of the time, had little to say, though he was not indifferent to painting and may (Nolhac hazards) have met Raphael. As for religion, he judged Roman behaviour by 'an evangelical ideal' which was foreign to Italians of that time; he may have exaggerated the evidences of irreligion. He recognized among some of the clergy 'true ministers of Christ, zealous prelates, learned and pious, worthy of their priesthood and their rank.' Nolhac believes (as at times Erasmus believed) that, had he remained at Rome (instead of heeding the call of Henry VIII in 1509), he would have been both happy and influential.[55]

Erasmus' relations with and debts to Italy have continued to be studied in the twentieth century. If some have emphasized his debts in an uncompromising, even exaggerated, way,[56] Augustin Renaudet in 1954 wrote rather of an Italian humanist influence diffused throughout Europe and accessible to Erasmus in his own country, in Paris, and, above all, in England.[57] Renaudet's *Erasme et l'Italie* is a late fruit of its author's long and productive labour on the biography of Erasmus and the history of humanism. The part of that labour most of interest to us is Renaudet's study (1916) of Erasmus' associations in Paris and his role in the humanist and early reforming movements there in the early years of the sixteenth century.[58]

Renaudet's *Préréforme et humanisme à Paris pendant les premières guerres d'Italie (1494–1517)* is a massive work recalling the diverse movements for reform in Paris in the last decade of the fifteenth century and the first two decades of the sixteenth. The term 'Préréforme' was intended to suggest a transitional time when continuity with the medieval past was still strong but also a time of preparation for both the Reformation and the Counter-Reformation. The usage is, naturally, debatable.[59] Renaudet has Erasmus moving in and out of the Parisian humanist and reform-

ing circles over the whole period; his connections there profoundly affected his own intellectual and spiritual development,
he in turn became a figure of influence among the Parisian intellectuals, representing one form of the reforming impulse. Renaudet's larger work had been preceded by a spare, sober study
of Erasmus' life (to 1517) based on Allen's first two volumes of
the correspondence.[60] There, too, he traces the links between the
man and the various environments through which he moved, not
least Paris. In that account it seems a critical moment when Erasmus, passing through Paris on his way to Italy, was pleased
'to find, in the general uncertainty of minds, hesitating between
the new teachings and the disciplines of the past, a freedom of
speaking and writing that was dear to him.'[61]

Renaudet's interest as a historian was primarily in the mental
life of the past. It was an interest as much in the psychological
as in the philosophical or the theological, and the latter less as
systems than as expressions of human aspiration.[62] The fluidity,
even the turbulence of its intellectual life made Paris at the beginning of the sixteenth century an appealing subject to him. He
saw the intellectual initiative as lying with the humanists and
their aspirations are at the centre of his study. But scholasticism
was not a spent force and the effects of the mystical revival of
the later Middle Ages were still being felt; intertwined with the
intellectual changes were the struggles for reform in the church
and, above all, in the orders, a fact recognized in Renaudet's rather
awkward organization of his book into parallel chapters on doctrines and reforms in the three periods, to 1494, 1494–1504,
1504–17.[63]

At his own arrival in Paris in the autumn of 1495, Erasmus
was, Renaudet says, no longer a medieval man. His enthusiasm
was wholly for the study of the ancient world. Yet his religious
belief and practice were rigorously traditional, as is revealed by
his devotion to Saint Geneviève, patroness of the city, and there
is evidence of continuing, if unavowed influence of his early
teachers among the Brethren of the Common Life. He was also
devoted to monastic reform. This mixture of humanism, religion,
and reform he shared with many of those among whom he moved
in Paris. With some aspects of the intellectual and spiritual revival
– Neoplatonism, an interest in the life of contemplation – he had
no sympathy.[64]

Renaudet shares the view that had, since Seebohm's book,

become a virtual orthodoxy, that the turning-point of Erasmus' life was his meeting with the so-called Oxford Reformers during his visit to England 1499–1500. There he found a serenity and balance of mind which the intellectual agitations of Paris had denied him. Henceforth his way was clear to him; already on his return to Paris in 1500 he was sketching the 'new theology,' biblical not scholastic, lay not clerical, companion and not enemy of the humanities.[65] Its first full expression was his *Enchiridion*. 'He no longer confounded the rules of the cloister with Christian holiness. He no longer thought that the perfect faithful ought to fly the world, and that the ethic of the gospel was unrealizable in the society of the living. The reform of the convents mattered less to him than the reform of the church, and the reform of the church less than that of the Christian society.'[66] Erasmus was for Renaudet advancing an alternative form of Christianity.

What is of interest for a study of Erasmus' Parisian connections is the contrast, a kind of counterpoint, which Renaudet makes between Erasmus and the other giant in the field of reform in France, Lefèvre d'Etaples, and that theme runs through the last half of his work. Lefèvre thought philosophically, he edited Aristotle and was influenced by the Neoplatonism of the Florentine school. At the same time he embraced the medieval mystical tradition and remained devoted to Catholic contemplative and ascetic practices. Renaudet's Erasmus, by contrast, taught a simple piety based directly on the Bible, free of elaborate ritual on the one hand and mystical excess on the other; it was a piety, not for the cloistered, but for a bourgeoisie living in the world and, consequently, could draw on human wisdom wherever found, even among the pagans. Yet, despite these contrasts, of which the two men themselves were aware, they were in effect working together through their biblical editions and commentaries. These, though not always perfectly done, put into the hands of contemporary Christians the means of judging the church and the clergy they knew. At this point – on Luther's appearance in 1517 with his more drastic biblicism – 'Préréforme' passed over into Reformation.[67]

It is important to recognize the subtlety of Renaudet's portrait of Erasmus, on which he continued to work, long after the period covered by this volume, with a refinement and sensitivity to literary and ethical values reminiscent of those other French authors on Erasmus in the nineteenth century who have been considered in an earlier chapter.[68] This Erasmus accepts the authority of revelation, recognizes the primary of grace, and is even drawn to the threshold of mysticism. Yet the dominant traits are those of the Enlightenment and liberalism. Renaudet writes of the 'modernism' of Erasmus, by which he means a prudent, a reverent scepticism, an affirmation of Christian liberty against traditional forms, a rationalist reserve about dogmatic definitions, even on central questions like the Trinity and the sacrament, or metaphysical reflections and speculations.[69] In the end he looked, says Renaudet, for a 'third church' free of medieval institutionalism and Lutheran dogmatism.[70] There is an echo here of Gibbon and Semler.

The Reformation in Germany had always bulked large in biographies of Erasmus. Yet the concentration had invariably been on Erasmus' attitude to and relations with Luther, culminating in the controversy over free will in 1525. There was a familiar set of sources, letters to, from, and about Luther, and the formal writings. A minor theme had been Erasmus' response to the Reformation in Basel and this had been developed, as we have seen, by a group of studies in the middle of the nineteenth century. At the end of the century scholars turned to the study of Erasmus' part in the war of pamphlets between Luther's supporters and opponents around 1520. That meant progress, not least because it recognized the Reformation as a movement whose cause could be advanced or retarded by controversy and struggle and not as the creation of one heroic man or, for that matter, of providence. For us its importance is in its depiction of Erasmus, not as a solitary scholar ironically observing the struggle at a distance or cringing, for fear of being caught up, in a corner, but as an effective, if in the end unsuccessful, campaigner.

Two writers in particular followed this line in the first years of this century, Max Richter (notably in his doctoral dissertation *Die Stellung des Erasmus zu Luther und zur Reformation in den Jahren 1516–1524*) and Paul Kalkoff. They had a common interest in Erasmus as propagandist and tactician in 1520–1, the critical years for Luther's relation to Rome and the empire. Of the two Richter makes the more modest claim for Erasmus and is closer to the traditional Protestant positions. It is indicative that, for Erasmus' views on church and dogma, he refers to Stichart and Lezius: Erasmus was a moralizing theologian, he looked for a

gradual enlightenment through learning and individual improvement. He was not the man for that decisive hour; his combination
of medieval Catholicism and humanist studies would never have
brought religious renewal and the 'rebirth of the German people.'[71]

Yet Max Richter can also pick up the language of Maurenbrecher, Karl Müller, and Wernle: Erasmus was 'the intellectual
great power of his age'; his main work was, not the revival of
antiquity, but the 'renaissance of Christianity'; one can speak of
'a specifically Erasmian reformation.' These expressions come from
the first chapter, 'Erasmus as Reformer,' of Richter's later, more
general work *Desiderius Erasmus und seine Stellung zu Luther auf
Grund ihrer Schriften*. Erasmus well understood the need to make
propaganda and win friends for his cause.[72] His policy in 1520–1
was mediation between the parties, which was essential for safe-
guarding and advancing his distinctive reform. To the task he
brought impressive skills; he had a cooler head for assessing the
circumstances than Luther. He won the interest of Frederick the
Wise of Saxony, Luther's prince, and of some at the imperial court.
His action was well prepared and thought out, but by the Diet
of Worms, with its outlawing of Luther, his plans had foundered.
Yet, despite setbacks and his own fearful and anxious disposition,
he returned to the struggle, especially in the time of Pope Adrian
VI (1522–3), keeping up his criticism of current abuses and
staunchly refusing violent suppression as the way of resolving
the German problem.[73]

Kalkoff attributes a larger influence to Erasmus and probes
more thoroughly the events and writings of 1520–1. Paul Kalkoff
(1858–1928) is one of the more original characters in the modern
history of Erasmus interpretation. He lived a relatively sedentary
life, teaching for forty years in a gymnasium in Breslau, and at
his retirement was appointed honorary professor of history at the
university there. In research he was passionate, restless, intense,
with an almost obsessive concentration (over forty years) on the
short but critical period of German history 1517–23. He said of
himself that he was born in the nineteenth century, lived in the
sixteenth, and died in the twentieth. His spoken word was inspiring to students but his writing was by contrast overstretched
and congested. He could push his conclusions beyond the point
his sources or the argument would allow.[74]

Despite these weaknesses, Kalkoff made a lasting contribution to the study of Erasmus and especially of his role in the critical time of Luther's confrontation with Rome. His main work on the subject was a long essay in the very first number of the *Archiv für Reformationsgeschichte* in 1904, 'Die Vermittlungspolitik des Erasmus und sein Anteil an den Flugschriften der ersten Reformationszeit' ('Erasmus' Mediating Policy and His Part in the Pamphlet War of the Early Reformation Period'). In the second half of 1520 (at a time when Luther had already been condemned at Rome, and a German diet to consider his case was imminent) Erasmus was, Kalkoff says, acting to protect Luther, to discredit his opponents, and to have the case referred to an impartial tribunal. His weapon was the anonymous pamphlet, an unusual recourse for him since, comments Kalkoff, anonymity, despite his naturally anxious temperament, was against his interest and his principles.[75]

Two works are in question. The first, *Acta Academiae Lovaniensis contra Lutherum*, Kalkoff describes as a 'little masterpiece of journalistic eloquence.' Its immediate purpose was to demonstrate that the papal bull against Luther was not authentic or was premature or at least not in binding form. It poured derision on Aleander, Erasmus' one-time colleague and recent rival, who was seeking the bull's implementation in northern Europe. This, says Kalkoff, was serious political action aimed at influencing opinion to force a reconsideration of Luther's case in both Rome and Germany.[76] The second pamphlet, *Consilium cuiusdam ex animo cupientis esse consultum et Romani Pontificis dignitati et Christianae religionis tranquillitati*, proposed an independent assessment of the case by impartial judges nominated by three European kings.[77] Here Erasmus was seeking a compromise which would check violence on both sides, preserve what was truly evangelical in Luther's teaching, and rebuff once and for all the friars and scholastic theologians, Luther's enemies and Erasmus' also. The preparation of the work itself required, according to Kalkoff, some compromise. On the difficult question of the authorship of the *Consilium*, Kalkoff decides for Erasmus but accepts also a collaboration between him and Johannes Faber, Dominican vicar-general and councillor to Emperor Maximilian I. Common action was possible for the two men at that moment but their outlooks generally were different; Faber, says Kalkoff, was closer than Erasmus to medieval Catholicism and his opposition of 1520 was determined by a residue of conciliar ideas and by German national grievances, neither of which touched Erasmus deeply.[78] The important point for us is Kalkoff's demonstration of the planned and persistent character of Erasmus' political action in 1520–1. This action, he adds, continued after the main effort at mediation was shipwrecked on Roman intransigence, represented by Aleander's book-burnings at Louvain and elsewhere, and by Luther's revolutionary pamphlets, especially the *Babylonian Captivity of the Church*; he encouraged friends and associates at Cologne to publish satirical sallies especially against Aleander.[79] The mutual enmity of Aleander and Erasmus is one of Kalkoff's themes and is developed at greater length in his contemporaneous work *Die Anfänge der Gegenreformation in den Niederlanden*.[80]

At the end of his long article on Erasmus' mediating policy, Kalkoff compares his activity with that of the editor of a modern political journal engaged in a well-prepared and far-reaching campaign to influence public opinion.[81] This was in part a return to Ranke's vision of Erasmus. It could be seen as the most substantial effort so far to free Erasmus from the image of solitary scholar, isolated and ineffective observer, 'man on his own.'

Despite Kalkoff's tendency to exaggerate and to claim certainty where the evidence was unsure, his picture of Erasmus in action at that time remains generally convincing. He also saw that this picture affected judgments on other participants in the drama of 1520–1, especially on Ulrich von Hutten. In works of 1920 Kalkoff reiterated his arguments of 1904 about Erasmus' role in the crisis: he worked with and for Luther, recognizing him as a powerful tool 'for the furthering of his own highest purposes, the purifying and deepening of the Christian religion by the standard of the earliest sources' (the extent of their theological agreement is overstated); he organized the campaign against scholastic theology and papal absolutism. Meanwhile Hutten was engaging in acts of terror, at critical times pursuing his own interests, continually damaging the cause by bloodthirsty invectives. Kalkoff's aim was to destroy the Hutten legend which went back to Herder. His contrast was between intelligent and principled (if, in the end, unsuccessful) political action and wild and fruitless posturing.[82] He was deliberately reversing a widely held picture; Erasmus became the effective, Hutten the ineffective historical actor.

Kalkoff's work brought a sense of historical reality to the depicting of Erasmus. That is not to say that his arguments were wholly convincing or all his conclusions justified, but he succeeded in placing Erasmus in the struggles of his time. Henceforth greater realism, a better sense of historical circumstance, was possible in accounts of the association and conflict between Luther and Erasmus. That topic had been treated often in the nineteenth century, as we have seen, but the treatment was mostly restricted to the personal relations between the two men and their theological differences, with the contrast in character or temperament a dominant theme. Kalkoff obliged students of the relationship to think politically about it. He advanced Maurenbrecher's initiative on that side.

This way of thinking appears in the work of the young French scholar André Meyer (1885–1908), *Etude critique sur les relations d'Erasme et de Luther*. His teachers, whose hopes were dashed by his early death, anticipated for Meyer a brilliant academic career in Germanic studies. The work on Erasmus and Luther was written during study years in Berlin, where the pamphlet literature of the Reformation era was readily available to him.[83] This is a remarkably mature work for a young man barely in his twenties. That is evident, not only in his judgment of Erasmus himself to which we will shortly return, but in his handling of the sources and his criticism of previous authors, especially the more partial Protestant writers.[84]

During the war of pamphlets (the time that interested Max Richter and Kalkoff), says Meyer, Erasmus and Luther were seen as working in the same cause. Their enemies in the old church (the 'dévots') condemned them together. At the same time Catholics, including his friends and supporters, were trying to persuade Erasmus to write against Luther. By clumsily provoking a quarrel, Hutten on the other side was pushing him in the same direction. In Meyer's view Erasmus had been the victim of a false situation, though the fault was not entirely his own.[85] He was not a wholehearted supporter of Luther's, and the Protestant image of adherence and betrayal is false. He had interests binding him to the old church, he feared for the effects of religious rebellion on good letters, he did not sympathize with the appeal (especially the national appeal) to the populace, and, above all, he did not intend to abandon the Catholic fold.[86]

Nevertheless, there was in the early stages a sense of common cause, though it was never complete. The Reformers, Meyer says, recognized their debt to the humanists and, above all, to Erasmus. Innovators always speak for their teachers and predecessors: 'Their [teachers'] sufferings make them act, they express their hatreds and hopes.' Luther and Erasmus did have common ideas at the beginning; they had common friends and enemies. In fact, their definitive judgments of one another were made early: Luther admired Erasmus but also had serious reservations; Erasmus always praised Luther for challenging church abuses but blamed his reckless language. The events of the early 1520s aggravated the critical tone on both sides. For Meyer the basis of Erasmus' position was his commitment to peace, 'the greatest of goods.' His struggle for peace and his deliberate neutrality demanded of him a firmness and moderation which have not been recognized enough.[87]

That moderation, Meyer concludes, persisted despite the break during the free-will controversy. Luther's bitter attacks and Erasmus' own distaste made it all the more praiseworthy. During the Diet of Augsburg (1530) he urged tolerance and pacification.[88] His appeal in the debate over free will was to reason, common sense, and classical morality against determinism. His devotion to public peace and the cause of learning was continuous.[89]

Meyer's Erasmus, Charles Andler says, shows more continuity in conduct, more courage in action, more coherence in thought, than is usually attributed to the historical figure.[90] Meyer believes that Wieland remains the best guide to his impressionable and nervous temperament. Erasmus' position seems ambiguous: 'To his misfortune he was the precursor and the enemy of the Reformation, the critic and the apologist for Catholicism.' We must, Meyer says, accept the sincerity of his attachment to Catholicism though he looked for a Catholicism purified and made more rational.[91] There is no more than a hint here of Renaudet's idea of the third church. Erasmus for Meyer was no freethinker; his religiosity was not profound but he was not indifferent.[92]

The interest of this book lies in its moderate judgment of Erasmus. That derives partly from Meyer's avowed attachment to the tradition of Wieland but also to his attempt to provide Erasmus with a realistic historical context, a sphere of activity, so to speak. The influence of Maurenbrecher is apparent. Meyer only partly succeeds but his interpretation of Erasmus is at least free of the intense preoccupation with character which we have found among Protestant (especially Lutheran) writers and which came from confessionalism but also, as we have often seen, from romanticism. The personality of Luther had weighed too heavily on that literature and become oppressive. The same cannot be said of the other great Reformer with whom Erasmus had contact, Huldrych Zwingli, or of the literature dealing with their relationship.

Erasmus' two biographers from Zürich in the last years of the eighteenth century, Johannes Gaudin and Salomon Hess, had referred to Zwingli's esteem for Erasmus and the time of cordial relations between the two men.[93] Before the end of the nineteenth century the pattern had been set of treating this relationship in a calm and reflective way, in contrast to the intense, often savage, and essentially adversary fashion of treating the Erasmus/Luther relationship.[94] The Reformed pastor Johann Martin Usteri (1848–90) published at Zürich in 1885 a judicious study of the relationship.[95] Investigation of Erasmus' influence, Usteri begins, is essential to understanding Zwingli's development as a Reformer. That influence, he says, has never been studied in a fundamental way. It would not lessen Zwingli's renown to acknowledge his debts to Erasmus although, Usteri adds (as one would expect), the Reformer of Zürich came to meet the needs of the time more deeply and centrally than his mentor. From the beginning Zwingli gave Erasmus highest praise, especially as a student of the Bible. Zwingli's reading demonstrates the influence: the *Enchiridion* made a deep impression upon him; he acknowledged above all the effect on his spiritual development of Erasmus' poem 'Expostulatio Iesu cum homine suapte culpa pereunte,' where Christ remonstrates with men for seeking their good outside himself (for Zwingli it pointed to Christ's role as sole mediator between God and man).[96]

Usteri's method is to study Zwingli's glosses and notes in the books of Erasmus he possessed and to seek parallels in their ideas. Gradually, he observes, Erasmus' criticisms of the existing church order fixed themselves in Zwingli's mind. That Zwingli's first Reformation tract concerned the free choice of foods indicates the effect of Erasmus' account of religion as essentially inward and ethical. On scripture as the one pure source of faith, Zwingli followed Erasmus exactly. At the beginning at least he accepted the *Enchiridion*'s call to allegorize the text. Again he began with Erasmus' conception of Christianity as essentially discipleship, imitation of Christ, but in time moved to a more Pauline position closer to Luther's. Nevertheless, Usteri adds in a qualification unusual in nineteenth-century Protestant literature, Erasmus too saw Christ as saviour and not merely as example.[97]

In another respect Usteri went beyond his contemporaries. He credited Erasmus with rehabilitating Christian social ideas overshadowed by ecclesiastical interests; ahead of the Reformation, he restored the sense of vocation in marriage, family, and worldly occupation. Usteri frees Erasmus from the charge of political simplicity or naïvety. 'He well knew to distinguish between the Christian norm and civil law. The latter would not make men morally perfect but avert malice and wrong.' His preaching of peace had been more commonly treated by nineteenth-century writers; Usteri emphasizes its importance for Zwingli who heavily marked his copy of the adage 'Dulce bellum inexpertis.'[98]

Theologically, Usteri says, Zwingli began with Erasmus' distinction between letter and spirit. Later he drew closer to Luther's distinction between law and gospel but never wholly accepted Luther's doctrine of the contradiction between the two or restricted the role of law to the exposing and condemning of sin. Usteri accepts that Erasmus' teaching on the sacrament was the foundation of Zwingli's. For Erasmus (while the real presence was neither denied nor stressed) 'the Lord's supper was valued as the feast of remembrance, covenant and community.'[99] Erasmus' writings, Usteri concludes, were rich in ideas which in the hands of more forthright and determined men became reforming deeds.[100] The eventual break between Erasmus and Zwingli was most clearly indicated by the adherence of the one to the doctrine of free will and the strong predestinarianism of the other.[101] Yet Zwingli drew from his mentor an openness and breadth of mind he never lost; he always regretted the break, while recognizing that Erasmus would never adopt the full Reformation position.[102]

The importance of Usteri's monograph lies partly in the seriousness with which it treats Erasmus' theology and partly in its identification of the Christian social element in his thought. Although Usteri emphasizes the development in Zwingli's thought, the comparison between him and Erasmus remains rather abstract; the connection between Erasmus' social ideas and Zwingli's program in Zürich is not explored. Nevertheless, the work presents a balanced, broadly convincing case which has not needed drastic revision. Its interest for us in this part of the discussion is in its demonstration of the influence of Erasmus and his reforming ideas, of how in Karl Müller's words he was among contemporaries a 'spiritual world power.'

That influence extended beyond the main centres of western and central Europe. Erasmus' connections with the political and intellectual élite of Poland were studied – for the doctorate of Breslau University – by the Poznan priest Kasimir von Miaskowski (b 1875). He gathered letters from the collections in Breslau, Leipzig, and Cracow.[103] His commentary does not explore Erasmus' Polish relationships in any depth but he does enough to demonstrate both Erasmus' appeal to leading figures in Poland and his interest in Polish affairs. These letters, he remarks, were not of peripheral interest to students of Erasmus or merely a source for Polish literary history in the sixteenth century. They demonstrate once again Erasmus' centrality to the history of his time; his own letters, in recounting European events from day to day, took the place of a modern newspaper.[104] The correspondents of Erasmus studied by Miaskowski belonged to the court and chancellery – and so were at or close to the centre of power – or were connected with the university at Cracow.[105]

The theme in this long section has indeed been the emergence among Erasmus scholars of the late nineteenth and early twentieth centuries of an awareness of Erasmus' role in the affairs of his age. The image of the eminent but solitary scholar was replaced by that of the mentor and patron of like-minded people throughout Europe. Networks of friendship and association appeared. This could be counted the single most important change in the interpretation of Erasmus at the threshold of modern scholarship. It was possible because of the success of more exact studies in Erasmus' correspondence (culminating in Allen's great edition), which gave scholars more confidence in tracing Erasmus' connections. The fading of confessional or denominational fervour, after its revival at the beginning of the nineteenth century, weakened the two-party model of religious history, which dominated many minds during that century. One could recognize, at least for the early years of the Reformation, the variety of options contemporaries faced, the diversity of their hopes, the opportunities activists and publicists had for political and cultural influence, for turning events their way. A more subtle picture replaced the broad categories which had often sufficed for Enlightenment and romanticism, light and darkness, the good cause and the bad, medieval and modern. A certain democratization brought forward the minor actors, the secondary historical agents; the history of humanism and Reformation was no longer written exclusively around the controversy of Erasmus and Luther but also introduced a multitude of pamphleteers, town clerks and royal secretaries, printers and physicians. All this meant a certain diminishing of Erasmus as a single figure but an enhancement of his historical significance.[106] One might say that the historical revolution of the nineteenth century came to fruition in Erasmus scholarship only in the last two decades of the century and thereafter.

II

It remains mysterious why commentators on Erasmus in the nineteenth century, the great age of constitutional debate in western Europe, showed so little interest in his political and social writings. Extensive study of them begins only with the crisis of the European political system during and after the First World War.[107] The dominance of the Reformation and theological issues must be considered part of the explanation. There is an anticipation of later treatments in two essays by Ludwig Enthoven of Strasbourg. One argues that the *Institutio principis christiani* is more than a derivative work and expresses a distinctively Erasmian spirit; though in form but a collection of aphorisms and in much of its content bound to its own time, it yet has lasting significance ethically and pedagogically.[108] The other deals with a question that had in various ways interested nineteenth-century writers: 'Erasmus Weltbürger oder Patriot?' In Erasmus there was, says Enthoven, an oscillation of feeling about his fatherland or any possible fatherland. He defended Holland against its critics but also himself passed unfavourable comments; he had a strong feeling for France, yet refused invitations to settle there; he took as self-evident his belonging to Germany, but his personal attachment was less patriotism than a response to the friendship and hero-worship of the German humanists. Both his principles and his personal experiences pointed Erasmus towards universalism, particularly the community of scholars.[109]

On one broadly social issue a substantial literature had appeared before or around the end of the nineteenth century, Erasmus' attitude to education. A number of these works still deserve a place beside modern scholarship, avoiding as they do summary judgments and seeking a balanced appreciation of the influences on Erasmus and his own aims. There had throughout the nineteenth century been a strong interest in pedagogy, especially in Germany. It derived from the hopes placed in education during the national revival of the Napoleonic era, reinforced by the influence of the great Swiss pedagogue Pestalozzi. The history of pedagogy by Karl von Raumer was representative of this movement. While studying in Paris in 1806 'in the midst of the haughty despisers of our German fatherland,' Raumer (1783–1865) read Pestalozzi and what Fichte said about Pestalozzi in his *Addresses to the German Nation*.[110] He combined natural science (he was professor of natural history and mineralogy at Erlangen) with a strong Protestant commitment (he joined in editing E.W. Hengstenberg's confessional paper the *Evangelische Kirchenzeitung*) and the intense patriotism of the liberation struggles.[111]

In his treatment of Erasmus in his *Geschichte der Pädagogik*, Raumer criticizes his equivocations over the Reformation and also the immorality of the *Colloquia*, compares his attitude to the study of nature unfavourably with Luther's, and declares this unhappy man without home, country, or church a poor instructor for children. All that was at the time of writing (1843) fairly predictable. Yet Raumer also recognizes Erasmus' denunciation of paganism in the *Ciceronianus* and sees his clear, decisive call for knowledge of real things and practical affairs as a force for good in pedagogy.[112]

An emphasis on the practical element in Erasmus' writing about education is characteristic of the writers we are considering. Albert Lange in K.A. Schmid's encyclopaedia of education speaks of Erasmus' 'verbal realism or realistic humanism' which he distinguishes, on the one hand, from the formal humanism of the Ciceronians with its call for strict verbal imitation and, on the other, from the experimentalism of Bacon and Comenius.[113] Humanist studies had for him, says Lange, a practical end: preparation for life, a stance attractive to Lange (1828–75), who himself had a neo-Kantian interest in the study of both nature and ethics and strong reforming inclinations of a social democratic kind.[114] Yet he remained within the limits of humanism, putting knowledge of words first and giving the Greeks pride of place in the knowledge of things.[115] Similarly, H.J. Kämmel (1813–81), who wrote the entry on Erasmus in the *Allgemeine deutsche Biographie* and was himself a teacher, directing the gymnasium at Zittau in Saxony for twenty-seven years, says (in his history of German education) that Erasmus' greatness lay in his making his scholarly work fruitful for life.[116] There was, he adds, a unity in his many-sided scholarly activity which would have had more lasting effects if events in Germany after 1517 had not turned minds in another direction.[117]

Erasmus' bent towards the practical is one of the themes of the first substantial monograph on Erasmus' educational thought, that of the French scholar Antoine Benoist (b 1846), *Quid de puerorum institutione senserit Erasmus* (1876). The educational priorities according to Erasmus should, Benoist says, be piety, civil manners, and good letters in that order. Under the second Erasmus intended not courtly conventions but what served the common life. There was for him a close connection between grammar and rhetoric and between rhetoric and moral philosophy; this principle, says Benoist, he put into effect in the *Adagia*. Writing must always be accommodated to the needs and circumstances of the time; he makes the point against the Ciceronians. Again, it is better for theological and philosophical debate to proceed by example and testimony than by speculative argument.[118]

Two other themes are apparent in Benoist's thesis, which is essentially a consolidation of Erasmus' views under topical headings. One is Erasmus' moderation as a reformer of education. He wished gradual correction rather than the sudden overthrow of present methods. Despite his dependence on the classical authors and his fierce denunciation of aspects of medieval culture, he actually borrowed much from medieval pedagogy. Even his hostility to dialectic had limits; he did not wish an exclusive domination for either rhetoricians or philosophers; dialectic should be a support and auxiliary to rhetoric.[119]

The other theme is Erasmus' dependence on classical predecessors. Benoist is here indicating Erasmus' limited originality. The point might be better put as a demonstration that he belonged to a succession of writers, ancient and contemporary, all moving in the same direction. Benoist shows how Erasmus' favourite topics had antecedents or correspondences in other writers: that education should begin early with the mother as first teacher (Xenophon, Plutarch, Quintilian); that there is no higher vocation than the teacher's (Plutarch, Filelfo, and also Luther); that the present brutal conduct of schools is deplorable (Filelfo, Budé);

and so on.[120] To his classicism Erasmus added what came from his own experience and temperament and his distinctive mixture of pre-Christian and Christian elements, above all the sense of building on, rather than striving against, nature, a capacity to see subjects from different angles (sometimes producing contradictions), and a wish that studies be loved for their own sake or for what they contributed to moral stability.[121] His own borrowings, Benoist concludes, were eclectic: 'Erasmian eloquence flows from every source.'[122]

Classicism, of which all writers naturally took Erasmus to be representative, was still dominant in European education in the third quarter of the nineteenth century; indeed classical studies, combined with a patriotic interest in German antiquities, had a revival in Germany around 1870.[123] A challenge to this movement and to the humanist tradition in education generally makes an unusual context for Erasmus. Friedrich Paulsen (1846–1908), after turning from theology and philosophy to pedagogy in the 1870s, began to question the assumptions underlying the prevailing neo-humanism. In his lectures at Berlin he argued for the autonomy of modern culture; the ancient languages and literatures were no longer an indispensable foundation. His students 'listened with rapt attention to these unheard of heresies emanating from a university chair.' Paulsen's book arguing the point (his *Geschichte des gelehrten Unterrichts auf den deutschen Schulen und Universitäten vom Ausgang des Mittelalters bis zur Gegenwart*) was, he says, greeted with a 'storm of indignation' by defenders of the classical gymnasium.[124]

For Paulsen, Erasmus belonged to an age when classicism was a living culture, when the ancients were more than objects of research (as they are, he says, in the present time). He was the first great representative of a purely humanist culture and formation (*Bildung*). The brief *De ratione studii* set the program for education and scholarship over the next century, one of those periods when classical culture was a living model to educated Germans. How, Paulsen asks, was the classical revival (in this, its earliest and healthy phase) affected by Luther's Reformation? Initially, he says, people looked for a general reform from Erasmus, and it is possible that this could have been carried through without breakdown or schism. As it turned out, young humanists became Protestant preachers and turned away from Erasmus; they could be heard denouncing reason and culture as the devil's work.

The classical revival was almost aborted, the storms of the Reformation nearly overwhelmed schools and universities, theological controversy chased humanist works from the market-place. It was the triumph of will (Luther) over intellect (Erasmus).[125] For Paulsen then the classical revival of Erasmus' time was not artificial like that of his own day; it was a response to the real needs of the age, though for a time retarded by a wave of anti-intellectualism.

Beside the classical revival of the 1860s and 1870s which Paulsen challenged, there was also at that time a renewed interest in the educational philosophy of Johann Herbart (1776–1841). One could speak of a 'vast Herbartian movement' seeking a 'complete reconstruction of German educational methods.'[126] Will, character, and intellect all have a place in the Herbartian scheme. Intellectual development and morality are not in Herbart's view at odds with one another; it is the will that chooses between the different presentations (*Vorstellungen*) in the mind. For Herbart the aims of education must be an active mental life offering a variety of presentations and a mature will for choosing between them. The end-product is a character formed for living constructively in present society.[127]

The Herbartian influence is apparent but not obtrusive in one of the better late nineteenth-century treatments of Erasmus, Johannes Gottfried Glöckner's *Das Ideal der Bildung und Erziehung bei Erasmus von Rotterdam* (1889). This work was presented as an *Habilitationsschrift* at Leipzig, at the time one of the centres for pedagogical studies (notably in the Herbartian mode). Glöckner (1861–1932) had been introduced to the educational thought of Herbart and the accompanying Kantian philosophy in studies at Leipzig in the early 1880s.[128]

This work has a balance and sobriety lacking in much nineteenth-century writing on Erasmus. Its subject, Glöckner insists, is Erasmus' educational ideal, not his pedagogy as a whole. This makes the treatment somewhat static. Glöckner is concerned with various balances in Erasmus' mind and, first, with the classic dilemma of the knowledge of words and the knowledge of things. Knowledge of words comes first; man has no more powerful or wonderful possession than speech; pure speech and wisdom are related without being simply dependent, the one on the other. However, eloquence does not mean merely beautiful speech; it means giving things their proper names. In a real sense, then, knowledge of things is primary.[129] Glöckner agrees with Raumer that Luther had a more ready appreciation of nature than Erasmus, but that did not mean he lacked any such appreciation.[130] The second balance is that between antiquity and Christianity. Erasmus believed, Glöckner says, in the necessary partnership of Christianity and learning but for him the moral and religious aim was determining ('Knowledge is good,' he had said; 'charity is better'). Christ is the object of all education. Glöckner rebuts the charge, often made against Erasmus in the nineteenth century, of moral superficiality; he is no mere teacher of propriety and decorum; the whole weight is on love to the neighbour.[131] For Erasmus, Glöckner adds, the Christian shapes and confines the classical: content must be put before form; form must be appropriate to content (hence his criticism of the Ciceronians). Similarly, the speculative philosophy of the ancients must be given only a modest place.[132]

The very practicality of Erasmus' educational ideal – recognized by Glöckner as by other writers of the time – demonstrates how serviceable the classical authors could be to Christianity. Education must complement book-learning with a practical-ethical teaching. Erasmus' cosmopolitanism, his attachment to the republic of letters, did not, Glöckner remarks, stand in the way of his seeing how education must serve the needs of particular states and communities. The practical, socially directed wisdom of the ancients would bear fruit at precisely this point.[133] Education directed at a calling, to which the classical wisdom contributed, would preserve the Christian from a purely intellectual-aesthetic preparation. Erasmus' ideal is, however, not restricted (Glöckner concludes) to the education of leaders or an aristocracy. It extends to a 'Volksbildung' of which the 'Volksschule' developed later by the Reformers was an expression.[134]

Glöckner's work is of interest for three reasons: it offers a believable account of Erasmus' thought, without one-sidedness, exaggeration, or caricature; it relates that thought to actual educational developments and may therefore be linked to the works discussed in the previous section of this chapter; it bears the stamp of its own time in the Herbartian associations apparent, above all, in the primacy given to moral formation (which in itself is not untrue to Erasmus). Another Leipzig dissertation, Hermann Tögel's *Die pädagogischen Anschauungen des Erasmus in ihrer psychologischen Begründung* (1896), is more avowedly Herbartian.[135]

Tögel's interest, as the title of his thesis makes clear, is in the psychological foundations of Erasmus' pedagogy. At the beginning he indicates two difficulties for this enquiry: Erasmus was no theoretical thinker and his views on psychological theory may have to be inferred; psychological theory itself was a creation of the eighteenth century and there could be anachronism in applying the expression to a sixteenth-century pedagogue. To the second objection Tögel replies that a concept appears in practice before it is worked out in theory.[136] His response to the first is more extended and leads him into a reflection on Erasmus' character, about which so much had been said in the nineteenth century.

'Erasmus was a man not of action but of reflection.' Through that bias of mind, says Tögel, he was disposed – Hamlet-like – to introspection and to reflecting on problems which a modern would call psychological. He mulled over the inner lives and experiences of others. He showed himself both a keen observer and a sensitive judge.[137] For a man of this character education could never be merely utilitarian, a gathering of useful information. Language was primary for him but only on the understanding that language and spirit are organically related; speech is an emanation of the spirit as the Logos is of God. These views help explain why Erasmus wrote so emphatically against the Ciceronians: language must not be mere imitation; it must express the individual personality. Hence piety rather than eloquence in itself must be seen as the end of education. On the distinctively Herbartian question of the relation of will and intellect Erasmus, Tögel says, writes with understanding but without resolving the problem.[138]

Indeed, he goes on, Erasmus' pedagogical thought cannot be reduced to a system. It has to be appreciated in its 'living many sidedness.' Its components – theoretical and practical, classical and Christian – are never in sharp contradiction but also never in complete accord. Overriding is his practical pedagogical concern, and that can produce deviations from positions (in theology, for example) which he would otherwise hold. His view of the soul can, says Tögel, be characterized as *Sensualismus*: the soul is an empty vessel waiting to be filled, a *tabula rasa*. Might this not lead, Tögel asks, to an overvaluing of education and be in conflict with the Christian doctrine of original sin? For Erasmus the pedagogical imperative – to take the individual student as far as possible – was primary.[139] The break from the corporate culture of the Middle Ages (Tögel here echoes Burckhardt) made this appreciation of the individual possible. Nevertheless Erasmus' individualism was in Tögel's view excessive. He had a weak sense for social structures and his belief that education could be the same for both sexes and all classes was anachronistically egalitarian.[140]

For Tögel Erasmus is an independent and distinctive figure in the history of education. He was plainly dependent on the ancients, especially on Plutarch and Quintilian, but the correspondences on matters of substance (in Tögel's view as in Benoist's) went beyond dependence and derived rather from a community of mind and spirit. Further, important ideas were Erasmus' own. He shared the strengths and weaknesses of humanist education but in the *Ciceronianus*, at least, surpassed his colleagues in psychological feeling. As for posterity, the ebbing of his influence under the Reformation was temporary. Tögel indicates anticipations in him of great figures of later times (and in some cases a direct influence): Comenius, Locke, Weigel, Pestalozzi, Rousseau. Besides, he concludes, not every influence can be demonstrated by citation: the traces of such a man will be deep, though sometimes hidden.[141]

The work by William Harrison Woodward (1855–1941) published at Cambridge in 1904 *Desiderius Erasmus concerning the Aim and Method of Education* is the high point and (in a sense) summation of the studies we have been considering. Woodward was then professor of education at Liverpool University, occupying a chair supported by and carrying the name of the city of Liverpool. It was a time of expansion in teacher education. His early studies at Christ Church, Oxford (like A.L. Smith's at Balliol) had combined classics and history; he was awarded second-class honours in classical moderations in 1874 and a first in history in 1877.[142] After pastoral work in the 1880s (he was vicar of St George's Everton from 1883), he returned to the academic world in 1891 as warden of a new teacher training institution established by University College, Liverpool (as it then was), becoming lecturer in education at the college itself in the following year.[143] Woodward's writings over the next fifteen years combined his various intellectual and academic interests: classics, history, education, and religion. He wrote history textbooks for schools, notably on the expansion of the British Empire; he wrote still valued works on the revival of classical education in the fifteenth and sixteenth centuries.[144] Like Erasmus he gave primacy to moral and religious aims in education, though the Erasmian ethic and that of a late Victorian or Edwardian Englishman were not in every way identical.[145] In one respect Woodward and Erasmus were more alike than might appear at first sight. The historian of Liverpool University reports 'Woodward, shrewd business man as well as historian, receiving telegrams from his broker at Senate meetings'; we now know that Erasmus was both a careful and a successful financier.[146]

Woodward relates Erasmus to a stage in the history of the classical revival. Apart from the Ciceronian aberration, the time of idolatry, imitation, and affectation had passed. Erasmus himself, Woodward says, had known such a stage in his earlier life but that too had passed. 'Gradually the New Learning became to him an instrument of life, actual and modern; a thing of use, to be adapted to intelligible needs, a source of illumination amid the hard experiences of ordinary men. In his maturity Erasmus showed himself a man of practical aims, with whom wisdom and scholarship were means to social well-being.' 'Modernity' in sixteenth-century terms meant Christian in character. A 'sense of reality,' says Woodward, saved Erasmus from neo-paganism. The real world then was a Christian world. The pre-eminence of the Christian was assumed.[147]

For Woodward Erasmus' mind and temperament were above all inclined to the practical and accessible. He moved 'freely only amidst ideas capable of easy verification and clear statement; mostly of a concrete order, of direct human interest, of definite applicability to life and action.' Hence he was attracted to the sober moralists rather than to the speculative thinkers of antiquity and his Christianity was plain, ethical, and unmystical. He had an 'instinct of proportion'; thus the true appreciation of antiquity excluded concentration on a single author, as with the Ciceronians.[148]

Only to one contemporary reality, says Woodward, was Erasmus unresponsive – nationality. This observation not only reveals the value Woodward himself places on patriotism, it also exposes a view of modern history which had bedevilled interpretations of Erasmus throughout the nineteenth century, the view that from as early as the sixteenth century nationality was the 'true mark' of modern history. For Woodward Erasmus' rejection of folk-tales, the stories of the Arthurian cycle, betrayed an indifference to popular sentiment.[149]

Nevertheless Woodward recognizes the essentially social character of Erasmus' thought. The reiteration of this point is the impressive feature of his presentation. For Erasmus, he says, the liberal education of the individual issues in social activity. The foundation is Erasmus' understanding of human nature and what Woodward, like Tögel, calls his psychology. Woodward's discussion of his (unoriginal) terminology (*natura, ratio, usus sive exercitatio*) may be summarized in the sentence: 'Nature gives potentialities, education transforms them into realities.' Here Woodward in his turn acknowledges the point of contact between Erasmus and Herbart. For both, the intellectual and the moral are in harness: 'Hence instruction (*eruditio, institutio*) is a most comprehensive force, operating upon a free will, whose determinations are easily fixed in the direction of reasonable action.'[150]

Woodward follows Erasmus' working out of this educational psychology (more a sound intuition than a full-fledged system)[151] in instructional practice; he touches on the home atmosphere, the qualities required in a master, moderation in discipline, and so on. Woodward, the trainer of teachers, appreciates Erasmus' sensitivity to the needs and standpoint of the child. More than once he comments on the modernity of his advice for the handling and encouraging of children. In this Woodward can present Erasmus as a guide rediscovered for his contemporaries. Modern and progressive in particular is the place he gave to the home in the education of children.[152] In another role Erasmus was associated with a long tradition and, so far as Woodward could see, an enduring one, though in fact its day was drawing to a close; that was as exponent – masterly exponent – of an education grounded in the languages and literatures of the ancient world. Of his book Woodward says in his preface: 'I have endeavoured to realise with precision the appeal which Antiquity made to Erasmus and the message which he believed it to convey to the modern world. Compared with this his share in the Lutheran conflict seems to me to be, in a serious appraisement of Erasmus, as unimportant as it was to himself distasteful.'[153] That was in its time an unusual judgment. Woodward describes the familiar outlines of Erasmus' advice on the teaching and learning of languages and on coming to terms with the ancient authors. He also recognizes the limitations of this purely literary culture. Here was an education lack-

ing in history (in any modern sense), in serious philosophy, and
– most sobering of all – in natural science. 'Next to their value
as literary adornment, natural phenomena had interest for Erasmus as analogies and parables for moral edification.' Yet the
expression 'purely literary' is misleading. The supreme end of
education for Erasmus as for Woodward was character. 'The nar-
rowing influence of a certain type of literary education, in the
direction, he means, of disqualifying the studious for active interests in life, he much deprecates. For "action" is the end of
education, with Erasmus not less than with the great Italian Masters of the Quattrocento.'[154]

There were substantial agreements among the writers on Erasmus and education around the end of the nineteenth century. To
repeat these at any length would be otiose. They are agreed that
for him the classical civilization was the substance of education,
the child was its end and subject, its aims and methods were
practical and sociable. The last, in particular, links this body of
writing with the works treated in the last section. In both, Erasmus
appears as active reformer, not distancing himself from the everyday problems of his age in the interests of learning or self-cul-
tivation but rather deeply enmeshed in its struggles. The books
on education also raise the question of Erasmus' modernity. That
is in the sense, not of the contemporary Christian society for
whose sake he challenged the Ciceronians, but rather of the world
inhabited by the writers themselves – on this side of the Enlightenment, the romantic movement and the scientific revolution. As
Paulsen was demonstrating, this spate of writing on Erasmus'
pedagogy was contemporaneous with challenges to the educational system founded on the languages and literatures of the
ancient world.[155] What could he have to say to the modern world
about the substance of education? Nevertheless, the sense for the
capacities and feelings of the growing child which struck these
writers as modern still impresses readers of Erasmus.

III

Erasmus' childhood, youth, and early manhood posed difficult
and (before the appearance of the first volume of P.S. Allen's
magisterial edition of the letters in 1906) virtually insoluble problems for the biographer and historian. Nevertheless serious debate about these problems had begun well before the end of the

nineteenth century. More important for our study of Erasmus interpretations is the place of beginnings in the historical thinking of the nineteenth century: later societies were thought to be in embryo in remote primitive communities; the whole man was found in the influences on and the experiences of the child and youth. Thus between 1860 and 1930 there was a body of writing on the young Erasmus to put beside the larger, more obsessed literature of the same period (and after) on the young Luther. The main question raised was the relative importance of the various influences on Erasmus' mind – a secularizing classical humanism, the pious movement centred in particular on the Netherlands and called the *devotio moderna*, or the ideas mediated by his English friends (be they Neoplatonism learned in Italy, biblical humanism home-grown in Oxford, or proto-Protestantism). Further, one asked: in what direction was his mind moving – from unguarded enthusiasm for pagan antiquity towards a commitment to religious renewal (thanks to John Colet and others); from medievalism (represented by his monastic vow and scholastic studies) towards more liberal and critical attitudes; from a search for personal cultivation and gratification in his studies to a sense of social responsibility? Those were among the possibilities.

At Brussels in 1864 Charles Ruelens of the royal library of Belgium reproduced photolithographically Erasmus' book of poems *Silva carminum* first published at Gouda in 1513. He added an introduction on Erasmus' youth and early works, presenting the whole in a beautiful format and including representations of Gouda and Steyn – places belonging to Erasmus' youth – from a late sixteenth-century atlas. Ruelens' work must be seen within that revival of interest in Erasmus in Belgium during the middle and later decades of the nineteenth century which we have discussed elsewhere.[156] He follows Erasmus' early life primarily from the *Compendium vitae* whose authenticity as an autobiography of Erasmus was soon to be sharply contested. He seeks at the same time to indicate what his experiences meant to Erasmus and so to fill in the larger picture of the world to which he belonged. Thus he lingers over the school at Deventer, which he associates fully with the Brethren of the Common Life and the piety they represented. The aim of such places, he says, was to be 'a school of mysticism rather than of profane studies.' Yet, despite their original intention the Brethren came to advance secular instruction and opened new horizons for many students. Teachers were led on by curiosity and eventually had word of the revival of letters in Italy. The rector of the school Alexander Hegius contributed more than any other to Erasmus' intellectual development (in view of Erasmus' own limited claim to acquaintance with Hegius in the *Compendium vitae*, this must be counted an exaggeration). Ruelens is on surer ground in recalling the prediction of Erasmus' future success by Jan Synthen, another teacher at the school, of whom Erasmus himself, however, said little.[157] Ruelens recounts without accepting the authenticity of the story (perhaps begun by Melanchthon) that the great humanist Agricola visited the school and also prophesied greatness for the young Erasmus.[158] The latter, says Ruelens concluding his discussion of that stage of his life, wrote his first poem – the *Carmen bucolicum* – at Deventer.[159]

The other stage treated by Ruelens is, of course, Erasmus' years in the monastery. In fact his essay begins with a history of the district and monastery at Steyn on the right bank of the Yssel, 'a land humid and unhealthy.' Unavoidably he follows Erasmus' own accounts of these years and also speaks of his earliest writings. Of the small studious group in the monastery Erasmus was the centre, although Ruelens recognizes the influence of another, older monk, Cornelis Gerard (a relative of Erasmus' friend Willem Hermans), who lived elsewhere.[160] Amid these associations Erasmus wrote his first attack on the (scholastic) 'barbarians,' cultivated his interest in Lorenzo Valla (the two, says Ruelens, were 'également savants, également frondeurs'), and established himself as a poet. In Ruelens' view the poetry is superior to the early prose. The *Oratio funebris in funere Bertae de Heyen* (c 1489), for example, was a very unequal work, essentially rhetorical, wavering between the cold and the sentimental and lacking 'that free manner, that spontaneity, that very lively spirit' characteristic of Erasmus' later works.[161] Many of his poems, Ruelens concludes, were also exercises but others express his deeper feelings, especially his affliction and regrets at the life of monastic constraint. He fulfilled the duties of that life but without a sense of vocation: 'the independence of his character, an instinct of superiority made him little disposed to passive obedience.'[162]

Ruelens' essay depicts an Erasmus familiar to nineteenth-century readers, the independent individual impatient of constraint. His contribution lay in a more leisurely treatment than appears even in the larger biographies of the man's early experiences and early writings. There is also a sense of local landscape and local community. A contribution of a different kind to the study of the young Erasmus was made by Johannes Benedictus Kan (1831–1902), rector for twenty-three years of the Gymnasium Erasmianum in Rotterdam (1873–96). It was of a critical and argumentative kind. Kan was a strong personality who powerfully advanced the interests of his school – through a building program and the promotion of coeducation, for example – and was also active in community organizations.[163] At the same time he wrote a series of brief studies (published in the *Programma litterarium* of his school or in the Rotterdam press) on Erasmus.[164] In the most important of these he raised issues about his parentage, birth, and childhood through a critical study of the *Compendium vitae*, his purported autobiography.[165]

It is necessary, Kan says, to examine critically sources which successive biographers, often aping one another, have slavishly followed. His purpose is to cast doubt on matters taken for granted and, incidentally, to arouse the interest of Rotterdamers in the story of their great countryman at a time when other countries are taking the lead in Erasmus studies.[166] His conclusion is that the *Compendium vitae* was a 'pious deception,' fabricated by friendly hands to protect Erasmus' reputation and, above all, to disguise the fact – Kan thought it a fact – that his father was a priest when he was conceived. The broken style of the piece and its use of the third person betrayed its character; its tone also was wrong, as in the inordinately unfavourable account of Erasmus' schooldays. The first editor of the work, Paullus Merula at Leiden, in the early seventeenth century was more deceived than deceiver.[167] Later – for a time – Kan took a harsher view of Merula (he then accused him of forging the document), but he did not persist in that judgment.[168]

Kan was naturally not satisfied with merely local publication of his views and circulated his papers among students of Erasmus in various countries. It was an early example of that community of scholars of which P.S. Allen was to become the centre and which was to expand (for good or ill) into the international scholarship of more recent times. He corresponded with men whose names are already familiar – Nève, Nolhac, Horawitz, Hartfelder – and with others soon to be known to us – Wilhelm Vischer, Arthur Richter, Max Reich, Joseph Lupton; he knit a bond between Rotterdam and Basel in the study of Erasmus. He did not convince all his correspondents.[169] He has not convinced later scholars; Allen accepted the authenticity of the *Compendium vitae*.[170] It has remained a puzzle and, though opinions have differed to the present, the balance seems to be in Merula's favour.[171] Nevertheless Kan had done a service in posing problems which future biographers must address. 'Eternal praise shall you receive,' Horawitz wrote to the Rotterdam schoolmaster, 'because you were the first to take this matter in hand.'[172]

Kan sought – through the publications of the school that bore his name in the city of his birth – to stir the interest of Rotterdamers in Erasmus. In the other Rhine city with a special place in his history Erasmus was, as we have seen, much studied.[173] Manuscripts in the university library at Basel relating to Erasmus' early life were published in 1876, partly in response to inquiries from Horawitz as he gathered materials for his projected biography of Erasmus, partly for a rectoral celebration. Years before as a young librarian Wilhelm Vischer had begun copying Erasmus manuscripts in the library.[174] In the meantime after notable service to the library, Vischer had turned more to history (he had become professor of history in 1874). As a historian he argued for the undoctrinaire, source-critical method of his German teachers, above all Georg Waitz at Göttingen (Vischer introduced the Rankean seminar to Basel).[175] His publication of the Erasmus sources was a congenial undertaking for Vischer: it produced hitherto unpublished materials; it made a Basel contribution to the development of exact studies on Erasmus; it recalled a figure with whom Vischer's conservative but humane temperament must have had some sympathy.

The documents published were significant ones in Erasmus' biography: the dispensations that he had sought in 1516 from Pope Leo X through his friend Andrea Ammonio, papal tax collector in England. They were from censures arising from Erasmus' abandonment of the habit of his order many years before and from the bars his illegitimacy put in the way of his holding benefices. The documents in the Basel library were the originals and once, of course, in Erasmus' possession.[176]

The interpretation of these documents depends on one's understanding of the earlier documents to which they were the response, above all the famous letter to Grunnius (a fictitious papal secretary), Erasmus' first attempt at an autobiography which had accompanied his appeal to Rome.[177] Vischer contends that this account of Erasmus' case and the purported reply of Grunnius were composed later and intended to leave the public with the impression that he was wholly emancipated from his order.[178] He argues further that the papal dispensation was important to Erasmus not as a defence against demands that he return to the monastery (such demands belonged to the past) but as a shelter in the storm awakened by his New Testament published some months before. Erasmus, Vischer concludes, saw that his relation to his order, his status as a monk (possibly one of apostasy), was a weak point in any enemy attack.[179] On the larger plane of Erasmus interpretations, which is our interest, Vischer relates Erasmus and these documents of his personal history to the public controversy in which he was engaged; it has Erasmus acting tactically, defensively, working on public opinion, clearing the ground of secondary issues. This publication, besides adding to knowledge of Erasmus' early life (notably of his relation to his order), contributes to the recognition of Erasmus as a public figure in his time. It touches the liberal tradition in the place it gives to Erasmus' search for independence.

We come to the book which has a fair claim to being the most influential work on Erasmus in the second half of the nineteenth century, Frederic Seebohm's *The Oxford Reformers John Colet, Erasmus, and Thomas More: Being a History of Their Fellow-Work*.[180] The unusual expression 'Fellow-Work' indicates the author's intention. It was, he says in the preface to the first edition of 1867, not to write three biographies but to trace the 'joint-history' of three men.[181] Hence also its form: the opening chapters demonstrate their convergence in the (incorrect) year 1498, and thereafter their activities are, so to speak, interleaved and, naturally, their meetings and correspondence treated at length.

The argument of the work may be concisely stated. At the very end of the fifteenth century there commenced at Oxford a movement for practical Christian reform. It stemmed from the experiences of John Colet, an English student and cleric of good family, on a journey to Italy in the 1490s. There he had studied the scriptures and observed both the deepest corruption of Christianity (in the papacy of Alexander VI) and the best promise of its renewal (in the revival of biblical and patristic learning and a Platonism warmed by the reforming zeal of Savonarola). But Colet was not only a scholar: 'he came back from Italy, not a mere Neo-Platonic philosopher or "humanist", but a practical Reformer.'[182]

The first overt act of the reform movement was his lectures on Paul's epistles at his return to Oxford, wherein he read Paul as a man addressing the practical needs of other men, avoided scholastic complexity in interpretation, and went for the literal sense of the text. Generally his outlook was progressive; breaking out of the closed world of the scholastics, he 'entered into the spirit of the new era.' He came to adhere to an alternative Christianity, concentrated on scripture and the apostles' creed, not averse to free enquiry, and summed up not in propositions but a person.[183]

Erasmus became involved in the reform movement (we are following the thread of Seebohm's argument) when he came to Oxford and immediately found friendship with Colet. His restless mind, too, was seeking freedom, though in so far as theology interested him at all he was still a scholastic. Colet's hope of 'fellow-feeling' turning into 'fellow-work' seemed dashed when Erasmus returned to Europe in 1500 with but a promise to support Colet when his own mind was matured. They lost touch but Erasmus had not forgotten. 'His intercourse with Colet at Oxford had changed the current of his thoughts, and the course of his life. Colet little knew by what slow and painful steps he had been preparing to redeem the promise he had made on leaving Oxford.'[184] The *Enchiridion* was a first demonstration of Erasmus' solidarity with Colet – in its insistence that religion consisted, not in scholastic dogma or in ceremony, but in 'a true self-sacrificing loyalty to Christ.' Fulfilment came in the writings of 1515–16, the *Adagia* of 1515 whose political essays showed that Erasmus was 'no mere bookworm' but a down-to-earth reformer and, supremely, the New Testament edition of 1516 which had the same purpose as Colet's lectures of twenty years before – to set a third alternative to Italian scepticism and the blind bigotry of the scholastic theologians. 'He believed, with Colet, that there *was* a Christianity which rested on facts and not upon speculation, and which therefore had nothing to do with the dogmatic theology of the Schoolmen on the one hand, and nothing to fear from free enquiry on the other.' Similarly, the *Utopia* of Thomas More disclosed 'the visions of hope and progress floating before the eyes of the Oxford Reformers' and their faith in the harmony of nature and religion.[185] Both Erasmus and More accepted Colet (become dean of St Paul's) as leader of the reform movement.

The nature of their program is already evident. The Oxford Reformers sought a church broad and tolerant as among the Utopians; their underlying assumption was that many points of doctrine are uncertain, 'mere hypotheses, which in their nature never *can* be verified.' This determined their reaction to Luther's Reformation which was dogmatically Augustinian. Seebohm has, in fact, a Gibbonian view of the Reformation: 'Even the Protestant Reformers, whilst on the one hand bravely breaking the yoke under which their ancestors had lived in bondage, ended by fixing another on the neck of their posterity.' They reimposed dogmas like the plenary inspiration of scripture and the necessity of ecclesiastical authority from which the Oxford Reformers, in going back behind Augustine and the 'patristic hypotheses,' had liberated themselves and others. The nineteenth century, Seebohm concludes, has had to start again on the quest for freedom; the sixteenth-century authorities refused the path opened by the Oxford Reformers and thus turned reform into dogmatic and violent revolution.[186]

Even on the book's own terms there are gaps in Seebohm's argument.[187] Colet's influence on Erasmus is taken for granted rather than demonstrated; it is certainly not weighed against other possible influences. Erasmus' life before his meeting with Colet is barely sketched. He came to that meeting on Seebohm's account virtually unformed.[188] Again, that Erasmus, Colet, and More were of one mind on issues of reform has, to a degree, to be taken on trust here. Their friendship is not, of course, in doubt, but that does not make them, as Seebohm wishes, a reforming circle, the instigators together of a movement ahead of and, for a time, rival to the Wittenberg Reformation. That hypothesis needed more searching investigation, to say the least.

One must then ask why the book had the influence it did. It carried conviction as a work of scholarship; annotation and referencing appear meticulous.[189] Further, in locating Erasmus in a congenial and active circle, a kind of reform party, Seebohm met an emerging need in Erasmus scholarship (considered earlier in this chapter), the need to place Erasmus in precise historical contexts. To make his English friendships the decisive experience of his life was naturally appealing to English patriotism. Actually in these views Seebohm had had predecessors in England, White Kennett and Samuel Knight in the eighteenth century and James Hamilton in his own time.[190] But in any case the argument for Colet as the primary influence on Erasmus' theological development was widely accepted among European scholars at the

end of the nineteenth century, largely on the strength of Seebohm's work. It met another need current in Erasmus scholarship,
the need to explain the outlook and commitments of the mature
Erasmus. Seebohm offered a plausible explanation when other
experiences of Erasmus in youth or earlier manhood remained
obscure, if not wholly in the dark. Over all, Seebohm's adherence
to the liberal tradition made his views appealing to his time. As
we have seen, he judged the Protestant Reformers much as Gibbon did. This is a version of the idea of the second reformation.
For Seebohm it was a constitutional reformation whose opportunity was denied or snatched away.

Seebohm (1833–1912) was a liberal banker and a Quaker. He
was active in liberal politics, notably in the campaigns for educational reform. He took a progressive view of history. 'He was
well acquainted with the critical work achieved by science and
philosophy, but he kept up his devotion to Christianity as the
moral guide in the history of the world.'[191] The combination is
reflected in the *Oxford Reformers*. The irony is that whereas in
Seebohm's other and most distinguished historical work (on the
medieval village community) he destroyed a Whig myth, that of
early Teutonic freedom and self-government,[192] in the *Oxford
Reformers* he created a myth (also liberal in complexion), that of
the Oxford reformation and – for students of Erasmus – of the
unique significance of his Oxford and London friends for Erasmus'
place in history. It proved persuasive and lasting.

Seebohm's lacunae were filled in a work which itself evoked
a sense of unfulfilled promise. Its author, Paul Mestwerdt
(1884–1914), was wounded in the first weeks of the Great War
and, after lingering for a month, died on 25 September 1914.[193]
His work – *Die Anfänge des Erasmus: Humanismus und 'Devotio
Moderna'* – was edited by Hans von Schubert, Mestwerdt's teacher,
and published in 1917 in the depths of the war. Schubert had
directed him to Erasmus when he returned to higher studies at
Heidelberg in 1912, following his military service and his earlier
theological studies at Heidelberg (with Troeltsch among others),
at Berlin (with Harnack), and at Göttingen (with Rudolf Otto).
His father, a Hanoverian pastor, wished an academic career for
his son as offering more personal freedom than the pastorate.
Paul Mestwerdt himself remained uncertain of his future direction
to the end.[194] He was absorbed by the question of individualism,
'the problem of a liberal church.' Unlike Harnack himself the

extreme liberals (Mestwerdt thought) had no sense of the church as community; he on the contrary thought the visible church a necessity: 'That may sound Catholic, but Protestantism is not simply the negation of Catholicism but a new position which runs parallel to it.'[195] This sense of both personal freedom and visible community Mestwerdt had in common with Erasmus. Otherwise Erasmus' personality was not attractive to him. After preparing a paper on More's *Utopia* for Hermann Oncken's seminar at Heidelberg, he declared it more rewarding to study an 'original' like More than Erasmus whose originality consisted in giving heightened expression to the concerns of his time. Like many of his nineteenth-century predecessors, Mestwerdt found in Erasmus indeterminateness of mind, whereas his own inclination was towards more concentrated personalities.[196]

The aim of Mestwerdt's book, which remained incomplete, was to present Erasmus' religious development 'genetically' up to the writings accompanying the New Testament edition, which embodied his mature program, and his encounter with the Reformation. That division was traditional.[197] Despite his expression 'genetisch,' Mestwerdt (because of his view of Erasmus' mind and personality) saw this development, not as the working out of an initial idea, but rather as the drawing in and moderating of various influences upon Erasmus. This determined the character of the book. It begins with substantial chapters on Italian humanism and the *devotio moderna* and comes to Erasmus' biography only after the halfway mark. The importance of the work lies precisely there, in the range of research that made it time-consuming and exhausting for Mestwerdt himself.[198] It brought into focus features of the background to Erasmus that had, of course, been recognized before but never fully studied and had been largely neglected by Seebohm, although (as we shall see) Mestwerdt agreed with Seebohm that Erasmus' encounter with Colet in England was to be decisive. Two ideas shaped Mestwerdt's work: the idea of development, that a program or body of ideas can be understood only by tracing it from its origins; the idea (especially applicable, Mestwerdt believed, to Erasmus' case) that a personality is formed by the succeeding and overlapping influences that are at work upon it and that must be balanced out if the individual is to arrive at a personal and distinctive standpoint. In Erasmus historiography there has, he believes, been too great a concentration on his position in the Reformation and he has been judged too much from an Augustinian standpoint. The liberals from Beard and Seebohm to Dilthey, Troeltsch, and Wernle linked him too closely to an Enlightenment kind of piety.[199]

The features of Italian humanism important for Erasmus' development were, Mestwerdt says, its universalism, its use of the historical-critical method, and its emphasis on the ethical and the practical in religion. Without rejecting the authority of Christian revelation, the humanists abandoned exclusiveness, held that truth had many expressions, and recognized the claims of profane life and the autonomy and validity of intellectual and cultural activities outside the church or religion. Already in Lorenzo Valla is to be found the idea (later expressed by both Erasmus and Luther) that baptism imposed the one obligation on all Christians and that there was no place for further vows.[200] It was Valla also who by the use of critical literary and historical methods offered the promise of recovering the intentions of the apostles and the Fathers by which the contemporary church should be judged. For him and other humanists the test of a religion or philosophy was its serviceability in real life. Christianity was ethic as well as dogma. Catholic piety had, of course, already recognized this. The new element, says Mestwerdt like Dilthey, was a moral self-consciousness that went beyond mere individualism; it was linked to the idea of human dignity and freedom.[201]

By contrast the *devotio moderna*, as expressed by lay communities (especially the Brethren of the Common Life) and monastic houses in the Netherlands, was 'purely religious'; its aim was to deepen and enliven personal religion in the traditional Catholic sense. Despite its obvious conservatism, however, the movement was in Mestwerdt's view open to new influences and itself a promoter of change. That was due to the inwardness of its piety, the emphasis (as in humanism) on the personal and the ethical; it could then seem indifferent to structures, ecclesiastical and dogmatic, and atheological. Its biblicism – 'the crucial positive characteristic of the devout theology' – was less a statement about the authority of scripture than a way of personal edification. The combination of conservatism and openness in the *devotio moderna* Mestwerdt styles a passive radicalism. On one side there was denial of the world, on the other opportunities for lay people in religious and social service which threatened, at least obliquely, the special place of the monastic life in the church.[202]

The *devotio moderna* could, therefore, in some of its aspects be a channel of humanism. The link was a common interest in the education of youth and in particular an education aimed at the moral development of the individual. Coming from different directions humanism and *devotio moderna* arrived, Mestwerdt says, at similar religious and ethical positions; they both regretted the fossilizing of Christianity in dogmas and structures and wished, above all through the study of the scriptures, to make piety more direct, personal, and practical. The seed of Italian humanism fell on prepared ground.[203]

The second part of Mestwerdt's book on Erasmus beginnings argues that at school and in the monastery – despite the negative account he himself gave of those experiences – Erasmus was able to draw from the channel linking humanism and the *devotio moderna*. He imbibed a conservative kind of humanism represented above all by Alexander Hegius, the rector of his school at Deventer. In the next stage of his life (in the service of the bishop of Cambrai), which was a time of relative freedom, he adopted a more independent humanism and exploited to the full the common ground between the humanist and devout inheritances. This phase found expression in his work against the barbarians (*Antibarbari*). A third stage, his studies in scholastic theology at Paris, appears in Mestwerdt's work as an anticlimax. The account of a further stage, his meeting with Colet and its outcomes, including the composition of the *Enchiridion*, which was to be the true climax of this volume, unhappily remained unwritten.[204]

Mestwerdt uses the critical work of the previous generation – that of Ruelens, Vischer, and Robert Fruin[205] – and the appearance in 1906 of the first volume of Allen's edition of Erasmus' correspondence to question the received account (based on Erasmus' own retrospective descriptions) of his early experiences and intellectual development. Above all he saw the letter to Grunnius as a reworked polemic against monasticism and of limited value as a source for Erasmus' biography. In fact, Erasmus (says Mestwerdt) owed more to the Brethren than he admitted – especially his enthusiasm for learning – and was more accepting of the monastic life than he later said. The monastery offered him opportunity for study, and the correspondence of the monastic years demonstrates the assurance he had already achieved in criticism of earlier forms of education and learning, his precocious critical sense already recognizing Valla's importance. At that time, he still shared the standpoint of Hegius: humanism was valued as a literary program and no claim was made for its moral autonomy. The *De contemptu mundi*, his most important work of those years, by and large represented that standpoint, although his avowed affinity with the practical and moral rather than the contemplative and mystical elements in the *devotio moderna* and his essentially pragmatic defence of monasticism (to the extent of seconding Valla's appeal to Epicurus) betokened a shift towards seeing issues of religion and learning more *sub specie humanitatis* and consequently towards a more autonomous humanism.[206]

The *Antibarbari* of 1494 took a long step in that direction. Mestwerdt underlines the influence upon it of Erasmus' friend Jacob Batt, town secretary of Bergen; in him (says Mestwerdt) he met for the first time a Renaissance man of the world. The setting of the dialogue was no longer monastic but civil and bourgeois.[207] The central theme was the relation of religion and learning and Batt the main speaker. To say that virtue and learning are two different things, Batt remarks, is to allot learning its own independent place. But is not the commendation of learning to Christians a break with the essential simplicity of the Christian religion and a return to the excessive intellectualism for which Erasmus (in line with both humanism and the *devotio moderna*) condemned the scholastics? Through Batt as mouthpiece Erasmus responds with a paradox: only one who has mastered learning can make a sacrifice of it for the sake of Christian simplicity. Mestwerdt describes this as 'an audacious paradox behind which there lies concealed a real solution to the problem of religion and culture.' The dialogue's conclusion represents for Mestwerdt a main stage in Erasmus' intellectual development: Christian truth and pagan truth are both of godly origin; Christianity and culture are not in contradiction or in a hierarchy; religion is in ceaseless dialogue with the independent expressions of human learning and culture.[208]

The final chapter of *Die Anfänge des Erasmus* as we now have it may be reported briefly. The Paris period, in Mestwerdt's view, represented no progress in Erasmus' struggle with the problem of religion and culture, piety and learning. His work in praise of marriage (*Encomium matrimonii*) continued the *Antibarbari*'s acceptance of the human and natural, indeed applied to sexuality the principle the latter applied to learning.[209] Otherwise his associations in Paris were with the representatives of a conservative humanism based in the monasteries; he wanted a church reform

346 The Nineteenth Century and After

in the spirit of the *devotio moderna*, not rigorist or merely traditional but at least open to humanism. On the negative side, Mestwerdt concludes, Paris confirmed the hostility to scholasticism instilled in Erasmus by both *devotio moderna* and humanism. The last surviving words of Mestwerdt's study indicate the course his argument would have taken in the missing chapters: 'The decisive impulse was given by Lord Mountjoy's invitation to accompany him to England and the consequent meeting with John Colet.'[210]

Mestwerdt's is a major work in the history of Erasmus scholarship. Erasmus is presented as the bearer, moderator, and furtherer of existing tendencies in humanism and the *devotio moderna* and as one promising to raise them (so to speak) to a higher power. Mestwerdt was the first to treat these tendencies at length in relation to Erasmus and to one another. For him neither Italian humanism nor the *devotio moderna* broke with the medieval Catholic religion but both moved out beyond its confines, posed the problem of the relation between Christianity and culture or learning, and suggested solutions. Through his experiences in youth and early manhood, his studies and associations, Erasmus took over the problem and sought a more integral solution. Like Seebohm Mestwerdt believed that only at the meeting with Colet did Erasmus finally absorb, master, and combine these tendencies in a distinctive way, thus becoming himself the teacher of his generation. But Mestwerdt's results were better balanced than Seebohm's (or would have been so if his work had been completed) because he took in view a range of influences and did not follow one channel alone. Erasmus' early work, he argues, revealed in differing proportions the influences upon him, the *De contemptu mundi* predominantly the devout, and the *Antibarbari* predominantly the humanist influences; gradually he was learning to knit together themes which both affirmed nature and the world and maintained the Christian faith. These ideas he would apply in time to problems of reform.

In summary the work's significance was twofold. First it placed the young Erasmus in a large historical context and thus overcame the too narrow concentration of previous biography. Second, while for Mestwerdt Erasmus lacked a strongly self-directed character and preferred to harmonize contrasting views rather than decide sharply among them,[211] he yet saw him as working through to a distinctive position full of promise for reform. That position was largely determined by two major intellectual or spiritual movements and was not merely imperfect Protestantism or imperfect Catholicism. The book remains of course, a great torso. Yet it defined orthodoxy on the young Erasmus for fifty years: his mind was formed by common strands from Italian humanism and *devotio moderna*, finally knit together by the Oxford theology of John Colet (as seen by Frederic Seebohm).[212]

IV

This work is concerned with interpretations of Erasmus from the Enlightenment to the 1920s. Its centre of interest lies in the uses – often in contemporary controversy – to which Erasmus' name and reputation have been put in succeeding generations. Interpretations appear here as assemblings of original material, past commentary, and personal judgment usually shaped to a present purpose. The work rests therefore on the assumption that there is a connection between the observers' own biographies and historical situations and their responses to the historical figure Erasmus. It takes its form from that assumption. It is a study of individual authors grouped by their commitments and associations, though it is recognized – in the titles of many chapters, for example – that the various groupings can be related to distinct problems in Erasmus interpretation; liberals confront Erasmus' scepticism, Protestant writers his attitude to the Reformation, Catholics his relation to the Catholic tradition, and so on. The relativism of this approach is qualified also by the recognition that there are indisputable advances in scholarship, for example in the identification, dating, arrangement, and publication of sources like Erasmus' letters. These are not the subject of this work but they require attention as they affect the history of Erasmus interpretation. We have already noted the increasing pace of such advances in the second half of the nineteenth century. Others are dealt with in this section, sometimes more briefly than the scale of the scholarly accomplishment might require; that is because attention here remains concentrated on Erasmus interpretations.

By the last part of the nineteenth century Erasmus studies generally were being conducted in a more scholarly and critical spirit. There were, as we have seen, more contacts between scholars and more exchanges in print. Two scholars may be taken as representative of this development, Ludwig Geiger (1848–1919) in

Germany and Robert Fruin (1823–99) in the Netherlands. Son of a Rabbi leader in the Jewish reform movement, himself a representative in Berlin affairs of the radical–liberal side of politics, Geiger, while a student in Paris, had translated Renan into German.[213] He was then a liberal and a rationalist. The important point is that by upbringing and conviction he stood outside the frameworks, the Protestant evangelical and the Catholic ultramontane, that had constrained Erasmus interpretation in Germany during the nineteenth century. Fruin, who held the chair of Dutch history at Leiden from 1860 to 1894, was also a liberal.[214] He represented above all a confident, critical historical positivism. His ideal was, from an unchallengeable knowledge of the sources, to achieve an exact understanding of events and processes, seen as 'neutral objects of observation.' 'Most of Fruin's writings were the result of his urge to correct the conceptions of others who knew less and were less critical.'[215] Though Erasmus was never a subject of primary interest for him, the ambiguous sources of Erasmus' biography and the excessively subjective and partisan literature about him were a tempting target.

In a review article of 1875 on recent writings on the history of humanism, Geiger set out conditions for a successful biography of Erasmus: a man so immersed in the history of his times must be placed in the widest historical context; the life and the work of a man whose writings arose so naturally out of events and experiences must not be treated separately. These specifications summed up the standpoint of the historical discipline as it had developed in the nineteenth century. They anticipated departures in Erasmus interpretation from Maurenbrecher on. But in Geiger's view none of the biographies he was reviewing came up to them. Durand de Laur, for example, failed on both counts: his treatment of historical context was thin and he handled life and works in two distinct parts; his division into chapters was arbitrary; he failed to master the bulk of his material and relied on over-long quotations. Drummond was superior on every count and especially in presenting well-rounded chapters where life and writings were discussed together, although he too quoted excessively. That of the three biographers of the 1870s Drummond was superior to Durand de Laur and Feugère was the common judgment of late nineteenth-century scholarship, and still stands. As for Stichart's work on Erasmus' views on church and Reformation, it exemplified in Geiger's view the fallacy of gathering excerpts without respect to logic or chronology.[216]

Despite his critical independence, Geiger shared the preferences and prejudices of his age. He made much of nationality and was at pains to prove Erasmus a German. A study of his relations with German humanism, Geiger adds, is a serious lack in contemporary scholarship.[217] Another need is for 'a penetrating psychological study.' Geiger's own characterization of Erasmus is not markedly different from others in the nineteenth century. Dominant in his expression was the satiric turn of the mouth. He had a volatile and impressionable nature in which feelings of love and hate quickly succeeded one another. He was touchy like other self-made men. The adulation of others and physical weakness combined to make him both confident and prudent. Geiger sums up his character with the expression from the *Letters of Obscure Men* which has been taken as title for this book: *homo pro se*.[218] The emphasis on independence and on nervous sensibility is reminiscent of Pattison's.

Above all Geiger puts the liberal view of Erasmus in its most advanced form. Essentially, says Geiger, he was an agnostic. His was not a Christian-Catholic, indeed not a religious, nature. In discussing the *Moriae encomium*, for example, the critic and historian should not be shy of going behind Erasmus' own disclaimers and uncovering intentions which he himself wished to conceal. This work was anticlerical and in a certain sense antireligious. The contradiction between Erasmus and Luther was not that between Catholic and Protestant but that between *philosophe* and theologian. Erasmus' biblical scholarship belonged, not to theology, but to philology and literary criticism. The distinction betrays the bias of Geiger's mind. Against Protestant charges of Erasmus' inconsistency before and after Luther's appearance, he accepts Hagen's case that he was a consistent freethinker, an exponent of humanist radicalism.[219]

Personal judgments are no so apparent in Fruin's 'Erasmiana.' Its purpose seems strictly scholarly. Like Geiger, Fruin considered Drummond's the best of the Erasmus biographies but thought the state of scholarship would remain unsatisfactory until the materials were better ordered and scholars began to trace Erasmus' development through the various editions of his works. Fruin argues in particular against Kan's rejection of the *Compen-*

dium vitae. One must, he remarks, distinguish between genuineness and credibility; the *Compendium* could contain inaccuracies
and even untruths and still be written by Erasmus. It does in fact,
Fruin goes on, include details that could have been known only
to Erasmus, not even to people as well informed as Merula and
his friends. Its form and style were consistent with Erasmus' purpose: to provide his friend Conradus Goclenius with notes for
defending his reputation in case of his death and, above all, to
put in the most favourable light the circumstances of his birth.
(These and Erasmus' apprehensions have, says Fruin, been illu-
minated by Vischer's publication.) Its reticences, notably about
Erasmus' older brother Pieter, confirm – for Fruin – its genuineness, if also Erasmus' lack of candour.[220]

The *Compendium vitae*, like the letter to Grunnius, had another
purpose: to demonstrate Erasmus' forced entry into, and his miserable experience of, the monastery as part of a strategy against
demands for his return. Fruin is sceptical about Erasmus' account:
his depiction of his guardians is implausible; his earliest correspondence shows that the cloister served Erasmus and his friends
as a training school in letters (the *De Contemptu mundi* confirms
the impression); indeed he could complete his studies in Paris
only because of his preparation in a Dutch cloister.[221]

Fruin's acumen and professionalism were persuasive on the
main issues, the authenticity of the *Compendium vitae* and the
prudence required in reading it and Erasmus' other autobiographical pieces. His arguments for ordering the texts and reading them
in context anticipate the age of exact scholarship. When Merula
published the *Compendium vitae*, Fruin says at one point, there
was of course no one around to challenge its assertions; 'only the
criticism of our day is called to separate the wheat from the chaff
and throw the chaff where it belongs.'[222]

Yet it would be mistaken to find no personal or subjective
element in Fruin's essay. There is here a coldness towards Erasmus that may arise from a critical examination of the texts but is
also, one suspects, a matter of temperament. After expressing (as
did Drummond) incredulity over Erasmus' account (in his letter
to Servatius Rogerus) of his abandonment at Bologna of the garb
of his order, Fruin remarks sarcastically: 'Here and everywhere
it is the same: what Erasmus has done contrary to his duty and
his well understood interest is the fault of circumstances and

wrong advice; he is himself never to blame.'[223] That is not a judgment of exact scholarship.

Fruin's noble hope for the ordering of the materials of Erasmus' life, especially his correspondence, was fulfilled only with the appearance in 1906 of the first volume of Allen's *Opus episto-larum*, a work 'carried on under the gloom of Indian summers and in high valleys in Kashmir.' Allen paid tribute to 'the toil of many predecessors, whose years have failed in preliminary preparations and into whose labours I have been permitted to enter.'[224] An early attempt – as gallant as it was unsuccessful – had been made in 1829 by the Schleswiger J. Gaye (as we have seen).[225] In the 1880s Horawitz not only gathered letters and published them himself but encouraged the works of others, including Vischer and Kan.[226] Erasmus scholars, as we have already noticed, were becoming a community. Of three serious contributions around the end of the century, two were German and one English – those of Arthur Richter (1891), Max Reich (1895), and F.M. Nichols, the first volume of whose English translation with commentary appeared in 1901. Allen acquired Reich's notes from his widow and shared Nichols' companionship on 'the ground in which I have been allowed to glean after him.'[227]

Both Richter (1862–1925) and Allen remarked that in these labours a literary was giving way to a historical arrangement of Erasmus' letters.[228] That registered the shift produced by the historical revolution of the nineteenth century. Richter's work dealing with the earliest and (as to dating) most difficult part of Erasmus' correspondence was a listing of 190 letters with summaries and some reference to the critical literature. Richter did not claim to offer a study of Erasmus' intellectual development. Yet the work contains notes of considerable interest. Thus Richter sees Erasmus' praise of Christian authors in a letter to Hendrik van Bergen of 7 November 1496 as indicative of his gradual change from mere humanist to theologian and enlightened reformer of the Catholic church; that means – against Maurenbrecher (and, we might add, Seebohm) – that the English visit at the end of the decade and Colet's influence produced not a new departure but a strengthening and confirmation of a change already well advanced.[229] In an appendix Richter challenges received opinion by arguing for Erasmus' knowledge of vernacular languages, notably Dutch and French; the comedy of manners he wrote depended on acquaintance with the language of the people.[230] Well before the appearance of Luther's German Bible Erasmus had spoken out for vernacular translations.[231] Though not attempting anything like a biography, Arthur Richter showed a sound critical sense on important issues. Nichols, who (like Allen) disagreed with particular datings, 'found ample occasion to appreciate his care and diligence in the illustration of his subject.'[232]

The Berlin dissertation of Max Reich (1866–1904) complemented Richter's work by dealing with letters from a later period of Erasmus' life, 1509–18. Every letter, he argues, if seen in its proper context, makes its contribution to understanding a historical character as volatile and controversial as Erasmus. Errors in received datings for the period 1509–18 ranged from one day to fifteen years.[233] In an accompanying narrative Reich touches on issues in Erasmus' biography. In particular he reconsiders the papal dispensation of 1516 which Vischer had published. It was intended, he says, to be a defence against enemies at Louvain who were working to destroy his credit at the Habsburg court in Brussels. Against Vischer Reich accepts the genuineness of the letter to Grunnius, though he sees it as edited and transmitted by Ammonio, Erasmus' friend in London.[234] The balance of opinion has favoured his argument for the letter's genuineness. Of his further view that Grunnius was a real person, he has convinced no one.[235]

While Richter and Reich represented professional scholarship and presented their work on Erasmus for higher degrees, Francis Morgan Nichols (1826–1915) was described by Allen as 'an amateur in the best sense of the word.'[236] Nevertheless he had served an apprenticeship in exact scholarship with his publication (1865) of the thirteenth-century law treatise attributed to John Britton. He became barrister-at-law at the Inner Temple in 1852. He had taken second-class honours in literae humaniores at Oxford in 1847 and was a fellow of Wadham College 1849–56. His other publications related to the Roman forum and to Lawford Hall, his home in Essex which had once belonged to Mountjoy, Erasmus' friend and patron. That connection led him to Erasmus.[237] He was approaching seventy when he began editing the letters. Allen and Nichols were cooperating early in the work of both of them; Allen was grateful in particular for Nichols' recognition of the significance of the Compendium vitae and the other biographical material.[238]

Allen's tribute to Nichols is fitting. The latter's publication was quickly overshadowed by that of his great successor, though it remained (up to the appearance of the Toronto edition) useful to English readers. As numerous notes of Allen's indicate, Nichols' work was skilfully done and his judgment was sound.

His object was to order the letters, and the result is presented summarily in a 'Chronological Register of the Epistles of Erasmus' (to December 1517).[239] There follow translations of letters to and from Erasmus in whole or in part, the principle of selection being biographical: 'No passage having an important bearing on the mind or history of the writer is suppressed.'[240] The linking commentary – some of its sections are small essays – assesses the value of the various letters for the student of Erasmus' life; in itself the commentary assembles the stuff of an Erasmus biography.

The substantial introduction begins with a comment on Erasmus as letter-writer: his is an 'inimitable epistolary style, the prevailing character of which is its lightness and flexibility, passing readily from grave to gay, and reflecting every shade of feeling, with a charming air of confidence in his correspondent.'[241] It finishes with an account of places especially associated with Erasmus and a translation (at least in part) of the prefaces of the published collections of Erasmus' letters up to Merula's of 1607. Much of it deals with issues that, since Vischer, Kan, and Fruin, had been crucial in Erasmus biography: the genuineness of the *Compendium vitae*, the value of the letters to Grunnius and Servatius Rogerus.

Nichols considers the broken style of the *Compendium vitae* exactly what a forger would have struggled to avoid. Like Fruin he finds recorded there (and in the letters accompanying it in Merula's publication) events and circumstances authenticated elsewhere and more likely to be known to the assumed author than to a fabricator a century later.[242] On balance Nichols accepts likewise (on internal evidence and because of contemporary reference to it) the authenticity of the important letter of 1514 to his one-time friend and present superior Servatius Rogerus, though it had not been published by Erasmus and was challenged by his executors.[243] He puts the letter to Grunnius in the category of 'epistolary fiction,' while accepting completely Erasmus' authorship and rejecting Vischer's case for later composition and Reich's for the actual existence of his correspondent.[244]

One may illustrate Nichols' shrewd scholarship from his handling of aspects of Erasmus' early history already identified by
biographers as of particular interest and importance. His school
at Deventer, Nichols observes, did not, despite the assertions of
various biographers, belong to the Brethren of the Common Life
but to the chapter of St Lebuin's church.[245] Like Drummond,
Nichols is sceptical of Erasmus' black depiction of his monastic
experience: his letters reveal, not discontent, but appreciation of
the opportunities he had for study.[246] He enters a gentle correction to the claim of Knight and Seebohm that, when he first came
to Oxford (for a stay shorter than had commonly been supposed),
Erasmus was an adherent of scholasticism and was converted to
a biblical theology by Colet. Certainly, as he reported to Jodocus
Jonas in a famous pen-portrait of Colet, the latter led him to doubt
the authority of Aquinas, but otherwise he was 'already distrustful
of the Scotists.' There is simple no evidence for the first part of
Gibbon's aphorism that he learned Greek at Oxford and taught
it at Cambridge.[247]

Nichols is a man of his age in taking a particular interest in
questions of character but his conclusions are both critical and
just. It was not the translator's fault, he had warned his readers,
'if in some of his pages Erasmus falls short of the ideal presented
by biographers, who have had more liberty in the selection of
their documents.' Erasmus was inclined to be inordinately suspicious of others and too protective of his own reputation. As for
the Compendium's claim that he had a hatred of lying, his correspondence is by no means innocent of fibs. However, 'he was
habitually honest in the expression of his opinions upon subjects
in which the interests of humanity or religion were concerned.
He could not be induced to sell his support to a cause which he
did not approve; and while cautious of his personal safety, he
never surrendered his independence of judgment.'[248] Circumstances and 'the mission of enlightenment' he knew he could
accomplish might excuse even the more grotesque flatteries of
his patrons, but Nichols' 'sense of kindness and good breeding'
was affronted by his irritable attack on his faithful friend Jacob
Batt.[249] The response was characteristic of one to whom Allen
attributed a 'grave courtesy,' a power of quiet concentration on
the work in hand and a 'sane and steady outlook upon life.'[250]

The most important event in the history of modern Erasmus
scholarship was the appearance from the Clarendon Press, Ox-

ford, in 1906 of the first volume of Allen's own *Opus epistolarum Des. Erasmi Roterodami denuo recognitum et auctum*. Allen (1869–1933) had decided to make a new edition of Erasmus' letters his life's work while competing (unsuccessfully) for the Chancellor's essay prize at Oxford in 1892–3.[251] The subject set was new to Allen – Erasmus. He had taken a first in classical moderations (1890) and a second in the more philosophical *literae humaniores* (1892).[252] Froude's lectures, which he heard in Oxford after returning from a year's travel in Australia and New Zealand, heightened his enthusiasm. He had begun the work in August 1893, a month after his twenty-fourth birthday. Allen's faith in his undertaking and his sense of vocation for scholarship recall Erasmus himself, though the two temperaments were very different. His Erasmian journeys and his international contacts (first with Ferdinand Vander Haeghen and R. Vanden Berghe of Ghent, editors of the *Bibliotheca Erasmiana*) began at once; in July 1894 he travelled to Rotterdam, Gouda, Mainz, Freiburg, Strasbourg, and Schlettstadt. Even when in 1897 he took up a five-year appointment as professor of history at the government college at Lahore, his commitment did not falter. 'Here we sit,' he wrote during a holiday in Kashmir in August 1899, 'happily beneath our trees, or in the tent-verandah if it rains, poring over Erasmus.' The following summer – 'a thick dust-pall over all' – he and his wife (he had married his cousin Helen Mary Allen in 1898 and she was to be his collaborator throughout) began cutting up two copies of the London edition of Erasmus' letters of 1642 to form the foundation of the new edition. Their return through ill-health (the voyage included visits to the libraries of Rome, Venice, and Basel) was accompanied by both promise and anxiety. Allen was dependent on an allowance from his father, Joseph Allen a London bill-broker, and on short-term appointments. The Clarendon Press, advised not least by Bishop Stubbs the great medievalist, accepted the first volume for publication, but at the same time came disturbing news of rival undertakings in Holland and Germany. Above all, Max Reich was said to be under commission from the Berlin Academy to publish all Erasmus' letters. The affair ended tragically with Reich's mental breakdown and death, the Press purchasing his papers in 1905 for £25.[253]

The appearance of the first volume was a triumph of both method and temperament. Allen had, says Garrod, 'a sense for method amounting to genius; and above all, whether by nature

or by discipline, he had serenity of mind.'[254] It was also a witness
– Allen's genius, devotion, and industry aside – to the international scholarship of the generation before 1914, the invisible
college of Erasmians to whose members Allen paid tribute in his
preface and notes.

The first volume came down to July 1514 and included the
autobiographical letter of that month to Servatius Rogerus. Attached were appendices, *inter alia* settling the authenticity of the
Compendium vitae, investigating the dating of the known events
of Erasmus' early life and of various early letters, detailing the
main editions of Erasmus' correspondence, and giving an account
of two major sources, the Deventer letter-book (enclosing letters
copied in 1517–18) and the Gouda manuscripts with their authoritative versions of Erasmus' writings (discovered by Allen in
a visit to Gouda in 1905).[255] Volume followed at even pace but
for the intervention of the Great War which enforced a nine-year
gap (1913 to 1922) between volumes III and IV and for a time
broke up the invisible college. Allen felt the calamity deeply.[256]
Volume VIII was in its last stages in 1933 when he was carried
off by illness, with which he had long struggled. Honours had
pressed on Allen in the 1920s;[257] in 1924 he was elected president
of Corpus Christi College, Oxford.

Our interest is in the vision Allen had of the man and historical
figure Erasmus. He published no biography; the notes to the *Opus
epistolarum* are reticent though not utterly devoid of matter for
judgment.[258] He left fragments of a biography begun at the insistence of a friend 'who begged that those who cannot read the
Latin might also be considered.'[259] In 1914 he published under
the title *Age of Erasmus* lectures delivered at Oxford and London
and modestly described as 'sketches of the world through which
Erasmus passed.'[260] In fact they conveyed marvellously the tex-
ture of sixteenth-century life, especially for those ambitious for
education or learning. A lecture 'Erasmus' delivered at the University of Liverpool and in Holland was published at Liverpool
in 1922. Other lectures and essays (some previously published,
some not) were gathered up after his death in *Erasmus: Lectures
and Wayfaring Sketches* (1934). The mode of these pieces is reflective, the sources always present but veiled, and the style easy
and clear, though sometimes heightened. The standpoint is a
justification of a lifetime of scholarly labour in its highest form
on the correspondence of Erasmus: 'it is only in periods when

the stream of personal record flows wide and deep that history begins to live, and that we have a chance to view it through the eyes of the actors instead of projecting upon it our own fancies and conceptions.'[261]

'He was of a free spirit, fully able to command itself but chafing at control by another.' This sentence from a fragment of his unfinished biography summarizes Allen's appreciation of Erasmus.[262] In another place he says that no one 'outside the ranks of the holy' served God more devotedly but the service had to be done in his own way.[263] Escape from external constraints and achievement of a productive self-mastery: these were the main themes of Erasmus' life. Early circumstances promised only confinement or limited opportunity. Hegius' teaching and the Brethren, with their voluntary obedience and 'sweet reasonableness,' gave glimpses of a way out but only momentarily. The monastery closed off every opportunity. Allen knew that the cloister offered a consoling and creative life to many but not to all. Erasmus was of 'those unhappy souls to whom seclusion had not brought peace.'[264] He had escaped fully only when he was settled in a vocation suited to his temperament and his capacities, and he was on the threshold of middle age before that happened.

The vocation was Christian learning and to it Erasmus' commitment was complete. After his contact with Colet he saw the need: 'a more concrete and historical study of the Bible' based on dependable texts; after his first contact with Froben (1514) he understood finally how the printing-press could make scholarship a public event, create a community of scholars, and bring him to leadership within it. But his temperament was not that of the modern scholar (indeed, one might add, of Allen himself), for whom the imperatives were patience, hastening slowly, and an even tenor of mind and spirit. He relied on his gift of 'swift divination.' 'His work was always done in heat, under the passion of his demand for knowledge. He read, he wrote, *tumultuarie, praecipitanter*. When he had formed a design, he liked to carry it out *uno impetu*.'[265]

The combination of settled purpose and quickness of sympathy and mind gave Erasmus his intellectual ascendancy. His thinking was not always profound but he had 'the power to grasp important truths and to present them with cogency in spontaneous, irresistible eloquence.' His personal style was fully apparent for the first time in the expanded edition of the *Adagia* of 1508:

expatiating as occasion arises on whatever interests him with complete absence of self-consciousness. Allen calls this (apparent also in his letters published, it would seem, without regard to the unfavourable light some would cast on his character) a 'vein of expansive self-revelation.'[266] His very manuscripts (and none better than Allen could say) reveal this expansive, fluent, conversational side of his personality; drafts of his correspondents' letters show every sign of painful composition; in his, whatever their object, 'the lines flow swiftly over the page, true and even, with hardly a word corrected.' Through all, says Allen, he is never tempted to shock for mere effect.[267]

On the vexing question of Erasmus' relations with the Reformers, Allen warns first against equating virulence of language with total enmity. Erasmus himself sought common ground. At the end he saw the Reformers as seditious and enemies of good order but he might, Allen says, have thought differently if he had been able to see the orderly lives of modern Protestant churches.[268] Allen, whose family but one generation back was prominent among the Quakers, had a warm appreciation of Erasmus' appeals for peace.[269] But he also shared the nineteenth-century Protestant view that something more than an Erasmian reform was necessary to deal with the real superstitions, 'the tender and beautiful phantasies' which deceived even the true-hearted.[270] There are, however, hints of an idea deriving from the Enlightenment, that Erasmus was raising more searching questions than Luther. 'For God to him was *Via, vita, veritas*; and Truth shirks no questions, however startling.'[271]

Allen was a Protestant Englishman whose mind was formed in the last years of the Victorian era.[272] ('The more we see of the centre of Christendom,' he wrote to his sister on his first visit to Rome, 'the more we are impressed with its paganism; and we shall be quite glad to get back to a Christian country.')[273] He was devoted to the Christian tradition but his theological formulation of it was liberal. He owed to a schoolteacher (James Wilson of Clifton College) his hatred of superstition and his belief that 'theologiam nisi liberam mortuam esse.'[274] At Corpus Christi he was a regular attender at chapel but omitted the clauses of the creed which his reason or conscience could not admit. He held with Erasmus that it was not prudent to hold for certain what could not be defended from scripture, and that it was not humble to reject petulantly what Christian thought had brought forth. To the sally that all this was too Erasmian, he replied that it was not possible to be too Erasmian.[275] His unshakeable regard for Froude fits into this pattern. To the end he considered Froude's the best biography of Erasmus. What, according to Garrod, outweighed the differences in background, temperament, and outlook between the older and the younger scholar was Allen's conviction that on the main issues of the Reformation Froude was right.[276] Allen's understanding of Erasmus as above all the pioneer of free Christian scholarship is connected with these convictions. His way of writing about Erasmus, a subject heavily burdened (as we know) with quick and self-righteous judgments, is also related to a personality singularly modest, uncensorious, and accepting of the best in his friends and associates and in humanity at large.[277]

While work proceeded on Erasmus' letters culminating in the splendour of Allen's edition, scholarship was advancing also on other fronts. One was Erasmus' relations with reforming movements in different parts of Europe (already considered in this chapter). Another was Erasmus' study of the biblical text. On that front the most important work to the 1920s was the investigation of Erasmus' first two editions of the New Testament and the controversies they aroused (*Die beiden ersten Erasmus–Ausgaben des Neuen Testaments und ihre Gegner*) by August Bludau (1862–1930). In its aim of relating the editions to the struggles of the period (1517–22), this study belongs to the body of writing just mentioned. It is reminiscent in this respect of Kalkoff's work. Bludau sees these as more than scholarly controversies; they gave to those long suspicious of Erasmus an opportunity to express their resentments. The longest and bitterest controversy was that with Edward Lee, an Englishman many years younger than Erasmus who was studying at Louvain, and to it Bludau devotes more than a quarter of his work. Lee was typical of Erasmus' critics in that his attack was both textual and doctrinal; he accused Erasmus of Arianism, for example.[278] He was much junior to Erasmus in both learning and reputation, though Bludau considers him more scholarly and a better character than Erasmus would admit. His notes against the New Testament edition had, says Bludau, an appearance of learning but often lacked substance. On Erasmus' side an inspired campaign was got up against Lee; it was virulent like the other pamphlet wars of the time and often unjust. Erasmus himself was bitter against Lee and at one stage, Bludau reports, rejected More's appeal for reconciliation. The affair, he concludes, speaks badly for Erasmus' character; 'a great scholar but a little man,' he says quoting Bezold.[279] Other controversies in Bludau's view, for example those with Lefèvre d'Etaples and Eck, demonstrated Erasmus' hypersensitivity and self-regard.[280]

An interest in Erasmus' personality traits, which associates Bludau with his nineteenth-century predecessors and even at places with the unfavourable Catholic tradition represented above all by Janssen, may also be found in the other part of his work, that concerned with the editions themselves. Erasmus was led to his biblical studies more by a historical–critical need than by any religious drive.[281] Bludau traces the growth of Erasmus' interest in the undertaking, mentions the encouragement of Colet and Jean Vitrier, Erasmus' intense Franciscan friend at Saint-Omer, and above all recognizes the importance of his chance discovery of Lorenzo Valla's notes to the New Testament; the preface to his edition of that work (1505) already set out the basic principle of his editions: biblical theology must be based on a philological study of the text without presuppositions. Further, Bludau makes some assessment of the manuscripts used by Erasmus; they were, he concludes, few in number and of modest value; Erasmus had a naïve faith in the Greek text he had produced.[282] He rates Erasmus' own annotations more highly; they were a 'rich treasure of philological notes over the language, text and style of the scripture,' along with theological and exegetical explanations often drawn from the Fathers.[283] On Erasmus' scholarly methodology Bludau has relatively little to say.[284]

He is most interested in Erasmus' larger aims and the wider context of his biblical work. This, he says at one point, was no mere scholarly undertaking; it was directed at practical reforms. Mingled in the annotations with issues of authorship, exegesis, and textual authenticity were satirical observations on church practices and political conditions. They thus became a more earnest version of the *Folly*. Erasmus, Bludau adds, hated precision in theology; the ideal held up in his notes was 'the greatest possible malleability, many-sidedness and vagueness.' The reference, one is not surprised to see, is to Janssen and Bezold.[285] In summary Bludau sees this as well short of a critical edition in the modern sense; nevertheless, it was 'eine grosse That,' not because it was a manifesto to the public (as Froude mistakenly thought), but because it prepared the way for critical scholarship on the biblical books. It also, Bludau does not deny, was a stimulus (especially through the annotations) to religious revolution; it armed for battle some whom Erasmus later was to contradict. At the personal level it expressed Erasmus' 'love for the study of the Bible and his zeal for the pure preservation of the word of God.'[286]

Much in this section and the preceding one has demonstrated that, even where issues of scholarship are primary and the scholarly achievements are great (in one case magisterial), Erasmus cannot be approached or interpreted without personal commitments, attachments, or antipathies entering in. Kan and Fruin, Geiger and Bludau, Nichols and Allen all have such personal stakes in Erasmus. Some derive from temperament, some from cultural formation, some from controversial commitments. Mixed with personal judgments are the broad patterns of interpretation traced in this book and their ideological overtones. Apart from the confessional (the Catholic and Protestant) patterns which were present almost from the beginning, there have been in this period – the late nineteenth and early twentieth century – the patterns deriving respectively from the Enlightenment and romanticism. They have been in many ways but not in all contradictory.

V

In the immediate postwar years the nineteenth-century pattern in Erasmus interpretation persisted. The preoccupations of liberalism remained in the Erasmus literature, perhaps encouraged by a tenuous optimism that came with the peace. One could see projects of the time as 'conceived in a climate of post-war optimism and international amity.'[287] Nevertheless, the disillusionment that the war had brought and the revolutionary mood it engendered provoked a reaction against the Enlightenment mentality of which Erasmus was taken to be representative. This renewed the appeal of the heroic and decisive, heard first in the romantic writers of the late eighteenth century. The dialectic is a familiar one. The two interpretations of Erasmus, the liberal and the romantic, the for and against, shared common ground. Both saw him essentially as an Enlightenment figure, rational, sceptical, and tolerant. For the one interpretation this made him progressive, constructive, an apostle of modernity. For the other he was either a destructive force (the Catholic medievalist view) or lacking in the power to create or mould the future (the Protestant confessional view).

Soon after the peace, in 1919 and 1920, two studies on the modernity of Erasmus appeared. One in the *English Historical Review* was by the Anglican church historian J.P. Whitney (1857–1939).[288] The other, *Der moderne Mensch in Erasmus* by Arthur Schröder, aimed to assess the Erasmian program from a Lutheran standpoint and so contained much that was familiar, but it was also fresh in relating Erasmus to an idea of modernity affected by the intellectual and cultural changes of the early twentieth century and, possibly, the catastrophe of the world war. In 1920 also, R.H. Murray (1874–1947) of Trinity College, Dublin, published his large and somewhat inchoate book *Erasmus and Luther: Their Attitude to Toleration*. The problem of toleration had been on the agenda of Erasmus scholarship since Bayle and was critical for liberals. Murray, who had been working on it for twenty years and used Acton's library among others, added: 'Life in Ireland inevitably suggests its study.'[289] In his Hulsean Lectures of 1921–2 at Cambridge, Leonard Elliott Binns characterized Erasmus, in a somewhat more limited arena than Schröder's or even Whitney's, as the man of the present hour.[290] In 1923 there appeared Preserved Smith's *Erasmus: A Study of His Life, Ideals and Place in History*, which may be taken as an apotheosis of the liberal tradition, and in the following year Johan Huizinga's *Erasmus*, a great, influential, and enigmatic work which resumes in itself the dialectic of nineteenth-century interpretations and may be seen as bringing that phase of Erasmus interpretation to an end. We will make a concise survey of these works as an epilogue to the present chapter and this book.

Whitney's concern is with the relation between medieval and modern in Erasmus. He was, Whitney says, formed by the Middle Ages. Thus the enquiring mind which some have thought particularly modern he shared with the scholastics, as also their willingness to accept authority when the debate was done.[291] But above all he was formed by those making a transition from medieval to modern, viz the Brethren of the Common Life. They worked for gradual change but were essentially progressive none the less.[292] Their influence was apparent above all in Erasmus' New Testament. 'Erasmus was its author, but the method he followed and the spirit in which he wrote were alike those of his early teachers, the pious and laborious Brethren of the Common

Lot. And so the dying Middle Ages were linked by their greatest product to the foundation of the Reformation age itself.'[293] But in some respects, Whitney continues, the modernity of Erasmus went beyond the Reformation. Luther was a scholastic to the end. 'Erasmus, on the other hand, postulated the free and full development of the individual, trained and disciplined, as the very foundation of theology.' Erasmus had a great respect for the religious tradition but his sense of individuality was modern. He had 'the mind of the more modern world, modern in its humour, modern in its gentleness, in its love of sound learning and of good letters.'[294] Whitney's awareness of the modern seems appropriate to a somewhat secluded theological seminary and 1920 a surprising year to speak of modern gentleness, but references to individuality and private judgment make the link with the Protestant Enlightenment's view of Erasmus and of the modern.[295]

Arthur Schröder's sense of modernity is more tough-minded than could emerge from Whitney's Anglican mildness. Modern man, he says, is a paradox and his traits are contradictory (he is rational and emotional, seeking both independence and authority, and so on); he is 'ein Mensch zwischen Ja und Nein.'[296] In his own time Erasmus was seen as a modern. Does the Erasmian type remain modern?[297] As a critic, Schröder answers, Erasmus knew how to be both sharp and prudent, to move between 'yea' and 'nay.' This indecisiveness was characteristically modern. There was no straight line from Erasmus to Nietzsche but Erasmus can be heard in the assertion of Karl Zimmermann, Nietzsche's follower, that the uncertainty of things is a proper confession of faith. Erasmus offers – to moderns – an attractive combination of rationalism and scepticism: 'The proud faith in the victorious power of the intellect is subdued by the insight into the relative nature of all human understanding.'[298] Although Schröder is diverted into the all-too-familiar contrast between Erasmus' scepticism and Luther's decisive faith, the suggestion of a harmony between his awareness of the variety of human opinions and the essential relativism of modern thought is at least fresh and thought-provoking.[299]

Similarly, Erasmus' cultural openness, his ethic of personal and social improvement based on the teachings of Christ and aimed, not at an élite, but at broad sections of society, his assimilation of religion to human culture correspond in Schröder's view to aspects of the modern outlook. Progress and change for him, especially change in religion towards greater inwardness and simplicity, were more important than maintaining the medieval inheritance. This is, of course, reminiscent of Dilthey, Wernle, and Troeltsch and, to a degree, of Mestwerdt, though Schröder unlike these predecessors judges Erasmus' modernism by a traditional Lutheran standard. While he defines the modern in the language of the early twentieth century, his identification of it in Erasmus recalls the old Enlightenment picture of Erasmus. He relates him to Luther much as the nineteenth-century Protestants did. Erasmus was, he concludes, modern in being a seeker rather than a finder, a sceptic and relativist; consequently he lacked force. There is an echo even of Adolf Müller: Erasmus was a man of intellect ('Verstandesmensch') rather than a man of religion and so could not be a true religious pioneer.[300]

Murray's is an ample and undisciplined work which is far from concentrated on the theme of its subtitle, the problem of toleration. Murray had a taste for aphorism and historical analogy which he indulged to excess in this book. Nevertheless the theme warrants the book's consideration at this point in our discussion and Murray's remarks upon it are of interest, though requiring extraction from a mass of surrounding matter. Erasmus, he says, while his devotion to the ideals of antiquity stood in the way of his adopting the modern idea of progress, nevertheless believed in the gradual overcoming of ignorance and the continuous growth and development of knowledge. These beliefs were for him supported by the doctrine of the Incarnation; Christianity was not embodied in settled dogmas but in a Person toward whom over time all creation moves. Thus he insisted on 'freedom from rigid definition.' There must be dogmas, but needless dogmatizing should be avoided. 'Erasmus felt with Montaigne that it is putting a high value on the opinions of a writer to burn men who do not see eye to eye with him.'[301]

The age of the Renaissance and Reformation promised progress towards toleration but that was hampered by the conflict between Luther and Erasmus. 'What,' Murray pleads, 'might not have been the forward step taken by toleration had they been able to combine? Why could not the wisdom of Erasmus be joined to the force of Luther? The one was Hellenic, the other Hebraic.' In part this is the standard nineteenth-century Protestant picture: the Hellenic philosopher against the Hebrew prophet, the one calling for time and patient labour for generations, the other for faith here and now, and Murray leans toward the second. But there is something fresh in his analogy between Erasmus and Edmund Burke. Both had been accused of changing their views for disreputable reasons, Erasmus after 1517, Burke after 1789. In fact, Murray says, these changes were more apparent than real; both remained committed throughout to 'balance, harmony, organic unity'; their thought remained the same, circumstances changed. Furthermore, despite their differences, Erasmus and Luther made complementary contributions to the progress of toleration. Erasmus' contribution as Murray describes it could be called liberal. Like Burke he combined a sense of the past with faith in future development. He also, while Luther was shaking the foundations of the existing church, 'contributed the mind that understands the many-sidedness of truth.'[302]

There is a trace here of Schröder's modern man. Generally Murray associates Erasmus with the liberal virtue of the open mind. He may thus be taken in support of the argument being put here that the postwar burst of writing about Erasmus (predominantly, one must say, in English) continued the liberal tradition of writing about him. In his Hulsean Lectures Leonard Elliott Binns also attributes an acceptance of the open mind to Erasmus; suspension of judgment, he believed, was often 'the only safe attitude in face of the many obscurities of existence.'[303] Binns is interested above all in the question: how may Christianity be adjusted with integrity to the intellectual requirements of the present time? It had preoccupied liberal Anglicans from the time of Thomas Arnold and Milman. There was, says Binns, a revolutionary and a conservative way. To the latter (Binns' preference) Erasmus was a guide. Against the revolutionary Luther he was a 'constitutional reformer.'[304] He stood for change with continuity – here Binns picks up Murray's analogy with Burke.[305] He was the type of reformer needed for the contemporary task of relating new knowledge to religious truth – patient, having convictions but not prejudices and both reverence for the past and refusal to be fettered by it.[306]

Personally Preserved Smith (1880–1941) had gone beyond the restatement of faith sought by Binns; by the time of his *Erasmus* he had abandoned all faith in the supernatural.[307] But he presented Erasmus as the apostle of theological restatement and to that extent his theme and Binns' were similar (though his book was much the more substantial as a work of scholarship). His unusual name came from a long line of Puritan forebears among whom, it should be added, a goodly proportion were accused of religious heterodoxy.[308] His father was suspended from his ministry in the Presbyterian church in Ohio for promoting the historical criticism of the Bible.[309] Much of his own education he owed to his father including a year of study in Europe at the age of fourteen when (he later claimed) he collected 'much of the material' for his books.[310] Those books included an acclaimed biography of Luther (1911), which was in the line of Protestant historiography in seeing the Reformation as the start of modern civilization and Luther as its herald, and the comprehensive *Age of the Reformation* (1920), which marked a shift by making the Reformation dependent on antecedent changes in the economy, society, and culture.[311] With *Erasmus* there was a return to biography but much of the book's intellectual impulse came (as we shall see) from Smith's interest in the intricate problem (as he called it) of the relations between Renaissance and Reformation.[312] In the year before its publication he was appointed professor of history at Cornell. That university's liberal tradition was congenial to him.[313]

The book is eminently readable. Smith's style is easy, fluent, conversational with an occasional more stately passage like that on letter writing which begins 'The epistle is at once a necessity, a comfort, and a luxury,' or that on Erasmus' own style: 'By whetting his words to a keen edge, he attained delicate polish and glow of supple beauty.'[314] In person Smith was witty in the manner of one who led a retiring and to a degree invalid life.[315] Evidences of this are not lacking in his work on Erasmus: two years after seeking from Erasmus the dedication of a work on preparation for death, Anne Boleyn's father went to execution and 'therefore had a very practical use for the work he had asked for.'[316] Lacunae might be noted in Smith's work, even by the standards of that time, notably an undervaluing of everything medieval, especially scholasticism, and a too brief treatment of Erasmus' work on the Fathers.[317] Yet on almost all issues he had come to terms fairly with recent and contemporary scholarship; one might mention the names of Mestwerdt, Kalkoff, Renaudet, Woodward, and Lindeboom by way of example, and Smith naturally avowed his debt to Allen. The book remained for a long time a good guide to the literature on Erasmus.[318] It was in narrative form, perhaps overladen with detail,[319] but over all directed at two general questions: What does modern liberal religion owe to Erasmus? How are Renaissance and Reformation related to his person and work?

For Christianity to have any future it must in Smith's view take an undogmatic form. Such a religion, a combination of the ethical and the reasonable, was now 'prevalent among large circles of our cultivated classes' (as he calls them). Erasmus was its forerunner and exponent: 'No writer before Voltaire has left behind him such a wreck of superstitions; few writers since the last Evangelists have bequeathed to posterity so much of ethical value.' Smith avows this position at the very beginning of his book.[320] Erasmus was not exactly the pioneer of liberal theology and undogmatic Christianity. He had a predecessor in Valla whom Smith treats as a radical; if not an atheist, he subjected religion to attacks of unparalleled daring. Further Valla was himself a representative figure; he was 'an incarnation of the intellectual Renaissance.'[321] On the other side Erasmus was influenced by the more mystical *devotio moderna* and Florentine Neoplatonism. Both pointed to an inner piety largely free of dogma and ceremony. This represents a heightening and to a degree a vulgarizing of Mestwerdt: 'Priest and sacrament shrank in importance before the new individualism.' The medieval background is foreshortened and the problem of influences not treated systematically. Erasmus discovered for himself, Smith says, the religion of Jesus and of the Sermon on the Mount. This is the conclusion of Wernle and Troeltsch, and Smith acknowledges a debt to the latter for his understanding of Erasmus' religion as essentially an ethic, infused with 'the spirit of free inquiry and of philosophic doubt.'[322]

On the broader question of the relations between Renaissance and Reformation, on which Robertson and Gibbon had differed a century and a half before, Smith diverged from Troeltsch. For the latter there were in Renaissance humanism anticipations of modern liberal religion, although the true break from the medieval order came with the Enlightenment. The Reformation belonged to the old world. For Smith the two, Renaissance and Reformation, were near allies and both were preparations for modern individualism and 'reactions against the asceticism and other-worldliness of the Middle Ages.'[323] Erasmus more than any other represented the common ground between them and eventually their divergences, which were due to external forces and above all the Reformation's association with popular, patriotic, and often violent movements.[324] Smith accepts that Erasmus' attitudes were more modern than those of the Reformers: 'He welcomed criticism and philosophy as aids to religion; they dreaded reason as a foe to faith.' The *Colloquia* propagated ideas which, beyond the Reformation, attracted Anabaptists, Arminians, Rabelais, and Montaigne. He prepared the way for the scientific study of the Bible, for the philological and historical criticism now freeing Christendom from 'the bondage of superstition and of the letter.'[325] Thus for Smith, as for Dilthey, Troeltsch, and Wernle, Erasmus anticipated the modern religious situation as the Reformers could never do. Yet in their own time Luther better than Erasmus understood what was required, the plain, vigorous, unyielding demand for reform. Erasmus' rejection of Luther's Reformation was, Smith concludes, a mistake in itself and a misfortune to the cause of liberalism.[326] This reversion to a tenet of Protestant historiography is not integrated in Smith's *Erasmus* with the more radical views owed to Troeltsch and Wernle. The biographer of Luther and the admirer of Erasmus sit together uneasily.

Smith does not attempt an integrated portrait of Erasmus. Indeed he finds more than one nature in the man; there is the author of the *Enchiridion*, there is the 'sportive mocker' who wrote the *Moriae encomium*. 'Matsys, the painter of serious, religious pictures, saw the one side of the man; Holbein, the merry portrait-painter and caricaturist, the other.' As well, he was responsive to different views and claims, able to see all sides of a question. His best qualities – tolerance and open-mindedness – stood him in ill stead in the Reformation conflicts.[327] But, Smith affirms, they would come into their own in a later and happier time. The progressive liberal undertone runs through this biography and, despite what is said above, gives it a kind of unity; the Erasmus who was wrong about the Reformation and Erasmus the herald of modern religious freedom do not need to be integrated – they represent different stages in the progress of humanity.

Smith's work may lack a final portrait of Erasmus but his admiration for his subject is essentially uncomplicated. His Erasmus, though a divided personality, appears relatively straightforward. Huizinga's *Erasmus* by contrast presents a figure over which light and shade play constantly. Three central chapters on Erasmus' mind and character break the narrative at the point where Erasmus' great influence over European culture began to decline under the impact of Luther and his cause. Fine threads there bind the mind and the character. Here in fact is one of the themes of Huizinga's book: Erasmus' inclinations were 'the correlates of his convictions.'[328]

Thus for Huizinga the dominant trait in Erasmus' character was delicacy, arising from physical weakness and expressed in fastidiousness, an obsession with cleanliness and purity. 'He has a violent dislike of stuffy air and smelly substances.' The intellectual correlate was a dislike of all that was overelaborated in medieval culture and religion and an attraction to 'the original and pure, all that is not yet overgrown or has not passed through many hands.' Hence the struggle over biblical criticism and the cry for a return to the unpolluted sources. Socially this trait found, according to Huizinga, a seemingly paradoxical expression: Erasmus' need for friendship as a way of reassuring and perhaps justifying himself and a longing for solitude, a 'maidenly coyness' (as he himself described it).[329]

As well, there was Erasmus' 'fervent desire of freedom,' to which Huizinga attaches a wish for rest: 'Without liberty, life is no life; and there is no liberty without repose.'[330] Hence Erasmus' restlessness under authority, his resistance to institutional demands, his refusal to take sides in the great struggle of his age, and hence, too, his fear of personal entanglements.

Finally, despite his sense – characteristic of the Renaissance – for the realities of the tangible world, Erasmus had an aversion for everything definite or decisive. He was 'the man of half-tones, of fine shadings, of the thought that is never completely expressed'; he was always aware of the imprecision in the meanings of words and 'the eternal ambiguity of human issues.'[331]

Huizinga's judgments of Erasmus' mind and his character are intertwined in what has so far been said. But he also makes a disjunction between mind and character; at least he awards them very different marks. A great mind but a little man: the distinction was a familiar one in the nineteenth century. Erasmus, Huizinga says, cannot be called one of the heroes of history. Was not this because 'his character was not on a level with the elevation of his mind'? He speaks indeed of the great Erasmus and the puny Erasmus. 'Let us try ever to see of that great Erasmus as much as the petty one permits.'[332]

The mind of the great Erasmus was in large measure liberal. There, too, Huizinga accepts a dominant judgment of the nineteenth century. Contemporaries saw him as 'the bearer of a new liberty of the mind.' He had moved beyond medieval Catholicism; he prefigured the Enlightenment. 'In Erasmus we already find the beginning of that optimism which judges upright man good enough to dispense with fixed forms and rules.' His educational ideals in their clear good sense 'foreshadow exactly those of the eighteenth century.'[333]

The earlier, more strictly biographical chapters of Huizinga's book, over which we cannot linger, deal with the experiences and associations that produced the mind and character just sketched. He draws on the scholarship of the previous generation as a selection of points indicates: Erasmus was not as unwilling a novice as he claimed; in the cloister he experienced the longings and frustrations of strongly sentimental friendships; he was not a careerist but followed the ideal of a free life; John Colet decided finally the bent of his many-sided mind; that bent was toward theology of a liberal kind, based on the Bible and free of scholastic complications.[334] By 1517 he seemed 'the international pivot on which the civilization of his age hinged.'[335]

The final chapters on the Reformation years trace the unravelling of his influence, his decline into ineffectiveness. The course of Huizinga's narrative does not run all one way: at Basel Erasmus 'approaches most closely to the ideal of his personal life'; the very surveillance to which arch-conservatives subjected him betrayed their fear of his standing and influence; the Ciceronianus of 1528 demonstrated both his Christian spirit and his undiminished wit and rhetorical power; he exercised a subterranean spiritual influence on the Anabaptists and in the Netherlands.[336] But otherwise he was crowded to the edge of the arena. Deep down that suited his nature, his double-sidedness and desire to keep aloof.[337] Though at times he had still the delusion of being at the centre of things, his grasp on the events and issues of his time weakened. He finished in an indeterminate conservatism.[338]

The relation of Huizinga (1872–1945) to his book has excited much discussion. It is overstated to say that his Erasmus is essentially a self-portrait, or at least that it tells us more of the author's mind than of his subject's.[339] Obviously its status as a work of scholarship speaks against that exaggeration. Huizinga worked closely with the sources, especially Allen's edition of the letters, as the notes to the Dutch edition demonstrate; one out-

come of his undertaking was a bond with the Allens themselves.[340] He tactfully persuaded the editor of the series ('Great
Hollanders') to which the book belonged, the Dutch-American
publisher Edward Bok, to withdraw a proposed introduction because it was absurdly remote from contemporary scholarship; he
resented Bok's removal of notes from the original English edition.[341] There is a certain Erasmian playfulness about Huizinga's
own account of the book's origins and what it meant to him:
'Many of my writings have been based on lecture notes or on
ideas that occurred to me in connection with them. Thus the
thought of writing about Erasmus – of whom I knew next to
nothing before 1920 – sprang directly from a lecture on the problem of the Renaissance. Soon afterwards, Edward Bok urged me
to make Erasmus the subject of a contribution to his series ...
Many people have expressed the view that here was a man after
my own heart. As far as I can tell, nothing could be farther from
the truth for, much though I admire Erasmus, he inspires me with
little sympathy and, as soon as the work was done, I did my best
to put him out of my mind.'[342] There is evidence that he had
been thinking more deeply about Erasmus and remained more
preoccupied with him than this suggests.[343]

There was an affinity of spirit between Huizinga and his subject.[344] In parts of the Erasmus portrait (the unwillingness to take
sides, the crippling sense of the ambiguities of existence) there is
perhaps an element of self-depreciation.[345] Reedijk warns against
exaggerating Huizinga's condemnation of Erasmus' character.[346]
Yet he was himself aware of differing from the Erasmians of his
time on that issue. To the Allens he wrote: 'One thing grieves
me: that you are sure to find my opinion of Erasmus too unfavourable. I could only present him as I saw him, still I am ready
to admit that, perhaps, after all has been said, your more sym-
pathising judgment must be the truer one, because it is founded
on the knowledge and the love of a life-work.'[347] Perhaps Kurt
Köster's expression of 'inner distance' best defines Huizinga's position when he was writing about Erasmus.[348] He was constantly
balancing strengths and weaknesses; that, he believed, was both
just and aesthetically satisfying.[349] Huizinga was more conscious
than most historians of effects in historical writing. The influence
upon him of the Dutch aesthetic movements of the last two decades of the nineteenth century has often been remarked. Histor-

ical understanding was, he said, 'like an evocation of images.'[350] He sought a subtlety in composition to achieve the balances, suggest the nuances, call up the images that he looked for. When all safeguards have been taken there is a drift in this appreciation of Erasmus away from the robust image projected by the late nineteenth- and early twentieth-century writers from Maurenbrecher to Kalkoff. The vigour in the personality has somehow been drained away; this is a 'delicate, aesthetic, hovering spirit,' a lover of secluded places.[351] He gives a faded, *fin de siècle* impression. Huizinga believed that his own time, like the sixteenth century (and, we might add, the time of Herder and the romantics), admired the 'ardently pious,' the heroic, those who pushed things to extremes. Erasmus lacked that dimension.[352] This is the element in the nineteenth-century dialectic in Erasmus interpretation which derived from the *Sturm und Drang* and romanticism; to it the appeal of the heroic in Huizinga responded.[353] But, it has been remarked, antinomies are characteristic of Huizinga's thought.[354] He gave full value to the other side of the nineteenth-century dialectic, that grounded in the Enlightenment and liberalism. Here is honoured above all the author of the *Praise of Folly* and the *Colloquies*; that is the Erasmus honoured by Huizinga.[355] His account of those works is among his best pages. Voltaire, too, had admired that Erasmus but we have not, of course, come full circle. Beside the massive advances in scholarship, we must recognize the religious components in Huizinga's picture of Erasmus to which both Protestant and Catholic predecessors had contributed. Yet the continuities are substantial enough for us to say that Huizinga's work rounds off the liberal tradition in Erasmus interpretation and within itself recapitulates the dialectic that had dominated the writings of the nineteenth century.

TWELVE

Conclusion

Between 1930 and 1980 an interpretation of Erasmus very different from that occupying us in the last section became dominant. In this interpretation Erasmus is seen above all as a serious Christian scholar and thinker. His relation to the Christian tradition has attracted attention. He appears as a Catholic Christian but, more broadly, as a figure ecumenical, devout, theological. This interpretation is not new. We have found anticipations of it, primarily but not exclusively on the Catholic side – in Imbart de la Tour, for example. They are present also in Schlottmann on the Protestant side. And even in the last two generations this interpretation, if dominant, has not occupied the whole field; the case of Joseph Lortz is a reminder of that.

In the same period the liberal interpretation has faded. The background hardly needs spelling out. The liberal confidences have waned. However, the current interpretation does not, as occurred in a different form in the nineteenth century, represent a revival of confessio......lism or a simple restoration of Christian confidence. Western society is one stage further removed from Christendom; the process of secularization has gone so far that the secularist debate is stilled. In these circumstances perhaps, it is easier to reclaim Christian figures from the past.

Between 1750 and 1920, the period covered by this book, issues posed during the Enlightenment were dominant in Erasmus interpretation. Indeed, one would say that the liberal interpretation was this era's favourite. Its essence was: Erasmus stood for a more open religion, for more critical scholarship, for a more tolerant society.

The limitations of this interpretation are apparent, above all a certain shallowness – Erasmus' thought seems too sunny, too much of a piece, too free of ambiguities. A simplifying process has gone on. One may state the principle: in assessing rival interpretations of a historical figure and his influence, it is complexity that carries conviction. That is a counterpart to the well-known principle of the harder reading in textual criticism, which Erasmus himself enunciated. Coleridge best exemplifies the virtues of complexity. Liberal simplification stemmed in part from the progressive idea of history, though whether Erasmus was to be found at the head of the march or behind among the quarrelsome camp-followers of the Reformers was often debated, as we have seen.

We cannot make a ready connection between the advances in Erasmus scholarship around the end of the nineteenth century, aspects of which we have sketched, and the more recent change in Erasmus interpretation. The persistence and persuasiveness of the liberal view are evidenced by the strong traces of it to be found in writers as distinguished and diverse as Allen, Renaudet, Lindeboom, Preserved Smith, and Huizinga, all of whom were masters of the new scholarship. The liberal interpretation cannot be simply rejected; the era of Erasmus interpretation studied in this book has a continuing interest.[1] The point may be demonstrated indirectly by reconsidering the nineteenth-century debates.

Erasmus interpretation was caught up in the strong reaction against Enlightenment values. The religious revival of the nineteenth century refastened old stereotypes: Erasmus was seen as the betrayer of the holy cause, be it medieval Catholic civilization or the rediscovered gospel. Curiously (as we have seen) the understanding of Erasmus among his critics was much like the Enlightenment's; his tolerance and moderation were now, however, condemned as weakness, evidence of an irresolute, unheroic, self-regarding character.[2] This view of Erasmus seems today less convincing than the liberal one; that is because it is much too negative. Erasmus' attractiveness to his contemporaries, his influence on them and on many of the next generation, is simply inexplicable on this view. The appreciation of Erasmus as an actor in the history of his time, as a force to be reckoned with, which began with Kampschulte and Maurenbrecher, was a product of liberal rather than confessional soil.

There are sides of Erasmus' complex mind and personality that can be fitted to the liberal image. There was an affable, sceptical, 'unparteiisch,' indeed a subversive Erasmus that must be mixed in with the theologian, writer of *spiritualia* and devoted Catholic Christian. This is the isolated Erasmus, the man on his own, of whom the authors of the *Epistolae obscurorum virorum* could say: 'Erasmus taketh his own part.'[3] This Erasmus balances the Erasmus of the great consensus, Erasmus of Christendom. His is the image recalled in these pages.

Abbreviations

꙱

ADB	*Allgemeine deutsche Biographie* 56 vols, 1875–1912
Allen	P.S. and H.M. Allen (eds) *Opus epistolarum Des. Erasmi Roterodami* 12 vols, Oxford 1906–58
Allibone	*A Critical Dictionary of English Literature and British and American Authors Living and Deceased from the Earliest Accounts to the Latter Half of the Nineteenth Century* 3 vols, Philadelphia 1891; *Supplement* by John Foster Kirk 2 vols, Philadelphia 1891–2
ARG	*Archiv für Reformationsgeschichte* 1903–
ASD	*Opera Omnia Desiderii Erasmi Roterodami* Amsterdam 1969–
Biographie nationale	*Biographie nationale de Belgique* 27 vols, 1866–
Contemporaries of Erasmus	Peter G. Bietenholz (ed) *Contemporaries of Erasmus: A Biographical Register of the Renaissance and Reformation* 3 vols, Toronto 1985–7
CWE	*The Collected Works of Erasmus* Toronto 1974–
DAB	*Dictionary of American Biography* 20 vols, 1928–36, and supplements
DBF	*Dictionnaire de biographie française* 1933–
Dict hist et biog	*Dictionnaire historique et biographique de la Suisse* 7 vols, Neuchatel 1921–34
DNB	*Dictionary of National Biography* 21 vols, 1921–2, and supplements
DTC	*Dictionnaire de théologie catholique* 15 vols, 1903–50
Gedenkschrift	*Gedenkschrift zum 400. Todestage des Erasmus von Rotterdam* Basel 1936
Hirsch	Emanuel Hirsch *Geschichte der neuern evangelischen Theologie im Zusammenhang mit den allgemeinen Bewegungen des europäischen Denkens* 4th ed, 5 vols, Gütersloh 1968

Hoefer	J.C.F. Hoefer (ed) *Nouvelle Biographie générale depuis les temps les plus reculés jusqu'à nos jours* 46 vols, 1853–66
HZ	*Historische Zeitschrift* 1859–
LB	Erasmus. *Opera omnia* ed J. LeClerc, 10 vols, Leiden 1703–6
Meinhold	Peter Meinhold *Geschichte der kirchlichen Historiographie* II, Munich 1967
Michaud	*Biographie universelle (Michaud) ancienne et moderne* founded by J.F. Michaud and L.G. Michaud, new ed, 45 vols, 1842–65
NDB	*Neue deutsche Biographie* 1953–
New Cath Enc	*New Catholic Encyclopedia* 15 vols, New York 1967
NNBW	*Nieuw Nederlandsch Biografisch Woordenboek* 10 vols, 1911–37
RE 3	*Realencyklopädie für protestantische Theologie und Kirche* 3rd ed, 21 vols (and Register), 1898–1909
RGG	*Die Religion in Geschichte und Gegenwart* 3rd ed, 6 vols (and Register), 1957–65
Scrinium Erasmianum	J. Coppens (ed) *Scrinium Erasmianum, Mélanges historiques publiés sous le patronage de l'Université de Louvain à l'occasion du cinquième centenaire de la naissance d'Erasme* 2 vols, Leiden 1969
Srbik	Heinrich Ritter von Srbik *Geist und Geschichte vom deutschen Humanismus bis zur Gegenwart* 3rd ed, 2 vols, Munich/Salzburg 1964
TRE	*Theologische Realenzyklopädie* Berlin/New York 1976–
Wulschner	Joachim Wulschner 'Erasmus von Rotterdam im 19. Jahrhundert. Sein Bild in der deutschen Literatur, vornehmlich gesehen in Hinblick auf seinen Gegenspieler Ulrich von Hutten' unpublished dissertation, Free University of Berlin 1955

Notes

✦

CHAPTER ONE

1 On these biographies, see my *Phoenix of His Age*, ch. 9.
2 Cf now M.A. Screech *Ecstasy and the Praise of Folly*.
3 See, eg, Wallace K. Ferguson *The Renaissance in Historical Thought: Five Centuries of Interpretation* 65 on Vasari.
4 *Phoenix of His Age* 236–47, 275–85. The same might be said – indeed in stronger terms – of the dissertation by Johannes Klefeker (ibid 221–4).
5 Ibid 253
6 Ibid xii, xiv
7 *The Education of a Christian Prince* CWE 27: 231

CHAPTER TWO

1 For a fuller summary of this period, see my 'Erasmus in the Age of Revolutions.'
2 There was some presentation of unfamiliar materials. J.F. Burscher published (at Leipzig between 1784 and 1802) important letters (written to Erasmus) in a series under the title *Spicilegia* (in 1802 F. Schoenemann republished them in a single volume). They were held thereafter at Leipzig University Library. The first of the letters is Ep 1067, from Wimpfeling 19 February 1520 (Allen IV 190–1). Cf F.L. Hoffmann 'Notes sur une série de lettres adressées à Érasme, soit par des Belges, soit par des personnes vivant temporairement en Belgique.'

CHAPTER THREE

1 Norman Hampson *The Enlightenment* 9

2 Peter Gay *The Enlightenment: An Interpretation,* 1: *The Rise of Modern Paganism* 4
3 *Erasmus ehedem und heute* 23
4 Hampson *Enlightenment* 86
5 Denis Diderot and Jean d'Alembert (eds) *Encyclopédie* I 650 a–b. On Arianism, see *Phoenix of His Age* index.
6 Cf R.N. Schwab and W.E. Rex *Inventory of Diderot's Encyclopédie* IV 916. It is odd that the article should have been attributed to Diderot himself (Preserved Smith *Erasmus* 436. Cf Kaegi 'Erasmus im achtzehnten Jahrhundert' 218).
7 John Lough 'Louis, Chevalier de Jaucourt (1704–80). A Biographical Sketch'
8 Quoted ibid 48
9 Ibid 60. Lough adds: 'yet amongst the thousands of articles which he turned out there are many which show beyond a doubt that he was by no means devoid either of originality or even of a sturdy independence of judgment.' That Jaucourt was in fact a staunch propagandist for the Enlightenment is made clear by George A. Perla 'La Philosophie de Jaucourt dans *l'Encyclopédie.*'
10 Quoted Lough 51
11 *Phoenix of His Age* 236–47
12 Gay *Enlightenment* 1: 294
13 *Encyclopédie* XIV 381 a
14 Ibid 380 a. Bayle's article in *Dictionnaire historique* XII 640–1.
15 Ibid 380 b – 381 a
16 *Dictionnaire historique* VI 238–9
17 *Encyclopédie* XIV 381 a. The piece concludes with a reference to Erasmus' writings in every *genre,* all composed with 'a purity and an admirable elegance' (ibid).
18 'Erasmus' 516
19 N.B. Tenhaeff *Erasmus en Voltaire als exponenten van hun tijd;* summary in Jean-Claude Margolin *Quatorze années de bibliographie érasmienne (1936–1949)* 214–15.
20 'I have sometimes thought of writing a dialogue of the dead in which Lucian, Erasmus, and Voltaire should mutually acknowledge the danger of exposing an old superstition to the contempt of the blind and fanatic multitude' (*Autobiography* 203).
21 *The Bridge of Criticism: Dialogues among Lucian, Erasmus, and Voltaire on the Enlightenment ... and on Its Meaning for Our Time.* Erasmus appears here as a foil to Voltaire.
22 Voltaire to Burigny, 10 May 1757 (*Correspondence* XXXI 159)
23 *Complete Works of Voltaire* 82 *Notebooks* II 563. The passage comes from the so-called Piccini Notebooks first published in Paris in 1802. Its authenticity may be accepted. The material dates to the period 1750–5 (ibid 81 *Notebooks* I 30–4).

24 Various fragments of the work had appeared since 1745 but the first edition proper was 1756. Succeeding editions (1761, 1769, 1775, 1785) added and corrected. The two passages where Erasmus is mentioned by name belong to 1761. Cf *Essay sur les moeurs* ed René Pomeau I lxvii–lxxiii.
25 Ibid II 209, 214
26 Ibid 213
27 Ibid 214, 216
28 Ibid 220–1
29 J.H. Brumfitt *Voltaire Historian* 62, 101, 163; J.B. Black *The Art of History* 36
30 Haydn Mason *Voltaire* 35
31 Brumfitt *Voltaire Historian* 123–4
32 Gembicki 'La Réforme allemande vue par Voltaire' 151–2; Trenard 'Voltaire, historien de la Réforme en France' 164. Voltaire made much use of Bayle and other encyclopaedists. Personal associations with liberal Protestants at Geneva strengthened the sceptical strain which had come from Bayle. But his literary dependences were mostly on Catholic historians of the seventeenth and eighteenth centuries – Bossuet, Maimbourg, Du Pin, and others. He does not seem to have used critical Protestant writers like Sleidan or Seckendorf (Gembicki ibid 149, 153; Trenard ibid 157–8). Concerning Erasmus, Burigny's work, which he knew, produced little effect.
33 René Pomeau *La Religion de Voltaire* 428–30, 436
34 'A l'auteur du livre des trois imposteurs' (1769) 404 (translation by R.S. Ridgway *Voltaire and Sensibility* 70n)
35 Pomeau *Religion de Voltaire* 315
36 Ute van Runset *Ironie und Philosophie bei Voltaire unter besonderer Berücksichtigung der 'Dialogues et entretiens philosophiques'* 182–3
37 *Dialogues et Anecdotes philosophiques* (ed Raymond Naves) 146–7
38 Ibid 148
39 Runset *Ironie und Philosophie* 55–8, 182–3
40 *Dialogues* 149, 151. For Naves' comment on the double role of the *philosophe*, see ibid 497–8.
41 Ibid 150–2. Cf Naves' note, ibid 498.
42 Runset *Ironie und Philosophie* 179
43 John Renwick *Marmontel, Voltaire and the* Bélisaire *affair* 120–4, 144, 308–9
44 Ibid 157, 174, 211
45 Ibid 189–91
46 *Dialogues et Anecdotes philosophiques* 172–4. Cf Naves' notes 502.
47 In his *Discourse of Free-Thinking* (1713) Anthony Collins, the English deist, used these words of Erasmus, possibly quoting them from Le Vayer. Voltaire read the *Discourse* probably in the 1730s

(Norman L. Torrey *Voltaire and the English Deists* 45–7). 'Sancte Socrates, ora pro nobis' comes from the colloquy 'The Godly Feast' (*Convivium religiosum*) (*Colloquies of Erasmus* 68).

48 *Dialogues* 176
49 'Lettre VI Sur Les Allemands,' in 'Lettres a S.A. Mgr Le Prince de *****' 1187
50 Ibid 1186
51 From a substantial literature, see, eg, Ernst Cassirer *The Philosophy of the Enlightenment* ch 5 'The conquest of the Historical World' and Gay *Enlightenment* 2: *The Science of Freedom* 368–96.
52 Manfred Schlenke 'Aus der Frühzeit des englischen Historismus'
53 An interest in the Arminian theologians did not mean a rejection of the Westminster Confession (John Erskine in his funeral oration on Robertson, quoted Mary Fearnley-Sander 'The Emancipation of the Mind' 103).
54 Ian D.L. Clark 'From Protest to Reaction: The Moderate Regime in the Church of Scotland' 207
55 Alexander Carlyle *Autobiography* 243
56 Jeremy J. Cater 'The Making of Principal Robertson in 1762'
57 Dugald Stewart *Account of the Life and Writings of William Robertson, D.D.* in *Works of William Robertson, D.D.* iii. Cf Clark 'Moderate Regime' 210, 213. He was famed for his reasonableness and was said never to be ruffled (Carlyle *Autobiography* 287–8).
58 Cf Fearnley-Sander 'Emancipation of the Mind' 93–5.
59 Felix Gilbert Introduction to Robertson *The Progress of Society in Europe* xiv
60 Schlenke 'Aus der Frühzeit' 110–16
61 Black *Art of History* 118, 131, 133. For comments on Robertson's work, see Allibone II 1827–8, 1830–1.
62 *Charles V* was 'composed with nobleness, with dignity, with elegance, and with judgment, to which there are few equals' (quoted Stewart *Life* xii).
63 Quoted ibid v
64 Ibid xvii
65 Black *Art of History* 139; Schlenke 'Aus der Frühzeit' 122. Cf Friedrich Meinecke *Die Entstehung des Historismus* 238. For an excellent discussion of Robertson's treatment of the Reformation, see now A.G. Dickens and John Tonkin *The Reformation in Historical Thought* 141–6.
66 *History of the Reign of the Emperor Charles V* in *Works* 454
67 Ibid 455-6, 461, 466
68 Ibid 462
69 *Charles V* in *Works* 457, 460, 466, 708
70 Ibid 466
71 *Scotland* in *Works* 39

72 *Charles V* in *Works* 708
73 Ibid 710
74 Ibid 467
75 *Phoenix of His Age* 225–6. There is also a reference to the Reformation history (1744–52) by Daniel Gerdes, the Calvinist professor of theology at Groningen. On Gerdes, Hoefer XX 206–7; *Mennonite Encyclopedia* II 480.
76 On Seckendorf, see *Phoenix* 210–13, on Jortin ibid 280–4.
77 *Charles V* in *Works* 467. The harsher judgments are closer to those of Jortin's predecessor Jean Le Clerc (*Phoenix* 254–6).
78 DNB XVI 1315
79 'Extracts from the Journal' in John, Lord Sheffield *The Miscellaneous Works of Edward Gibbon, Esq.* 446–9. 'It is a work of great reading. As M. de Burigny proposed connecting with his history, a general account of the sciences and religion during his time, he has very deeply considered his subject. His style and reflections are suited to a man of sense and modesty, who neither pretends to, nor possesses the least share of genius. Upon the whole, the book is a perfect contrast to most fashionable French ones, since it is useful without being brilliant' (ibid 446–7). Note that this text differs slightly from Charles Butler's quotation (*Phoenix of His Age* 294–5).
80 Andrew Lossky 'Gibbon and the Enlightenment' 12; Joseph M. Levine *Humanism and History: Origins of Modern English Historiography* 184–5
81 'Extracts from the Journal' 447
82 Ibid
83 Ibid 449. Cf *Decline and Fall* 7: 136–7 for Gibbon's remarks on the elements of servility and liberation in the revival of letters in Italy.
84 *Decline and Fall* 2: 370n; 3: 395n; 7: 135. The first refers to Erasmus' delineation of Hilary, the second to his biography of Chrysostom, the third to his part in transmitting Greek learning to northern Europe. For a modern judgment on the Chrysostom biography, see Peter G. Bietenholz *History and Biography in the Work of Erasmus of Rotterdam* 96.
85 *Decline and Fall* 3: 396n
86 Ibid 4: 97. 1 John 5: 7: 'For there are three that bear record in heaven, the Father, the Word, and the Holy Ghost: and these three are one' is a late interpolation but accepted into the Vulgate. Erasmus, finding it in no early source, omitted it from his New Testament of 1519 but, in response to criticism, incorporated it again when a (dubious) manuscript including it was produced (John B. Payne *Erasmus: His Theology of the Sacraments* 56–7, 257).
87 'Extracts from the Journal' 447

88 Ibid
89 *Dictionnaire historique* VI 217
90 'Extracts from the Journal' 448
91 *Decline and Fall* 6: 122, 131
92 Fearnley-Sander 'Emancipation of the Mind' 158–9
93 For what follows, *Decline and Fall* 6: 131–3.
94 The idea has been reiterated in our time by H.A. Enno van Gelder *The Two Reformations in the 16th Century*.
95 *Decline and Fall* 6: 134. The first reference was to the doctrine of atonement, whose gradual but complete overthrow Priestley anticipated (*History of the Corruptions* I 275–6); the second was to the alliance of throne and altar (ibid II 484).
96 *Autobiography* 84, 89, 97
97 'From my childhood I had been fond of religious disputation' (ibid 82).
98 Joseph Ward Swain *Edward Gibbon the Historian* 65; Gerhart B. Ladner 'The Impact of Christianity' 64; Owen Chadwick 'Gibbon and the Church Historians' 221
99 Paul Turnbull 'The "Supposed Infidelity" of Edward Gibbon.' Cf David Dillon Smith 'Gibbon in Church.'
100 *Autobiography* 203
101 Ibid 181: '... his trumpet of sedition may at length awaken the magistrates of a free country.' Gibbon's reference to Priestley in chapter LIV had been written some time between July 1784 and May 1786, three to five years before the revolution in France. Joseph Priestley – Unitarian divine, educator, scientist – had, in *An History of the Corruptions of Christianity* (1782), challenged Gibbon to debate what Priestley considered his confusions between the essence of Christianity and its corruptions, among which Priestley counted doctrines which had been thought fundamental, like the Trinity (*History of the Corruptions* II 455–6, 461; cf Basil Willey *The Eighteenth Century Background* 188). Gibbon was unusually touchy about Priestley – to the extent of aligning himself with Priestley's orthodox critic and defender of the Anglican establishment, Samuel Horsley, bishop of St David's (*Autobiography* 181; on the Priestley–Horsley debate, see Leslie Stephen *History of English Thought in the Eighteenth Century* I 367–73). Priestley's 'sedition' consisted of the proclamation of liberal individualism and, later, of sympathy for the French Revolution. In religious matters he was open to persuasion (the norms of scripture and the primitive church safeguarded); he had (like many in the dissenting congregations) advanced from Calvinism to Unitarianism; it was his taste for theological controversy which made him uncongenial to Gibbon who handled him quite unfairly (cf DNB XI 362). On Priest-

ley's own views of the Reformation, which in some points paral-
leled Gibbon's, see G.H. Williams 'Joseph Priestley on Luther.'

102 See my 'Erasmus in the Age of Revolutions.'

103 Cf D.M. Low *Edward Gibbon 1737–1794* 264–5.

104 In the 1760s thirty-one universities had between them only 7000
students, the median student body being 220 (Charles E. McClelland *State, Society, and University in Germany 1700–1914* 28).

105 McClelland *State, Society, and University* 34–9

106 Josef Engel 'Die deutschen Universitäten und die Geschichtswissenschaften' 262, 265

107 Herbert Butterfield *Man on His Past: The Study of the History of
Historical Scholarship* 39–44

108 Hampson *Enlightenment* 59–61. On the German Enlightenment
and its social background, see Hajo Holborn *A History of Modern
Germany 1648–1840* 305–15 and W.H. Bruford *Germany in the
Eighteenth Century: The Social Background of the Literary Revival.*

109 Karl Aner *Die Theologie der Lessingzeit* 3–4. For a sharp critique of
too systematic a use of the terms 'orthodoxy,' 'pietism,' 'Enlightenment' and a reminder that thinkers grouped under these heads
are very diverse, see Dominique Bourel 'Orthodoxie, piétisme,
Aufklärung.'

110 Brucker had studied at Jena with J.F. Buddeus who represented a
transition from orthodoxy to pietism and early Enlightenment
(NDB 2: 647; on Buddeus RGG 1: col 1469).

111 *Historia critica philosophiae* VI *Appendix* 695

112 Ibid IV 85–6, VI 695

113 On Brucker and Diderot's use of him in the *Encyclopédie*, see Gay
Enlightenment 1: 365–8. Cf Ferguson *Renaissance in Historical
Thought* 108.

114 See *Phoenix of His Age* passim.

115 RGG 4: cols 1157–8; Meinhold II 11–30; Hirsch II 354–70; Karl
Heussi *Die Kirchengeschichtsschreibung Johann Lorenz von Mosheims*

116 Heussi *Kirchengeschichtsschreibung* 53–6

117 *Versuch einer unparteyischen und grundlichen Ketzergeschichte* I 22

118 Ibid 13. On Arnold, see *Phoenix of His Age* 215–20.

119 Meinhold II 11; Heussi *Kirchengeschichtsschreibung* 21–38

120 *Insitutionum historiae ecclesiasticae antiquae et recentioris libri quatuor* 608–28 (Eng trans *An Ecclesiastical History* I 764–93)

121 *Institutionum* 626n

122 *An Ecclesiastical History* I 790

123 *Institutionum* 647 (my translation)

124 Ibid 643–4, 650–1

125 Ibid 690 (*An Ecclesiastical History* II 82), 704–8

126 Karl Heussi *Johann Lorenz von Mosheim* 22–41. On Hamburg, see Jean-Claude Margolin 'La Religion d'Erasme et l'Allemagne des Lumières' 202–4.
127 Heussi *Mosheim* 46, 96–7
128 Ibid 1, 233–5; Hirsch II 360
129 Meinhold II 80–9, 97–110, 596–7; Hirsch V 57–9; RGG 5: cols 403–4, 1545–6
130 Herbert Gutschera *Reformation und Gegenreformation innerhalb der Kirchengeschichtsschreibung von Johann Matthias Schröckh* 1–2, 12–13
131 Meinhold II 80–5
132 Ibid 81; Gutschera *Reformation und Gegenreformation* 3, 14
133 Johann Matthias Schröckh *Christliche Kirchengeschichte* 30: 273
134 Gutschera 2n
135 Friedrich Lücke *Dr. Gottlieb Jakob Planck* 30–2
136 Aner *Die Theologie der Lessingzeit* 139–40
137 Lücke *Planck* 39–42
138 M. Maeder 'Notice sur la vie et les écrits de Théophile-Jacques Planck' 136
139 Meinhold II 98–9
140 *Geschichte der Entstehung, der Veränderungen und der Bildung unsers protestantischen Lehrbegriffs* I xiii–xvii
141 *Einleitung in die Theologische Wissenschaften* 2: 233
142 Meinhold II 99–104
143 Cf Lücke *Planck* 27
144 As one would expect, Schröckh proceeds biographically, relying on the standard lives of Erasmus, and by an analysis of his works.
145 *Christliche Kirchengeschichte seit der Reformation* 1: 49–50
146 *Geschichte* I 8, 14, 20–3
147 Ibid 24–7
148 *Christliche Kirchengeschichte* 30: 277, 280
149 *Christliche Kirchengeschichte seit der Reformation* 1: 54–61
150 *Christliche Kirchengeschichte* 30: 290
151 Planck *Geschichte* I 338–44. Cf Schröckh *Christliche Kirchengeschichte seit der Reformation* 1: 204–7, 244–5.
152 *Christliche Kirchengeschichte seit der Reformation* 1: 311–12, 314; Planck *Geschichte* II 111–13
153 *Geschichte* II 137
154 *Christliche Kirchengeschichte seit der Reformation* 1: 546
155 The problem of the 'forerunners' has remained in Reformation historiography. See H.A. Oberman *The Forerunners of the Reformation.*
156 Leopold Zscharnack 'Reformation und Humanismus im Urteil der deutschen Aufklärung' 161–7

157 The translation was actually by a friend, a pastor in Braun-
schweig. It was fully revised by Henke (*Das Leben des Desiderius
Erasmus von Rotterdam ... Aus dem Französischen des Herrn von
Burigny* I iii).

158 Ibid I xii, xxiii, II 29

159 NDB 8: 526; RGG 3: 221; Hirsch V 11–14; Aner *Die Theologie der
Lessingzeit* 140; Meinhold II 90–3, 593

160 *Das Leben* I xxiv, xxvi, xxviii–ix, 286–7, II 93–6

161 Ibid I vii–x, 479, II 423

162 Ibid II 555–7. On Simon, see *Phoenix of His Age* 174–9.

163 Ibid II 558, 562, 565, 568, 580–8

164 Ibid I xxix–xxxiii, II 32–3

165 Hirsch IV 49

166 *Neue Versuche, die Kirchenhistorie der ersten Jahrhunderte mehr
aufzuklären* 2–8

167 Goffried Hornig *Die Anfänge der historisch-kritischen Theologie* 11;
Hirsch IV 86; Meinhold II 41

168 *Versuch eines fruchtbaren Auszugs der Kirchengeschichte* 2: a3^r

169 Hornig *Die Anfänge* 9, 12, 126; Hirsch IV 88–9

170 *Lebensbeschreibung von ihm selbst abgefasst* II 119–24, 233–4

171 Cf Hirsch IV 53–5; Hornig *Die Anfänge* 24–5; Leopold Zscharnack
Lessing und Semler 178–80.

172 *Desiderii Erasmi Roterod: Ratio seu Methodus verae theologiae: Recensuit et illustravit S. Io. Semler* vii–viii

173 Aner *Die Theologie der Lessingzeit* 102–7

174 *Ratio* xvii

175 'Hic primus et unicus tibi sit scopus, ... ut muteris, ut rapiaris, ...
ut transformeris in ea, quae discis' (*Ausgewählte Werke*, ed Holborn 180). Cf Marjorie O'Rourke Boyle *Erasmus on Language and
Method in Theology* 73.

176 *Lebensbeschreibung* II 235–9

177 *Versuch* II 221–2; *Neue Versuche* 43

178 *Institutio ad doctrinam christianam liberaliter discendam* 27–9

179 *Liber de sarcienda ecclesiae concordia* (1533)

180 *Versuch* 400. Cf Hornig *Die Anfänge* 133–4.

181 Hornig *Die Anfänge* 130; Meinhold II 41

182 On the Bohemians, Moravians, and Waldensians and on the philosophers – Aristotelians and Platonists – who stood outside the
authoritarian church, *Versuch* II a7^r–a8^v; on Valla, *Neue Versuche*
43; on the Greek exiles from Constantinople, *Institutio* 26–7.

183 Quoted in Meinhold II 62. Cf Hornig *Die Anfänge* 146–7.

184 *Versuch* II b2^r–b3^r

185 'Alia iam est formula colligendorum et tuendorum civium, cuius
ius et fas a Theologis non requiritur' (*Ratio* xv).

186 *Ratio* xi–xvi. Cf Hirsch IV 69–72, 79; Meinhold II 41, 45; *TRE* IV

601. Semler recognized his debts to Gottfried Arnold (*Neue Versuche* 93–4). There were significant differences between them, especially Semler's more developed historical sense (Hirsch IV 73).
187 *Ratio* viii–xi. I have here treated Semler after Planck although the latter was by far the younger man. In important respects Planck was Semler's pupil (cf Hirsch IV 88). Nevertheless, in his interpretation of Erasmus, Semler was more 'advanced' and indeed the high point of the theological Enlightenment.
188 *Phoenix of His Age* 20, 227
189 Holborn *History of Modern Germany* 282; T.C.W. Blanning *Joseph II and Enlightened Despotism* 58
190 Quoted Saul K. Padover *The Revolutionary Emperor: Joseph II of Austria* 147
191 R.A. Kann *A History of the Habsburg Empire 1526–1918* 187
192 Quoted Blanning *Joseph II* 188. For Erasmus on the history of monasticism, see 'Letter to Paul Volz' in John C. Olin *Christian Humanism and the Reformation: Selected Writings* 125–8.
193 Kann *Habsburg Empire* 191
194 Paul P. Bernard *The Origins of Josephinism: Two Studies* 42
195 Srbik 131–2; Arnold Berney 'Michael Ignaz Schmidt'
196 Berney 'Michael Ignaz Schmidt' 213–14
197 *Geschichte der Deutschen* 5–6. For volume 5 I use the second edition, Ulm 1788, for volume 6 the first, Ulm 1785.
198 Ibid 5: 54–5
199 Ibid 6: chs 22–3, 287–315: 'Was theoretische und praktische Religion durch die Reformation gewonnen'; 'In wie weit die Aufklärung dadurch befördet worden.'
200 Ibid 6: 288–9. Erasmus to Mountjoy, Anderlecht, (c 5 July?) 1521, Allen Ep 1219, IV 542–5.
201 Ibid 6: 290–4. Semler had, of course, frankly identified himself with Erasmus.
202 Ibid 6: 294–300
203 Ibid 6: 305–13
204 *Allgemeine deutsche Bibliothek* 72 (1787): 240, 245–6
205 [J.F. Gaum] *Luther und die Reformation* 17, 19, 134
206 Bainton *Erasmus of Christendom* 198–202, 211–16; Hajo Holborn *Ulrich von Hutten and the German Reformation*
207 Werner Kohlschmidt *A History of German Literature* 11; Roy Pascal *The German Sturm und Drang* 16–17
208 Kohlschmidt 3–5
209 'Hutten' in *Der Teutsche Merkur* July 1776: 3–34, *Sämmtliche Werke* (henceforth SW) 9: 476–96. In the late eighteenth century the essay was mistakenly attributed to Goethe and the error persisted. Thus F.K. von Moser in *Patriotisches Archiv für Deutschland* 7 (1787) and the English translation by Anthony Aufrere *A Tribute*

to the Memory of Ulrich von Hutten London 1789. See Robert T. Clark Jr *Herder: His Life and Thought* 448. Zscharnack repeats the error (Reformation und Humanismus' 162).

210 'Hutten' 4–8, SW 9: 477–9
211 'Hutten' 11–12, SW 9: 481–2. For Erasmus' attitude to the letters, see Epp 622, 637 in CWE 5: 65–7, 83–5. The story that Erasmus laughed so much at the letters that he burst an abscess is retailed by Bayle; it was said to demonstrate one of the benefits of reading (*Dictionnaire historique* VI 241).
212 'Hutten' 18–28, SW 9: 486–92
213 'Hutten' 29–30, SW 9: 492–3
214 SW 1: 359–60, 371–2. Of course, Herder accepted the study of the classics as essential for every educated person. He rejected the domination of Latin and consequent emasculation, as he saw it, of German. His target was Christian Adolf Koltz of Halle, a Latin poet and representative of what he saw as a sterile classical tradition (Clark *Herder* 72–3).
215 Cf Kaegi 'Erasmus im achtzehnten Jahrhundert' 221–2.
216 'Vom Erkennen und Empfinden den zwo Hauptkräften der Menschlichen Seele' (MS 1775 SW 8: 307–8). In this essay Herder rejected the assumption that cognition and sensation were distinct faculties in favour of a unitary, vitalistic psychology, by which knowing and feeling were subject to mutually dependent laws (Clark *Herder* 217–18, 227; cf Pascal *Sturm und Drang* 164–6, Kaegi 'Erasmus im achtzehnten Jahrhundert' 222–3).
217 Cornelius Sommer *Christoph Martin Wieland* 36–7; Friedrich Sengle *Wieland* 407–17. Cf Wieland to Fritz Jacobi 2 November 1775: 'The *Merkur* shall above all make its fortune among the middling sort of people and does so' (quoted Sengle 407). The success of the journal was considerable; in its first year a printing of 2500 copies was insufficient (Sommer *Wieland* 37).
218 'Zusatz des Herausgebers' 34–7, SW 9: 496–7
219 Wieland to Merck 13 June 1777 (quoted Clark *Herder* 248)
220 Sengle *Wieland* 299–314; Sommer *Wieland* 37
221 The Holbein profile, reversed, appeared in the October number and, in December, 'Ein Fragment über den Charakter des Erasmus von Rotterdam' 262–72.
222 'Ein Fragment' 262–4
223 Ibid 264–6
224 Ibid 267–72
225 *Wieland* 315, 317. Lieselotte E. Kurth-Voigt has remarked on their common appreciation of the multiple ways of observing reality and of the validity of differing points of view, in *Perspectives and Points of View: The Early Works of Wieland and Their Background* 32, 35, 129–30.

226 Cf Kaegi 'Erasmus im achtzehnten Jahrhundert' 223–6.
227 Clark *Herder* 264
228 'Über den Einfluss der schönen in die höhern Wissenschaften'
    (1781) SW 9: 305–6. Others of this kind among the moderns were
    de Thou, Montaigne, Sidney, Shaftesbury, Machiavelli, Sarpi, and
    Grotius.
229 *Briefe, das Studium der Theologie betreffend* SW 10: 187, 252
230 'Briefe an Theophron' (1781, but not published until 1808 in the
    first complete edition of Herder's works edited by Müller) SW 11:
    169–70. Cf Clark *Herder* 279–81.
231 Kohlschmidt *History of German Literature* 247
232 F.M. Barnard *Herder's Social and Political Thought* 86–7, 91–3,
    104–5
233 Ibid 75
234 Clark *Herder* 367–9
235 SW 17: 67–8
236 Quoted Clark *Herder* 393
237 From a late MS, SW 18: 332
238 SW 20: 69. Kaegi refers the remark to the death of Erasmus but
    that of Luther makes more sense ('Erasmus im achtzehnten Jahr-
    hundert' 226).
239 'Denkmal Ulrichs von Hutten' reprinted in *Zerstreute Blätter*
    (1793) SW 16: 273–93
240 Herder's preface at SW 16: 133–4
241 Ibid 290
242 Ibid 281n
243 Sommer *Wieland* 40
244 Sengle *Wieland* 440. Bernd Weyergraf charges Wieland with
    equivocation: '[He] wavered between a radical bourgeois critique
    of absolutism and fears of a bourgeois revolution' (*Der skeptische
    Bürger* xii, 9).
245 *Wielands Werke* 15: 772
246 See my 'Erasmus in the Age of Revolutions.' My text was com-
    pleted before I became aware of the finely argued work by Wil-
    helm Kreutz *Die Deutschen und Ulrich von Hutten: Rezeption von
    Autor und Werk seit dem 16. Jahrhundert*. Kreutz demonstrates that
    in their handling of Hutten in the original essays, Wieland uses a
    distancing language, Herder a language of total commitment to
    his subject (*Die Deutschen und Ulrich von Hutten* 63–73).
247 Cf *Phoenix of His Age* 300–1.
248 There is no extended reference to Erasmus in the writings of G.E.
    Lessing. The Vienna thesis by Gerhard Forsthuber, 'Erasmus und
    Lessing: Eine Untersuchung über die Beziehungen zwischen Hu-
    manismus und Frühklassik,' is concerned with parallels in the life
    and thought of the two men and treats them as representatives of

the intellectual movements mentioned in the subtitle. It lists various minor references by Lessing to Erasmus at p. 128. On Lessing's attitude to the Reformation, see E.W. Zeeden *Martin Luther und die Reformation im Urteil des deutschen Luthertums* I 281.

CHAPTER FOUR

1 On Enlightenment influences, Paul Wernle *Der schweizerische Protestantismus im XVIII. Jahrhundert* I 470, 478–80; on history, Richard Feller and Edgar Bonjour *Geschichtsschreibung der Schweiz vom Spätmittelalter zur Neuzeit* II 431–3, 453–4.
2 Wernle *Schweizerische Protestantismus* I 539. Cf ibid II 408; Kaegi 'Erasmus im achtzehnten Jahrhundert' 214–15.
3 'La Journée des Quatre Sapins' (quoted in Kaegi 215–16)
4 *Religiöse Gespräche der Todten* 102–21. On Wegelin, see *Dict hist et biog* VII 251; ADB 41: 423–4. Constrained by the orthodox atmosphere of St Gallen, he accepted a call to Frederick the Great's Berlin in 1765.
5 Quoted in Feller and Bonjour *Geschichtsschreibung* II 540
6 *Lob der Narrheit aus dem Lateinischen des Erasmus von Rotterdam*, übersetzt ... von Wilhelm Gottlieb Becker
7 *Dict hist et biog* III 334
8 *Leben des Erasmus* 174. In other places (41, 86n) Seckendorf and Semler are mentioned. Erasmus' early life is written from Beatus Rhenanus, the *Compendium vitae*, the letter to Servatius Rogerus, Bayle, and Jortin. For the Swiss Reformation, there is reference to the seventeenth-century Zürich historian J.H. Hottinger and to the *Histoire de la réformation de la Suisse* of Abraham Ruchat (1678–1750), professor at Lausanne, who did original work on the Reformation in French-speaking Switzerland (see Feller and Bonjour II 528–31).
9 Johannes Gaudin *Leben des Erasmus* viii, 33, 39–40, 146
10 Erasmus to Luigi (Aloysius) Marliano 25 March 1521 (Allen Ep 1195 IV 461)
11 Gaudin *Leben* 43, 77–80, 134n, 139
12 Ibid 72–3
13 Ibid 65, 85–95
14 Ibid 98, 108, 118–23, 148
15 From a long appendix on Erasmus and the Reformation ibid 188–236, at 193–210. Cf Wulschner's remark: 'Erasmus appears in Gaudin as a kind of frustrated Luther' (Wulschner 36).
16 Gaudin *Leben* 234
17 Ibid 42, 54, 152–6
18 Cf Wulschner 37
19 On the Hess family, NDB 9: 1–3; on Salomon Hess, Wernle *Der*

schweizerische Protestantismus II 383–4, *Dict hist et biog* IV 89, RE[3] 7 801; on Johann Jakob, Albert Schweitzer *Quest for the Historical Jesus* 29–31.

20 Salomon Hess *Erasmus von Rotterdam nach seinem Leben und Schriften* I ix–x, 506

21 Ibid I 56. On Knight, see *Phoenix of His Age* 270–3.

22 Hess I 73–5, 79–81, 115, 127

23 Ibid I 159, 218

24 Ibid I 182. Le Clerc at *Bibliothèque choisie* (1705) V 185 (see *Phoenix of His Age* 251).

25 Hess I 233, 270, 331, 408, 459, 470–1. At 469–70 Hess touches on the seventeenth- and eighteenth-century controversies about Erasmus among French Catholics.

26 Ibid I 512

27 Ibid II viii. In this section of his work Hess aims at a full account of Erasmus' various opponents; he used MS collections by Johann Jakob Simmler (1716–88), editor of the *Sammlung alter und neuer Urkunden zur Beleuchtung der Kirchen-Geschichte vornämlich des Schweizerlandes* 1759–63 (ibid II v; cf *Dict hist et biog* VI 194; Wernle *Schweizerische Protestantismus* II 382–3; Feller and Bonjour *Geschichtsschreibung* II 432).

28 Hess II vi–vii

29 Ibid II 8, 51, 79–81

30 Ibid II, 60, 78–9, 192, 316

31 Ibid II 505, 508–10, 512–13, 519–21, 522–3

32 *Leben des Desiderius Erasmus.* The book was published under the pseudonym A.G. and in a series edited by J.F.W. Tischer.

33 Wulschner 45

34 Wagner *Leben* iv–vii

35 Ibid iii–iv, 1–3

36 Ibid 4–7, 9, 11–12

37 Ibid 19–20. Wagner follows Hess in identifying Colet's influence.

38 Ibid 21, 27–8, 36–8, 46

39 Ibid 22–5, 48–9, 61–2

40 Ibid 62, 77, 85, 88–90, 102–3, 108–9, 115–16, 119

41 Ibid 130–3, 139–41

42 Ibid 163–4

43 *Encyclopedia of Philosophy* 8: 16. On the place of the common-sense philosophy in Scottish education and culture, see George Elder Davie *The Democratic Intellect: Scotland and Her Universities in the Nineteenth Century* ch 11.

44 John Veitch 'Memoir of Dugald Stewart' xxxix. Stewart was from 1785 professor of moral philosophy at Edinburgh after already occupying the chair of mathematics conjointly from 1775 (DNB XVIII

1169–73; cf Fearnley-Sander 'Emancipation of the Mind 192–202). His teaching was polymathic. When once standing in for the professor of natural philosophy he described himself as 'employed in premeditating two lectures – the one on the Air Pump, and the other on the Immortality of the Soul' (Veitch lvi).

45 Veitch 'Memoir' xxxvi–vii, xlix

46 Quote Veitch ixn

47 *Dissertation: Exhibiting the Progress of Metaphysical, Ethical, and Political Philosophy, since the Revival of Letters in Europe* 487, 497

48 Ibid 25, 27. The tendency here will be understood if it is recognized that Stewart's hero in this part of his discussion is Bacon. When Stewart was at Edinburgh 'intellectual life in the University was nourished in great measure by the writings of Bacon and Newton' (Veitch 'Memoir' xi).

49 *Dissertation* 27–8

50 Ibid 28–9, 31–3, 36–41

51 Ibid 27–8

52 Stewart praised Gibbon's delineation of Erasmus' character (ibid 57n).

53 Ibid 530 (from an additional note on More)

54 The similarity with Robertson's views has been noted (Fearnley-Sander 'Emancipation of the Mind' 229–30).

55 'The Prospect of Perpetual and Universal Peace to be Established on the Principles of Christian Philanthropy' in *Works* VI 351–70

56 DNB XI 334–6; Allibone I 1044–5; 'Biographical Preface' in *Works* I vi–vii, x. Knox, said the *Edinburgh Review*, deserved respect for his 'rare independence of mind' and 'his steady adherence, through the worst of times, to the cause of liberty' (quoted Allibone I 1045).

57 'Biographical Preface' ii

58 *Annual Register 1821* 242. Cf 'Biographical Preface' x.

59 J.E. Cookson *The Friends of Peace: Anti-War Liberalism in England, 1793–1815* 5–9, 32–3. A history and full description of Knox's work as it appears in an edition of 1795 has been provided by Emile V. Telle 'In the Wake of Erasmus of Rotterdam: An Outcry for Perpetual and Universal Peace in England in 1793–1795.' This edition included translations (by Knox) of *Querela pacis* and a second adage *Aut regem aut fatuum nasci oportere.* Cf F. Vander Haeghen et al *Bibliotheca Belgica* II 370–1; Margaret Mann Phillips 'Erasmus and Propaganda' 13–15. Knox aimed at a free translation of *Dulce bellum inexpertis* which he came across by chance (*Antipolemus* xiv). Both the 1794 and 1795 editions (the first used by me, the second by Telle, though the same pagination is used in both) included some letters of Erasmus and other sources (ibid

112–82; cf Telle 'In the Wake' 116–18). Telle's article, which I read after preparing my own text, also includes a treatment of Knox's debts to Erasmus and his Erasmianism generally.

60 *Antipolemus* v–vii

61 Ibid vii–ix

62 Ibid x–xiv. Erasmus, says Knox, spoke freely to the princes of his time and was graciously received. Today – 'in days of BOASTED LIBERTY' – he would be sent to Botany Bay (ibid 139).

63 Ibid xvii–xx, xxii, xxxiii–v

64 Knox takes care to avow his attachment to the constitution, while adding that reforms are needed (ibid xlii). While sharing the wit of Voltaire and Rousseau, Erasmus had 'the advantage of them in *two* points, in sound LEARNING, and in RELIGION' (ibid xxxix). Cf Jortin on Voltaire (*Phoenix of His Age* 279).

65 *Phoenix of His Age* 180

66 Jean Marie Louis Coupé (1732–1818) associated Erasmus' reputation with the need for peace, less from sympathy with the Revolution than from post-revolutionary exhaustion. In 1797 under the Directory he wrote a 'Notice' on Erasmus in his periodical *Les Soirées littéraires*. Both Erasmus' experience and his own demonstrated, he believed, that troubled times threw good letters into disfavour. While Coupé has some interesting things to say about Erasmus as a writer, his portrait generally is a pale and sometimes careless repetition of Burigny's. Erasmus appears as a pleasant and honourable littérateur, rather like Coupé himself (*Soirées* VII 5–7 and 'Erasme' passim; on Coupé, see Hoefer XII cols 173–4).

67 *Essay on the Spirit and Influence of the Reformation of Luther* 15–16. I use the translation by James Mill but refer also to the original *Essai sur l'esprit et l'influence de la Réformation de Luther* for significant references to Erasmus.

68 Michaud 43: 505–12; Yvonne Knibielher 'Réforme et Révolution d'après Charles de Villers.' His German sojourn changed his view of the revolution as the *Essai* reveals (cf Knibielher 'Réforme et Révolution' 173).

69 *Essay* 25, 31–4 (*Essai* 22–4)

70 *Essay* 35–48

71 Ibid 93, 104, 313, 399

72 He also uses the argument beloved of the Whig historians that Protestant countries were to the fore in social and intellectual progress (see, eg, ibid 330).

73 DNB XIII 383

74 J.H. Burns 'The Light of Reason: Philosophical History in the Two Mills' 4–5; Alexander Bain *James Mill: A Biography* 51–2

75 *Essay* i–iii

76 Ibid 15n. Frappell connects the English predilection for putting the blame on the *philosophes* with Burke; Mill accepts their influence without drawing Burke's conservative conclusion (Frappell, 'Interpretations of the Continental Reformation' 122).

77 *Essay* 34–5

78 Thus he finds no meaning in Villers' idea of the discordance of form and spirit in medieval Christendom (ibid 48n). On Mill's resistance to Kant and German philosophy generally, see Elie Halévy *The Growth of Philosophic Radicalism* 436.

79 *Essay* 354n

80 *Watchman* 9–10

81 Ibid 28. Cf Introduction xxviii, xxxix.

82 *Watchman* Introduction xl–xli. Cf Basil Willey *Nineteenth Century Studies* 8. He later spoke more kindly of Godwin (*Watchman* 197n).

83 *The Friend, Collected Works* 4.I editor's Introduction xxxvi.

84 Ibid xciii

85 The 1818 edition of the *Friend* appears as volume 4.I of the *Collected Works*. The 1809–10 version is printed as an appendix in volume 4.II. The passage on Erasmus which interests us is identical in both versions, apart from changes in capitalization. The whole essay is at 4.I 129–34 and 4.II 111–14.

86 *Friend Collected Works* 4.I 130–1

87 Ibid 131–2

88 Ibid 132–3

89 Ibid 134. For Coleridge on Luther, see Gordon Rupp *Righteousness of God* 49–50; L.O. Frappell 'Interpretations of the Continental Reformation in Great Britain during the Nineteenth Century' ch II; and, above all, Frappell 'Coleridge and the "Coleridgeans" on Luther.'

90 *Friend Collected Works* 4.I 148–53

91 Ibid 156

92 Coleridge *Aids to Reflection* xv–xvi

93 *Friend Collected Works* 4.I 156

94 James D. Boulger *Coleridge as Religious Thinker* 8–9, 35, 58, 60, 66, 75–6; J. Robert Barth *Coleridge and Christian Doctrine* 15–24; Willey *Nineteenth Century Studies* 27–38; Frappell 'Coleridge and the "Coleridgeans"' 308–10

95 *The Philosophical Lectures* 305–8. The lectures as published by Kathleen Coburn in 1949 derive from a verbatim report checked against other sources, including Coleridge's notebooks.

96 Editor's Introduction 27. An observer said of Lecture x: 'The cursory history of these times with an occasional levelling on the principal personages was all Mr C. attempted' (quoted ibid 30).

97 Ibid 37

98 The development of philosophy is 'an organic growth for Coleridge' (ibid 42).

99 *Philosophical Lectures* 284

100 Ibid 290–1, 294, 316–17

101 Ibid 300, 305

102 Ibid 308

103 Ibid 284

104 *Table Talk and Omniana* 336

105 Ibid 228–9

106 *Literary Remains* 4 57. Coleridge there agreed with Luther that Erasmus' mockery would not defeat the papal enemy head-on but it was 'an excellent pioneer and an excellent *corps de reserve.*' He was not uncritical of the Reformers: 'As soon as men began to call themselves names, all hope of further amendment was lost.' The English Reformers made a fatal error, that of 'clinging to court and state, instead of cultivating the people' (*Table Talk* 55, 106).

107 *Works of Samuel Johnson* I *Diaries, Prayers, and Annals* 11n, 22–3

108 James Boswell *Life of Johnson* ed G.B. Hill and L.F. Powell I 97, 99. Mathurin Cordier (1479–1564), the teacher of Calvin, published colloquies for schoolboys. J. Clarke's selection with English translations was first published at Nottingham in 1720 (Vander Haeghen *Bibliotheca Erasmiana* series 1 47).

109 *Works* I 194–5. Erasmus' distinction is from *Modus orandi Deum* (ASD V-1 140). On Baudius, see *Phoenix of His Age* 131.

110 *Works* I 198. Cf Boswell *Life of Johnson* V 466 and Allen VII 283. The *Epistola consolatoria* was first published at Basel in 1527. A final, much later reference is to the differences on transubstantiation between Erasmus and Chrysostom, whom Johnson took to be unorthodox on the question (*Works* I 365).

111 Johnson to Mrs Thrale, 6 October 1777, *Letters of Samuel Johnson* Letter 554, II 220

112 Johnson to Richard Brocklesby, 21 July 1784, ibid Letter 979, III 185

113 William Bowles (1755–1826) in his memoranda of Johnson's conversation at Heale, Bowles' residence in Wiltshire (*Life of Johnson* IV Appendix J 524).

114 Ibid III 84. Johnson 'would never consent to disgrace the walls of Westminster Abbey with an English inscription' (ibid 85).

115 From a catalogue prepared by Johnson early in life under the title 'Designs' and once in the possession of George III (*Life of Johnson* IV 381–4, 549).

116 *Works* III *The Rambler* 'Introduction' xxiii, xxvii

117 *Works* IV 213–14. 'No totum' etc. is from the opening sentence of the preface to Thomas More. That Erasmus wrote more than an-

other might hope to read was a commonplace of the Erasmus literature.

118 Note the title of B.H. Bronson's influential essays, 'Johnson Agonistes' (Donald J. Greene *Samuel Johnson: A Collection of Critical Essays* 30–45).
119 Albert C. Outler *John Wesley* 146–7
120 Cf *Phoenix of His Age* ch 3.
121 Rupert Davies and Gordon Rupp (eds) *A History of the Methodist Church in Great Britain* I 176–9
122 DNB VIII 312–14; Bernard Semmel *The Methodist Revolution* 52
123 'Zelotes and Honestus Reconciled; Or, The Third Part of An Equal Check to Pharisaism and Antinomianism' (1775), quoted Semmel 84–5
124 The *History* was begun by Joseph Milner with some contribution from Isaac. The latter revised and extended the work after his brother's death (1797), using his notes. Joseph did not reach beyond the early stages of the Luther affair. There is no point in distinguishing the work of the two authors; the brothers, between whom there was an intense attachment, shared the same outlook, though markedly different in personality (DNB XIII 465; J.D. Walsh 'Joseph Milner's Evangelical Church History' 176, 186).
125 DNB XIII 465; Walsh 184–5; John H. Overton and Frederick Relton *The English Church from the Accession of George I to the End of the Eighteenth Century* 194
126 *History of the Church of Christ* iii, v. John Newton's church history (1770) had already taken this approach as its title indicates: *A Review of Ecclesiastical History, so far as it concerns the progress, declensions and revivals of evangelical doctrines and practice, with a brief account of the spirit and methods by which vital and experimental religion have been opposed in all ages of the church* (cf Walsh 177).
127 Ford K. Brown *Fathers of the Victorians: The Age of Wilberforce* 80
128 *History* iv
129 John Lawson *A Town Grammar School through Six Centuries: A History of Hull Grammar School against Its Local Background* 167
130 Quoted Brown *Fathers of the Victorians* 421
131 Robert Isaac and Samuel Wilberforce *The Life of William Wilberforce* I 4, II 228
132 Quoted Brown *Fathers of the Victorians* 53
133 DNB XIII 456–9
134 *Essays in Ecclesiastical Biography* II 359
135 Wilberforce *Life* I 87, 381
136 G.R. Balleine, quoted Brown *Fathers of the Victorians* 291
137 Stephen *Essays* II 366
138 Ibid 360, 364

398 Notes to pages 99–102

139 *History of the Church of Christ* 660, 662–3, 670
140 Ibid 666–7
141 Ibid 673–4, 697
142 Ibid 855–6
143 Ibid 858–9, 861–2, 865
144 Ibid 887–9. Milner insisted that the Church of England, to whose establishment he was unreservedly committed, rejected Pelagianism (Article IX).
145 *Essays* II 362–3
146 There is one qualification: Beausobre's book, *Histoire de la Réformation, ou origine et progrès du Luthéranisme, dans l'Empire & les Estats de la confession de Augsbourg, depuis 1517 jusqu'en 1530,* was published posthumously (Berlin 1785). Beausobre fled France in 1685. He worked on the history throughout his exile which was spent (from 1693) at Berlin under the patronage of the Prussian court (DBF 5 cols 1181–2).
147 Walsh 'Joseph Milner's Evangelical Church History' 183. It is well known that the work's conception of the constant renewal of the church by effusions of the Holy Spirit influenced Newman (*Apologia pro Vita Sua* 22–3).
148 The same judgment, but from the side of old Dissent, is to be found in *The Life of Philip Melanchthon* by Francis Augustus Cox (2nd ed 1817). 'The learned, witty, vacillating, avaricious and artful Erasmus' was at the head of the party which understood the abuses of the papacy but was unwilling to break with it and sympathized with the aims of the Reformers but refused to join them (34–5). Cox (1783–1853), from an old Baptist family, was Baptist minister at Hackney for forty-two years. (See DNB IV 1336; Allibone I 441.) Between the first (1815) and second editions of *Melanchthon* he moderated his expressions on Erasmus in response to criticism from some 'literary friends' and in an appendix quoted Jortin somewhat to Erasmus' defence (567–9).
149 See John Walsh 'Origins of the Evangelical Revival,' especially 148–53.
150 On Lavater see Wernle *Schweizerische Protestantismus* III 221–84; RGG 4: cols 243–4; Hirsch IV 185–92; Christian Janentzky *Johann Caspar Lavater;* John Graham *Lavater's Essays on Physiognomy: A Study in the History of Ideas;* Julius Forssman *J.K. Lavater und die religiösen Strömungen des achtzehnten Jahrhunderts.*
151 Lavater described portrait painting as 'the most natural, the most human, the noblest and most useful art' – and the most difficult (*Physiognomische Fragmente* II 78).
152 Wernle III 247–8; Janentzky *Lavater* 59
153 *Physiognomische Fragmente* I a3ᵛ, 13, 45, 57. Cf Graham *Lavater's Essays* 39–40.

154 *Physiognomische Fragmente* I 52, II 5
155 Wernle III 224–6, 233, 243–4; Forssman *J.K. Lavater* 76, 91–2
156 Janentzky *Lavater* 43, 56–7; Wernle III 229
157 Quoted Janentzky 58
158 Cf Wernle III 231, 272
159 *Physiognomische Fragmente* II 267–8
160 On the arbitrary character of physiognomy and its deceptive precision, see Graham 46, Forssman 82. On the enormous popularity of the work in the nineteenth century, Graham 11, 61–2. The *Gentleman's Magazine* of February 1801 said: 'In Switzerland, in Germany, in France, even in Britain, all the world became passionate admirers of the Physiognomical Science of Lavater ... In the enthusiasm with which [his books] were studied and admired, they were thought as necessary in every family as even the Bible itself' (quoted Graham 61).
161 Karl Barth *Protestant Thought: From Rousseau to Ritschl* 306
162 The 'Einleitung in das Studium der Kirchengeschichte' of 1806 is published as an appendix in Friedrich Schleiermacher *Geschichte der christlichen Kirche* 623–31.
163 Brian Gerrish 'Schleiermacher and the Reformation: A Question of Doctrinal Development' 155; Jerry F. Dawson *Friedrich Schleiermacher: The Evolution of a Nationalist* 132–7
164 Schleiermacher *Geschichte* vii; Hanna Jursch *Schleiermacher als Historiker* 10–11
165 Quoted Gerrish 'Schleiermacher and the Reformation' 149. Cf Jursch *Schleiermacher* 51–3.
166 Schleiermacher *Geschichte* 15, 21–2. Cf Jursch *Schleiermacher* 61, 65.
167 Schleiermacher *Geschichte* 5
168 Ibid 22, 26. Cf Jursch *Schleiermacher* 63.
169 Schleiermacher *Geschichte* 45
170 Jursch *Schleiermacher* 65; Hirsch IV 524–6
171 Barth *Protestant Thought* 332
172 Werner Schultz *Schleiermacher und der Protestantismus* 23, 27–8
173 Quoted Gerrish 'Schleiermacher and the Reformation' 157. Cf Hirsch V 157–8.
174 Schleiermacher *Geschichte* 574–5
175 Ibid 576, 582–3
176 Ibid 584–8, 594, 603, 622
177 ADB XXII 764–83
178 Allen Ep 1161 IV 380–3
179 'Heldenmüthiges ungedrucktes Schreiben Ulrichs von Hutten' 5. Moser mistakenly attributes Herder's essay to Goethe (ibid 7).
180 Ibid 6–7, 10–12, 14, 19
181 Allen Ep 1445 V 451–3

182 'Heldenmüthiges ungreducktes Schreiben' 17–18, 20
183 Lutz Winckler *Martin Luther als Bürger und Patriot*
184 On Rotermund, see Winckler *Martin Luther* 81. On his view of the Reformation, ibid 20.
185 *Erneuertes Andenken der Männer die für und gegen die Reformation Lutheri gearbeitet haben* 1: 284–6
186 Ibid 286–7, 290. Rotermund's references are to Beatus Rhenanus, Melchior Adam, Du Pin, Le Clerc, Burigny and Henke, Hess, Wagner, and Schröckh (ibid). He lists (290–308) separate editions of Erasmus' works in chronological order, with brief notes on some, especially German translations. It is interesting that Erasmus is not mentioned in Rotermund's essay on Hutten, who is presented more as a satirist than a national hero (537–42).
187 Cf Winckler *Martin Luther* 30.
188 *Luther und seine Zeitgenossen* 66–8
189 Ibid 48–50, 52, 63, 77–8, 90
190 Winckler *Martin Luther* 35, 40, 49–50
191 *Ulrichs von Hutten Leben: Fortsetzung der Reformatoren* Leipzig 1803
192 *Ulrich von Hutten nach seinem Leben, seinem Karakter und seinen Schriften geschildert* Nuremberg 1823 (quoted Wulschner 43).
193 *Ulrich von Hutten gegen Desiderius Erasmus und Desiderius Erasmus gegen Ulrich von Hutten* 11–12, 15, 34, 41–5, 55, 57–60
194 *Der Streit zwischen Ulrich von Hutten und Erasmus von Rotterdam* vi, viii–ix, xii, 60. The book contains translations of the two men's writings against one another with some associated correspondence. There are introductions and substantial notes to each document. Cf Kreutz *Die Deutschen und Ulrich von Hutten* 95–6.
195 *Der Streit* 1–3, 59, 146–7, 156
196 [Jos. Heller] *Vertheidigung des grossen Erasmus von Rotterdam gegen ungegründete Beschuldigungen desselben durch die Anhänger Huttens* iv–vi
197 Ibid ix–x, 12, 17, 34–5, 45
198 Ibid 86–93. The rationalist theologian H.E.G. Paulus (1761–1851) in his journal *Sophronizon* defended Erasmus against the reproach of handling Hutten unfairly in his *Colloquia*, eg, by presenting him as the syphilitic nobleman in 'The Unequal Marriage,' but also defended the morals and integrity of Hutten himself ('Zur richtigeren Beurtheilung Hulderichs von Hutten und Erasmus').
199 This is an extended version of my treatment in 'Erasmus and the Mediating School' 307–9.
200 For what follows, see 'Leben des Verfassers' in A. Schottmüller *Luther: Ein deutsches Heldenleben* vii–xvii. By the time of this Luther biography, Müller had changed his name to Schottmüller by adding his mother's surname to his father's.

201 In a review of Rudhart's biography of Thomas More (*Theologische Studien und Kritiken* III 4: 900)

202 In a review of Mayerhoff's biography of Reuchlin (ibid IV 3: 608–9)

203 See preface to his biography, *Leben des Erasmus von Rotterdam: Mit einleitenden Betrachtungen über die analoge Entwickelung der Menschheit und des einzelnen Menschen* iii–iv.

204 *Erinnerungen an einen Heimgegangenen* 7, 9–10, 19, 24, 31

205 *Leben des Erasmus* 3–4, 10, 30, 52, 77–81. Though Italy emerged from ignorance and barbarism during the fifteenth century, studies there were restricted to the classics for their own sake (ibid 155–6).

206 Ibid 216, 221–2

207 Ibid 120, 236, 239–40. The judgment – made in a comment on the morality of the *Colloquies* – is shockingly unfair in view of Erasmus' repeated and lifelong condemnation of mere outward observance in religion and life.

208 Ibid 261

209 Ibid 196–7, 283, 321, 381

210 Ibid 96–7, 109–13

211 Ibid 100, 108–9, 203–4. A Dutch reviewer who shared Müller's general (Protestant) view of the period nevertheless considered his judgments on Erasmus' character too harsh and those on his works too little related to the age (P.J.L. Huet *Drie brieven aan eenen vriend, over een Hoogduitsch Werk*). A reviewer in the *Zeitschrift für die Geistlichkeit des Erzbisthums Freyburg* (1828) made a more vigorous rebuttal of Müller and defence of Erasmus' character, his approach to Christian renewal and reform, and his unpartisan stand in the Reformation struggles (extracts in 'Nogmaals iets over Erasmus').

CHAPTER SIX

1 Pl. Lefèvre 'La lecture des oeuvres d'Erasme au sein du bas clergé durant la première moitié du XVIe siècle'

2 R.W. Scribner *For the Sake of Simple Folk: Popular Propaganda for the German Reformation* 104–5

3 Heinz Holeczek *Erasmus Deutsch* 1: 20, 23, 28, 36

4 Irene Collins *The Government and the Newspaper Press in France 1814–1881* 58–9

5 E.K. Bramsted and K.J. Melhuish *Western Liberalism* 401–6

6 Collins ch VIII; Kurt Koszyk *Deutsche Presse im 19. Jahrhundert* ch VIII

7 Veit Valentin *1848 Chapters of German History* 328

8 Paul Joachimsen in Introduction to *Deutsche Geschichte im Zeitalter der Reformation* lxvii

9 Leonard Krygier *Ranke: The Meaning of History* 41
10 Theodore von Laue *Leopold Ranke: The Formative Years* 12–13;
Krygier *Ranke* 48–9
11 Letters to his brother Heinrich 18 February 1824, 26 November
1835 (*Das Briefwerk* 53–4, 271). Cf Krygier 69–70, 77.
12 Krygier *Ranke* 151–8
13 *Deutsche Geschichte* I 3–4, 155–60
14 Ibid 164. Cf *History of the Reformation* I 121.
15 Ibid 165–7, 171–6
16 'Der erste grosse Autor der Opposition in modernem Sinne' (ibid
176; cf *History* I 130).
17 *Deutsche Geschichte* I 176–7
18 Ibid 177–8
19 Krygier *Ranke* 29–30
20 *Deutsche Geschichte* I 179–80
21 *History* I 133
22 As the expressions indicate: 'voll Feinheit der Beobachtung, Laune
um den Mund, von etwas furchtsamer Haltung ...' (*Deutsche Geschichte* I 180). Lavater's expressions included: '(a) Die furchtsame
... Stellung. (b) Das Launigte im Munde. (c) Das Feine in Blicke'
(*Physiognomische Fragmente* II 267). An English editor mentions
the direct influence of 'Holbein's well-known portrait' (*History* I
133 n2).
23 He noted, but in a somewhat inappropriate context, Erasmus' remark that he had striven to make good letters – in Italy almost
pagan – speak of Christ (*Deutsche Geschichte* I 179 n2). The remark is in a letter of 9 September 1526 to Andrzej Krzycki (Andrew Cricius): '... ut bonae litterae, quas scis hactenus apud Italos
fere paganas fuisse, consuescerent de Christo loqui' (Allen Ep
1753 VI 414).
24 *Deutsche Geschichte* I 183–90. Cf Joachimsen Introduction lii–iii.
25 On Hagen, ADB 10 341–3.
26 *Deutschlands literarische und religiöse Verhältnisse* II viii
27 The first volume had the subtitle 'Mit besonderer Rücksicht auf
Wilibald Pirkheimer.' Reviewers of the first volume convinced
him of the book's general character (II v–vi).
28 G.P. Gooch *History and Historians in the Nineteenth Century* 68;
Charles E. McClelland *State, Society, and University in Germany
1700–1914* 147
29 I follow in part my discussion in 'Erasmus in the Nineteenth Century: The Liberal Tradition' 211–13 (permission granted by Renaissance Society of America).
30 *Verhältnisse* I 278–9; III 20
31 Ibid 301–; II ix–x
32 Ibid I 254–7

33 Ibid 306, 309, 316, 320–1
34 Ibid 408
35 Ibid III 13–26, 36–9
36 Ibid II ix–x; III vii–ix
37 Ibid III 247–50
38 Ibid 69, 75–6, 86–7
39 Ibid 43, 65–7

CHAPTER SEVEN

1 Cf A.E. Douglas 'Erasmus as a Satirist' in T.A. Dorey (ed) *Erasmus* 32.
2 See Marjorie O'Rourke Boyle *Rhetoric and Reform: Erasmus' Civil Dispute with Luther.*
3 For what follows, see Sainte-Beuve 'Ecrivains critiques contemporains'; Nisard 'Lettre au Directeur de la Revue des Deux Mondes'; Hoefer XXXVIII cols 93–6; J. Barbey d'Aurevilly *Les quarante médaillons de l'Académie* 94–8; J.-C. Margolin 'Sardou, traducteur des *Colloques* d'Erasme.'
4 'Lettre' 498
5 'Ecrivains critiques contemporains' 273–4
6 'Lettre' 501–2, 505
7 Mansfield 'Erasmus in the Nineteenth Century: The Liberal Tradition' 204–7. I again in part, with permission, follow this text.
8 Nisard 'Erasme' 538
9 Ibid 261, 264–5
10 Ibid 268, 270, 280–1
11 Ibid 286–9, 293
12 Ibid 295–6
13 Ibid 383, 387–9, 396–8
14 Ibid 407–8, 410–11. It is sad, Nisard adds, to see the best minds of an age devoured by such sterile controversies. This is no embarrassment to the historical fatalists 'who interest Providence in all men's follies' and produce good out of evil, but he would prefer to believe that 'there are actions as well as lives lost without fruit in the work of humanity' (ibid 411).
15 Ibid 422–3
16 Ibid 385–7. Nisard is possibly criticizing Villers.
17 Ibid 510, 513–17
18 Ibid 545–9
19 Ibid 534–5, 539–43
20 G.P. Gooch *History and Historians* 172–3
21 Ibid 170
22 See Paul Viallaneix *La Voie royale: Essai sur l'idée de peuple dans l'oeuvre de Michelet.*
23 *Histoire de France* VII 192, 195, 197–9. Is the reference to Erasmus'

'Saint Socrates, pray for us' in the colloquy 'Convivium Religiosum' (*Colloquies*, ed Thompson, 67–8)?
24 *Histoire de France* VII ii, iv–v, ix. Cf Ferguson *Renaissance in Historical Thought* 174–8, 192.
25 *Histoire de France* VII xciii, cxxxii–iv. Cf Taine *Essais de critique et d'histoire* 334.
26 *Histoire de France* VIII xi–xv, 83, 85–6, 92, 92, 109
27 *Mémoires de Luther, écrits par lui-même*. The work was composed mostly in 1828–9, but first published in 1835.
28 *Mémoires* ix–xii
29 See Irène Tieder *Michelet et Luther: Histoire d'une rencontre*. For other comments on the change in Michelet's view of Luther, Gabriel Monod *La Vie et la pensée de Jules Michelet* I 351 and O.A. Haac *Les Principes inspirateurs de Michelet* 52, 69.
30 *Histoire de France* VIII 97–8, 100, 113–14
31 Cf Tieder *Michelet et Luther* 167 and Viallaneix *La Voie royale* 347.
32 *Histoire de France* VII 203–4
33 Michelet *Journal* 14 August 1838, 24–5 August 1843 I 286, 528–31. Monod considered these the finest pages of Michelet's journal (*La Vie et la pensée* II 162).
34 *Mémoires de Luther* 61–3, 215–16. We find the same characterization in a note in Michelet's 'Journal des idées' of March 1829, ie when he was preparing the *Mémoires*: 'C'est, avec moins d'esprit et de force, le Voltaire du temps. D'un temps où l'on ne pouvait pas tout dire: de là, aussi, moins d'esprit' (*Ecrits de jeunesse* 245).
35 *Histoire de France* VIII 414. Passages Michelet has in mind include: 'the human race is propagated by the part [of the body] which is so foolish and funny that it cannot even be mentioned without a snicker. That is the sacred fount from which all things draw life ...' 'What is it about babies that makes us hug and kiss and cuddle them? ... Nothing but the allurement of folly ...' (*Praise of Folly* 18, 20). By contrast, Luther re-created the family, breaking the tyranny of the priest and restoring sex, marriage, and the family to nature (*Histoire de France* VIII 102–6).
36 *Histoire de France* VII 204–5
37 DBF 13 cols 1218–19; Feugère *Erasme* x–xi
38 Feugère 206–7
39 Ibid 302–5, 317–19
40 Ibid 207–8, 216–22, 236
41 Ibid 29, 46, 122
42 Ibid 237–43, 278
43 Ibid 319–20, 324–5, 328–9, 377–9
44 Ibid 343–7, 354–8, 365–74, 407, 434
45 Ibid 124, 236
46 Ibid 207–8

47 Ibid 1–2
48 Ibid 215–16, 244
49 Ibid 57, 249
50 Ibid 76, 91, 96
51 Ibid 248–59, 277, 285, 291–2
52 Ibid 163–4, 175
53 Ibid 7–9, 17, 19, 197–202
54 Ibid 450–1. He had 'ni le flegme ni l'esprit positif' of his Dutch compatriots.
55 Ibid 203, 452–3
56 *Göttingische gelehrte Anzeigen*, 1875, II 1258–9
57 Michelet, said Taine, 'considère l'histoire comme une école populaire de patriotisme et de morale' (*Essais* 338).
58 Two more famous authors wrote sympathetically of Erasmus, broadly from an Enlightenment standpoint. Sainte-Beuve defended him against a charge of indecisiveness made by the famous preacher Lacordaire. He would, he said, never cease to revindicate under Erasmus' name 'the right of a refined and mitigated good sense, of a reason that regards, that observes, that chooses, that has no wish to believe more than it does believe,' the right, in short, of neutrals against dogmatists and fanatics (*Causeries du Lundi* 239–40; Eng trans E.J. Trechmann 192). As a young man, Victorien Sardou, later the author of *Tosca*, translated Erasmus' *Colloquia*; in his preface (published only in 1924), Sardou presents Erasmus as the *philosophe* of the gospel, as one seeking a reform moderate, tolerant, essentially moral and devout but opening the way for modern liberalism ('Erasme et ses *Colloques*' 492–4, 497, 502–3; cf J.-C. Margolin 'Sardou' 160).
59 DBF II col 660
60 *Erasme* iv–xi, 418–19
61 Ibid xi–ii. A work still relevant, says Amiel, in view of Lourdes and La Salette and the infallibility decree of 1870 (ibid 92).
62 Ibid 160, 174, 217, 256, 358, 446
63 Ibid 36, 38, 85, 147–9, 334–5
64 Ibid 246, 301
65 Ibid 338, 443–5
66 Ibid 161, 197–8, 261–2, 265, 318
67 Ibid 12–13, 34, 201, 242, 250
68 Mansfield 'Erasmus in the Nineteenth Century' 209

CHAPTER EIGHT

1 Erasmus 'On the Freedom of the Will' and Luther 'On the Bondage of the Will' in E. Gordon Rupp and Philip S. Watson (eds) *Luther and Erasmus: Free Will and Salvation* 37, 109

2 Marjorie O'Rourke Boyle *Rhetoric and Reform: Erasmus' Civil Dispute with Luther* 17–30. Cf Harry J. McSorley *Luther: Right or Wrong?* 279–82.

3 W.E.H. Lecky *History of the Rise and Influence of the Spirit of Rationalism in Europe* I xix. Cf Frappell 'Interpretations of the Continental Reformation' 157–8.

4 J.W. Burrow *A Liberal Descent: Victorian Historians and the English Past* 28–35

5 L.O. Frappell 'The Reformation as Negative Revolution or Obscurantism Reaction: The Liberal Debate on the Reformation in Nineteenth-Century Britain' 289, 306

6 DNB VIII 980–2, at 981 (Leslie Stephen)

7 J. W. Burrow *Liberal Descent* 30–2

8 G.P. Gooch *Historical Surveys and Portraits* 149

9 Cf T.P. Peardon *The Transition in English Historical Writing 1760–1830* 210.

10 *Introduction to the Literature* I Preface xiv

11 ibid xii

12 See, eg, notes, ibid 292, 297, 300–1, 308–9, 361, 363.

13 Ibid 232, 234, 237, 245, 247

14 Ibid 283–4. On this quarrel, see *Contemporaries of Erasmus* I 215–16.

15 *Introduction* I 276, 285

16 On this concluding passage of the essay, which does not fit easily with the rest of the text, see ASD II.6 425n.

17 *Introduction* I 285–91

18 Ibid 290

19 Ibid 292–5

20 Ibid 366. As a result, Hallam goes on, we can confidently allocate to our contemporaries allegiances in the sixteenth century and attribute nineteenth-century allegiances to figures from that time, including Luther and Erasmus. He admits, nevertheless, that we are too apt to judge past figures by consequences they could not have foreseen (ibid 366–7).

21 Ibid 381–2

22 Ibid 299, 383

23 Ibid 298, 304–7. As for Hutten, Herder's partiality was unreasonable; Jortin, on the other hand, was too contemptuous, 'but this is nearer justice than the veneration of the modern Germans' (ibid 297).

24 Ibid 364

25 Ibid 358–61

26 Ibid 359, 364

27 He was especially contemptuous of Isaac Milner, who 'rarely does justice to any one who did not servilely follow Luther.' He re-

jected all three terms of F.A. Cox's description of Erasmus as 'vacillating, avaricious, and artful.' He accepted Erasmus' basic consistency: 'his religious creed was nearly that of the moderate members of the church of Rome.' As for artfulness, how can it be attributed to a man 'perpetually involving himself by an unguarded and imprudent behaviour' (ibid 361n)?

28 Ibid 330–1, 405
29 Macaulay said: 'He is a hanging judge. His black cap is in constant requisition' (quoted Gooch *History and Historians* 275).
30 Cf Frappell ('Reformation as Negative Revolution' 303): 'Unlike most liberals, Pattison had come to believe that enlightenment is dearly won and easily lost, and a regression to obscurantism always a possibility.'
31 Mark Pattison *Memoirs* 100–1, 208
32 V.H.H. Green *Oxford Common Room: A Study of Lincoln College and Mark Pattison* 118. I have again been following in part my discussion in 'Erasmus in the Nineteenth Century: The Liberal Tradition.'
33 John Sparrow *Mark Pattison and the Idea of a University* chs 2, 3. In his first chapter, Sparrow discusses the purported representations of Pattison by nineteenth-century novelists, Rhoda Broughton (*Belinda*), George Eliot (*Middlemarch*), and Mrs Humphrey Ward (*Robert Elsmere*).
34 Of himself in the 1850s, Pattison said: 'brooding, melancholy, taciturn, and finally pessimist' (*Memoirs* 307). John Morley thought him remarkably destitute of nerve ('On Pattison's Memoirs' *Works* VI 240–1).
35 Dean Church, quoted in Sparrow *Pattison* 58
36 Pattison 'Erasmus' 515–16. Thus, Pattison avers, he was at his weakest in the free-will controversy.
37 Ibid 516–17
38 Morley 'On Pattison's Memoirs' 256
39 'Erasmus' 513
40 I pass over the physiognomic exercises deriving from Lavater and the idealist strictures of Adolf Müller.
41 'I cannot travel by railway without working out in my mind a better timetable than that in use' (*Memoirs* 254).
42 'Erasmus' 515
43 Ibid 516
44 The other subjects were Bentley, Casaubon, Grotius, Lipsius, More, Macaulay. Pattison once envisaged writing a history of learning since the Renaissance; he completed a life of Casaubon but the larger project, eventually centred on Joseph Scaliger, was never completed (Sparrow *Pattison* 27).
45 'With this abundance of choice, in which the same story is told

by a score of writers in English, French, and German, and in every variety of style, we can hardly say, as Sydney Smith did in 1812, that "a life of Erasmus is a desideratum" ' ('Erasmus' 518). This was to underestimate the unresolved problems in Erasmus' biography.

46 It is a rewriting of four articles which appeared in the Unitarian journal. *Theological Review*, between 1867 and 1870. Drummond had been a student at the Unitarian Manchester College 1854–7. A year of study on the Continent as a Hibbert Fellow, 1869–70, assisted the Erasmus biography. He was minister of St Mark's Unitarian Church, Edinburgh, for fifty years and published works on theological and public issues until well into this century (H. McLachlan *The Unitarian Movement in the Religious Life of England* I 265).

47 *Erasmus* I 31

48 Ibid I 8–11, 21

49 Ibid II 342–9

50 Eg, Gustave Masson, *Revue des questions historiques* xv (1874) 243–4. Marcus Dods thought Drummond too preoccupied with the evangelicals and his attacks on them lacking in dignity (*Erasmus and Other Essays* 5).

51 *Erasmus* I 3, vii; II 367–9. Masson, who otherwise admired the biography, thought the identification with the Broad Church 'quite simply absurd.' The views of Mr Jowett and Dean Stanley would have made Erasmus as well as Luther recoil with horror (*Revue des questions historiques* xv 244).

52 *Erasmus* I 239, 346–8

53 Ibid I 85

54 Ibid I 56, 255. The latter incident refers to Erasmus' accident on a horse in August 1514, given by Drummond as August 1515 (Ep 301, CWE 3 8–12). Drummond allows for the possibility that the whole was essentially a comic anecdote.

55 Ibid II 249, 338, 355–7, 361–4

56 Ibid II 180–6 (on the preface to the Hilary edition), 365

57 Ibid I 113–15, 185, 200, 260, 404–5. In his chapter on the *Adagia*, Drummond remarks that Erasmus was the earliest of the sixteenth-century writers to vindicate the right of rebellion, but his pages on the 'Sileni Alcibiadis' and the 'Scarabeus aquilam quaerit' are essentially paraphrase (ibid I 291–306).

58 Ibid II 2, 12, 66–7, 110, 349–50, 355

59 John Colet may be taken as an example (ibid I 70–1, 88–90): 'But if Colet found in Erasmus far greater intellectual vigour, profounder learning, more extensive knowledge of the world than he could pretend to, and a biting humour which he did not possess, Erasmus found in him on the other hand, a deep earnestness, a

gravity and holy fervour which were not in his own nature, and of the want of which he may have been conscious' (88–9). For contemporary reviews, see Ludwig Geiger (*Göttingische gelehrte Anzeigen* 1873) and Marcus Dods (*Erasmus and Other Essays* 7). There is justice in Herbert McLachlan's clumsily expressed remark of 1934: 'As the work of a little-known writer on one of the greatest figures in the history of European literature, published sixty years ago and still retaining its pride of place, this life of Erasmus is amongst the unique products of Nonconformist scholarship in the mid-Victorian age' (*Unitarian Movement* I 266).

60 *Theological Review* X (1873) 410–11, 416
61 DNB 1901–10 Supplement; C. Kegan Paul *Memories* 264
62 His Hibbert lectures were published in the Luther anniversary year of 1883 as *The Reformation of the 16 Century in its Relation to Modern Thought and Knowledge*. A *Martin Luther and the Reformation in Germany* was published posthumously.
63 DNB XXII (Supplement) 154–5; Charles Dorfman 'Foreword' *Reformation of the 16th Century* v–xxi; H. McLachlan 'Charles Beard, B.A., LL.D.' in *Records of a Family 1800–1903: Pioneers in Education, Social Service and Liberal Religion* 36–75
64 DNB II 14
65 *Reformation of the 16th Century* 343
66 At Nottingham in April 1876 he said: 'Are Priestley and Channing yours? not less are Augustine and Paul; for you Wesley sings and Keble; Barclay expounds the deep things of the Spirit, à Kempis teaches the imitation of Christ' (quoted McLachlan *Records* 47). Cf Gladstone's comment (John Morley *The Life of William Ewart Gladstone* II 114).
67 'Except in the sense in which complete is opposed to partial truth, there is no fear lest the twentieth century should contradict the nineteenth' (*Reformation of the 16th Century* 403).
68 Ibid 34, 147–8
69 Ibid 36, 52. One recalls Nisard's monk, 'lowering his heavy eyelids before the light like a bird of the night before the day,' and Hallam's giant of Ignorance, sending out 'his dark hosts of owls and bats.' Later, Froude said of the monks: 'They were children of darkness, and they dreaded daylight like bats and owls' (*Life and Letters of Erasmus* 73).
70 *Reformation of the 16th Century* 37
71 Ibid 63–73
72 Ibid 149–51. Erasmus' handling of 1 John 5:7 is well known (see John B. Payne *Erasmus: His Theology of the Sacraments* 56–7 and cf *Phoenix of His Age* 54, 235–6, 272). On Romans 9:5, see Payne 57.
73 *Reformation of the 16th Century* 148–9, 151–3. Cf B.A. Gerrish *Grace and Reason: A Study in the Theology of Luther* 24–5 and Mar-

jorie O'Rourke Boyle 'Stoic Luther: Paradoxical Sin and Necessity' 91–2.
74 *Reformation of the 16th Century* 163–4, 166, 168, 170. Here Beard quotes extensively from Luther, including the passage from the Galatians commentary beginning: 'It is a quality of faith that it wrings the neck of reason and strangles the beast, which else the whole world, with all creatures, could not strangle' (ibid 163).
75 Ibid 340. On one point, at least as seen in the *Enchiridion*, Erasmus is the more conservative – in his preference for allegorical interpretation (ibid 120).
76 Ibid 406
77 Ibid 143–5, 163–8
78 'The catholicity of his sympathies and his ability to discern agents of moral progress under a variety of forms separates Beard's from the more common liberal idea of the Reformation' (Frappell 'Interpretations of the Continental Reformation' 370). Cf note 66 above.
79 *Memoirs* 215
80 Herbert Paul *Life of Froude* ch 1; Waldo Hilary Dunn *James Anthony Froude: A Biography* I chs 1–6
81 Cf Basil Willey 'J.A. Froude' 106. For a balanced judgment of the *History of England,* see A.G. Dickens and John Tonkin *The Reformation in Historical Thought* 167 and G.R. Elton 'J.A. Froude and His History of England.'
82 Owen Chadwick *The Victorian Church* I 533–4, 537
83 Dunn *Froude* I 10
84 'The Oxford Counter-Reformation' 239, 242
85 Dunn *Froude* I 72–3. Cf Willey 'Froude' 107.
86 Burrow *Liberal Descent* 236, 240, 242
87 In Froude, the idea of progress is qualified by the Carlylean catastrophic view of history, a recurring pattern of decay, destruction, and renewal (ibid 252–7).
88 Quoted Dunn *Froude* I ix
89 *Short Studies on Great Subjects* I 47–8, 51–2, 59–61, 74
90 Ibid 83–4, 86–7
91 Ibid 134–5
92 Ibid 114, 118
93 *On Heroes, Hero-Worship and the Heroic in History* 157
94 *Life and Letters of Erasmus* 431
95 Ibid v
96 Ibid 233. The account was in a letter to Beatus Rhenanus (Ep 867 CWE 6: 112–26).
97 *Life and Letters* 297
98 Lecture VIII. The translation is at 156–74.
99 Ibid 145

100 Ibid 89
101 Ibid 54–5. M.M. Phillips comments that satire is present in the
first edition, if in a rudimentary form (*Adages* 52).
102 *Life and Letters* 227–8
103 Ibid 2, 4, 19, 23–4
104 Ibid 44–7. Erasmus' report of the conversation is in a letter to Johannes Sixtinus (Ep 116 CWE 1: 229–33).
105 *Life and Letters* 51, 63
106 Ibid 34, 63, 92, 100, 102, 104, 126
107 Ibid 71–2. An early literary endeavour had been a contribution on
St Neot to Newman's *Lives of the Saints* (Dunn *Froude* I 78–80).
108 *Life and Letters* 39, 147
109 Ibid 127, 146. Froude mistakenly attributes the chill in Loyola's
devotions to the New Testament edition (ibid 130). The culprit
was, of course, the *Enchiridion*.
110 Ibid 190–3. Liberals were affronted by Froude's defence of the
stringencies of Tudor government in his *History of England* (Burrow *Liberal Descent* 237–9).
111 *Life and Letters* 212–14
112 Ibid 214, 239, 258, 281, 287
113 Ibid 328–9, 334, 342. Froude was sympathetic to Charles v and at
one time planned a full study of him (Paul *Life* 298, 426).
114 *Life and Letters* 353–4, 423
115 Ibid 404
116 'Oxford Counter-Reformation' 293–302
117 *Life and Letters* 322. Cf M.A. Screech *Ecstasy and the Praise of
Folly*.
118 P.S. Allen *Erasmus: Lectures and Wayfaring Sketches* 60. Allen also
refers to the 'many blunders in points of fact and detail,' which a
good secretary might have served to avert. Although, according to
Dunn, who studied Froude's notes, the lectures were revised more
than once before delivery and again, thoroughly, before publication (*Froude* II 586), there is evidence of haste under pressure of
time and perhaps failing powers. Much was made of inaccuracies
in translating or paraphrasing, especially by William Samuel Lilly,
the Catholic writer, who dealt with Froude in his essay 'The New
Spirit of History' (*Essays and Speeches* 212–15) and, above all, in
an article in the *Quarterly Review* in 1895 reviewing seven works
on Erasmus (including Nisard's, Feugère's, and Amiel's), all more
or less favourably except for Froude's. Lilly rightly identified
avoidable chronological blunders, eg the misdating of the *Moria*
and of a letter from Henry VIII to Erasmus (*Life and Letters* 98;
Lilly 'Erasmus' 18n). He saw that Froude had misunderstood the
story about Loyola's reaction to Erasmus ('Erasmus' 23n). Lilly's
charges of mistranslation were justified in important cases. Cf Al-

len Ep 2443 IX 165 with Lilly's translation ('Erasmus' 28) and
Froude's (*Life and Letters* 385); Allen Ep 1183 IV 439 with *Life and
Letters* 286. Nevertheless, the validity of Froude's paraphrases
generally was confirmed in a study of them made by P.S. Allen
and R.W. Lee (Dunn *Froude* II 633). Cf Paul *Life* 406–8. Further,
on some important points modern scholarship would side with
Froude rather than with Lilly. Thus Froude's favourable judgment
of the *Enchiridion* is met by Lilly's absurd remark: 'a judgment so
surprising as to induce a doubt whether Mr. Froude can have
really read it' ('Erasmus' 13). Generally, Lilly's picture of Froude
as a brilliant word-painter, abounding 'in sage sayings, in racy reflections, in caustic criticisms' ('Erasmus' 4) but congenitally incapable of telling the truth, is grossly intemperate (*Essays and
Speeches* 213). One should conclude by recalling that Froude encouraged Allen, who was in his mid-twenties at the time of the
Oxford professorship, in his editing of the letters of Erasmus, and
that must be counted his greatest contribution to Erasmus scholarship (Dunn *Froude* II 583–4).
119 Burrow *Liberal Descent* 257

CHAPTER NINE

1 Erika Rummel *Erasmus' Annotations on the New Testament* ch 4
2 Joseph Lortz *The Reformation in Germany* I 144–56; and Lortz 'Erasmus – kirchengeschichtlich.' Cf my 'Erasmus, Luther and the
Problem of Church History' 49–52.
3 John C. Olin 'Interpreting Erasmus' 67. Cf Louis Bouyer *Autour
d'Erasme*.
4 Marcel Bataillon 'La situation présente du message érasmien' 7;
Donald Nugent 'The Erasmus Renaissance'
5 How legitimate for a church historian is Lortz's question: 'Has
Erasmus really encountered the Master?' ('Erasmus – kirchengeschichtlich' 310)?
6 On the confrontation of church and revolution, see Owen Chadwick *The Secularization of the European Mind in the Nineteenth
Century* 121–2.
7 DNB III 497–9; *New Cath Enc* 2: 915
8 Charles Butler *Reminiscences* I 5, 9
9 Bernard Ward *Dawn of the Catholic Revival in England, 1781–1803* I
91. Cf Martin Haile and Edwin Bonney *Life and Letters of John
Lingard 1771–1851* 39.
10 Cf *Reminiscences* II 132.
11 For what follows, see Edward Norman *The English Catholic
Church in the Nineteenth Century* ch 1, and Joan Connell *The Roman Catholic Church in England 1780–1850: A Study in Internal
Politics* 55–79.

12 Haile and Bonney *Lingard* 124, 167
13 It is said that Butler retracted some opinions at the end of his life
    after the passage of the emancipation act in 1829 (DNB III 498;
    New Cath Enc 2: 915).
14 DNB III 497
15 *Life of Erasmus* 41
16 Ibid 73–4
17 Ibid 1, 26–7
18 Ibid 34–5, 39–41, 50, 67
19 In his colloquy 'A Pilgrimage for Religion's Sake' (Thompson *Col-
    loquies* 285–312)
20 *Life of Erasmus* 96, 127. Butler refers to Erasmus' eloquent and
    feeling description of the charms of Englishwomen but, in his sol-
    emn way, overlooks the kisses of which others made so much
    (ibid 64).
21 Ibid 168
22 Ibid 153–4
23 Ibid 147, 150–2
24 Ibid 183, 185, 188–9, 192. Milton's line is from *Paradise Lost* Book
    2.
25 Ibid 194, 214. Butler remarks that Catholics believe that there
    could be no deficiency in the faith of the church but, at the time
    of Luther's appearance, a reformation was needed in discipline
    and morals (ibid 184n).
26 *Les pèlerinages de Suisse* [1839] in *Oeuvres complètes* 2: 221–3. On
    Veuillot, see Philip spencer *Politics of Belief in Nineteenth-Century
    France* 108–9, 211–18
27 Victor Conzemius 'Vorwort,' Ignaz von Döllinger, Lord Acton *Brief-
    wechsel 1850–1890* I xv
28 Döllinger to Acton 7 February 1881 ibid III 230. Acton had been
    pressing Döllinger on the question which obsessed him, moral
    judgments on historical figures: would Newman and the mild Hane-
    berg have acted differently from persecutors like Pius V and Bor-
    romeo if they had lived in their time and situation? Sensibly,
    Döllinger replied: 'About that I cannot say: I do not know – it is
    possible – but who will wish to judge men after mere possibili-
    ties.' For himself, if he were living in that time, he would be an
    Erasmus.
29 NDB 4 21
30 'Döllinger's Historical Work' in Lord Acton *History of Freedom and
    Other Essays* 384
31 NDB 4 23; Friedrich Heyer *The Catholic Church from 1648 to 1870*
    159; Georges Goyau *L'Allemagne religieuse: Le Catholicisme
    (1800–1848)* II 387–92
32 Heyer 124

33 Cf Acton 'Döllinger's Historical Work' 394–5. See also Dickens and Tonkin *Reformation in Historical Thought* 181–3.

34 *Die Reformation, ihre innere Entwicklung und ihre Wirkungen im Umfange des Lutherischen Bekenntnisses* I 1–3

35 Ep 967 CWE 6: 365–72

36 *Die Reformation* 4–6

37 Ibid 10–11, 13–14, 16–18

38 Notice, however, that he wrote two biographies of Catholic figures of the sixteenth century, *John Fisher* (1860) and *Reginald Pole* (1874).

39 Wilhelm Kosch (ed) *Das Katholische Deutschland* II col 2076; *Biographisches Jahrbuch und Deutscher Nekrolog* V 301–2

40 Heyer *Catholic Church* 126–31, 173

41 'Erasmus und sein theologischer Standpunkt' 531–4

42 Ibid 534–6. Kerker quotes, *inter alia*, Erasmus' expression to Beda: 'ut inciperent tandem bonae literae Christum sonare.'

43 Ibid 537–40. The nineteenth-century reader, Kerker says, is surprised to find in the *Ciceronianus* a picture of humanist circles in the age of Leo X like that of contemporary paganism given by the abbé Gaume in his famous book, *Le ver rongeur des sociétés modernes* (Eng trans *Paganism in Education*). Curiously, Gaume speaks of Erasmus' fanatical favour for Cicero: in another age, a Christian, priest, and religious would have blushed to express himself so (*Paganism in Education* 95).

44 'Erasmus' 541–7. Erasmus' report of Colet's condemnation of Aquinas reveals his own distaste for the great scholastic (ibid 544–5). This report is in a letter to Justus Jonas 13 June 1521 (Allen Ep 1211 IV 520; Eng trans John C. Olin [ed] *Christian Humanism and the Reformation* 172–3).

45 'Erasmus' 548–51

46 Ibid 551–2

47 'Erasmus will der Freiheit eine Gasse' (ibid 560n).

48 Ibid 547

49 Ibid 553, 557, 559–62

50 Ibid 564–5

51 The one full modern study of the subject is Christian Dolfen *Die Stellung des Erasmus von Rotterdam zur scholastichen Methode*. Cf C.J. de Vogel 'Erasmus and His Attitude towards Church Dogma,' J.-P. Massaut 'Erasme et Saint Thomas,' Charles Trinkaus 'Erasmus, Augustine, and the Nominalists,' and Brendan Bradshaw 'The Christian Humanism of Erasmus.' The subject needs assessment in the light of the re-evaluation of late scholasticism as in H.A. Oberman *The Harvest of Modern Theology*.

52 An earlier example is the edition of Erasmus' *Paraclesis* by Joseph Widmer (1779–1844), canon and professor of moral and pastoral

theology at Lucerne (ADB 42: 361–2; *Dict hist et biog* VII 305). Widmer was the pupil and friend of Johann Michael Sailer (1751–1832), the irenic bishop of Regensburg and pioneer of modern pedagogy and pastoral theology (*New Cath Enc* 12: 851–2). Sailer himself, in one of his pedagogical works, commended Erasmus as one who, like other great thinkers of the past, had anticipated future needs and could be the healer of the sickness of contemporary society (*Ueber Erziehung für Erzieher, oder Pädagogik* II 87; cf Wulschner 'Erasmus von Rotterdam im 19. Jahrhundert' 18). Widmer's edition of the *Paraclesis* includes the Latin text and a German translation and twelve essays on theological and pastoral themes suggested by Erasmus' little work, in which Erasmus is quoted, as one author among a number, in support of Widmer's reflections. In his foreword Widmer calls Erasmus a truly classical writer, since he combined Catholicity, unusual learning, and warm piety. His aim was to purify theology and lead it back to the divine sources. There were some reproachable expressions in his works but they must be read in the light of the times. Otherwise, he shows the present how faith in Catholic doctrine and submission to authority can be associated with intellectual capacity and freedom of spirit (*Paraklesis* iii–vi, ix–xi). This is an Erasmus for the Catholic revival of the early nineteenth century, before the rise of neo-scholasticism and ultramontanism.

53 ADB XV 64–6; Wilhelm Kosch (ed) *Das Katholische Deutschland* II col 1989
54 John Patrick Dolan *The Influence of Erasmus, Witzel and Cassander in the Church Ordinances and Reform Proposals of the United Duchies of Cleve during the Middle Decades of the Sixteenth Century*
55 Cf R.W. Scribner 'The Erasmians and the Beginning of the Reformation in Erfurt.'
56 *Die Universität Erfurt in ihrem Verhältnisse zu dem Humanismus und der Reformation* I 226–8
57 Ibid 229–39, 244–7, 251, 254
58 *De Erasmi Roterodami studiis irenicis* 1–2
59 Ibid 3. Woker's chronology seems awry, since Erasmus was in close association with his English friends in 1499–1500, long before the writing of the *Moriae encomium.*
60 Ibid 3–7
61 Ibid 8–11
62 Ibid 4–5, 13–17
63 Ibid 21–6, 29–30, 32
64 Ibid 27–8, 31, 33–42. Woker has an appendix on Erasmus' part in the Cleves ordinances (ibid 46–8).
65 Ibid 42. We hear 'eum concordiae felicitatem paene lyrico motu decantentem.'

66 There are references, among others, to Knight, von der Hardt, Seckendorf, Planck, Adolf Müller, and the contemporary Protestant writer F.O. Stichart.

67 A minor example is the thesis defended at the Sorbonne in February 1863 *Erasmus Roterodamus morum et litterarum vindex* by T.-A. Desdevises du Dezert (1822–91), later professor of geography at Clermont and Caen. The aim was to present Erasmus as 'moderate, self-controlled, always directing his life justly and honestly.' In the Lutheran affair he sought reconciliation, without compromising the faith, but was assailed by both sides (*Erasmus Roterodamus* 9–10, 14–20, 59–60; on Desdevises du Dezert, see DBF 10 col 1039).

68 G. Marin 'Erasme et son nouvel historien' 229

69 Ibid; Ludwig Geiger in *Göttingische gelehrte Anzeigen* 49 (1872) 1922–9

70 Durand de Laur *Erasme* I 680–1. Thus, he attributes Erasmus' first visit to England to its correct year (1499), a point on which Feugère and Froude were mistaken.

71 Durand de Laur is described as 'ancien professeur de rhétorique au lycée de Versailles.' His book was long in preparation, much interrupted by teaching duties, and finally completed after premature retirement (*Erasme* I iv).

72 A contemporary Félix Nève compared the two writers thus: Feugère proceeded 'par fines et discrètes analyses, au lieu de sommaires développés et d'abondantes citations.' He praised Feugère *inter alia* for the 'finesse dans ses appreciations littéraires' ('Erasme d'après ses nouveaux historiens' 260).

73 *Erasme* I 3, 21–2. Hermans' letter is at CWE 1 Ep 33 62–4.

74 *Erasme* I 7–11. Durand de Laur remarks that the letter to Grunnius should be read with a 'certain reserve' (ibid 13). He considers the pictures of Erasmus' brother Peter and his principal guardian Winckel 'une exagération volontaire et calculée' (note B ibid 679). The self-interested friend was Cornelis of Woerden whom Durand de Laur confuses (a common confusion) with Cornelis Gerard (note C ibid 680; cf *Contemporaries of Erasmus* I 341).

75 *Erasme* I 13–14, 20–1, 24, 41

76 Ibid 16, 44–5, 57

77 Ibid 156, 216, 231, 269. Compared with Budé, 'Erasme fit paraître plus de grâce et de fine ironie, mais moins de candeur' (ibid 231).

78 Ibid 201

79 Ibid viii, 298, 302–3, 386

80 Erasmus lacked 'l'héroisme de l'apostolat' (ibid 327).

81 On his relations with Adrian VI, see ibid 366, 374, 376.

82 Ibid 406, 471, 674. Durand de Laur refers to a report that Erasmus said from time to time: 'Mater mei, memento mei.' See below.

83 Erasmus agitated, Durand de Laur says at one point, a question
   still passionately debated in the nineteenth century, the temporal
   possessions of the papacy. He failed to ask whether the pope
   could have dignity and independence without them (ibid II 309).
84 Ibid II 42–4
85 *Adagia* at ibid 48–50; *Colloquia* 56–7; translations 61, 64; *Antibarbari* 90–3. Durand de Laur was unusual among nineteenth-century writers in giving prominence to the *Antibarbari*.
86 Ibid 97–114
87 Ibid 140–8. It should be noted, however, that Durand de Laur has
   a chapter on the *Ciceronianus* under the title 'Erasme modérateur
   de la Renaissance' (ibid ch 3).
88 Ibid 172–3. Durand de Laur himself seems at times strongly anti-
   scholastic (see ibid 9).
89 Ibid 39. The reference is to his role as educational reformer.
90 Ibid 211–13, 262, 272–3, 284
91 Ibid 289–90, 301. Durand de Laur rightly attributed the *Julius exclusus* to Erasmus on the basis of both internal and circumstantial
   evidence (ibid note L 589–91).
92 Ibid 326
93 Ibid 538–9. His secular learning, according to Durand de Laur,
   also lacked a certain rigour. Paraphrasing came more naturally
   than translating to 'cet esprit improvisateur, abondant et facile'
   (ibid 529, 536).
94 Ibid 540–7
95 Ibid 383. Cf Boyle *Rhetoric and Reform*.
96 *Erasme* II 430–3
97 Ibid 527. Durand de Laur wrote the section on war before 1870:
   war, he said, had not disappeared but it had become rarer and
   nobler than in Erasmus' time. The 'savage war' which devastated
   France in 1870 left him chastened but undaunted; in the spirit of
   his age, he commented: progress is not continuous, there can be
   set-backs but progress is soon resumed and at an accelerated pace
   (ibid 521n).
98 Ibid I x–xi
99 See, eg, Henri Pirenne *Histoire de Belgique* VII 99–105, 177–92.
100 The old University of Louvain, founded in the fifteenth century,
    was suppressed by the French republican authorities, then occu-
    pying Belgium, in 1794. In 1833 Pope Gregory XVI issued a papal
    brief opening the university again (*New Cath Enc* 8: 1035).
101 *Biographie nationale* 5 cols 650–70
102 'Particularités sur le séjour d'Erasme, à Bâle, et sur les derniers
    moments de cet homme célèbre' 462–8, 475
103 They were an unsigned manuscript letter located in the imperial
    library in Vienna, a letter from Tielmann Gravius of Cologne to

Erasmus Schets, and one from Eustace Chapuys also to Schets. They are respectively Epp 3134, 3136, 3140 in Allen XI 341–3, 345, and 351. The first was probably a circular letter sent by Henry Stromer to various friends of Erasmus (ibid 342). The second and third letters were in de Ram's possession when he wrote his article and subsequently were part of the so-called Nève collection, whose history Allen describes in Appendix XVII (VI 492–3).

104 'Note sur Lambert Coomans' 437–8. On Coomans, see *Contemporaries of Erasmus* I 336; Franz Bierlaire *La Familia d'Erasme: Contribution à l'histoire de l'humanisme* 100; Henri de Vocht 'Le dernier "Amanuensis" d'Erasme.' Coomans was not in fact a priest when he served as Erasmus' last *famulus* (de Vocht 179–80).

105 The book was L. van Gorkom *Beschryvinge der stad en vryhed van Turnhout* (Malines 1790). De Vocht identifies the documents as two seventeenth-century compositions. He accepts the story of Erasmus' dying words to Coomans ('Le dernier "amanuensis"' 183–5). It is rejected by more recent scholarship (*Contemporaries of Erasmus* I 336; Reedijk 'Das Lebensende des Erasmus' 29–33).

106 'Note' 439–40

107 *Bibliographie nationale: Dictionnaire des écrivains belges et catalogue de leurs publications* 1830–80 III 329

108 Of errors of fact, one might notice that Rottier has Erasmus' mother not long surviving his birth (she 'n'avait pu survivre au deshonneur') and Agricola in charge of Erasmus' studies at the school at Deventer (*La Vie et les travaux* 15). The Hamburg savant F.L. Hoffmann said, with some irony, that Rottier's qualities of style, Catholic zeal, disdain for the Reformation, and ease in making a critique of Erasmus' works could not compensate for 'le défaut d'ordre, les contradictions, les lacunes' ('Notes sur une série de lettres addressées à Erasme' 278n). De Ram and two other assessors had made similar criticism of a first version of the memoir in 1853 (*Bulletins de l'Académie Royale* XX II 73–84).

109 *La vie et les travaux* 3–4, 96, 168

110 Ibid 75–6, 174

111 Ibid 43–4, 83–6, 134–7

112 Ibid 21, 46–7

113 Ibid 186

114 *Biographie nationale* 41 cols 591–8. Cf T.J. Lamy 'Notice sur la vie et les travaux de Félix-Jean-Baptiste-Joseph Nève' (discussion of Nève's work on Erasmus at 566–9).

115 *La Renaissance des lettres et l'essor de l'érudition ancienne de Belgique* 11

116 Ibid 1, 9–11. Nève adds solemnly: 'Peut-on discuter avec le panégyriste et l'imitateur de Rabelais?' (ibid 9).

117 Ibid 12–14

118 Shown by Johannes Janssen (see below)
119 *La Renaissance des lettres* 4–7
120 Ibid 1–3, 15. The study of the sixteenth century confirms the idea of authority which safeguards human liberty and dignity (ibid 3).
121 Ibid vii. Nève wrote a history of the Trilingual College at Louvain (1856) which also attributed this role to Erasmus (ibid v–vi).
122 'Recherches sur le séjour et les études d'Erasme en Brabant' 52, 57, 131
123 Ibid 53, 62, 133–4
124 Ibid 55, 137
125 Ibid 139–43. The theologians concerned were Dorp, Briart, Latomus, and Driedo. Cf *Contemporaries of Erasmus* 1, 2; Henry de Vocht *History of the Foundation and Rise of the Collegium Trilingue Lovaniense 1517–1550* I; Jacques Etienne *Spiritualisme érasmien et théologiens louvanistes*.
126 'Recherches' 145–50
127 Ibid 152–4. Nève uses Erasmus' lettres to Erasmus Schets gathered by de Ram and included in the Nève collection (see note 103 above).
128 Note Nève's comparison of Feugère and Durand de Laur (note 72 above). Interesting also is his remark that Nisard, if rewriting, would have to take more account of Erasmus' reticences and reserves ('Erasme d'après ses nouveaux historiens' 258).
129 Ibid 261
130 Eg Baron Leys who saw Erasmus as 'la personification de la science et l'idée philosophique' and whose subjects included 'Erasmus in his study,' 'Erasmus at the Habsburg court,' and 'Erasmus reading to Margaret of Austria and Charles V' (Edouard Fétis 'Notice sur Jean-Auguste-Henri Leys' 230).
131 'Erasme d'après ses nouveaux historiens' 262–71
132 Ibid 272–7. Nève judges Feugère the best commentator on these themes (ibid 273).
133 Ibid 278–82, 286. Nève – with the letters to Erasmus Schets, Erasmus' banker, in mind – adds that a *desideratum* of Erasmus research is a study of his finances. Erasmus, he says, has been wrongly accused of avarice (ibid 282–4). On Schets, see Eckhard Bernstein 'Erasmus' Money Connection: The Antwerp Banker Erasmus Schets and Erasmus of Rotterdam, 1525–36.'
134 Ludwig Freiherr von Pastor *Tagebücher – Briefe – Erinnerungen* 53. Later Pastor said that Döllinger's fate deeply affected Janssen ('Zur Charakteristik Janssens' 88).
135 On Janssen, NDB 10: 343–4 (Jedin); ADB 50: 733–41 (Pastor); Sbrik II 57–63; Dickens and Tonkin *Reformation in Historical Thought* 183–4; Pastor 'Zur Charakteristik Janssens.'
136 Pastor 'Zur Charakteristik Janssens' 92

137 Sbrik II 58
138 Pastor 89
139 *History of the German People at the Close of the Middle Ages* III 1, 4, 7
140 Ibid 14
141 Ibid 8–12
142 Ibid 13, 19
143 Ibid 15–16, 21, 25
144 Ibid 12n
145 I refer to the notes in the seventh German edition, *Geschichte des deuschen Volkes seit dem Ausgang des Mittelalters* II.
146 Cf Gerhard Ritter 'Die geschichtliche Bedeutung des deutschen Humanismus' 434 and Lewis W. Spitz *The Religious Renaissance of the German Humanists* 3–4.
147 *History of the Popes from the Close of the Middle Ages* VII 422
148 'Een portret van Erasmus' 1–2
149 Ibid 3–4, 7–9, 18, 35
150 Ibid 19–20, 26
151 Ibid 6, 15, 19
152 Ibid 28, 32–3, 50, 53, 58
153 The philologian and printer Alphonse Diepenbrock (1862–1921); I owe the last remarks to the essay by Johannes Trapman 'Le Latin mystique de Remy de Gourmont (1892) et son influence aux Pays-Bas.'
154 Review of Janssen *Theologische Quartalschrift* 62 (1880) 661–4, 667–8, 671–4. On original sin, Funk concedes that Erasmus used mistaken expressions in interpreting particular passages, eg Romans 5:12, but on the main question he stood with the church; he was wrongly reproached with Pelagianism (ibid 674).
155 Ibid 665, 667, 669, 672–3. On Plitt and Stichart, whom Funk also mentions, see ch 10 below.
156 Ibid 676
157 Ibid 666. On Marsollier, see *Phoenix of His Age* 187–91.
158 *An meine Kritiker* and *Ein zweites Wort an meine Kritiker*
159 *An meine Kritiker* 3, 101
160 Ibid 8–9. On Ebrard, who spent his teaching career at Zürich and Erlangen, see NDB 4: 269–70, ADB 48: 248–50, and Schweitzer *The Quest of the Historical Jesus* 116–17. In dogmatic terms, Ebrard, who first made a name by an attack on D.F. Strauss, was associated with the so-called mediating theology which was to a degree sympathetic to Erasmus (see ch 10 below and my 'Erasmus and the Mediating School').
161 *Die Objectivität J. Janssen's urkundlich beleuchtet* 46–7
162 *Erasmus redivivus* I ch 2
163 ADB 31: 561–7. Schlottmann's career was clouded by controversies

over fraudulent archaeological finds in Moab which he mistakenly accepted.

164 Ibid 566; *Erasmus redivivus* I vii, ix
165 *Erasmus redivivus* I viii–ix, 1–2, 8–12, 21
166 Ibid 24–5. From the past, Schlottmann mentions in particular Fabricius (cf *Phoenix of His Age* 221–4). Of writers already known to us, he mentions Ranke, Drummond, Nisard, Feugère, and Durand de Laur. For Ullmann, Maurenbrecher, Horawitz, and Pennington, who are also mentioned, see below.
167 *Erasmus redivivus* I 117–19, 121–2, 126, 132–3, 137–9, 144–7
168 Ibid 156–7. A comparison with Humboldt is not developed.
169 Ibid 158–60, 169–70
170 Ibid 177, 196, 202–6, 225–35, 256, 260, 262
171 Ibid 282–5, 310–16
172 Cf Marjorie O'Rourke Boyle *Erasmus on Language and Method in Theology.*
173 *Erasmus redivivus* I 320
174 The *Kulturkampf* was already drawing to a close when Schlottmann completed the first volume of his book in September 1882 (Koppel S. Pinson *Modern Germany: Its History and Civilization* 189).
175 DTC V pt 1 col 395. I follow in part, with permission, my discussion in 'Erasmus, Luther and the Problem of Church History.'
176 Ibid col 394
177 Ibid col 396
178 One was W.S. Lilly, Froude's critic and for many years secretary of the Catholic Union of Great Britain (on Lilly *Who's Who 1911*). See his 'Erasmus' 31–5.
179 DNB *Supplement 1922–30* 330–2
180 David Knowles *The Historian and Character and Other Essays* 240–63
181 *Eve of the Reformation* 155
182 Ibid 169, 199–202
183 Gertrude Himmelfarb *Lord Acton: A Study in Conscience and Politics* 154; W.H. McNeill 'Introduction,' in Lord Acton *Essays in the Liberal Interpretation of History* xiv–vi
184 It had appeared in the *Home and Foreign Review*, an independent Catholic quarterly, which replaced the monthly *Rambler*, when the latter faced censure from Catholic officialdom, though the *Review* soon shared the same fate (Himmelfarb *Lord Acton* 58).
185 'Ultramontanism' 193
186 'The Catholic Academy' 282. This essay was first published in the *Rambler* in September 1861.
187 Ibid 283–7
188 'Fra Paolo Sarpi' 253

189 'The History of Freedom in Christianity' 79, 85
190 'Acton-Creighton Correspondence' 360
191 Ibid 359. Johannes Gropper was Erasmus' disciple and an irenic Catholic theologian involved in the reunion discussions of the 1530s and 1540s. Acton criticized primarily the mildness of the Anglican Creighton's treatment of the moral failings, and especially the intolerance, of the Renaissance papacy: 'The inflexible integrity of the moral code is, to me, the secret of the authority, the dignity, the utility of history' (ibid 365). It was this insistence on inflexible moral judgments by the historian that had separated him from Döllinger. The review, as finally published in the *English Historical Review* in 1887, though milder than the first version which occasioned the correspondence quoted, stuck to this main point ('A History of the Papacy during the Period of the Reformation'). On Acton and Creighton, see Himmelfarb *Lord Acton* 158-62, David Mathew *Lord Acton and His Times* 329-35.
192 *Lectures on Modern History* 19
193 Ibid 92-4, 101, 104
194 Cf Herbert Butterfield on 'Lord Acton and the Nineteenth-Century Historical Movement,' in *Man on His Past* 62-99.
195 See Dermont Fenlon '*Encore une Question*: Lucien Febvre, the Reformation and the School of *Annales*' 75-7.
196 See Elizabeth G. Gleason 'On the Nature of Sixteenth-Century Italian Evangelism: Scholarship, 1953-1978,' the notes to Fenlon '*Encore une Question*,' and Heather M. Vose 'More Light on Sixteenth-Century *Evangélisme*: A Study in Cross and Spirit.'
197 Note Imbart de la Tour's remark in an unfinished preface to volume IV of *Les Origines*: 'L'histoire a une grande vertu d'apaisement' (quoted Jacques Chevalier, Préface, xi). On Imbart de la Tour, see also Ferguson *Renaissance in Historical Thought* 264-6.
198 *Les Origines* III vi
199 Ibid x
200 Ibid 70, 75
201 Ibid 82, 104. I again follow in part my discussion in 'Erasmus, Luther and the Problem of Church History.'

CHAPTER TEN

1 'Compendium vitae' CWE 4: 410
2 On Erasmus and the Reformers, see eg Boyle *Rhetoric and Reform*, Karl Heinz Oelrich *Der späte Erasmus und die Reformation*, and Cornelis Augustijn *Erasmus en de Reformatie: Een onderzoek naar de houding die Erasmus ten opzichte van de Reformatie heeft aangenomen*. On the terms 'Reformation' and 'Protestant,' see R.W. Scribner *The German Reformation* 1-5.

3 *Phoenix of His Age* 66–7
4 Cf my 'Erasmus in the Age of Revolutions.'
5 TRE X 209; RGG II col 623
6 RE³ XII 637–43; André Encevré 'Image de la Réforme chez les protestants français de 1830 à 1870' 185; Suzanne Stelling-Michaud (ed) *Le Livre du Recteur de l'Académie de Genève* 4: 512–13
7 Encevré 'Image de la Réforme' 184, 188
8 *History of the Reformation* I 1, 4, 9
9 Ibid 84, 87
10 Ibid 82, 84–5, 88. I have compared the second French edition (Paris/Geneva 1838) with the translation by Henry Beveridge (Glasgow n.d.) which is based on the French edition of 1842. Merle d'Aubigné's avowed references on Erasmus in both editions are Burigny, Müller, Le Clerc, and Nisard, whose judgment he considers mistaken (*History of the Reformation* I 93).
11 Ibid 89–93
12 RGG IV col 1119; Daniel Robert *Genève et les églises réformées de France de la 'Réunion' (1798) aux environs de 1830* 55–9
13 Marius Addi *Essai sur Erasme: Ses rapports avec la Réformation* (1869); W. Bauer *Etude sur Erasme et ses rapports avec la Réforme* (1878); Paul Boyer *Erasme: Ses rapports avec la Réforme* (1886).
14 Bauer *Etude* 8–9; Addi *Essai* 11–13; Boyer *Erasme* 14–15
15 Addi *Essai* 7; Bauer *Etude* 16; Boyer *Erasme* 47–51, 54
16 Boyer *Erasme* 31, 61–2
17 See ch 4 above.
18 J.A. Venn *Alumni Cantabrigiensis* Part II (1752–1900) V 85
19 *Life and Character of Erasmus* 190
20 Ibid 11, 59–60, 181, 184, 223
21 Ibid 60–2, 155, 203, 210, 212, 313, 343, 376–8
22 Ibid 373
23 Ibid xii. The famous bishop of Lincoln, Christopher Wordsworth (1807–85), contributed a preface to Pennington's book. It defended the English Reformation and the Anglican *via media*, a middle course between 'the temporizing moderation of an Erasmus and the rash courage of a Luther.' The *via media* alone provides security in the struggle between ultramontanism and unbelief now threatening Europe with destruction (x–xi). Wordsworth himself cultivated contacts with Döllinger and the old Catholics (DNB XXI 925). Erasmus, he says, contributed to the distinctive character of the English Reformation, especially through his biblical and patristic studies (vi). He and Luther complemented one another. This is not exactly Pennington's approach.
24 *Geschichte der teutschen Reformation* I 225. On Marheineke, see

ADB 20: 338–40, Bornkamm *Luther im Spiegel der deutschen Geistesgeschichte* 79.

25 On Plitt, see ADB 26: 304–7; RE³ XV 486–9. On Hofmann, see Bornkamm *Luther im Spiegel* 58. Plitt's judgments on other authors on Erasmus were set by Lutheran orthodoxy. Thus, he says, Hagen could not offer a satisfactory judgment because of his religious views. Similarly, Kerker, whose theology was deficient, ie inadequately biblical, could not further discussion on Erasmus ('Desiderius Erasmus in seiner Stellung zur Reformation' 480, 514). Actually, despite their theological and ecclesiastical differences (the one neo-scholastic, the other Lutheran), the judgments of Plitt and Kerker have, to the modern observer, much in common and each had a substantial influence on his particular audience.

26 'Desiderius Erasmus in seiner Stellung zur Reformation' 480–2

27 Ibid 483–4, 488

28 Ibid 488, 490, 493–7, 506–7, 514

29 ADB 36: 164–5. On Stichart's book, cf Georg Gebhart *Die Stellung des Erasmus von Rotterdam zur römischen Kirche* 25n.

30 *Erasmus von Rotterdam: Seine Stellung zu der Kirche* vi, 6–8

31 Ibid 397–8

32 Ibid 20, 23, 27, 33, 132, 179, 198–227

33 Ibid 27, 162n

34 Ibid 305

35 Ibid 235, 243, 248–9, 253–6, 265–6, 272–5

36 Ibid 293–301, 307, 339

37 A possible exception to the standard orthodox rejection of Erasmus is Johann Valentin Henneberg's *Erasmus von Rotterdam für Prediger seiner und unserer Zeit* (1822), a collection in translation of excerpts from Erasmus' book on preaching, *Ecclesiastes*. Its tone is pietistic and somewhat conservative; Henneberg seeks, he says, the approval of the thoughtful, prudent people of his time who share his own conviction that, in preaching as in other matters, not everything new is good or everything old bad (*Erasmus von Rotterdam für Prediger* viii). For himself he had long found Erasmus' writings instructive and agreeable (ibid vii). Erasmus clearly saw that the better nurture of religion among the people depended on improvement in the clergy and especially better preaching (ibid 2–4). It is unusual to find in works of this tone Erasmus warmly commended as a model. Nevertheless, other books on preaching of the late eighteenth and early nineteenth centuries referred to by Henneberg also mention Erasmus with praise (cf Wulschner 53).

38 Ernest Lieberkühn, the author of an oration delivered at Jena in July 1836, argued for Erasmus as a pioneer of freedom of thought,

either in association with Luther or beyond him (*De Erasmi Roter-odami ingenio ac doctrina quid valuerint ad instaurationem sacrorum* 3–4, 13–15). A more scholarly dissertation than Lieberkühn's was that defended by the young scholar from Schleswig, Johannes Gaye (born 1804), at Kiel on 14 November 1829, *Disquisitionis de vita Desiderii Erasmi specimen ab ann. nat. usque ad annum 1517.* Gaye has studied at Kiel and Berlin, where he had attended lectures by, among others, Hegel, Marheineke, Ranke, and Schleiermacher ('Vita' in *Disquisitionis ... specimen* 103–4). Obviously, Gaye will have less to say about Erasmus' relation to the Reformation than Lieberkühn, though the problem bulks quite large in his dissertation, by anticipation as it were. This dissertation is essentially in annalistic form, with an attempt to put in order Erasmus' correspondence as it appears in the third volume of the Leiden edition, an attempt which is serious and scholarly without being notably successful. (Cf Arthur Richter *Erasmus – Studien* 4.) His characterization is of one who lived essentially for himself and his studies, who was nevertheless highly susceptible to external influences, fluctuating in his human relations, and very reluctant to become involved in public affairs or, indeed, the common life (see, eg, *Disquisitionis ... specimen* 26–7, 73n, 83, 88–9). This criticism seems to underestimate Erasmus' capacity for friendship and his passionate concern for the public good as he understood it. For Gaye, Erasmus – against his will – prepared the Reformation: thus his New Testament edition prepared minds for reformation as nothing before it, taking Erasmus, as the needs of the age required, beyond the limits he had set himself (ibid 94). He was not in himself an initiator. He was then as a reformer like the ancient sceptics, who could point out the failings of the old without having a new system to offer (ibid 31–2). These judgments associate Gaye more with orthodox Protestant opinion on Erasmus than with Lieberkühn's rather ill-considered liberalism.

39 ADB 6: 197–8
40 H.A. Erhard 'Erasmus' 157, 159–60, 169. On Colet's influence, Erhard anticipates Seebohm's influential work.
41 Ibid 161–2
42 Ibid 162–3. I call them 'debatable' contentions because they overlook the themes of freedom and individual development present in Erasmus' educational writings. Cf J.-C. Margolin's remark: 'One of the elements of the psychology and pedagogy of Erasmus, which appears, moreover, in his whole work as in every manifestation of his character, is the sense of *freedom* profoundly united to the sense and recognition of the *individual* as such' (*Declamatio de pueris statim ac liberaliter instituendis Etude* 43).
43 'Erasmus' 168, 172

44 Ibid 173–4
45 Eg, in his account of the *Ratio verae theologiae* and *Ecclesiastes* (ibid 172–3)
46 Ibid 178–80, 188–9, 191–5
47 Ibid 196
48 RGG VI cols 1362–4; H. Stephan *Geschichte der evangelischen Theologie seit dem deutschen Idealismus* 188–201; F. Schnabel *Deutsche Geschichte im neunzehnten Jahrhundert* IV 496–9; O. Pfleiderer *The Development of Theology in Germany since Kant and Its Progress in Great Britain since 1825*; M. Pattison 'Present State of Theology in Germany' 237–48. I follow in part my discussion in 'Erasmus and the Mediating School.'
49 Stephan *Geschichte* 112. Cf Pfleiderer *Development of Theology* 281 and A. Harnack 'August Neander.'
50 See ch 4 above.
51 W. Beyschlag 'D. Carl Ullmann: Eine biographische Skizze' 15–16. Further on Ullmann, see ADB 39: 196–9, RE³ XX 204–11.
52 Review of Müller 181–2, 200–2
53 Beyschlag 'Ullmann' 18–19, 32–3
54 Hence his *Reformatoren vor der Reformation* (1841–2). For a critical comment, see H.A. Oberman *Forerunners of the Reformation* 32–3. Ullmann planned a biography of Erasmus as a sequel but the plan remained unfulfilled (Beyschlag 48).
55 Review 206–7. Ullmann regretted that Müller had not made more use of the *Ratio verae theologiae* and the *Ecclesiastes*.
56 Ibid 203–4
57 Beyschlag 22
58 Review 202–4
59 K.F.A. Kahnis 'Schlusswort' *Zeitschrift für die historische Theologie* 619; Illgen 'Vorrede' xii; B. Lindner 'Erinnerung an den verewigten Präses der historisch-theologischen Gesellschaft zu Leipzig Domherrn Professor Dr. Chr. Fr. Illgen' 19
60 Wilhelm Ernest Eberhardi 'Warum blieb Desiderius Erasmus, Luthers freisinniger Zeitgenosse, katholik? Eine unparteiische Untersuchung' 99–100, 103–4, 147–9
61 Ibid 127–8, 130, 134–5, 139–40
62 Ibid 115–16, 121–2, 146
63 Wulschner calls Eberhardi's standpoint unique in its time (Wulschner 60). The *Zeitschrift für historische Theologie* carried another article on this theme, Wilhelm Chlebus 'Erasmus und Luther.' It is more representative of Protestant opinion. Chlebus makes a sharp contrast in character and aims between Erasmus and Luther.
64 DNB XIII 448–51
65 W.E.H. Lecky 'Henry Hart Milman, D.D., Dean of St. Paul's' 257.

Stanley described Milman's work as 'the first decisive inroad of
German theology into England' (ibid 260).

66 *History of Christianity from the Birth of Christ to the Abolition of
Paganism in the Roman Empire* 3 vols (1840); *History of Latin
Christianity: including that of the Popes to the Pontificate of Pope
Nicholas V,* 6 vols (1854–5). On the plan for a history of Teutonic
Christianity, see Duncan Forbes *The Liberal Anglican Idea of History* 76, 166.
67 Quoted Arthur Milman *Henry Hart Milman, D.D., Dean of St.
Paul's* 143–4
68 Quoted ibid 227–8
69 Forbes *Liberal Anglican Idea* 75
70 Lecky 'Henry Hart Milman' 257
71 'Life of Erasmus' 2. Milman does not refer further to Erasmus'
writings on marriage.
72 Ibid 35, 41–2
73 Lecky 'Henry Hart Milman' 260–1
74 'Life of Erasmus' 52. Milman's comments on previous writers include: Hess is 'laborious but heavy'; Müller labours so hard not to
be partial to Erasmus that he falls into 'the opposite extreme'; Nisard is 'lively and clever,' but, 'as is M. Nisard's wont, too showy,
and wanting in grave and earnest appreciation.' He considers Erhard's the best study (ibid 4). Acton reviewed Milman's own
work when it was reprinted in *Savonarola, Erasmus, and Other Essays* (1870). He considered the republication a tribute to Milman's
position 'as a classic in the debateable land between scholarship
and polite literature.' I have again followed my 'Erasmus in the
Nineteenth Century: The Liberal Tradition.'
75 DNB 1922–30 779–81. Smith was later a famous tutor at Balliol
and in 1916 master.
76 [M.F. Smith] *Arthur Lionel Smith Master of Balliol (1916–1924): A
Biography and Some Reminiscences by His Wife* 21, 78
77 Ibid 75–6
78 *Erasmus, Humourist, Scholar, Divine: An Essay in Biography and
History* 1, 8, 11, 13–14
79 Cf [M.F. Smith] *Arthur Lionel Smith* 17 ('he really had no childhood that he could remember, and no home-life, surely a blank
in life which can never be filled up'). On Erasmus' origins, Smith
refers to Charles Reade's *The Cloister and the Hearth* as 'a work of
real research and dramatic power' (*Erasmus* 4).
80 *Erasmus* 54–5, 67
81 Ibid 56
82 Marcus Dods *Erasmus and Other Essays* 9
83 DNB VIII 1072; R. Buick Knox 'James Hamilton and English Presbyterianism' 286–90

84 William Arnot *Life of James Hamilton D.D. F.L.S.* 497; Robert Naismith *Memoir of Rev. James Hamilton, D.D. F.L.S.* 67. Hamilton edited a monthly periodical 1851–9 (Knox 291). Controversy
surrounded his work on a Presbyterian hymn-book (Naismith 67).

85 The lecture was to an audience of 'earnest and high-minded
youths' (the Young Men's Christian Association) in a series delivered at Exeter Hall 1860–1 (*Lectures* iv); the essays were first published in *Macmillan's Magazine* 1865.

86 'Early Years of Erasmus' 470. Unlike most biographers of Erasmus
known to him, who supported 1467, Hamilton argued for 1465 as
Erasmus' year of birth (ibid 471–2). He recognized, as does modern scholarship, that Erasmus in later life pushed back the date
but, unlike modern scholars, he took this at face value (cf A.C.F.
Koch *The Year of Erasmus' Birth*). The earlier date made more
plausible (in his view) Erasmus' achievements in studies as a boy.
Hamilton accepted – above all, on the basis of the letter to Grunnius – the existence of his older brother ('Early Years' 470n).

87 'Erasmus' in *Lectures* 381–2, 402

88 'Early Years' 478–9, 488–9, 493–4

89 Hamilton sticks to the mistaken notion of visits to England in
1497 and 1498 ('Erasmus in England' 501n). He also repeats the
story beloved of English nineteenth-century writers that Erasmus
learned Greek at Oxford (ibid 502). The expression 'learned Greek
at Oxford and taught it at Cambridge' is Gibbon's, referring to
Knight's life of Erasmus (*Decline and Fall* 7: 135n). Cf Allen App
VI I 592.

90 'Erasmus in England' 505

91 Ibid 517–18n. On Knight, see *Phoenix of His Age* 270–1.

92 'Erasmus in England' 524. On Stillingfleet, see *Phoenix of His Age*
263–4. Hamilton's own reference at this point is to Merle d'Aubigné.

93 *Lectures* 396–7, 404

94 Knox 'James Hamilton' 288–9, 292–5, 298–9

95 DNB Supplement 1901–11 I 510–12

96 P.C. Simpson *Life of Principal Rainy* II 110

97 *Erasmus and Other Essays* 55–8, 62

98 Ibid 23–4, 41–3, 46, 50, 54–5, 64–7

99 Ibid 5–7. Dods praises Seebohm's book without sharing its theological presuppositions (ibid 3–4). He adopts Seebohm's view of
Colet as a latitudinarian (ibid 59) which is not that of modern
scholarship. It is characteristic that Dods praises Froude for a
sense of humour unique among Erasmus' biographers (ibid 8).

100 Ibid 2

101 Ibid 13, 19, 21–2

102 Ibid 14–15, 17, 25–6, 28, 30

103 The lecture 'Erasmus' by John Meiklejohn (in a series in 1885 on the pre-Reformers and Reformers under the auspices of the liberally inclined United Presbyterian Church) shares these characteristics.

104 *University Addresses* 57. On Caird, DNB XXII Supplement 368–9.

105 *University Addresses* 77–8

106 Ibid 79–82, 84–5, 87

107 Ibid 60. For Erasmus' biography, Caird referred his listeners to Drummond and Feugère.

108 The Genevan thesis by François Bungener *Erasme: Son role et son oeuvre en face de la Réformation* (1869) is close to the British liberal Protestant interpretations. A second Genevan thesis by Amédée Salles (1877) takes the same standpoint but presents a darker view of Erasmus' personality (in the manner of Lavater and Müller). Here the nineteenth century's dominant (liberal) view of Erasmus' theology and its dominant (romantic) view of his personality are in contradiction. One may interpolate here a reference to the Strasbourg thesis of 1853 by D.Ch. Teutsch (*Controverse entre Luther et Erasme sur le libre arbitre*). It is, theologically, more substantial than that of Salles but follows somewhat the same pattern; the account of the debate inclines towards Erasmus but, on his behaviour and role in history, the standard Protestant judgment is offered.

109 'Erasmus von Rotterdam: Ein Beitrag zur Gelehrtengeschichte des sechszehnten Jahrhunderts' 489–90

110 ADB 6: 353–5; *Dict hist et biog* III 19. On the Zürich reforms ibid VII 510–11, 521; *New Cambridge Modern History* X 80–1.

111 'Erasmus von Rotterdam' 504–5, 513

112 Ibid 569

113 Ibid 532. The reference is to the Hilary preface.

114 Ibid 522, 542–5, 550, 571

115 Ibid 562–5

116 The comparison with Karl Hagen whose writing on Erasmus belongs to the same atmosphere is of interest (see ch 6 above).

117 Edgar Bonjour *Die Universität Basel von den Anfängen bis zur Gegenwart 1460–1960* 370. On Hagenbach ADB 10: 344–5; RE³ 7: 335–8; James I. Good *History of the Swiss Reformed Church since the Reformation* 412–14; Bonjour *Die Universität Basel* 373–4.

118 'Erasmus von Rotterdam in Basel 1516–1536' 5–6, 8–9, 11, 14–16

119 On Stockmeyer *Dict hist et biog* VI 369, on Amerbach *Contemporaries of Erasmus* 1: 42–6.

120 Emanuel [sic] Stockmeyer 'Erasmus in seinen Briefen an Bonifacius Amerbach' 73. Cf Allen I App VII 598, 602. On Merian Bonjour *Die Universität Basel* 370.

121 'Erasmus in seinen Briefen' 82–3, 89–91, 94–5

122 Ibid 74–5, 92–4, 113
123 *Dict hist et biog* VI 386; Bonjour 643–4
124 *Basler Taschenbuch* I iv
125 'Erasmus von Rotterdam zu Basel' 47 and n, 48–52, 55–9. For Erasmus' advice to the Basel council of January 1525, see Allen Ep 1539 VI 7–10; for a concise history of the Basel Reformation, see Hans R. Guggisberg *Basel in the Sixteenth Century* ch II.
126 'Erasmus von Rotterdam zu Basel' 63–4, 68–71. Streuber gives an accurate account of Erasmus' seal, the god Terminus, and its motto 'Concedo nulli' (ibid 76).
127 Ibid 74–5
128 RE³ 7: 338; Andreas Lindt *Protestanten-Katholiken Kulturkampf* 95–6; Werner Kaegi *Jacob Burckhardt: Eine Biographie* I 442
129 *Vorlesungen über Wesen und Geschichte der Reformation* 162–5. Ranke had referred to this shuddering at the name of death (*Deutsche Geschichte* I 180). O. Schottenloher has remarked that the reiteration of this statement of Ranke's, without troubling oneself about the context of Erasmus' own words, demonstrates the superficial and self-righteous way Erasmus has been judged. What Erasmus said (CWE Ep 867 6: 126) was that as a youth he trembled at the name of death but now he feared death little and did not measure men's happiness by their length of life (*Erasmus im Ringen um die humanistische Bildungsform: Ein Beitrag zum Verständnis seiner geistigen Entwicklung* 40).
130 *Vorlesungen* 166–7, 172–4. Hagenbach recounts the story of the pantomime said to have been played before Charles V at Augsburg in 1530: Reuchlin and Erasmus brought dry tinder which it needed Luther to light. It was first used, he says, by Maius *Vita Reuchlini* 1687 (ibid 170–1).
131 'Erasmus' 115–117, 120; *Vorlesungen* 175
132 RE³ 18: 735–7 (O. Kirn); Anton Bettelheim (ed) *Biographisches Jahrbuch und deutscher Nekrolog* V (1903) 297–300; Bonjour *Die Universität Basel* 308–9
133 'Erasmus' 280
134 Ibid 282; *Erasmus Stellung zur Reformation hauptsächlich aus von seinen Beziehungen zu Basel aus beleuchtet* 12–14
135 *Erasmus Stellung* 5–6
136 Ibid 15; 'Erasmus' 284
137 *Erasmus Stellung* 16, 25–7; 'Erasmus' 284–5
138 *Erasmus Stellung* 29. On Stähelin I have followed my 'Erasmus and the Mediating School.'
139 Cf Guggisberg *Basel in the Sixteenth Century* 73–4.
140 See *Phoenix of His Age* ch 4. Cf Oene Noordenbos *In het voetspoor van Erasmus* and Johan Lindeboom 'Erasmus' Bedeutung für die Entwicklung des geistigen Lebens in den Niederlanden.'

141 A. Ypeij and I.J. Dermout *Geschiedenis der Nederlandsche Her-vormde Kerk* I (Breda 1819) 18, 31 (quoted C. Augustijn *Erasmus en de Reformatie* 2).

142 N. Swart 'Erasmus: Het luisterrijkst voorbeeld van verwonnen zwarigheden' 411–13. The author Nicolaas Swart (1779–1843) was minister in the Remonstrant brotherhood in Amsterdam from 1808. He had been influenced by Kantian philosophy, was a leader in the Maatschappij tot Nut van het Algemeen, and wrote much for young people. The didactic tone of his essay on Erasmus is not then surprising (NNBW X col 999).

143 'Erasmus geenszins de eerste en grootste hervormer der christelijke kerk, volgens zijne eigene schriften enz' 291, 293, 296

144 J.J.F. Noordziek *Erasmus: Eene voorlezing* 4–5, 8–9, 11, 15, 26. On Noordziek, see NNBW IV col 1033.

145 Ph. de Vries 'The Writing and Study of History in the Netherlands in the 19th Century' 252–3. His own judgment on Erasmus was consistent with these convictions: 'he cared more for the honour of men than the honour of God' (quoted J. Lindeboom 'Erasmus in de waardeering van het Nageslacht' 119).

146 E.H. Kossmann *The Low Countries 1780–1940* 289

147 Ibid 290. Cf D. Nauta 'De Reformatie in Nederland in de Historiografie' 54–5.

148 *Verhandeling over Erasmus als nederlandsch kerkhervormer* 6–7. Glasius was in fact an established historian, author of two works on the church history of the Netherlands. In the 1850s he was to publish the biographical dictionary *Godgeleerd Nederland* (1851–6) and later a history of the Dordrecht synod. In 1883 he was president of the synod of the Reformed Church (NNBW III cols 469–70).

149 *Verhandeling over Erasmus* 9–10

150 Ibid 176–7, 180–2

151 Ibid 177–9, 183–4

152 Ibid 211–20

153 Ibid 186–90, 199–200. Piety cannot be denied, as Müller wishes, to one who held the Bible so dear, who aroused others to living a Christian life, and who urged trust in God's love in Christ and death to worldly desires (ibid 194–8).

154 Ibid 254, 270, 277, 280–1. Note the discussion of Geert Groote (258–9), Thomas à Kempis (267–70), Wessel Gansfort (272–6).

155 Ibid 281–3, 300, 302, 308–9

156 Ibid 365–8, 370–3, 382–3

157 Ibid 347–8, 353–4

158 Lucien Febvre 'Une question mal posé: Les origines de la réforme française et le problème des causes de la réforme'

159 Of other Dutch commentators on Erasmus, I might mention, less for the substance than for the place and the person, the *Oratio de*

Desiderii Erasmi in doctrinam moralem meritis by Cornelis Fransen
van Eck (1764–1830). This oration was delivered at Deventer in
1804 on the occasion of the author's laying down the office of
rector of the Athenaeum in that city (where, of course, Erasmus
had gone to school). Erasmus emerges as an enlightened moralist,
if naturally falling short of his successors Grotius and Leibniz
(ibid 13). Van Eck himself was a liberal thinker who faced opposition at Deventer during the social conflicts of the revolutionary
era but surmounted them to remain pastor there until 1828
(NNBW I cols 787–8).
160 Other biographers in the series were H.E. Jacobs (Luther), J.W.
Richard (Melanchthon), H.M. Baird (Beza), S.M. Jackson (Zwingli),
W. Walker (Calvin), H. Cowan (Knox).
161 *Desiderius Erasmus* 338
162 DAB 21 (Supplement 1) 285–6
163 *Desiderius Erasmus* iii
164 Ibid xv, 3, 18, 33, 48, 141
165 Ibid 450
166 Ibid 65–8
167 Ibid xxi
168 Ibid 109, 160, 256, 435, 461
169 Ibid 110–11, 462
170 Ibid 400–1
171 Ibid 297, 330–2, 445
172 Ibid 463
173 His bibliographical note does not mention Maurenbrecher's work.
174 David Friedrich Strauss (1808–74), author of the great *Life of Jesus*, wrote in the later part of his life (after miserable experiences
in the 1848 revolution) a life of Hutten. His contrast between humanism and Reformation is in the Protestant historical tradition.
The former was 'large-minded but faint-hearted,' the latter a narrower but more concentrated force. However, he warns that in
the maturing of a crisis like the Reformation precursors appear at
a disadvantage. Erasmus should be seen against his original background, the classical revival. In religion, says Strauss, he had a
strong practical, if not mystical, sense and always laid stress on
'the real meaning and significance of things' (*Ulrich von Hutten:
His Life and Times* 316, 346). Later he was misled by his dread of
revolution (ibid 341–2; cf Wulschner 78–9).
175 This phrase is used by T.M. Lindsay (1843–1914), whose *History
of the Reformation* offers the most odious, if – in some ways –
most memorable version of this dialectic. Erasmus, Lindsay says,
was 'always writing for effect, and often for effect of a rather sordid kind ... He had the ingenuity of the cuttle-fish to conceal
himself and his real opinions, and it was commonly used to pro-

tect his own skin.' Lindsay, principal of the Free Church theological college at Glasgow (see DNB 1912–21: 338–9), recognized at the same time Erasmus' faithfulness to his own idea of reformation and his genuine and noble horror of war. In the Holbein portraits he finds nothing masculine and a primness suggesting 'descent from a long line of maiden aunts' (*History* I 172–3, 175, 177).

176 Henry Goodwin Smith 'The Triumph of Erasmus in Modern Protestantism' 64, 69–76
177 Ibid 74–5
178 Ibid 65, 76–8, 81–2
179 'Auffassung und Analyse des Menschen im 15. und 16. Jahrhundert' 16–18
180 Ibid 42–4. There are echoes here of Hagen, indeed of Ranke.
181 Ibid 56, 58, 70, 73. On Dilthey's interpretation of Luther, see Heinrich Bornkamm *Luther im Spiegel der deutschen Geistesgeschichte* 100–3.
182 'Auffassung und Analyse' 74–7
183 *Zur Charakteristik* 15
184 Ibid 12, 16–20
185 Ibid 20–1, 24, 65–6, 69–71
186 Ibid 27–30. Faith, however, is not to be taken in the Reformation sense; for Erasmus as for medieval theologians, says Lezius, the heart of faith is love (ibid 31).
187 Ibid 35, 39, 41, 43–5
188 Ibid 46–9
189 Note the title of J. von Walter's essay 'Das Ende der Erasmus-renaissance' (1936).
190 On Müller, who saw church history simply as part of general history, see RGG IV cols 1171–2; Meinhold II 366–70, 596.
191 *Kirchengeschichte* II 1: 205–9
192 Ibid 303, 306. Müller does not deny that Erasmus continued to have an influence on both the old and new churches (ibid 307).
193 'Meine Bücher' 7–8. Cf Wilhelm Pauck *Harnack and Troeltsch: Two Historical Theologians* 59–62. For a critique from a Lutheran standpoint, see Walter Bodenstein *Neige des Historismus: Ernst Troeltschs Entwicklungsgang* 92–101. There has recently been a revival of interest in Troeltsch. See, eg, Robert G. Rubanowice *Crisis in Consciousness: The Thought of Ernst Troeltsch* xxi–ii.
194 'Protestantisches Christentum und Kirche in der Neuzeit' 473–5, 478. This paragraph is taken, with amendments, from my 'Erasmus in the Nineteenth Century.'
195 Edgar Bonjour *Die Universität Basel* 509; Richard Feller and Edgar Bonjour *Geschichtsschreibung der Schweiz* 788; Meinhold II 362–5, 599

196 *Die Renaissance des Christentums im 16. Jahrhundert* 17, 33, 41
197 Ibid 22–3, 26
198 Ibid 3–7, 8–16
199 Ibid 27, 29–30
200 *Calvins Jenseits-Christentum in seinem Verhältnisse zu den religiösen Schriften des Erasmus* 3
201 The main works are *De Praeparatione ad mortem, De contemptu mundi, Declamatio de morte, Enarratio Psalmi 38.*
202 *Calvins Jenseits-Christentum* 74
203 Ibid 6–7, 16, 30–2, 34, 38, 61–3
204 Ibid 5, 17, 47, 55–6
205 *Die religiösen Reformbestrebungen des deutschen Humanismus* 3, 9–11, 15
206 See, eg, Bernd Moeller 'Religious Life in Germany on the Eve of the Reformation.'
207 Hermelink's distinction is between this more constructive form of scholasticism and the sophistry of the 'nominalist' school. It is now unconvincing and, as well, Hermelink underestimates the complexity of late-medieval scholasticism. For criticism, see H.A. Oberman *Masters of the Reformation: The Emergence of a New Intellectual Climate in Europe* 33. This relates to Hermelink's history of the theological faculty at Tübingen (1906), the work which secured his habilitation at Leipzig. Hermelink (1877–1958) was later professor of church history at Kiel, Bonn, and Marburg (NDB 8: 667–8).
208 *Die religiösen Reformbestrebungen* 22
209 Ibid 24–5, 31–2, 34, 46
210 'Verhältnis von "via antiqua" und "via moderna" zu Humanismus und Reformation. – Religiös-theologische Bedeutung des Erasmus' 769, 772–4
211 *Theologische Literaturzeitung* 11 (1903) cols 336–8. Köhler's view here is shared by Karl Zickendraht in his study of the free-will controversy: Erasmus was much less interested in the specific theological issue than in challenging the place of dogma in religion generally and in the reform movement in particular (*Der Streit zwischen Erasmus und Luther über die Willensfreiheit* 26).
212 See ch 11.
213 'Die neueste Beurteilung des Erasmus' 136–40. On Walter, Lutheran professor of church history at Breslau (1909–17), see RGG VI col 1543; Meinhold II 388–93, 596.
214 'Die neueste Beurteilung' 140–50
215 Concrete study of these connections had already begun in the nineteenth century, as displayed in the Belgian and Basel writers.
216 Lindsay also speaks of the old Erasmus as 'absolutely alone, friendless, and without influence' (*History of the Reformation,* I

173); but later he demonstrates his considerable influence in England, on Zwingli and the Reformed churches generally (ibid II 9–13).

217 Adolf von Harnack in his great history of dogma accepted that Erasmus and the radical reformers rather than Luther were the precursors of the modern mind (*Lehrbuch der Dogmengeschichte* III 811); but humanism, despite its contribution to historical criticism, was not fruitful in the history of theology or dogma in the strict sense. Dilthey's view that Erasmus was the founder of theological rationalism was correct but forced: 'Erasmus is too many-sided and too uncertain in principles to have founded anything other than methods' (ibid 515).

218 Gustav Wolf *Quellenkunde der deutschen Reformationsgeschichte* I *Vorreformation und Allgemeine Reformationsgeschichte* 373–4

CHAPTER ELEVEN

1 Wolf *Quellenkunde* 369–71
2 Ibid 367
3 Gooch *History and Historians* 134–5
4 ADB 52: 244–8; Gustav Wolf *Wilhelm Maurenbrecher: Ein Lebens- und Schattenbild* 11–12, 16; Maurenbrecher *Geschichte der katholischen Reformation* I v–vii. Maurenbrecher's estimation of his predecessors is instructive: Ranke, who had been his teacher at Berlin in 1858, Hagen, Döllinger, and Kampschulte still deserved attention: Drummond was more useful than Feugère or Durand de Laur. As we shall see, he acknowledged his debt to Seebohm and thought Woker's monograph on Erasmus' irenicism a rounding out of Seebohm's study of his 'fellow-work' with Colet and More. Protestant studies of his relations with Luther were all deficient in assuming the absolute correctness of the Lutheran position, 'without examining or judging Erasmus in his own terms.' As for Janssen and Kerker, no one would look for impartiality there; certainly no one would find it (*Geschichte der katholischen Reformation* I 387–8n).
5 *Geschichte* I 119–25, 128
6 Ibid 131–5, 153–4, 243–5, 265–70, 349–50, 352
7 Ibid 354–6, 361–3
8 C. Weizsäcker, review of Maurenbrecher in *Göttingische gelehrte Anzeigen* 1881
9 *Almanach der kaiserlichen Akademie der Wissenschaften* 39 (1889): 190–3; Alphons Lhotsky *Geschichte des Instituts für österreichische Geschichtsforschung 1854–1954* 99–100; Allen I v
10 ADB 50: 24–5; *Zeitschrift für die Geschichte des Oberrheins* NF VIII (1893): 538–41 (Gustav Knod)

11 Gustav Knod 540–1
12 'Ueber die "Colloquia" des Erasmus von Rotterdam' 55, 61–2, 73, 75. Despite these remarks, Horawitz's essay is disappointing in that it remains largely expository and relates the work in no consistent way to the age.
13 Ibid 120–1
14 'Erasmiana. I' 389–91
15 'Desiderius Erasmus von Rotterdam und die Päpste seiner Zeit' 133, 150, 159–62
16 See *Contemporaries of Erasmus* I, II, and especially I 177–8 (on Botzheim).
17 'Der humanistische Freundeskreis des Desiderius Erasmus in Konstanz' 15
18 To Marcus Laurinus 1 February 1523 Allen Ep 1342 V 213–15
19 'Der humanistische Freundeskreis' 24–8
20 'Erziehung und Unterricht im Zeitalter des Humanismus' 75
21 Cf Wolf *Quellenkunde* 373–4.
22 Gisbert Beyerhaus 'Friedrich von Bezold' 316, 318–19; NDB 2: 211; Bornkamm *Luther im Spiegel der deutschen Geistesgeschichte* 50–1; Srbik II 172–3
23 *Geschichte der deutschen Reformation* 230–3, 238–9
24 Ibid 236–7, 241–2
25 Ibid 228, 288, 292
26 *Het Land van Rembrand: Studien over de Noordnederlandsche Beschaving in de Zeventiende Eeuw* I 281–3. Huet assumes that Erasmus' father was a priest at the time of his conception.
27 Ph. de Vries 'The Writing and Study of History in the Netherlands in the 19th Century' 264–5
28 *Het Land van Rembrand* I 257–63, 282
29 Ibid 232
30 NNBW VI cols 823–7; Kossmann *Low Countries 1780–1940* 296, 309
31 *Het Land van Rembrand* 238–9. The names mentioned include that of J.H. Scholten, the Leiden theologian who had been Huet's teacher in the 1840s.
32 Ibid 286–7, 333–4
33 Ibid 285, 291, 297, 307, 329
34 Ibid 339–41
35 *Erasmus en Leiden* 83
36 *Erasmus en de Nederlandsche Reformatie* 7–8, 10–11, 22
37 Ibid 11–13
38 Ibid 16–19
39 Ibid 19–26
40 *Erasmus en Leiden* 83; *Wie is Dat? 1956* 382. From 1914 to 1952

Lindeboom was professor of church history and the history of dogma at Groningen.

41 *Erasmus: Onderzoek naar zijne theologie en zijn godsdienstig gemoedsbestaan* 10. I have not seen Lindeboom's *Het bijbelsch humanisme in Nederland* (1913) which deals with the representatives of that tendency. The subject continued to interest him as is apparent from his 'Erasmus' Bedeutung für die Entwicklung des geistigen Lebens in den Niederlanden' of 1952.

42 Thus Erasmus was not the 'Voltaire of the sixteenth century' (*Erasmus* 3).

43 *Erasmus* 7, 13, 17, 19–20, 23–5

44 Ibid 8, 37–45, 82–5, 88

45 Ibid 8, 60, 63–6, 80

46 Ibid 156–60, 163–4, 174–7, 195–6, 200. For later discussions of the idea of a distinctive Netherlands reform movement, including criticism of Pijper and Lindeboom for overstating the case, see D. Nauta 'De Reformatie in Nederland in de Historiografie' 66–71.

47 In a much later essay Lindeboom speaks appreciatively of the Erasmus interpretations of Dilthey and Troeltsch ('Erasmus in de waardeering van het nageslacht' 129–30).

48 Augustin Renaudet *Erasme et l'Italie* xi

49 *Erasme en Italie* 16–21, 34–7

50 Ibid 87–9. Erasmus to Augustine Steuchus 27 March 1531 Allen Ep 2465 IX 206. I quote the translation by F.M. Nichols *Epistles of Erasmus* I 460–1.

51 *Erasme en Italie* 1, 4–5n, 5, 90

52 Ibid 21, 23. On Bombasius (Bombace), see *Contemporaries of Erasmus* I 163–5.

53 *Erasme en Italie* 32, 40, 44, 52, 70–1. On Venice cf Deno John Geanakoplos *Greek Scholars in Venice* ch 9 'Desiderius Erasmus: Associate of the Greek Scholars of Aldus' Academy.'

54 *Erasme en Italie* 73, 95. The contemporaneous article by Edward H.R. Tatham also, against Seebohm, takes a positive view of Erasmus' Italian experiences ('Erasmus in Italy').

55 *Erasme en Italie* 65–6, 69, 76–80, 90. Nolhac completed his work with a selection of letters of Erasmus (hitherto mostly unpublished) from two Roman collections, the Vatican and the Barberini libraries (ibid 97–132).

56 Raymond Marcel 'Les Dettes d'Erasme envers l'Italie' 171 ('in my view, all his works, without exception, are only the logical consequence of the various initiatives of the Italian humanists').

57 *Erasme et l'Italie* 101 ('His Italy remains the English Italy of Oxford, that of Colet, Grocyn, and Linacre; all an Italian England to which he owed the essential element in his genius'). All this is

462 Notes to pages 311-17

438 Notes to pages 311-17

438 Notes to pages 311-17

part of the debate about Erasmus' intellectual origins which See-bohm had begun and to which we will return.

58 An early example of the kind of study we are considering related to France was Antoine Péricaud's brief *Erasme dans ses rapports avec Lyon* (1843). It begins with Erasmus' stunning account of the amenities of the inns of Lyon in the colloquy 'Inns' (*Diversoria*). He had visited the city on the way to Italy in 1506. It is concerned mostly with his relations with the humanists of Lyon.

59 L. Febvre 'Un historien de l'humanisme: Augustin Renaudet' xv

60 In the form of an article over two numbers of the *Revue historique* CXI–CXII (1912–13): 'Erasme: Sa vie et son oeuvre jusqu'en 1517 d'après sa correspondence.'

61 'Erasme: Sa vie et son oeuvre' CXI 261

62 Febvre 'Un historien de l'humanisme' x–xii. Renaudet himself said: 'L'histoire n'a pour moi qu'un intérêt psychologique: c'est pourquoi j'ai choisi l'histoire religieuse – et n'en sortirai pas' (quoted ibid xi).

63 *Préréforme* preface. On the organization of *Préréforme*, cf Febvre xix.

64 *Préréforme* 265, 279, 289; 'Erasme' CXI 236, 245–6

65 *Préréforme* 385–9, 394; 'Erasme' CXI 246–8, 250–1

66 *Préréforme* 435

67 *Préréforme* 698–701. On weaknesses in Erasmus' New Testament edition, see ibid 680–2.

68 Ch 7

69 *Etudes* 146, 176, 182–3 and ch IV

70 *Erasme et l'Italie* 175. Catholic writers have sharply criticized Renaudet's conceptions of Erasmus' 'modernism' and the 'third church.' See Louis Bouyer *Autour d'Erasme*, especially ch XI. Cf J.K. McConica 'Erasmus and the Grammar of Consent' 77–8.

71 *Die Stellung* 9, 11, 19, 75

72 *Desiderius Erasmus* 1–3

73 *Die Stellung* 16, 24, 27–8, 37–8, 40, 42–3

74 NDB 11: 63–4; A.O. Meyer in HZ 138 (1928): 449–50

75 'Die Vermittlungspolitik' 2–3

76 Ibid 23, 26, 50–1

77 Both the *Acta* and the *Consilium* are in Wallace K. Ferguson (ed) *Erasmi Opuscula* at, respectively, 304–28 and 338–61.

78 'Die Vermittlungspolitik' 10–11, 14–17. On Faber, see *Contemporaries of Erasmus* II 4–5; on the authorship of the *Consilium*, see Ferguson *Erasmi Opuscula* 343–8 and Heinz Holeczek *Erasmus Deutsch* I 151–8 (where the four German versions of the work are also discussed). Both Ferguson and Holeczek accept the essentials of Kalkoff's argument for Erasmus as author.

79 'Die Vermittlungspolitik' 59, 64, 67, 73
80 *Die Anfänge* I 65–8, 83–90, II 39–47. Kalkoff exaggerates Aleander's role in driving Erasmus from Louvain and the Netherlands
   (cf Imgard Höss NDB 11: 63).
81 'Die Vermittlungspolitik' 75
82 'Erasmus und Hutten in ihrem Verhältnis zu Luther.' Kalkoff published a large work on Hutten in 1920. For a critique, see Kreutz
   Die Deutschen und Ulrich von Hutten 206–17.
83 Preface to *Etude critique* by Charles Andler vi–vii, x
84 *Etude critique* 2, 157–8
85 Ibid 63–81
86 Ibid 53–61
87 Ibid 5, 15–19, 23, 31
88 Ibid 142–4
89 Ibid 89, 99–100
90 Ibid, preface, xii
91 Ibid 55, 88–9, 159–61
92 Ibid 3–4
93 Gaudin 146, Hess II 170–1
94 For modern examples of such treatment, see *Contemporaries of Erasmus* 3: 481–6 (Fritz Büsser); Gottfried W. Locher 'Zwingli und
   Erasmus' and 'Zwingli and Erasmus'; Joachim Rogge *Zwingli und
   Erasmus: Die Friedensgedanken des jungen Zwingli;* E.W. Kohls 'Erasmus und die werdende evangelische Bewegung des 16. Jahrhunderts' 208–14.
95 On Usteri *Dict hist et biog* VI 787. He became professor of theology at Erlangen in 1889.
96 *Zwingli und Erasmus: Eine reformationsgeschichtliche Studie* 6–10.
   The poem is found in C. Reedijk (ed) *The Poems of Desiderius Erasmus* 291–6 (Zwingli's acknowledgment, 293). The importance of
   the poem had already been recognized by Zwingli scholars (eg
   J.C. Mörikofer *Ulrich Zwingli nach den urkundlichen Quellen* I 27).
97 *Zwingli und Erasmus* 11–19
98 Ibid 21–3
99 Ibid 24–5, 30. Cf Payne *Erasmus: His Theology of the Sacraments* ch
   VIII.
100 *Zwingli und Erasmus* 33
101 Ibid 25. For a modern view of Zwingli's predestinarianism and its
    limits, see J.V. Pollet *Huldrych Zwingli et la Réforme en Suisse
    d'après les recherches récentes* 47–9.
102 *Zwingli und Erasmus* 34, 38
103 He used the Rhediger collection at Breslau, which Horawitz had
    first calendared ('Erasmiana' III, IV), the Burscher collection at Leip-
    zig (cf ch 2 note 2 above), and a rich archive at Cracow gath-

ered in the eighteenth century for preparation of a history of Poland, including copies of unpublished *Erasmiana* (on the latter, cf Allen IX 316).

104 *Die Korrespondenz des Erasmus von Rotterdam mit Polen* ii–iii
105 For the grouping of Erasmus' Polish admirers, cf Maria Cytowska 'Erasme en Pologne avant l'époque du Concile de Trente' 11. Cf Claude Backvis 'La Fortune d'Erasme en Pologne.'
106 I have not attempted to survey the literature on all parts of Europe. A notable omission has been Spain. Relevant study began with two articles, A. Helfferich's 'Beitrag zu dem brieflichen Verkehr des Erasmus mit Spanien: Nach handschriftlichen Quellen' (1859) and Ed. Boehmer's 'Erasmus in Spanien' (1862) which prints two letters of the Spanish translator of the *Enchiridion* (one to Erasmus) and touches on the enthusiasm for and attacks on his work (cf Marcel Bataillon *Erasme et l'Espagne* 205–6, 241–2, 302).
107 The first studies by L.K. Born, who was later (1936) to publish an edition of the *Institutio principis christiani*, belong to 1928 and 1930. The first substantial monographs are by E.C. Bagdat (on the *Querela pacis*), A.W. de Jongh, and F. Geldner and belong to 1924, 1927, and 1930 respectively.
108 'Über die Institutio principis christiani des Erasmus' 315, 329. O. Herding considers Enthoven's article still worth reading (ASD IV–1 119).
109 'Erasmus Weltbürger oder Patriot?' 207–10, 213–15. Later studies on the same theme include Johan Huizinga 'Erasmus über Vaterland und Nationen' and Craig Thompson 'Erasmus as Internationalist and Cosmopolitan.'
110 *Memoirs of Eminent Teachers and Educators in Germany* 10
111 ADB 27: 420–3
112 *Geschichte der Pädagogik vom Wiederaufblühen klassischer Studien bis auf unsere Zeit* I 80–2, 88, 90–1
113 'Erasmus' 230. On the pre-Baconian character of Erasmus' pedagogy and his influence on Comenius, see Margolin *Erasme Declamatio* 113–14 and 'The Method of "Words and Things" in Erasmus's *De Pueris Instituendis* (1529) and Comenius's *Orbis Sensualium Pictus* (1658).'
114 NDB 555–7
115 'Erasmus' 231
116 *Geschichte des deutschen Schulwesens im Übergange vom Mittelalter zur Neuzeit* 329. On Kämmel, ADB 15: 51–6.
117 'Erasmus' 168, 171
118 *Quid de puerorum institutione* 8, 13, 89–91, 113–14, 123
119 Ibid 31–2, 44, 119–20, 124. Erasmus' attitude to dialectic is summed up thus: 'non semper ei hostis, nunquam ei socius est.'
120 Ibid 5, 16–17, 20, 36

121 Ibid 38–9, 43, 45, 140, 143
122 Ibid 110
123 Margolin *Erasme Declamatio* 314, 326
124 *Autobiography* 280–2, 313
125 *Geschichte des gelehrten Unterrichts* v–vi, 1–2, 38–9, 103, 130–3. There are signs here of Lavater's continuing influence: 'War Luther ganz Wille, so war Erasmus ganz Intellekt, wie es die Natur auf die beiden Physiognomien mit grosser, man möchte fast sagen erschreckender Deutlichkeit geschrieben hat' (ibid 132).
126 *Encyclopedia of Education* 4: 353
127 Ibid 349–51, Margolin *Erasme Declamatio* 75, 321
128 NDB 6: 462–3. Glöckner taught systematic and historical pedagogics and pedagogical psychology at Leipzig 1890–4. Failing to make the academic career he sought, he became pastor of the German congregation at Helsinki (1894–1910).
129 *Das Ideal* iii, 16–20
130 Ibid 19n
131 Ibid 30–4. 'Knowledge is good, charity is better' is from *Antibarbari* (CWE 23: 73).
132 *Das Ideal* 48, 57
133 Ibid 82–4
134 Ibid 44, 92, 97
135 Tögel (b. 1869) studied theology at Leipzig and Halle and then *Pädagogik* (*Die pädagogischen Anschauungen* iii).
136 Ibid 2–4
137 Ibid 17, 129
138 Ibid 21–3, 27–8, 30
139 Ibid 31, 35, 37–8, 44–5. On Erasmus' 'empirisme,' its 'banal' reiteration (philosophically speaking) of Aristotle, and its anticipation of Locke, see Margolin *Erasme Declamatio* 45, 69.
140 Ibid 8–9, 46–7
141 Ibid 116–24
142 Thomas Kelly *For Advancement of Learning: The University of Liverpool 1881–1981* 116; *Honours Register of the University of Oxford 1883* 596
143 Joseph Foster *Alumni Oxonienses: The Members of the University of Oxford, 1715–1886* IV 1606; Kelly *For Advancement of Learning* 77. Cf Margolin *Erasme Declamatio* 281.
144 His *Vittorino da Feltre and Other Humanist Educators: Essays and Versions* and his *Studies in Education during the Age of the Renaissance, 1400–1600*, as well as the work on Erasmus, were reissued in the 1960s in the Columbia series 'Classics in Education.'
145 Erasmus would not have taken kindly to works celebrating the expansion of empire. Cf Margolin *Erasme Declamatio* 284n.
146 Kelly 171; Eckhard Bernstein 'Erasmus' Money Connection: The

Antwerp Banker Erasmus Schets and Erasmus of Rotterdam, 1525–36'
147 *Desiderius Erasmus* 31, 34, 51
148 Ibid 36–7, 54
149 Ibid 35, 64
150 Ibid 81–2
151 '... it is characteristic of him to work intuitively towards right methods whose psychological validity he had no means of proving' (ibid 105).
152 Ibid 155–6. Cf Margolin *Erasme Declamatio* 285–6.
153 *Desiderius Erasmus* xxviii. The distinguished classicist R.C. Jebb (1841–1905) delivered the Rede lecture on Erasmus at Cambridge in 1890. He did not dwell on his services to classical scholarship but marked the practical character of his educational activity: 'he took the most profitable authors of antiquity, – profitable in a moral as well as a literary sense, – chose out the best things in them, – and sought to make these things widely known, – applying their wisdom or wit to the circumstances of his own day' (*Erasmus* 36). Cf Jebb 'The Classical Renaissance' *Cambridge Modern History* I 570. On Jebb, see DNB Supplement 1901–11 306–9.
154 *Desiderius Erasmus* 147–8, 160
155 In his Romanes lecture at Oxford in 1899, R.C. Jebb spoke of humanist education as 'in its essentials a type which satisfied the western world for four hundred years,' and added, 'the generation has not yet passed away which first saw its claims seriously challenged' (*Essays and Addresses* 517).
156 See ch 9 above.
157 *Silva carminum* vii–iii, x–xii. On the Brethren and the school at Deventer in Hegius' time, see Post *Modern Devotion* 576–9; on Synthen *Contemporaries* III 303.
158 *Silva carminum* xix–xx. Ruelens had the story from Melchior Adam (cf *Phoenix of His Age* 98–9). See Erasmus' own account in his letter to Botzheim (Allen I 2). Cf *Contemporaries* I 16; *Phoenix of His Age* 18n, 91.
159 *Silva carminum* xviii. On the history of the text and its publication, see Reedijk *Poems* 131–5.
160 *Silva carminum* i–iii, xxi–v. Modern scholarship has recognized the importance of Cornelis Gerard's friendship (cf *Contemporaries* II 88–9; *Erasmus en Leiden* 15–17; Charles Béné *Erasme et Saint Augustin* 37; Reedijk *Poems* 49–54).
161 *Silva carminum* xxvi, xxix–xxx, xxxv–viii. The *Oratio funebris* is at LB VIII 551–60. Cf Reedijk's introduction to two associated epitaphs (*Poems* 159).
162 *Silva carminum* xli–ii.

163 NNBW III cols 664–5; N. van der Blom 'Rector, schoolhistoricus, vir Erasmianus.'
164 See *Catalogus van geschriften over leven en werken van Desiderius Erasmus aanwezig in de Bibliotheek der Gemeente Rotterdam* 14–15 and index.
165 This 'Erasmiana' appeared first in *Nieuwe Rotterdamsche Courant* 3 December 1877. I use the French translation by L. Paul Delinotte, Kan's colleague at the school.
166 Kan/Delinotte 'Erasmiana' 186–7, 190
167 Ibid 197, 200, 203–5. On Merula, see *Phoenix of His Age* 125–7.
168 The first chapter of his 'Erasmiana' of 1881 ('De P. Merulae fide') accused Merula of fraud. Apprised of a manuscript in Vienna of the mid-sixteenth century, Kan published it with other documents in 1894 (in *Erasmiani gymnasii programma litterarium*). Cf Allen I 46; van der Blom 'Rector, schoolhistoricus, vir Erasmianus' 174. Its existence excluded the possibility of fraud by Merula. Roland Crahay who contested the authenticity of the *Compendium vitae* exculpated Merula ('Recherche sur le "Compendium vitae" attribué à Erasme' 14, 150).
169 I owe knowledge of this correspondence to N. van der Blom's paper 'Rotterdam and Erasmus' 248–9.
170 Allen I 575–8
171 For a modern discussion, see CWE 4: 400–3.
172 Quoted van der Blom 'Rotterdam and Erasmus' 248
173 See ch 10 above.
174 Vischer *Erasmiana* 3–4
175 *Dict hist et biog* VII 152; ADB 40: 70–1; Bonjour *Die Universität Basel* 462, 688–9
176 Epp 517–18 CWE 4: 188–97
177 Ep 447 ibid 6–32
178 *Erasmiana* 20. Modern editors have accepted this status for Grunnius' reply but have thought the letter reshaped rather than composed later (Allen II 292; J.K. McConica CWE 4: 7). They were first published by Erasmus in 1529.
179 Allen believes to the contrary that Erasmus was seeking safety from renewed attempts to return him to the monastery (II 292).
180 I use the third edition of 1887.
181 *Oxford Reformers* x
182 Ibid 16–17, 74
183 Ibid 4, 33–4, 39, 41, 103–5
184 Ibid 95, 97, 102–3, 106–7, 127–8, 135–6, 160
185 Ibid 173, 312, 321, 325–6, 355, 390
186 Ibid 462, 491–2, 494, 496, 508–10
187 'On the book's own terms,' ie without reference to modern litera-

ture on Colet and More. J.H. Lupton's life of Colet (1887) accepts
Seebohm's view of his relationships with Erasmus and More (*Life
of John Colet, D.D.* 95n). He presents Colet and Erasmus as complementary characters, the latter versatile and expansive, the former concentrated and of 'undivided purpose' (ibid 109). Actually
Lupton sees Colet less as the initiator of a reform movement than
as a connecting link between medieval and modern (ibid 265–6).
John B. Gleason's *John Colet* (1989) has made Seebohm's interpretation of Colet untenable, while demonstrating that it derived in
part from Erasmus and appealed to Victorian liberal, modernist,
or Broad Church feelings. Colet emerges as a reformer of a severely conservative cast, puritanical, antihumanist, antirationalist,
and morally absolutist. To understand Seebohm's influence, it is
necessary, as I have suggested, to appreciate how his scheme, no
matter how wrong-headed, met a need in Erasmus interpretations
at the end of the nineteenth century, in Europe as well as in England.

188 Albert Hyma in particular criticized the neglect of Erasmus' debts
to the *devotio moderna* and the Brethren of the Common Life
(*Youth of Erasmus* 126).

189 Allen described Seebohm's book as 'a careful and illuminating
monograph' (*Erasmus: Lectures and Wayfaring Sketches* 60). Gleason shows that Seebohm and Lupton slid over passages that
made untenable their hailing of Colet (in his Oxford lectures) as a
pioneer of the historical interpretation of scripture (*John Colet*
171–9).

190 See *Phoenix of His Age* 269–71 and ch 10 above. It should be
noted that Seebohm had already indicated the importance he
gave to Colet in an article of 1859 on More ('Sir Thomas More
and the Reformation' 107–9).

191 DNB 1912–21 488–90

192 The primary work was *The English Village Community examined in
its Relations to the Manorial and Tribal Systems ... An Essay in Economic History* (London 1883). Cf Allibone *Supplement* II 1328 and
Paul Vinogradoff 'Frederic Seebohm.'

193 *Die Anfänge des Erasmus* xxvii (C.H. Becker's 'Paul Mestwerdt: Ein
Bild seines Lebens und seiner Persönlichkeit.' What follows concerning Mestwerdt's life and from his correspondence is drawn
from this sketch).

194 He wondered, he wrote to his father, whether he would be better
working at 'einer anderen, unmittelbarer in das Leben eingreifen-
den Tätigkeit' (ibid xxvi).

195 Ibid xvii–iii

196 Ibid xxiv, 9. Cf Becker's comments (ibid xxvi–ii).

197 Ibid xxv, 9

198 Cf ibid xxiv.

199 Ibid 1, 3–4. Mestwerdt adds that even Drummond, whose biography was the best, did not attempt a systematic account of the origin and development of Erasmus' religious ideas, while Durand de Laur simply assumed his originality (ibid 8).

200 Ibid 37–9, 64–6

201 Ibid 31–2, 54–62

202 Ibid 83–7, 112, 118–19, 123–4, 128–9, 134–5

203 Ibid 139–44, 147–8. For criticism of Mestwerdt's view of the *devotio moderna*, especially for overestimating its openness to humanism, see R.R. Post *The Modern Devotion* 6–8.

204 Mestwerdt intended his first volume to finish at the *Enchiridion* and a second to deal with the period from it to the New Testament edition, by which time Erasmus had arrived at his distinctive program (*Die Anfänge* 15–16).

205 For Fruin's critical work, see below.

206 *Die Anfänge* 188–9, 191–2n, 200–5, 210–11, 215, 229, 233–6

207 Ibid 242–3, 251–2. On Batt, see *Contemporaries* I 100–1.

208 *Die Anfänge* 260–6, 269, 272–3

209 Ibid 309–10

210 Ibid 291, 302–3, 333–6

211 Ibid 197–9

212 Otto Schottenloher's *Erasmus im Ringen um die humanistische Bildungsform* (1933) works still within Mestwerdt's framework though departing from his scepticism about Erasmus' own records of his youth. The framework has since been loosened most by downgrading of the influence and importance of the Brethren as in Post's *Modern Devotion*, though Post has in turn overstated his case. James D. Tracy's *Erasmus: The Growth of a Mind*, which is the modern counterpart of Mestwerdt's book, is more prudent about tracing connections between Erasmus and his various *milieux* and organizes a chronological account of his intellectual development around 'the fundamental thought structures of Erasmus' reform program,' viz *humanitas*, *libertas*, and *simplicitas* (14). But note his 'Against the "Barbarians": The Young Erasmus and His Humanist Contemporaries,' which agrees with Mestwerdt over the 'secular' tone of the *Antibarbari* and the importance of Valla's influence. One ought not to finish this section on the young Erasmus without recalling that one of the best-known historical romances of the nineteenth century, Charles Reade's *The Cloister and the Hearth* (1861), deals with the love and adventures of Erasmus' father and finishes with a remark that some contemporary writers on Erasmus might well have heeded: history 'has written half a dozen lives of him. But there is something left for her yet to do. She has no more comprehended magnum Eras-

mum, than any other pigmy comprehends a giant, or partisan a judge.' For Reade's sources, including Erasmus' works and earlier biographies, see A.M. Turner *The Making of the Cloister and the Hearth*.

213 NDB 6: 144–5; *Encyclopaedia Judaica* VII cols 161–2
214 Ph. de Vries 'The Writing and Study of History in the Netherlands in the 19th Century' 260–3; *Erasmus en Leiden* 74–5; NNBW VII 452–6
215 de Vries 262. It has been remarked that late in life Fruin returned to an earlier appreciation of the place of subjectivity (NNBW VII 454).
216 'Neue Schriften zur Geschichte des Humanismus' 76–80, 82–3. Geiger praised Kampschulte's work and that of Woker, his student (ibid 72, 84).
217 Ibid 71–3; *Renaissance und Humanismus* 527–8
218 'Neue Schriften' 73–5; *Renaissance und Humanismus* 530, 532
219 'Neue Schriften' 84; *Renaissance und Humanismus* 541–2, 545
220 'Erasmiana' 85–7, 89, 92–8
221 Ibid 103–9, 115
222 Ibid 111
223 Ibid 110. Lindeboom overlooks these criticisms of Erasmus in concluding, from a parallel Fruin made between Erasmus and Grotius as opponents of religious fanaticism, that his opinion of him was essentially a favourable one ('Erasmus in de Waardeering van het Nageslacht' 128–9).
224 Allen I v
225 See above ch 10, n 38
226 Horawitz published in the *Sitzungsberichte der kaiserlichen Akademie der Wissenschaften* four articles on Erasmus' letters under the title 'Erasmiana' (1878, 1879, 1882, 1884). In addition, he published – under the title *Erasmus von Rotterdam und Martinus Lipsius: Ein Beitrag zur Gelehrtengeschichte Belgiens* – a codex of letters acquired in 1881 and deriving from the convent at Louvain to which Lipsius (Maarten Lips), a younger friend of Erasmus, belonged; it had probably been prepared under his supervision (*Erasmus von Rotterdam und Martinus Lipsius* 3–4). Horawitz rightly thought these letters a useful supplement to the work of Nève and others on Erasmus' associations with Belgium (ibid 17). Lips cooperated especially in Erasmus' patristic work. On the later history of the codex, see Allen IV xxvii. Scrutiny convinced Allen that Horawitz had done his work well.
227 Allen I vi
228 *Erasmus-Studien* 3; Allen I vi
229 *Erasmus-Studien* 23. The reference is to Ep 49 (CWE 1: 99–105).

230 *Erasmus-Studien* xix–xx. Allen agreed (*Erasmus: Lectures and Wayfaring Sketches* 77).
231 *Erasmus-Studien* xxiv. In another appendix Richter dealt with Erasmus' birth-year which he put at 1466 (ibid xviii).
232 Nichols *Epistles* I lviii–ix
233 *Erasmus von Rotterdam: Untersuchungen zu seinem Briefwechsel und Leben in den Jahren 1509 bis 1518* i, iii
234 Ibid 25–9
235 See Allen II 293. Cf Nichols I lx–ii.
236 Introduction *Epistles* III v
237 Joseph Foster *Alumni Oxoniensis* III 1022; *Honours Register of the University of Oxford 1883* 244; *Epistles* III vi
238 *Epistles* III vi–ii. He was seventy-five when the first volume appeared in 1901. A second volume covering letters between 1510 and 1517 appeared in 1904. Volume III, which was not part of Nichols' original design, covered the rich correspondence of 1517–18; it was completed some years before his death but published only in 1918 by his son.
239 *Epistles* I (1)–(33)
240 Ibid I vi
241 Ibid I xix–xx
242 Ibid I xlvi–ii, li–ii. Allen considered these arguments decisive (Appendix 1 I 576).
243 *Epistles* I xli–iv, II 139–40. Cf Allen I 564–5, CWE 2: 294.
244 *Epistles* I lx–iii
245 Ibid I 16–17. His knowledge of Deventer Nichols owed to J.C. van Slee, pastor and librarian in the city.
246 Ibid I 88. For a modern statement of Erasmus' satisfaction with his monastic experience, see R. De Molen 'Erasmus as Adolescent' 20–1.
247 *Epistles* I 224
248 Ibid I vi, xlviii, lxxi–ii, 18–19
249 Ibid I 308. The letter concerned is 146 (CWE 2: 18–21).
250 *Epistles* III x–xi. It is perhaps also characteristic that Allen himself treated this same correspondence with gentle irony: 'we must needs think more highly of Erasmus, if his friend could accept such treatment at his hand and not be wounded' (*Age of Erasmus* 116).
251 For what follows I have used three pieces by H.W. Garrod: DNB 1931–40: 5–6, 'Compendium vitae P.S. Allen,' and 'Percy Stafford Allen 1869–1933,' together with the *Letters of P.S. Allen* edited by his wife. Of the judges for the essay competition, Garrod says: 'They were likely to bring to their task no kind of prejudice and no knowledge of the subject' ('Percy Stafford Allen' 382n).

252 H.M. Allen says: 'For philosophy he had little interest. It was history and scholarship which stirred his imagination' (*Letters* 10).
253 Ibid 21, 24, 29–30, 38–9
254 'Percy Stafford Allen' 385. He began by making a catalogue of the letters in the Leiden edition with an *auctarium* of known letters not found there (*Letters* 12). Transcripts of letters made in the libraries which held them went without further copying to the printer; the proofs were checked against the original in the library. Every library was then visited at least twice ('Compendium vitae P.S. Allen' xiv). The text had priority and note-writing followed (*Letters* 55).
255 'Compendium vitae P.S. Allen' ix
256 Ibid xiv. On 5 August 1914 he wrote to his friend Aurel Stein: 'Armageddon has come, and we are overwhelmed with shame for Europe' (*Letters* 123). Only in that year was his lecture 'Force and Fraud' published, indicating at one point the distance civilization had come since the savageries of the sixteenth century (*Age of Erasmus* 178).
257 For example: 1922 honorary doctorate of Leiden University; 1923 election to British Academy; 1928 fellowship of Netherlands Academy
258 Garrod remarks that one would not learn here what kind of man Erasmus was; the material is 'presented with a scrupulosity and bareness which sometimes achieves the effect of a *suppressio veri*. Often the reader sighs for something of Froude's partisanship' (DNB 1931–40: 6).
259 H.M. Allen's preface to *Erasmus: Lectures and Wayfaring Sketches* v. I have not included Allen's entry 'Erasmus' in NNBW 5: 159–71.
260 *Age of Erasmus* 8
261 Ibid 7
262 'Young Erasmus' 27
263 *Age of Erasmus* 66
264 'Young Erasmus' 26, 29. Cf the lecture 'Monasteries' in *Age of Erasmus*.
265 *Erasmus: Lectures and Wayfaring Sketches* 31, 56 (from a lecture on 'Erasmus' Services to Learning' first delivered to the British Academy 1925).
266 *Erasmus: A Lecture* 15, 19. Cf 'Young Erasmus' 30–1.
267 *Erasmus: A Lecture* 15–16
268 *Erasmus: Lectures and Wayfaring Sketches* 58–9, 87; *Erasmus: A Lecture* 20–1. Erasmus' appeal for moderation and reconciliation in another setting is reported in 'Erasmus and the Bohemian Brethren,' a paper presented to an international historical congress in London in 1913 and published in *Age of Erasmus* 276–99.
269 *Erasmus: Lectures and Wayfaring Sketches* 65; *Age of Erasmus* 164–6

270 *Erasmus: A Lecture* 22
271 *Erasmus: Lectures and Wayfaring Sketches* 72–3
272 I can claim here only to be offering a sketch. A full study is a *desideratum*. We now have the precious memoir by Margaret Mann Phillips, published posthumously: 'P.S. Allen: A Lifetime of Letters.' It contains a personal recollection but also a brief biography full of charm and an account (from the voluminous papers in the Bodleian Library) of Allen's work on the edition.
273 *Letters* 27
274 'Compendium vitae P.S. Allen' v
275 Ibid xii; 'Percy Stafford Allen' 392–3
276 DNB 1931–40 5
277 'Compendium vitae' xii–iii; 'Percy Stafford Allen' 393: 'He could never be persuaded that the men and women about him were not a great deal better and nobler than they were.'
278 *Die beiden ersten Erasmus-Ausgaben* 106
279 Ibid 87–8, 107, 112–17; Bezold *Geschichte der deutschen Reformation* 228. On this controversy, see *Contemporaries of Erasmus* 2: 311–14. Cf Robert Coogan 'The Pharisee against the Hellenist: Edward Lee versus Erasmus.'
280 *Die beiden ersten Erasmus-Ausgaben* 67, 72
281 Ibid 2
282 Ibid 3–5, 14–15, 143–4. Bludau makes use of earlier commentators on the textual history of the New Testament: John Mill (1645–1707), J.J. Wettstein (1693–1754), F.J. Delitzsch (1813–90), F.H.A. Scrivener (1813–91), E. Reuss (1804–91). For a modern, more favourable judgment on Erasmus' manuscripts, see Jerry H. Bentley *Humanists and Holy Writ* 124–38.
283 *Die beiden ersten Erasmus-Ausgaben* 51
284 Bentley 114n
285 *Die beiden ersten Erasmus-Ausgaben* 13–14, 51–5. For a modern assessment, see Rummel *Erasmus' Annotations on the New Testament*.
286 *Die beiden ersten Erasmus-Ausgaben* 19, 32–3, 143–5. Erasmus' Latin translation of the text (a late addition to his plans) Bludau considers 'klar und durchsichtig' and combining reasonably close adherence to the original with elegance of Latin expression (ibid 43).
287 C. Reedijk 'Huizinga and His *Erasmus*: Some Observations in the Margin' 419
288 Whitney was professor of ecclesiastical history, King's College, London, 1908–18, and Dixie professor of ecclesiastical history at Cambridge, 1919–39. He was known for his attractive character, wide sympathies, and depth of learning (DNB 1931–40: 904–5).
289 *Erasmus and Luther* v

290 Binns (born 1885) published the lectures as *Erasmus the Reformer: A Study in Restatement* (1923).
291 'Erasmus' 21–2
292 Ibid 3. Whitney overestimates the scholarly progress made by the Brethren: 'Latin they had conquered and towards Greek they advanced.'
293 Ibid 13. In 1920 Whitney thought 'Common Lot' the correct title; when he republished 'Erasmus' in his *Reformation Essays* in 1939, he reverted to the more familiar 'Common Life.'
294 'Erasmus' 18, 25
295 Thus Erasmus' view of the papacy was 'that combination of respect for authority and of regard for private judgment which is so typical of Erasmus' (ibid 25n).
296 *Der moderne Mensch in Erasmus* 6
297 Ibid 11. Schröder remarks that, in view of the widely differing opinions about Erasmus and indeterminacy in the concept of the modern itself, one can only work towards an answer to this question and not expect to be decisive (ibid 19).
298 Ibid 20–4, 42–3
299 Schröder is aware of the dangers of anachronism; Erasmus' valuing of extra-Christian culture, he remarks, is not modern cultural relativism but rather its assimilation to Christian culture and above all to the Christian humanist way of thinking (ibid 45).
300 Ibid 59, 63–5, 70–3, 78–9
301 *Erasmus and Luther* vi, 25–7, 35
302 Ibid 86, 193, 285, 351, 353–4, 391–2
303 *Erasmus the Reformer* 62
304 Ibid vii–ix. The phrase 'constitutional reformer' appealed to English writers. Binns, like many before him, believed that Erasmus would have approved of the English Reformation and the Anglican church (ibid 93).
305 Ibid xii–iii. Binns dedicated his work to his teachers Mandell Creighton and J.N. Figgis who presumably represented for him the balance of the Anglican tradition and Anglican scholarship.
306 Ibid 102–4
307 On Smith, see DAB Supplement Three 1941–1945: 725–6 (W.K. Ferguson); William Gilbert 'The Work of Preserved Smith'; John A. Garraty 'Preserved Smith, Ralph Volney Harlow, and Psychology'; Craig R. Thompson 'Three American Erasmians' 12–23.
308 Gilbert 354
309 On Henry Preserved Smith (1847–1927), see DAB 17: 278–9. He was later (1898–1906) professor of biblical literature at Amherst and librarian of Union Theological Seminary, New York (1913–25).

310 *American Scholar* VI (1937) 127 (in an author's note to an article by Smith 'Erasmus, Enemy of Pedantry')

311 Cf Thompson 16–18. Garraty remarks that Smith's initial choice of biography was conservative, since the so-called new history associated with (among others) the name of James Harvey Robinson, with whom Smith had studied at Columbia, excluded biography as an outmoded form ('Preserved Smith, Ralph Volney Harlow, and Psychology' 457). He later (1913) tried something new in 'Luther's Early Development in the Light of Psycho-analysis' (published in the *American Journal of Psychology*) but did not repeat the experiment. Some would have thought Erasmus a promising subject (cf Nelson H. Minnich and W.W. Meissner 'The Character of Erasmus').

312 *Erasmus* xii

313 Thompson 14. The founding president of Cornell, Andrew Dickson White (1832–1918), famous scholar, administrator, and diplomat, saw Erasmus as the pioneer of the scientific investigation of the Bible (*A History of the Warfare of Science with Theology in Christendom* II 303, 314). While attending the Hague peace conference in 1899 and after gazing at Erasmus' statue at Rotterdam, he wrote: 'If my life were long enough I would gladly use my great collection of Erasmiana in illustrating his services to the world. To say nothing of other things, the modern "Higher Criticism" has its roots in his work' (*Autobiography* II 324). White's collection was left to Cornell (Smith *Erasmus* 429).

314 *Erasmus* 202, 318

315 DAB Supplement Three 726; Thompson 14. Smith had to battle with tuberculosis from his youth.

316 *Erasmus* 285

317 Thompson 20

318 The present inquiry owes much to his concluding chapter on Erasmus interpretation.

319 Smith's own criticism of his work (Gilbert 359).

320 *Erasmus* xi–ii

321 Ibid 15–16

322 Ibid 53–4, 424, 439. Smith thought Amiel and Froude went too far in attributing to Erasmus 'a complete and scoffing rationalism' (ibid 323).

323 Ibid 321

324 Ibid 4, 324, 378

325 Ibid 55, 159, 301. Like Murray Smith finds lacking a full idea of development (ibid 169).

326 Ibid 244, 439

327 Ibid 149, 244–5

328 *Erasmus of Rotterdam* 117
329 Ibid 109, 117, 123
330 Ibid 106
331 Ibid 105, 114–16, 127
332 Ibid 117, 129
333 Ibid 100, 107
334 Ibid 10–12, 15, 17, 30, 33, 101
335 Ibid 99
336 Ibid 151, 168, 170–2, 178
337 Ibid 142, 145. For that reason he could not, says Huizinga, have played the role Kalkoff attributed to him.
338 Ibid 167, 180, 184
339 Ernest W. Nelson 'Recent Literature Concerning Erasmus' 88
340 'My Path to History' 275
341 C. Reedijk 'Huizinga and His *Erasmus*: Some Observations in the Margin' 417–20. Huizinga wrote in Dutch and the work was translated by F.J. Hopman (1877–1932). On him, ibid 421–2.
342 'My Path to History' 274–5
343 J. Margolin 'Huizinga et les recherches érasmiennes' 116–17. He had, for example, published in 1921 an article on Erasmus and Dante. He returned to Erasmus with various essays in the commemorative year 1936.
344 Reedijk 'Huizinga' 426
345 Dutch critics in the 1930s criticized him for his reputed reluctance or inability to take sides (R.L. Colie 'Johan Huizinga and the Task of Cultural History' 616. Cf E.H. Gombrich 'Huizinga's *Homo Ludens*' 143).
346 Reedijk 427
347 *Erasmus* (Dutch edition) v–vi
348 Kurt Köster *Johan Huizinga 1872–1945* 33
349 Cf *Erasmus en Leiden* 76–8.
350 'My Path to History' 269. Huizinga was influenced by the German studies of the 1890s on intellectual and cultural history, eg Dilthey's (Köster 'Der Historiker Johan Huizinga' xxiv–v).
351 *Erasmus of Rotterdam* 131. Huizinga points out that familiar talk among friends in a country garden was a Renaissance ideal (104).
352 Ibid 188–9. For the appeal of mysticism to Huizinga and its effect on his judgment of Erasmus' indifference to much in the medieval Catholic tradition, see Johannes Trapman 'Le Latin mystique de Remy de Gourmont (1892) et son influence aux Pays-Bas' 48–9.
353 Emmanuel Stoffers 'Erasmus in de twintigste eeuw' 316
354 Karl J. Weintraub *Visions of Culture* 210–11. Cf E.H. Kossmann 'Postscript' 225–6.
355 Margolin 'Huizinga' 122; Stoffers 314

CHAPTER TWELVE

1 Note Margolin's comparison of the 'fundamentally religious interpretation' of Erasmus in the 1970s with Huizinga's 'intellectualist
and liberal point of view.' He remarks that both views have a
subjective element ('Huizinga et les recherches érasmiennes'
129-31).
2 For criticism of this line, see Richard Newald *Erasmus Roterodamus*
3-6.
3 Ulrich von Hutten, et al *On the Eve of the Reformation: Letters of
Obscure Men* 224

Bibliography

BIBLIOGRAPHIES

Bibliographie nationale: Dictionnaire des écrivains belges et catalogue de leurs publications 1830–80 III, Brussels 1897

Catalogus van geschriften over leven en werken van Desiderius Erasmus aanwezig in de Bibliotheek der Gemeente Rotterdam Rotterdam 1936/7

Hoffmann, F.L. 'Essai d'une liste d'ouvrages et dissertations concernant la vie et les écrits de Didier Érasme de Rotterdam (1518–1866)' *Le Bibliophile Belge: Bulletin trimestriel publié par la Société des Bibliophiles de Belgique* II (1866): 129–60, 241–51

– 'Notes sur une série de lettres adressées à Érasme, soit par des Belges, soit par des personnes vivant temporairement en Belgique et qui ne se trouvent pas dans le 3e vol. des Oeuvres Complètes d'Érasme' *Bulletin du Bibliophile belge* XV (1859): 273–97

Margolin, J.-C. *Douze années de bibliographie érasmienne (1950–1961)* Paris 1963

– *Quatorze années de bibliographie érasmienne (1936–1949)* Paris 1969

– *Neuf annés de bibliographie érasmienne (1962–1970)* Paris and Toronto 1977

Vander Haeghen, F. *Bibliotheca Erasmiana* Ghent 1893, reprint Nieuwkoop 1961

Vander Haeghen, F., R. Vanden Berghe, and T.J.I. Arnold *Bibliotheca Erasmiana* in *Bibliotheca Belgica* 27 vols, Ghent 1891–1922; reprinted in 6 vols, Brussels 1964. 'Erasmus' vol II

Wolf, Gustav *Quellenkunde der deutschen Reformationsgeschichte.* I *Vorreformation und Allgemeine Reformationsgeschichte* Gotha 1915

PRIMARY PRINTED SOURCES AND WORKS ON ERASMUS c 1750–1920

Acton, John, Lord review of Milman in *North British Review* LIII (1871): 603–4

- 'Acton-Creighton Correspondence' in *Essays on Freedom and Power* ed Gertrude Himmelfarb, Glencoe, Ill. 1948, 357–73
- 'The Catholic Academy' in *Essays on Church and State* ed Douglas Woodruff, London 1952, 279–90
- 'Döllinger's Historical Work' in *History of Freedom and Other Essays* London 1907, 375–435
- 'Fra Paolo Sarpi' in *Essays on Church and State* 251–9
- 'The History of Freedom in Christianity' in *Essays on Freedom and Power*, 58–87
- 'A History of the Papacy during the Period of the Reformation' in *Historical Essays and Studies* ed John Neville Figgis and Reginald Vere Laurence, London 1907, 426–41
- *Lectures on Modern History* New York 1961
- 'Ultramontanism' in *Essays in the Liberal Interpretation of History* ed W.H. McNeill, Chicago 1967, 160–213
Addi, Marius *Essai sur Érasme: Ses rapports avec la Réformation* Montauban 1869
Allard, H.J. 'Een portret van Erasmus' *Studien op godsdienstig, wetenschappelijk en letterkundig gebied* new series, 14 (1882): 1–69
Allen, H.M. (ed) *Letters of P.S. Allen* Oxford 1939
Allen, Percy Stafford *The Age of Erasmus: Lectures Delivered in the Universities of Oxford and London* Oxford 1914
- *Erasmus: A Lecture Delivered for the Genootschap Nederland–Engeland, and for the English Association in Holland, and in the Library of the Department of Education at the University of Liverpool* Liverpool 1922
- *Erasmus: Lectures and Wayfaring Sketches* Oxford 1934
- 'The Young Erasmus' in *Gedenkschrift* 25–33
Almanach der kaiserlichen Akademie der Wissenschaften (Vienna) 39 (1889): 190–3
Amiel, Emile *Erasme: Un libre-penseur du XVIe siècle* Paris 1889
The Annual Register, or a View of the History, Politics, and Literature, of the Year 1821 London 1822
Arnot, William *Life of James Hamilton D.D. F.L.S.* Edinburgh 1870
Barbey d'Aurevilly, J. *Les quarante médaillons de l'Académie* Paris 1864
Bauer, W. *Etude sur Erasme et ses rapports avec la Réforme* Montauban 1878
Bayle, Pierre *Dictionnaire historique et critique* VI, XII Paris 1820
Beard, Charles *The Reformation of the 16th Century in Its Relation to Modern Thought and Knowledge* Ann Arbor 1962
Becker, C.H. 'Paul Mestwerdt: Ein Bild seines Lebens und seiner Persönlichkeit' in Mestwerdt *Die Anfänge des Erasmus*
Becker, Gottfried Wilhelm *Luther und seine Zeitgenossen oder Ursachen, Zweck und Folgen der Reformation* Leipzig 1817
Becker, Wilhelm Gottlieb (ed) *Lob der Narrheit aus dem Lateinischen des*

Erasmus von Rotterdam, übersetzt und mit Anmerkungen begleitet Basel
1780
Benoist, A. *Quid de puerorum institutione senserit Erasmus* Paris 1876
Bettelheim, Anton (ed) *Biographisches Jahrbuch und deutscher Nekrolog*
v (1903): 297–302
Beyerhaus, Gisbert 'Friedrich von Bezold' HZ 141 (1929): 315–26
Beyschlag, W. 'D. Carl Ullmann: Eine biographische Skizze' *Theolo-
gische Studien und Kritiken* (1867): Ergänzungsheft Gotha 1867
Bezold, Friedrich von *Geschichte der deutschen Reformation* Allgemeine
Geschichte in Einzeldarstellungen, ed Wilhelm Oncken, III.1, Berlin
1890
Binns, Leonard Elliott *Erasmus the Reformer: A Study in Restatement.
Being the Hulsean Lectures Delivered before the University of Cam-
bridge for 1921–1922* London 1923
Bludau, August *Die beiden ersten Erasmus-Ausgaben des Neuen-Testa-
ments und ihrer Gegner* Biblische Studien VII.5, Freiburg im Breisgau
1902
Boehmer, Ed. 'Erasmus in Spanien' *Jahrbuch für romanische und en-
glische Literatur* 4 (1862): 158–65
Boswell, James *Life of Johnson* ed. G.B. Hill, revised and enlarged by
L.F. Powell, 6 vols, Oxford 1934–50 (vols V, VI, 2nd ed, 1964)
Boyer, Paul *Erasme: Ses rapports avec la Réforme* Montauban 1886
Brucker, Johann Jakob *Historia critica philosophiae* 2nd ed, IV *A tempore
resuscitatarum in occidente literarum ad nostra tempora* VI *Appendix
accessiones, observationes, emendationes, illustrationes atque supple-
menta exhibens* Leipzig 1766–7
Bungener, François *Erasme: Son role et son oeuvre en face de la Réforma-
tion* Geneva 1869
Busken Huet, Conrad *Het Land van Rembrand: Studien over de Noord-
nederlandsche Beschaving in de Zeventiende Eeuw* I, Haarlem 1920
Butler, Charles *The Life of Erasmus: With Historical Remarks on the State
of Literature between the Tenth and Sixteenth Centuries* London 1825
– *Reminiscences* 4th ed, I, London 1824, II 1827
Caird, John *University Addresses: Being Addresses on Subjects of Aca-
demic Study Delivered to the University of Glasgow* Glasgow 1898
Carlyle, Alexander *Autobiography of the Rev. Dr Alexander Carlyle of
Inveresk, 1722–1805* ed J.H. Burton, Edinburgh/London 1860
Carlyle, Thomas *On Heroes, Hero-Worship and the Heroic in History*
London and Glasgow n.d.
Chlebus, Wilhelm 'Erasmus und Luther' *Zeitschrift für die historische
Theologie* XV (1845): 3–82
Coleridge, Samuel Taylor *Aids to Reflection* 5th ed, ed H.N. Coleridge,
London 1843
– *Collected Works* general ed Kathleen Coburn, 2 *The Watchman* ed

Lewis Patton, London/Princeton 1970; 4 *The Friend* ed Barbara E. Rooke, London/Princeton 1969
- *Literary Remains* ed H.N. Coleridge, 4 vols, London 1836–9
- *The Philosophical Lectures* ed Kathleen Coburn, London 1949
- *Table Talk and Omniana* ed T. Ashe, London 1896
Coupé, Jean Marie Louis 'Erasme: Notice sur sa personne et sur ses ouvrages' in *Les soirées littéraires, ou Mélanges de Traductions nouvelles des plus beaux morceaux de l'Antiquité; de Pièces instructives et amusantes, tant françaises qu'étrangères, qui sont tombées dans l'oubli; de Productions, soit en vers, soit en prose, qui paraissent pour la première fois en public; d'Anecdotes sur les Auteurs et sur leurs écrits etc* VII, Paris 1797, 155–216
- 'Lettres latines d'Erasme, de Melanchthon, de Morus, de Vivès' in ibid XX, Paris 1800, 101–255
Cox, Francis Augustus *The Life of Philip Melanchthon: Comprising an Account of the Most Important Transactions of the Reformation* 2nd ed, London 1817
De Ram, Pierre-François-Xavier 'Particularités sur le séjour d'Erasme, à Bâle, et sur les derniers moments de cet homme célèbre' *Bulletin de l'Académie Royale des Sciences et Belles-Lettres de Bruxelles* IX, pt 1 (1842): 462–75
- 'Sur les rapports d'Erasme avec Damien de Goes' ibid, pt 2: 431–6
- 'Note sur Lambert Coomans, secrétaire d'Erasme' ibid: 437–40
- 'Rapport' on Rottier's *mémoire Bulletins de l'Académie Royale des Sciences, des Lettres et des Beaux-Arts de Belgique* XX (1853): 73–84
Desdevizes du Dezert, Théophile-Alphonse *Erasmus Roterodamus: Morum et litterarum vindex* Paris 1862
Diderot, Denis, and Jean d'Alembert (eds) *Encyclopédie, ou Dictionnaire raisonné des sciences, des arts et des métiers, par une société de gens de lettres* I, Paris 1751, XIV, XVII, Neufchastel 1765
- *Table analytique et raisonné des matières contenues dans les XXXIII volumes in-folio du Dictionnaire des sciences, des arts et des métiers, et dans son supplément* I, Paris/Amsterdam 1780
Dilthey, Wilhelm 'Auffassung und Analyse des Menschen im 15. und 16. Jahrhundert' in *Gesammelte Schriften* II, Leipzig/Berlin 1914
Dods, Marcus *Erasmus and Other Essays* London 1891
Döllinger, Johan Joseph Ignaz von, and Lord Acton *Briefwechsel 1850–1890* ed Victor Conzemius, I, Munich 1963, III 1971
Döllinger *Die Reformation, ihre innere Entwicklung und ihre Wirkungen im Umfange des Lutherischen Bekenntnisses* 2nd ed, I, Regensburg 1848
Drummond, Robert Blackley *Erasmus: His Life and Character as shown in His Correspondence and Works* 2 vols, London 1873
Durand de Laur, H. *Erasme: Précurseur et initiateur de l'esprit moderne* 2 vols, Paris 1872

Eberhardi, Wilhelm Ernst 'Warum blieb Desiderius Erasmus, Luthers freisinniger Zeitgenosse, Katholik? Eine unparteiische Untersuchung' *Zeitschrift für die historishe Theologie* IX (1839): 99–151

Ebrard, J.H.A. *Die Objectivität J. Janssen's urkundlich beleuchtet* Erlangen 1882

Eck, Cornelis Fransen van *Oratio de Desiderii Erasmi in doctrinam moralem meritis* Deventer 1831

Emerton, Ephraim *Desiderius Erasmus of Rotterdam* New York/London 1899

Enthoven, Ludwig 'Über die Institutio principis christiani des Erasmus: Ein Beitrag zur Theorie der Fürstenerziehung' *Neue Jahrbücher für das klassische Altertum, Geschichte und deutsche Literatur und für Pädagogik* 24 (1909): 312–29

– 'Erasmus Weltbürger oder Patriot?' ibid 29 (1912): 205–15

Erasmus, Desiderius *Ausgewählte Werke* ed Hajo Holborn and Annemarie Holborn, Munich 1933

– *Christian Humanism and the Reformation: Selected Writings* ed John C. Olin, 3rd ed, New York 1987

– *The Colloquies of Erasmus* ed Craig R. Thompson, Chicago/London 1965

– *Erasme: Declamatio de pueris statim ac liberaliter instituendis: Etude critique, traduction et commentaire* ed J.-C. Margolin, Geneva 1966

– *Erasmi Opuscula: A Supplement to the Opera Omnia* ed Wallace K. Ferguson, Hague 1933

– *Erasmi Roterodami Silva carminum antehac nunquam impressorum: Gouda, 1513: Reproduction photo-lithographique: Avec notice ... par M.Ch. Ruelens* Brussels 1864

– 'On the Freedom of the Will' (and Martin Luther 'On the Bondage of the Will') in *Luther and Erasmus: Free Will and Salvation* ed E. Gordon Rupp and Philip W. Watson, Library of Christian Classics XVII, London 1969

– *Poems* ed C. Reedijk, Leiden 1956

– *The Praise of Folly* ed Clarence H. Miller, New Haven/London 1979

– *Ratio seu Methodus verae theologiae: Recensuit et illustravit D.Io.Sal.Semler* Halle 1782

'Erasmus geenszins de eerste en grootste hervormer der christelijke kerk, volgens zijne eigene schriften enz.' *Vaderlandsche letteroefeningen* 1821: 289–96

Erhard, H.A. 'Erasmus' in *Allgemeine Encyklopädie der Wissenschaften und Künste* 36, ed J.S. Ersch and J.G. Gruber, Leipzig 1842, 155–212

Escher, Heinrich 'Erasmus von Rotterdam: Ein Beitrag zur Gelehrtengeschichte des sechszehnten Jahrhunderts' *Historisches Taschenbuch* new series, IV (1843): 487–574

Fétis, Edouard 'Notice sur Jean-Auguste-Henri Leys' *Annuaire de l'Aca-*

démie Royale des Sciences, des Lettres et des Beaux-Arts 38 (1872): 201–37

Froude, James Anthony *Life and Letters of Erasmus: Lectures Delivered at Oxford 1893–4* London 1897
- 'The Oxford Counter-Reformation' in *Short Studies on Great Subjects* 4 vols, London 1891, IV, 231–360
- 'Times of Erasmus and Luther' in ibid I, 39–153

Fruin, Robert 'Erasmiana' *Bijdragen voor vaderlandsche Geschiedenis en Oudheidskunde* new series, X (1880): 85–118

Funk, Frank Xavier, review of Janssen in *Theologische Quartalschrift* 62 (1880): 660–79

Gasquet, F.A. *The Eve of the Reformation* London 1900

[Gaudin, Johannes] *Leben des Erasmus* Zürich 1789

[Gaum, J.F.] *Luther und die Reformation: Aus Michael Ignaz Schmidts Geschichte der Deutschen: Mit Anmerkungen begleitet* 1783

Gaume, John Joseph *Paganism in Education* London 1852

Gaye, Johannes *Disquisitionis de vita Desiderii Erasmi specimen ab ann. nat. usque ad annum 1517* Kiel 1829

Geiger, Ludwig, review of Drummond in *Göttingische gelehrte Anzeigen* 1873 II 48: 1908–20
- review of Durand de Laur in ibid 1872 II 49: 1921–63
- 'Neue Schriften zur Geschichte des Humanismus' HZ 33 (1875): 49–125
- *Renaissance und Humanismus in Italien und Deutschland* Allgemeine Geschichte in Einzeldarstellungen II.8, Berlin 1882

Gibbon, Edward *The Autobiography of Edward Gibbon* ed Dero A. Saunders, New York 1961
- *The History of the Decline and Fall of the Roman Empire* ed J.B. Bury, 7 vols, London 1909–14
- *The Miscellaneous Works of Edward Gibbon, Esq., with Memoirs of His Life and Writings, Composed by Himself* ed John, Lord Sheffield, London 1837

Glasius, B. *Verhandeling over Erasmus als nederlandsch kerkhervormer* Hague 1850

Glöckner, G. *Das Ideal der Bildung und Erziehung bei Erasmus von Rotterdam* Dresden 1889

Godet, P. 'Erasme' DTC V, pt 1, cols 388–97

Hagen, Karl *Deutschlands literarische und religiöse Verhältnisse im Reformationszeitalter* 3 vols, Erlangen 1841–4

Hagenbach, Karl Rudolf 'Erasmus von Rotterdam in Basel 1516–1536' *Neujahrs-Blatt für Basels Jugend* VII (1827): 3–16
- 'Erasmus' in *Realencyklopädie für protestantische Theologie und Kirche* 4, Stuttgart/Hamburg 1855, 114–21
- *Vorlesungen über Wesen und Geschichte der Reformation* 2nd ed, Leipzig 1851

Hallam, Henry *Introduction to the Literature of Europe, in the Fifteenth, Sixteenth, and Seventeenth Centuries* I, 5th ed, London 1855

Hamilton, James 'Early Years of Erasmus' in *Works* IV, London 1873, 469–96

– 'Erasmus in England,' in ibid, 497–524

– 'Erasmus' in *Lectures Delivered before the Young Men's Christian Association, in Exeter Hall, from November, 1860, to February, 1861* London 1861, 379–407

Harnack, Adolf *Lehrbuch der Dogmengeschichte* 4th ed, III, Tübingen 1910

Hartfelder, Karl 'Desiderius Erasmus von Rotterdam und die Päpste seiner Zeit' *Historisches Taschenbuch* 6th series, XI (1892): 121–62

– 'Erziehung und Unterricht im Zeitalter des Humanismus' in *Geschichte der Erziehung vom Anfang an bis auf unsere Zeit* II.2, ed K.A. Schmid, Stuttgart 1889, 1–150

– 'Der humanistische Freundeskreis des Desiderius Erasmus in Konstanz' *Zeitschrift für die Geschichte des Oberrheins* new series, VIII (1893): 1–33

Helfferich, Adolph 'Beitrag zu dem brieflichen Verkehr des Erasmus mit Spanien: Nach handschriftlichen Quellen' *Zeitschrift für die historische Theologie* 29 (1859): 592–616

[Heller, Jos.] *Vertheidigung des grossen Erasmus von Rotterdam gegen ungegründete Beschuldigungen desselben durch die Anhänger Huttens* Bamberg 1824

Henneberg, Johann Valentin *Erasmus von Rotterdam für Prediger seiner und unserer Zeit: Ein Auszug aus dessen klassischem Werke*: Ecclesiastes, sive de ratione concionandi, Erfurt and Gotha 1822

Herder, Johann Gottfried 'Hutten' *Der Teutsche Merkur* July 1776: 3–34

– *Sämmtliche Werke* ed Bernhard Suphan, 33 vols, Berlin 1877–99, 1913

Hermelink, Heinrich *Die religiösen Reformbestrebungen des deutschen Humanismus* Tübingen 1907

[Hess, Salomon] *Erasmus von Rotterdam nach seinem Leben und Schriften* 2 vols, Zürich 1790

The Honours Register of the University of Oxford Oxford 1883

Horawitz, Adalbert 'Erasmiana I' *Sitzungsberichte der kaiserlichen Akademie der Wissenschaften Philosophisch-Historische Classe* Vienna 90 (1878): 387–457

– 'Erasmiana II' ibid 95 (1879): 575–609

– 'Erasmiana III' ibid 102 (1882): 755–98

– 'Erasmiana IV' ibid 108 (1884): 773–856

– *Erasmus von Rotterdam und Martinus Lipsius: Ein Beitrag zur Gelehrten-geschichte Belgiens* Vienna 1882

– 'Über die "Colloquia" des Erasmus von Rotterdam' *Historisches Taschenbuch* 6th series VI (1887): 53–121

Huet, P.J.L. *Drie brieven aan eenen vriend, over een Hoogduitsch werk: Leven van Erasmus door Adolf Müller* Amsterdam 1829
Huizinga, Johan H. *Erasmus of Rotterdam* London 1952
– *Erasmus* Haarlem 1924
– 'Erasmus über Vaterland und Nationen' in *Gedenkschrift*, 34–49
– 'My Path to History' in *Dutch Civilisation in the Seventeenth Century and Other Essays* London 1968, 244–76
Hülsen, Helene von *Erinnerungen an einen Heimgegangenen* Berlin n.d.
Hume, David *The History of England from the Invasion of Julius Caesar to the Revolution in 1688* 6 vols, New York 1879, III
Hutten, Ulrich von, et al *On the Eve of the Reformation: Letters of Obscure Men*, trans Francis Griffin Stokes, ed Hajo Holborn, New York 1964
Illgen, Christian Friedrich 'Vorrede' *Zeitschrift für die historische Theologie* I (1832): x–xiv
Imbart de la Tour, Pierre *Les Origines de la Réforme* III *L'Evangélisme (1521–38)* Paris 1914
Janssen, Johannes *An meine Kritiker* Freiburg im Breisgau 1883
– *Ein zweites Wort an meine Kritiker* Freiburg im Breisgau 1883
– *Geschichte des deutschen Volkes seit dem Ausgang des Mittelalters* 7th ed, II, Freiburg im Breisgau 1882
– *History of the German People at the Close of the Middle Ages* III, London 1900
Jebb, R.C. 'The Classical Renaissance' in *Cambridge Modern History* I, Cambridge 1902
– *Erasmus* 2nd ed, Cambridge 1897
– *Essays and Addresses* Cambridge 1907
Johnson, Samuel *Letters of Samuel Johnson with Mrs. Thrale's Genuine Letters to Him* ed R.W. Chapman, 3 vols, London 1952
– *The Works of Samuel Johnson* (Yale edition) I, *Diaries, Prayers, and Annals* ed E.L. McAdam Jr with Donald and Mary Hyde; III, IV *The Rambler* ed W.J. Bate and Albrecht B. Strauss, New Haven/London 1958, 1969
Kahnis, K.F.A. 'Schlusswort' *Zeitschrift für die historische Theologie* 45 (1875): 617–28
Kalkoff, Paul *Die Anfänge der Gegenreformation in den Niederlanden* 2 vols, Halle 1903–4
– 'Erasmus und Hutten in ihrem Verhältnis zu Luther' HZ 122 (1920): 260–7
– 'Die Vermittlungspolitik des Erasmus und sein Anteil an den Flugschriften der ersten Reformationszeit' ARG I (1903–4): 1–83
Kämmel, H.J. 'Erasmus' in ADB VI, Leipzig 1877, 160–80
– *Geschichte des deutschen Schulwesens im Übergange vom Mittelalter zur Neuzeit* Leipzig 1882
Kampschulte, F.W. *Die Universität Erfurt in ihrem Verhältnisse zu dem Humanismus und der Reformation* I, Trier 1858

Kan, J.-B. 'Erasmiana' *Bulletin du bibliophile et du bibliothécaire* 1878, 185–211, French trans L. Paul Delinotte (offprint Gemeentebibliotheek, Rotterdam)
– 'Erasmiana' in *Erasmiani Gymnasii Programma Litterarium* Rotterdam 1881, 1–8
Kegan Paul, C., review of Drummond in *The Theological Review: A Journal of Religious Thought and Life* X (1873): 405–16
– *Memories* 1899
Kerker, Moritz 'Erasmus und sein theologischer Standpunkt' *Theologische Quartalschrift* 41 (1859): 531–66
Kieser, Carl *Der Streit zwischen Ulrich von Hutten und Erasmus von Rotterdam; ein Beitrag zur Charakteristik Ulrichs von Hutten und seiner literarischen Zeitgenossen* Mainz 1823
Knod, Gustav, obituary of Hartfelder in *Zeitschrift für die Geschichte des Oberrheins* new series, VIII (1893): 538–41
Knox, Vicesimus *Anti-polemus: Or, the Plea of Reason, Religion, and Humanity, against War: A Fragment: Translated from Erasmus; and addressed to aggressors* London 1794
– 'The Prospect of Perpetual and Universal Peace to be Established on the Principles of Christian Philanthropy' in *Works* VI, London 1824, 351–70
– *Works* I, London 1824 'Biographical Preface,' i–xv
Köhler, W., review of Schultze in *Theologische Literaturzeitung* 11 (1903): cols 335–8
Lamy, T.J. 'Notice sur la vie et les travaux de Félix-Jean-Baptiste-Joseph Nève,' *Annuaire de l'Académie Royale des Sciences, des Lettres et des Beaux-Arts de Belgique* 60 (1894): 499–584
Lange, Albert 'Erasmus' in K.A. Schmid (ed) *Encyklopädie des gesammten Erziehungs- und Unterrichtswesens* 2nd ed, II, Gotha 1878, 223–32
Lavater, Johann Caspar *Physiognomische Fragmente, zur Beförderung der Menschenkenntniss und Menschenliebe* I, II, Leipzig/Winterthur 1775–6
Lecky, W.E.H. 'Henry Hart Milman, D.D., Dean of St Paul's' in *Historical and Political Essays* London 1908, 249–74
– *History of the Rise and Influence of the Spirit of Rationalism in Europe* I, London 1884
Lévesque de Burigny *Vie d'Erasme, dans laquelle on trouvera l'histoire de plusieurs hommes célèbres avec lesquels il a été en liaison, l'analyse critique de ses ouvrages, & l'examen impartial de ses sentiments en matière de religion* 2 vols, Paris 1757
Lezius, Friedrich *Zur Charakteristik des religiösen Standpunktes des Erasmus* Gütersloh 1895
Lieberkúhn, E.G.F. *De Erasmi Roterodami ingenio ac doctrina quid valuerint ad instaurationem sacrorum* Jena 1836
Lilly, William Samuel 'Erasmus' *Quarterly Review* 180 (1895): 1–35

- *Essays and Speeches* London 1897
Lindeboom, Johannes *Erasmus: Onderzoek naar zijne theologie en zijn godsdienstig gemoedsbestaan* Leiden 1909
- 'Erasmus' Bedeutung fur die Entwicklung des geistigen Lebens in den Niederlanden' ARG 43 (1952): 1–12
- 'Erasmus in de waardeering van het Nageslacht' *Bijdragen voor vaderlandsche Geschiedenis en Oudheidskunde* 7th series, VII (1936): 117–31
Lindner, Bruno 'Erinnerung an den verewigten Präses der historisch-theologischen Gesellschaft zu Leipzig Domherrn Professor Dr. Chr. Fr. Illgen' *Zeitschrift für die historische Theologie* XV (1845): 1–45
Lindsay, Thomas M. *A History of the Reformation* 2nd ed, 2 vols, Edinburgh 1907–8
Lücke, Friedrich *Dr. Gottlieb Jakob Planck: Ein biographischer Versuch* Göttingen 1835
Lupton, J.H. *Life of John Colet, D.D. Dean of St Paul's and Founder of St. Paul's School* 2nd ed, London 1909
Maeder, M. 'Notice sur la vie et les écrits de Théophile-Jacques Planck, professeur en théologie à l'Université de Goettingue' in *Essais et fragments de philosophie et de théologie, publiés par plusieurs professeurs du Séminaire protestant et de la Faculté de Théologie de Strasbourg* 1, pt 2 (1838): 75–141
Marheineke, Philipp *Geschichte der teutschen Reformation* Berlin 1816
Marin, G. 'Erasme et son nouvel historien' *Revue des questions historiques* XV (1874): 228–34
Masson, Gustave, review of Drummond in *Revue des questions historiques* XV (1874): 243–4
Maurenbrecher, Wilhelm *Geschichte der katholischen Reformation* I, Nördlingen 1880
Meiklejohn, John 'Erasmus' in *The Reformers: Lectures Delivered in St. James' Church, Paisley, by Ministers of the United Presbyterian Church, Graduates of the University of Glasgow* Glasgow 1885, 142–90
Memoirs of Eminent Teachers and Educators in Germany; with Contributions to the History of Education from the Fourteenth to the Nineteenth Century ed Henry Burnard, New York 1863
Merle d'Aubigné, J.H. *Histoire de la Réformation du seizième siècle* 2nd ed, I, Paris/Geneva 1838
- *History of the Reformation in the Sixteenth Century* trans Henry Beveridge, I, Glasgow n.d.
Mestwerdt, Paul *Die Anfänge des Erasmus: Humanismus und 'Devotio Moderna'* Studien zur Kultur und Geschichte der Reformation II, Leipzig 1917
Meyer, A.O., obituary of Kalkoff in HZ 138 (1928): 449–50

Meyer, André *Etude critique sur les relations d'Erasme et de Luther* Paris 1909

Miaskowski, Kasimir von *Die Korrespondenz des Erasmus von Rotterdam mit Polen* Posen 1901

Michelet, Jules *Ecrits de jeunesse* ed Paul Viallaneix, Paris 1959

– *Histoire de France au seizième siècle* VII *Renaissance* VIII *Réforme*, Paris 1855

– *Journal* ed Paul Viallaneix, I, Paris 1959

– *Mémoires de Luther, écrits par lui-même* Brussels 1837

Milman, Arthur *Henry Hart Milman, D.D. Dean of St Paul's: A Biographical Sketch* London 1900

Milman, Henry Hart 'Life of Erasmus' *Quarterly Review* 106 (1859): 1–58 (reprinted in *Savonarola, Erasmus and Other Essays* London 1870)

Milner, Joseph *The History of the Church of Christ; from the Days of the Apostles, till the famous Disputation between Luther and Miltitz, in 1520: Continued after the Same Plan by the Rev. Isaac Milner, D.D. F.R.S.* London 1847

Moser, Friedrich Karl von 'Heldenmüthiges ungedrucktes Schreiben Ulrichs von Hutten an Erasmus von Rotterdam' *Patriotisches Archiv für Deutschland* 7 (1787): 5–32

Mosheim, Johann Lorenz von *Institutionum historiae ecclesiasticae antiquae et recentioris libri quatuor* Helmstedt 1755. Eng trans *An Ecclesiastical History, Antient and Modern, from the Birth of Christ, to the Beginning of the Present Century: in which the Rise, Progress, and Variations of Church Power are considered in their Connexion with the State of Learning and Philosophy, and the Political History of Europe during that Period* ed Archibald Maclaine, 2 vols, London 1765

– *Versuch einer unparteyischen und gründlichen Ketzergeschichte* 2nd ed, Helmstedt 1748

Müller, Adolf *Leben des Erasmus von Rotterdam: Mit einleitenden Betrachtungen über die analoge Entwickelung der Menschheit und des einzelnen Menschen* Hamburg 1828

– [as Schottmüller, Adolf] 'Leben des Verfassers' in *Luther: Ein deutsches Heldenleben* Berlin n.d. [1862]

– reviews in *Theologische Studien und Kritiken* III (1830): 899–907; IV (1831): 607–12

Müller, Karl *Kirchengeschichte* II, Tübingen/Leipzig 1902

Murray, Robert H. *Erasmus and Luther: Their Attitude to Toleration* London 1920

Naismith, Robert *Memoir of Rev. James Hamilton D.D. F.L.S. Regent Square, London, Model Student, Preacher, and Pastor* London [1896]

Nève, Félix 'Erasme d'après ses nouveaux historiens' *Revue catholique* XXXIX (1875): 257–86

- 'Recherches sur le séjour et les études d'Erasme en Brabant' ibid XLI
  (1876): 44–72, 128–58
- *La Renaissance des lettres et l'essor de l'érudition ancienne de Belgique*
  Louvain 1890
Newman, John Henry *Apologia pro Vita Sua: Being a History of His Religious Opinions* London 1890
Nichols, Francis Morgan *The Epistles of Erasmus from His Earliest Letters to His Fifty-first Year* 3 vols, London 1901–18 (vol III under title:
  ... *to His Fifty-third Year*)
Nisard, J.M.N. Désiré 'Erasme' *Revue des deux mondes* 4th series, III
  (1835): 253–300, 381–423, 509–50 (also in *Etudes sur la Renaissance*
  2nd ed, Paris 1864)
- 'Lettre au Directeur de la Revue des Deux Mondes' ibid VIII (1836):
  495–506
'Nogmaals iets over Erasmus' *Vaderlandsche letteroefeningen* II (Amsterdam 1830): 90–100
Nolhac, Pierre de *Erasme en Italie: Etude sur un épisode de la Renaissance* 2nd ed, Paris 1898
Noordziek, J.J.F. *Erasmus: Eene voorlezing* Hague 1841
Pastor, Ludwig Freiherr von *Aus dem Leben des Geschichtschreibers Johannes Janssen 1829–91 mit einer Charakteristik Janssens* Cologne
  1929
- *History of the Popes from the Close of the Middle Ages* VII, London
  1908
- *Tagebücher – Briefe – Erinnerungen* ed Wilhelm Wühr, Heidelberg
  1950
Pattison, Mark 'Erasmus' in *The Encyclopaedia Britannica: A Dictionary
  of Arts, Sciences and General Literature* 9th ed, VIII, Edinburgh 1878,
  512–18
- *Memoirs* London 1885
- 'Present State of Theology in Germany' in *Essays* II, Oxford 1889,
  237–48
Paulsen, Friedrich *An Autobiography* ed Theodor Lorenz, New York
  1938
- *Geschichte des gelehrten Unterrichts auf den deutschen Schulen und
  Universitäten vom Ausgang des Mittelalters bis zur Gegenwart: Mit be-
  sonderer Rücksicht auf dem klassischen Unterricht* Leipzig 1885
Paulus, H.E.G. 'Zur richtigeren Beurtheilung Hulderichs von Hutten
  und Erasmus' *Sophronizon oder unparteyisch-freymüthige Beiträge zur
  neuren Geschichte, Gesetzgebung und Statistik der Staaten und Kirchen*
  4 (1822): 60–71
Pennington, A.R. *The Life and Character of Erasmus* London 1875
Péricaud, Antoine *Erasme dans ses rapports avec Lyon* Lyon 1843
Pijper, F. *Erasmus en de Nederlandsche Reformatie* Leiden 1907

Planck, Gottlieb Jakob *Einleitung in die Theologische Wissenschaften* 2, Leipzig 1795
- *Geschichte der Entstehung, der Veränderungen und der Bildung unsers protestantischen Lehrbegriffs vom Anfang der Reformation bis zu der Einführung der Concordienformel* 2nd ed, I, II, Leipzig 1791–2
Plitt G.L. 'Desiderius Erasmus in seiner Stellung zur Reformation' *Zeitschrift für die gesammte lutherische Theologie und Kirche* 27 (1866): 479–514
Priestley, Joseph *An History of the Corruptions of Christianity* 2 vols, Birmingham 1782 (facsimile in *The Life and Times of Seven Major British Writers. Gibboniana* x, New York/London 1974)
Ranke, Leopold von *Das Briefwerk* ed W.P. Fuchs, Hamburg 1949
- *Deutsche Geschichte im Zeitalter der Reformation, Sämmtliche Werke* I, Leipzig 1873. Eng trans Sarah Austin, ed Robert A. Johnson *History of the Reformation in Germany* I, London 1905 (reprint New York 1966)
Raumer, Karl von *Geschichte der Pädagogik vom Wiederaufblühen klassischer Studien bis auf unsere Zeit* 4th ed, I, Gütersloh 1872
Reade, Charles *The Cloister and the Hearth: A Tale of the Middle Ages* Modern Library edition, New York n.d.
Reich, Max *Erasmus von Rotterdam: Untersuchungen zu seinem Briefwechsel und Leben in den Jahren 1509 bis 1518* Trier 1895
Renaudet, Augustin *Erasme et l'Italie* Geneva 1954
- 'Erasme: Sa vie et son oeuvre jusqu'en 1517 d'après sa correspondance' *Revue historique* CXI ((1912): 225–62; CXII (1913): 241–74
- *Etudes érasmiennes 1521–1529* Paris 1939
- *Préréforme et humanisme à Paris pendant les premières guerres d'Italie (1494–1517)* 2nd ed, Paris 1953
Richter, Arthur *Erasmus-Studien* Dresden 1891
Richter, Max *Desiderius Erasmus und seine Stellung zu Luther auf Grund ihrer Schriften* Leipzig 1907
- *Die Stellung des Erasmus zu Luther und zur Reformation in den Jahren 1516–1524* Leipzig 1900
Robertson, William *The History of the Reign of the Emperor Charles V* in *The Works of William Robertson D.D.* London 1837, 305–712
- *The History of Scotland* in ibid 1–304
- *The Progress of Society in Europe: A Historical Outline from the Subversion of the Roman Empire to the Beginning of the Sixteenth Century* ed Felix Gilbert, Chicago/London 1972
Rotermund, Heinrich Wilhelm *Erneuertes Andenken der Männer die für und gegen die Reformation Lutheri gearbeitet haben* I, Bremen 1818
Rottier, Eugène *La vie et les travaux d'Erasme, considérés dans leurs rapports avec la Belgique* Mémoires couronnés et Mémoires des savants

étrangers, publiés par l'Académie Royale des Sciences, des Lettres et des Beaux-Arts de Belgique VI, Brussels 1855

Ruelens, Charles 'Notice sur la jeunesse et les premiers travaux d'Erasme' in *Erasmi Roterodami Silva carminum* ... Brussels 1864, i–xliv

Sailer, Johann Michael *Ueber Erziehung für Erzieher, oder Pädagogik* II, in *Sämmtliche Werke* ed Joseph Widmer, VII, Sulzbach 1831

Sainte-Beuve, Charles-Augustin *Causeries du Lundi* 4th ed, I, Paris n.d. (Eng trans E.J. Trechmann, London n.d.)

– 'Ecrivains critiques contemporains: *Les Poètes latins; – Précis de l'histoire de la littérature française,* par M. Nisard' *Revue des deux mondes* 4th series, VIII (1836): 270–86

Salles, Amédée *Erasme et son traité du libre arbitre* Geneva 1877

Sardou, Victorien 'Erasme et ses Colloques' *Revue des deux mondes* 7th series, 21 (1924): 481–511

Schleiermacher, Friedrich *Geschichte der christlichen Kirche: Aus Schleiermachers handschriftlichem Nachlasse und nachgeschriebenen Vorlesungen* ed E. Bonnell, *Sämmtliche Werke,* Abtheilung 1 (Zur Theologie) 11, Berlin 1840

Schlottmann, Constantin *Erasmus redivivus sive de Curia Romana hucusque insanabili* 2 vols, Halle 1883, 1889

Schmidt, Michael Ignaz *Geschichte der Deutschen* 1st ed, VI, Ulm 1785; 2nd ed, IV, V, Ulm 1787–8

Schröckh, Johann Matthias *Christliche Kirchengeschichte* 30, Leipzig 1800

– *Christliche Kirchengeschichte seit der Reformation* 1, Leipzig 1804

– review of Schmidt in *Allgemeine deutsche Bibliothek* 72 (1787): 219–52

Schröder, A *Der moderne Mensch in Erasmus: Eine Untersuchung zur Frage nach der christlichen Weltanschauung* Leipzig 1919

Schulze, Martin *Calvins Jenseits-Christentum in seinem Verhältnisse zu den religiösen Schriften des Erasmus* Görlitz 1902

Seebohm, Frederic *The Oxford Reformers John Colet, Erasmus, and Thomas More: Being a History of Their Fellow-Work* 3rd ed, London 1887

– 'Sir Thomas More and the Reformation' *North British Review* XXX (1859): 102–36

Semler, Johann Salomo *Institutio ad doctrinam christianam liberaliter discendam* Halle 1774

– *Lebensbeschreibung von ihm selbst abgefasst* II, Halle 1782

– *Neue Versuche, die Kirchenhistorie der ersten Jahrhunderte mehr aufzuklären* Leipzig 1788

– *Versuch eines fruchtbaren Auszugs der Kirchengeschichte* II, Halle 1774

Smith, Arthur Lionel *Erasmus, Humourist, Scholar, Divine: An Essay in Biography and History* Oxford 1874

Smith, Henry Goodwin 'The Triumph of Erasmus in Modern Protestantism' *Hibbert Journal* 3 (1905): 64–82
Smith M.F. *Arthur Lionel Smith Master of Balliol (1916–1924): A Biography and Some Reminiscences by His Wife* London 1928
Smith, Preserved *Erasmus: A Study of His Life, Ideals and Place in History* New York 1962 (first published 1923)
– 'Erasmus, Enemy of Pedantry' *American Scholar* VI (1937): 85–92,
127
Stähelin, Rudolf 'Erasmus' in *Realencyklopädie für protestantische Theologie und Kirche* 2nd ed, 4, Leipzig 1879, 278–90
– *Erasmus Stellung zur Reformation hauptsächlich von seinen Beziehungen zu Basel aus beleuchtet* Basel 1873
Stelling-Michaud, Suzanne *Le Livre du Recteur de l'Académie de Genève
(1559–1878)* 4 *Notices biographiques des étudiants* H-M Geneva 1975
Stephen, James *Essays in Ecclesiastical Biography* 2 vols, London 1849
Stewart, Dugald 'Account of the Life and Writings of William Robert-
son D.D.' in *The Works of William Robertson D.D.* London 1837, i–xxxi
– *Dissertation: Exhibiting the Progress of Metaphysical, Ethical, and Political Philosophy, since the Revival of Letters in Europe* in *Collected
Works* ed Sir William Hamilton, I, Edinburgh 1854
Stichart, Franz Otto *Erasmus von Rotterdam: Seine Stellung zu der Kirche
und zu den kirklichen Bewegungen seiner Zeit* Leipzig 1870
Stockmeyer, Emanuel 'Erasmus in seinen Briefen an Bonifacius Amer-
bach' *Schweizerisches Museum für Historische Wissenschaften* 3 (1839):
73–113
Stolz, Johann Jakob (ed) *Ulrich von Hutten gegen Desiderius Erasmus,
und Desiderius Erasmus gegen Ulrich von Hutten: Zwey Streitschriften
aus dem sechszehten Jahrhundert* Aarau 1813
Strauss, David Friedrich *Ulrich von Hutten: His Life and Times* London
1874
Streuber, Wilhelm-Theodor 'Erasmus von Rotterdam zu Basel' *Basler
Taschenbuch* I (1850): 45–80
Swart, N. 'Erasmus: Het luisterrijkst voorbeeld van verwonnen zwa-
righeden' *Vaderlandsche letteroefeningen* 1824: 397–414
Taine, H. *Essais de critique et d'histoire* Paris 1858
Tatham, Edward H.R. 'Erasmus in Italy' *English Historical Review* X
(1895): 642–62
Teutsch, D.Th *Controverse entre Luther and Erasme sur le libre arbitre*
Strasbourg 1853
Tögel, Hermann *Die pädagogischen Anschauungen des Erasmus in ihrer
psychologischen Begründung* Dresden 1896
Troeltsch, Ernst 'Meiner Bücher' in *Gesämmelte Schriften* IV, Tübingen
1925, 3–18
– 'Protestantisches Christentum und Kirche in der Neuzeit' in Paul

Hinneberg (ed) *Die Kultur der Gegenwart* I IV.1, Leipzig/Berlin 1922, 431–792

- 'Verhältnis von "via antiqua" und "via moderna" zu Humanismus und Reformation. – Religiös-theologische Bedeutung des Erasmus' in *Gesämmelte Schriften* IV, 762–74

Ullmann, Carl, review of Adolf Müller in *Theologische Studien und Kritiken* 2 (1829): 178–208

- *Reformers before the Reformation, principally in Germany and the Netherlands* 3rd ed, I, Edinburgh 1863

Usteri, Johann Martin *Zwingli und Erasmus: Eine reformationsgeschichtliche Studie* Zürich 1885

Veitch, John 'Memoir of Dugald Stewart' in Dugald Stewart *Collected Works* ed Sir William Hamilton, X, Edinburgh 1858, i–clxxvii

Veuillot, Louis *Les pèlerinages de Suisse* in *Oeuvres complètes* II, Paris 1924

Villers, Charles *Essai sur l'esprit et l'influence de la Réformation de Luther* 2nd ed, Paris 1804

- *Essay on the Spirit and Influence of the Reformation of Luther* ed James Mill, London 1805

Vischer, Wilhelm *Erasmiana: Programm zur Rectoratsfeier der Universität Basel* Basel 1876

Voltaire, Francois-Marie Arouet *Anecdote sur Bélisaire par l'abbé Mauduit, qui prie qu'on ne le nomme pas* in *Dialogues et Anecdotes philosophiques*, ed Raymond Naves, Paris 1966, 172–6

- *Conversation de Lucien, Erasme, et Rabelais dans les champs élysées* in ibid 146–52

- *Correspondance* ed Theodore Besterman, XXXI, Geneva 1958

- *Essai sur les moeurs et l'esprit des nations et sur les principaux faits de l'histoire depuis Charlemagne jusqu'à Louis XIII* ed René Pomeau, 2 vols, Paris 1963

- *Lettres à S.A. Mgr Le Prince de ***** sur Rabelais et sur d'autres auteurs accusés d'avoir mal parlé de la religion chrétienne* Lettre VI 'Sur les Allemands' in *Mélanges* ed Jacques van den Heuvel, Paris 1961, 1186–9

- *Notebooks* 2 vols, *Complete Works of Voltaire* 81–2 ed Theodore Besterman, Geneva/Toronto 1968

[Wagner, Gottlieb Heinrich Adolf] *Leben des Desiderius Erasmus* Leipzig 1802

Walter, Johannes von 'Das Ende der Erasmusrenaissance' in *Christentum und Frömmigkeit: Gesämmelte Verträge und Aufsätze* Gütersloh 1941, 153–62

- 'Die neueste Beurteilung des Erasmus' in ibid, 132–52

Weizsäcker, C., review of Maurenbrecher in *Göttingische gelehrte Anzeigen* 1881 II 27–8: 833–51

Wernle, Paul *Die Renaissance des Christentums im 16. Jahrhundert*
Tübingen/Leipzig 1904
White, Andrew Dickson *Autobiography* New York 1905
- *A History of the Warfare of Science with Theology in Christendom* II,
New York 1960
Whitney, J.P. 'Erasmus' *English Historical Review* XXXV (1920): 1–25
- *Reformation Essays* London 1939
Widmer, Joseph *Paraklesis des Erasmus von Rotterdam, oder Ermahnung
zum Studium der christlichen Philosophie* Lucerne 1820
Wieland, Christoph Martin 'Ein Fragment über den Charakter des Er-
asmus von Rotterdam' *Der Teutsche Merkur* December 1776: 262–72
- 'Nachricht von Ulrich von Hutten' ibid February 1776: 174–85
- *Werke* 15 *Prosaische Schriften* II 1783–1794 ed Wilhelm Kurrelmeyer,
Berlin 1930
- 'Zusatz des Herausgebers' *Der Teutsche Merkur* July 1776: 34–7
Wilberforce, Robert Isaac and Samuel *The Life of William Wilberforce* 5
vols, London 1838
Woker, P. *De Erasmi Roterodami studiis irenicis: Dissertatio historica* ...
Paderborn 1872
Woodward, W.H. *Desiderius Erasmus concerning the Aim and Method of
Education* Cambridge 1904
Zickendraht, Karl *Der Streit zwischen Erasmus und Luther über die Wil-
lensfreiheit* Leipzig 1909

SECONDARY LITERATURE AND MODERN WORKS ON
ERASMUS

Aner, Karl *Die Theologie der Lessingzeit* Hildesheim 1964
Augustijn, Cornelis *Erasmus en de Reformatie: Een onderzoek naar de
houding die Erasmus ten opzichte van de Reformatie heeft aangenomen*
Amsterdam 1962
Backvis, C. 'La Fortune d'Erasme en Pologne' *Colloquium Erasmianum*
Mons 1968, 173–202
Bain, Alexander *James Mill: A Biography* London 1882
Bainton, Roland H. *Erasmus of Christendom* New York and London
1969
Barnard, F.M. *Herder's Social and Political Thought: From Enlightenment
to Nationalism* Oxford 1965
Barth, J. Robert SJ *Coleridge and Christian Doctrine* Cambridge, Mass.
1969
Barth, Karl *Protestant Thought: From Rousseau to Ritschl* New York
1959
Bataillon, Marcel *Erasme et l'Espagne: Recherches sur l'histoire spirituelle
du XVIᵉ siècle* Paris 1937

- 'La situation présente du message érasmien' in *Colloquium Erasmianum* Mons 1968, 3–16
Béné, Charles *Erasme et Saint Augustin ou influence de Saint Augustin sur l'humanisme d'Erasme* Geneva 1969
Bentley, Jerry H. *Humanists and Holy Writ: New Testament Scholarship in the Renaissance* Princeton 1983
Bernard, Paul P. *The Origins of Josephinism: Two Studies* Colorado College Studies 7, Colorado Springs 1964
Berney, Arnold 'Michael Ignaz Schmidt: Ein Beitrag zur Geschichte der deutschen Historiographie im Zeitalter der Aufklärung' *Historisches Jahrbuch* 44 (1924): 211–39
Bernstein, Eckhard 'Erasmus' Money Connection: The Antwerp Banker Erasmus Schets and Erasmus of Rotterdam, 1525–36' *Erasmus in English* 14 (1985–6): 2–7
Bierlaire, Franz *La familia d'Erasme: Contribution à l'histoire de l'humanisme* Paris 1968
Bietenholz, Peter G. *History and Biography in the Work of Erasmus of Rotterdam* Geneva 1966
Black, J.B. *The Art of History: A Study of Four Great Historians of the Eighteenth Century* London 1926 (reprint New York 1965)
Blanning, T.C.W. *Joseph II and Enlightened Despotism* London 1970
Blom, Nicolaas van der 'Rotterdam and Erasmus: Some Remarks' in *Erasmus of Rotterdam: The Man and the Scholar* ed J. Sperna Weiland and W.Th.M. Frijhoff, Leiden 1988, 240–52
- 'Rector, schoolhistoricus, "vir Erasmianus"' in *Grepen uit de geschiedenis van het Erasmiaans Gymnasium 1328–1978* Rotterdam 1978
Bodenstein, Walter *Neige des Historismus: Ernst Troeltschs Entwicklungsgang* Gütersloh 1959
Bonjour, Edgar *Dei Universität Basel von den Anfängen bis zur Gegenwart 1460–1960* Basel 1960
Bornkamm, Heinrich *Luther im Spiegel der deutschen Geistesgeschichte* Göttingen 1955
Boulger, James D. *Coleridge as Religious Thinker* New Haven 1961
Bourel, Dominique 'Orthodoxie, piétisme, Aufklärung' *Dix-huitième Siècle* 10 (1978): 27–32
Bouyer, Louis *Autour d'Erasme* Paris 1955
Boyle, Marjorie O'Rourke *Erasmus on Language and Method in Theology* Toronto 1977
- *Rhetoric and Reform: Erasmus' Civil Dispute with Luther* Cambridge, Mass. 1983
- 'Stoic Luther: Paradoxical Sin and Necessity' ARG 73 (1982): 69–93
Bradshaw, Brendan 'The Christian Humanism of Erasmus' *Journal of Theological Studies* 33 (1982): 411–47
Bramsted, E.K., and K.J. Melhuish *Western Liberalism: A History in Documents from Locke to Croce* London/New York 1978

Bronson, B.H. 'Johnson Agonistes' in *Samuel Johnson: A Collection of Critical Essays,* ed Donald J. Greene, 30–45

Brown, Ford K. *Fathers of the Victorians: The Age of Wilberforce* Cambridge 1961

Bruford, W.H. *Germany in the Eighteenth Century: The Social Background of the Literary Revival* Cambridge 1959

Brumfitt, J.H. *Voltaire Historian* Oxford 1958

Burns, J.H. 'The Light of Reason: Philosophical History in the Two Mills' in *James and John Stuart Mill/Papers of the Centenary Conference* ed John M. Robson and Michael Laine, Toronto 1976, 3–20

Burrow, J.W. *A Liberal Descent: Victorian Historians and the English Past* Cambridge 1981

Butterfield, Herbert *Man on His Past: The Study of the History of Historical Scholarship* Boston 1960

Cassirer, Ernst *The Philosophy of the Enlightenment* Princeton 1951

Cater, Jeremy J. 'The Making of Principal Robertson in 1762: Politics and the University of Edinburgh in the Second Half of the Eighteenth Century' *Scottish Historical Review* 49 (1970): 60–84

Chadwick, Owen 'Gibbon and the Church Historians' in *Edward Gibbon and the Decline and Fall of the Roman Empire* ed G.W. Bowersock, John Clive, Stephen R. Graubard, Cambridge, Mass. 1977, 219–31

– *The Secularization of the European Mind in the Nineteenth Century* Cambridge 1975

– *The Victorian Church* 2 vols, London 1966, 1970

Chevalier, Jacques 'Préface' to Pierre Imbart de la Tour, *Les Origines de la Réforme* IV, Paris 1935, v–xiii

Clark, Ian D.L. 'From Protest to Reaction: The Moderate Regime in the Church of Scotland, 1752–1805' in *Scotland in the Age of Improvement: Essays in Scottish History in the Eighteenth Century* ed N.T. Phillipson and Rosalind Mitchison, Edinburgh 1970, 200–24

Clark, Robert T. Jr *Herder: His Life and Thought* Berkeley/Los Angeles 1955

Colie, R.L. 'Johan Huizinga and the Task of Cultural History' *American Historical Review* LXIX (1964): 607–30

Collins, Irene *The Government and the Newspaper Press in France 1814–1881* Oxford 1959

Connell, Joan *The Roman Catholic Church in England 1780–1850: A Study in Internal Politics* Philadelphia 1984

Coogan, Robert 'The Pharisee against the Hellenist: Edward Lee versus Erasmus' *Renaissance Quarterly* 39 (1986): 476–506

Cookson, J.E. *The Friends of Peace: Anti-War Liberalism in England, 1793–1815* Cambridge 1982

Crahay, Roland 'Recherches sur le "Compendium vitae" attribué à Erasme' *Humanisme et Renaissance* 6 (1939): 7–19, 135–53

Cytowska, Maria 'Erasme en Pologne avant l'époque du Concile de Trente' *Erasmus in English* 5 (1972): 10–16

Davie, George Elder *The Democratic Intellect: Scotland and Her Universities in the Nineteenth Century* Edinburgh 1961

Davies, Rupert, and Gordon Rupp (eds) *A History of the Methodist Church in Great Britain* I, London 1965

Dawson, Jerry F. *Friedrich Schleiermacher: The Evolution of a Nationalist* Austin/London 1966

De Molen, R. 'Erasmus as Adolescent: "Shipwrecked am I, and lost, 'mid waters chill"' *Bibliothèque d'Humanisme et Renaissance* XXXVIII (1976): 7–25

Dickens, A.G., and John Tonkin *The Reformation in Historical Thought* Cambridge, Mass. 1985

Dolan, John Patrick *The Influence of Erasmus, Witzel and Cassander in the Church Ordinances and Reform Proposals of the United Duchies of Cleve during the Middle Decades of the Sixteenth Century* Münster 1957

Dolfen, Christian *Die Stellung des Erasmus von Rotterdam zur scholastischen Methode* Osnabrück 1936

Dorey, T.A. (ed) *Erasmus* London 1970

Dunn, Waldo Hilary *James Anthony Froude: A Biography* 2 vols, Oxford 1961, 1963

Elton, G.R. 'J.A. Froude and His History of England' in *Studies in Tudor and Stuart Politics and Government* III, Cambridge 1983, 391–412

Encevré, André 'Image de la Réforme chez les protestants français de 1830 à 1870' in *Historiographie de la Réforme* ed Philippe Joutard, Paris 1977, 182–204

Encyclopedia of Education 10 vols, 1971, vol 4

Encyclopaedia Judaica Berlin 1928–34, VII

Encyclopedia of Philosophy 8 vols, New York/London 1967, vol 8

Engel, Joseph 'Die deutschen Universitäten und die Geschichtswissenschaften' HZ 189 (1959): 223–378

Enno van Gelder, H.A. *The Two Reformations in the 16th Century: A Study of the Religious Aspects and Consequences of Renaissance and Humanism* Hague 1961

Erasmus en Leiden: Catalogus van de tentoonstelling gehouden in het Academisch Historisch Museum te Leiden van 23 oktober tot 19 december 1986 Leiden 1986

Etienne, Jacques *Spiritualisme érasmien et théologiens louvanistes* Louvain 1956

Fearnley-Sander, Mary 'The Emancipation of the Mind: A View of the Reformation in Four Eighteenth Century Historians' unpublished PHD thesis, University of Western Australia 1977

Febvre, Lucien 'Une question mal posée: Les origines de la réforme

française et le problème des causes de la réforme' in *Au Coeur reli-
gieux du XVIe siecle* Paris 1957, 3–70
– 'Un historien de l'humanisme: Augustin Renaudet' in *Mélanges Augustin Renaudet: Bibliothèque de l'Humanisme et Renaissance* XIV
(1952): vii–xxii
Feller, Richard, and Edgar Bonjour *Geschichtsschreibung der Schweiz
vom Spätmittelalter zur Neuzeit* 2nd ed, 2 vols, Basel/Stuttgart 1979
Fenlon, Dermot '*Encore une Question*: Lucien Febvre, the Reformation
and the School of *Annales' Historical Studies: Papers read before the
Irish Conference of Historians* IX, Belfast 1974, 65–81
Ferguson, Wallace K. *The Renaissance in Historical Thought: Five Centuries of Interpretation* Cambridge, Mass. 1948
Forbes, Duncan *The Liberal Anglican Idea of History* Cambridge 1952
Forsthuber, Gerhard 'Erasmus und Lessing: Eine Untersuchung über
die Beziehungen zwischen Humanismus und Frühklassik' unpub-
lished doctoral dissertation, University of Vienna 1953
Foster, Joseph *Alumni Oxoniensis: The Members of the University of Ox-
ford, 1715–1886* III, IV, Kraus reprint, Nendeln/Liechtenstein 1968
Frappell, L.O. 'Coleridge and the "Coleridgeans" on Luther' *Journal of
Religious History* 7 (1973): 307–23
– 'Interpretation of the Continental Reformation in Great Britain dur-
ing the Nineteenth Century' unpublished PHD thesis, Macquarie
University 1972
– 'The Reformation as Negative Revolution or Obscurantist Reaction:
The Liberal Debate on the Reformation in Nineteenth-Century Brit-
ain' *Journal of Religious History* 11: 289–307
Garraty, John A. 'Preserved Smith, Ralph Volney Harlow, and Psy-
chology' *Journal of the History of Ideas* 15 (1954): 456–65
Garrod, H.W. 'Compendium Vitae P.S. Allen' in Allen VIII v–xx
– 'Percy Stafford Allen 1869–1933' *Proceedings of the British Academy*
XIX (1933): 381–407
Gay, Peter *The Bridge of Criticism: Dialogues among Lucian, Erasmus,
and Voltaire on the Enlightenment – on History and Hope, Imagination
and Reason, Constraint and Freedom – and on Its Meaning for Our
Time* New York 1970
– *the Enlightenment: An Interpretation* 1: *The Rise of Modern Paganism*,
2: *The Science of Freedom* London 1973
Geanakoplos, Deno John *Greek Scholars in Venice: Studies in the Dis-
semination of Greek Learning from Byzantium to Western Europe* Cambridge, Mass. 1962
Gebhart, Georg *Die Stellung des Erasmus von Rotterdam zur römischen
Kirche* Marburg an der Lahn 1966
Gembicki, Dieter 'La Réforme allemande vue par Voltaire' in *Historiographie de la Réforme* ed Philippe Joutard, Paris 1977, 148–55

Gerrish, Brian A. *Grace and Reason: A Study in the Theology of Luther* Oxford 1962
– 'Schleiermacher and the Reformation: A Question of Doctrinal Development' *Church History* 49 (1980): 147–59
Gilbert, William 'The Work of Preserved Smith' *Journal of Modern History* 23 (1951): 354–65
Gleason, Elisabeth G. 'On the Nature of Sixteenth-Century Italian Evangelism: Scholarship, 1953–1978' *Sixteenth Century Journal* 9 (1978): 3–26
Gleason, John B. *John Colet* Berkeley/Los Angeles/London 1989
Gombrich, E.H. 'Huizinga's *Homo Ludens*' in *Johan Huizinga 1872–1972: Papers Delivered to the Johan Huizinga Conference Groningen 11–15 December 1972* ed W.R.H. Koops, E.H. Kossmann, Gees van der Plaat, Hague 1972, 133–54
Gooch, G.P. *Historical Surveys and Portraits* London 1966
– *History and Historians in the Nineteenth Century* Boston 1959
Good, James I *History of the Swiss Reformed Church since the Reformation* Philadelphia 1913
Goyau, Georges *L'Allemagne religieuse: Le Catholicisme (1800–1848)* II, Paris 1905
Green, V.H.H. *Oxford Common Room: A Study of Lincoln College and Mark Pattison* London 1957
Greene, Donald J. (ed) *Samuel Johnson: A Collection of Critical Essays* Englewood Cliffs 1965
Guggisberg, R. *Basel in the Sixteenth Century* St Louis 1982
Gutschera, Herbert *Reformation und Gegenreformation innerhalb des Kirchengeschichtsschreibung von Johann Matthias Schröckh* Goppingen 1973
Haac, O.A. *Jules Michelet* Boston 1982
– *Les Principes inspirateurs de Michelet: Sensibilité et Philosophie d'Histoire* New Haven/Paris 1951
Haile, Martin, and Edwin Bonney *Life and Letters of John Lingard 1771–1851* London n.d.
Halévy, Elie *The Growth of Philosophic Radicalism* London 1949
Hampson, Norman *The Enlightenment* Harmondsworth 1968
Harnack, Adolf 'August Neander' in *Reden und Aufsätze* I, Giessen 1904, 195–218
Heussi, Karl *Johann Lorenz von Mosheim: Ein Beitrag zur Kirchengeschichte des achtzehnten Jahrhunderts* Tübingen 1904
– *Die Kirchengeschichtsschreibung Johann Lorenz von Mosheims* Gotha 1904
Heyer, Friedrich *The Catholic Church from 1648 to 1870* London 1969
Himmelfarb, Gertrude *Lord Acton: A Study in Conscience and Politics* London 1952
Holborn, Hajo *A History of Modern Germany 1648–1840* London 1965

– *Ulrich von Hutten and the German Reformation* New Haven 1937
Holeczek, Heinz *Erasmus Deutsch* I, Stuttgart–Bad Cannstatt 1983
Hornig, Gottfried *Die Anfänge der historisch–kritischen Theologie: Johann Salomo Semlers Schriftverständnis und seine Stellung zu Luther* Göttingen 1961
Hyma, Albert *Renaissance to Reformation* Grand Rapids 1951
– *The Youth of Erasmus* Ann Arbor 1930
Janentzky, Christian *Johann Caspar Lavater* Frauenfeld/Leipzig 1923
Joachimsen, Paul, Introduction to Ranke's *Deutsche Geschichte im Zeitalter der Reformation* I, Munich 1925, v–cxvii
Jursch, Hanna *Schleiermacher als Historiker* Jena 1933
Kaegi, W. *Erasmus ehedem und heute 1469–1969* Basel 1969
– 'Erasmus im achtzehnten Jahrhundert' in *Gedenkschrift*, 205–27
– *Jakob Burckhardt: Eine Biographie* I, Basel 1947
Kann, Robert A. *A History of the Habsburg Empire 1526–1918* Berkeley/Los Angeles/London 1974
Kelly, Thomas *For Advancement of Learning: The University of Liverpool 1881–1981* Liverpool 1981
Knibielher, Yvonne 'Réforme et Révolution d'après Charles de Villers' in *Historiographie de la Réforme* ed Philippe Joutard, Paris 1977, 171–81
Knowles, David *The Historian and Character and Other Essays* Cambridge 1964
Knox, R. Buick 'James Hamilton and English Presbyterianism' *Journal of the United Reformed Church Historical Society* 2 (1978–82): 286–307
Koch, A.C.F. *The Year of Erasmus' Birth* Utrecht 1969
Köster, Kurt *Johan Huizinga (1872–1945)* Oberursel (Taunus) 1947
– 'Der Historiker Johan Huizinga' in Johan Huizinga *Geschichte und Kultur: Gesammelte Aufsätze* et Kurt Köster, Stuttgart 1954
Kohls, E.W. 'Erasmus und die werdende evangelische Bewegung des 16. Jahrhunderts' in *Scrinium Erasmianum* I, 203–19
Kohlschmidt, Werner *A History of German Literature 1760–1805* London 1975
Kosch, Wilhelm (ed) *Das Katholische Deutschland: Biographisch-bibliographisches Lexikon* II, Augsburg n.d.
Kossmann, E.H. *The Low Countries 1780–1940* Oxford 1978
– 'Postscript' in *Johan Huizinga 1872–1972* ed W.R.H. Koops, E.H. Kossmann, Gees van der Plaat, Hague 1972, 223–34
Koszyk, Kurt *Deutsche Presse im 19. Jahrhundert* Geschichte der deutschen Presse II, Berlin 1966
Kreutz, Wilhelm *Die Deutschen und Ulrich von Hutten: Rezeption von Autor und Werk seit dem 16. Jahrhundert* Munich 1984
Krygier, Leonard *Ranke: The Meaning of History* Chicago 1977

Kurth-Voigt, Lieselotte E. *Perspectives and Points of View: The Early Works of Wieland and Their Background* Baltimore/London 1974

Ladner, Gerhart B. 'The Impact of Christianity' in *The Transformation of the Roman World: Gibbon's Problem after Two Centuries* ed Lynn White Jr, Berkeley/Los Angeles 1966, 59–91

Laue, Theodore von *Leopold Ranke: The Formative Years* Princeton 1950

Lawson, John *A Town Grammar School through Six Centuries: A History of Hull Grammar School against Its Local Background* London 1963

Lecler, Joseph *Histoire de la tolérance au siècle de la Réforme* 2 vols, Paris 1955

Lefèvre, Pl. 'La Lecture des oeuvres d'Erasme au sein du bas clergé durant la première moitié du XVIᵉ siècle' *Scrinium Erasmianum* I, 83–91

Levine, Joseph M. *Humanism and History: Origins of Modern English Historiography* Ithaca and London 1987

Lhotsky, Alphons *Geschichte des Instituts für österreichische Geschichtsforschung 1854–1954* Graz/Köln 1954

Lindt, Andreas *Protestanten–Katholiken Kulturkampf* Zürich 1963

Locher, Gottfried W. 'Zwingli und Erasmus' in *Scrinium Erasmianum* II, 325–50

– 'Zwingli and Erasmus' *Erasmus in English* 10 (1979–80): 2–11

Lortz, Joseph 'Erasmus – kirchengeschichtlich' in T. Steinbüchel and T. Müncker (eds) *Aus Theologie und Philosophie: Festschrift für Fritz Tillmann zu seinem 75. Geburtstag* Düsseldorf 1950, 271–86

– *The Reformation in Germany* I, London/New York 1968

Lossky, Andrew 'Introduction: Gibbon and the Enlightenment' in *The Transformation of the Roman World: Gibbon's Problem after Two Centuries* ed Lynn White Jr, Berkeley/Los Angeles 1966, 1–29

Lough, John 'Louis, Chevalier de Jaucourt (1704–1780): A Biographical Sketch' in *The* Encyclopédie *in Eighteenth-Century England and Other Studies* Newcastle upon Tyne 1970, 25–70

Low, D.M. *Edward Gibbon 1737–1794* New York 1937

Mansfield, Bruce 'Erasmus and the Mediating School' *Journal of Religious History* 4 (1967): 302–16

– 'Erasmus in the Age of Revolutions' in *Erasmus of Rotterdam: The Man and the Scholar* ed J. Sperna Weiland and W.Th.M. Frijhoff, Leiden 1988, 228–39

– 'Erasmus in the Nineteenth Century: The Liberal Tradition' *Studies in the Renaissance* XV (1968): 195–219

– 'Erasmus, Luther and the Problem of Church History' *Australian Journal of Politics and History* VIII (1962): 41–56

– *Phoenix of His Age: Interpretations of Erasmus c 1550–1750* Toronto 1979

Marcel, Raymond 'Les Dettes d'Erasme envers l'Italie' *Actes du*

Congrès Erasme Rotterdam 27–29 Octobre 1969 Amsterdam/London 1971, 159–73

Margolin, Jean-Claude 'Huizinga et les recherches érasmiennes' in *Johan Huizinga 1872–1972* ed W.R.H. Koops, E.H. Kossmann, Gees van der Plaat, Hague 1972, 116–32

– 'The Method of "Words and Things" in Erasmus's *De Pueris Instituendis* (1529) and Comenius's *Orbis Sensualium Pictus* (1658)' in *Essays on the Works of Erasmus* ed Richard L. de Molen, New Haven/London 1978, 211–20

– 'La Religion d'Erasme et l'Allemagne des Lumières' ARG 72 (1981): 197–231

– 'Sardou, traducteur des *Colloques* d'Erasme' in *Recherches érasmiennes* Geneva 1969, 128–61

Mason, Haydn *Voltaire* London 1975

Massaut, J.-P. 'Erasme et Saint Thomas' in *Colloquia Erasmiana Turonensia* 2 vols, Paris 1972, 581–612

Mathew, David *Lord Acton and His Times* London 1968

McClelland, Charles E. *State, Society, and University in Germany 1700–1914* Cambridge 1980

McConica, J.K. 'Erasmus and the Grammar of Consent' in *Scrinium Erasmianum* II, 77–99

McLachlan, H. *Records of a Family 1800–1903: Pioneers in Education, Social Service and Liberal Religion* Manchester 1935

– *The Unitarian Movement in the Religious Life of England* I *Its Contribution to Thought and Learning 1700–1900* London 1934

McNeill, W.H. 'Introduction' to Acton *Essays in the Liberal Interpretation of History* Chicago 1967

McSorley, Harry J. *Luther: Right or Wrong? An Ecumenical–Theological Study of Luther's Major Work, The Bondage of the Will* New York 1969

Meinecke, Friedrich *Die Entstehung des Historismus* Munich 1965

The Mennonite Encyclopedia 4 vols, Scottdale Pa. 1955–9

Minnich, Nelson H., and W.W. Meissner 'The Character of Erasmus' *American Historical Review* 83 (1978): 598–624

Moeller, Bernd 'Religious Life in Germany on the Eve of the Reformation' in *Pre-Reformation Germany* ed Gerald Strauss, London 1972, 13–42

Mörikofer, J.C. *Ulrich Zwingli nach den urkundlichen Quellen* I, Leipzig 1867

Monod, Gabriel *La Vie et la pensée de Jules Michelet (1798–1852)* 2 vols, Paris 1923 (reprint Geneva/Paris 1975)

Morley, John *The Life of William Ewart Gladstone* II, London 1908

– 'On Pattison's Memoirs' in *Works* VI, London 1921, 235–67

Nauta, D. 'De Reformatie in Nederland in de Historiografie' *Serta Historica* II (1970): 49–66

Nelson, Ernest W. 'Recent Literature Concerning Erasmus' *Journal of Modern History* 1 (1929): 88–103

Newald, Richard *Erasmus Roterodamus* Freiburg im Breisgau 1947

New Cambridge Modern History x *The Zenith of European Power 1830–70* Cambridge 1960

Noordenbos, Oene *In het voetspoor van Erasmus* Hague 1941

Norman, Edward *The English Catholic Church in the Nineteenth Century* Oxford 1984

Nugent, Donald 'The Erasmus Renaissance' *The Month* CCXXIX (1970): 36–45

Oberman, H.A. *The Harvest of Medieval Theology* Cambridge, Mass. 1963

– *Forerunners of the Reformation: The Shape of Late Medieval Thought* London 1967

– *Masters of the Reformation: The Emergence of a New Intellectual Climate in Europe* Cambridge 1981

Oelrich, Karl Heinz *Der späte Erasmus und die Reformation* Münster 1961

Olin, John 'Interpreting Erasmus' in *Six Essays on Erasmus* New York 1979, 57–73

Outler, Albert C. *John Wesley* New York 1964

Overton, John H., and Frederic Relton *The English Church from the Accession of George I to the End of the Eighteenth Century 1714–1800* London 1906

Padover, Saul K. *The Revolutionary Emperor: Joseph II of Austria* London 1967

Pascal, Roy *The German Sturm und Drang* Manchester 1953

Pauck, Wilhelm *Harnack and Troeltsch: Two Historical Theologians* New York 1968

Paul, Herbert *The Life of Froude* London 1905

Payne, J.B. *Erasmus: His Theology of the Sacraments* 1970

Peardon, T.P. *The Transition in English Historical Writing 1760–1830* New York 1933

Perla, Georges A. 'La Philosophie de Jaucourt dans l'*Encyclopédie*' *Revue de l'histoire des religions* CXCVII (1980): 59–78

Pfleiderer, O. *The Development of Theology in Germany since Kant and Its Progress in Great Britain since 1825* London 1890

Phillips, Margaret Mann *The 'Adages' of Erasmus: A Study with Translations* Cambridge 1964

– 'Erasmus and Propaganda: A Study of the Translations of Erasmus in England and France' *Modern Language Review* 37 (1942): 1–17

– 'P.S. Allen: A Lifetime of Letters' *Erasmus of Rotterdam Society Yearbook Nine (1989)*, 91–105

Pinson, Koppel S. *Modern Germany: Its History and Civilization* 2nd ed, New York 1966

Pirenne, Henri *Histoire de Belgique* VII *De la révolution de 1830 à la guerre de 1914* 2nd ed, Brussels 1948

Pollet, J.V. *Huldrych Zwingli et la Réforme en Suisse d'après les recherches récentes* Paris 1963

Pomeau, René *La Religion de Voltaire* Paris 1969

Post R.R. *The Modern Devotion: Confrontation with Reformation and Humanism* Leiden 1968

Reedijk, C. 'Huizinga and His *Erasmus*: Some Observations in the Margin' in *Hellinga: Festschrift/Feestbundel/Mélanges* Amsterdam 1980, 413–34

– 'Das Lebensende des Erasmus' *Basler Zeitschrift für Geschichte und Altertumskunde* 57 (1958): 23–66

Renwick, John, *Marmontel, Voltaire and the* Bélisaire *Affair* Studies on Voltaire and the Eighteenth Century, ed Theodore Besterman, CXXI, Banbury, Oxfordshire 1974

Ridgway, R.S. *Voltaire and Sensibility* Montreal/London 1975

Ritter, Gerhard 'Die geschichtliche Bedeutung des deutschen Humanismus' HZ 127 (1923): 393–453

Robert, Daniel *Genève et les églises réformées de France de la 'Réunion' (1798) aux environs de 1830* Geneva/Paris 1961

Rogge, Joachim *Zwingli und Erasmus: Die Friedensgedanken des jungen Zwingli* Stuttgart 1962

Rubanowice, Robert G. *Crisis in Consciousness: The Thought of Ernst Troeltsch* Tallahassee 1982

Rummel, Erika *Erasmus* Annotations *on the New Testament: From Philologist to Theologian* Toronto 1986

Runset, Ute van *Ironie und Philosophie bei Voltaire unter besonderer Berücksichtigung der 'Dialogues et entretiens philosophiques'* Geneva 1974

Rupp, Gordon *The Righteousness of God: Luther Studies* London 1953

Schlenke, Manfred 'Aus der Frühzeit des englischen Historismus: William Robertsons Beitrag zur methodischen Grundlegung der Geschichtswissenschaft im 18. Jahrhundert' *Saeculum* 7 (1956): 107–25

Schnabel, F. *Deutsche Geschichte in neunzehnten Jahrhundert* 2nd ed, IV, Freiburg 1951

Schottenloher, Otto *Erasmus im Ringen um die humanistische Bildungsform: Ein Beitrag zum Verständnis seiner geistigen Entwicklung* Münster 1933

Schultz, Werner *Schleiermacher und der Protestantismus* Hamburg/Bergstedt 1957

Schwab, R.N. and W.E. Rex *Inventory of Diderot's Encyclopédie* IV, Studies on Voltaire and the Eighteenth Century, ed Theodore Besterman, XCI, Banbury, Oxfordshire 1972

Schweitzer, Albert *The Quest of the Historical Jesus: A Critical Historyof Its Progress from Reimarus to Wrede* 3rd ed, London 1954

Screech, M.A. *Ecstasy and the Praise of Folly* London 1980

Scribner, R.W. 'The Erasmians and the Beginning of the Reformation in Erfurt' *Journal of Religious History* 9 (1976): 3–31

– *For the Sake of Simple Folk: Popular Propaganda for the German Reformation* Cambridge 1981

– *The German Reformation* London 1986

Semmel, Bernard *The Methodist Revolution* London 1974

Sengel, Friedrich *Wieland* Stuttgart 1949

Simpson, P.C. *Life of Principal Rainy* 2 vols, London 1909

Smith, David Dillon 'Gibbon in Church' *Journal of Ecclesiastical History* 35 (1984): 452–63

Sommer, Cornelius *Christoph Martin Wieland* Stuttgart 1971

Sparrow, John *Mark Pattison and the Idea of a University* Cambridge 1967

Spencer, Philip *The Politics of Belief in Nineteenth-Century France* London 1954

Spitz, Lewis W. *The Religious Renaissance of the German Humanists* Cambridge, Mass. 1963

Stephan, H. *Geschichte der evangelischen Theologie seit dem deutschen Idealismus* 2nd ed, Berlin 1960

Stephen, Leslie *History of English Thought in the Eighteenth Century* 2 vols, New York 1962

Stoffers, Emanuel 'Erasmus in de twintigste eeuw: een terugblik op de Erasmusbiografieën van deze eeuw in zijn 450ste sterfjaar' *Theoretische Geschiedenis* 13 (1986): 309–31

Swain, Joseph Ward *Edward Gibbon the Historian* London/New York 1966

Telle, Emile V. 'In the Wake of Erasmus of Rotterdam: An Outcry for Perpetual and Universal Peace in England in 1793–1795' *Erasmus of Rotterdam Society Yearbook Three (1983)*, 104–29

Thompson, Craig R. 'Erasmus as Internationalist and Cosmopolitan' ARG 46 (1955): 167–95

– 'Three American Erasmians' *Erasmus of Rotterdam Society Yearbook Four (1984)*, 1–36

Tieder, Irène *Michelet et Luther: Histoire d'une rencontre* Paris 1976

Torrey, Norman L. *Voltaire and the English Deists* New Haven 1930

Tracy, James D. 'Against the "Barbarians": The Young Erasmus and His Humanist Contemporaries' *Sixteenth Century Journal* 11 (1980): 3–22

– *Erasmus: The Growth of a Mind* Geneva 1972

Trapman, Johannes 'Le Latin mystique de Remy de Gourmont (1892) et son influence aux Pays-Bas' *Septentrion* 15 (1986): 45–9

Trenard, Louis 'Voltaire, historien de la Réforme en France' in *Historiographie de la Réforme* ed Philippe Joutard, Paris 1977, 156–70

Trinkaus, Charles 'Erasmus, Augustine and the Nominalists' ARG 67 (1976): 1–32

Turnbull, Paul 'The "Supposed Infidelity" of Edward Gibbon' *Historical Journal* 5 (1982): 23–41

Turner, A.M. *The Making of the Cloister and the Hearth* Chicago 1938

Valentin, Veit *1848. Chapters of German History* London 1940

Venn, J.A. *Alumni Cantabrigiensis* pt II (1752–1900) V, Cambridge 1953

Viallaneix, Paul *La Voie royale: Essai sur l'idée de peuple dans l'oeuvre de Michelet* Paris 1959

Vinogradoff, Paul 'Obituary: Frederic Seebohm (1833–1912)' in *Collected Papers* I, Oxford 1928, 272–6

Vocht, Henry de 'Le dernier "Amanuensis" d'Erasme' *Revue d'Histoire ecclésiastique* XLV (1950): 174–86

– *History of the Foundation and Rise of the Collegium Trilingue Lovaniense 1517–1550* I, Louvain 1951

Vogel, C.J. de 'Erasmus and His Attitude towards Church Dogma' in *Scrinium Erasmianum* II, 101–32

Vose, Heather M. 'More Light on Sixteenth-Century *Evangélisme*: A Study in Cross and Spirit' *Journal of Religious History* 14 (1987): 256–68

Vries, Ph. de 'The Writing and Study of History in the Netherlands in the 19th Century' *Acta Historiae Neerlandica* III (1968): 247–65

Walsh, John 'Origins of the Evangelical Revival' in G.V. Bennett and J.D. Walsh *Essays in Modern English Church History in Memory of Norman Sykes* London 1966, 132–62

– 'Joseph Milner's Evangelical Church History' *Journal of Ecclesiastical History* 10 (1959): 174–87

Ward, Bernard *The Dawn of the Catholic Revival in England, 1781–1803* 2 vols, London 1909

Weintraub, Karl J. *Visions of Culture* Chicago/London 1966

Wernle, Paul *Der schweizerische Protestantismus im XVIII. Jahrhundert* 3 vols, Tübingen 1923–5

Weyergraf, Bernd *Der skeptische Bürger: Wielands Schriften zur Französischen Revolution* Stuttgart 1972

Who's Who 1911

Wie is Dat? 1956

Willey, Basil *The Eighteenth Century Background: Studies on the Idea of Nature in the Thought of the Period* London 1965

– 'J.A. Froude' in *More Nineteenth Century Studies: A Group of Honest Doubters* London 1956, 106–36

– *Nineteenth Century Studies: Coleridge to Matthew Arnold* London 1949

Williams, George Hunston 'Joseph Priestley on Luther' in *Interpreters of Luther: Essays in Honour of Wilhelm Pauck* ed Jaroslav Pelikan, Philadelphia 1968, 121–58

Winckler, Lutz *Martin Luther als Bürger und Patriot: Das Reformationsjubiläum von 1817 und der politische Protestantismus des Wartburgfestes* Lübeck and Hamburg 1969

Wolf, Gustav *Wilhelm Maurenbrecher: Ein Lebens-und Schattenbild* Berlin 1893

Zeeden, Ernst Walter *Martin Luther und die Reformation im Urteil des deutschen Luthertums* 2 vols, Freiburg 1950

Zscharnack, Leopold *Lessing und Semler: Ein Beitrag zur Entstehungsgeschichte des Rationalismus und der kritischen Theologie* Giessen 1905

– 'Reformation und Humanismus im Urteil der deutschen Aufklärung: Zur Charakteristik der Aufklärung des 18. Jahrhunderts' *Protestantische Monatschefte* 12 (1908): 81–103, 153–71

Index

Abelard, Peter 149

Acta Academiae Lovaniensis contra Lutherum 316

Acton, John Emeric Edward Dalberg: on Döllinger 192; and Döllinger 229, 413n 28, 422n 191; and Catholicism 229; on ultramontanism 229–30; on church and learning 230; on Erasmus and learning 230; on Erasmus as Catholic reformer 230–1; on Erasmus and Renaissance 231–2; on Erasmus and Luther 232; on history and moral standards 232, 422n 191; Murray uses library of 362

Adam, Melchior 39, 101, 400n 186, 442n 158

Addi, Marius: on Erasmus 242–3

Addison, Joseph 95

Adrian VI, pope 215, 315

Agricola, Rudolf 335, 418n 108

Albigensians 33

Aldine academy 311

Aldus Manutius 310

Aleander, Girolamo 148, 193, 302, 316–17, 439n 80

Alexander VI, pope 338

Allard, Hermann Jozef: recalls Janssen 220; on Erasmus' character 220–1

Allen, Helen Mary 355

Allen, Joseph 355

Allen, Percy Stafford: work prepared for in nineteenth century 122; on Froude 184, 359, 411n 118; accepts *Compendium vitae* 337, 356; on predecessors 351; and Nichols 352–3; edits Erasmus' correspondence 355–6; method and temperament of 355–6, 448n 254; writings on Erasmus 356–7; on Erasmus as free spirit 357; on Erasmus' vocation 357; on Erasmus' personality 357–8; on Erasmus and Reformers 358; outlook of 358–9; personality of 359, 447n 250, 448n 258, 449n 277; interests of 448n 252; on Great War 448n 256; honours 448n 257; P. Smith's debt to 366; and Huizinga 371

Alva, Fernando Alvarez de Toledo, duke of 67

Amerbach, Bonifacius 267, 274

Amiel, Emile: and classical tradition 148; on Erasmus and modern religion 148; on Eras-

mus' writings 149; on Erasmus and Reformation 149; on Erasmus' political writings 149–50; on Lavater and A. Müller 150
Ammonio, Andrea 337, 352
Anabaptists 157, 368, 370
Anglicanism 93, 96, 97, 423n 23, 450n 305 (see also England, Church of)
Antwerp, synod of 280
Aquinas, Thomas 218, 354, 414n 44
Archiv für Reformationsgeschichte 316
Arianism 5, 15–16, 168, 173 (see also Socinians)
Aristotle 41, 66, 79, 140, 313, 441n 139
Arminians 6, 34, 41, 96, 368, 382n 53 (see also Remonstrants)
Arminius, Jacobus 96
Arnold, Gottfried 39, 42, 43, 388n 186
Ashbourne 94
Augsburg, Diet of (1530) 201
Augsburg Confession 51, 245
Augustine 52, 66, 99, 190, 287, 340, 409n 66
Augustinianism 66, 273, 290, 340
Australia and New Zealand 355
Austria 211 (see also Habsburg dynasty)
'Awakening' 8, 240, 276

Babylonian Captivity of the Church 317
Bacon, Francis 324, 393n 48
Baechem, Nicolaas 214
Balliol College, Oxford 258
Barclay, Robert 409n 66
Basel: Erasmus' death in 5, 48; attachment to Erasmus in 6; Bayle and Jaucourt on 17; Hutten at 58, 60; Erasmus and 70,

268; Gaudin on Erasmus and Reformation in 72; Erasmus and Hutten at 114; Nisard on Erasmus' last years in 139; Michelet on 142; Veuillot on 191; Durand de Laur on Erasmus' death in 205; De Ram on Erasmus and 210; theological faculty in 266; Hagenbach and 266; Hagenbach on Erasmus and 267; Stockmeyer and 267; University of 267–8; Stockmeyer on Erasmus and 268; Streuber and 269; Reformation in 274; Wernle at 288; Kan and 336; Vischer publishes Erasmus MSS at 337; Allen at 355; Huizinga on Erasmus at 370
Basler Taschenbuch 269
Basler Zeitung 269
Batt, Jacob 345, 354
Baudius, Dominic 94
Bauer, W.: on Erasmus 242–3
Bayle, Pierre 6, 16–18, 21, 25, 35, 92, 138, 144, 155, 189, 391n 8
Beard, Charles: life and outlook 171; on Reformation 171–2; on Erasmus 172–3; on Luther and Erasmus 173–4; on Erasmus and modern thought 174; on two Reformations 173, 185; Emerton and 282; Mestwerdt on 343
Beard, John Relly 171
Beatus Rhenanus 54, 63, 165, 189, 300, 310, 391n 8
Beausobre, Isaac de 101, 398n 146
Becker, Gottfried: on Erasmus, Hutten, and Reformation 111
Belgium: Catholics and 209; Rottier on Erasmus and 211; Nève on Erasmus and 214; claim to

Erasmus 215; writers on Erasmus in 216; Ruelens and Erasmus' revival in 334 (*see also* Burgundy, Netherlands)
Bélisaire 23
Bellarmine, Robert 144
Benoist, Antoine: on Erasmus' priorities in education 325; on Erasmus' moderation 325; on Erasmus' predecessors 325–6
Bentley, Richard 407n 44
Bergen, Hendrik van 351 (*see also* Cambrai, bishop of)
Bergen 345
Berlin 348; Academy 355; University of 104, 115, 127, 171, 199, 240, 244, 266–7, 281, 318, 341, 425n 38
Bern 129
Beza, Theodore 17
Bezold, Friedrich von: work compared with Ranke's 303; on Erasmus as reformer 303; and Drummond 303–4; on Erasmus' character 304; and Maurenbrecher 304; Bludau and 360
biblical studies: Henke on Erasmus and 48–9; Semler and 50; Herder on Erasmus and 65; Schleiermacher on 106; Becker on 111; in late-medieval universities 128; Beard on Erasmus and 173; Durand de Laur on Erasmus and 207; Erhard on 249; Milman on Erasmus and 257; Hamilton on Colet and Erasmus and 261; Dods and 262; Dods on Erasmus and 262–3; Glasius on Erasmus and 278; in Reformed church 280; Dilthey on Erasmus and 286; Bezold on Erasmus and 303; Renaudet on Lefèvre d'Etaples, Erasmus and

313; Usteri on Erasmus and 320; Seebohm on Colet and 338–9; Geiger on Erasmus and 349; Allen on Erasmus and 357; Bludau on Erasmus and 359–61
Bibliotheca Reformatoria Neerlandica 306
Binns, Leonard Elliott: on Erasmus as reformer 362, 365
Bismarck, Otto von 298
Bludau, August: on Erasmus' controversies 359; on Erasmus' character 359–60; on Erasmus' biblical studies 360, 449n 286; on Erasmus and reform 360–1; and earlier commentators 449n 282
Boehmer, Ed 440n 106
Bohemians 387n 182, 448n 268
Bok, Edward 371
Boleyn, Thomas 366
Bologna 310, 350
Bombasius, Paolo 310
Bonn, University of 199, 200, 217, 223, 266, 434n 207
Borromeo, Carlo 413n 28
Bossuet, Jacques Benigne 35, 135, 381n 32
Boswell, James 93–4
Botzheim, Johann von 302
Bowles, William 396n 113
Boyer, Paul: on Erasmus 242–3
Brabant 210, 211, 213, 215
Brant, Sebastian 305
Braunschweig 39, 387n 157
Bremen 110
Breslau 288, 292, 322, 439n 103
Brethren of Common Life 40, 190, 260, 277, 306, 312, 334, 343, 354, 357, 362–3, 450nn 292–3 (*see also devotio moderna*)
Brighton 81

British and Foreign Evangelical Review 262
Britton, John 352
Broad Church 166, 177, 408n 51 (*see also* latitudinarians)
Broughton, Rhoda 407n 33
Brucker, Johann Jakob: and Protestant tradition 38; on Erasmus 38–9; and earlier writers 39; and Hallam 155
Brunswick manifesto 82
Brussels 240, 334, 352
Brutus 67, 79
Bucer, Martin 142
Buddeus, Joannes Franciscus 385n 110
Budé, Guillaume 155, 205, 206, 325, 416n 77
Bungener, François 429n 108
Burckhardt, Jakob 270
Burgundy 16, 211, 215
Burigny *see* Lévesque de Burigny
Burke, Edmund 36, 276, 365, 395n 76
Burns, Robert 78
Burscher, Johann Friedrich 379n 2, 439n 103
Butler, Charles: life and background 188; and Catholic emancipation 188–9; his *Life of Erasmus* 189; as Catholic interpreter of Erasmus 190; on Erasmus' works 190–1; on Erasmus and Luther 191; and Erasmus 191

Cain 180
Caird, John: on Erasmus and learning 263; on Erasmus on religion and culture 264; and Milman 264
Calvin, John 6, 20, 33, 199, 239, 292, 396n 108
Calvinism 16, 96, 274, 276, 307, 384n 101 (*see also* Reformed church)

Cambrai, bishop of 165, 180, 344 (*see also* Bergen, Hendrik van)
Cambridge 16, 90, 94, 98, 243, 330, 354, 428n 89
Canterbury 190
Carlisle 98
Carlyle, Thomas 176, 178, 258
Casaubon, Isaac 407n 44
Castellio, Sebastian 96
Catholic emancipation 188–9
Catholic Reformation 298
Cato 147
Centre party 223
Channing, William Ellery 409n 66
Charles V, emperor 17, 27, 54, 55, 107, 163, 183, 201, 249, 411n 113
Charters 1815, 1830 149
Chartist movement 171
Chillingworth, William 34
Chlebus, Wilhelm 426n 63
Christ Church, Oxford 330
Chrysostom 383n 84, 396n 110
Cicero 32, 94, 138, 196, 414n 43
Cincinatti 284
Clarendon Press 354–5
Clarke, John 94, 396n 108
classics 81, 135, 148, 326
Cleves, Duchy of 199, 202, 300
Clifton College 358
Cloister and the Hearth 427n 79, 445n 212
Coleridge, Samuel Taylor: equal sympathy for Luther and Erasmus 12; on French Revolution 86; and the *Friend* 86–7; on history 87; compares Erasmus and Voltaire, Luther and Rousseau 87–9; on 'Understanding' and 'Reason' 90–1; lectures on history of philosophy 91, 395n 96; on Reformation 91; on Erasmus and Luther 92, 396n 106; distinctive interpretation

118; A.L. Smith and 258; Dods and 263

Colet, John: Erasmus and 5; Hess on Erasmus and 73; A. Müller on 116; Amiel on 149; Drummond on 408n 59; Butler on Erasmus and 190; Woker on Erasmus and 200; Durand de Laur on 204; Erhard on Erasmus and 249; Hamilton on 261; Dods on 428n 99; Emerton on Erasmus and 282; K. Müller on 289; Wernle on Erasmus and 291; Seebohm on Italian journey of 338; Seebohm on lectures of 339; Seebohm on Erasmus and 339–40; Gleason on 444n 187; A. Richter on Erasmus and 351; Nichols on Erasmus and 354; Allen on Erasmus and 357; Huizinga on Erasmus and 370

Collins, Anthony 381n 47

Cologne 201, 293, 317

Columbus, Christopher 141, 231, 241

Comenius, Johann Amos 324, 330

Condillac, Etienne de 149

Consilium cuiusdam ex animo cupientis esse consultum 316

Constance 302

Constance, Council of 231

Coomans, Lambert 210, 418n 105

Coornheert, Dirk Volkerts 286

Copernicus, Nicolaus 141, 231

Cordier, Mathurin 94, 396n 108

Cornelis of Woerden 416n 74

Cornelius, Carl Adolf von 199

Cornell University 366, 451n 313

Corpus Christi College, Oxford 356, 358

Côte d'Or 148

Coupé, Jean Marie Louis 394n 66

Cox, Francis Augustus 398n 148, 407n 27

Coxe, William 70

Cracow 322, 439n 103

Cramer, Samuel 306

Cranmer, Thomas 96

Creighton, Mandell 230–1, 450n 305

Creuzer, Georg Friedrich 253

Cudworth, Ralph 42

Dante 230, 263, 452n 343

Darwin, Charles 260

death, Erasmus and 128, 271, 292, 430n 129

deists 144, 286

Demosthenes 60, 138

De Ram, Pierre François-Xavier: life and work 209–10; on Erasmus and Basel 210; on Erasmus' death 210

Dermout, Isaac Johannes 275

Descartes, René 148

Desdevizes du Dezert, Théophile-Alphonse 416n 67

Deventer 165, 190, 204, 260, 279, 334, 344, 354, 356, 418n 108, 432n 159, 447n 245

devotio moderna 260, 334, 343–4, 367 (see also Brethren of Common Life)

De Wette, Wilhelm Martin Leberecht 266

dialectic 325, 440n 119

Dictionnaire de théologie catholique 227

Diderot, Denis 15–16, 380n 6

Dilthey, Wilhelm: on Renaissance and Reformation 285; on Erasmus 285–6; on Reformation 286; on Erasmus' religion 286; Troeltsch and 290; assessment of 295; Harnack on 435n 217; Mestwerdt on 343; Schröder and 364; P. Smith and 368

Dods, Marcus: on Hamilton 259;
and biblical criticism 262; on
Erasmus' religion 262; on
Drummond 262, 408n 50; on
Erasmus' character 263
dogma 170, 196–7, 228, 284–5,
286, 340, 364, 367, 434n 211,
435n 217
Döllinger, Ignaz von: and first
Vatican Council 192; Catholic
views of 192; his history of
Reformation 192–3; on Eras-
mus 193–4; on Erasmus and
Luther 193; on Erasmus and
Reformation 193–4; and Acton
413n 28; Kerker and 196;
Schlottmann on 224; C.
Wordsworth and 423n 23;
Maurenbrecher on 435n 4; and
Bezold 303
Dordrecht, synod of 42, 431n
148
Douai 188, 190
Dresden 246
Drummond, Robert Blackley: life
of 408n 46; compared with
Hallam and Pattison 164, 166;
on Erasmus' character 165–6;
anachronism in 166; on Eras-
mus' religion 166–8; compares
Erasmus with Jerome 167; on
Erasmus' works 168; on Eras-
mus and Reformation 168–9,
185; Kegan Paul and 170;
Janssen and 219; Pennington
and 244; A.L. Smith and 258;
Caird refers to 429n 107; Mest-
werdt on 445n 199; Geiger on
348; Nichols and 354
Du Pin, Louis Ellies 381n 32,
400n 186
Durand de Laur, H.: his work on
Erasmus 202–3, 205–6, 416n
71; compared with Feugère
203, 416n 72; as moderate

Catholic 203; on Erasmus' life
203–4; on Erasmus' personality
204–5; on Erasmus and Luther
205; on Erasmus and Renaissance 206; on Erasmus' influence 206; on Erasmus' religion
206–8; on free-will controversy
208; on Erasmus and modern
world 208–9; Mestwerdt on
445n 199; Geiger on 348
Durandus 196

Eberhardi, Wilhelm Ernest: on
Erasmus and Luther 255; on
Erasmus' character 255; Glasius on 279
Ebernburg 108
Ebrard, August 222–3
Eck, Cornelis Fransen van: oration on Erasmus 431n 159
Eck, Johann Maier von 360
Eckhart, Johannes (Meister) 51
ecumenism 8, 224
Edinburgh, University of 26, 85,
392n 44, 393n 48
education: Erhard on Erasmus
and 250, 425n 42; in nineteenth-century Germany 324;
K. von Raumer on Erasmus
and 324; Lange on Erasmus
and 324; Kämmel on Erasmus
and 324–5; Benoist on Erasmus and 325–6; Paulsen on
classical 326; Paulsen on Erasmus and 326; Herbartian influence on 327–9; Glöckner on
Erasmus and 327–8; Tögel on
Erasmus and 329–30; Wood-
ward on Erasmus and 332–3;
Jebb on Erasmus and 442n
153
Egmond see Baechem, Nicolaas
Egmont, Lamoraal van, count of
67
Eichhorn, Johann Gottfried 155

Eliot, George 407n 33
Emerton, Ephraim: career and
  work on Erasmus 281–2; on
  Erasmus' personality 282; on
  Erasmus and Reformation 282;
  on Erasmus and nature 283;
  contradiction in 283–4; on Erasmus and Luther 283–4
Encyclopaedia Britannica 164
Encyclopédie: and Erasmus 7; article on Arianism in 15; article
  on Rotterdam in 15–18 (see
  also Jaucourt, Louis de)
England: Erasmus' visits to 17;
  toleration in 34; Catholic
  emancipation in 188–9; liberal
  Protestant interpretations in
  256; Hamilton on Erasmus'
  visits to 428n 89; Lindsay on
  Erasmus' influence in 435n
  216
England, Church of 96, 175–6,
  398n 144 (see also Anglicanism)
English Historical Review 362,
  422n 191
Enlightenment: documents of 7;
  theology of 8; and Reformation 11; defined 14; and history 25; in Scotland 26; in
  Germany 37–8; and Protestantism 46; Semler and 388n
  187; Gaudin uses language of
  70; and Christianity 93; and
  Lavater 102; Schleiermacher's
  debt to 108; Erasmus interpretation in 118, 121–2, 374;
  Michelet's Erasmus and 143;
  Hallam and historiography of
  156; interpretation of Reformation in 238–9; Troeltsch on
  289–90, 294
Enlightenment, Protestant: judgment of Erasmus in 69; and
  Lavater 103; influence of in

1817 110
Enthoven, Ludwig: on Erasmus'
  political writings 323; on Erasmus' universalism 323
Eobanus Hessus 199
Epicurus 66, 345
Epistolae obscurorum virorum 59,
  67, 201, 349, 389n 211
Erasmus' birth date 428n 86,
  447n 231
Erasmus' works
– Adagia 139, 142, 143, 149,
  155–6, 162, 179, 206, 242, 247,
  263, 311, 339, 357, 408n 57
– Annotationes 74, 173, 360
– Antibarbari 206, 344, 345–6,
  417n 85, 445n 212
– Ciceronianus 31, 94, 139, 145,
  159, 195, 263, 324, 325, 328,
  330, 331, 370, 414n 43, 417n
  87
– Colloquia 93, 136, 144, 149,
  158–9, 162, 179, 190, 206, 219,
  301, 307, 324, 368, 372, 401n
  207, 404n 23, 405n 58
– Compendium vitae 165, 189,
  334–5, 336–7, 349–50, 352,
  356
– correspondence 8, 158, 298,
  301, 344, 351–9
– De concordia 52, 71, 107, 202
– De contemptu mundi 345–6,
  350
– De libero arbitrio 52, 208, 259,
  286 (see also free-will controversy)
– De pueris instituendis 250
– De ratione studii 250
– Dulce bellum inexpertis 17, 81,
  201, 321
– Ecclesiastes 144, 426nn 45 and
  55
– Enchiridion 45, 76–7, 94, 116,
  130, 144, 168, 179, 190–1, 207,
  211, 219, 221, 222, 243, 250–1,

261, 282, 290, 291, 313, 320,
339, 344, 368, 411n 109, 412n
118, 440n 106
– *Encomium matrimonii* 70, 345
– *Epistola consolatoria* 94
– *Epistola contra pseudevangelicos*
194
– *Institutio christiani matrimonii*
145, 283
– *Institutio principis christiani*
168, 323
– *Julius exclusus* 179, 263, 417n
91
– *Methodus* 144
– *Moriae encomium* 3, 38, 70, 73,
92, 95, 127, 130–1, 142, 143–4,
149, 156, 162, 168, 179, 191,
199, 200, 207, 211–12, 219,
222, 227, 229, 241, 248, 283,
286, 307, 349, 360, 368, 372,
411n 118, 415n 59
– *Novum Testamentum* 41, 50,
73–4, 107, 144, 162, 180–1,
190, 200, 234, 241, 243, 261,
262, 266, 290, 338, 339,
359–60, 362, 411n 109, 438n
67
– *Oratio funebris in funere Bertae
de Heyen* 335
– *Paraclesis* 414n 52
– *Paraphrases* 45, 65, 92, 261
– poems 320, 334–5
– *Querela pacis* 168, 202
– *Ratio verae theologiae* 45, 50–3,
206–7, 307, 426nn 45 and 55
– *Spongia* 60, 67, 112
Erfurt, University of 199
Erhard, Heinrich August: on Erasmus and Reformation 249,
251; career of 249; on Erasmus
and Reuchlin controversy 250;
on Erasmus and learning 250;
on Erasmus' religion 250–1;
assessment of 251; on religious
reconciliation 252; Milman on

427n 74
Erlangen, University of 129,
244–5, 303, 324, 420n 160
Ersch, Johann Samuel 249
eschatology 292
Escher, Heinrich: in Zürich 265;
rejects A. Müller 265; on Erasmus' religion 265–6; on Erasmus and Luther 266; on
Erasmus' qualities 266; Streuber praises 269
Eton 170
evangelicals 96–8, 118, 239–40,
243–4, 248, 261, 408n 50
Evangelische Kirchenzeitung 324
Exeter College, Oxford 170

Faber, Johannes 316–17
Fabri, Johannes 302
Fabricius, Johann Albert 39, 41
family: Michelet on 404n 35;
Feugère on Erasmus and 145;
Milman on 257; Usteri on Erasmus and 321
Fathers 127, 144, 222, 224, 290,
303, 366
Febronius, Justinius 54
Fénelon, François de Salignac de
la Mothe 66
Feuerbach, Ludwig Andreas 130
Feugère, Gaston: on Erasmus'
theological writings 143–4; on
Erasmus' political writings
144–5; on Erasmus' ethical
writings 145; on Renaissance
and scholasticism 146; on Ref-
ormation 146–7; on Erasmus'
personality 147; Geiger on
147, 348; Nève on 416n 72,
419n 132; Caird refers to 429n
107
Feugère, Léon-Jacques 143
Fichte, Johann Gottlieb 50, 324
Figgis, John Neville 450n 305
Filelfo, Francesco 325

Fletcher, John 96
Flugschriften 124, 129, 131
Foxe, John 97
France: influence on eighteenth-
  century Germany 37; Herder
  in 59; revolutions of 1830 in
  124, 134–5; nineteenth-century
  writers in 134, 151; Amiel on
  classical tradition and 148; En-
  thoven on Erasmus and 323
  (*see also* French Revolution)
Francis I, king of France 5
Francke, August Hermann 96
Frankfurt 217; Assembly 129
Franklin, Benjamin 66
Frederick II (the Great), king of
  Prussia 108
Frederick the Wise, elector of
  Saxony 315
Free Christian Union 170
free-will controversy 46, 52, 61,
  66, 75, 77, 100, 132, 138, 142,
  191, 208, 225, 242, 255, 259,
  283, 284, 319, 407n 36, 434n
  211
Freiburg 210, 268, 355
French Revolution: and German
  Reformation 7; parallel with
  Reformation 12; Gibbon on 36;
  Wieland on 67; Herder on 68;
  Stewart on 81; Knox and 82;
  Villers on 84, 394n 68; Mill on
  86; Coleridge on 86; Michelet's
  History of 140; Hallam on Ref-
  ormation and 154, 157
Friedrich Wilhelm III, king of
  Prussia 105
Friend 86–7, 91
Froben, Johann 210, 267, 357
Fronde 83
Froude, Hurrell 175
Froude, James Anthony: com-
  pared with Pattison 175; life
  and experience 175–6; and Er-
  asmus 176–7; lectures on Eras-

mus 177, 178; on Luther
  177–8, 185; and Carlyle 178;
  on Erasmus' works 179; on
  Erasmus' life 179–80; on
  Erasmus' finances 180; on
  Erasmus' reform program 181;
  on Erasmus and Luther 182–3;
  on Erasmus' last years 183; on
  Erasmus and Reformation 183;
  on appeal of Erasmus 184; on
  religion 184; Allen and 184,
  355, 359, 411n 118, 448n 258;
  Bludau and 360
Froude, Margaret 176
Fruin, Robert: Mestwerdt uses
  344; as historian 348; on Erasmus scholarship 349; on *Compendium vitae* 349–50; on
  Erasmus in monastery 350; assessment of 350–1; Lindeboom
  on 446n 223
Funk, Frank Xavier: critique of
  Janssen 221–2; on Erasmus
  222

Gallicanism 55, 188
Garrod, H.W. 359
Gasquet, Francis Neil (Dom Ai-
  dan): career and writings 228;
  on Erasmus 228–9
Gaudin, Johannes: background of
  70; on Erasmus and enlighten-
  ment 70–1; on Reformation 71;
  on Erasmus' controversies 71;
  on Basel Reformation 72; on
  Erasmus' character 72; com-
  pared with A. Müller 114
Gaum, Johann Ferdinand 58
Gaume, John Joseph 414n 43
Gay, Peter 18
Gaye, Johannes: on Erasmus'
  correspondence and character
  351, 425n 38
Geertruidenberg 277
Geiger, Ludwig: on Feugère

147–8; background of 348; on
Erasmus biography and biographers 348; on Erasmus' nationality 349; on Erasmus'
character 349; on Erasmus' religion 349
Geneva 16, 239, 240, 242, 306,
381n 32
George, duke of Saxony 193
George III, king of England 396n
115
Gerard, Erasmus' father 436n 26,
445n 212
Gerard, Cornelis 204, 335, 442n
160
Gerdes, Daniel 155
Germany: Voltaire on Reformation in 19–20; universities in
37, 385n 104; Enlightenment
in 37–8; Schmidt on history of
54–5; Villers and 83; nationality issue in 109, 111–12; Erasmus and public opinion in
123; 1848 revolution in 124,
129; Ranke on late medieval
reform movements in 126;
Hagen on reform movements
129; Nève on schools in 213;
Janssen on fifteenth-century
conditions in 217–18; Janssen
on humanists in 218; history
in 244; Stähelin on Erasmus
party in 273; Wernle on Erasmus' influence in southern
291; Hermelink on humanism
in 293–4; Maurenbrecher on
Erasmus' influence in 300; Kalkoff on history of 1517–23
315; Enthoven on Erasmus
and 323; classical revival
in 326; Geiger on Erasmus
and 349
Ghent 211, 355
Gibbon, Edward: on dialogue between Erasmus and Voltaire

18, 36; on Erasmus and learning 31–2; on Erasmus' character 32; on Erasmus and
Reformation 32–3; on Paulicians 33; on Reformers 33–4;
on Erasmus and second reformation 34–5; on Priestley
35–6, 384nn 95 and 101; and
Christianity 35–6; on revolution in France 36; on Erasmus
and revolution 36; compared
with Robertson 36–7; and Hallam 158; and Beard 173–4; and
Froude 181; A.L. Smith and
258; on Erasmus' Greek 428n
89; Dilthey and 286; and Renaudet 314; Seebohm and
340–1
Giberti, Gian Matteo 230
Giessen 288
Glasgow, University of 259, 263
Glasius, Barend: background of
277, 431n 148; on Erasmus'
reform program 277–8; on Erasmus and Reformation 279;
on Erasmus and Netherlands
reforming tradition 279; on Erasmus' character 279; on Erasmus' influence in Netherlands
280; assessment of 280
Gleason, John B. 444nn 187 and
189
Glöckner, Johannes Gottfried:
Herbartian 327; on Erasmus'
educational ideal 327–8; assessment of 328; career of
441n 128
Goclenius, Conradus 350
Godet, P.: on Erasmus' character
227; on Erasmus' religion
227–8
Godwin, William 86, 395n 82
Goethe, Johann Wolfgang von
59, 229, 266, 388n 209
Goldsmith, Oliver 94

Görres circle 192
Göttingen, University of 37, 39, 42, 43, 83, 288, 341
Göttingische gelehrte Anzeigen 294
Gouda 334, 355, 356
Gourmont, Remy de 221
Great War 323, 341, 356, 361
Greek studies 127, 155, 206, 310, 354
Gregory XVI, pope 417n 100
Grimani, Domenico, cardinal 310
Grocyn, William 437n 57
Groen van Prinsterer, Gulielmus 276
Groningen school 277–8
Gropper, Johannes 231
Grotius, Hugo 18, 34, 66, 67, 70, 277, 390n 228, 407n 44, 432n 159
Gruber, Johann Gottfried 249
Grunnius, letter to 165, 180, 204, 260, 337, 344, 352–3, 416n 74, 443n 178
Gymnasium Erasmianum, Rotterdam 336

Habsburg dynasty 54, 352
Hagen, Karl: career of 129; on fifteenth-century reform movements 129–30; on Erasmus and reform movements 130–1; on Luther and reform movements 131; on Erasmus' character and significance 132; compared with Ranke 132–3; Janssen and 219; Plitt on 424n 25; Escher compared with 429n 116; Dilthey and 286, 433n 180; Maurenbrecher on 435n 4; Geiger and 349
Hagenbach, Karl Rudolf: influences on 266–7; and Basel 266; on Erasmus and Basel 267; Schleiermacher and 266, 270–1; and mediating theology

270; Burckhardt on 270; on Erasmus' character 271; and liberal Protestant interpretations 271; on Erasmus and Reformation 271–2; Glasius on 279
Hague 277, 451n 313
Hallam, Henry: life and personality 154; on Reformation and French Revolution 154, 157; on Erasmus' character 155–6, 158; on Erasmus' political writings 156; on Luther 157; and Drummond 164, 166; on Erasmus and Reformers 185; A.L. Smith and 258
Halle, University of 37, 38, 50, 51, 223, 253, 265, 389n 214
Hamann, Johann Georg 59
Hamburg 41, 240
Hamilton, James: life of 259–60; writings on Erasmus 260; on Erasmus' psychology 260; on influences on Erasmus 260; on Colet and Erasmus 261; on Erasmus' religion 261; and Seebohm 340
Haneberg, Daniel Bonifacius von 413n 28
Hanover 37, 43
Hardt, Hermann von der 30, 39, 54, 155, 416n 66
Hare, Julius 157
Harnack, Adolf von: on Erasmus 435n 217; and Mestwerdt 341
Hartfelder, Karl: on Erasmus and papacy 302; on Erasmus and Constance humanists 302; assessment of 302–3; on Erasmus' influence 303; Kan and 336
Harvard University 281
Hayley, William 36
Hackfeld 112
Hegel, Georg Wilhelm Friedrich 50, 115, 195, 253, 425n 38

Hegelianism 8, 243, 244
Hegius, Alexander 40, 278, 279,
335, 344, 357
Heidelberg 129, 253, 254, 288,
301, 341–2
Helfferich, Adolph 440n 106
Heller, Jos. *see Vertheidigung des
grossen Erasmus*
Helmstedt 39
Helsinki 441n 128
Helvétius, Claude-Adrien 149
Helwig, Christopher 93
Hengstenberg, Ernst Wilhelm
324
Henke, Heinrich Philipp Konrad:
and Protestant tradition 46; on
Burigny 47; on Erasmus' theol-
ogy 47–8; on Erasmus as re-
former 48–9; relativism in 49;
Rotermund refers to 400n 186
Henneberg, Johann Valentin: on
Erasmus' *Ecclesiastes* 424n 37
Henry VIII, king of England 5,
176, 180, 311, 411n 118
Herbart, Johann 327–9, 332
Herder, Johann Gotfried: life of
59; on Hutten and Erasmus
59–60; on Latin and German
60–1, 389n 214; on Luther and
Erasmus 60–1; on determinism
61; on humanities 64–5; on Erasmus' biblical studies 65; on
universalism and *Humanität*
65; and French Revolution
65–6; changed view of Erasmus 66–7; revises Hutten article 67; on Lavater 103; Moser
on 109; influences Hagenbach
266; Kalkoff and 317
Hermans, Willem 204, 335
Hermelink, Heinrich: on humanism and *via antiqua* 293; on
Erasmus and medieval spirituality 293–4; Troeltsch on 294
Herzog, Johann Wernhard 268

Hess, Johann Jakob 72–3
Hess, Salomon: and Zürich 72;
on Erasmus' friends and enemies 73; on Erasmus as enlightened critic 73–4; on
Erasmus and Luther 74–5; Rotermund refers to 400n 186;
and Müller 114; Milman on
427n 74
Hibbert Journal 284
Hilary 74, 383n 84
Historisches Taschenbuch 264,
300
history: in Enlightenment 25; in
German universities 37; Mos-
heim and 39; in nineteenth-
century Protestantism 244; and
Erasmus scholarship 351; Huizinga on 371–2 (*see also* Whig
historians)
Hofmann, Johannes Christian
Konrad von 245
Hofstede de Groot, Petrus 278
Holbein, Hans, the Younger 17,
62, 103–4, 117, 165, 227, 368,
433n 175
Holland 34, 41, 276–7, 305, 323
(*see also* Netherlands)
Home and Foreign Review 421n
184
Homer 66, 140
Hontheim, Johann Nicolaus von
see Febronius, Justinius
Hopman, Frederick Jan 452n 341
Horace 64
Horawitz, Adalbert: career
300–1; Allen on 301; on *Colloquia* 301, 436n 12; on Erasmus
as reformer 301–2; and Ranke
302; and Maurenbrecher 302;
assessment of 302; Kan and
336–7, 351; and Erasmus' correspondence 351, 446n 226;
Allen on 446n 226
Horsley, Samuel 384n 101

Hottinger, Johann Heinrich 391n 8
Huet, Conrad Busken: on Erasmus as Netherlander 304–5; on Netherlands religion 305; on Luther 305; on Erasmus' psychology 306
Huizinga, Johan: summation of nineteenth-century interpretations 362, 372; on Erasmus' mind and character 369; on Erasmus' liberalism 369–70, 372; on Erasmus' biography 370; on Erasmus and Reformation 370; relation to his book 370–1; and Erasmus 371; and Allens 371; and historical writing 371–2; and heroic 372; criticism of 452n 345; and Dilthey 452n 350; Margolin on 453n 1
Hull 97
humanism 4, 46, 153, 187, 195, 197, 218, 222–3, 293, 312, 324, 343 (see also Renaissance, revival of learning)
Hume, David 27
Hummelberg, Michael 302
Hus, John 33, 111
Hutten, Ulrich von: and romanticism 12; Voltaire on 18; Robertson on 29; and Erasmus 58; Herder on 59–60; Wieland on 61–3; Gaudin on 71; Wagner on 76–7; Moser on 108–9; Becker on 111; biographies of after wars of liberation 112; Kieser condemns 112–13; symbol in age of revolution 114; Paulus on 400n 198; Hagen on 132; Hallam on 406n 23; Erfurt humanists and 199; Strauss on 432n 174; Maurenbrecher on 299; Kalkoff on 317
Huysmans, J.-K. 221

Hyma, Albert 444n 188
Illgen, Christian Friedrich 254–5
Imbart de la Tour, Pierre: on évangélisme 233; on Catholicism 233, 235; on French church 234; on Erasmus and reform 234; on Erasmus and liberty 235; anticipated by Glasius 280
indulgences 231
Inner Temple 352
Institut de France 83, 85
Ireland 362
irenicism 200, 270, 275
Irving, Edward 259
Italy: Erasmus' visit to 17; A. Müller on 401n 205; Feugère on Renaissance in 146; neo-Thomism in 195; Kerker on humanism in 197; Rottier on Erasmus and 211; Troeltsch on German humanism and 294; Nolhac on Erasmus' experiences in 310–11; influence on Erasmus of 310, 437nn 54 and 56; Renaudet on Erasmus and 311; Seebohm on Colet in 338; Mestwerdt on humanism in 343
Jansenists 51
Janssen, Johannes: life and commitments 217; patriotism of 217; on fifteenth-century Germany 217–18; on two humanist generations 218; on Erasmus 218–19; assessment of 219–20; Funk's critique of 221–2; defends objectivity 222; Ebrard's critique of 222–3; Schlottmann's critique of 223; Godet and 227; Gasquet and 229; Imbart de la Tour compared with 234–5; Wolf on 297; Maurenbrecher on 435n

4; Bezold and 303–4; Bludau
and 360
Jaucourt, Louis de: background
of 15; and *Encyclopédie* 15;
plagiarizes Bayle 15–17; on Erasmus 17–18; and Enlightenment 380n 9 (*see also Encyclopédie*)
Jebb, Richard Claverhouse: on
Erasmus and education 442n
153; on humanist education
442n 155
Jena 129, 385n 110, 424n 38
Jerome 167, 190
Jesus, religion of 47, 282, 290,
293, 307, 367 (*see also* Sermon
on the Mount)
Jesus College, Cambridge 90
Johnson, Samuel: praises Knox
81; interest in Erasmus 93–4;
on classical tradition 94; on Erasmus 94–5
Joly, Claude 83
Jonas, Jodocus 354
Jortin, John 6, 30, 81, 90, 93,
101, 155, 169, 189, 258, 391n
8, 406n 23
Joseph II, emperor of Austria
53–4
Journal des Débats 135
Jowett, Benjamin 408n 51
Julius II, pope 5, 310

Kaegi, Werner 15
Kalkoff, Paul: career and outlook
315; on Erasmus' mediating
policy 1520 316–17; on Hutten
317; assessment of 317–18;
and Maurenbrecher 318; Bludau and 359; P. Smith and
366
Kämmel, Heinrich Julius: on Erasmus and education 324–5
Kampschulte, Friedrich Wilhelm:
life of 199; on Erfurt Univer-

sity and Erasmus 199–200;
Wolf on 297; Maurenbrecher
on 435n 4
Kan, Johannes Benedictus: per-
sonality of 336; on *Compen-
dium vitae* 336–7; and Erasmus
scholars 336–7; Fruin on
349–50
Kant, Immanuel 59, 83, 90, 327,
395n 78
Karl August, duke of Weimar 59
Kashmir 351, 355
Kaunitz, Wenzel Anton, chancel-
lor of Austria 54
Keble, John 409n 66
Kegan Paul, Charles: on Drum-
mond and Erasmus 170, 185
Kennett, White 340
Kerker, Moritz: career and back-
ground of 194; on humanism
and scholasticism 195, 197; on
Erasmus and scholasticism
195–7; assessment of 198;
Nève and 213; Janssen on 219;
Plitt on 424n 25; Mauren-
brecher on 435n 4
Kiel, University of 41, 425n 38,
434n 207
Kieser, Carl: condemns Hutten
112–13; on Erasmus 113
Kingsley, Charles 170
Kingsley, Mary 176–7
kissing, by English noblewomen
17, 413n 20
Klefeker, Johannes 49, 379n 4
Kleinsüssen 194
Knight, Samuel 73, 93, 189, 261,
340, 354, 416n 66
Knox, Vicesimus: as advocate of
peace 81; and classical culture
81; on Erasmus and war 81–3
Köhler, Walter: on Schulze and
Erasmus 294
Koltz, Christian Adolf 389n 214
Königsberg 59

Köster, Kurt 371
Kulturkampf 217, 223, 226, 298, 421n 174

La Mothe Le Vayer, François de 24, 381n 47
Lange, Albert: on Erasmus and education 324
La Sallette 405n 61
Latin 60–1, 64, 94, 105, 139, 145, 159, 161, 195, 246, 265
latitudinarians 34, 42, 101 (see also Broad Church)
Lausanne Academy 70
Lavater, Johann Caspar: predecessor of Hess 73; physiognomic studies of 102, 398n 151; life of 102–3; on religion 103; influence of 103; on Erasmus 103–4; and hostile Protestant tradition 104; popularity of 399n 160; A. Müller and 117; Ranke and 128, 402n 22; Feugère and 147; Amiel sceptical of 150; Drummond and 165; Godet and 227; Erhard and 250; Escher and 266; Bezold and 304
Lawford Hall 352
Lecky, William Edward Hartpole 152, 256–7
Le Clerc, Jean 6, 32, 34, 36, 39, 42, 73, 75, 102, 155, 164, 267, 400n 186, 423n 10
Lee, Edward 214, 359–60
Lee, R.W. 412n 118
Lefèvre d'Etaples, Jacques 234, 313, 360
Leibniz, Gottfried Wilhelm von 24, 224, 225, 432n 159
Leiden 16, 94, 260, 436n 31
Leipzig 254, 281, 293, 322, 327, 379n 2, 434n 207, 439n 103
Leo X, pope 5, 19, 141, 223, 224, 225, 337, 414n 43

Lessing, Gotthold Ephraim 144, 390n 248
Letters of Obscure Men see Epistolae obscurorum virorum
Lévesque de Burigny, Jean 6–7, 18, 32, 42–3, 47, 48, 73, 74, 155, 189, 383n 79, 400n 186, 423n 10
Lezius, Friedrich: on Erasmus' religion 287–8; assessment of 288; and Dilthey 288; on Erasmus and Reformation 288; M. Richter and 314
L'Hôpital, Michel de 192
liberalism: dominant 8, 373; and religion 152; and Reformation 153; and Erasmus interpretation 153, 239, 248–9; Catholic 236; Protestant 256, 263, 271; Anglican 257; in Switzerland 264; H.G. Smith on Erasmus and Protestant 285; Mestwerdt and 341–2; preoccupations of continue after Great War 361; P. Smith on Erasmus, Luther, and 368; fading of 373; limitations of Erasmus interpretation in 373–4; persistence and persuasiveness of 374
Lichfield 93, 94
Lieberkühn, Ernest: on Erasmus 424n 38
Lilly, William Samuel: criticizes Froude 411n 118; on Erasmus 421n 178
Linacre, Thomas 437n 57
Lincoln College, Oxford 160
Lindeboom, Johannes: career of 307, 436n 40; on Erasmus and Netherlands tradition 307, 309; on Erasmus' consistency 308; on Erasmus' theology 308; on Erasmus' religious personality 308–9; on Dilthey and Troeltsch 437n 47; assessment

of 309, 437n 46; P. Smith and
366
Lindsay, Thomas M.: on Erasmus
432n 175, 434n 216
Lips, Maarten 446n 226
Lipsius, Justus 407n 44
Liverpool 171, 330; University of
330–1, 356
Locke, John 78, 330
London 352, 355, 356
Lortz, Joseph 186, 373
Louis XIV, king of France 242
Louis Philippe, king of France
135
Lourdes 405n 61
Louvain, University of 209, 212,
213, 214, 217, 317, 352, 359,
417n 100, 439n 80
Loyola 144, 191, 411nn 109 and
118
Lübeck 41, 83
Lucian 21–2, 36, 144, 168
Luden, Heinrich 129
Lupton, Joseph: Kan and 336; on
Colet and Erasmus 444n 187;
criticism of 444n 189
Luther, Martin: Erasmus and
5–6; and romanticism 12; Voltaire on 19–20; Robertson on
28–9; Planck and Schröckh on
45–6; Semler on 51–2; Schmidt
on 55–7; Herder on 60–1; Wieland on 63; Gaudin on 71;
Hess on 74–5; Wagner on
76–7; Villers on 84; Coleridge
on 87, 89–90; Milner on 99; A.
Müller on 116–17; Hagen on
131; Nisard on 138; Michelet
on 141; Amiel on 149; Table
Talk of 155; Drummond on
169; Beard on 173–5; Froude
on 177–8; Butler on Erasmus
and 191; Döllinger on Erasmus
and 193; Woker on Erasmus
and 201; Durand de Laur on

Erasmus and 205; Acton on
Erasmus and 232; Montauban
thesis-writers on Erasmus and
242; Pennington on Erasmus
and 244; Erhard on Erasmus
and 251; Eberhardi on Erasmus and 255; Stähelin on 273;
Emerton on Erasmus and
283–4; H.G. Smith on liberal
Protestants and 284–5; Dilthey
on 286; Wernle on Erasmus
and 291; Hermelink on 294;
Maurenbrecher on Protestant
studies of 435n 4; Maurenbrecher on 299; Huet on 305;
Lindeboom on Erasmus and
308–9; M. Richter on Erasmus
and 1520–1 315; Kalkoff on
Erasmus and 1520 316–17;
and Erasmus literature 320; on
education 325; Geiger on Erasmus and 349; Whitney on Erasmus and 363; Murray on
Erasmus and 364–5; P. Smith
on Erasmus and 368
Lutheran church 105, 131,
244–5, 305
Luther anniversary 1817 109–10,
240
Lyon 438n 58

Macaulay, Thomas Babington
154, 407n 29, 407n 44
Machiavelli, Niccolò 231, 390n
228
Madeley, Shropshire 96
Magdeburg Centuries 97
Maimbourg, Louis 381n 32
Mainz 355; archbishop of 193
Maitland, Samuel Roffey 97
Mallet, Edme 15
Manchester 171
Marburg 272, 434n 207
Marcus Antoninus 66
Marheineke, Philipp Conrad: on

Erasmus 244; Gaye student of
425n 38
Marmontel, Jean François 23
Marsollier, Jacques 222
Matsys, Quentin 368
Maurenbrecher, Wilhelm: on
Catholic Reformation 298; on
Erasmus and reform 299; on
Erasmus' influence 299–300;
on Erasmus and mediation
300; on Erasmus' character
300; influence of 300; A. Rich-
ter and 351
Maurer, Hans Rudolf 70
Maurice, Frederick Denison 170
Maximilian I, emperor 55, 316
mediating theology: described
252; and Erasmus 254, 255–6;
in Switzerland 270
Meiklejohn, John 429n 103
Melanchthon, Philipp 6, 24, 39,
45, 51–2, 66, 194, 223, 245,
254, 301
Melishofer, Johann 302
Merian, Emanuel 268
Merle d'Aubigné, Jean Henri: life
and reputation 240; on the
Reformation 240; on Erasmus
240–1; influence of 241–2;
Stockmeyer and 269; congenial
to Dutch Calvinists 274; Glasius on 279
Merula, Paullus 336–7, 350, 353,
443n 168
Mestwerdt, Paul: life and studies
341; and liberalism 341–2; and
Erasmus 342; and Seebohm
342, 346–7; aim and approach
of 342; on Italian humanism
343; on devotio moderna 343–4;
on Erasmus' early development 344, 346; on Erasmus
and monasticism 344–5; on
Antibarbari 345; on Erasmus in
Paris 345–6; assessment of

346–7; and recent scholarship
445nn 203 and 212; Schröder
and 364; P. Smith and 366
Methodism 96
Meyer, André: maturity of 318;
on Erasmus and Luther
318–19; on Erasmus' moderation 319; on Erasmus and Catholicism 319
Miaskowski, Kasimir von: on Erasmus and Poland 322
Michelet, Jules: on Christianity
140; on Renaissance 140–1; on
Luther and Reformation 141;
on Erasmus 141–3; Feugère
compared to 145; Amiel on
149; Nève on 213
Middle Ages 19, 39, 69, 79, 116,
125, 140, 143, 153, 187, 194–6,
213, 218, 221, 286–7, 294, 363
Mill, James: background of 85;
compares Erasmus and philosophes 85; compares Reformation and French Revolution 86
Milman, Henry Hart: career and
writings 256, 426n 65; on Reformation 256–7; on Erasmus
and Reformation 257–8; A.L.
Smith and 258; Caird and 264
Milner, Isaac: career and personality 98–9; on free-will controversy 100–1; on Erasmus'
levity 101; contribution to History 397n 124; Hallam on 155,
406n 27
Milner, John 189
Milner, Joseph: plan for History
97; life of 97–8; on Luther 99;
on Erasmus 99–100; contribution to History 397n 124;
James Stephen on 101; Hallam
on 155; Pennington and 243
Milton, John 191
Moderates, Church of Scotland
25–6

modernism 314, 438n 70
modernity 4, 153, 208–9, 264, 294, 296, 305, 331, 333, 362–4, 368, 450nn 297 and 299
Möhler, Johann Adam 195
monastery, Erasmus in: Nisard on 136; Drummond on 165; Durand de Laur on 204; Hamilton on 260; Ruelens on 335; Vischer on 337; Mestwerdt on 344; Fruin on 350; Nichols on 354; Huizinga on 370
monks: in Josephine reforms 54; Nisard on 136–7; Hallam on 156; Milman on Erasmus and 257; Hamilton on Erasmus and 260; Dilthey on Erasmus and 285; Lezius on Erasmus and 287; late medieval reform movements among 312–13
Montaigne, Michel 95, 142, 144, 364, 368, 390n 228
Montauban, Protestant Faculty at 241–2
Moravians 106, 387n 182
More, Thomas: biographies of 4; Erasmus and 5; Stewart on 80; Hallam on 156, 158; Pattison on 407n 44; Woker on Erasmus and 200; Gasquet on 229; Seebohm on 339–40; and Lee 359
Morhof, Daniel Georg 155
Morley, John 164
Moser, Friedrich Karl von: character of 108; on Hutten 108–9; on Erasmus 109; on Herder 109
Moses 275
Mosheim, Johann Lorenz von: as historian 39–40; on revival of learning 40; on Erasmus 40–1; connections with Holland and England 41–2; Milner on 97; and Hallam 155
Mountjoy, William Blount, baron

55, 180, 346, 352
Müller, Adolf: compared with Gaudin and Hess 114; life and outlook of 114–15; dicta of 115–16; on Renaissance and Reformation 116; on Erasmus and Luther 116–17; on Erasmus' character 117; reviews of 401n 211; Feugère and 147; Woker and 416n 66; Janssen and 219, 222; Merle d'Aubigné refers to 423n10; Stichart and 248; Erhard and 250; Milman on 427n 74; Escher rejects 265; Stockmeyer and 268; Streuber on 269; influences Hagenbach 271; congenial to Dutch Calvinists 274; Glasius on 279, 431n 153; Bezold and 304; Schröder and 364
Müller, Georg 65
Müller, Karl: on Erasmus' religion 289; and Dilthey 289; on church history 433n 190; on Erasmus' influence 433n 192
Munich University 192, 303
Münster 217
Müntzer, Thomas 88
Murray, Robert H.: work on toleration 362; on Erasmus and dogmas 364; on Erasmus and Luther 364–5; compares Erasmus with Burke 365; P. Smith and 451n 325
Mutian, Conrad 199
mysticism 51, 287, 306, 309, 312, 452n 352

Naigeon, Jacques André 16
Napoleon 43, 104, 111, 114, 242, 305
Napoleonic wars 7, 43, 109, 115, 239
nationalism 7, 12, 109, 111–12, 324, 349

National Scotch Church, Regent
Square 259
nature, Erasmus on 283, 324,
326, 328, 332, 333, 345
Neander, August 223, 240,
252–3, 266
neologians 38, 51
Neoplatonism 91, 290–1, 312–13,
334, 338, 367
neo-scholasticism 8, 144, 195
Netherlands: southern 5; Froude
on 179; Rottier on Erasmus
and 211; Allard on Erasmus
and 220; medievalism in 221;
differences over Erasmus in
274–5; Calvinist revival in 276;
reforming tradition in 279;
Huet on Erasmus and 304–5;
Huet on higher education in
305; Huet on religion in 305;
Pijper on reforming movement
in 306–7; Lindeboom on Erasmus and 307, 309; Huizinga
on Erasmus and 370
Nève, Félix: compares Feugère
and Durand de Laur 416n 72;
polymath 213; Catholic commitment of 213–14; on Renaissance and Reformation 213–
14; on Erasmus and Luther
214–15; on Erasmus' Christianity 215; on Erasmus as social critic 215–16; on Erasmus'
writings 216; Kan and 336;
Horawitz supplements work of
446n 226
Newcastle 177
New College, Edinburgh 259
Newman, John Henry 160, 175,
181, 263, 398n 147
Newton, Isaac 98, 393n 48
Nichols, Francis Morgan: life and
works 352; on Erasmus' correspondence 353, 447n 238; on
Compendium vitae and letters

to Servatius Rogerus and
Grunnius 353; on Erasmus'
early history 354; on Erasmus'
character 354; Allen on 354
Nicolai, Christoph Friedrich 38
Nietzsche, Friedrich 363
Nisard, Jean M.N. Désiré: and
revolution of 1830 134–5; and
romantics 135; on Erasmus
and monks 136–7; on Eras-
mus' character 136–7; on Erasmus and Luther 137–9; on
Erasmus' writings 139; Feugère
attracted to 143; Nève on 419n
128; Merle d'Aubigné on 423n
10; quoted by Montauban thesis-writers 242; Milman on
427n 74
Nolhac, Pierre de: Renaudet on
309–10; on Erasmus' Italian
experiences 310–11; on influence of Italy on Erasmus 310;
Kan and 336
Noordziek, Jan Jacobus Frederik:
on Erasmus' humour 276
North Wales 94
Nottingham 396n 108, 409n 66
Nyon 70

Ochs, Peter 70
Ockham, William of 196
Oecolampadius, Johannes 33, 72,
275
old Catholics 199, 201, 215,
423n 23
Oncken, Hermann 342
Oriel College, Oxford 159–60
Ortwinus Gratius 60
Otto, Rudolf 341
Oxford 159–60, 176, 180, 330,
334, 338–41, 354, 356, 428n
89, 437n 57
'Oxford Reformers' 261, 272, 299,
313, 339–41 (*see also* See-
bohm, Frederic)

papacy 19, 44, 52, 125–6, 295,
302, 422n 191, 450n 295 (see
also Rome, church of)
Paris 124, 126, 167, 180, 311–13,
345, 350
Pascal, Blaise 96, 145, 242
Pastor, Ludwig von: and Janssen
216–17; on Erasmus 220
Pattison, Mark: on Erasmus and
Voltaire 18, 161; life and outlook 159–60; and Erasmus 160;
on Erasmus' anticlericalism
160–1; on Erasmus' learning
161; on Erasmus' usefulness
162; on Erasmus' psychology
162–3; Drummond compared
with 164; Froude compared
with 175; on Erasmus as sceptic 185; Dilthey and 286;
Geiger and 349
Paul III, pope 183, 234
Paul, Saint 90, 92, 167, 290–1,
293, 409n 66
Paulicians 33
Paulinism 290
Paulsen, Friedrich: on classicism
326; on Erasmus and classical
education 326; on Erasmus
and Reformation 326–7
Paulus, Heinrich Eberhard Gottlob 400n 198
Pelagianism 100–1, 225, 273,
308, 398n 144, 420n 154
Penn, William 66
Pennington, Arthur Robert:
career 243; on Erasmus and
Reformation 243–4; and Drum-
mond 244
Péricaud, Antoine: on Erasmus
and Lyon 438n 58
Pestalozzi, Johann Heinrich 324,
330
Petrarch 306
Pflug, Julius 202
Phillips, Margaret Mann 449n

272
philosophes 14, 23–4, 31, 85,
394n 76
Pico della Mirandola 195
Pieter, Erasmus' brother 136,
350, 416n 74, 428n 86
pietists 42, 51, 108
Pijper, Fredrik: on Netherlands
reforming movement 306–7;
on Erasmus' influence 307;
and liberal theologians 307;
critique of 437n 46
Pindar 66
Pio, Alberto, prince of Carpi 193
Pirckheimer, Willibald 129, 402n
27
Pius V, pope 192, 413n 28
Planck, Gottlieb Jakob: career of
43; as historian 43; on Reformation 43–4; on Erasmus
44–6; compared with Schröckh
45–6; and Henke 48; Semler's
pupil 388n 187; praised by
Gaudin 70; Woker refers to
416n 66
Plato 66, 140, 291, 292
Plitt, Gustav Leopold: career and
• background 244–5; on Reformation 245; on humanism and
Erasmus 245–6; on Erasmus
and Reformation 246; Stockmeyer and 269
Plutarch 325, 330
Poland 322, 440n 103
Possevino, Antonio 144, 155
Post, Regnerus Richardus 445nn
203 and 212
Poznan 322
Presbyterian church 366
press, newspaper 124
Priestley, Joseph 35, 384nn 95
and 101, 409n 66
printing 79, 111, 155, 357
progress, idea of: in Enlightenment 14; Mosheim on 39;

Stewart on 79; Villers on 83; Coleridge on 86; ingredient of liberalism 152–3; Beard on 171; Froude on 181; Durand de Laur on 417n 97; Plitt on 245; Seebohm on 341; and Erasmus interpretation 374

providence 38–9, 84, 157, 239, 240, 247, 314, 403n 14

Prussia 104–5, 115, 217, 298

public opinion: Erasmus and 123; importance appreciated by Ranke 124; in late-medieval Germany 126; Hagen and Ranke on 133; Nisard on Erasmus and 136; Hallam on Luther and 157; Kalkoff on Erasmus and 317; Vischer on Erasmus and 337

Puritans 261, 366

Pythagoras 66

Quakers 341, 358

Quarterly Review 256

Queen's College, Cambridge 98

Quintilian 196, 325, 330

Rabelais, François 18, 22, 368, 418n 116

Rambler (Acton) 421n 184

Rambler (Johnson) 95

Ranke, Leopold von: eighteenth-century writers close to 25; anticipated by Robertson 27; and public opinion 124; and historical vocation 124–5; on general theories and revolutionary politics 125; on papacy and reform 125–6; on Erasmus' early life 126–7; on Erasmus as critic 127–8; on Erasmus' character 128; on Luther 128; compared with Hagen 132–3; Nisard and 139; Hallam on 155; Döllinger reply to 192; Kampschulte stu-

dent of 199; Merle d'Aubigné and 241; Gaye student of 425n 38; Dilthey and 433n 180; Wolf on 297; Maurenbrecher and 298, 435n 4; Kalkoff returns to 317

rationalism 38, 46, 173, 286, 294

Raumer, Friedrich von 264

Raumer, Karl von: and pedagogy 324; on Erasmus 324

Reade, Charles *see Cloister and the Hearth*

Reedijk, Cornelis 371

Reformation: consequences of 4; Erasmus and 6; debates reopened 8; and Enlightenment 11; Bayle on Erasmus and 16; Voltaire on 19–20; Robertson on 27–9; Gibbon on 33–4; Mosheim on 41; Schröckh on 42; Planck on 43–4; forerunners of 46, 275, 386n 155; Schmidt on 55–7; Wieland on Erasmus and 62–3; Protestant Enlightenment on Erasmus and 69, 248–9; Gaudin on 71; Stewart on 79–80; Villers on 84–5; Mill on 86; Coleridge on 91, 396n 106; in Luther anniversary 1817 110; and liberalism 153; Hallam on 154, 157; Drummond on 168–9; Kegan Paul on 170; Beard on Renaissance and 171; Froude on Erasmus and 183; Döllinger's history of 192–3; Nève on 213–14; interpretation of 238–9; Merle d'Aubigné on 240; Montauban thesis-writers on 242; Erhard on Erasmus and 251; Glasius on Erasmus and 279; alternative interpretations of Erasmus and 280–1; Emerton on Erasmus and 282; Lezius on Erasmus and 288;

Bezold on 304; and controversy 314; early years of 322;
Paulsen on Erasmus and
326–7; Allen on 358–9; P.
Smith on 366, 367–8; Huizinga
on Erasmus and 370
Reform Bill 1832 154, 176
Reformed church 6, 105, 280,
305, 431n 148, 435n 216 (see
also Calvinism)
Reich, Max: Kan and 336; on Erasmus' correspondence 352;
and Vischer 352; on letter to
Grunnius 352; Nichols on 353;
Allen and 355
Reinhardsgrimma 246
Remonstrants 274, 277, 280 (see
also Arminians)
Renaissance 29, 89, 93, 111, 116,
140, 146–7, 172, 206, 213, 231,
258, 283, 308 (see also humanism, revival of learning)
Renan, Ernest 148, 348
Renaudet, Augustin: on 'Préréforme' in Paris 311; on Erasmus and Parisian intellectuals
312; as historian 312, 438n 62;
on 'Oxford Reformers' 313; on
Lefèvre d'Etaples and Erasmus
313; and Enlightenment 314;
on modernism of Erasmus 314,
438n 70; Meyer and 319; P.
Smith and 366
Restoration 7, 12, 112, 118,
123–4
Reuchlin, Johann 18, 29, 38, 45,
77, 106, 111, 128, 199, 201,
205, 212, 249–50
Réveil see 'Awakening'
revival of learning 28–9, 40, 57,
79, 86, 91, 128, 155, 189,
229–30, 383n 83, 402n 23 (see
also humanism, Renaissance)
revolution of 1688 153
revolutions of 1830 124–5,

134–5, 209, 211
revolutions of 1848 124, 129,
171, 192, 256
Richter, Arthur: Kan and 336; on
Erasmus' correspondence 351;
on Erasmus' development 351;
on Erasmus and vernaculars
351–2; Nichols on 352
Richter, Max: on Erasmus' religion 314–15; on Erasmus as
reformer 315; on Erasmus' policy 1520–1 315
Riga 59, 60
Robertson, William: as Moderate
leader, Church of Scotland
25–6; as historian 26–7; on
Reformation 27–9; and Scottish
Enlightenment 28; on revival
of learning 28–9; on Erasmus'
influence 29–30; on Erasmus
and Luther 30–1; and Gibbon
31, 36–7; never ruffled 382n
57; and Planck 46
Robespierre, Maximilien 88
Robinson, James Harvey 451n
311
Roe, R.H. 258
romanticism 12, 75, 83, 121, 135,
192, 239, 276–7, 361, 372
Rome 310–11, 316, 337, 355
Rome, church of: Gibbon's conversion to 35; Mosheim on
40–1; Gaudin on 71; Mill on
85; Michelet on 140; Drummond on Erasmus and 167;
Janssen and 217; and German
empire 217, 223; Escher on
Erasmus and 266; Stockmeyer
on Erasmus and 268; Lindeboom on Erasmus and 308;
Kalkoff on intransigence of
1520 317; Allen on 358 (see
also papacy)
Rotermund, Heinrich Wilhelm:
on Erasmus and Reformation

110–11; debts to earlier writers 400n 186
Rotterdam: *Encyclopédie* article on 15–18; Voltaire on Erasmus' statue in 24; Kan and 336; Allen at 355; A.D. White and Erasmus' statue in 451n 313
Rottier, Eugène: Erasmus, amateur enthusiasm for 211; on Erasmus and Netherlands 211; on Erasmus' religion 211–12; errors of fact 418n 108
Rousseau, Jean-Jacques 87–9, 92, 142, 330, 394n 64
Ruchat, Abraham 391n 8
Ruelens, Charles: and Erasmus revival in Belgium 334; on Erasmus' schooling 334–5; on Erasmus in monastery 335; assessment of 335–6; Mestwerdt uses 344

sacraments: Erhard on Erasmus and 251; Lezius on Erasmus and 288; Usteri on Erasmus and Zwingli and 321
Sailer, Johann Michael 415n 52
Sainte-Beuve, Charles Augustin 135, 405n 58
St Gallen 70
St Genevieve 147, 167, 312
St George's, Everton 330
St Lebuin's church, Deventer 354
Saint-Omer 360
St Pierre, Jacques Henri Bernardin de 66
Salles Amédée: on Erasmus' theology and personality 429n 108
Sardou, Victorien 405n 58
Sarpi, Paolo 66, 101, 155, 230, 390n 228
Sauvage, Jean, chancellor of Burgundy 214

Savonarola, Girolamo 257, 338
Saxony 19, 107, 306, 325
Scaliger, Joseph 407n 44
Scaliger, Julius Caesar 17
scepticism 35, 152, 207, 286, 363, 425n 38
Schets, Erasmus 419nn 127 and 133
Schleiermacher, Friedrich Ernst Daniel: and Semler 50; on religion 104; and Prussia 105; as church historian 104–5; on history of Christianity 105–6; on Reformation 106; on Erasmus 107–8; influences A. Müller 115; and Ranke 127; Hagen compared with 132; Gaye student of 425n 38; and mediating theologians 252; and Ullmann 253; and Hagenbach 266
Schlettstadt 355
Schlottmann, Constantin: and *Kulturkampf* 223; career of 223, 420n 163; on church since Reformation 224; on Erasmus 224–5; on Erasmus' influence 225; on Erasmus and Luther 225–6; assessment of 226
Schmid, Karl Adolf 303, 324
Schmidt, Michael Ignaz: German history of 54–5; on Habsburg dynasty 55; Febronian 55; on Erasmus and Reformation 55–7; on Luther 56; on Protestant freedoms 56–7; on Reformation and Enlightenment 57; Schröckh on 57–8; Gaum on 58; and Hallam 155
scholasticism: Erasmus and 5, 186–7; Brucker on 38; Villers on 84; Coleridge on 91; Schleiermacher on 105; Feugère on 146; Amiel on 149; Beard on 172; nineteenth-cen-

tury revival of 187; Butler on
Erasmus and 190; Kerker on
humanism and 195; Kerker on
Erasmus and 195–7; Woker on
Erasmus and 201; Durand de
Laur on Erasmus and 207; Milman on Erasmus and 257;
Hermelink on humanism and
293; in late fifteenth-century
Paris 312; Ruelens on Erasmus
and 335; Seebohm on Colet
and 339; Mestwerdt on Erasmus and 346; Nichols on Erasmus and 354; P. Smith
undervalues 366
scholasticism, Protestant 52, 57,
66–7, 138
Scholten, Jan Hendrik 436n 31
Schottenloher, Otto: on Erasmus
and death 430n 129; and Mestwerdt 445n 212
Schröckh, Johann Matthias: career of 42; as historian 42; on
Erasmus 44–6; compared with
Planck 45–6; and Henke 48;
on Schmidt 57–8; Rotermund
refers to 400n 186
Schröder, Arthur: on Erasmus
and modernity 363–4
Schulze, Martin: on Erasmus'
pessimism 292; on Erasmus
and Calvin 292–3; compared
with Dilthey, Troeltsch, and
Wernle 292–3; Köhler on 294;
assessment of 296
Scotland: Church of 25–6; Enlightenment in 26; Robertson's
History of 27; common-sense
philosophy in 78, 85; disruption in Church of 261; Free
Church of 262
Scotus, John Duns 196
Seckendorf, Veit Ludwig von 30,
101, 155, 381n 32, 391n 8,
416n 66

secularization 8, 145, 373
Seebohm, Frederic: Hamilton anticipates 261; Dods on 428n
99; Maurenbrecher and 299,
435n 4; purpose and form of
Oxford Reformers 338; on Colet
in Italy 338; on Colet's lectures
339; on Erasmus and Colet
339–40; on 'Oxford Reformers'
and Reformation 340; critique
of 340, 444nn 187–9; influence
of 340–1; and liberal tradition
341; career and background
341; Mestwerdt and 342, 347;
A. Richter and 351; Nichols
corrects 354
Semler, Johann Salomo: and
Protestant tradition 46; compared with Mosheim 49–50;
and historical-critical method
50; and Schleiermacher 50;
debt to Erasmus 50–1; and
radical neologians 51; on Erasmus 51–3; on inner religion
53; mentioned by Gaudin
391n 8; Lavater on 103; and
Renaudet 314
Sepulveda, Juan Gines de 193
Sermon on the Mount 148, 290,
307, 367 (see also Jesus, reli-
gion of)
Servatius Rogerus 218, 220, 260,
350, 353, 356, 391n 8
Servetus, Michael 15
Shaftesbury, Anthony Ashley
Cooper 390n 228
Shakespeare, William 142
Sickingen, Franz von 60
Sidney, Philip 390n 228
Simancas 298
Simon, Richard 48
Sleidan, Johannes 101, 155, 381n
32
Smith, Arthur Lionel: liberal
Protestant 258; on Erasmus

258–9; on Erasmus and Luther 259; later career 427n 75; Hamilton and 260
Smith, Henry Goodwin: on Erasmus and liberal Protestantism 284–5
Smith, Henry Preserved 366, 450n 309
Smith, Preserved: upbringing and writings of 365–6; style of 366; and recent scholarship 366; on Erasmus and undogmatic Christianity 367; on relation between Renaissance and Reformation 367–8; portrait of Erasmus 368; on Amiel and Froude 451n 322
Smith, Sydney 408n 45
Société évangelique de Genève 239
Society of Jesus 5, 41, 55, 57, 224
Socinians 35, 286 (see also Arianism)
Socrates 66, 79, 149, 308
Sorbonne 23, 101
Spain 298–9, 440n 106
Stähelin, Rudolf: on Hagenbach 270; influences on 272; and Basel 272; on Erasmus' influence 272; and Seebohm 272–3; on Erasmus and Reformation 273–4
Stanley, Arthur Penrhyn 408n 51, 427n 65
Stein, Aurel 448n 256
Stephen, James 98, 101
Stewart, Dugald: on Robertson 27; career of 392n 44; and common-sense philosophy 78; on idea of progress 79; on revival of letters 79; on Reformation 79–80; on Erasmus 80–1; on French Revolution 81; praises Gibbon 393n 52; com-

pared with Robertson 393n 54; Mill admires 85; Beard and 171
Steyn 334–5
Stichart, Franz Otto: Woker uses 416n 66; Janssen uses 219; on Erasmus and church 247; on Erasmus' character 247; on Erasmus' religion 248; M. Richter and 314; Geiger on 348–9
Stillingfleet, Edward 261
Stockmeyer, Immanuel: career of 267; on Erasmus and Amerbach 268; on Erasmus and Basel 268; on Erasmus and Reformation 268–9
Stolz, Johann Jakob: on Hutten and Erasmus 112
Strasbourg 251, 323, 355, 429n 108
Strauss, David Friedrich 130, 265, 420n 160, 432n 174
Streuber, Wilhelm Theodor: and Basel 269; life of 269; on Erasmus and Basel Reformation 269–70
Stubbs, William 355
Sturm and Drang 59, 61, 103
Sturminster Marshall, Dorset 170
Swabia 194
Swart, Nicolaas: on Erasmus 275; career and outlook of 431n 142
Swift, Jonathan 22, 166
Switzerland: French invasion of 70; Reformation in 210; liberalism in 264; mediating theology in 270; Wernle on Erasmus' influence in 291
Sybel, Heinrich von 298
Synthen, Jan 335

Tatham, Edward H.R. 437n 54
Tauler, Johann 51
Tell, William 67

Terminus 104, 430n 126
Tetzel, Johann 231
Teutsch, D. Christian: on Erasmus and Luther 429n 108
Teutsche Merkur 61, 389n 217
Theological Review 170, 408n 46
Theologische Literaturzeitung 294
Theologische Quartalschrift 194
Theologische Studien und Kritiken 254
Thijm, Alberdingk 217
Third Republic 148
Thirty Years' War 56, 57
Thomas à Kempis 117, 260, 305, 409n 66
Thou, Jacques-Auguste de 101, 390n 228
Tögel, Hermann: Herbartian 328–9; on Erasmus' psychology 329; on Erasmus' pedagogy 329–30; on Erasmus' influence 330; career of 441n 135; and Woodward 332
toleration 14, 23, 54, 229, 275, 280, 284, 286, 362, 364–5
Torresani, Andrea, of Asola 310
Tracy, James D. 445n 212
Tractarianism 159–60, 175–6, 181
Treitschke, Heinrich von 290
Trent, Council of 5, 41, 187, 190, 235
Trilingual College 214
Trinitarian text 32, 383n 86
Trinity 5–6, 34, 168, 173, 222, 248
Trinity College, Dublin 362
Troeltsch, Ernst: on Reformation and modern world 289–90; and humanist theology 290; on Hermelink 294; on Erasmus' modernity 294; assessment of 295; Huet and 305; and Mestwerdt 341, 343; Schröder and 364; P. Smith and 367–8

Tübingen, University of 43, 194, 288, 293, 434n 207
Tudor despotism 153, 176, 411n 110
Tunbridge School 81

Ullmann, Carl: and A. Müller 253; theology of 253; on Erasmus 253–4; Glasius on 279
ultramontanism 187, 205, 229, 236
Unitarianism 86, 170–1, 384n 101
United Presbyterian Church 429n 103
universities: in eighteenth-century Germany 37, 385n 104; new learning in 128
Usteri, Johann Martin: on Zwingli's debt to Erasmus 320; method of 320; on Erasmus' social and political ideas 321; on theology of Erasmus and Zwingli 321
Utopia 339, 342
Utterby, Lincolnshire 243

Valla, Lorenzo 48, 73, 116, 204, 249, 287, 303, 335, 343–5, 360, 367, 445n 212
Vanden Berghe, R. 355
Vander Haeghen, Ferdinand 355
Varro 196
Vatican Council, first 192, 199, 205, 217, 223–4, 230, 247
Vatican Council, second 186
Venice 310, 355
vernaculars 32, 145, 250, 265, 351–2
Vertheidigung des grossen Erasmus 113–14
Veuillot, Louis: on Erasmus 191–2; and first Vatican Council 192
Via antiqua 293

Vienna 55, 301, 443n 168
Villers, Charles: and German
idealism 83; on French Revolution 84, 394n 68; on Erasmus
and Reformation 84–5; Nisard
criticizes 139; Pennington and
243
Virgil 140
Vischer, Wilhelm: Kan and 336;
publishes Erasmus MSS 337;
interpretations of 338; Mestwerdt uses 344; Horawitz and
351; Reich and 352; Nichols
and 353
Vitrier, Jean 360
Volksschule 328
Voltaire, François Marie Arouet
de: and Erasmus 7; compared
with Erasmus 18, 161; on Erasmus in notebooks 18; in *Essai sur les moeurs* 19–20; on
papacy 19; on German Reformation 19–20; as historian 20;
on Erasmus in 'Conversation
de Lucien, Erasme, et Rabelais'
21; on Rabelais 22; on Erasmus in *Anecdote sur Bélisaire*
23–4; in *Sur les allemands*
24–5; Wieland and 62; Knox
on 394n 64; Coleridge on
87–9, 92; Nisard on Erasmus
and 136, 139; Michelet on Erasmus and 142, 143, 404n 34;
Janssen on Erasmus and 219;
Allard on Erasmus and 221;
Schlottmann on Erasmus and
225; Dilthey on Erasmus and
285; Bezold on Erasmus and
304; Huet on 306; Lindeboom
on Erasmus and 437n 42; P.
Smith on Erasmus and 367
Vulgate 41, 49, 162

Wadham College, Oxford 352
Wagenseil, Christian Jacob 112

Wagner, Gottlob Heinrich Adolf:
on Erasmus' character 76; on
Erasmus' works 76–7; on Eras-
mus and Reformation 76–7;
Rotermund refers to 400n 186;
Hutten biography 112
Waitz, Georg 337
Waldensians 387n 182
Walter, Johannes von: career
434n 213; and Maurenbrecher,
K. Müller, Wernle, Troeltsch,
Lezius, and Hermelink 295; on
Erasmus as late medieval fig-
ure 295; and Schulze 295
war: Knox on Erasmus and 81–3;
Feugère on Erasmus' writings
on 144; Durand de Laur on
417n 97
Ward, Mrs Humphrey 407n 33
Warham, William 180
Wartburg 110, 240
Watchman 86
Wegelin, Jakob 70
Weigel, Erhard 330
Weimar 59, 62, 255
Wernle, Paul: and Dilthey and
Troeltsch 290; on Christian
renaissance 290; on Erasmus'
reform program 290–1; on Er-
asmus' influence 291; assess-
ment of 295–6; Mestwerdt on
343; Schröder and 364; P.
Smith and 367–8
Wesley, John 96, 258, 409n 66
Westminster Abbey 94, 396n 114
Westminster Confession 382n 53
Westphalia 199, 200
Whig historians 153, 176, 179,
341, 394n 72
White, Andrew Dickson: and Er-
asmus 451n 313
Whitney, James Pounder: on me-
dieval and modern in Erasmus
362–3; career and character
449n 288

Widmer, Joseph 414–15n 52
Wieland, Christoph Martin: and
Teutsche Merkur 61; and Sturm
und Drang 61–2; on Hutten
and Erasmus 61–3; and Herder
62, 64; on Erasmus and Refor-
mation 62–3; on Erasmus'
character 63; and French Revo-
lution 67, 390n 244; compared
with Erasmus 389n 225; Gau-
din and 72; Hess refers to 75;
Moser and 109; Meyer and 319
Wilberforce, William 97–8
William of Orange 274, 307
Wilson, James 358
Winckel, Pieter 416n 74
Wiseman, Nicholas, cardinal 230
Wittenberg 340; University of 42
Witzel, Georg 199, 202
Woker, Philipp: career of 200; on
Erasmus' irenicism 200; on Erasmus and church 201; on Erasmus and Luther 201–2; on
Erasmus' search for peace 202;
assessment of 202; Mauren-
brecher on 435n 4
Wolf, Friedrich A. 265
Wolf, Gustav 296–7
Wolff, Christian 24, 38, 54
Wolsey, Thomas 193
Woodward, William Harrison:
career of 330; writings of
330–1; on Erasmus and classi-
cal revival 331–2; on Erasmus
and nationality 331–2; on Erasmus' psychology 332, 442n
151; on Erasmus and the child

332; on Erasmus on education
and social action 332–3
Wordsworth, Christopher: on Er-
asmus and Luther 423n 23
Worms, Diet of 58, 201, 315
Württemberg 194
Würzburg 55
Wyclif, John 33, 111

Xenophon 325

Ypeij, Annaeus 275

Zeitschrift für die historische
Theologie 254
Zeno 66
Zickendraht, Karl 434n 211
Zimmermann, Karl 363
Zittau 325
Zürich: Enlightenment theology
and historical interests in 70;
Hess family in 72; Lavater and
103; liberal reforms in 264;
Escher in 265; Pijper on influence of 306; Zwingli as Reformer of 320
Zwingli, Huldrych: Gibbon on
33; Semler on Erasmus and 52;
as forerunner of Enlightenment 70; Michelet on 142; De
Ram on Reformation of 210;
and English Reformation 261;
Dilthey on 286; Lindsay on Erasmus and 435n 216; Gaudin
and Hess on Erasmus and 320;
Usteri on debt to Erasmus 320;
on theology of Erasmus and
321

Erasmus Studies

𝕏

A series of studies concerned with Erasmus and related subjects

1 *Under Pretext of Praise: Satiric Mode in Erasmus' Fiction*
  Sister Geraldine Thompson
2 *Erasmus on Language and Method in Theology*
  Marjorie O'Rourke Boyle
3 *The Politics of Erasmus: A Pacifist Intellectual and His Political Milieu*
  James D. Tracy
4 *Phoenix of His Age: Interpretations of Erasmus c 1550–1750*
  Bruce Mansfield
5 *Christening Pagan Mysteries: Erasmus in Pursuit of Wisdom*
  Marjorie O'Rourke Boyle
6 *Renaissance English Translations of Erasmus: A Bibliography to 1700*
  E.J. Devereux
7 *Erasmus as a Translator of the Classics*
  Erika Rummel
8 *Erasmus' Annotations on the New Testament: From Philologist to Theologian*
  Erika Rummel
9 *Humanist Play and Belief: The Seriocomic Art of Desiderius Erasmus*
  Walter M. Gordon
10 *Erasmus: His Life, Works, and Influence*
  Cornelis Augustijn
11 *Interpretations of Erasmus, c 1750–1920: Man On His Own*
  Bruce Mansfield